# The New International Lesson Annual

## 2009–2010

### September–August

Abingdon Press
Nashville

THE NEW INTERNATIONAL LESSON ANNUAL 2009–2010

*Copyright © 2009 by Abingdon Press*

All rights reserved.
No part of this work may be reproduced or transmitted in any form or by any means, electronic or mechanical, including photocopying and recording, or by any information storage or retrieval system, except as may be expressly permitted by the 1976 Copyright Act or in writing from the publisher. Requests for permission can be addressed to Abingdon Press, P.O. Box 801, 201 Eighth Avenue South, Nashville, TN 37202-0801, or e-mailed to permissions@abingdonpress.com.

*This book is printed on acid-free paper.*

ISBN 978-0-687-65158-0

ISSN 1084-872X

09 10 11 12 13 14 15 16 17 18—10 9 8 7 6 5 4 3 2 1

MANUFACTURED IN THE UNITED STATES OF AMERICA

# PREFACE

Ancient sages tell us, "A journey of a thousand miles begins with a single step." We are so glad that you have taken the first step on a journey that will enable you to better understand God's Word so that you can live more faithfully as a Christian disicple. Our journey together will help us explore what it means to be a covenant community; demonstrate how Christ is the fulfillment of prophecy; examine teachings about community; and discern the nature and foundations of the Christian commitment we are called to live today. As you study each week, you will join countless Bible students around the world who use resources based on the work of the Committee on the Uniform Series, known by many as the International Lesson Series.

Although adult learners often use *The New International Lesson Annual*, it is mainly designed for teachers of adults who want a solid biblical basis for each session and a teaching plan that will help them lead their classes. The following features are especially valuable for busy teachers who want to provide in-depth Bible study experiences for their students. Each lesson includes the following sections:

**Previewing the Lesson** highlights the background and lesson scriptures, focus of the lesson, three goals for the learners, a pronunciation guide in lessons where you may find unfamiliar words or names, and supplies you will need to teach.

**Reading the Scripture** includes the Scripture lesson printed in both the *New Revised Standard Version* and the *New International Version*. By printing these two highly respected translations in parallel columns, you can easily compare them for in-depth study. If your own Bible is another version, you will then have three translations to explore as you prepare each lesson.

**Understanding the Scripture** closely analyzes the background scripture by looking at each verse. Here you will find help in understanding concepts, ideas, places, and persons pertinent to each week's lesson. You may also find explanations of Greek or Hebrew words that are essential for understanding the text.

**Interpreting the Scripture** looks at the lesson scripture, delves into its meaning, and relates it to contemporary life.

**Sharing the Scripture** provides you with a detailed teaching plan. It is divided into two major sections: *Preparing to Teach* and *Leading the Class*.

In the *Preparing to Teach* section, you will find a devotional reading related to the lesson for your own spiritual enrichment and a "to do" list to prepare your mind and classroom for the session.

The *Leading the Class* portion begins with "Gather to Learn" activities designed to welcome the students and draw them into the lesson. Here, the students' stories and experiences or other contemporary stories are highlighted as preparation for the Bible story. The next three headings of *Leading the Class* are the three "Goals for the Learners." The first goal always focuses on the Bible story itself. The second goal relates the Bible story to the lives of the adults in your class. The third goal prompts the students to take action on what they have learned. You will find a variety of activities under each of these goals to help the learners fulfill them. The activities are diverse in nature and may include among other strategies: listening, reading, writing, speaking, singing, drawing, interacting with others, and meditating. The lesson ends with "Continue the Journey," where you will find closing activities, preparation for the following week, and ideas for students to commit themselves to action during the week, based on what they have learned.

In addition to these weekly features, each quarter begins with the following helps:

- **Introduction to the Quarter** provides you with a quick survey of each lesson to be studied during the quarter. You will find the title, background scripture, date, and a brief summary of each week's basic thrust. This feature is the first page of each quarter.
- **Meet Our Writer,** which follows the quarterly introduction, provides biographical information about each writer, including education, pastoral and/or academic teaching experience, previous publications, and family information.
- **The Big Picture**, written by the same writer who authored the quarter's lessons, is designed to give you a broader scope of the materials to be covered than is possible in each weekly lesson. You will find this background article immediately following the writer's biography.
- **Close-up** gives you some focused information, such as a timeline, chart, overview, short article, or list that you may choose to use anytime during the quarter, perhaps even repeatedly.
- **Faith in Action** provides ideas related to the broad sweep of the quarter that the students can use individually or as a class to act on what they have been studying. These ideas are usually intended for use beyond the classroom.

Finally, two annual features are included:

- **List of Background Scriptures** is offered especially for those of you who keep back copies of *The New International Lesson Annual*. This feature, which follows the Contents, will enable you to locate Bible background passages used during the current year at some future date.
- **Teacher enrichment article** is intended to be useful throughout the year, so we hope you will read it immediately and refer to it often. This year's article, "The Church as a Teaching Community," will challenge you to provide a variety of educational settings and strategies to enable the learners to be informed, transformed, and conformed to the image of Christ. You will find the article following the List of Background Scriptures.

We truly appreciate your feedback. Please send your questions and comments to me. I invite you to include your e-mail address and/or phone number. I will respond as soon as your message reaches my home office in Maryland.

Dr. Nan Duerling<br>
Abingdon Press<br>
PO Box 801<br>
Nashville, TN 37202

We are blessed to have you among our *New International Lesson Annual* community. May God grant you wisdom and grace as you study and lead others to a broader understanding of the Bible and a deeper relationship with our Lord Jesus Christ.

Nan Duerling, Ph.D.<br>
Editor, *The New International Lesson Annual*

# CONTENTS

FIRST QUARTER

## Covenant Communities
September 6–November 29, 2009

### UNIT 1: LEADERS IN THE COVENANT COMMUNITY
(September 6-27)

### UNIT 2: AN OPEN INVITATION TO COVENANT LIVING
(October 4-25)

## UNIT 3: THE NEW COVENANT COMMUNITY
### (November 1-29)

## SECOND QUARTER

# Christ, the Fulfillment
### December 6, 2009–February 28, 2010

## UNIT 1: THE PROMISED BIRTH FULFILLED
### (December 6-27)

## UNIT 2: EVIDENCES OF JESUS AS MESSIAH
### (January 3-31)

## THIRD QUARTER

# Teachings on Community
## March 7–May 30, 2010

## UNIT 1: COMMUNITY WITH A MISSION
### (March 7-28)

## UNIT 2: TEACHINGS OF JESUS
### (April 4-25)

## UNIT 3: TEACHINGS OF THE CHURCH
### (May 2-30)

### FOURTH QUARTER

# Christian Commitment in Today's World
### June 6–August 29, 2010

### UNIT 1: THE NATURE OF CHRISTIAN COMMITMENT
### (June 6-27)

### UNIT 2: THE FOUNDATION OF CHRISTIAN COMMITMENT
### (July 4-25)

## UNIT 3: THE MARKS OF CHRISTIAN COMMITMENT
### (August 1-29)

# LIST OF BACKGROUND SCRIPTURES, 2009–2010

## Old Testament

| | | | |
|---|---|---|---|
| Joshua 1 | September 6 | Ruth 4:13-17 | December 6 |
| Judges 6–8 | September 13 | Isaiah 7:13-17 | December 13 |
| Ezra 9 | September 20 | Jonah 1:1-3 | March 7 |
| Nehemiah 2 | September 27 | Jonah 3:1-9 | March 7 |
| Ruth 1:1-16 | March 21 | Jonah 3:10–4:11 | March 14 |
| Ruth 2–3 | March 28 | | |

## New Testament

| | | | |
|---|---|---|---|
| Matthew 1:1-17 | December 6 | Acts 28 | August 29 |
| Matthew 1:18-25 | December 20 | Philippians 1 | August 1 |
| Matthew 2 | December 27 | Philippians 2:1–3:1a | August 8 |
| Matthew 3 | January 3 | Philippians 3:1b–4:1 | August 15 |
| Matthew 4:1-11 | January 10 | Philippians 4:2-14 | August 22 |
| Matthew 5:17-20 | April 18 | Philippians 4:15-23 | August 29 |
| Matthew 9:27-34 | January 17 | Colossians 1 | May 2 |
| Matthew 11:2-6 | January 17 | Colossians 2:1-1-19 | May 9 |
| Matthew 11:25-30 | January 24 | Colossians 3 | May 16 |
| Matthew 13:54-58 | January 31 | 1 Thessalonians 1 | June 6 |
| Matthew 15:21-28 | February 7 | 1 Thessalonians 2 | June 13 |
| Matthew 16:13-27 | February 14 | 1 Thessalonians 3 | June 20 |
| Matthew 17:1-12 | February 21 | 1 Thessalonians 4:1-12 | June 27 |
| Matthew 22:34-40 | April 18 | 1 Thessalonians 4:13–5:28 | July 4 |
| Matthew 26:6-13 | February 28 | 2 Thessalonians 1 | July 11 |
| Mark 1:35-45 | October 4 | 2 Thessalonians 2 | July 18 |
| Mark 5:1-20 | October 11 | 2 Thessalonians 3 | July 25 |
| Mark 7:24-30 | October 18 | Philemon | May 23 |
| Mark 10:17-31 | October 25 | 1 Peter 1 | November 1 |
| Luke 1:26-38 | December 13 | 1 Peter 2:1-17 | November 8 |
| Luke 4:16-30 | January 31 | 1 Peter 4 | November 15 |
| Luke 14:7-24 | April 25 | 2 Peter 1:3-15 | November 22 |
| John 13:21-30 | April 4 | 2 Peter 3 | November 29 |
| John 16:16-24 | April 4 | 1 John 2:7-17 | April 11 |
| John 20:11-16 | April 4 | Jude | May 30 |

# THE CHURCH AS A
# TEACHING COMMUNITY

## Setting the Stage for Teaching and Learning

During 2009–2010 we will study much about the church as a covenant community where the teachings of Jesus come alive as members seek to live out their commitment to him. The Spirit moves as the Spirit will, so we recognize that not all teaching and experiences with God can be programmed to occur on schedule. Yet, as the church, we have a responsibility to ensure that people of all ages have the opportunity to learn, for a disciple is a learner. Teaching and learning occur not only for the benefit of the individual but also for the body of Christ as a whole.

Think for a moment about the teaching opportunities that your church offers. Are the sermons biblically-based and able to connect with how you live daily as a Christian disciple? Does your church nurture its children in Sunday school classes and in other programs such as vacation Bible school and weekday child care or preschool programs? Is there a confirmation program that teaches youth who they are, whose they are, and how they fit into the life of the church? Are adults encouraged to continue learning and growing through Sunday school classes, short term Bible studies, missionary projects, Advent and Lenten studies, and other opportunities? Do learners of all ages have opportunities not only to learn in classroom settings but also to go beyond the church walls to witness and serve?

In this article we will explore two questions: *why is it important for the church to be a teaching community,* and *what opportunities are there for such teaching?*

Why does the church teach? The end purpose of Christian education is not *information.* Yes, we need information. But that is our starting point, not our goal. We study information with open hearts and minds so that it may *transform* us. Ultimately, we pray that through continuing transformation we may become *conformed* to the image of Christ that dwells within us. Conformation in Christ, then, is the real goal of Christian education.

With that goal in mind, you would think that all Christians would want to participate in teaching and learning activities. But have you heard anyone say, "I went to Sunday school as a child. I learned the Bible stories then, so I don't need to attend Sunday school as an adult"? Unfortunately, there are many who think that what they learned in third grade will carry them through all the trials and challenges that life throws at them as adults. But let's be honest: which of us in third grade really understood the implications of the stories of Abraham being told to take his wife and leave their home to answer God's call, or the huge responsibilities that Moses was called to bear in order to lead the Hebrew people out of slavery, or the power and significance of Pentecost? Who at age eight could begin to grasp the significance of Jesus' transfiguration, prayer in Gethsemane, crucifixion, or resurrection?

While teaching children and youth are essential ministries of the church, adults must also be encouraged to go deeper and wider in the Bible. Not all stories are suitable for third graders, so as adults we encounter those familiar stories and others as well: David and

Bathsheba; Abraham's willingness to sacrifice Isaac; and Peter's confession that Jesus was the Messiah, followed by his denial of the Lord, not once but three times. We confront the wars that the Israelites fought, the betrayal of Jesus, and the desertion of Jesus by his disciples. We recognize not only that "Jesus Loves Me" but also that Jesus will return in glory to judge the living and the dead. Even if we were exposed to some of these stories as children, I daresay that most of us had no real understanding of their meaning.

So how, as a teaching community of faith, do we help adults engage the Scriptures in ways that enable them to go deeper and wider? What do we say and do in order to provide adult disciples with information that can lead to transformation and conformation to the image of Christ?

One way, of course, is through Sunday school classes. Traditionally, classes have been formed, often with younger adults, who grow together through the years. Some churches have a class for men and another for women. Congregations may offer a class for married couples. Classes that follow these models often stay together for decades. In some settings, these approaches still work, but there are many other options as well. Churches are recognizing that many people cannot or do not want to make long-term commitments to one group. Work obligations, changing interests, and short-term residency in a community often prompt people to seek a class with a defined beginning and end.

Short-term studies focused on a theme, book of the Bible, season of the church year, or life issue bring together people with a common interest. These learners study the topic and then disperse after the agreed-upon number of sessions. Studies that run six to thirteen weeks provide an excellent opportunity for adults to concentrate on a topic of interest and also to get in the habit of studying with other adults. While some groups prefer to have a single leader or a team of two or three, others rotate leaders. Even a single leader may bring in guest teachers. In some cases, a core group will bond and continue to study a variety of topics on a short-term basis while some students come and go. A church that offers a variety of short-term studies throughout the year will likely have a vibrant teaching ministry.

Not all Christian education must occur on Sunday morning. Classes scheduled on weekdays provide opportunities for folks who want more study time or who are unavailable on Sunday mornings. Classes that meet at night may draw working adults or parents whose children or teens are participating in evening activities at the church. Groups that gather during the day tend to include parents whose children may be in school or attend your church preschool. Daytime groups are also popular with older adults who may not drive at night. A Saturday morning study group that includes breakfast may also attract students.

Although the church building is often chosen for convenience as the meeting place, Christian education can occur in many other venues. Some congregations have tried online discussion groups for Bible study with varying degrees of success. Many churches have study groups in members' homes. This plan works well where you have a contingent of people living in a small area. The host family may or may not be the leaders of the group. Other classes may meet for breakfast in a restaurant. Some businesses allow ecumenical lunchtime studies in a conference room, provided that no employee feels coerced to attend. Prisons often have classes and may invite community groups to assist in leading them. Folks who enjoy recreational vehicles may hold a study at a campground. The list of possible places for education is limited only by one's imagination.

Most of us are accustomed to learning from books. But CDs, DVDs, computer-based learning, field trips, experiential learning where students actually do something, peer teaching of a small group, and one-on-one mentoring are also exciting possibilities. While some groups will prefer to listen to a lecturer, others will thrive on a variety of interactive activities that allow them to share their experiences and raise their questions. No one way is "correct," but some ways tend to attract more people than others.

## The Bible and Life Class: A Case Study

My own class of about twenty-five students is one of three adult Sunday school classes in our church. With learners ranging in age from sixty to ninety, the Bible and Life Class has been together almost twenty years, but is always open to new people. Lively discussion and thought-provoking questions are the order of the day. A true United Methodist group, we gather at the refreshment table for some brief fellowship before class begins. We study a wide range of topics to expand our theological horizons. We also have studied spiritual disciplines so that we might grow closer to Christ as we spend time alone with him during the week. We care for one another, laugh together, and agree to disagree with others whose theology and life experiences may differ. Many of us are leaders, so we try to put what we learn into practice as we undertake our respective responsibilities in the church, community, and workplace. Our name was deliberately chosen to reflect our goal of bringing the Bible and its teachings into all aspects of our daily lives.

Our class tends to prefer books that run thirteen to twenty-six weeks, but our "policy" is that the course runs as long as we want it to. Even a book with a stated timeframe, such as *Three Months with Matthew* by Justo Gonzalez, captured our interest so much that we spent almost a year on it! We devoted six months to The Letter of James, which only has five chapters, analyzing its meaning and considering how the contemporary church does—and does not—live up to James' ideal and how we could be more intentional about following his teachings. As part of that study, we also considered Elsa Tamez's book *The Scandalous Message of James: Faith Without Works Is Dead* to see how Christians in Third World countries might interpret James and how their interpretations can inform our own.

We are blessed to have a talented professional artist in our class, so using a text based on art housed in the National Gallery of Art depicting the life of Christ, we looked at "Jesus Through the Eyes of the Artist." The book and scanned pictures that were projected by computer onto a large screen made for lively discussion. We concluded that course with a bus trip to the National Gallery in Washington, D.C., which is about forty-five minutes from our church. Seeing Jesus depicted by different people in different cultures and historical periods broadened our horizons about who Jesus is and how others perceive him, both visually and in the Scriptures.

By using the lectionary-based curriculum, *Scriptures for the Church Season,* during Lent, we were able to more fully immerse ourselves in preparations for Holy Week and Easter. Since most of our class members attend church before Sunday school, we combined our study with a talk-back on the sermon that prompted us to engage more fully in worship.

We have also completed *Jesus in the Gospels,* part of the second generation of the DISCIPLE series. To do this long-term study, which requires two and a half hours per session, we covenanted to meet for an extended period on Sunday for class and then attend the worship service after Sunday school. This series combined reading at home with videos with some class discussion and a lot of small group work. We did stick closely to the schedule as set forth for this course and at the end of the thirty weeks agreed that we had learned more about and grown closer to Jesus as a result of this in-depth study of our Lord as portrayed in the four Gospels.

A number of years ago we studied curriculum from Habitat for Humanity. When that course ended we asked ourselves, "Now what can we do?" As a result, we got our church and several other congregations involved in building not one but several Habitat houses in our county—and sent money so that other homes could be built internationally. We shared our learning by organizing others, raising funds, recruiting volunteers, and participating in construction.

Last summer our class agreed to take a break from our studies, and we learned even while we did that. Our church gives the teachers of children and youth time off during the summer and invites other church members to lead classes on a rotating schedule. Many of our class members agreed to work with the children and youth, thereby sharing not only our knowledge but also our love of Christ with younger disciples in the church. Some members of our class returned to grades they had taught many years ago. I decided to try an age group I had never taught and learned that three- and four-year-olds are fun to be with and eager to learn about Jesus.

As I write this article, we have just begun a series of lessons on rabbinic Christianity with a Jewish rabbi affiliated with the Baltimore-Washington Conference of The United Methodist Church. We are intrigued by how Jesus' role as a rabbi and knowledge of the Hebrew Scriptures inform his teachings in ways that we have never been exposed to before.

## Your Classes as a Teaching Community

Should your class do what my class has done? No. You and your group need to work in ways that are best for you. My point in sharing this information about the Bible and Life Class of Linthicum Heights United Methodist Church is to suggest that there are many ways to teach and learn in the community of faith. And, as noted previously, lessons are learned in many ways in many settings. Sunday school is an important time for such learning to occur, but it is hardly the only time. Often, it is the catalyst for action beyond the church walls.

The major question you and other adult Christian education leaders in your church need to ask is this: *are we providing a variety of opportunities to draw in as many people as possible so that they might not only learn about Jesus but more importantly come to know him in a deep and personal way that empowers them to follow him?*

If your church needs to expand your opportunities, talk with some adults who do not attend Sunday school or other venues for adult education. What questions are they asking? What are the cries of their hearts? How can you answer these questions and respond to the cries by offering new educational opportunities? Who will lead these groups? Where and when will they meet? How long will they covenant to study together? What books or other media will be most appropriate? What kinds of activities outside of class can support and reinforce their study?

Although none of us can truly know the heart of another, we can see fruit in one another's lives. As you think about those who participate in adult education, do you perceive the "love, joy, peace, patience, kindness, generosity, faithfulness, gentleness, and self-control" that Paul described in Galatians 5:22-23? Do you see people who perform the acts of mercy that Jesus did and expects us to do: feeding the hungry, tending the sick, visiting the prisoner, and assisting those who are most vulnerable? Do you see the power of the Holy Spirit at work as lives are healed and changed? If you see these signs, then it seems likely that your church is truly a teaching community where people are learning in the school of Jesus how to be faithful disciples who are conformed to his image.

# First Quarter
## Covenant Communities

SEPTEMBER 6, 2009—NOVEMBER 29, 2009

During the fall we will explore the theme "Covenant Communities." Examining Scripture from both the Old and the New Testaments, we will get acquainted with people whom God chose as covenant leaders, overhear the invitations God offered to enter into community, witness people's responses to these invitations, and examine the nature of God's new covenant community.

Unit 1, "Leaders in the Covenant Community," considers four people—Joshua, chosen to lead the people into the Promised Land; Gideon, called to deliver the people from the threat of the Midianites and Amalekites; Ezra, a priest called to intercede on behalf of the recently returned exiles; and Nehemiah, instructed by God to gather people to rebuild the walls of Jerusalem. Each in his own way was called to lead the Israelites into covenant with God. The unit begins on September 6 with "Joshua: A Leader for the People," which explores Joshua 1 to recognize a strong and courageous leader. Judges 6–8 provides the background for the session on September 13 that looks at a very unlikely leader in "Gideon: A Deliverer for the People." Ezra 9 is the backdrop for the lesson on September 20 where "Ezra: A Priest for the People" recognizes Israel's sins and helps get the people back on course with God. The unit ends on September 27 with "Nehemiah: A Motivator for the People," which recognizes how a leader overcomes problems as discussed in Nehemiah 2.

Unit 2, "An Open Invitation to Covenant Living," includes four lessons from the Gospel of Mark that show Jesus interacting with people and inviting them to live in covenant with God. Mark 1:35-45, the text for October 4, describes how people are "Looking for Jesus." On October 11, Mark 5:1-20 records the story of a demon-possessed person restored to wholeness by "Recognizing Jesus." A Gentile woman approaches Jesus on behalf of her daughter in "Begging to Get In," the session for October 18 from Mark 7:24-30. "Opting Out!" the lesson for October 25, recounts the familiar story in Mark 10:17-31 of the rich man whose consuming passion for his possessions became a stumbling block to answering Jesus' invitation.

The five lessons of Unit 3, "The New Covenant Community," explore the letters of 1 and 2 Peter to discern qualities of those who are part of God's covenant community. "A Holy People," the lesson for November 1 that is based on 1 Peter 1, calls the covenant people to a lifestyle of holiness. On November 8 we turn to 1 Peter 2:1-17 to read that those in the covenant community are "A Chosen People." Being part of the covenant community is not always easy, as we see in "A Suffering People," the session for November 15 from 1 Peter 4 that helps us face opposition. "A Faithful People," as described on November 22 in 2 Peter 1:3-15, assures believers that God has given us all we need to live godly lives. The quarter concludes on November 29 with an investigation of 2 Peter 3 where "a hopeful people" are promised that the best is yet to come.

# Meet Our Writer

## THE REVEREND JANICE CATRON

Janice Catron is a Christian educator and ordained minister in the Presbyterian Church (USA), currently pastoring at John Knox Presbyterian Church in Louisville, Kentucky. Prior to moving to this congregation, she served on the national staff of the Presbyterian Church (USA) for fourteen years in various positions related to education and publication. In conjunction with her publishing house work, Rev. Catron was a member of the Committee of the Uniform Series. She also taught as adjunct faculty at Louisville Presbyterian Theological Seminary.

A native of Mississippi, the Reverend Catron received her B.S. from Millsaps College, M.A. from Emory University, M.Div. from Louisville Presbyterian Theological Seminary, and did her doctoral work at the University of Chicago. In addition to writing for *The New International Lesson Annual*, Janice is the author of *Job: Faith Remains When Understanding Fails* and *God's Vision, Our Calling: Hope and Responsibility in the Christian Life*.

Janice and her husband, Gordon Berg, live in Louisville, where he provides information technology support for a nonprofit educational and counseling facility for emotionally-challenged teenage girls. When not working, Janice and Gordon enjoy watching movies together, playing on the computer, and spoiling their cat.

# THE BIG PICTURE: LIFE IN THE COVENANT COMMUNITY

This quarter includes lessons from across biblical history that explore what it means to live within God's covenant community. Drawing on texts from both Testaments, these sessions explore such questions as:

- What distinguishes members of the Christian church from other groups?
- How can we support and strengthen a growing and effective faith?
- How can we encourage others to keep persevering when problems seem insurmountable?

Along the way, we will examine the covenant community from many angles. Leading and following, healing and being healed, serving and witnessing—all are part of what we experience within the company of faith.

Underlying all these lessons are two basic concepts. The first is that, as part of the *covenant* community, we are in a unique relationship with God that involves both privilege and responsibility. We come into this relationship at God's invitation, through grace and grace alone, and as a result we receive a multitude of blessings. By entering into this covenant relationship, however, we also agree to abide by God's terms, which, as Jesus showed us, means dedicating ourselves to a life of love.

The second concept follows necessarily on the heels of the first: we are a covenant *community*. Life as a child of God cannot be lived in isolation. Faith expresses itself in and through our connection to others, just as love does. Thus, the Bible consistently speaks of faith in terms of how it is lived out in the community itself *and* in terms of how the community lives in the world. The focus of this quarter will be the same.

## Life as God's Covenant Community

If we take the Bible as a whole, we get a very definite picture of what it means to be God's covenant community. For example, we are those called by God, bonded by God, and transformed by God. In looking ahead to the lessons in this quarter, three other elements particularly come to mind.

First, the biblical concepts of both *covenant* and *community* recognize that we human beings are *a people of connection*. We are created for relationships, and we cannot survive, much less thrive, without them. Moreover, we do best when we build and maintain the kinds of relationships that God has always intended for us—healthy and loving associations that reflect genuine respect and honor for the other person and for God.

Second, as a covenant community, we are *a people of promises*. Our identity starts with the divine promise: "I will take you as my people, and I will be your God" (Exodus 6:7). Beyond that, God also promises a multitude of other blessings—to redeem us, to care for us, to strengthen us, to guide us, to be with us, and more. In turn, we make promises to God and to Jesus Christ that include putting them first in our lives, following their teachings, and treating others with the same love and regard that our Creator and Savior show to us. These promises make us, shape us, and keep us as a covenant community.

Finally, the Bible affirms that we are *a people of the Spirit*. God does not leave us to struggle in this world alone. For generations, the Spirit of God came to prophets and other leaders to guide the ancient community of faith, and that same Spirit comes to us now as an ongoing connection to the risen Christ. Through the power of the Spirit, we receive gift upon gift—encouragement and consolation when we are anxious or grieving, strength when we are weak, guidance and direction when we are confused, and a connection to the divine presence when we face human loneliness. All this is God's gift to us, and it is especially manifest in the way we nurture, support, and sometimes gently challenge one another within the community of faith. As the lessons for this quarter will show, the Spirit is also very much in evidence when the community of faith joins together in ministry to people in need, regardless of who they are.

## Unit 1: Leaders in the Covenant Community

Our study begins with a look at some magnificent leaders from the Old Testament. In part, this is to show that the history of the covenant community and God's relationship to people of faith does not start with the New Testament! Those of us who cherish a relationship with God through Jesus Christ are actually part of a divine activity that spans all time. God's intention for us and for the world shaped the creation of all that is, and that same intention will shape what occurs at the final return of the Messiah. Along the way, God chose to reveal glimpses of this plan through the Hebrew people, especially their prophets, and that same revelation continues on today through the church. We look back to the great Hebrew leaders of our past to remind ourselves of our roots, but even more to remind ourselves of God's ongoing, steadfast love for the covenant community.

The four people highlighted in Unit 1—Joshua, Gideon, Ezra, and Nehemiah—were selected because they serve another purpose as well. None of them was perfect, yet God accomplished wonderful things through them. In their flaws we can easily see ourselves, and in their stories we can see reassurance of how God can use us too. We can also see through these lessons that, within the faith community, good leaders share the following traits:

- They trust God.
- They know they are ordinary people.
- They are honest about their failings and diligently seek God's grace and forgiveness through prayer.
- They help others commit to works for the common good.

The four lessons of Unit 1 focus on the above characteristics as key to becoming a leader who lives out faithfulness in his or her relationship with God. More than that, though, these lessons invite us to consider the ways in which such attitudes and behaviors are marks of good discipleship in general—and therefore something to which we should all aspire.

## Unit 2: An Open Invitation to Covenant Living

Unit 2 builds on the understanding that God's covenant is lived out only in community. Here we look at four passages from the Gospel of Mark in which Jesus responds to people in varying ways, all designed to allow them to enter into God's community should they choose. Through these stories of healing and invitation, Mark gives us an idea of what Jesus offers to all. Moreover, we see Jesus himself modeling what the role of the church should be as it lives out its own covenant faithfulness to God as a community of proclamation, healing, hospitality, and commitment.

The Gospel of Mark is the earliest of the four included in Scripture. Many scholars believe the author lived in Galilee or Syria during the time of the Roman-Jewish War (A.D. 66–73), which began when a group of Jewish Zealots tried to establish their nation's independence. Rome crushed the rebellion at great cost to the people of Israel; along with all the other damage, the Temple was destroyed. If this dating is accurate, then the traumatic events of the war explain why Mark witnesses to Jesus Christ by focusing on such mighty deeds as healing, exorcism, and so on. By highlighting these miracles, Mark makes it inescapably clear that the realm of God is breaking into the world of human activity *now*.

Another characteristic of Mark's Gospel is what some scholars call "the messianic secret." More than any other Gospel, Mark stresses occasions when Jesus instructs people not to share what he has done for them. Occasionally this appears to be the result of his growing popularity, and some scholars therefore surmise that Jesus, already hounded by crowds, perhaps has no wish to add to the number of those who seek him. We can certainly understand Jesus' need for time alone to pray and to reenergize himself spiritually, yet it is hard to accept the suggestion that he would somehow try to limit the number of people he can help. Why would Jesus, Son of God sent to save the world, keep anyone from coming to him for healing or other forms of restitution?

Other scholars maintain that a better answer to Jesus' desire for secrecy arises when we look at the entirety of his actions and teachings in Mark. Jesus clearly wanted to avoid any misunderstanding about who he was and what he came to do. To acknowledge and proclaim him as the Messiah may be the truth, but it could also be misleading. There were too many expectations of the Messiah to be a national hero, leading the people to a military victory over Rome, for people to accept easily the role Jesus was to play. Jesus the Christ came to be a suffering servant, a sacrifice offered up for our sakes, but that message would quickly be denied by those who looked for a warrior leader. Thus, Mark indicates that Jesus wanted the truth about himself to be withheld until after the crucifixion and resurrection, because only then would people be able to understand the Messiah's true mission.

The four lessons of this unit explore ways in which Christ's mission and purpose—no longer secret but now good news to be proclaimed—continue to find expression through the ministry of the church today. In addition, they invite us to consider the ways in which we keep covenant faithfulness as disciples of Jesus by remembering we are Christ's body in the world, getting out into the world with our ministry and our witness, being both persistent and expectant, and, most of all, keeping a sound relationship with God as our top priority.

## Unit 3: The New Covenant Community

Our final unit turns to the letters of 1 and 2 Peter and what they have to say regarding the qualities of people who are part of God's covenant community. Among other things, we learn from these writings that Christians are:

- those whom God calls to be holy, as God is holy.
- those who embody Christ in the world.
- those who are to respond in certain ways when we suffer for the sake of the gospel.
- those who have been given a new name (identity) and a new status by God.
- those who anticipate the celebration of Christ's birth *and* of his return.

For both books, authorship poses a big question. In the case of 1 Peter, some scholars argue against the apostle Peter being the writer. They base their view chiefly on two lines of thought: (1) the somewhat eloquent Greek language exceeds what we would expect of a mere Galilean fisherman; and (2) the letter talks about a rather serious persecution, which suggests a date sometime after Peter's martyrdom, when Roman political authorities set themselves against the church. Other scholars are quick to point out, however, that these are not weighty arguments. One can still assume that the apostle Peter wrote the letter by taking into account two things. First, the letter was physically written by a secretary, Silvanus (5:12), whose name suggests a Greek heritage. He could easily have "translated" Peter's rougher Greek into the smooth language of the letter. Second, the persecution mentioned in the letter does not match the organized efforts that came later under Rome. Here the persecution seems to be privately not publicly instigated (1:6; 3:14-16; 4:12-14), and it is social but not political (2:13-17). Based on this, the lessons in Unit 3 assume that the apostle Peter is the author of 1 Peter.

It is much more difficult, however, to assign the authorship of 2 Peter to the apostle. First, the language is very different from that of the other letter, although use of a different scribe could account for this. Second, and more compelling, the letter bears internal evidence that it came from a time after Peter's death in A.D. 64. The first generation of Christian leaders has already died (3:4) and Paul's letters have been formed into a collection (3:15-16), something that did not occur as far as we know until the end of the first century. Finally, the early church itself did not agree that Peter was the author of this letter. The first mention of this debate is in the writings of Origen (about 185–about 254), who refers to one acknowledged letter of Peter's and a second letter whose apostolic authorship is in doubt. Thus, the last two lessons of this quarter, which focus on 2 Peter, assume that someone other than the apostle was the author.

While questions of authorship may seem like unimportant academic trivia on one level, such inquiries are important in establishing a likely date for the letters' composition. The date matters because it helps us recreate the social and political setting of the original audience, which in turn helps us understand the problems they faced in living as God's covenant community at that time. By putting these people of faith in their context, we can better see what they have to teach us about faithful living in today's world.

Writing in the mid-first century to believers who were beginning to feel social pressure to abandon the moral and ethical code of Christianity, 1 Peter stresses and celebrates the hope that Christians have because of Christ's resurrection (1:3-9) and builds on that hope as the reason we must live lives of holiness, manifestly different and better than those who are not Christians (1:13-21). To live in such a way, we must depend on God's grace and be in community with one another (2:1-10). Even so, faithful living sometimes will lead to suffering for Christ's sake, in the midst of which we must bear witness to the hope that we have in him (3:13-18; 4:1-2). Throughout everything, our common life is to be marked by love, humility, and resistance to evil (4:7-11; 5:1-11).

The author of 2 Peter addresses more dire concerns that arose a generation or two later. The purpose of the letter is to encourage Christians who are struggling with a perceived delay in the promised Second Coming of Christ (3:1-13), with false teaching (2:1-3), and with the effort to maintain their faith in the midst of the growing reality of persecution (3:14-18).

Although sent in response to two particular situations two millennia ago, these letters have much to say to us about how faith, love, and hope shape our life as a covenant community. Together with the other lessons from Units 1 and 2, they remind us that we are indeed called to be the people of God. We are those set apart for the special purpose of being "ministers of a new covenant" (2 Corinthians 3:6). We are those whom God has invited to take part in bringing salvation to the world by healing brokenness, tearing down walls, reaching across breaches, and forging a connection where there hasn't been one before. We are the body of Christ. "To him be the glory both now and to the day of eternity. Amen" (2 Peter 3:18).

# Close-Up: Map of Ancient Jerusalem

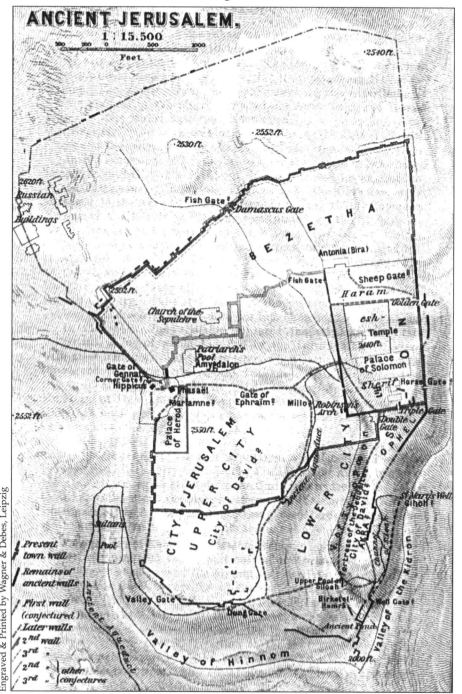

ANCIENT JERUSALEM.

1 : 15.500

Feet

·2540 ft.

·2552 ft.

·2530 ft.

·2620 ft.
Russian
Buildings

Fish Gate?

Damascus Gate

B E Z E T H A

Antonia (Bira)

·2590 ft.

Fish Gate

Sheep Gate?

H a r a m

Golden Gate

Church of the
Sepulchre

esh -

Temple
zion

Patriarch's
Pool
Amygdalon

Palace
of Solomon

Gate of
Gennath
Corner Gate?
Hippicus

Sherif

Horse Gate

Phasael
Mariamne?

Gate of
Ephraim?

Millo?

Robinson's
Arch

Triple Gate

·2552 ft.

Palace
of Herod

·2550 ft.

C I T Y   O F   J E R U S A L E M
U P P E R   C I T Y
City   of   David?

Double
Gate

L O W E R   C I T Y
City of David
ACRA

O P H E L

Fortress of the Jebusites

St Mary's Well
Gihon

Sultan's
Pool

Valley Gate

Dung Gate

Upper Pool of
Siloah

Birket el
Hamra

Ancient Pool

Well Gate?

·2100 ft.

Valley   of   Hinnom

Valley   of   the   Kidron

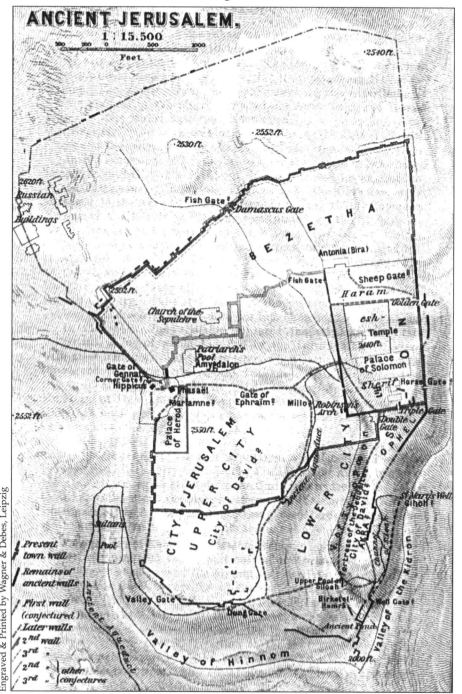

Present
town wall
Remains of
ancient walls
First wall
(conjectured)
Later walls
2nd wall
3rd "
2nd "
3rd " } other
conjectures

Engraved & Printed by Wagner & Debes, Leipzig

# FAITH IN ACTION:
# INVITING OTHERS TO CHRIST

During this quarter we will see how people responded to Jesus. "Everyone [was] searching" for Jesus, including a leper, according to Mark 1:35-45. A Gentile woman of Syrophoenicia begged Jesus to free her daughter of the demons that bound her. People of all stripes came to Jesus, even a rich man, though Mark 10:17-31 reports that he turned away from Jesus because he was unwilling to part with his possessions.

Jesus offered healing and wholeness to those who would follow him. As the church, the body of Christ, we too offer an invitation to all people to come to Jesus. Discuss these questions with the class or assign questions to small groups to discern how your congregation is inviting others to Christ and welcoming them into the covenant community.

(1) Do we intentionally let the neighborhood know who we are and why we exist? Do our members invite new residents to attend? Do we advertise our services and activities in the local media? Are our children and youth encouraged to invite friends from school to join them on Sunday?

(2) Does our building seem welcoming to people? Are entrances and rooms well marked? Are there ramps, elevators, or other means of including those who have mobility issues? Is our sound system adequate even for parishioners with hearing impairments? Do we have large-print bulletins and hymnals for those who are visually impaired?

(3) Do our greeters, ushers, and all members welcome others and make them feel at home? Do members speak to visitors, introduce them to others, and include them in conversations? Do we invite visitors to Sunday school and other activities? Do we ask for contact information so that we can get in touch during the week?

(4) Do we encourage newcomers to become active in the covenant community? Does the leadership of the church welcome new members and find meaningful roles for them to play on committees? Do our choirs, ushers, and other small groups welcome those who come?

(5) Do the ministries we engage in enrich and excite people? In other words, do others see us as a vibrant faith community or as one focused on survival? Are we reaching out to serve others, or reaching inward just to keep the doors open? Do our ministries include people of all ages? Do they include people from any ethnic, educational, or socioeconomic group that chooses to come?

(6) Do we encourage our pastor(s) to preach biblically based sermons that challenge us to be an empowered covenant community? Do we support our clergy in other ways that are obvious even to newcomers?

(7) Do our members live as Spirit-empowered disciples who bear fruit for the kingdom of God? Where do you see evidence of this kind of covenantal living in your faith community? How can you affirm the benefits of this fruit?

Invite the groups to report on their findings if you chose that option. Based on this information, encourage the class to begin to discern ways that it can help the church continue to become the kind of covenant community to which people will be attracted.

## UNIT 1: LEADERS IN THE COVENANT COMMUNITY
# JOSHUA: A LEADER FOR THE PEOPLE

---

### PREVIEWING THE LESSON

**Lesson Scripture:** Joshua 1:1-11, 16-17
**Background Scripture:** Joshua 1
**Key Verse:** Joshua 1:9

### Focus of the Lesson:
In the midst of change and uncertainty, we need leaders who can guide us in the right direction. What are the characteristics of such leaders? Joshua, who succeeded Moses, was a strong, courageous leader whose obedience to God enabled the people to cross the Jordan into the Promised Land.

### Goals for the Learners:
(1) to discover God's directions and promises to Joshua.
(2) to identify characteristics that make them effective leaders of God's people.
(3) to commit themselves to support their current church leaders and cultivate their own leadership traits.

### Pronunciation Guide:
Euphrates (yoo fray' teez)
Hittite (hit' tite)
Manasseh (muh nas' uh)

### Supplies:
Bibles, newsprint and marker, paper and pencils, hymnals

---

### READING THE SCRIPTURE

NRSV
Joshua 1:1-11, 16-17
¹After the death of Moses the servant of the LORD, the LORD spoke to Joshua son of

NIV
Joshua 1:1-11, 16-17
¹After the death of Moses the servant of the LORD, the LORD said to Joshua son of

Nun, Moses' assistant, saying, [2]"My servant Moses is dead. Now proceed to cross the Jordan, you and all this people, into the land that I am giving to them, to the Israelites. [3]Every place that the sole of your foot will tread upon I have given to you, as I promised to Moses. [4]From the wilderness and the Lebanon as far as the great river, the river Euphrates, all the land of the Hittites, to the Great Sea in the west shall be your territory. [5]No one shall be able to stand against you all the days of your life. As I was with Moses, so I will be with you; I will not fail you or forsake you. [6]Be strong and courageous; for you shall put this people in possession of the land that I swore to their ancestors to give them. [7]Only be strong and very courageous, being careful to act in accordance with all the law that my servant Moses commanded you; do not turn from it to the right hand or to the left, so that you may be successful wherever you go. [8]This book of the law shall not depart out of your mouth; you shall meditate on it day and night, so that you may be careful to act in accordance with all that is written in it. For then you shall make your way prosperous, and then you shall be successful. [9]**I hereby command you: Be strong and courageous; do not be frightened or dismayed, for the LORD your God is with you wherever you go."**

[10]Then Joshua commanded the officers of the people, [11]"Pass through the camp, and command the people: 'Prepare your provisions; for in three days you are to cross over the Jordan, to go in to take possession of the land that the LORD your God gives you to possess.'"

[16]They answered Joshua: "All that you have commanded us we will do, and wherever you send us we will go. [17]Just as we obeyed Moses in all things, so we will obey you. Only may the LORD your God be with you, as he was with Moses!"

Nun, Moses' aide: [2]"Moses my servant is dead. Now then, you and all these people, get ready to cross the Jordan River into the land I am about to give to them—to the Israelites. [3]I will give you every place where you set your foot, as I promised Moses. [4]Your territory will extend from the desert to Lebanon, and from the great river, the Euphrates—all the Hittite country—to the Great Sea on the west. [5]No one will be able to stand up against you all the days of your life. As I was with Moses, so I will be with you; I will never leave you nor forsake you.

[6]"Be strong and courageous, because you will lead these people to inherit the land I swore to their forefathers to give them. [7]Be strong and very courageous. Be careful to obey all the law my servant Moses gave you; do not turn from it to the right or to the left, that you may be successful wherever you go. [8]Do not let this Book of the Law depart from your mouth; meditate on it day and night, so that you may be careful to do everything written in it. Then you will be prosperous and successful. [9]**Have I not commanded you? Be strong and courageous. Do not be terrified; do not be discouraged, for the LORD your God will be with you wherever you go."**

[10]So Joshua ordered the officers of the people: [11]"Go through the camp and tell the people, 'Get your supplies ready. Three days from now you will cross the Jordan here to go in and take possession of the land the LORD your God is giving you for your own.'"

[16]Then they answered Joshua, "Whatever you have commanded us we will do, and wherever you send us we will go. [17]Just as we fully obeyed Moses, so we will obey you. Only may the LORD your God be with you as he was with Moses."

## UNDERSTANDING THE SCRIPTURE

**Joshua 1:1.** The Book of Joshua begins with the significant phrase, "After the death of Moses . . ." (1:1). In these few words, we are reminded of two key elements that set the text for Joshua's call.

First, the people who have wandered in the wilderness for so long have just lost their most significant leader. Moses was the one through whom God acted to bring them out of Egypt; Moses was the one who met God on the mountain of Sinai and brought down the law; and Moses was the one who guided them each step of the way to their new home. Later scriptures would honor Moses as "unequaled for all the signs and wonders that the LORD sent him to perform . . . and for all the mighty deeds and all the terrifying displays of power that [he] performed in the sight of all Israel" (Deuteronomy 34:11-12).

At the same time, we need also to remember that Moses was far from perfect. In fact, God had denied Moses entry into the land because of an event that happened during the wilderness wanderings (Numbers 20:1-13). At one point when the people were rebellious due to thirst, Moses and his brother Aaron sought relief from God. Moses then failed to follow God's instructions to the letter. Water came from a rock as God intended, but under circumstances that could be attributed to Moses' action rather than God's miraculous intervention. For this, God declared that Moses would not cross the Jordan. Unfortunately, neither would the adult generation of the people that left Egypt. As a result of their disobedience, they had been denied that privilege, too.

So, ironically, while the people mourn the death of Moses, that event also signals a cause for celebration—they can enter the land at last. Joshua had been commissioned by Moses himself to be the one to lead the people forward on this final stage of their journey (Deuteronomy 34:9).

Thus, Joshua 1:1 establishes that Joshua has the hard task of following an extraordinary predecessor *and* that both God and Moses considered him able to do so. This confidence is affirmed by the author of the book, who refers to Joshua as Moses' "assistant" (NRSV) or "aide" (NIV). Joshua had been under Moses' direct training for some time, handling the spiritual and legal affairs of the people on that great man's behalf, so that he can feel better equipped to say yes now that God's call has come.

**Joshua 1:2-9.** God's call to Joshua harkens back to Moses fairly often. It is as if God is aware of the grief and uncertainty caused by the death, and God wants to help Joshua now step into his new leadership role. God begins with the acknowledgement, "My servant Moses is dead" (1:2); in other words, he is telling Joshua clearly that now is the time for action. God also reassures Joshua that the promise made to Moses will be kept (1:3) and that God will be with Joshua as with Moses (1:5).

In exchange, God asks Joshua to be diligent in keeping the law that was entrusted to Moses (1:7), and to help the people stay faithful as well. The "book of the law" (1:8) they are to follow probably refers to Deuteronomy (see Deuteronomy 31:24-26). This obedience, which is all God asks, is critically important. The people's success in the land will depend on it.

Taken together, these verses help us see the outline of a covenant agreement between God and Joshua. The covenant is not formally ratified, but its terms are clear. God is offering Joshua the same covenant relationship that Moses once had—a precious commodity for this new leader!

That promise made to Moses includes establishing the people within the land. Notice how carefully the borders of the land are described and how surprising some of them are. These boundaries include the wilderness of Sinai to the south, the mountain range of Lebanon to the north, the Euphrates River to the east, and the Mediterranean Sea to the west. While historical Israel never occupied an area this large, the boundaries reflect a tradition that David's territory reached these points (see 2 Samuel 8:3, for example). They also anticipate a day when David's kingdom will be restored and established forever—the theological point being that the future event stretches back beyond David to promises made to Joshua, Moses, and Abraham (see Genesis 12:1-3).

God tells Joshua to "be strong and courageous" (1:6, 7, 9), rather than "frightened and dismayed" (1:9). This encouragement echoes the first account of Joshua's commissioning, found in Deuteronomy 31:1-8, where the same phrases occur.

**Joshua 1:10-15.** Joshua responds to God's call with obedient action. He sends his officers throughout the camp with word that the people are to prepare to enter Canaan in three days' time. Special provision is made for the tribes of Reuben and Gad and half the tribe of Manasseh because their promised territory lies "beyond the Jordan" (1:14)—that is, on the east side of the Jordan, rather than on the west side with the other tribes. Following the details of an agreement made between these tribes and Moses (Numbers 32), Joshua agrees that their wives, children, and cattle can stay on the eastern side in relative safety if the warriors agree to help the other Israelites fight for the land west of the Jordan. Once the west side is secured, these men will be allowed to go back home to their families.

**Joshua 1:16-18.** The folk of the eastern (or Transjordan) tribes agree. Moreover, they promise to obey Joshua completely, just as they had Moses. In this way, they affirm Joshua's authority as their new leader. They also echo the language of Joshua's call, thus emphasizing the trust that God will be with him and the need for him to be strong and courageous.

## INTERPRETING THE SCRIPTURE

### Joshua's Challenge

Have you ever thought about how hard it is for a new pastor to come to a congregation that has enjoyed a long-term relationship with a beloved minister? No matter how skilled he or she is, there will inevitably be a comparison to the treasured predecessor. Over time, of course, this changes (at least in healthy congregations), but it can make the first few years of a ministry quite challenging. Still, this in nothing compared to what Joshua faced.

In this opening lesson for the quarter, we find Joshua presented with the difficult task of following a leader *par excellence*. He had been trained by Moses and affirmed as someone who followed God's laws, but it is hard to imagine that he truly felt up to the task at hand. After all, he is now the one expected to lead the people across a river into hostile territory in hopes of establishing a home there. Stepping back and looking at the bigger theological picture, he is the one entrusted to fulfill the promise made to Abraham back in Genesis 12, *and* he is the one to whom God looks to keep the people on track spiritually as well as geographically. Even Moses himself had failed in this particular leadership role from time to time. How is someone who is *not* Moses ever supposed to do it?

### God's Promises

In examining Joshua as a faithful participant in God's covenant, we may at first assume that he represents a level of leadership that few of us could ever attain. After all, his character was forged during many years of wandering in the wilderness, and he had served as an apprentice leader to no less a person than Moses himself. Who among us can boast a resumé like that?

Nevertheless, there is much in Joshua's call that applies to us all. Notice, for example, that the passage begins with God's promises rather than with Joshua's credentials. The starting place for each of us lies in God's willingness and ability to work through us, not in any particular confidence that we may have in ourselves.

Notice also the nature of the promises that God makes. First is the guarantee that what God intends to be achieved *will* be achieved. Joshua is invited to be a participant in helping God's plan be realized, but the text leaves no doubt that the actual power at work is God's and God's alone.

Second, God promises to be with Joshua throughout the journey to come. No doubt Joshua felt overwhelmed by the loss of Moses and the tasks that lay ahead, but God makes it clear that there is a spiritual support network in place to help this new leader get through it all. "I will not fail you or forsake you," says God in verse 5. Other ways of translating this Hebrew text reflect language that we might associate with a parent reassuring a young child:

- "I will not leave or abandon you."
- "I will not drop you (meaning, I will keep holding you in my arms)."
- "I will not relax my attention to you."

God promises to be consistently (and persistently!) present and attentive, never leaving Joshua to feel left alone or neglected.

In light of these revelations, any hesitation that Joshua might have felt concerning his own ability to accomplish God's ends is irrelevant—and so it is with us. When God calls us to join in holy work, whatever it may be, we carry with us these same two reassuring promises: (1) that the accomplishment of God's goals rests on God's power and not our own, and (2) that God will be right beside us, helping and guiding, every step of the way.

*Rising to the Call*

Although reminding ourselves of God's promises is certainly the best way to begin any response to a call to God's service, the Bible never pretends that following through on a call is easy. Indeed, God's speech to Joshua anticipates one of the major difficulties that leaders face within the faith community.

Three times God lifts up to Joshua the need to "be strong and courageous" in the days ahead (see 1:6, 7, 9). It is as if God is warning Joshua that some days this will be a challenge! Indeed, verse 9 anticipates there will be times when Joshua might be inclined to give up, feeling less than adequate to the task at hand. The Hebrew of this verse indicates that terror and dread, coupled with a sense of being emotionally shattered, are possible outcomes if Joshua does not maintain his grounding in God.

Given this, we might wonder why Joshua would commit to following through with this call to serve as a leader of God's people in such a difficult time. The answer might lie in the language of the charge itself to "be strong and courageous." Taken together in all their levels of meaning, the two verbs indicate a process: Joshua is to *become* strong and courageous by holding fast to his trust in God and acting in that trust. In other words, it is through the practice—the spiritual discipline, we might say—of actively trusting God that Joshua will grow in the strength and courage necessary to do as God asks.

For those of us who strive to be loyal participants in God's covenant today, this is an important insight. Faithful disciples are not necessarily strong or courageous people. The mark of a faithful disciple is, instead, a willingness to trust God and to keep working toward God's goals despite fear of failure or doubts about one's personal abilities.

*What More Can We Do?*

Given the above insights from the text, what clues to do we see for actions we can put into practice?

First, Joshua's story challenges us to accept God's call to leadership, whenever and however it may come to us, despite any insecurities we may feel as to our own abilities. The text assures us that we are never alone when we serve God in this way, for God journeys with us and provides what we need.

Beyond this, however, God's speech in the text suggests that all leaders face times of doubt or discouragement. Surely those who serve on your church's governing board, those who serve as teachers, and those who serve as leaders in other ways—even as pastor—worry occasionally about being up to the task. There are times they must wonder if they are doing enough or if they are making a difference as God intends.

So, Joshua's story reminds us that we have a ministry in caring for those who lead and serve us. We can help those who lead us to "be strong and courageous" by encouraging them through acknowledgements of their service and by expressing our thanks. Think about sending a card or even an e-mail to your lay and clergy leaders, or just taking a moment to say "You're appreciated!" when passing by them in a hallway. Our support and gratitude, shared openly and generously, is perhaps the best gift we can give to those who lead us in faithful response to God's covenant call.

---

# SHARING THE SCRIPTURE

*Preparing Our Hearts*

Meditate on this week's devotional reading, found in 1 Timothy 2:1-6. In these instructions regarding prayer, we are told in verse 2 to pray for "all who are in high positions." Notice that the reason that we are to uphold these leaders is "so that we may lead a quiet and peaceable life in all godliness and dignity" (1:2). Add the names of political, business, civic, and church leaders to your prayer list. Lift these individuals up to God on a regular basis.

Pray that you and the adult learners will recognize the importance of praying for your leaders and do so as often as possible.

*Preparing Our Minds*

Study the background scripture from Joshua 1 and the lesson scripture from Joshua 1:1-11, 16-17. As you read, consider the characteristics of leaders who can guide us in the right direction.

Write on newsprint:
❑ traits listed under "Identify Characteristics That Make the Learners Effective Leaders of God's People"
❑ information for next week's lesson, found under "Continue the Journey."
❑ activities for further spiritual growth in "Continue the Journey."

Read the "Introduction," "The Big Picture" and "Faith in Action" articles for this quarter, which immediately precede this lesson. Note that the map for Close-up, which also precedes this lesson, will help you with the lesson for September 27. Decide how you will use the information from these supplemental resources as you lead this quarter's sessions.

## LEADING THE CLASS

*(1) Gather to Learn*

❖ Welcome the class members and introduce any guests.

❖ Pray that those who have gathered today will be ready to hear and heed God's word for them.

❖ Share with the class the comparison Andrew Roberts makes between two leaders during World War II: Adolph Hitler, whose leadership style Roberts asserts is "charismatic" and Winston Churchill, whose style is "inspirational" (http://www.bbc.co.uk/history/worldwars/wwtwo/hitler_churchill_03.shtml). **"Churchill was the model of the inspirational politician, not the charismatic one. . . . Of the two men, Hitler was actually kinder to his immediate staff than Churchill was to his. . . . Churchill was loved by his staff because he was 'saving civilisation', not because of his off-hand way of treating them. . . . Although Hitler might have been a better people-manager in some ways, his tendency to attempt to micro-manage the Third Reich once the war broke out led directly to his downfall. . . . Churchill did the absolute opposite. . . . Once the war was underway he managed to concentrate on the bigger picture. . . ."**

❖ Ask: **What aspects of this description challenge your beliefs about good leaders? What aspects affirm your beliefs?**

❖ Read aloud today's focus statement: **In the midst of change and uncertainty, we need leaders who can guide us in the right direction. What are the characteristics of such leaders? Joshua, who succeeded Moses, was a strong, courageous leader whose obedience to God enabled the people to cross the Jordan into the Promised Land.**

*(2) Discover God's Directions
and Promises to Joshua*

❖ Choose two volunteers, one to read Joshua 1:1-11 and the other to read Joshua 1:16-17.

❖ Ask these questions:
   **(1) What kinds of concerns do you think Joshua would have had?**
   **(2) How might God address these**

**concerns?** (See "God's Promises" and "Rising to the Call" in Interpreting the Scripture).
   **(3) How did the people affirm God's call of Joshua?**
   **(4) In what ways do you affirm the call of God's leaders—both lay and clergy—within your congregation?**

*(3) Identify Characteristics That Make the Learners Effective Leaders of God's People*

❖ Post these traits of effective leaders of God's people, which have been gathered from many sources. Distribute paper and pencils and ask the students to write the traits from this list that they think they possess. They may have other traits to add.
   ■ Has a personal relationship with Jesus Christ
   ■ Courageous
   ■ Dependable
   ■ Decisive
   ■ Enthusiastic
   ■ Has a clear sense of justice
   ■ Is able to promote a vision
   ■ Can make others feel important
   ■ Knows how to listen
   ■ Willing to encourage others
   ■ Knowledgeable
   ■ Takes initiative
   ■ Follows the golden rule

❖ Ask the adults to talk with a small group about the traits they have identified and listed. Encourage the students to affirm each other's gifts.

❖ **Option:** Omit the personal lists, if the class members know each other well. Instead, ask them to call out the names of class members who demonstrate a particular trait. List the names beside the traits on newsprint. Likely, the adults will be able to see that the class has all of these traits, although not every individual may have each one.

❖ Conclude by discussing these questions:

(1) Given the needs in our congregation for leadership, and given the number of leadership traits we have represented in our class, why do you think many people are unwilling to assume leadership roles?

(2) What clues does Joshua's story give us for helping those who are reluctant take on leadership responsibilities?

*(4) Commit to Supporting the Learners' Church Leaders and Cultivate Their Own Leadership Traits*

❖ Read aloud "What More Can We Do?" from Interpreting the Scripture.

❖ Distribute paper and pencils if you have not already done so. Challenge the students to list at least one way they will try to support your pastor and other church leaders. Also challenge them to identify and write one way that they will use their own leadership talents in God's service within the next month.

❖ Close this portion by asking the students to read to each other today's key verse, Joshua 1:9, as a word of encouragement.

*(5) Continue the Journey*

❖ Pray that today's participants will recognize their own gifts for leadership and boldly answer God's call for service when they hear it.

❖ Read aloud this preparation for next week's lesson. You may also want to post it on newsprint for the students to copy.

■ Title: Gideon: A Deliverer for the People

■ Background Scripture: Judges 6–8

■ Lesson Scripture: Judges 6:1-3, 7-14

■ Focus of the Lesson: When situations seem hopeless, we assume there is nothing we can do. How can we face threats to our well-being—even our very existence—with confidence? The story of Gideon, the self-described weakest member of the weakest family in Israel, demonstrates that God calls and equips ordinary people to bring about extraordinary changes.

❖ Challenge the students to complete one or more of these activities for further spiritual growth, which you will write on newsprint for the students to copy.

(1) Write a note to your pastor or another church leader this week affirming his or her gifts and graces for leadership. Give an example of how this leadership has had a positive impact on your faith journey.

(2) Research some cults, such as those of Jim Jones of the People's Temple or David Koresh of the Branch Davidians. Ponder why people may be so mesmerized by a leader that they are willing to commit suicide at their leader's command. What criteria do you have for determining how much loyalty you will give to a leader?

(3) Recall that Moses had mentored Joshua long before he was entrusted with the leadership of the people. Whom can you mentor to step into a leadership role you have? Contact this person and see how you can work together.

❖ Sing or read aloud "Be Still, My Soul."

❖ Conclude today's session by leading the class in this benediction, based on 1 Peter 2:9: Go forth with the assurance that you are part of "a chosen race, a royal priesthood, a holy nation, God's own people, in order that you may proclaim the mighty acts of him who called you out of darkness into his marvelous light."

UNIT 1: LEADERS IN THE COVENANT COMMUNITY

# GIDEON: A DELIVERER FOR THE PEOPLE

## PREVIEWING THE LESSON

**Lesson Scripture:** Judges 6:1-3, 7-14
**Background Scripture:** Judges 6–8
**Key Verse:** Judges 6:14

### Focus of the Lesson:
When situations seem hopeless, we assume there is nothing we can do. How can we face threats to our well-being—even our very existence—with confidence? The story of Gideon, the self-described weakest member of the weakest family in Israel, demonstrates that God calls and equips ordinary people to bring about extraordinary changes.

### Goals for the Learners:
(1) to explore the account of Gideon, a judge (military leader) whom God raised up to defeat the Midianite oppressors of the Israelites.
(2) to identify ways God can work through seemingly unlikely people to accomplish great things.
(3) to answer God's call.

### Pronunciation Guide:
Abiezrite (ay bi ez' rite)            Midianite (mid' ee uh nite)
Amalekite (uh mal' uh kite)           Ophrah (of' ruh)
Amorite (am' uh rite)                 Oreb (or' eb)
Asherah (uh shiyhr' uh)               Penuel (peh nyoo uhl)
Baal (bay' uhl) or (bah ahl')         Succoth (suhk' uhth)
ephod (ee' fod)                       Zalmunna (zal muhn' uh)
Ephraim (ee' fray im)                 Zebah (zee' buh)
Jerrubaal (ji ruhb bay' uhl)          Zeeb (zee' uhb)
Joash (joh' ash)

### Supplies:
Bibles, newsprint and marker, paper and pencils, hymnals

## READING THE SCRIPTURE

NRSV
Judges 6:1-3, 7-14

[1]The Israelites did what was evil in the sight of the LORD, and the LORD gave them into the hand of Midian seven years. [2]The hand of Midian prevailed over Israel; and because of Midian the Israelites provided for themselves hiding places in the mountains, caves and strongholds. [3]For whenever the Israelites put in seed, the Midianites and the Amalekites and the people of the east would come up against them.

[7]When the Israelites cried to the LORD on account of the Midianites, [8]the LORD sent a prophet to the Israelites; and he said to them, "Thus says the LORD, the God of Israel: I led you up from Egypt, and brought you out of the house of slavery; [9]and I delivered you from the hand of the Egyptians, and from the hand of all who oppressed you, and drove them out before you, and gave you their land; [10]and I said to you, 'I am the LORD your God; you shall not pay reverence to the gods of the Amorites, in whose land you live.' But you have not given heed to my voice."

[11]Now the angel of the LORD came and sat under the oak at Ophrah, which belonged to Joash the Abiezrite, as his son Gideon was beating out wheat in the wine press, to hide it from the Midianites. [12]The angel of the LORD appeared to him and said to him, "The LORD is with you, you mighty warrior." [13]Gideon answered him, "But sir, if the LORD is with us, why then has all this happened to us? And where are all his wonderful deeds that our ancestors recounted to us, saying, 'Did not the LORD bring us up from Egypt?' But now the LORD has cast us off, and given us into the hand of Midian." **[14]Then the LORD turned to him and said, "Go in this might of yours and deliver Israel from the hand of Midian; I hereby commission you."**

NIV
Judges 6:1-3, 7-14

[1]Again the Israelites did evil in the eyes of the LORD, and for seven years he gave them into the hands of the Midianites. [2]Because the power of Midian was so oppressive, the Israelites prepared shelters for themselves in mountain clefts, caves and strongholds. [3]Whenever the Israelites planted their crops, the Midianites, Amalekites and other eastern peoples invaded the country.

[7]When the Israelites cried to the LORD because of Midian, [8]he sent them a prophet, who said, "This is what the LORD, the God of Israel, says: I brought you up out of Egypt, out of the land of slavery. [9]I snatched you from the power of Egypt and from the hand of all your oppressors. I drove them from before you and gave you their land. [10]I said to you, 'I am the LORD your God; do not worship the gods of the Amorites, in whose land you live.' But you have not listened to me."

[11]The angel of the LORD came and sat down under the oak in Ophrah that belonged to Joash the Abiezrite, where his son Gideon was threshing wheat in a winepress to keep it from the Midianites. [12]When the angel of the LORD appeared to Gideon, he said, "The LORD is with you, mighty warrior."

[13]"But sir," Gideon replied, "if the LORD is with us, why has all this happened to us? Where are all his wonders that our fathers told us about when they said, 'Did not the LORD bring us up out of Egypt?' But now the LORD has abandoned us and put us into the hand of Midian."

**[14]The LORD turned to him and said, "Go in the strength you have and save Israel out of Midian's hand. Am I not sending you?"**

## UNDERSTANDING THE SCRIPTURE

**Judges 6:1-10.** Gideon's call follows a pattern that runs throughout the Book of Judges. The cycle is: (1) the people turn away from God, (2) after God removes divine protection, the people suffer at the hands of other groups, (3) the people cry to God for help, and (4) God sends a warrior-hero to save them. Usually the people then live for some years of peace before the cycle starts all over.

In this case, the people have been under regular attack for some years, especially at planting and harvest times, from three named groups. First are the Midianites, whose territory was south of Canaan, perhaps in the Sinai Peninsula or northwestern Arabia. These folk were descendants of Abraham (Genesis 25:2-4), and Moses' father-in-law Jethro was a priest of Midian. The Amalekites, descended from Esau (Genesis 36:12), were a nomadic tribe with a long history of conflict with the Israelites (see Numbers 14:42-45; 1 Samuel 15:2). The people of the East are seen as a general enemy in certain prophetic books (Isaiah 11:14; Jeremiah 49:28; Ezekiel 25:1-10).

After years of having their food supply destroyed, Israel cries out to God for help. God then sends a prophet to remind the people of how they have deserted their Lord despite all that God has done for them in the past.

**Judges 6:11-16.** The text moves quickly from the people's inexcusable behavior to God's mercy. The "angel of the LORD" goes to deliver Gideon's call personally.

**Judges 6:17-24.** Gideon does not agree immediately to God's call. First he asks for proof of the identity of the stranger before him. Gideon prepares a meal offering and becomes convinced when the food is consumed by a sudden flame from a rock and the mysterious stranger disappears. At this point, Gideon becomes afraid, but God reassures him. He then builds an altar to God on the spot.

**Judges 6:25-32.** Gideon's first task is to tear down sacred symbols of the fertility gods Baal and Asherah that his father had put up. He does so secretly at night, out of fear of the reaction of his family and the townspeople. The next day, the people discover he is the culprit and demand his death. Gideon's father, Joash, stands by him, though, and defends him against the crowd. The actions of that day lead to Gideon receiving the nickname of Jerubbaal, which means "let Baal fight with him."

**Judges 6:33-40.** When the enemies of Israel amass for another attack, Gideon calls various tribes to fight with him. For two nights before the attack, he tests God by asking for miraculous signs of a guaranteed victory. The first night, a sheepskin is soaked in dew while the ground stays dry. Needing more reassurance, Gideon asks for the opposite on the next night. The ground is wet but the skin is dry, so Gideon agrees to go forward with the attack.

**Judges 7:1-25.** In order to leave no doubt as to the source of the impending victory, God tells Gideon to reduce the troop numbers by letting the fearful go home. According to verse 3, only 10,000 of the original 32,000 remain. God then reduces this number through another weeding process: All the men are to drink at a stream, but only those who drink a certain way are to stay. With only three hundred men left, there will be no doubt that any victory comes at the hand of God (7:7).

To bolster Gideon's confidence, God sends him to the enemy camp to overhear an account of a dream that predicts a Midianite defeat. Fortified by this news, Gideon worships God and then devises a clever and deceptive plan of attack. He and his men surround the Midianite camp in the middle of the night and shock the enemy out of sleep by smashing jars, blowing trumpets, and holding torches high.

Disoriented and confused, the Midianites believe themselves to be outnumbered so they run. Gideon's men are able to hunt down and kill most of them. The defeat of two key Midianite military leaders, Oreb and Zeeb, by the warriors of Ephraim seals the victory (7:25).

**Judges 8:1-3.** The tribe of Ephraim complains about not being invited to the main fight. Peace is restored, however, when Gideon points out the significance of their killing the main Midianite captains.

**Judges 8:4-17.** Joshua then leads his troops across the Jordan to the east to continue pursuit of the Midianites. Two towns, Succoth and Penuel, refuse to give food or rest to his troops, yet the exhausted warriors are able to defeat their remaining enemies in an ambush. Gideon chases and captures the two Midianite kings, after which he returns to Succoth and Penuel to punish the people there for their lack of aid.

**Judges 8:18-21.** For the first time, we learn that Gideon may have a personal motive for his actions: the two Midianite kings, Zebah and Zalmunna, had killed his brothers at Mount Tabor (see 4:6). Gideon then orders his young son to kill the two, but the boy is afraid. No longer hesitant to act himself, Gideon performs the deed.

**Judges 8:22-28.** The Israelites beg Gideon to become their king, but he refuses on the basis that God alone is the people's ruler. This does not stop Gideon from taking a nice reward, though—the gold earrings of the defeated enemy, as well as the clothing and other items of the two kings. Gideon then melted the earrings down and made an ephod. Exactly what this term means is unclear. In later Judaism, an ephod is part of the priestly vestments, but here it seems to be an idol or image of some kind. In any event, it becomes a source of idolatry for Gideon, his family, and his town, which is an ironic end to the life of a man who started his call by tearing down an altar to Baal.

**Judges 8:29-35.** The account of Gideon's life ends with a mention of his sons and record of his death and burial. Not surprisingly, we then read of the people's rapid return to Baal worship. This starts the next phase of the cycle that runs throughout Judges of apostasy, punishment, and eventual deliverance.

---

## INTERPRETING THE SCRIPTURE

### *Understanding the Text*

This week we read about Gideon and his call to leadership. The call is unexpected, both because it comes in an unusual way and because Gideon himself is a somewhat unlikely hero. This latter detail, however, brings home a significant point: God calls ordinary people to do extraordinary things.

Gideon's story is set in a particular context designed to heighten the unusual aspect of his selection by God. The immediate setting is a time of war, and the larger context establishes this theologically as part of God's ongoing attempt to engage the people in a covenant relationship.

Judges 6:1-3 describe the immediate situation. For seven years Israel has been at the mercy of the Midianites and other peoples who live to the east. These roving armies come primarily in the spring, when the planting and harvest take place, because that is when roads are most passable—and because disrupting Israel's food supply is one way to weaken them further. Finding themselves outmatched militarily, the Israelites have resorted to hiding in rough territory where it is hard for armies to follow or to conduct extensive searches.

When the people call out for divine deliverance (6:7), God sends a prophet to remind the people of what led to these circumstances. The prophet's message, recorded in verses 8-10, establishes the larger theological context for what comes next.

Following a pattern that runs throughout the Book of Judges, we see that the people had fallen into sinful ways and deserted God. This, in turn, led God to withdraw all divine protection, allowing the people to become prey to their neighbors. After a period of suffering and oppression, they have now cried out to God for help. As before, God will now raise up someone to save the people so they can have peace and prosperity again—at least until the cycle starts all over. The leaders described as "judges" functioned more like military leaders in times of crisis. The full meaning of the term in the Book of Judges is more like "deliverer" or "savior," in the sense of one who rescues another.

This brings us to the call of the current hero-to-be, Gideon. Alone among all the "judges," his call comes from the lips of an angel. Much later, an angel will appear to the mother of Samson to alert her to her son's special call, but Samson himself does not encounter this divine being.

Like angels elsewhere in the Hebrew Bible, this messenger resembles a human male so closely that Gideon does not know the difference at first. The angel is also identified so strongly with the presence of God that the text, confusingly to modern minds, refers to this being as "the LORD" in verse 14. We are not to become bogged down in logical paradoxes. The text merely wants to make clear that Gideon's call is directly from God and is not to be disputed as such.

### An Odd Choice

One might assume that the role of God's angel is to convince us, the audience, of the validity of Gideon's call, but the text itself suggests another possibility. More than any other judge, Gideon seems initially less suitable and less inclined to serve. Perhaps the presence of the angel was to ensure that Gideon would not shake off the call by convincing himself that it was not real.

The irony of God's selection of Gideon runs throughout verses 11-14. The angel addresses our hero-elect as "you mighty warrior" (6:12) while he is in the midst of the mundane task of threshing wheat at a place carefully chosen to keep him away from the danger of a Midianite attack. Although threshing was normally done on a hard surface at the top of a hill to catch the breeze, Gideon is in a winepress—a cave-like depression carved out of the side of a rock.

If we read slightly further, into verse 15, we see why Gideon is taking these precautions, and even more why he is an unlikely leader for God's people at this time. "My clan is the weakest in Manasseh," he declares, "and I am the least in my family."

Yet, God's plan for Gideon encompasses even this. "Go with what strength you have," says God in essence, "and leave the rest to me." Clearly the importance of trusting God, discussed in the lesson for September 6, takes on added significance for those of us who start out with limited resources and reserves!

### People Like Us

The church is largely composed of ordinary people just like Gideon—people whose families are not rich or powerful, people who spend large parts of each day trying to get the basics accomplished without drawing undue trouble to themselves, and people who are certainly not expecting a sudden divine call to a difficult task. Yet it is to this group of ordinary people that God turns, time and again, with the invitation to take part in God's plans.

In Gideon's story, we are reminded that our call to serve God is not about us per se. It is about God's ability to work in and through us in spite of, and even *because of* who we are. By working through ordinary folk like us, God's power and grace become unmistakable. As the apostle Paul so beautifully put it: "We have this treasure in clay jars, so that it may be made clear that this extraordinary power belongs to God and does not come from us" (2 Corinthians 4:7).

I am reminded of a very tiny urban church that received an extraordinary call, much as Gideon did. They were on the verge of closing the church doors: the youngest of their twelve members was in her sixties, there was little money for a pastor and less for upkeep on the aging building, and no one felt capable of dealing with the increased violence of their changing neighborhood. Then one day an angel came with a message from God.

In this case, the angel was their new pastor, who had a vision and a dream for that little church. Like Gideon, the people at first thought there must be some mistake, and they insisted on signs from God as verification this call was real. Those signs came, and with some fear and trembling the congregation set out to do what God was asking of them.

Today, ten years later, that little church has close to seventy members, two pastors, and a restored building that is designated as a historical landmark. What matters to them, however, is that they also have several vital programs that are essential to supporting families (and especially children) in their neighborhood, and each year they are adding more.

Ten years ago, God said to this little church, "Go in this might of yours and deliver the people of your neighborhood from the hand of despair; I hereby commission you." They answered this call and are at it still. During this time, they have become the last remaining mainline congregation in their area, but they mean to stay. They have discovered what Gideon learned: that when the power of God is behind what we do, miracles are bound to happen. Knowing this, when God calls, how can we say no?

---

## SHARING THE SCRIPTURE

### Preparing Our Hearts

Meditate on this week's devotional reading, found in 1 Corinthians 1:26-31. Here Paul explains that God calls the "foolish" (1:27) and "weak" (1:27) to fulfill God's purposes. As we will see in today's lesson, Gideon certainly fits that description. How about you? What has God called you to do? If you are able to do it in your own power, ponder whether or not God has really called you to that specific task. If, however, you need to rely on the power of the Holy Spirit to do the job, then God has likely called you in your weakness and endowed you with power from on high.

Pray that you and the adult learners will continue to listen for God's call and be ready to serve, especially in those challenging situations where you know that you cannot undertake the task in your own power.

### Preparing Our Minds

Study the background from Judges 6–8 and lesson scripture, Judges 6:1-3, 7-14. Ponder how we can face threats to our well-being—even our very existence—with confidence.

Write on newsprint:
- ❑ information for next week's lesson, found under "Continue the Journey."

❑ activities for further spiritual growth in "Continue the Journey."

Prepare a lecture for "Explore the Account of Gideon, a Judge (Military Leader) Whom God Raised Up to Defeat the Midianite Oppressors of the Israelites."

## LEADING THE CLASS

### (1) Gather to Learn

❖ Welcome the class members and introduce any guests.

❖ Pray that those who have gathered today will look for God in unexpected people and places.

❖ Read this story from a publication of Gordon College to the class: **The Reverend Heather Blackstone met with family members after a tragic accident involving a car and train that killed eleven people and seriously injured many others. Heather recalled the immediate aftermath: "As a chaplain I was supposed to offer hope in a hopeless situation." Because of the way she handled this situation, the Glendale (California) Police Department invited her to serve as chaplain, an honor she humbly accepted. When asked about her approach to ministry with people in grief, Heather replied: "[E]very ministry needs the person to be completely hollowed out so God can work. In my first experience as a chaplain, I was drained and clueless as to how to handle the situation, and yet somehow I was able to get through it while God moved in me . . . at some point God took over and dragged me through. Even though most situations aren't that extreme, it reminded me of God's presence and that God is always that active; I need to step aside."**

❖ Ask: **How does Heather's response support the idea that people can take action even in apparently hopeless situations?**

❖ Read aloud today's focus statement: **When situations seem hopeless, we assume there is nothing we can do. How can we face threats to our well-being—even our very existence—with confidence? The story of Gideon, the self-described weakest member of the weakest family in Israel, demonstrates that God calls and equips ordinary people to bring about extraordinary changes.**

### (2) Explore the Account of Gideon, a Judge (Military Leader) Whom God Raised Up to Defeat the Midianite Oppressors of the Israelites

❖ Choose a volunteer to read Judges 6:1-3, 7-14.

❖ Read aloud the first paragraph of Judges 6:1-10 from Understanding the Scripture to make clear (a) the cycle described there and (b) why God needed to send a military leader to deliver the people.

❖ Tell the rest of the story by presenting a brief lecture based on information through the end of chapter 8 from Understanding the Scripture.

❖ Discuss these questions:
(1) **Had you known Gideon, his work, and his family, what would you have said when you heard that God had chosen him to lead the Israelites against the Midianites?**
(2) **What comparisons do you see between the way Gideon responded to his call and the way Moses responded to God?**
(3) **What does Gideon's call reveal to you about how God works and who God calls?** (Be sure to note that God called a very unlikely candidate, one with no military experience and no traits that would lead one to suspect he would make a great leader.)

❖ Sum up this portion of the lesson by reading or retelling "An Odd Choice" from Interpreting the Scripture.

*(3) Identify Ways God Can Work Through Seemingly Unlikely People to Accomplish Great Things*

❖ Distribute paper and pencils. Ask the students to list as many "unlikely servants" as they can in two minutes. These may be biblical characters or other historical or known contemporary figures who have worked for God.

❖ Invite volunteers to read several names from their lists.

❖ Discuss what each "unlikely servant" had to overcome and how she or he was able to make a contribution worthy of the kingdom of God.

*(4) Answer God's Call*

❖ Read aloud "People Like Us." Invite the class to respond to the story of how a declining church reacted to its pastor's vision.

❖ Divide the class into small groups. Give each group a sheet of newsprint and ask them to think about what God may be calling this class or church to do right now. Suggest that they write that call and consider ways that the call could be answered.

❖ Bring the groups together so that each one can report.

❖ Recommend that students who hear a call that resonates with them covenant together to pray about this call. Challenge them to stay in touch and act on this call as they feel led over the coming weeks.

*(5) Continue the Journey*

❖ Pray that today's participants will be willing to answer God's call, trusting that God will guide them.

❖ Read aloud this preparation for next week's lesson. You may also want to post it on newsprint for the students to copy.

 ■ Title: Ezra: A Priest for the People
 ■ Background Scripture: Ezra 9
 ■ Lesson Scripture: Ezra 9:5-11, 15

■ **Focus of the Lesson: Sin, wherever it may be found, seems so prevalent that we often do not know how to deal with it. What should be our response to sin? The priest Ezra, who had opened his heart and mind to God's teachings, diligently taught the people the laws of God and responded to sin among the Israelites by fervently praying for God's forgiveness and grace.**

❖ Challenge the students to complete one or more of these activities for further spiritual growth, which you will write on newsprint for the students to copy.

  (1) **Research the period of the judges, which extends from about 1200 B.C. to 1020 B.C., when Saul was made king. What characteristics do you note about the people who were called to be judges, that is, military leaders?**

  (2) **Read the entire Book of Judges, paying special attention to the cycle of disobedience, help from God, and a return to sin. In what ways do you perceive this cycle to be continuing today?**

  (3) **Recognize that God's promise to give the land to Israel is a source of continuing conflict between the Israelis and Palestinians. Read about this conflict. Ponder how you think God would want to resolve this issue today.**

❖ Sing or read aloud "Jesus Calls Us."

❖ Conclude today's session by leading the class in this benediction, based on 1 Peter 2:9: **Go forth with the assurance that you are part of a chosen race, a royal priesthood, a holy nation, God's own people, in order that you may proclaim the mighty acts of him who called you out of darkness into his marvelous light.**

UNIT 1: LEADERS IN THE COVENANT COMMUNITY

# Ezra: A Priest for the People

---

## PREVIEWING THE LESSON

**Lesson Scripture:** Ezra 9:5-11, 15
**Background Scripture:** Ezra 9
**Key Verse:** Ezra 9:6

### Focus of the Lesson:

Sin, wherever it may be found, seems so prevalent that we often do not know how to deal with it. What should be our response to sin? The priest Ezra, who had opened his heart and mind to God's teachings, diligently taught the people the laws of God and responded to sin among the Israelites by fervently praying for God's forgiveness and grace.

### Goals for the Learners:

(1) to explore the story of Ezra, who offered confession for the sins of the Israelites.
(2) to recognize the spiritual depth and maturity necessary to be a prayerful leader.
(3) to repent and to offer prayers of confession for unfaithfulness to God.

### Pronunciation Guide:

Ammonite (am' uh nite)               Jeshua (jesh' yoo uh)
Artaxerxes (ahr tuh zuhrk' seez)     Moabite (moh' uh bite)
Canaanite (kay' nuh nite)            Sheshbazzar (shesh baz' uhr)
Darius (duh ri' uhs)                 Zechariah (zek uh ri' uh)
Haggai (hag' i)                      Zerubbabal (zuh ruhb' uh buhl)
Hittite (hit' tite)

### Supplies:

Bibles, newsprint and marker, paper and pencils, hymnals

---

## READING THE SCRIPTURE

NRSV
Ezra 9:5-11, 15

⁵At the evening sacrifice I got up from my fasting, with my garments and my mantle

NIV
Ezra 9:5-11, 15

⁵Then, at the evening sacrifice, I rose from my self-abasement, with my tunic and

torn, and fell on my knees, spread out my hands to the LORD my God, ⁶and said,

"O my God, I am too ashamed and embarrassed to lift my face to you, my God, for our iniquities have risen higher than our heads, and our guilt has mounted up to the heavens. ⁷From the days of our ancestors to this day we have been deep in guilt, and for our iniquities we, our kings, and our priests have been handed over to the kings of the lands, to the sword, to captivity, to plundering, and to utter shame, as is now the case. ⁸But now for a brief moment favor has been shown by the LORD our God, who has left us a remnant, and given us a stake in his holy place, in order that he may brighten our eyes and grant us a little sustenance in our slavery. ⁹For we are slaves; yet our God has not forsaken us in our slavery, but has extended to us his steadfast love before the kings of Persia, to give us new life to set up the house of our God, to repair its ruins, and to give us a wall in Judea and Jerusalem.

¹⁰"And now, our God, what shall we say after this? For we have forsaken your commandments, ¹¹which you commanded by your servants the prophets, saying, 'The land that you are entering to possess is a land unclean with the pollutions of the peoples of the lands, with their abominations. They have filled it from end to end with their uncleanness.' . . . ¹⁵O LORD, God of Israel, you are just, but we have escaped as a remnant, as is now the case. Here we are before you in our guilt, though no one can face you because of this."

cloak torn, and fell on my knees with my hands spread out to the LORD my God ⁶and prayed:

"O my God, I am too ashamed and disgraced to lift up my face to you, my God, because our sins are higher than our heads and our guilt has reached to the heavens. ⁷From the days of our forefathers until now, our guilt has been great. Because of our sins, we and our kings and our priests have been subjected to the sword and captivity, to pillage and humiliation at the hand of foreign kings, as it is today.

⁸"But now, for a brief moment, the LORD our God has been gracious in leaving us a remnant and giving us a firm place in his sanctuary, and so our God gives light to our eyes and a little relief in our bondage. ⁹Though we are slaves, our God has not deserted us in our bondage. He has shown us kindness in the sight of the kings of Persia: He has granted us new life to rebuild the house of our God and repair its ruins, and he has given us a wall of protection in Judah and Jerusalem.

¹⁰"But now, O our God, what can we say after this? For we have disregarded the commands ¹¹you gave through your servants the prophets when you said: 'The land you are entering to possess is a land polluted by the corruption of its peoples. By their detestable practices they have filled it with their impurity from one end to the other.'

¹⁵"O LORD, God of Israel, you are righteous! We are left this day as a remnant. Here we are before you in our guilt, though because of it not one of us can stand in your presence."

---

## UNDERSTANDING THE SCRIPTURE

**Introduction.** The account of Ezra and his leadership tells part of the story of the return from exile. This momentous event in Israel and Judah's history seems to have happened in four stages:

(1) The initial return was led by Sheshbazzar under Cyrus's decree (539–538 B.C.). Work on the Temple was begun, but it stopped due to local pressure.

(2) Another return, led by Zerubbabal,

occurred under Darius I (522–486 B.C.). Encouraged by the prophets Haggai and Zechariah, this group completed rebuilding the Temple despite opposition.

(3) Ezra then led a return under Artaxerxes I (465–424 B.C.), and he brought with him a version of the Mosaic law that was to become the standard for the community.

(4) The last stage of the return was under Artaxerxes II (404–358 B.C.). This group was led by Nehemiah, who had already been to Jerusalem twice during the reign of Artaxerxes I on a mission to rebuild the city walls. Part of Nehemiah's ongoing role was also to establish approved worship practices in the restored community.

Ezra 5:1–6:22 records events from the second of these returns. Here we learn of the efforts of Zerubbabal and Jeshua to rebuild the Temple. We read the details of the opposition against them and also of the supportive arguments provided by Haggai and Zechariah. This section of Ezra ends with verification by King Darius that the Temple project has royal permission dating back to King Cyrus and with the celebration of both the Temple dedication and a special Passover by all the people.

Ezra's own story does not start until chapter 7, which tells of his commission by King Artaxerxes. A letter from the king recorded here outlines Ezra's fourfold charge. He is to lead a group of Jews back to Jerusalem (7:13), deliver official gifts to the Temple (7:15-18), check up on how people in and around Jerusalem are complying with the Mosaic law (7:14), and appoint magistrates and judges to teach and uphold the law (7:25).

Ezra 8 then describes the journey to Jerusalem. First comes a long list of priests and laypeople who went back with Ezra, followed by an account of Ezra's efforts to get Levites and Temple servants to go as well. The trip itself goes smoothly, though, and Ezra and his entourage offer a sacrifice shortly after their arrival.

**Ezra 9:1-4.** Ezra soon encounters a problem. City officials come to tell him that the people, including priests and Levites, have married women from various neighboring nations. Ezra immediately begins a ritual of extreme mourning and repentance because he is so appalled by this revelation.

We need to recall that in Ezra's time these Canaanite, Hittite, Ammonite, Moabite, and Egyptian women were considered non-Jewish because of their bloodline, and so were their children. It did not matter if they had been faithfully worshiping the Jewish God and practicing the Mosaic law—they were considered a threat to the purity of Jewish religion. Israel and Judah had fallen away from worshiping God in the past through the influence of folk who introduced them to other religions, and Ezra worried that this would happen again. His fear will lead to drastic action in chapter 10, when he demands that the men divorce their non-Jewish wives and cast them out, along with their children.

**Ezra 9:5-15.** Faced with what he sees as a momentous sin on the part of the people, Ezra offers an urgent prayer of confession on their behalf. He begins with a summary of the covenant relationship up until now. First, he gives a brief summation of Israel's sins throughout history that led to the exile. Then he recaps God's acts of grace and mercy in preserving a remnant, allowing them to prosper under Persian rule, and granting them a second chance in this return to Jerusalem. After setting this historical context, Ezra moves to the current sin of the people.

Ezra describes the present sin as forsaking commandments given through the "servants the prophets." Here, Ezra is likely referring to texts in books written by Moses, a man whom many Israelites (including Ezra) thought of as a powerful prophet. Deuteronomy 7:3, for example, expressly forbids marriage with these outsiders. Note that some of the nations listed in Deuteronomy 7:1 also appear in Ezra 9:1.

Ezra is convinced that the current marriages represent a serious breach with God.

What's more, this breach involves the whole community. Everyone bears the responsibility for letting these marriages take place and for letting them continue. Ezra's clearly expressed fear is that God will at last take offense and not forgive again. As Ezra sees it, by sanctioning these marriages the community has created the possibility that they may be completely destroyed by the God who has so far preserved them.

Ezra's prayer presents a challenge for those of us who study it today. The exclusiveness that Ezra demanded is counter to the hospitality and acceptance that we see modeled in Christ. Ezra put up strict social and religious walls to keep his community pure; Jesus tore down these walls to create a new community of love.

Thus, as we approach this text, it helps to remember two things. First, Ezra's view was not universally accepted by the Jews of his day or those of later generations. Many scholars think the books of Ruth and Jonah, with their unavoidable messages of God's love for foreigners, came to prominence during Ezra's time as a protest against his harsh theological perspective. Second, regardless of what we think of Ezra's interpretation of the law, we can see value in his prayer as a model of public confession and accountability. The rest of our lesson will focus on this.

## INTERPRETING THE SCRIPTURE

### Ezra's Example

In the previous lesson, we explored how God calls ordinary people to leadership, sometimes with extraordinary results. This week's lesson shows a leader who recognizes and confesses sin on behalf of the people and himself so that they might be restored to a right relationship with God.

Ezra himself is someone with a highly impressive resumé. He was a priest descended from the line of Aaron and a trusted court official under the Persian king Artaxerxes I. On his return to Jerusalem, he had the full authorization of the Persian government to reestablish worship of the Jewish God and adherence to the law of Moses as he saw fit. Yet, despite this outstanding list of achievements, Ezra was a man who knew when to be humble before God. His personal and political record makes his prayer of confession even more powerful.

When leaders are very good at what they do, and especially when God has used them to accomplish wonderful things, we have a tendency to place them on a pedestal. We start to think that these folk are better than the rest of us—somehow more gifted or special, somehow less imperfect.

There are two dangers from this line of thinking that our text addresses. First, we may come to believe that we ourselves can never fill leadership roles because we are not good enough. Second, once we are in a leadership role, we may be drawn into the temptation to let praise go to our heads, causing us to commit the sin of pride. In worst cases, this pride can lead us to a form of spiritual blindness in which we can no longer see any of our faults or shortcomings.

Ezra stands as a model against both ways of thinking. He knew himself to be less than perfect; in fact, he knew himself to be a sinner. Rather than see this as a reason to refuse the call to leadership, though, he said yes to God and faced his failings another way.

When we look at Ezra in this text, we see three things about how a mature church leader deals with sin. Briefly stated, these are:

(1) Mature leaders are honest with themselves when they fail to live up to what God asks.

(2) Mature leaders do not try to hide their mistakes or shortcomings. They acknowledge them and seek God's forgiveness through prayer.

(3) Mature leaders serve this same function for the community as a whole. They help the community face sin honestly and seek forgiveness from God and one another.

Ezra's example shows how a mature leader can help a community heal and then move forward. He also shows the importance of helping people understand the significance of *sin* and *repentance* as they affect our discipleship.

### The Problem of Sin

Let's face it. Sin is no longer popular.

This was first brought to my attention many years ago by a seminary professor who had a passionate addiction to a particular soap opera. His afternoon class routinely started ten minutes late because he would stay home until the end of the show and then race over the two blocks to campus. We could always tell whether it was a good episode by his mood when entering the room.

One afternoon, he burst through the door exclaiming, "What ever happened to *sin*?" It seems that a character in the show had committed several egregious acts, including sleeping with a married man and deliberately becoming impregnated by him. When confronted by her mother over this behavior, the character replied, "I made a mistake." And so it was that our class was launched into an impromptu discussion on the growing loss of a sense of sin in our society.

Over time, this professor's concern proved well founded. Many churches today wrestle with whether to include a prayer of confession and, if so, how to word it so that people are not too offended. After all, as one member of a congregation's worship committee once put it, "Confessing sin is such a downer!"

Yet if we abandon the language and the concept of sin, how are we to understand the human condition? How are we to describe the actions and attitudes that damage our relationships with God and with others? And how will we ever see a way to restore those relationships to what they should be?

### Dealing with Sin

Leaders like Ezra help us name our sin for what it is. They help us acknowledge it and deal with it appropriately. By examining Ezra's actions in the text, we can see an outline for how to accomplish this.

*First, Ezra approaches the problem through prayer.* He could have opted to preach to the people instead and leave it at that, but such action would not have been enough. By beginning with prayer, he invites God into the process of reconciliation and forgiveness from the start.

*Second, Ezra does not abuse the prayer privilege.* He could have worded the prayer in such a way as to distance himself from the others, sending a message about their behavior but not his own. Instead, Ezra identifies himself as one of those who have sinned. He does not stand apart from the people, point fingers, and say only how bad they have been. Rather, he prays openly and honestly in front of the congregation about his own guilt and shame, and then moves into a corporate prayer on behalf of the whole community.

*Third, Ezra grounds the motivation for confession and repentance in God's own covenant faithfulness.* He reminds the people that it was by God's grace that a remnant survived at all. By God's grace, they have a place to worship and a reason to rejoice. By God's grace, they have returned home and have a chance at a new life. Throughout the exile and return, God has remained constant in covenant love for the people. Given this, how can they not repent of their sins and ask forgiveness? Ezra helps the people realize what they stand to lose if they do not seek reconciliation with God.

*Finally, Ezra roots the act of confession and repentance firmly in the worship life of the community.* A prayer such as his could have been given any place and any time, but Ezra chose his setting carefully. The prayer comes during a normal time for worship ("at the evening sacrifice," 9:5), but *outside* of the sanctuary (see 10:1). Ezra will not enter into the presence of God until all has been made right, both on his own behalf and on behalf of all the people. Through this action, he uses the traditional practices and rituals of the congregation to make a powerful theological point. The people's reaction indicates that they are indeed struck on a visceral level that perhaps would not have been achieved by words alone (see 10:1-5).

Ezra challenges the church today to take sin more seriously—not from the standpoint of condemning others but from a sincere desire to be made right with God. When we think of everything God feels for us, everything God so longs to give us, and everything God is willing to accomplish through us, how can we not be moved to respond?

---

## SHARING THE SCRIPTURE

### *Preparing Our Hearts*

Meditate on this week's devotional reading, found in Psalm 32:1-5. In these verses the psalmist points out the happiness that comes to those who confess their sins and receive God's forgiveness. Note in verses 3 and 4 the profound effect unconfessed sin has on our bodies. Even though he lacked sophisticated medical knowledge, the psalmist understands how the mind and body interact to create physical ailments when sinful thoughts and actions remain bottled up inside us.

Pray that you and the adult learners will recognize and confess sins to God, who promises to forgive us.

### *Preparing Our Minds*

Study the background from Ezra 9 and lesson scripture, Ezra 9:5-11, 15. Consider what our response to sin should be.

Write on newsprint:
❑ the four italicized comments in "Dealing with Sin" in the Interpreting the Scripture section.
❑ information for next week's lesson, found under "Continue the Journey."
❑ activities for further spiritual growth in "Continue the Journey."

Prepare an introductory lecture on the Book of Ezra from Understanding the Scripture to orient the adults for the section "Explore the Story of Ezra, Who Offered Confession for the Sins of the Israelites."

Be aware as you research this lesson that scholars disagree as to how the books of Ezra and Nehemiah are to be read, because they were originally in one book. Different scholars may use different dates for events.

Recognize that the focus of today's lesson is on Ezra as a leader, not on his proclamation calling for Israelite men to divorce their foreign wives and give up the children of these unions. This proclamation was made in a peculiar historical context and great care needs to be exercised in ensuring that the text is not used inappropriately.

### LEADING THE CLASS

#### *(1) Gather to Learn*

❖ Welcome the class members and introduce any guests.

❖ Pray that those who have come will open their hearts and minds to the message from God's Word that we will study.

❖ Read "The Problem of Sin" from Interpreting the Scripture.

❖ Invite the class members to discuss the questions in the final paragraph of the reading. If the class is large, divide into groups so that more people can participate.

❖ Read aloud today's focus statement: **Sin, wherever it may be found, seems so prevalent that we often do not know how to deal with it. What should be our response to sin? The priest Ezra, who had opened his heart and mind to God's teachings, diligently taught the people the laws of God and responded to sin among the Israelites by fervently praying for God's forgiveness and grace.**

*(2) Explore the Story of Ezra, Who Offered Confession for the Sins of the Israelites*

❖ Introduce the story of Ezra by reading "Introduction" and Ezra 9:1-4 from Understanding the Scripture, or present the lecture you have prepared.

❖ Select a volunteer to read Ezra 9:5-11, 15.

❖ Invite the students to examine Ezra's prayer by looking in their Bibles and answering these questions:

(1) **How did Ezra prepare himself to offer this prayer?** (Ezra 9:5—He fasted, tore his garment as a sign of grief and repentance, and assumed an attitude of prayer.)

(2) **Why is Ezra "too ashamed and embarrassed to lift [his] face" to God?** (Ezra 9:6-7—The people have a long history with God that is deeply scarred by sin.)

(3) **How has God responded to the people?** (Ezra 9:8-9—God has been very gracious to the people, giving them new life and the opportunity to return home.)

❖ Explore Ezra's traits as a mature

leader by reading or retelling "Ezra's Example."

❖ Note that Ezra is a priest and, according to 1 Peter 2:9, every believer is also a priest. Ask the students to comment on how they see themselves as priests. (Perhaps some have never thought of themselves in this way.) You may want to use the definition of "priest" from the *Merriam Webster Online Dictionary* as **"one authorized to perform the sacred rites of a religion especially as a mediatory agent between humans and God."**

❖ Choose a student to read aloud Hebrews 4:14-16, which is part of a discussion of Jesus as our great high priest. Note especially verse 16, which clearly invites us to approach God in prayer: **"Let us therefore approach the throne of grace with boldness, so that we may receive mercy and find grace to help in time of need."**

❖ Talk about ways in which your church members intercede for the church, community, and nation. For example, many churches use a weekly prayer of confession. Some churches have groups of pray-ers, linked via the telephone or e-mail, who intercede for those requesting prayer. Point out that such prayers are undertaken by those who fit the definition of a priest.

❖ Conclude this portion of the session by inviting the students to comment on any other traits they see in Ezra that make him a spiritually mature leader.

*(3) Recognize the Spiritual Depth and Maturity Necessary to Be a Prayerful Leader*

❖ Read the four italicized comments that explain how Ezra acted as a prayerful leader under "Dealing with Sin" in Interpreting the Scripture. Post these comments on newsprint so that everyone can see them.

❖ Encourage the students to respond to these comments by agreeing, disagreeing, and adding other ideas that help describe a prayerful leader.

❖ **Option:** Read the entire section entitled "Dealing with Sin."

❖ Provide a few moments of quiet time for the students to assess their own maturity as a prayerful leader and then silently ask God's help in growing in their faithfulness.

### (4) Repent and Offer Prayers of Confession for Unfaithfulness to God

❖ Make a list on newsprint of corporate sins that the class believes the church is guilty of committing. Focus on sins of the church in general, not any particular congregation or denomination. Sins committed by individuals are definitely not to be mentioned. (Note that some students may have different ideas as to what constitutes a sin in the church. List all ideas but do not allow a debate to derail the lesson.)

❖ Distribute paper and pencils. Encourage the adults to each write a prayer confessing, on behalf of the church, at least one of the sins they have identified.

❖ Invite volunteers to read their prayers. If possible, ask the students to form a prayer circle to read these petitions.

❖ Conclude this portion of the session by challenging the class members to continue to offer prayers of confession during the week for the sins of the church.

### (5) Continue the Journey

❖ Pray that all who have come today will continue to pray that where the church has gotten off course, God will forgive and set them aright by grace.

❖ Read aloud this preparation for next week's lesson. You may also want to post it on newsprint for the students to copy.
  - ■ **Title: Nehemiah: A Motivator for the People**
  - ■ **Background Scripture: Nehemiah 2**

■ **Lesson Scripture: Nehemiah 2:5, 11-20**

■ **Focus of the Lesson: Life's problems sometimes threaten to immobilize us. Where can we find encouragement to move in the right direction again? The story of Nehemiah shows us that God sends dedicated leaders who pray for change and motivate people to move in God's direction.**

❖ Challenge the students to complete one or more of these activities for further spiritual growth, which you will write on newsprint for the students to copy.

  **(1)** **Offer prayer this week on behalf of your congregation by confessing some sin or weakness you see manifest in this group. Include yourself as Ezra did. Ask for and receive God's forgiveness.**

  **(2)** **Identify mature leaders in your congregation and denomination. What traits do these people share? In what ways can you follow their example? If you believe that you are one of the mature leaders, how can you mentor others to follow in your footsteps?**

  **(3)** **Do whatever you can to help your congregation, or a group within the congregation, get back on course if they have strayed from their purpose of serving and proclaiming the good news.**

❖ Sing or read aloud "It's Me, It's Me, O Lord."

❖ Conclude today's session by leading the class in this benediction, based on 1 Peter 2:9: **Go forth with the assurance that you are part of a chosen race, a royal priesthood, a holy nation, God's own people, in order that you may proclaim the mighty acts of him who called you out of darkness into his marvelous light.**

UNIT 1: LEADERS IN THE COVENANT COMMUNITY

# NEHEMIAH: A MOTIVATOR FOR THE PEOPLE

---

## PREVIEWING THE LESSON

**Lesson Scripture:** Nehemiah 2:5, 11-20
**Background Scripture:** Nehemiah 2
**Key Verse:** Nehemiah 2:18

### Focus of the Lesson:
Life's problems sometimes threaten to immobilize us. Where can we find encouragement to move in the right direction again? The story of Nehemiah shows us that God sends dedicated leaders who pray for change and motivate people to move in God's direction.

### Goals for the Learners:
(1) to explore Nehemiah's plan to rebuild the walls of Jerusalem.
(2) to relate Nehemiah's approach to motivating people with their way of motivating others.
(3) to motivate members of the congregation to undertake a project for God.

### Pronunciation Guide:
Ammonite (am' uh nite)          Kedar (kee' duhr)
Artaxerxes (ahr tuh zuhrk' seez)     Sanballat (san bal' at)
Geshem (gesh' uhm)           Susa (soo' suh)
Hanani (huh nay' ni)          Tobiah (to bi' uh)
Horonite (hor' uh nite)

### Supplies:
Bibles, newsprint and marker, paper and pencils, hymnals

---

## READING THE SCRIPTURE

NRSV

Nehemiah 2:5, 11-20

⁵Then I said to the king, "If it pleases the king, and if your servant has found favor

NIV

Nehemiah 2:5, 11-20

⁵[A]nd I answered the king, "If it pleases the king and if your servant has found favor

with you, I ask that you send me to Judah, to the city of my ancestors' graves, so that I may rebuild it."

[11]So I came to Jerusalem and was there for three days. [12]Then I got up during the night, I and a few men with me; I told no one what my God had put into my heart to do for Jerusalem. The only animal I took was the animal I rode. [13]I went out by night by the Valley Gate past the Dragon's Spring and to the Dung Gate, and I inspected the walls of Jerusalem that had been broken down and its gates that had been destroyed by fire. [14]Then I went on to the Fountain Gate and to the King's Pool; but there was no place for the animal I was riding to continue. [15]So I went up by way of the valley by night and inspected the wall. Then I turned back and entered by the Valley Gate, and so returned. [16]The officials did not know where I had gone or what I was doing; I had not yet told the Jews, the priests, the nobles, the officials, and the rest that were to do the work.

[17]Then I said to them, "You see the trouble we are in, how Jerusalem lies in ruins with its gates burned. Come, let us rebuild the wall of Jerusalem, so that we may no longer suffer disgrace." [18]**I told them that the hand of my God had been gracious upon me, and also the words that the king had spoken to me. Then they said, "Let us start building!"** So they committed themselves to the common good. [19]But when Sanballat the Horonite and Tobiah the Ammonite official, and Geshem the Arab heard of it, they mocked and ridiculed us, saying, "What is this that you are doing? Are you rebelling against the king?" [20]Then I replied to them, "The God of heaven is the one who will give us success, and we his servants are going to start building; but you have no share or claim or historic right in Jerusalem."

in his sight, let him send me to the city in Judah where my fathers are buried so that I can rebuild it."

[11]I went to Jerusalem, and after staying there three days [12]I set out during the night with a few men. I had not told anyone what my God had put in my heart to do for Jerusalem. There were no mounts with me except the one I was riding on.

[13]By night I went out through the Valley Gate toward the Jackal Well and the Dung Gate, examining the walls of Jerusalem, which had been broken down, and its gates, which had been destroyed by fire. [14]Then I moved on toward the Fountain Gate and the King's Pool, but there was not enough room for my mount to get through; [15]so I went up the valley by night, examining the wall. Finally, I turned back and reentered through the Valley Gate. [16]The officials did not know where I had gone or what I was doing, because as yet I had said nothing to the Jews or the priests or nobles or officials or any others who would be doing the work.

[17]Then I said to them, "You see the trouble we are in: Jerusalem lies in ruins, and its gates have been burned with fire. Come, let us rebuild the wall of Jerusalem, and we will no longer be in disgrace." [18]**I also told them about the gracious hand of my God upon me and what the king had said to me.**

**They replied, "Let us start rebuilding."** So they began this good work.

[19]But when Sanballat the Horonite, Tobiah the Ammonite official and Geshem the Arab heard about it, they mocked and ridiculed us. "What is this you are doing?" they asked. "Are you rebelling against the king?"

[20]I answered them by saying, "The God of heaven will give us success. We his servants will start rebuilding, but as for you, you have no share in Jerusalem or any claim or historic right to it."

## UNDERSTANDING THE SCRIPTURE

**Introduction.** The first seven chapters of Nehemiah probably come from a personal memoir, depicting people and events through Nehemiah's own perspective. We know that he was an official at the court of Artaxerxes I in Susa, and that he traveled to Jerusalem in 445 B.C. to be the governor of the Persian province of Judea. His great accomplishment, the beginnings of which we study in this lesson, was rebuilding the walls and gates of Jerusalem despite great opposition (including attempted assassination).

Nehemiah and his crew were able to complete the rebuilding of the walls in fifty-two days in spite of massive problems (Nehemiah 6:15). These walls gave Jerusalem the protection and security its people desperately needed. Nehemiah served twelve years as governor and then returned to Babylon.

He returned to Jerusalem "after some time" (Nehemiah 13:6) and instituted several important religious reforms. These included closing the city on the Sabbath so that no trading could take place, making sure the Levites received their proper support through Temple tithes, and forbidding mixed marriages.

The first chapter of Nehemiah describes a period of his life in Susa, one of the three capitals of the Persian Empire. During November–December, his brother Hanani brings some visitors from Judah to see Nehemiah. When asked about the state of things in Jerusalem, they give a grim report. The city's walls are destroyed and its gates burned, and the people are in great distress.

Hearing this, Nehemiah mourns and makes confession on the people's behalf. He asks God to remember the promises made to Moses and to bring about the restoration of the people. Despite this prayer, however, Nehemiah apparently remains distressed for some time. Our text for this lesson picks up some four months later, yet his sadness is still strong enough to be visible.

**Nehemiah 2:1-8.** The chapter begins in the month of Nisan, the equivalent of our March–April. No explanation is offered as to why this conversation between the king and Nehemiah takes place so much later after the events recorded in chapter 1.

Nehemiah enters the presence of the king in his role as the royal cupbearer. This was a position of great honor and trust. The cupbearer sampled wine for the king to assure the quality of its taste and also to test for poisoning, and then poured the wine to be drunk by the king himself. Because poison was a somewhat popular form of assassination in the ancient Near East, only the most trusted of servants handled the king's food and drink. Moreover, cupbearers served as a more physical form of bodyguard as well; they often guarded the royal living quarters.

When the king sees Nehemiah's sadness and asks as to the cause, Nehemiah explains (with great fear, 2:2) that his distress is over conditions in "the city, the place of my ancestors' graves" (2:3). Notice that Nehemiah does not call Jerusalem by name in the presence of the king, either here or later in 2:5. This might be because he knew of the city's reputation for rebellion among Persian officials (see Ezra 4:9-16), and he was worried that the king would be sensitive to mention of it.

In any event, Nehemiah's language shifts the concern from the political realm to the personal one. The king not only agrees to this request for a trip to Judah but he also sends Nehemiah as governor (5:14).

Scholars looking for an explanation of the king's extraordinary generosity suggest three possibilities. First, the king may have wanted to impress his wife, who was sitting near him (2:6). Second, the time these events take place is at the beginning of the year according to certain ancient calendars. Perhaps the king responded so generously because this represented a form of New Year's gift. Finally, maybe the king's motivation was just what the text suggests—a fondness and respect for Nehemiah, spurred by God in answer to Nehemiah's prayer.

Nehemiah leaves for Jerusalem with a military guard, royal credentials, and an abundant supply of lumber from the royal forest. The wood is to aid in the repairs of the city walls and gates, and also to allow Nehemiah to build or repair a house for his own use.

**Nehemiah 2:9-10.** Along the way, Nehemiah presents the king's letters on his behalf to the governors of "Beyond the River," a province west of the Euphrates. Now we learn of two foreign officials who are not happy to hear of Nehemiah and his mission: Sanballat and Tobiah.

Sanballat was governor of Samaria, and Tobiah may have been governor of Ammon or an assistant to Sanballat. Nehemiah never acknowledges any titles, however; he only refers to them as "the Horonite" and "the Ammonite" (2:10).

**Nehemiah 2:11-16.** In 2:11, Nehemiah calls Jerusalem by name for the first time. After being in the city three days, he makes a secret inspection of the walls at night. Beginning and ending at the Valley Gate, he covers the entire circumference of the walls in a counter-clockwise direction. Verses 12 and 16 underscore that he is careful to let no one know what he is doing, other than the few men who accompany him, and that no one besides himself yet knows his plans for the city.

**Nehemiah 2:17-20.** Nehemiah calls the priests, nobles, officials, Jews, "and rest that were to do the work" (2:16) to repair the holy city. He mentions Jerusalem by name often now, as if to provide additional inspiration to those whom he addresses: *Jerusalem* lies in ruins and *Jerusalem's* gates need rebuilding. Roused by Nehemiah's ardor and urgency, all the people commit to the restoration project.

Verse 19 then reintroduces the theme of opposition. Sanballat, Tobiah, and Geshem (the king of Kedar, whose title is also omitted by Nehemiah) try to stop the project by slandering it as a first step leading to rebellion. In answering them, Nehemiah calls on the ultimate authority: "the God of heaven" (2:20). Moreover, he uses God's name to draw a line between his opponents and the people of the city. According to Nehemiah, Sanballat and his cronies have no civic, legal, or religious rights in Jerusalem.

---

# INTERPRETING THE SCRIPTURE

*Nehemiah's Story*

In the previous lesson, we saw how Ezra helped the people name their sin and seek forgiveness from God. In this lesson, we will see how Nehemiah helped the restored community commit themselves to a large and difficult task for the common good.

Nehemiah is introduced as a Jew who has gained a high position in the court of the Persian king Artaxerxes. His role reflects great trust of him on the king's part, and it seems the king holds a great liking for him as well. Accordingly, the king agrees to Nehemiah's request to return to Jerusalem (2:6), something Nehemiah came to desire after learning that Jerusalem's wall and gates had been destroyed.

Three days after reaching the city, Nehemiah makes a secret inspection of the walls and gates by night (2:11-16). What he learns confirms his fears and moves him to action. Calling the city officials together, Nehemiah tells them to rebuild the wall, setting this command in the context of both God's and Artaxerxes' favor (2:17-18). Any resistance is omitted from the text, because the officials agree immediately and enthusiastically—"Let us start building!" (2:18). The chapter closes with Sanballat and foreign officials trying to stop the project, first through ridicule and then through the accusation of treason (2:19). Nehemiah boldly counters not only with the affirmation that the Jews are following God's will but also with the prediction that these opponents will be left with no rights regarding Jerusalem (2:20).

### The Power of a Word

There are a lot of philosophical debates over which single word may be the most powerful in any given language. Usually people lobby for "yes," "no," or "if." In his current circumstances, though, Nehemiah might have made a strong argument for the word "but." That one syllable can stop cold the most rational argument or the most visionary plan, with little hope for advancement.

Reading the list of objections that Nehemiah encountered over rebuilding the wall and the gates, we see embarrassingly familiar elements. Thankfully, we also see suggestions for how to motivate ourselves beyond these.

The first problem Nehemiah faces is *"but we've never done this before."* For the existing community, this was true enough: the people who returned from exile had no experience at massive city undertakings such as this. They had never planned or built such a large public structure. They really did not know where to begin. Add to this the fact that the destroyed wall and gates had been suffering ongoing damage for decades while the people were in exile, plus twenty years after their return. We can see how the people might have been overwhelmed into a state of inertia.

Nehemiah deals with the problem by first assessing the work to be done. He sees the wall and gates for himself, so that he can honestly evaluate the task that lies ahead. Armed with this information, he can then speak knowledgeably and with authority to the community.

Notice how well Nehemiah then handles this next step. When he addresses those living in Jerusalem, he does not belittle them or attack them for their lack of action so far. Rather, he inspires them by sharing his vision of what God has in mind. He invites them to see the possibilities of their home through God's eyes. He shifts them from a feeling of helplessness and indecision to a state of excitement and energy, all by moving their attention from themselves to God.

### When Conflict Occurs

Yet in Nehemiah's time, just as in our own, congregations wrestled regularly with two difficult realities: most people do not like change, and most people will go to some lengths to avoid conflict. Thus, despite the people's enthusiasm, it is not long before Nehemiah hears *"but there will be a fight over this."*

The threat presented by Sanballat, Tobiah, and Geshem reminds us that God's plans often face resistance by those who feel they have something to lose in the outcome. For example, modern churches sometimes find themselves treated with hostility by neighbors who oppose the building of a homeless shelter or a drug-treatment clinic because "it will ruin the neighborhood." More to our shame, we even face opposition to some valid new visions from within our own faith communities. Handling such conflict in a healthy manner is a part of moving forward as God asks.

Note that Nehemiah does not let conflict stop his work in God's name. Rather, he deals with his opponents in ways that we can admire. First, he makes sure the truth is always aired so both sides can hear it. In addition, he couples practical solutions to the opposition with active prayer that the matter may be resolved (see 4:9). More than anything, Nehemiah stands firm in his belief that God will work out everything. This trust gives him the strength to withstand all the difficulties that others place in his path.

### The Importance of Trust

If we read on in chapter 5, we see that Nehemiah eventually encounters the familiar challenge of *"but we don't have the resources."* In their initial excitement, the people poured all their time, energy, and material goods into the rebuilding project. Over time, however, problems developed: homes began to be in disrepair because of the lack of available material, food became scarce because people were not working the fields, and poverty was on the rise because of high taxes.

Nehemiah addresses this by helping the people analyze the situation more accurately. The problem is not a lack of resources but selfishness on the part of some officials. There are, in fact, enough resources of time and energy and wealth to give the people what they need *and* to rebuild the city—but not enough to keep some folk at the level of luxury to which they have become accustomed.

Because of his own level of personal integrity and that of others with whom he works, Nehemiah is able to change the system to one that is more equitable. Just as important, he uses this opportunity to remind the people of a vital truth. When God calls us to accomplish a purpose, then God will provide all that we need to do so. Any apparent lack of resources should make us take a closer look at ourselves, rather than leading us to abandon God's project.

Understanding the power of a word, Nehemiah counters each "but" with a call to trust. If the people trust God's vision and intent for them, then the wall and gates will be rebuilt even if the people have to learn how to do it as they go. If the people trust God to provide what they need, then limited resources are not an issue. If the people trust God to accomplish the divine ends, then no opposition can win in the end. Thus, with a simple word, Nehemiah challenges us to reevaluate every barrier we may see to stepping forward in actions to which God calls us on behalf of the good of all.

## SHARING THE SCRIPTURE

### Preparing Our Hearts

Meditate on this week's devotional reading, found in Isaiah 62:1-7. In this psalm in which the writer celebrates Jerusalem's exoneration after its defeat by the Babylonians, we read in verse 6 that God will post sentinels on the walls. This reading relates to today's text from Nehemiah, who motivates the returned Israelites to rebuild those shattered walls. Where in your life are there pieces lying in ruins? Who or what can encourage you to pick up these pieces and rebuild?

Pray that you and the adult learners will find the encouragement you need to restore the broken parts of your lives.

### Preparing Our Minds

Study the background from Nehemiah 2 and lesson scripture from verses 5, 11-20. Think about where we can find encouragement to move in the right direction when life's problems have threatened to immobilize us.

Write on newsprint:
- ❑ information for next week's lesson, found under "Continue the Journey."
- ❑ activities for further spiritual growth in "Continue the Journey."

Plan how you will present the information in the "Introduction" as suggested for "Explore Nehemiah's Plan to Rebuild the Walls of Jerusalem."

Sketch on newsprint the outline of the city walls found on the Close-up page for this quarter.

## LEADING THE CLASS

### (1) Gather to Learn

❖ Welcome the class members and introduce any guests.

❖ Pray that each person who has come today will be motivated by the power of the Holy Spirit.

❖ Read aloud this story of Rudy Ruettiger, which was made into a 1993 movie entitled *Rudy*: **Rudy was the third of fourteen children born to a family in an Illinois steel town. He had high ambitions; some would say unreasonably high ambitions. Diagnosed with dyslexia while in junior college, Rudy had to work very hard with his teachers and tutors just to earn the "B" average necessary to transfer to Notre Dame in the fall of 1974. Once there, this five-foot six-inch, 165-pound guy had the audacity to try out to play football for the renowned Fighting Irish. He worked extremely hard to earn the respect of his coaches and teammates, playing every practice as if it were a league game. Although he had to sit on the bench until the last game of his college career, in the one chance that he had he proved himself to be a real hero.**

❖ Discuss with the class the character traits that it takes for someone with the odds so stacked against him to move forward and achieve his dreams.

❖ Read aloud today's focus statement: **Life's problems sometimes threaten to immobilize us. Where can we find encouragement to move in the right direction again? The story of Nehemiah shows us that God sends dedicated leaders who pray for change and motivate people to move in God's direction.**

### (2) Explore Nehemiah's Plan to Rebuild the Walls of Jerusalem

❖ Read or share in a brief lecture the information under "Introduction" in Understanding the Scripture.

❖ Choose a volunteer to read Nehemiah 2:5, 11-20. Invite the class to read in unison "Let us start building" in verse 18.

❖ Show the sketch you have made on newsprint of the walls of Jerusalem as reconstructed by Nehemiah. Using a different colored marker than the sketch, trace Nehemiah's route as recorded in 2:13-16. You will find Valley Gate, Dung Gate, and Fountain Gate on the sketch. The valley referred to in verse 15 is the Kidron Valley. Note that Nehemiah did not inspect the northern wall due to the debris but rather returned the way that he had come.

❖ Ask the adults to look again at verses 17-18 and discuss how Nehemiah motivates the people. (Be sure to point out that Nehemiah states that God inspired him to act and that the king had supported him. The people then saw that this project was for "the common good" and so made an enthusiastic commitment to it.)

❖ Read or retell "When Conflict Occurs" to help the students understand how Nehemiah confronted the very real threat from Israel's neighbors.

### (3) Relate Nehemiah's Approach to Motivating People with the Way Learners Motivate Others

❖ Brainstorm with the group answers to this question, which you will record on newsprint: **What are the characteristics of someone who can motivate people?** (Here are some possible answers: *has a vision, goal-oriented, enthusiastic, dedicated, able to inspire people and make them feel passionate about an idea, able to make people feel that they are important and have something to contribute.*)

❖ Encourage the students to identify the traits Nehemiah exhibited by placing an asterisk (*) next to them on the list.

❖ Distribute paper and pencils. Ask the students to list the traits that enable them to motivate others.

❖ Invite students to work with a partner to discuss these traits and to encourage their partners to use the traits they have identified. Consider how each partner may be like Nehemiah.

### (4) Motivate Members of the Congregation to Undertake a Project for God

❖ Challenge the students to think of some small but important projects that they could undertake to "spruce up" the church building and grounds. Here are some ideas: *clean closets, paint a Sunday school room, plant or weed a garden, houseclean the church kitchen.*

❖ Encourage the students to select one or two of these projects to work on together. Provide time for the class (or small groups) to consider what they hope to accomplish and how they will go about meeting their goal. Include as many ways to participate as possible so that all will feel included. (For example, the person who provides lunch is just as important as the person wielding a paint brush.)

❖ Conclude this activity by asking for a show of hands of those who will participate in the project.

❖ **Caveat:** Depending on how your church operates, you may need to secure official approval from a group, trustees for example, to do what you are proposing. However, most churches are happy to have volunteers willing to tend the building and grounds. A persuasive motivator in the class may need to go before the official body to get its blessings.

### (5) Continue the Journey

❖ Pray that each participant will motivate other people, even as they find others who motivate them to act on behalf of God.

❖ Read aloud this preparation for next week's lesson. You may also want to post it on newsprint for the students to copy.

■ Title: Looking for Jesus

■ **Background Scripture: Mark 1:35-45**

■ **Lesson Scripture: Mark 1:35-45**

■ **Focus of the Lesson: We often seek out people we believe can help us solve our problems. Where can we find such people? The people of Galilee realized that Jesus had the words of life and a healing touch that they sought, so they went looking for him.**

❖ Challenge the students to complete one or more of these activities for further spiritual growth, which you will write on newsprint for the students to copy.

(1) Think about projects that need to be done in your own church or community. What steps can you take to motivate others to participate? Take at least one of those steps this week.

(2) Visit a devastated place in or near your community. Offer whatever encouragement and help you can to those who need to rebuild as a result of fire or other catastrophe.

(3) Recall that Nehemiah was resourceful in getting the king to give him the supplies that he would need for the building project. Who could you contact to provide something needed for the church? Could you persuade a good seamstress to make new curtains for a room, or a carpenter to build storage shelves? Contact this person and try to motivate him or her to act.

❖ Sing or read aloud "All My Hope Is Firmly Grounded."

❖ Conclude today's session by leading the class in this benediction, based on 1 Peter 2:9: **Go forth with the assurance that you are part of a chosen race, a royal priesthood, a holy nation, God's own people, in order that you may proclaim the mighty acts of him who called you out of darkness into his marvelous light.**

## UNIT 2: AN OPEN INVITATION TO COVENANT LIVING
# LOOKING FOR JESUS

---

### PREVIEWING THE LESSON

**Lesson Scripture:** Mark 1:35-45
**Background Scripture:** Mark 1:35-45
**Key Verse:** Mark 1:37

### Focus of the Lesson:
We often seek out people we believe can help us solve our problems. Where can we find such people? The people of Galilee realized that Jesus had the words of life and a healing touch that they sought, so they went looking for him.

### Goals for the Learners:
(1) to unpack a narrative about Jesus and the disciples when they ministered to those who sought help.
(2) to be aware that they can turn to God when they are in need.
(3) to help someone who is searching for a relationship with God.

### Supplies:
Bibles, newsprint and marker, paper and pencils, hymnals

---

### READING THE SCRIPTURE

NRSV
Mark 1:35-45

<sup> </sup>35In the morning, while it was still very dark, he got up and went out to a deserted place, and there he prayed. 36And Simon and his companions hunted for him. **37When they found him, they said to him, "Everyone is searching for you."** 38He answered, "Let us go on to the neighboring towns, so that I may proclaim the message there also; for that is what I came out to do." 39And he went throughout Galilee, proclaiming the message in their synagogues and casting out demons.

NIV
Mark 1:35-45

35Very early in the morning, while it was still dark, Jesus got up, left the house and went off to a solitary place, where he prayed. 36Simon and his companions went to look for him, **37and when they found him, they exclaimed: "Everyone is looking for you!"**

38Jesus replied, "Let us go somewhere else—to the nearby villages—so I can preach there also. That is why I have come." 39So he traveled throughout Galilee, preaching in their synagogues and driving out demons.

[40]A leper came to him begging him, and kneeling he said to him, "If you choose, you can make me clean." [41]Moved with pity, Jesus stretched out his hand and touched him, and said to him, "I do choose. Be made clean!" [42]Immediately the leprosy left him, and he was made clean. [43]After sternly warning him he sent him away at once, [44]saying to him, "See that you say nothing to anyone; but go, show yourself to the priest, and offer for your cleansing what Moses commanded, as a testimony to them." [45]But he went out and began to proclaim it freely, and to spread the word, so that Jesus could no longer go into a town openly, but stayed out in the country; and people came to him from every quarter.

[40]A man with leprosy came to him and begged him on his knees, "If you are willing, you can make me clean."

[41]Filled with compassion, Jesus reached out his hand and touched the man. "I am willing," he said. "Be clean!" [42]Immediately the leprosy left him and he was cured.

[43]Jesus sent him away at once with a strong warning: [44]"See that you don't tell this to anyone. But go, show yourself to the priest and offer the sacrifices that Moses commanded for your cleansing, as a testimony to them." [45]Instead he went out and began to talk freely, spreading the news. As a result, Jesus could no longer enter a town openly but stayed outside in lonely places. Yet the people still came to him from everywhere.

---

## UNDERSTANDING THE SCRIPTURE

**Introduction.** The text for today comes from the end of Mark's first chapter. Prior to these verses, John the Baptist sets the stage for Jesus' appearance and Jesus' ministry gets quickly underway.

Unlike Matthew or Luke, Mark's Gospel does not begin with a genealogy or by establishing an historical date. Mark's Gospel starts with the proclamation of the good news by John the Baptist that One is coming who will baptize the people with the Holy Spirit. The themes of John's call to repentance and Jesus' ability to draw people into communion with God will run throughout the rest of the Gospel.

John's prophetic activity is followed by Jesus' own baptism (1:9-11) and a brief description of his temptations in the wilderness (1:12-13). This prologue section then ends with Jesus going to Galilee to preach and perform great deeds after John has been arrested (1:14-15).

Verse 15 is especially important for understanding the rest of Mark's Gospel because it summarizes the theological message of the book: "The time is fulfilled, and the kingdom of God has come near; repent, and believe in the good news." The four stories from Mark that we will consider in Unit 2 each reflect this proclamation in some way, as does Mark overall.

Verses 16-20 record the call of Jesus' first disciples, and verses 21-34 follow this with four vignettes that fall on a single day. These accounts are important because they characterize events that will occur repeatedly throughout Jesus' ministry.

First, Jesus preaches at the synagogue in Capernaum, and his authority amazes those who hear him. For the rest of his life, Jesus' sense of God-given authority—as well as the content of what he teaches and preaches—will amaze, astonish, and sometimes anger people.

While still at the synagogue, a man with an unclean spirit accosts Jesus. Jesus expels the spirit, providing the crowd with one more example of his authority, and the people are even more amazed. This is followed by the healing of Simon's mother-in-law that same day. Although this event took place in a private home and not in a public setting like the synagogue, word of the healing spreads quickly.

Jesus' day ends with a familiar scene: crowds of people have tracked him down in the hopes that he can cure their diseases or cast out their demons. Mark records that he helped as many as he could, perhaps indicating that some were still waiting when he quit from exhaustion. This scene, in which "the whole city" (1:33) was gathered around the house where Jesus stayed, sets the stage for where this week's passage begins.

Before we turn to the rest of Mark 1, however, it might be helpful to say a word about the end of verse 34. There Jesus commands the demons he has cast out not to speak, because they might reveal who he is. This same directive to keep silent will come up in this lesson and others, and it always seems a bit odd.

This particular command occurs in Mark's Gospel far more than any other, and many scholars refer to it as "the messianic secret" because it is specifically aimed at keeping Jesus' identity as the Messiah unknown. But why would Jesus want to keep this a secret? As Mark tells it, Jesus is concerned about people misunderstanding who he is and what he has come to accomplish. After all, Jesus knows that popular expectations for the Messiah include a military leader who will lead the nation to victory over Rome and an otherworldly figure who will immediately usher in the Day of the Lord to the destruction of this world. If Jesus can only keep the truth about himself secret until after his death and resurrection, Mark proposes, then people will be able to understand his real mission.

**Mark 1:35-39.** The next morning, Jesus understandably slips away from the crowds for some private time. He seeks time alone with God to renew his spirit after a grueling yesterday and to fortify himself for the tasks that lie in his immediate future. All the Gospels show that prayer time was important to Jesus and that he worked hard at carving out that time for himself.

Verses 36-37 show how difficult it was for Jesus to get the time he needed. His disciples hunt Jesus down in the remote and deserted place he has chosen for prayer, apparently so they can urge him to return to town. Why? Because everyone is searching for him. One can almost hear Jesus sigh at this point.

Instead of returning to town, though, Jesus chooses to move on. His mission is to spread the good news, and he cannot do that by staying in one place. So we read that he went throughout Galilee preaching, teaching, and casting out demons.

**Mark 1:40-45.** At some point during this journey, a man with a severe skin condition approaches Jesus and begs to be made clean. While English versions traditionally translate the Hebrew term as "leprosy," this could have been one of several other skin ailments. Archeological evidence suggests that the term does not refer to modern-day leprosy (or Hansen's Disease) because skeletal evidence from biblical times shows no trace of this malady.

We may be surprised at the wording of the man's request, expecting him rather to ask for healing in a more direct way, but Mark uses this language deliberately. The issue is not so much curing a disease as restoring the man completely—spiritually as well as physically. Only if the man is pronounced "clean" can he return to worship and to his community, and this is his real request.

Acting with compassion toward the man, Jesus cures him and then commands him to go to a priest to complete his purification. He also tells the man not to reveal what really happened. In his excitement, however, the man does the opposite and spreads the news of what Jesus has done. The account ends with Jesus becoming so sought after that he has to hide from crowds.

# INTERPRETING THE SCRIPTURE

### Background to the Story

This week's story falls in a series of accounts of Jesus' healing ministry. We are in the first chapter of Mark's Gospel, yet Jesus' popularity and fame have already grown to challenging proportions because of the miracles he has performed. Crowds chase after Jesus everywhere, and time for himself has become a precious commodity. Thus, the second passage for today starts with a sense of irony—Jesus, who desperately seeks isolation and cannot get it, is sought out by a man with a skin disease who passionately desires to have his forced isolation overcome.

It is unclear in our passage whether Jesus is alone or with others when the ailing man approaches him. Neither does the passage tell us much about the man apart from mentioning his illness. We know nothing of how long he has suffered from this affliction, whether he has a family, or even what his name is. We know only that he has a skin condition deemed by the priests to be dangerous enough to warrant declaring him "unclean" (see Leviticus 13–14)—and that he believes Jesus has the power to heal him.

Mark's original audience would have supplied a few other details as they heard this story. They knew that to be unclean meant to be cast out of all society and denied entry into places of worship. They knew that people diagnosed with leprosy had to live outside the city, near the garbage dump, because scraps there were their only source of food. They knew that such people could no longer have contact with their friends or families and that they were required to shout out "Unclean, unclean!" whenever they moved about so that no one would accidentally touch them. They knew that anyone who did touch such a person was automatically declared unclean as well and faced a rigorous examination by the priests. Plus, many of Mark's audience would have assumed, as did most people of that time, that anyone who contracted such a horrible skin disease was being punished by God for a sin that he or she committed.

### A Healing Moment

The man approaches Jesus, kneels before him, and begs, "Make me clean!" On one level, he is certainly asking Jesus to cure him of his disease. On a deeper level, however, he is asking Jesus to make him spiritually and emotionally whole. He is asking Jesus to take action that will restore him to the social and religious life of his community.

Jesus is moved to compassion by this man's plea, and so he grants the request. More than that, he does so in a way designed to express his compassion directly and meaningfully. No doubt Jesus could have spoken a word from a discreet distance, and the man would have been cured. Instead, he reaches out and touches the man *before* the healing takes place, thus joining the man's unclean status, and then accomplishes the miracle. It is hard for us to comprehend what an amazing sign of acceptance this was—or how much that one touch might have meant to a person who had forcibly foregone human contact for so long.

In responding to the man in this way, Jesus sends a message to all who claim to be his disciples. We live in a society that still creates and isolates "lepers." This shows in all the ways someone might feel unwanted and unwelcome if they do not have the right physical appearance, social skills, sexual orientation, skin color, or educational background. Jesus challenges us not only to feel compassion for those who are outcast, but to reach out and touch them in ways that can let healing begin.

*Two Commands*

Jesus tells the man to go straight to a priest so that he can be declared "clean." In so doing, Jesus is encouraging the man both to honor the law of Moses and to do what is necessary to restore himself fully to his family, friends, and worshiping community. Jesus wants the man to gain the true benefit of his cure—reentry into the community of faith—just as soon as possible.

No doubt Jesus had in mind Leviticus 13 and 14, which are full of instructions for dealing with skin conditions that can cause one to be declared unclean. These chapters also describe the steps one has to take in order to come back into the covenant community. The purification process lasted for eight days. This came after any physical cure, so clearly the ritual is concerned with spiritual purification. Persons who were no longer diseased had to be sanctified (that is, made holy) before they could rejoin God's holy people. Moreover, part of the process involved anointing the person with blood from a sacrificial animal and with oil that had been consecrated for the purpose. The application of the blood symbolized coming back into life from a state of death, while the application of the oil celebrated and confirmed this restored status.

In a very real sense, Jesus had already achieved the gift of new life for the man he cured, but he knows that the rituals of the community must be observed if the man is to be allowed to go home. Thus he commands the man to find a priest and start the process as soon as possible.

Notice that Jesus also commands the man not to tell what happened. This could be because he does not want to detract from God as the power behind the miracle, or because he does not want to add to the crowds that are hunting for him. More likely, though, Jesus may be concerned that anyone hearing this story would think only of his ability to physically heal and cure, thereby seeking only that from him. For Jesus, the spiritual element is every bit as important as the physical. He has come to mend hearts as well as bones, to cure sickness of the soul as well as of the body. Everything he does is designed to reconnect us to God and to one another, but that gospel message could be easily lost among a crowd of desperate people looking only for a miracle doctor.

*On This Day . . .*

This lesson is made even more poignant for us when we consider that today is World Communion Sunday. Around the globe, from time zone to time zone, congregations will join in conscious awareness of one another as we gather at the Lord's Table. It is a day to remember that God's covenant community is larger than just the folk we see each week in our own church.

The practice of World Communion Sunday also serves as a reminder that each of us comes to Christ's table at his invitation. We gather at the table as those for whom Jesus has felt compassion, those whom he has touched, and those whom he has healed. We gather as those who have been brought into the loving family of God through the grace and mercy of our Lord.

Perhaps today is a good day for us to pray on behalf of Christ's church that we may all remember we are called to be Christ's body in the world. We are the ones through whom he chooses to welcome those who are unwanted, to reach out to those who are alone, and to remove the barriers that separate us from one another. Surely people would "[come] from every quarter" (1:45) to be part of a community like that!

## SHARING THE SCRIPTURE

### Preparing Our Hearts

Meditate on this week's devotional reading, found in Ezekiel 34:11-16. Here we see a portrait of God as the good shepherd. Note in verse 16 that God will "bind up the injured" and "strengthen the weak." Think about how God has strengthened you and cared for you, especially in times of illness or injury. What do you tell others about such care? Share a word of witness with someone who needs to know that God is the good shepherd.

Pray that you and the adult learners will give thanks for the care that God has given and continues to provide for them.

### Preparing Our Minds

Study the background and lesson scripture, both found in Mark 1:35-45. Think about who you turn to when you have a problem to solve.

Write on newsprint:
❑ names of animals for "Gather to Learn."
❑ information for next week's lesson, found under "Continue the Journey."
❑ activities for further spiritual growth in "Continue the Journey."

Review the suggested readings from Understanding the Scripture and Interpreting the Scripture and decide how you will present them to the class.

### LEADING THE CLASS

#### (1) Gather to Learn

❖ Welcome the class members and introduce any guests.
❖ Pray that those in attendance will truly seek Jesus this day.
❖ Invite the students to assess how they generally confront problems by categorizing themselves as one of the following animals. Post newsprint with the animals listed and then read the description for each animal. Learners may have other animals to add.

■ **Ostrich—I hide my head in the sand if there is a problem.**
■ **Beaver—I keep gnawing away at the problem and hope that I can build a protective barrier.**
■ **Turtle—I withdraw into myself and hope my shell will protect me from the situation.**
■ **Lion—I "roar" about the problem to everyone who will listen and act aggressively.**
■ **Hamster—I run faster on my treadmill but don't seem to get any further in solving the problem.**
■ **Sheep—I follow along with my herd and trust someone else to figure out the solution.**
■ **Dog—I survey the situation and try to dig my way out.**
■ **(Other animal and ways this animal may respond.)**

❖ Allow a few moments to discuss approaches that seem most effective in solving problems, including seeking out help.
❖ Read aloud today's focus statement: **We often seek out people we believe can help us solve our problems. Where can we find such people? The people of Galilee realized that Jesus had the words of life and a healing touch that they sought, so they went looking for him.**

#### (2) Unpack a Narrative about Jesus and the Disciples When They Ministered to Those Who Sought Help

❖ Read or retell "Introduction" from Understanding the Scripture to set the stage for today's readings.
❖ Invite a volunteer to read about Jesus' preaching tour in Galilee from Mark 1:35-39.

■ Discuss these questions.
- **(1) What does this passage tell you about Jesus?**
- **(2) What does it tell you about the disciples?**
- **(3) What does it suggest to you about the people who have heard or want to hear Jesus?**

■ Select several volunteers to role-play a conversation between the disciples as they search for Jesus and then with Jesus once they find him.

■ Debrief the roleplay by asking the observers to identify the concerns/needs the disciples had and the concerns/needs that Jesus had.

❖ Choose someone to read Mark 1:40-45, which tells the story of Jesus cleansing a leper.

■ Draw a distinction between leprosy, which we know as Hansen's Disease, and skin ailments referred to as leprosy in the Bible by reading the first paragraph under Mark 1:40-45 in Understanding the Scripture.

■ Read or retell "A Healing Moment" in Interpreting the Scripture to help the class members understand the extent of the man's request when he asks Jesus to heal him.

■ Reread this sentence: **We live in a society that still creates and isolates "lepers."** Encourage the adults to identify groups of people that seem to be contemporary "lepers." Discuss *why* people feel this way about these groups and *how* the church can go about inviting them back into the mainstream of society.

■ **Option:** Assign half of the class to read Leviticus 13 and the other half to read Leviticus 14 to see what would have been expected of the healed leper in order to rejoin society. Both groups are to report their findings to the entire class.

■ Look at the two commands Jesus gives in Mark 1:44. Explain the reasons for these commands by reading or retelling "Two Commands" in Interpreting the Scripture.

*(3) Be Aware That the Learners Can Turn to God When They Are in Need*

❖ Point out that the leper had obviously heard about Jesus and had great faith that he could cleanse him. This leper recognized that he could turn to God, in the person of Jesus, when he needed help.

❖ Distribute paper and pencils. Invite the adults to reflect on this quotation by Erwin W. Lutzer (1941– ): **Human problems are never greater than divine solutions.** Encourage the class members to recall concrete examples of times when they faced difficulties and God provided a solution to the problem. Ask them to write (or think about) why they turn to God in times of need and how they see God working in their lives.

❖ Enlist volunteers to share their reflections with the class or a small group.

*(4) Help Someone Who Is Searching for a Relationship with God*

❖ Lead the class in reading aloud today's key verse, Mark 1:37.

❖ Ask the students to identify in their minds, but not name aloud, someone who they believe is searching for God.

❖ Brainstorm with the class ways that the students may be able to help those who are seeking such a relationship. Ideas may include: *discussing one's own experiences with the seeker; inviting the seeker to church, Sunday school, or another venue where he or she may encounter God; acting as Christ's disciple by assisting this person with problems he or she is facing.*

❖ Conclude this portion of the lesson by challenging the students to act, in the power of the Holy Spirit, to help the people they have identified to find Christ in their lives.

*(5) Continue the Journey*

❖ Pray that today's participants will continue to seek Jesus in their own lives and lead others to do so as well.

❖ Read aloud this preparation for next week's lesson. You may also want to post it on newsprint for the students to copy.

- ■ **Title: Recognizing Jesus**
- ■ **Background Scripture: Mark 5:1-20**
- ■ **Lesson Scripture: Mark 5:1-13, 18-20**
- ■ **Focus of the Lesson: At times, our problems are so overwhelming and sometimes cause such alienation that we do not know where to turn. What help is available? Mark's account of the Gerasene demoniac demonstrates that Jesus is able to break the chains that bind and isolate us and bring us back into community.**

❖ Challenge the students to complete one or more of these activities for further spiritual growth, which you will write on newsprint for the students to copy.

**(1) Keep an eye on local newspapers** and other media to discern who in your community is being excluded or pushed to the margins. Do whatever you can to help these persons find the inclusive, healing power of Christ.

**(2) Continue to search for a deeper relationship with Christ by devoting additional time this week to prayer and meditation.**

**(3) Go to a place where today's "lepers" are likely to be found. Consider group homes for the mentally challenged, soup kitchens, homeless shelters, facilities for HIV/AIDS patients. Do whatever you can to minister to needs there.**

❖ Sing or read aloud "Seek the Lord."

❖ Conclude today's session by leading the class in this benediction, based on 1 Peter 2:9: **Go forth with the assurance that you are part of a chosen race, a royal priesthood, a holy nation, God's own people, in order that you may proclaim the mighty acts of him who called you out of darkness into his marvelous light.**

UNIT 2: AN OPEN INVITATION TO COVENANT LIVING
# RECOGNIZING JESUS

---

## PREVIEWING THE LESSON

**Lesson Scripture:** Mark 5:1-13, 18-20
**Background Scripture:** Mark 5:1-20
**Key Verse:** Mark 5:19

### Focus of the Lesson:
At times, our problems are so overwhelming and sometimes cause such alienation that we do not know where to turn. What help is available? Mark's account of the Gerasene demoniac demonstrates that Jesus is able to break the chains that bind and isolate us and bring us back into community.

### Goals for the Learners:
(1) to explore Jesus' encounter with a person bound by unclean spirits.
(2) to recognize ways they may be in bondage so as to open themselves to Jesus' liberating healing.
(3) to identify and find ways to assist those persons who live in isolation at the edges of society.

### Pronunciation Guide:
Decapolis (di kap' uh lis)        Gerasa (ger' uh suh)
Gadara (gad' uh ruh)           Gergesa (ger' guh sa)
Gadarenes (gad' uh reens)      Gergesene (ger' guh seen)
Gerasene (ger' uh seen)         Jairus (jay i' ruhs)

### Supplies:
Bibles, newsprint and marker, paper and pencils, hymnals, optional meditative music and appropriate player

---

## READING THE SCRIPTURE

NRSV
Mark 5:1-13, 18-20

¹They came to the other side of the sea, to the country of the Gerasenes. ²And when he had stepped out of the boat, immediately a

NIV
Mark 5:1-13, 18-20

¹They went across the lake to the region of the Gerasenes. ²When Jesus got out of the boat, a man with an evil spirit came from the

man out of the tombs with an unclean spirit met him. ³He lived among the tombs; and no one could restrain him any more, even with a chain; ⁴for he had often been restrained with shackles and chains, but the chains he wrenched apart, and the shackles he broke in pieces; and no one had the strength to subdue him. ⁵Night and day among the tombs and on the mountains he was always howling and bruising himself with stones. ⁶When he saw Jesus from a distance, he ran and bowed down before him; ⁷and he shouted at the top of his voice, "What have you to do with me, Jesus, Son of the Most High God? I adjure you by God, do not torment me." ⁸For he had said to him, "Come out of the man, you unclean spirit!" ⁹Then Jesus asked him, "What is your name?" He replied, "My name is Legion; for we are many." ¹⁰He begged him earnestly not to send them out of the country. ¹¹Now there on the hillside a great herd of swine was feeding; ¹²and the unclean spirits begged him, "Send us into the swine; let us enter them." ¹³So he gave them permission. And the unclean spirits came out and entered the swine; and the herd, numbering about two thousand, rushed down the steep bank into the sea, and were drowned in the sea.

¹⁸As he was getting into the boat, the man who had been possessed by demons begged him that he might be with him. ¹⁹But Jesus refused, and said to him, **"Go home to your friends, and tell them how much the Lord has done for you, and what mercy he has shown you."** ²⁰And he went away and began to proclaim in the Decapolis how much Jesus had done for him; and everyone was amazed.

tombs to meet him. ³This man lived in the tombs, and no one could bind him any more, not even with a chain. ⁴For he had often been chained hand and foot, but he tore the chains apart and broke the irons on his feet. No one was strong enough to subdue him. ⁵Night and day among the tombs and in the hills he would cry out and cut himself with stones.

⁶When he saw Jesus from a distance, he ran and fell on his knees in front of him. ⁷He shouted at the top of his voice, "What do you want with me, Jesus, Son of the Most High God? Swear to God that you won't torture me!" ⁸For Jesus had said to him, "Come out of this man, you evil spirit!"

⁹Then Jesus asked him, "What is your name?"

"My name is Legion," he replied, "for we are many." ¹⁰And he begged Jesus again and again not to send them out of the area.

¹¹A large herd of pigs was feeding on the nearby hillside. ¹²The demons begged Jesus, "Send us among the pigs; allow us to go into them." ¹³He gave them permission, and the evil spirits came out and went into the pigs. The herd, about two thousand in number, rushed down the steep bank into the lake and were drowned.

¹⁸As Jesus was getting into the boat, the man who had been demon-possessed begged to go with him. ¹⁹Jesus did not let him, but said, **"Go home to your family and tell them how much the Lord has done for you, and how he has had mercy on you."** ²⁰So the man went away and began to tell in the Decapolis how much Jesus had done for him. And all the people were amazed.

---

## UNDERSTANDING THE SCRIPTURE

**Introduction.** Mark 5 describes three events—an exorcism, a healing, and a raising from the dead—that occurred on a preaching tour in which Jesus went across the Sea of Galilee and back again. The first account, which tells of the encounter with the Gerasene man, occurs in Gentile territory on the eastern side of the sea. Jesus then goes back across the water to an unidentified Jewish waterfront town. Here he performs the miracles of healing the woman with a hemorrhage and raising Jairus's daughter.

Bible scholars are quick to point out that Mark deliberately places these stories immediately after the calming of the storm at sea (4:35-41). In this way, Mark shows in quick succession the power of the Messiah over four cosmic elements:

- *the destructive forces of chaos,* represented by the storm and waves
- *evil,* represented by the demons
- *physical frailty,* represented by the woman's disease
- and even *death* itself.

Set in this context, we see the story of the Gerasene man as a meaningful witness to Jesus as the Messiah, the One whose coming signifies the breaking-in of God's realm and power to our world here and now.

**Mark 5:1.** The exact location of this encounter is unknown. Mark 5:1 and Luke 8:26 place the tombs in the region of the Gerasenes, while Matthew 8:28 refers to the local area of the Gadarenes. In addition, some ancient copies of the Gospels have a variant reading that reflects a third tradition; they read "Gergesenes."

Taken together, all these references point to three possible cities as the place where Jesus went—Gerasa, Gadara, and Gergesa. Of these, Gerasa is the least likely choice because it lies almost thirty miles from the Sea of Galilee. Gadara is much closer, only ten miles away, but there are no nearby cliffs. The third city, Gergesa, is the least known but the best candidate. It is located close to the shore and near the only steep cliff on that side of the sea. Whichever city was the site of this exorcism, we know that it was within Gentile territory.

**Mark 5:2-5.** Mark introduces the man from the tombs in a way designed to show him both as someone to be feared and as someone to be pitied. He is wild, out of control, and capable of violence toward himself and others. At the same time, one cannot help thinking of him as starving, unprotected from the elements, and terribly alone.

Scholars debate whether the man was Jewish or Gentile. True, Jesus met him in Gentile territory, but the text says he returned to his home "in the Decapolis" (5:20). The Decapolis was a territory rather than a city; the term refers to a federation of ten city-states throughout the Gentile region east of the Jordan. Because this area included some large Jewish settlements as well, it is impossible to say for sure what the man's heritage was.

For Mark, at least, this detail did not matter. The point of the encounter in his Gospel is not related to the man's identity as a Jew or a Gentile but to Jesus' identity as the Messiah.

**Mark 5:6-13.** The demons possessing the man recognize Jesus for who he is, and they immediately try to negotiate with him so as to avoid being cast out. "Legion," which is the name for a company of six thousand Roman soldiers, asks Jesus "not to send them out of the country." In this time and place, divine beings were understood to live in a particular location. "Legion" did not want to move to a new location. They ask instead to be sent into the nearby herd of pigs. The choice is interesting because according to Jewish law pigs are unclean.

Jesus agrees to their request, but this leads to an ironic and darkly humorous twist in the outcome. The unclean spirits, sporting the Roman (and therefore Gentile) name of "Legion," get sent into unclean, Gentile-owned animals—and the whole lot end up drowning in the sea. Mark's original audience of Jewish Christians would have found this funny, fitting, and perhaps deeply satisfying.

**Mark 5:14-17.** The swineherds then run away to spread the news of what happened, but Mark does not elaborate on what they said. What we *do* know is that people came to see for themselves, and they witnessed the formerly possessed man "sitting there, clothed and in his right mind" (5:15).

Witnesses at the scene tell what happened, and then we are hit by something unexpected. The people *beg* Jesus to leave their neighborhood. Mark does not offer an explicit explanation for this reaction, but Luke says that "they were seized with great fear" (8:37). The townspeople, having just been rid of one powerful force they could not control, apparently do not want to risk allowing another into the area, however benevolent it seems.

**Mark 5:18-20.** The story ends with another twist, this time on the traditional formula for becoming a disciple. Usually we see Jesus call out to someone, "Follow me"; then we see the person go with him (see, for example, Mark 1:16-20). Here, the opposite happens. The cured man calls out to Jesus, begging to be allowed to go with him, but Jesus denies his request.

Why does Jesus say no to this man? Some commentators think the reason may be that only the Twelve were intended to have the close relationship with Jesus that the man seems to be seeking (see 3:14). Others, however, suggest that Jesus simply has a different call in mind for this person. After all, he did say to the man, "Go home to your friends, and tell them how much the Lord has done for you, and what mercy he has shown you" (5:19).

Seen from this latter perspective, the cured man becomes a disciple who follows Jesus *spiritually* rather than physically. He serves his Lord by proclaiming the good news as he has been asked to do. Isn't this what we, as disciples in Christ's community today, are also called to do?

---

## INTERPRETING THE SCRIPTURE

### A Life Destroyed

This week's passage presents a man who is even more isolated than the person with leprosy whose cure we studied last week—and who is certainly in as much torment. Yet, as the story unfolds, we see once again Jesus' ability to heal any affliction and, in this case, his power to overcome whatever binds a person in isolation, fear, and self-destruction. With the freed man—who was at last restored to his family, faith community, and town—we also celebrate the way Christ continues to heal through the blessing of our membership in the family of God.

Our story begins with Jesus and his disciples going to a place where everything is wrong, at least by traditional Jewish standards. Indeed, the possibilities for becoming "unclean" here definitely outnumber the single risk presented in the previous lesson. First, verse 1 establishes that they have crossed the Sea of Galilee and entered Gentile territory. As if this is not bad enough, the boat lands near a graveyard (5:2) and the grazing place of a large number of pigs (5:11). Then, added to these other conditions unacceptable to pious Jews, a man possessed by an evil spirit runs toward their party to speak with Jesus.

The picture of the man from the tombs is disturbing. Whether you consider him demon-possessed or mentally ill, he presents a frightening image. Violently strong and prone to conduct conversation by shouting at the top of his lungs, he carries the marks of places where he has deliberately cut and bruised himself. Verse 15, which describes the townspeople as surprised to see him clothed, suggests that his normal state was to wear little or no clothing. It is no wonder that the people tried to chain him so he could not run free.

Yet, when we think about it, the picture of this man is also very pathetic. Here is someone who has been kept in chained solitude by others, possibly even friends and family, and completely cut off from loving human contact. For who knows how long, his only companions among the corpses in the graveyard have been the spirits that possess him. No doubt over the years, the loneliness and isolation added to his condition; they certainly did not help it. No wonder he ran to Jesus.

### An Identity Confirmed

In today's world, many of us take great care to guard against identity theft. We are warned through commercials, e-mails, and letters how to avoid having someone steal our personal information and then use it for their own personal gain. The financial problems that would then ensue seem almost small, though, compared to the level of identity theft that the Gerasene man has endured.

Taken over by forces beyond his power to control, this man no longer has a sense of self at all. He doesn't even have a name—when Jesus asks for one, only the spirits reply. They are "Legion" (a Roman military term designating a unit of about six thousand); the man himself is nameless. It is as if he no longer exists except as a vessel for the spirits' presence in the world.

Yet these spirits, who have apparently destroyed this man's identity completely, have no trouble recognizing who Jesus is. They address him immediately as the "Son of the Most High God" (5:7) and acknowledge his power over them. They see what the humans around Jesus do not, as yet: that the power of God has come fully into the world at last, and from now on nothing will be the same.

Indeed, that turns out to be true for the tormented man. Jesus releases him from the forces that control him, thus restoring him to life. From now on, nothing will be the same, and that is good news such as only God can create. From now on, the man will be able to laugh and love, care and serve,

worship and pray—all within the company of others that he so longed to have.

### A New Life Given

Up until now in this story we have seen Jesus acquiesce to what the evil spirits ask of him. At the start of their impromptu meeting, "Legion"—speaking through the unwilling host—shouts out, "do not torment me" (5:7), and Jesus doesn't. Then the spirits beg Jesus not to send them out of the area (5:10), and again he complies. They make a final request that Jesus send them into the herd of swine (5:12), which he does.

Given this, it may come as a bit of a surprise when Jesus denies the only request made to him by the cured man (5:18-19). Brought back to the wholeness of life at last, the man wants only to be with Jesus, so he begs to be allowed to accompany him. Jesus refuses, though, and sends the man away.

Then comes another surprise. Instead of telling the man to keep quiet about what has happened, as usually happens in Mark's Gospel, Jesus charges him to go home and tell what the Lord has done. The man does as Jesus asks, and then some: he spreads the news throughout the whole area.

In the original Greek, Jesus tells the man to go to his household and speak to the people there. Perhaps Jesus did not want the family to suffer any more. After all, they had waited a long time, perhaps with little or no hope, for this man to be restored to them. Surely they would grieve to learn that, although now restored to himself, he was still not to be a part of them.

Or perhaps Jesus wanted to help this man, who now knew himself to be a part of the household of God, discover and grow into his role in this new family. By leaving Jesus, at whose side he felt accepted and safe, the man freed himself to serve the Lord through evangelism and mission. By going when and where Jesus sent him, the man became the means by which others could discover their own invitation to join the family of God.

Like the restored man, we too need to go away sometimes from the place where we feel comfortable. Rather than sitting inside the familiar walls of our church, in the familiar same old pew, we need to step out into the world. Rather than spiritually lingering beside Jesus, basking in the comfort that brings us, we need to go where he sends us, when he sends us.

In an article in *Christian Century* (May 29, 2007) entitled "The Poured-out Church," noted Episcopalian preacher Barbara Brown Taylor refers to this as "leaving church," and she highly recommends it:

Leaving church, I believe, is what church is for[—]leaving on a regular basis, leaving to see what God is up to in the world and joining God there, delivering all the riches of the institution to those who need them most, in full trust that God will never leave the church without all that it needs to live.

# SHARING THE SCRIPTURE

### *Preparing Our Hearts*

Meditate on this week's devotional reading, found in Luke 7:18-23. As you contemplate this passage, ask yourself: How do I know who Jesus is? What signs enable me to recognize him? Luke reports that the disciples of John have been sent to ask Jesus if he, or another, is the One they are waiting for. Jesus answers by telling John's disciples to report on what they have seen and heard Jesus do. How would you introduce others to Jesus so that they too could clearly recognize him as the Messiah?

Pray that you and the adult learners will be ever alert to the marvelous words and deeds of Jesus that are enacted in your presence.

### *Preparing Our Minds*

Study the background from Mark 5:1-20 and the lesson scripture from verses 1-13, 18-20. Consider the help available to you when problems are so overwhelming that you do not know where to turn.

A word of caution as you approach this session: some members of the class, or those they love, may have battled or continue to battle with mental illness. While it is appropriate to note that a relationship with Christ can help one dealing with such illness, be very careful not to create the impression that one who is truly related to Christ cannot become mentally ill.

Write on newsprint:
- ❑ information for next week's lesson, found under "Continue the Journey."
- ❑ activities for further spiritual growth in "Continue the Journey."

Select meditative music and have the appropriate player on hand if you opt to use this music for "Recognize Ways the Learners May Be in Bondage So As to Open Themselves to Jesus' Liberating Healing."

### LEADING THE CLASS

### *(1) Gather to Learn*

❖ Welcome the class members and introduce any guests.

❖ Pray that those who have gathered today will find peace and joy as they recognize the living Christ in their midst.

❖ Read this story to the class: **When Willard State Hospital in upstate New York, which opened in 1869 to treat mentally ill patients, closed in 1995, a treasure trove of patients' lives was left behind in suitcases that had been long stored in the attic. A book by Darby Penney and Dr.**

Peter Stastny, *The Lives They Left Behind: Suitcases from a State Hospital Attic*, reveals in words and photographs the lives of several of those patients. Whatever the specific diagnosis that prompted their admission to Willard, these patients were alienated and isolated from those around them. The hospital seemed to be their only source of help. Yet, treatments in vogue at the time of their illness generally made little difference. Very few were able to rejoin their families and communities.

❖ Ask: **How do people today view those who suffer from mental illness? What attempts are made to help them return to the mainstream of life?**

❖ Read aloud today's focus statement: **At times, our problems are so overwhelming and sometimes cause such alienation that we do not know where to turn. What help is available? Mark's account of the Gerasene demoniac demonstrates that Jesus is able to break the chains that bind and isolate us and bring us back into community.**

*(2) Explore Jesus' Encounter with a Person Bound by Unclean Spirits*

❖ Select three volunteers to read the parts of Jesus, the demoniac/unclean spirits, and the narrator in Mark 5:1-13, 18-20.

❖ Talk with the class about the isolation this demoniac must feel, given his mental situation and where he lives. Use "A Life Destroyed" from Interpreting the Scripture if you prefer to do a lecture.

❖ Point out, using information from Mark 5:6-13 in Understanding the Scripture, that the demons recognize Jesus and try to negotiate with him.

❖ Look again at Mark 5:18-20. Ask: **Why does Jesus deny this man's request to go with Jesus?** Use information from these verses in Understanding the Scripture to provide several explanations.

❖ Distribute paper and pencils. Invite the adults to work with a partner or in a small group to write a prayer of thanksgiving that this man, now released from demons, might have offered. If time permits, encourage several volunteers to read their prayers aloud.

*(3) Recognize Ways the Learners May Be in Bondage So As to Open Themselves to Jesus' Liberating Healing*

❖ Provide time for the learners to think about ways they may see themselves in bondage. Perhaps they feel trapped by poverty, or are in an abusive situation, or have a chronic illness that limits their actions, or have a challenging family member for whom they are responsible. As an option, play a meditative, instrumental selection that will allow the adults to focus their thoughts.

❖ Conclude this time with this guided imagery as learners sit with eyes closed.

■ **See yourself with Jesus in a place that is special to you. Notice the sights, sounds, and aromas of this place as you see him walk toward you.** (pause)

■ **Envision yourself kneeling before Jesus as he asks, "Son or daughter, what can I do for you?"** (pause)

■ **Speak silently to Jesus, sharing whatever burden that has shackled you.** (pause)

■ **Feel, see, and hear these chains break as Jesus pronounces you liberated and healed.** (pause)

■ **Offer a silent prayer of praise and thanksgiving. Try to be as specific as possible about how this deliverance will change your life.** (pause)

■ **Covenant with Jesus to go and tell others how his mercy has changed your life.** (pause)

■ **Open your eyes when you are ready.** (Pause until most class members have indicated their readiness to move on.)

*(4) Identify and Find Ways to Assist Those*
*Persons Who Live in Isolation at the*
*Edges of Society*

❖ Point out that although mental illness often isolates people from society and reality itself, there are many people today who live in isolation for other reasons. List on newsprint groups of people (not individuals) who appear to be isolated from the mainstream. Here are some groups to consider: *those with HIV/AIDS, homeless persons, poor people, people with infirmities that keep them homebound, prisoners, people separated from families due to war.*

❖ Discern together one or more groups of people that the class may be able to assist. Discuss steps that the class can take to help these people move from isolation to community.

❖ Covenant together to enact whatever steps you have outlined.

*(5) Continue the Journey*

❖ Pray that all who have gathered will recognize Jesus and through him be restored to health and wholeness.

❖ Read aloud this preparation for next week's lesson. You may also want to post it on newsprint for the students to copy.

■ **Title: Begging to Get In**
■ **Background Scripture: Mark 7:24-30**
■ **Lesson Scripture: Mark 7:24-30**
■ **Focus of the Lesson: We are sometimes astonished by the faith and** tenacity that people exhibit. What motivates people to maintain such an attitude? The woman of Syrophoenicia believed that Jesus could heal her daughter, so she persisted despite Jesus' challenging questions.

❖ Challenge the students to complete one or more of these activities for further spiritual growth, which you will write on newsprint for the students to copy.

(1) **Visit, if possible, someone who suffers from mental illness or has emotional problems. Do whatever you can to let this person know that he or she is valued and loved.**

(2) **Do an Internet search on "Christian faith and mental health" to learn more about the role that faith can play in achieving and sustaining mental health.**

(3) **Go forth, just as the newly delivered demoniac was commissioned to do, to tell others about what God has done for you and the mercy God has shown.**

❖ Sing or read aloud "He Touched Me."

❖ Conclude today's session by leading the class in this benediction, based on 1 Peter 2:9: **Go forth with the assurance that you are part of a chosen race, a royal priesthood, a holy nation, God's own people, in order that you may proclaim the mighty acts of him who called you out of darkness into his marvelous light.**

## UNIT 2: AN OPEN INVITATION TO COVENANT LIVING
# BEGGING TO GET IN

---

### PREVIEWING THE LESSON

**Lesson Scripture:** Mark 7:24-30
**Background Scripture:** Mark 7:24-30
**Key Verse:** Mark 7:26

### Focus of the Lesson:

We are sometimes astonished by the faith and tenacity that people exhibit. What motivates people to maintain such an attitude? The woman of Syrophoenicia believed that Jesus could heal her daughter, so she persisted despite Jesus' challenging questions.

### Goals for the Learners:

(1) to explore the narrative of Jesus' encounter with the Syrophoenician woman.
(2) to appreciate the role of tenacious faith in their own lives.
(3) to recount times when they needed a strong faith and to share how God worked in their lives during those times.

### Pronunciation Guide:

Syrophoenician (si roh fi nish' uhn)
Tyre (tire)

### Supplies:

Bibles, newsprint and marker, paper and pencils, hymnals

---

### READING THE SCRIPTURE

NRSV
Mark 7:24-30

²⁴From there he set out and went away to the region of Tyre. He entered a house and did not want anyone to know he was there. Yet he could not escape notice, ²⁵but a woman whose little daughter had an unclean spirit immediately heard about him,

NIV
Mark 7:24-30

²⁴Jesus left that place and went to the vicinity of Tyre. He entered a house and did not want anyone to know it; yet he could not keep his presence secret. ²⁵In fact, as soon as she heard about him, a woman whose little daughter was possessed by an evil spirit

and she came and bowed down at his feet. <sup>26</sup>**Now the woman was a Gentile, of Syrophoenician origin. She begged him to cast the demon out of her daughter.** <sup>27</sup>He said to her, "Let the children be fed first, for it is not fair to take the children's food and throw it to the dogs." <sup>28</sup>But she answered him, "Sir, even the dogs under the table eat the children's crumbs." <sup>29</sup>Then he said to her, "For saying that, you may go—the demon has left your daughter." <sup>30</sup>So she went home, found the child lying on the bed, and the demon gone.

came and fell at his feet. <sup>26</sup>**The woman was a Greek, born in Syrian Phoenicia. She begged Jesus to drive the demon out of her daughter.**

<sup>27</sup>"First let the children eat all they want," he told her, "for it is not right to take the children's bread and toss it to their dogs."

<sup>28</sup>"Yes, Lord," she replied, "but even the dogs under the table eat the children's crumbs."

<sup>29</sup>Then he told her, "For such a reply, you may go; the demon has left your daughter."

<sup>30</sup>She went home and found her child lying on the bed, and the demon gone.

---

## UNDERSTANDING THE SCRIPTURE

**Introduction.** Mark 7:1-13 contains a theological debate between Jesus and the scribes and Pharisees regarding the nature of defilement, followed by Jesus teaching the crowd about the same concept. The scribes and Pharisees want to uphold Jewish tradition by maintaining that everyone should adhere strictly to the laws governing food preparation. To do anything else is to become ritually unclean, profane rather than holy.

Jesus counters this argument by saying that our attitudes affect our holiness far more than unfeeling observance of a law does. He accuses the scribes and Pharisees of breaking God's law at their convenience by interpreting ancient laws in ways that let them be ignored. Their actions show that they do not really love God or others, and that alone is enough to show themselves as less than holy.

In Mark 7:14-16 Jesus summarizes this theme by teaching a crowd about what constitutes defilement. We hear Jesus continue this discussion with his disciples in verses 17-23.

The debate over what defiles a person sets a powerful context for this week's passage. Jesus has just maintained that only what's in the heart determines whether a person is living out God's call to holiness, yet he is about to meet a Gentile woman—a person whom traditional Jews considered far from holy based on both her race and her gender. In her request of aid for her daughter, the issue will shift from the debate of whether defilement relates to what's "within" or what's "without" to the far more critical question of whether Jesus' ministry is only for those "within" the bounds of Judaism—or if it is also for those who are "without."

At the time Mark wrote, Jewish and Gentile Christians were still learning how to be a community together. Thus, Mark wanted to make very clear that *both* groups were called by Jesus, loved by Jesus, and saved by Jesus. To help make this point, he follows the meeting with the Syrophoenician woman with two other accounts of Jesus' care for Gentiles. Mark 7:31-37 tells of the healing of a man in a Gentile area who is deaf and mute, and Mark 8:1-10 records a miracle feeding of four thousand people in the wilderness.

**Mark 7:24-26.** Jesus has gone off to the

region of Tyre, which was a major Phoenician seaport. At one time, relations between Tyre and Israel were very good. The Bible records that King Hiram of Tyre, who had been a friend of King David's, sent workers and cedar timbers at King Solomon's request to aid in building the Temple (1 Kings 5:1-12). Over the years, however, that changed, and relations between the Hebrew community and the people of this area became very strained. Thus, the primary motive for choosing this site seems to be Jesus' hope that few people will recognize him.

Indeed, Mark indicates that Jesus has gone to this Gentile area to get a break from all the people seeking him out. He quietly enters a house in Tyre with the intention of maintaining a low profile so that no one will know he is in town. Yet somehow his fame had reached the Gentiles here already, and someone recognizes him. Word spreads quickly; we are told that a certain woman hears of him "immediately" (7:25). This woman's small daughter is possessed by an unclean spirit, so perhaps interested parties hurried to her with news of the miracle worker's arrival.

The woman approaches Jesus, bows down at his feet, and begs him to rid her daughter of the demon. In this, she mirrors the action of the man whom Jesus cured of a skin disease (lesson for October 4) and the man that Jesus freed from demon possession (lesson for October 11). They too approached Jesus, knelt before him, and begged for help. Unlike them, however, the woman is not begging for help for herself. Her request is for her daughter, and perhaps that is why the Greek form of the verb for "beg" in 7:26 carries the sense of a repeated and persistent action. This mother will not stop making her plea until there is absolutely no hope left.

**Mark 7:27-30.** Jesus' reply to the woman seems quite harsh to modern readers. He apparently rebuffs her, stating in essence that he has come to feed God's "children" (Israel) and not the "dogs" (Gentiles).

Church members and scholars alike have wrestled over these words and wondered what Jesus really intended by saying them. Some of the more common suggestions are:

(1) Jesus really did believe his mission was to teach and minister to the Jews, and that somehow the Gentiles would come in later under the missionary efforts of the church.

(2) Jesus needed this time of retreat and did not want to draw attention to himself by another miracle.

(3) Jesus acted this way for the disciples' sake, so they would face their own prejudice and be challenged to overcome it.

(4) Jesus and the woman were verbally sparring with each other, but in a friendly way. Proponents of this view point out that the word translated "dog" is a diminutive form that could indicate a pet held in affection.

The first two views do not fit Jesus' actions throughout the rest of Mark and the other Gospels, and the latter two suggestions are problematic in other ways. For example, while Jesus says harsh things to others on occasion, it is never to teach the disciples a lesson at an innocent person's expense. Likewise, even if we shift the word "dog" to "pet," it still sounds condescending. So none of the above perspectives quite seem to address the matter satisfactorily.

A fifth suggestion offered by a few scholars seems more fitting with the rest of Mark's Gospel. Perhaps Jesus speaks as he does to ensure that his role as the Messiah will not be misunderstood as it applies to Jews and to Gentiles. (More is said on this as follows.)

Regardless of Jesus' motive in speaking as he does, the women's motive is clear: she wants help for her daughter, and she knows Jesus can give it. Her persistence, grounded as it is in faith, pays off. She replies to Jesus' seeming rebuff with a clever answer that apparently meets with his approval. Then and there he proclaims the daughter to be set free. The woman returns home to find that it is so.

# INTERPRETING THE SCRIPTURE

### An Intrusive Encounter

At the start of the passage for this week, it's easy to feel sorry for Jesus. He has been hounded by crowds from the start of his ministry, and, despite his best efforts, people seem bent on misinterpreting his mission. Time alone to pray and recoup his spiritual energy has become a challenge, and one gets the sense that Sabbaths are not exactly a day of rest for him anymore (see, for example, 2:23–3:6 and 6:1-6). So, in what seems almost an act of desperation, he heads off to the area around the city of Tyre.

Like the Decapolis (mentioned in last week's lesson), this area was primarily Gentile but contained a number of Jewish settlements. It is likely that Jesus went to a home in one of these Jewish areas. The only detail Mark makes very clear is Jesus' motive: he wanted a place where he could hide out for awhile (7:24). Yet, after traveling all those miles to find a place where he could be inconspicuous, he is still sought out—and by a Gentile woman, no less!

Mark's original audience would have understood immediately that this woman is trespassing into Jesus' space in more ways than one. First, there is a level of audacity in seeking him out, uninvited, within the confines of another person's home—especially the home of someone she probably does not know. (What's more, the text hints that Jesus was staying inside to avoid encounters like this.) Second, as a Gentile, she knows that her presence will be unwelcome to a practicing Jew. Finally, and perhaps most of all, the woman knows that, as a female, to come unbidden and unattended into the presence of a man who is not a family member is shockingly disgraceful behavior. That one act alone is enough to bring shame on both her and Jesus.

Seen from this perspective, we can appreciate that the woman does not exactly present herself in a way designed to impress Jesus or even to get him to look on her favorably. She is desperate, however, and her need overcomes all thoughts of social propriety.

### A Surprising Model of Faith

As socially shocking as the woman's behavior is, the rest of her actions are surprisingly befitting to a person of faith. Here, where we might least expect to find it, are expressions of humility, trust, and hope. First, the woman bows down before Jesus, as have others in Mark's Gospel who recognize his authority as being from God. Then, she begs him to rescue her small daughter from the demons that possess her, and she shows absolute confidence that he has the power to do so.

When Jesus throws up a seeming barrier to the child's deliverance, the woman responds with a theological insightfulness that pleases him. She does not accept at face value a proposed theology that limits Jesus' mission or his power to one group alone; neither does she argue against it. Rather, she affirms God's apparent priorities and asks merely to have her child included in them. She shows us that sometimes we can broaden the whole mission of the church simply by taking that first step to reach out to a single person we have excluded until now.

This Gentile mother also teaches us about persistence and trust. She reminds us to keep pressing for healing and wholeness wherever they are needed and to keep working for what is just and right. She reminds us that to stop pressing is to let the demonic forces win. Most of all, she reminds us the basis for this persistence is trust—trust that God in Christ has the power and the desire to tend to us and our needs. Knowing this, *believing* this, frees us to then focus on the needs of others, which is what discipleship and ministry are all about.

### Bread for the World

We are still left with the question of why Jesus initially responds to the woman as he does. Here is a mother whose child is in pain, requiring deliverance that a regular physician or priest cannot provide, and she has sought the one person who can help. Here is Jesus, the same man who was moved to compassion by an outcast in the lesson for October 4 and who granted the request of demons in the lesson for October 11, and he responds, "Let the children be fed first, for it is not fair to take the children's food and throw it to the dogs" (7:27).

Some scholars have proposed that Mark's use of the messianic secret may be the clue to understanding this problematic saying. Throughout his Gospel, Mark has Jesus tell people not to spread the news about who he is or what he has done *so that people will not jump to the wrong conclusion about who the Messiah is and what defines his mission.* Jesus knows that only after the crucifixion and resurrection will people be able to understand a Messiah who comes as a Suffering Servant and not as a national hero.

In that same vein, then, perhaps Jesus is making sure this Gentile woman understands his mission clearly. If she does, it will lessen the chance that helping her might confuse the issue. He knows that by helping her he will blur some boundaries, and that's okay—but it is *not* okay for his identity to

also become blurred in the process. Jesus has come as the Jewish Messiah, the one expected by the prophets and promised by God, and he cannot afford for his role or purpose to be misconstrued.

So Jesus throws down the theological gauntlet of his identity to see if she will understand and accept it. She does. In fact, the woman upholds it. Her response to Jesus shows that she understands that because he *is* the Messiah of Israel, then he is also the One who God promised would save the world. His mission may not put her or her daughter at the center, but it does include them somewhere within its boundaries. In her own way, she affirms Jesus as the bread of heaven who "gives life to the world" (John 6:33), and she takes that to mean even folk like her will be granted the mercy of a crumb of it. In her faith, she trusts a single crumb to be enough.

Because of her insight, persistence, and trust, Jesus gives the woman the "crumb" for which she desperately begs—her daughter is freed from the demon's possession. His mission as the Jewish Messiah is still intact, and he will soon return to Galilee and renew his efforts to call the Jews back into a right relationship with God. Yet, in this act of using his healing mercies on behalf of the woman and her daughter, we see that Jesus was willing to respond positively to faith wherever he encountered it. We see the beginnings of a mission to the Gentiles that, thanks be to God, has brought far more than crumbs of grace to us all.

---

## SHARING THE SCRIPTURE

### Preparing Our Hearts

Meditate on this week's devotional reading, found in 2 Corinthians 8:1-7. Paul writes to the church in Corinth, asking them

to be generous in their financial giving for the struggling mother church in Jerusalem. He cajoles them by pointing out how generous the poverty-stricken churches in Macedonia have been. God's mercy and grace have been poured out, and Paul wants people to respond to that mercy and grace by helping brothers and sisters in need. How do you respond to those who need help? In what ways do you share with others the mercy and grace that God has lavished upon you? What action can you take this week to share more of God's goodness with others?

Pray that you and the adult learners will be alert for instances of God's mercy in your own lives and the lives of others.

### Preparing Our Minds

Study the background and lesson scripture, both of which are from Mark 7:24-30. Think about what motivates some people to maintain an attitude of faith and tenacity.

Write on newsprint:

❏ Scripture assignments and questions for "Appreciate the Role of Tenacious Faith in the Learners' Lives."

❏ information for next week's lesson, found under "Continue the Journey."

❏ activities for further spiritual growth in "Continue the Journey."

### LEADING THE CLASS

### (1) Gather to Learn

❖ Welcome the class members and introduce any guests.

❖ Pray that all who have come today will be open to the leading and teaching of the Holy Spirit.

❖ Read this story circulating on the Internet that has been attributed to Paul Harvey concerning the persistence of a small bold boy: **Before entering a grocery store, a mother instructed her young son not to ask for chocolate chip cookies because he wasn't going to get any. When they reached the cookie aisle, the boy asked, "Mom, can I have some chocolate chip cookies?" to which she replied that** she had told him not to even ask. **Having forgotten something in that aisle, the mother circled back and the boy again asked for chocolate chip cookies—and was again denied. Finally, at the checkout counter the desperate lad stood up and shouted, "In the name of Jesus, may I have some chocolate chip cookies?" Shoppers laughed, applauded, and due to their generosity, the boy and his mother left with twenty-three boxes of chocolate chip cookies.**

❖ Ask: **What does this story suggest about persistent faith, even when the answer seems to be "no"?**

❖ Read aloud today's focus statement: **We are sometimes astonished by the faith and tenacity that people exhibit. What motivates people to maintain such an attitude? The woman of Syrophoenicia believed that Jesus could heal her daughter, so she persisted despite Jesus' challenging questions.**

### (2) Explore the Narrative of Jesus' Encounter with the Syrophoenician Woman

❖ Read or retell the section entitled "Introduction" in Understanding the Scripture to set the stage for today's lesson.

❖ Choose three volunteers, each of whom has a different translation of the Bible, to read Mark 7:24-30. Encourage the students to listen carefully for different wording in these translations that shade the meaning of the story.

❖ Ask someone to tell the story from the point of view of the mother. Suggest that the storyteller include answers to these questions. Why did she approach Jesus? What did she think that she, a Gentile woman, might be able to get from Jesus? What concerns, if any, did she have about defying social conventions?

❖ Ask another volunteer to tell the story from the point of view of Jesus. Suggest that the storyteller include answers to these questions. How was he feeling before the woman arrived? Why did he initially deny her request? What might he have learned about his own mission as a result of this encounter?

❖ Use Mark 7:27-30 in Understanding the Scripture to help the class understand possible interpretations of Jesus' initial attempt to turn this woman away. Ask: **Which of these explanations seems most plausible to you? Do you have another possible explanation?**

❖ Conclude this portion of the lesson by reading or retelling "A Surprising Model of Faith" to help the class see what lessons this Gentile mother might teach them.

*(3) Appreciate the Role of Tenacious Faith in the Learners' Lives*

❖ Divide the class into groups and distribute paper and pencils. Assign one of these stories in which Jesus commends someone's faith to each group. If the class is large, you may assign the same story to more than one group or add other examples. Post the assignments on newsprint.

■ Matthew 8:5-13    **Jesus Heals a Centurion's Servant**
■ Matthew 9:2-8    **Jesus Heals a Paralytic**
■ Mark 5:25-34    **Jesus Heals a Woman**
■ Luke 7:36-50    **Jesus Forgives a Sinful Woman**
■ Luke 17:11-19    **Jesus Cleanses Ten Lepers**
■ Luke 18:35-43    **Jesus Heals a Blind Beggar**

❖ Post these questions on newsprint for each group to answer.

(1) **What does this main character need from Jesus?**

(2) **To what lengths does the character (or friends) seem willing to go to have this need met? What risk is this character taking?**

(3) **If there are spectators, do any act as if the person in need does not deserve Jesus' compassion and grace? Why do you think some people feel this way? What do Jesus' actions reveal about his willingness to be merciful?**

(4) **In what way(s) do you see the main character(s) in your assigned story as being similar to the Syrophoenician woman?**

(5) **What does this story teach you about Jesus' response to people of faith?**

❖ Invite a speaker from each group to report to the class.

❖ End this portion of the lesson by asking the class: **What impact do these stories have on your faith?**

*(4) Recount Times When the Learners Needed a Strong Faith and Share How God Worked in Their Lives During Those Times*

❖ Ask the students to tell a partner about a time when they needed a strong faith and found that God worked in their lives.

❖ Bring the class together and thank the students for sharing their stories. Invite the class to discuss these questions.

(1) **In what ways are our stories similar to the stories of the Syrophoenician woman and the other characters we have encountered today?**

(2) **What does this Gentile mother's story reveal to us about who God is ready to include in the Kingdom?**

(3) **What do we need to do as individuals and as a class to let those on the outside know that God—and we—welcome them?**

❖ Close this part of the session by inviting the students to meditate silently on these questions: **On a scale of one to ten, how do I rate my own degree of faith in**

God? If I believe my faith is insufficient, what help do I need from God to increase it?

### (5) Continue the Journey

❖ Break the silence by praying that today's participants will give thanks for the grace and mercy of God even as they continue to grow in their faith.

❖ Read aloud this preparation for next week's lesson. You may also want to post it on newsprint for the students to copy.

- ■ Title: Opting Out!
- ■ Background Scripture: Mark 10:17-31
- ■ Lesson Scripture: Mark 10:17-31
- ■ Focus of the Lesson: People wonder whether eternal life exists and how they may obtain it. What leads to eternal life? Jesus teaches that to become true followers and so inherit eternal life we must submit our possessions and ourselves to God.

❖ Challenge the students to complete one or more of these activities for further spiritual growth, which you will write on newsprint for the students to copy.

(1) Read a book or an article about how strong faith helped an individual or group deal with difficult circumstances. How does this faith encourage you?

(2) Support, in whatever way you can, someone who is having difficulty. Listening carefully to concerns and offering prayer are important ways of letting people know you—and God—care.

(3) Write in your spiritual journal about a time when you faced a challenging situation and persevered with God until a solution came.

❖ Sing or read aloud "There's a Wideness in God's Mercy."

❖ Conclude today's session by leading the class in this benediction, based on 1 Peter 2:9: Go forth with the assurance that you are part of a chosen race, a royal priesthood, a holy nation, God's own people, in order that you may proclaim the mighty acts of him who called you out of darkness into his marvelous light.

## UNIT 2: AN OPEN INVITATION TO COVENANT LIVING
# OPTING OUT!

---

### PREVIEWING THE LESSON

**Lesson Scripture:** Mark 10:17-31
**Background Scripture:** Mark 10:17-31
**Key Verse:** Mark 10:21

### Focus of the Lesson:
People wonder whether eternal life exists and how they may obtain it. What leads to eternal life? Jesus teaches that to become true followers and so inherit eternal life we must submit our possessions and ourselves to God.

### Goals for the Learners:
(1) to delve into Mark's version of a rich person's encounter with Jesus.
(2) to recognize that they must wholeheartedly focus on God, not allowing anything else to take priority.
(3) to make a commitment to give their lives and possessions completely to God.

### Supplies:
Bibles, newsprint and marker, paper and pencils, hymnals, optional pictures illustrating wealth, tape

---

### READING THE SCRIPTURE

NRSV
Mark 10:17-31

¹⁷As he was setting out on a journey, a man ran up and knelt before him, and asked him, "Good Teacher, what must I do to inherit eternal life?" ¹⁸Jesus said to him, "Why do you call me good? No one is good but God alone. ¹⁹You know the commandments: 'You shall not murder; You shall not commit adultery; You shall not steal; You shall not bear false witness; You shall not defraud; Honor your father and mother.'"

NIV
Mark 10:17-31

¹⁷As Jesus started on his way, a man ran up to him and fell on his knees before him. "Good teacher," he asked, "what must I do to inherit eternal life?"

¹⁸"Why do you call me good?" Jesus answered. "No one is good—except God alone. ¹⁹You know the commandments: 'Do not murder, do not commit adultery, do not steal, do not give false testimony, do not defraud, honor your father and mother.'"

20He said to him, "Teacher, I have kept all these since my youth." 21**Jesus, looking at him, loved him and said, "You lack one thing; go, sell what you own, and give the money to the poor, and you will have treasure in heaven; then come, follow me."** 22When he heard this, he was shocked and went away grieving, for he had many possessions.

23Then Jesus looked around and said to his disciples, "How hard it will be for those who have wealth to enter the kingdom of God!" 24And the disciples were perplexed at these words. But Jesus said to them again, "Children, how hard it is to enter the kingdom of God! 25It is easier for a camel to go through the eye of a needle than for someone who is rich to enter the kingdom of God." 26They were greatly astounded and said to one another, "Then who can be saved?" 27Jesus looked at them and said, "For mortals it is impossible, but not for God; for God all things are possible."

28Peter began to say to him, "Look, we have left everything and followed you." 29Jesus said, "Truly I tell you, there is no one who has left house or brothers or sisters or mother or father or children or fields, for my sake and for the sake of the good news, 30who will not receive a hundredfold now in this age—houses, brothers and sisters, mothers and children, and fields, with persecutions—and in the age to come eternal life. 31But many who are first will be last, and the last will be first."

20"Teacher," he declared, "all these I have kept since I was a boy."

21**Jesus looked at him and loved him. "One thing you lack," he said. "Go, sell everything you have and give to the poor, and you will have treasure in heaven. Then come, follow me."**

22At this the man's face fell. He went away sad, because he had great wealth.

23Jesus looked around and said to his disciples, "How hard it is for the rich to enter the kingdom of God!"

24The disciples were amazed at his words. But Jesus said again, "Children, how hard it is to enter the kingdom of God! 25It is easier for a camel to go through the eye of a needle than for a rich man to enter the kingdom of God."

26The disciples were even more amazed, and said to each other, "Who then can be saved?"

27Jesus looked at them and said, "With man this is impossible, but not with God; all things are possible with God."

28Peter said to him, "We have left everything to follow you!"

29"I tell you the truth," Jesus replied, "no one who has left home or brothers or sisters or mother or father or children or fields for me and the gospel 30will fail to receive a hundred times as much in this present age (homes, brothers, sisters, mothers, children and fields—and with them, persecutions) and in the age to come, eternal life. 31But many who are first will be last, and the last first."

---

## UNDERSTANDING THE SCRIPTURE

**Introduction.** The story of Jesus and the little children (10:13-16) forms one bookend for our text this week. The other is the story of James and John seeking places of honor in the future time of Jesus' glory, immediately after he has predicted his death and resurrection for the third time (10:32-45).

Together, these accounts provide a fertile setting for Jesus' encounter with the rich man and his subsequent teachings to the disciples. We are reminded that disciples are to trust God as completely as a child does *and* that following Jesus means setting all other priorities in second place. This theological framework helps us explore Jesus' words to the rich man through the lens that Mark had in mind.

**Mark 10:17-22.** Verse 17 brings us to the story of the rich man. Although most people think of it as the story of the rich young ruler, only Luke says he was a ruler (18:18), and only Matthew says he was young (19:20). The critical point, held by all three Gospel writers, is that he was rich.

As Mark presents it, the account begins almost as a parody of the ones we have studied so far. Four times now a person has run up to Jesus, knelt before him, and asked for something. The first three begged for healing, wholeness, and restoration to the community of faith. Now, on this last occasion, we see a rich man ask for instructions as to how to get eternal life—the place where healing, wholeness, and restoration to a full relationship with God are available forever—only to discover that he may not decide to pursue it after all.

The difference? The three people before this man knew they had lost everything, and no price was too high to pay to get what they longed for. This rich man, however, has virtually everything he could wish for, and he definitely sees some costs as too much to pay.

Jesus leads the man to confront the dilemma by forcing a moment of choice: "Sell what you own, and give the money to the poor . . . then come, follow me" (10:21). The man is often seen as the only person recorded who refuses this invitation. Although the text does not explicitly say what he ultimately did, the clear implication is that he walked away and never returned.

The incident of the rich man raises the problem of our own attitude toward material possessions. The ruler was a devout person, concerned about his relationship with God, and ready, within limits, to receive advice or correction about that relationship. In answer to Jesus' initial teaching, the man declared he had kept all the commandments that were mentioned. No doubt he expected to receive praise for his virtues, but instead Jesus asserted that he lacked one thing. Did Jesus mean love or generosity? If the ruler had been more generous would Jesus have asked him to sell all and give to the poor before coming to follow him?

Thus we come to the central problem. Does this passage condemn wealth in general or the man's attitude toward his riches? Human nature being what it is, we naturally prefer the latter interpretation, and it may be correct. There is no evidence that Jesus asked all who believed in him to abandon all their possessions and their families, although this may have been partially true for the Twelve.

**Mark 10:23-27.** Reflecting on the reaction of the man, Jesus comments on how difficult it is for those with wealth to enter the kingdom. In verse 25 we read the well-known saying: "It is easier for a camel to go through the eye of a needle than for someone who is rich to enter the kingdom of God."

Scholars have attempted to soften the impact of the saying in a couple of ways. Some have thought that Jesus referred to a common and well-known practice of travelers in those days. All cities were surrounded by high protective walls, not just against invading armies but against organized groups of thieves that wandered the countryside. During the day the gates in the wall were open, but at night they were closed. Should travelers arrive at the walls at night, it would be unsafe to camp outside, and they would demand a special opening of the gates to enter. A trick of the thief gangs was to load a camel with huge bags on both sides, beg entrance at the gate, then rush in when the gates were opened wide to admit the laden beast. In defense of that maneuver, many cities cut a second gate next to the first, this one a tiny gate called the "needle's eye." In order to enter, the camel had to be unloaded, kneel down and be pushed from behind and pulled from the front. No thief could sneak in.

The other approach is to point out that the word for "camel" is almost identical with the word for "rope" or "hawser." Some suggest that this was the metaphor Jesus used: "It is easier for a rope to go through the eye of a needle than for a rich man to enter the kingdom." However, lest we let ourselves off the hook too easily, we need to wrestle with the implication of taking Jesus' words at face value.

**Mark 10:28-31.** The conversation now shifts from the problem of the wealthy and the realm of God to the issue of the disciples' destiny and their rewards. Peter speaks for the group and reminds Jesus that the Twelve have "left everything" to follow Jesus. (This does not seem to have been the consistent practice in the first-generation church. First Corinthians 9:3-6 indicates that Peter (Cephas) and other itinerant preachers were accompanied by their wives.)

Jesus' reassuring response to Peter's question involves a twofold promise in verse 30. First, there is the promise for "in this age." The promise is that those who had made such sacrifices would receive "a hundredfold" more. Second, there is a promise of "eternal life" in the age to come. Taken in context with the previous verse, this means that those who have made sacrifices in terms of family life will receive blessings through fellowship in the Christian community.

---

## INTERPRETING THE SCRIPTURE

### Some Key Questions

The passage for this week falls within a section of Mark that focuses on discipleship (8:22–10:52). Much of this section serves as a sort of catechism in which Jesus teaches his followers about what they must do to follow him. The verses for this lesson highlight the dangers of riches, the necessity of putting God first, and the costs and gains of following Christ.

The three sections of this week's text hinge on the two questions presented here:

What must I do to inherit eternal life?

Who, then, can be saved?

Before we can adequately address them, however, we need to understand what these questions are *really* asking. Neither is about living on forever after one is dead or about somehow getting a spiritual passport stamped so one can enter heaven. Rather, these questions are rooted in a Jewish tradition concerning the age to come.

The Jews of Jesus' day expected God to usher in a new age when the time was right. They hoped and prayed that event would come in their lifetime. Although the prophets often talked of the "day of the LORD" as a time of judgment, they also described it as a turning point for all creation. The old would pass away, and the new heaven and new earth would be a true fresh start for humanity. The righteous would be blessed with peace, prosperity, well-being, and joy—and the unrighteous would be punished at last. From that time on, God's justice would shape the world.

Both the rich man and the disciples are curious about aspects of this age that God will bring, and so they turn to Jesus for insights and explanations. On a surface level, they are asking about who gets in, and how. Jesus reveals, however, that there is another question underlying this one: if I do get in, what can I take with me?

Fittingly enough given the theme of the text, Jesus addresses the last question first. "If you get in," he says in essence, "you can't take anything with you. Those who enter the realm of God when it comes in full enter that new life as newborn babes, and like any newborn they must enter with nothing. You can't take your earthly riches with you, and neither can you take your old attachments, whether these are to things or people." The answer of *who* gets in and *how* flows from this: those who are willing to leave everything else behind, and do so, are those who enter the new life.

### Our Salvation

Jesus does not stop there, however. He goes on to describe what happens next. This rebirth is into God's own family—and it is available *now*, as are the privileges and responsibilities that go along with membership. Moreover, the clue as to the nature of what we gain and what we are to give is embedded in the word "salvation."

In the Greek, "salvation" has several different meanings that all relate to our life in the new age as those who are saved. In secular use, the term encompasses:

- being made whole, often in the sense of being restored to a community;
- being kept, both in the sense of being protected and of being kept from getting lost; and
- benefiting, especially in terms of receiving and maintaining wholeness as individuals and as a community.

Certainly this was a comforting message to the Christians in Mark's day, as it is to us. Yet, salvation does not stop at what we *gain*; it also involves what we are expected to *give*. Thus the New Testament adds a fourth, more outwardly focused meaning to the Greek word:

- to gain the ability and the desire to be of benefit to others, especially by bringing God's peace and wholeness to them. (See Acts 13:47 for an example.)

To be saved is to enter into God's realm here and now—and it is also to be called to the servant ministry that marks all the citizens (and family members) of that realm.

### But What about Our Wealth?

The disciples were astounded when Jesus told the rich man to sell all he had. Partly, this surprise comes from the idea that being blessed by God included wealth, a notion that had become firmly entrenched in most of the Jews' theology. They might have been surprised as well, though, because this was not a demand that Jesus made of all his followers. The Lord and his closest disciples were supported in their travels by well-off believers (especially women; see Matthew 27:55-56) who provided for them financially, just as missionaries like Paul would be supported in years to come by Lydia and others (Acts 16:14-15, 40).

The disciples were stunned on this occasion to hear wealth presented as a burden, not a blessing, and their surprise invites us to take an even closer look at the text. We know that Jesus did not condemn people for having enough to live on, and it appears that he did not routinely condemn people for having more than enough. So what is the real issue? It seems that the state of his finances has become more important to this man than the state of his soul, and radical steps will have to be taken if he is to change that inner sense of priorities.

The story ends with Peter, famous for saying the wrong thing, pointing out that the disciples had left home and followed Jesus. Once again, he has failed to see the true point, so Jesus sets the story straight, reversing the sequence suggested by Peter. In effect, Jesus says, "It is not about leaving this or that, but just putting *me* first, that is all. Let *me* be the most important focus of your life—not your own efforts at righteousness. I, in turn, will bless you and fulfill all your needs."

Isn't this what Jesus says to us all? Thank goodness, throughout the ages, many faithful followers have gotten the message and taken it to heart. In *Matthew* of the Westminster Bible Companion series, noted commentator Tom Long reminds us that, for some, this does mean giving up everything and leaving home; for others, living as children of God comes in another way:

Some followers of Jesus leave their families and their homes to travel to distant fields of mission, and others leave their families and homes on Thursday evenings to tutor street kids. Some leave lucrative careers to become hospice workers and schoolteachers in troubled schools; others refuse to close on deals they know will hurt other people and decline to climb the corporate ladder by stepping on somebody's back.

The call to follow Jesus comes in as many varieties as there are disciples. There is no single life's work that is the one and only way to serve him. Nor it there one rigid set of criteria that apply to us all—except for the most basic one of all. In all that we do, and certainly in all that we treasure, nothing should mean more to us than the Lord of all life.

---

# SHARING THE SCRIPTURE

*Preparing Our Hearts*

Meditate on this week's devotional reading, found in Proverbs 11:1-7. Among these sayings, we find in verse 4, "Riches do not profit in the day of wrath." We are probably all aware that we cannot take our material possessions with us, yet we want to be prepared for each day by being sure that we have enough. In today's lesson we will examine the relationship of a rich man to his money. Before you read today's scripture lesson, think about the role possessions play in your life. Suppose you were to lose every material thing you own. What difference would that make to you?

Pray that you and the adult learners will learn how to live according to God's covenant.

*Preparing Our Minds*

Study the background and lesson scripture, found in Mark 10:17-31. Ponder your beliefs about eternal life and how one may obtain it.

Write on newsprint:

❏ information for next week's lesson, found under "Continue the Journey."

❏ activities for further spiritual growth in "Continue the Journey."

Locate pictures symbolizing wealth in magazines, junk mail, or other sources from which you can clip. Large homes, expensive cars, yachts, a private airplane, designer jewelry, and luxurious clothing are possibilities. Cut these pictures for use as an optional activity in "Recognize That as Believers the Learners Must Wholeheartedly Focus on God, Not Allowing Anything Else to Take Priority."

## LEADING THE CLASS

*(1) Gather to Learn*

❖ Welcome the class members and introduce any guests.

❖ Pray that those who are present will be willing to open themselves to covenant living and all its rewards.

❖ Discuss this question: **If someone asked you, "What must I do to inherit eternal life," how would you reply?** (Note that there may be students who do not have a ready answer because they question the notion of eternal life themselves. Accept their questions.)

❖ Read aloud today's focus statement: **People wonder whether eternal life exists, and how they may obtain it. What leads to eternal life? Jesus teaches that to become true followers and so inherit eternal life we must submit our possessions and ourselves to God.**

*(2) Delve into Mark's Version of a Rich Person's Encounter with Jesus*

❖ Choose readers to present Mark 10:17-31 as a drama. One will read the narrator's portion, another act as the rich man, a third will read the words of Jesus, and another the words of Peter. Ask the entire class to read the words of the disciples in verse 26: "Then who can be saved?"

❖ Read or retell "Some Key Questions" from Interpreting the Scripture to help the students understand what the rich man really wanted to know and understand.

❖ Make this point again: **Jesus says, in essence, "If you get in you can't take anything with you."** Invite the students to respond to this point by answering this question: **Why do we seek that which has no value in the kingdom of God?**

❖ Ask the class to read in unison today's key verse, Mark 10:21.

❖ Provide time for silent meditation on these questions: **We know that the rich man went away grieving because of his wealth. How would you have responded to Jesus? What evidence in your life supports your answer?**

*(3) Recognize That as Believers the Learners Must Wholeheartedly Focus on God, Not Allowing Anything Else to Take Priority*

❖ Brainstorm with the class symbols of wealth and list these on newsprint.

❖ **Option:** Have pictures from magazines of some things that students will likely name. Tape these pictures to the newsprint as the related symbol of wealth

(such as a large home or expensive car) is named.

❖ Talk about what level of riches constitutes "wealth." (Point out that compared with much of the rest of the world, average-income citizens of the United States are considered wealthy.)

❖ Raise the issue that wealth has long been seen as a sign of God's blessing. As an option, read the first and second paragraph from "But What about Our Wealth?" in Interpreting the Scripture.

❖ Invite two groups of two or three people each to support or refute this statement in an informal debate: **It is impossible for the wealthy to be good Christians.** Set a time limit.

❖ Encourage the class to respond to the ideas presented, noting how these ideas support or challenge their beliefs. Some students may find that they have changed their minds about the place of the wealthy in the kingdom of God.

❖ **Option:** Read paragraphs five and six from Mark 10:17-22 in Understanding the Scripture to add to the discussion.

*(4) Make a Commitment to Give Lives and Possessions Completely to God*

❖ Encourage the students to follow in their Bibles as you read aloud Jesus' words about the priority of God in our lives as found in Matthew 6:24-34.

❖ Distribute paper and pencils. Suggest that the students each write a prayer in which they ask God to help them put whatever material goods they have in their proper perspective so that their priority and focus is on God. Their prayer may also include words of confession if they, like the rich man, have been focused on what they have and not who they are in relation to Jesus. Invite the students to read their prayers silently, but not to share them with the rest of the class.

### (5) Continue the Journey

❖ Pray that those in attendance will give themselves completely to God.

❖ Read aloud this preparation for next week's lesson. You may also want to post it on newsprint for the students to copy.

- ■ **Title: A Holy People**
- ■ **Background Scripture: 1 Peter 1**
- ■ **Lesson Scripture: 1 Peter 1:13-25**
- ■ **Focus of the Lesson: The world is a sordid place where people try to step up and over others in order to get ahead. Why, then, should we want to become holy people? First Peter says that God's people should be holy because God is holy.**

❖ Challenge the students to complete one or more of these activities for further spiritual growth, which you will write on newsprint for the students to copy.

(1) **Consider prayerfully how you steward the material resources entrusted to you. What truly is your attitude toward your money and possessions? As you consider Jesus' words to the rich man, what if any changes do you need to make to focus more clearly on God?**

(2) **Recall that in this week's lesson Jesus told Peter about the benefits the disciples would receive in this life and in the life to come. What are the most important reasons that you have for following Christ? What benefits do you perceive?**

(3) **Give away something of value to you, if possible. See this gift not as charity but as a way of drawing closer to Christ.**

❖ Sing or read aloud "We Give Thee But Thine Own." If you do not have access to a hymnal that includes the words to this 1864 hymn by William W. How, you may want to read them line by line and ask the class to echo them as a reminder that all that we have and all that we are belongs to God:

**We give Thee but Thine own,**
**Whate'er the gift may be;**
**All that we have is Thine alone,**
**A trust, O Lord, from Thee.**

❖ Conclude today's session by leading the class in this benediction, based on 1 Peter 2:9: **Go forth with the assurance that you are part of a chosen race, a royal priesthood, a holy nation, God's own people, in order that you may proclaim the mighty acts of him who called you out of darkness into his marvelous light.**

UNIT 3: THE NEW COVENANT COMMUNITY
# A HOLY PEOPLE

---

## PREVIEWING THE LESSON

**Lesson Scripture:** 1 Peter 1:13-25
**Background Scripture:** 1 Peter 1
**Key Verses:** 1 Peter 1:15-16

### Focus of the Lesson:
The world is a sordid place where people try to step up and over others in order to get ahead. Why, then, should we want to become holy people? First Peter says that God's people should be holy because God is holy.

### Goals for the Learners:
(1) to explore the teachings on holiness found in 1 Peter 1.
(2) to identify examples of holy living within their congregation.
(3) to find ways to be holy in all their conduct.

### Pronunciation Guide:
Aquila (ak' wi luh)
Bithynia (bi thin' ee uh)
Cappadocia (kap uh doh' shee uh)
Pontus (pon' tuhs)

### Supplies:
Bibles, newsprint and marker, paper and pencils, hymnals

---

## READING THE SCRIPTURE

NRSV
1 Peter 1:13-25

[13]Therefore prepare your minds for action; discipline yourselves; set all your hope on the grace that Jesus Christ will bring you when he is revealed. [14]Like obedient children, do not be conformed to the desires that you formerly had in ignorance.

NIV
1 Peter 1:13-25

[13]Therefore, prepare your minds for action; be self-controlled; set your hope fully on the grace to be given you when Jesus Christ is revealed. [14]As obedient children, do not conform to the evil desires you had when you lived in ignorance.

<sup>15</sup>Instead, **as he who called you is holy, be holy yourselves in all your conduct;** <sup>16</sup>**for it is written, "You shall be holy, for I am holy."**

<sup>17</sup>If you invoke as Father the one who judges all people impartially according to their deeds, live in reverent fear during the time of your exile. <sup>18</sup>You know that you were ransomed from the futile ways inherited from your ancestors, not with perishable things like silver or gold, <sup>19</sup>but with the precious blood of Christ, like that of a lamb without defect or blemish. <sup>20</sup>He was destined before the foundation of the world, but was revealed at the end of the ages for your sake. <sup>21</sup>Through him you have come to trust in God, who raised him from the dead and gave him glory, so that your faith and hope are set on God.

<sup>22</sup>Now that you have purified your souls by your obedience to the truth so that you have genuine mutual love, love one another deeply from the heart. <sup>23</sup>You have been born anew, not of perishable but of imperishable seed, through the living and enduring word of God. <sup>24</sup>For

"All flesh is like grass
    and all its glory like the flower
        of grass.
The grass withers,
    and the flower falls,
<sup>25</sup>  but the word of the Lord endures
        forever."
That word is the good news that was announced to you.

<sup>15</sup>But **just as he who called you is holy, so be holy in all you do;** <sup>16</sup>**for it is written: "Be holy, because I am holy."**

<sup>17</sup>Since you call on a Father who judges each man's work impartially, live your lives as strangers here in reverent fear. <sup>18</sup>For you know that it was not with perishable things such as silver or gold that you were redeemed from the empty way of life handed down to you from your forefathers, <sup>19</sup>but with the precious blood of Christ, a lamb without blemish or defect. <sup>20</sup>He was chosen before the creation of the world, but was revealed in these last times for your sake. <sup>21</sup>Through him you believe in God, who raised him from the dead and glorified him, and so your faith and hope are in God.

<sup>22</sup>Now that you have purified yourselves by obeying the truth so that you have sincere love for your brothers, love one another deeply, from the heart. <sup>23</sup>For you have been born again, not of perishable seed, but of imperishable, through the living and enduring word of God. <sup>24</sup>For,

"All men are like grass,
    and all their glory is like the flowers of
        the field;
the grass withers and the flowers fall,
<sup>25</sup>    but the word of the Lord stands
        forever."
And this is the word that was preached to you.

## UNDERSTANDING THE SCRIPTURE

**1 Peter 1:1-2.** First Peter addresses Christians who were scattered throughout the Near East, outside of Palestine. These Christians were probably Gentile, and they were certainly under persecution, although it is not clear from the letter why that was the case.

The names of the five provinces in verse 1 indicate regions throughout modern-day Turkey. Acts records that some of the devout Jews who experienced the first Pentecost were residents of Cappadocia, Pontus, and Asia (Acts 2:9), and that Paul and his companions went through Galatia twice (16:6;

18:23). Aquila, who with his wife Priscilla was Paul's partner in mission, was a native of Pontus (18:2).

**1 Peter 1:3-12.** Peter begins the body of his letter by laying out the theological foundation for all that will follow. Believers in Christ are called to a certain way of life as individuals and as a community, a way of life that includes hope and joy in the midst of troubles as well as adhering to God's moral standards. The basis for all of this is the new life that we have in Christ.

Much as Jesus used parables to describe the realm of God, Peter uses analogies from everyday life to try and explain the divine mystery of this new life. First, because it is a new life with a whole new set of benefits, he describes it in terms of a rebirth into a family where one is now eligible for a new inheritance (1:3-4). Then he uses the image of gold to help explain the preciousness of this new life and its formation process; like gold, these Christians will be refined by fire (1:6-7).

Without denying the problems these Christians are facing and will continue to face, Peter nevertheless manages to set their existence within a framework of positive certainties. All they do rests on Christ's resurrection victory over death (1:3), the ongoing protection of the power of God (1:5), and the guaranteed outcome of salvation (1:9). They will have all they need in this present world and an even greater reward in the age to come. Considering this, Peter implies that they will be able to withstand all that the world throws at them and more.

To help bolster their confidence in these promises, Peter then points to the message of the prophets (1:10-12). For generations, the people of God had gifted individuals who spoke God's intention to redeem the world through a Messiah. Now, with hindsight, the church sees that promise has come true, and it is also able to trust the other promises that God made through the prophets. Salvation for the world is at hand, although no one (not even the angels, 1:12)

understands exactly how it works. The church does not need to understand it completely, however; all the church needs to do is trust this message of salvation to be true and live out their hope accordingly.

**1 Peter 1:13-16.** The rest of 1 Peter 1 forms an appeal to holiness on the part of the community of faith. Verse 13 grounds this appeal in Christ's return, which the author of the letter apparently expects to be within the span of a lifetime.

The call to action involves three elements of preparation before a single deed takes place (1:13). Believers are first to ready themselves mentally, emotionally, and spiritually. Only in this way will they be able to live out the call to holiness (that is, the call to be set apart solely for God's use).

The first command underscores the urgency of the situation. Peter calls on these Christians to "prepare your minds for action." The literal translation is "gird up the loins of your mind for action." The image is of a person gathering up the bottom portion of a long robe so that it will not impede movement, something that was done when one intended to run or (as is probably the intention here) start out walking on a long journey.

The following call to "discipline yourselves" literally translates "keep yourselves completely sober." This is not an injunction against drinking, as we might assume. In Peter's culture, the phrase was used idiomatically to indicate a basic orientation of one's emotions and desires. To "stay sober" was to avoid the impulse to give in to any pleasures offered by the secular world that might draw one away from God. It referred to the kind of self-control a trained athlete, for example, would have. Those who have had training are to serve as role models for others.

Christians are able to accomplish these first two goals by setting their hope on the fulfillment of Christ's grace. In other words, they are to live in the certainty that Christ has already bestowed grace on them. They are also to embody the conviction that Christ's grace will take on a new and greater manifestation in the age to come. This spiritual assurance will give them what they need to stay mentally and emotionally able to act faithfully.

Verses 14-16 then express this same thought with different images. The believers are like children who are growing in knowledge, and their obedience to the heavenly parent will help them achieve "holiness" (in its sense of "being set apart for God").

**1 Peter 1:17-21.** Peter makes it clear that the only way to move into the new life in Christ is to abandon the old life completely. To underscore the obligation these folk owe to God, Peter uses more images from every-day life. The believers are described as exiles, freed captives, and beneficiaries of a sacrifice—all of whom owe their salvation to God, who had planned redemption in Christ since before creation (1:20; see Colossians 1:26).

**1 Peter 1:22-25.** Peter closes by describing our new life as one that brings a new family, one we are to embrace in mutual love. This God-established community is as much a new creation as our own new life. Moreover, just as all creation came into being by the spoken word of God, so Christians enter new life through this same creative force. This is good news indeed, because human beings are frail creatures, but the word that works through them "endures forever" (1:25; Isaiah 40:6-8).

---

## INTERPRETING THE SCRIPTURE

### We Are All Saints

Today is All Saints' Day, and we could not pick a better time in the liturgical year to begin a study on 1 and 2 Peter. Part of the theological purpose of this day, of course, is to remember all those who have gone before us in the faith—that "great cloud of witnesses" celebrated in Hebrews 12:1 who surround us, inspire us, and wait for us in God's realm. The *other* theological goal of this day, however, is to remind us that we are all saints, surprising as that may seem. We are the ones called by God to be holy as God is holy.

First Peter describes our life in Christ through several images, of which holiness is only one. Two key metaphors that run throughout the book are those of membership in God's family and citizenship in God's realm. Our verses for today grow from the former: our call to holiness is based on our new identity as children in the household of God.

Holding on to this identity was critical for Peter's original audience. Those Christians faced the usual challenges related to daily life, illness, depression, and death, but they also had to endure more than that. First, these Christians were surrounded by a culture that in no way reflected or honored their own lifestyles and priorities. The temptation to somehow walk in both worlds or to abandon the Christian life altogether had to be faced every day. In addition, Peter addresses Christians who are already (or who are about to be) facing persecution. Peter knew they needed all the encouragement they could get to hold fast to their faith.

### Being Holy

At first glance, the call to be holy may not appear like a great way to inspire a people already under stress. After all, it seems fairly impossible. Even under good conditions, most of us feel less than holy on a regular basis. We have a pretty clear notion of what holiness is, after all, and it doesn't seem to match our own attitudes or behavior often. Based on what we read in Scripture, however, Peter believed differently.

The concept of "holiness" in this letter comes from an understanding rooted in Hebrew Scripture and carried forward into the early church. When Peter encourages readers to "be holy," he quotes Leviticus 19:2. Understanding that reference will help us understand what Peter had in mind.

To be "holy" in the Hebrew language is to be "set apart for a specific purpose," and so God's people always understood themselves to be. Significantly, the ancient Hebrews, weak and insignificant, were chosen only because God loved them (Deuteronomy 7:7-8), yet they always maintained this relationship was for a larger purpose. Indeed, God called them for nothing less than the salvation of the world (Isaiah 49:6).

When we see holiness in this light, it takes on a new aspect. Being holy is not being perfect, nor is it being inhumanly good. It is not even, as some Christians have believed over the centuries, being pious to the point of severity and grimness. Rather, being holy involves setting our faith and hope on God (1:21) and loving others "deeply from the heart" (1:22). It is a state of being that encompasses all God intends for us, including thankfulness, joy, and peace.

### Exiles in This World

Having described the call to holiness as part of our new life as brothers and sisters in God's household, Peter now refers to God as an impartial judge (1:17). At first glance, the description of "Father" and "judge" do not seem compatible. In volume 12 of *The New Interpreter's Bible*, David L. Bartlett argues that this ambiguous verse may be interpreted in two ways, which do not necessarily exclude each other. The first possibility, which is closer to the meaning rendered in the NIV, is this: "Since the one

you already call 'Father' is also the impeccably fair judge, be sure that you live in appropriate fear of God's judgment." A second possibility, which is closer to the meaning of the NRSV, states: "Since the one who judges all impartially is the one you are invited to call 'Father,' though you rightly fear God, your fear can include confident reverence." Whichever way this verse is read, it is still clear that we are in a relationship with God and are called to live responsibly within that relationship.

These images of God as parent and judge are more than a theological attempt to define God. As Peter sees it, these images are essential to understanding our life in the world. He describes the Christian community as undergoing a period of "exile" (1:17). Generically, this word refers to people who are traveling in a foreign nation, without any of the rights they have in their homeland. Literally, the word means to be alongside the borders of one's own home. In other words, Peter pictures Christians as people who live on the edge of God's realm—not yet fully in it but with all the rights and responsibilities of citizenship nonetheless. Based on this citizenship, we look to the standards of God and not those of the world in determining right from wrong, and we find ourselves able to follow them because of the ransom that freed us. Moreover, we find ourselves reassured, time and again, that we are not just part of God's realm but part of God's own household.

### Living Saints

The word translated as "holy" in this passage appears elsewhere in the New Testament as "saint." We tend to think of saints as some select group of Christians, but in the biblical meaning every Christian is called to be a saint. This concept is celebrated in a great hymn by Lesbia Scott called "I Sing a Song of the Saints of God," which identifies some pretty unlikely characters. On the list are a shepherdess and soldier, a doctor and a queen, and folk that we might meet anywhere and anytime.

The hymn calls to mind all the saints that we have known and admired throughout our lifetime—family members, Sunday school teachers, and so on. As the song points out, what they have in common is *not* background or position or any of the other categories we use to group people. What they have in common is a life dedicated to God and to Jesus Christ.

In the passage for today, Peter points out a few other characteristics that identify God's saints. Simply listed, we see that such folk show their holiness—in this case, meaning they bear witness to their faith—in at least four ways:

1. They take action on God's behalf (1:13).
2. They exercise self-control (1:13).

3. They manifest a deep love for others (1:22).

4. Perhaps most important of all, they base everything they do on their hope in the grace of Jesus Christ (1:13).

Today, as we celebrate all the folk who have modeled holiness in this way, we are invited to explore what it means for us to be similarly "set apart." For example, do we give strangers a reason to comment on our joy or our kindness? Do we go about the tasks of each day with a sense of peace that communicates itself to others? Do the people among whom we live and work see us as different in some way that makes them want to share in our experience? We are set apart to live in service to God, and in so doing we witness to God. That is the blessed opportunity of being a saint.

---

## SHARING THE SCRIPTURE

### *Preparing Our Hearts*

Meditate on this week's devotional reading, found in Deuteronomy 7:6-11. Here in the wilderness Moses reminds the people that they are "a people holy to the LORD" (7:6). They have been called out and chosen to be God's "treasured possession" (7:6). How do you see yourself as called and set apart to live a holy life? Do you feel that you are living up to this call? If not, what changes of heart, attitude, and behavior do you need to ask God to help you make?

Pray that you and the adult learners will see yourselves as the holy, set apart, treasured people that God claims you are.

### *Preparing Our Minds*

Study the background in 1 Peter 1 and the lesson scripture from verses 13-25. Consider why, in a world where people step up and over others to get ahead, we should want to become holy people.

Write on newsprint:
❑ list of four ways that people show holiness, found in the third paragraph of "Living Saints," for "Find Ways to Be Holy in All Conduct."
❑ information for next week's lesson, found under "Continue the Journey."
❑ activities for further spiritual growth in "Continue the Journey."

Be prepared to read or retell portions of Understanding the Scripture to open the section entitled "Explore the Teachings on Holiness Found in 1 Peter 1."

### LEADING THE CLASS

### *(1) Gather to Learn*

❖ Welcome the class members and introduce any guests.

❖ Pray that everyone who is present today will be challenged to live the kind of holy life that befits their calling as children of God.

❖ Read this information aloud: **Scandals have rocked the corporate world in the United States, especially in the early years of this century. Activities at Adelphia, Tyco, Arthur Andersen (Accounting), Enron, and World Com were major news stories. Executives and others entrusted with the money and lives of employees and shareholders looked out for themselves and their own gain. Due to their greed, many people lost not only jobs but also their retirement and savings. "Corporate" and "ethics" seemed like words not usually used in the same sentence.**

❖ Ask: **How are Christians called to demonstrate different values and lifestyles than these?**

❖ Read aloud today's focus statement: **The world is a sordid place where people try to step up and over others in order to get ahead. Why, then, should we want to become holy people? First Peter says that God's people should be holy because God is holy.**

*(2) Explore the Teachings on Holiness Found in 1 Peter 1*

❖ Read or retell 1 Peter 1:1-2 and 3-12 from Understanding the Scripture to lay the groundwork for today's session.

❖ Select a volunteer to read aloud 1 Peter 1:13-25.

❖ Divide the class into groups of three or four. Note that verse 25 says that the Word of the Lord is the good news that is announced to us. Invite the groups to discuss how they hear these verses of the lesson dcripture in 1 Peter 1 as good news. What specifically about these verses is good news to them?

❖ Bring everyone together and read "Being Holy" in Interpreting the Scripture

to help the class understand the meaning of holiness.

❖ Conclude this part of the lesson by asking: **How does this call to holiness, which is indeed good news, affect the way you live your life each day?**

*(3) Identify Examples of Holy Living within the Learners' Congregation*

❖ **Option:** Invite the students to look at the hymn "I Sing a Song of the Saints of God." Allow them time to silently read this hymn, which you will sing or read in unison at the end of class. Encourage them to comment on the kinds of people portrayed as the saints of God in this hymn. Where do they see themselves?

❖ Read the first and second paragraphs of "Living Saints" in Interpreting the Scripture.

❖ Point out that the church of the twenty-first century in the United States is for the most part culturally "at home." This stands in sharp contrast to the counter-culture of the early church where believers were focused on living in the image of Christ. In those days, the church and surrounding culture looked very different from one another. Brainstorm answers to this question with the students: **In what ways is our church living according to the counter-cultural demands of the New Testament, which call us to holy living?**

❖ Invite the adults to share with the class (or in small groups) the challenges they face in living this counter-cultural holy life when the surrounding culture pressures them to conform to society's norms?

*(4) Find Ways to Be Holy in All Conduct*

❖ Read aloud the third and fourth paragraphs of "Living Saints" in Interpreting the Scripture.

❖ Post newsprint showing the four characteristics of those who show their holiness and bear witness to their faith.

❖ Distribute paper and pencils. Set a time limit. Ask the learners to list as many ways as they can think of to take action on God's behalf, exercise self-control, and show love for others.

❖ Call time and go around the room, asking each student to name one item on his or her list. If time permits, go around more than once.

❖ Encourage the class members to write on their paper one or two ways they will try this week to be more holy in their conduct.

*(5) Continue the Journey*

❖ Pray that everyone who has gathered today will seek to be holy and recognize that holiness requires them to conform to the ways of Jesus, not to the ways of the world.

❖ Read aloud this preparation for next week's lesson. You may also want to post it on newsprint for the students to copy.

- **Title: A Chosen People**
- **Background Scripture: 1 Peter 2:1-17**
- **Lesson Scripture: 1 Peter 2:1-10**
- **Focus of the Lesson: The way we live sends a clear signal about who we are and what we believe. What distinguishes members of the Christian church from other groups? Peter teaches that we are "a royal priesthood," a "holy nation," whose purpose is to declare God's mighty acts.**

❖ Challenge the students to complete one or more of these activities for further spiritual growth, which you will write on newsprint for the students to copy.

(1) **Study Colossians 1:15-23. What similarities do you note between this text and today's lesson from 1 Peter? What else can you glean from Colossians concerning your own holiness?**

(2) **Look up the words "holy" and "holiness" in a Bible concordance. Check some of the chapters and verses. What does the Bible teach about holiness in relation to God and in relation to the way God's people are called to live?**

(3) **Practice living as one who is redeemed by Christ and whose "faith and hope are set on God" (1 Peter 1:21).**

❖ Sing or read aloud "I Sing a Song of the Saints of God."

❖ Conclude today's session by leading the class in this benediction, based on 1 Peter 2:9: **Go forth with the assurance that you are part of a chosen race, a royal priesthood, a holy nation, God's own people, in order that you may proclaim the mighty acts of him who called you out of darkness into his marvelous light.**

UNIT 3: THE NEW COVENANT COMMUNITY
# A Chosen People

---

## PREVIEWING THE LESSON

**Lesson Scripture:** 1 Peter 2:1-10
**Background Scripture:** 1 Peter 2:1-17
**Key Verse:** 1 Peter 2:9

### Focus of the Lesson:
The way we live sends a clear signal about who we are and what we believe. What distinguishes members of the Christian church from other groups? Peter teaches that we are "a royal priesthood," a "holy nation," whose purpose is to declare God's mighty acts.

### Goals for the Learners:
(1) to explore Peter's teachings on the duties and obligations of Christians.
(2) to examine what "being chosen" really means in their lives.
(3) to commit to living out their "chosenness" and proclaiming God's amazing deeds to others.

### Supplies:
Bibles, newsprint and marker, paper and pencils, hymnals

---

## READING THE SCRIPTURE

NRSV
1 Peter 2:1-10

¹Rid yourselves, therefore, of all malice, and all guile, insincerity, envy, and all slander. ²Like newborn infants, long for the pure, spiritual milk, so that by it you may grow into salvation—³if indeed you have tasted that the Lord is good.

⁴Come to him, a living stone, though rejected by mortals yet chosen and precious in God's sight, and ⁵like living stones, let yourselves be built into a spiritual house, to

NIV
1 Peter 2:1-10

¹Therefore, rid yourselves of all malice and all deceit, hypocrisy, envy, and slander of every kind. ²Like newborn babies, crave pure spiritual milk, so that by it you may grow up in your salvation, ³now that you have tasted that the Lord is good.

⁴As you come to him, the living Stone—rejected by men but chosen by God and precious to him—⁵you also, like living stones, are being built into a spiritual house to be a

NOVEMBER 8

be a holy priesthood, to offer spiritual sacrifices acceptable to God through Jesus Christ. [6]For it stands in scripture:

"See, I am laying in Zion a stone,
    a cornerstone chosen and precious;
and whoever believes in him will not be
    put to shame."

[7]To you then who believe, he is precious; but for those who do not believe,

"The stone that the builders rejected
    has become the very head of the
        corner,"

[8]and

"A stone that makes them stumble,
    and a rock that makes them fall."

They stumble because they disobey the word, as they were destined to do.

[9]**But you are a chosen race, a royal priesthood, a holy nation, God's own people, in order that you may proclaim the mighty acts of him who called you out of darkness into his marvelous light.**

[10] Once you were not a people,
    but now you are God's people;
once you had not received mercy,
    but now you have received mercy.

holy priesthood, offering spiritual sacrifices acceptable to God through Jesus Christ. [6]For in Scripture it says:

"See, I lay a stone in Zion,
    a chosen and precious cornerstone,
and the one who trusts in him
    will never be put to shame."

[7]Now to you who believe, this stone is precious. But to those who do not believe,

"The stone the builders rejected
    has become the capstone,"

[8]and,

"A stone that causes men to stumble
    and a rock that makes them fall."

They stumble because they disobey the message—which is also what they were destined for.

[9]**But you are a chosen people, a royal priesthood, a holy nation, a people belonging to God, that you may declare the praises of him who called you out of darkness into his wonderful light.** [10]Once you were not a people, but now you are the people of God; once you had not received mercy, but now you have received mercy.

---

## UNDERSTANDING THE SCRIPTURE

**1 Peter 2:1-3.** The passage for this week continues where 1 Peter 1 ended. The first three verses (2:1-3) begin with (NIV) or include (NRSV) the word "therefore," which ties them closely to what comes before (1:22-25). Thus, the current passage's focus on Christian behavior is set firmly in our identity as those who have been born anew into the family of God.

First, Peter maintains his Christian audience needs to abandon the ways of their old life, which includes giving up its attitudes and practices (2:1). Only then can they receive the pure, spiritual nourishment they need. Continuing the metaphor of these Christians as newborn babies, Peter compares this nourishment to mother's milk.

They are to "long for" this spiritual food in the same way an infant desires and even demands its physical sustenance. This image may reflect an early church ritual as well as a common theological concept—as early as the second century, newly baptized converts were fed with milk to symbolize their new birth and childlike faith in God, and this milk was given along with honey (see Exodus 3:8).

**1 Peter 2:4-7.** The image of a new birth now shifts to that of a new building (2:4-10) and a new people. Interestingly enough, Peter's language and metaphors throughout this section all come from the Hebrew Scriptures.

In verses 4-5, Peter transitions from the image of babes to that of "living stones" formed into a spiritual dwelling place for God. (The Greek word used here means a stone that has been dressed for construction use, not a raw rock.) As the building blocks of the church, Christians must "be built into a spiritual house" (2:5). The passive form of the verb suggests that becoming part of the building is something that is done to and for us, not the outcome of our own efforts. To further support this understanding, we read that the "chosen and precious" cornerstone for this building is no less than Christ himself (2:6-7; see also Psalm 118:22; Isaiah 28:16), who controls the design of the whole building.

**1 Peter 2:8.** Peter then injects a word of caution. This same cornerstone that supports and directs the structure of our living temple is also a stone over which some stumble (2:8a). This seems straightforward enough, but the verse goes on to add "They stumble because they disobey the word, as they were destined to do" (2:8b).

How are we to understand these words? Is Peter really saying that God forces some people to "stumble," creating a condition under which they cannot be saved? Surely, given all the biblical witness to God's nature, this cannot be the case. What then could Peter mean?

First of all, it may help to consider other valid translations of this text. The Greek is a little ambiguous, so its true sense is hard to capture in English. For example, one way the verse can be translated is, "They stumble because they disobey the word, onto which they also were placed." Those who accept this reading understand Peter to say that not all people who have been given the foundation of God's Word and the cornerstone of Christ choose to keep that as their spiritual base. When these folk choose not to obey God—in the language of the metaphor, when they step off the word and cornerstone on which they stand—then they stumble.

Another valid (although not quite as literal) translation, which takes into account grammatical connections, reads, "According to God's plan, they stumble when they disobey the word." Those who prefer this reading interpret it to mean that God's plan is not that some should disobey and therefore stumble but that God's plan is for stumbling to always be a consequence of disobedience. This interpretation fits well with theological views throughout the Hebrew Scriptures that maintain God lets us suffer the consequences of our bad choices so that we might learn from our mistakes and come to repent. In this interpretation, as in the one above, the stumbling is not necessarily permanent; there is still opportunity for salvation if the person will believe and walk in the way of faith.

**1 Peter 2:9-10.** The metaphor of the building then turns into a temple wherein we serve as "a royal priesthood" (2:9) able to approach God (2:10), to bring others to God (2:9b), and to present the "spiritual sacrifices" (2:5) of our very selves (see also Romans 12:1).

This section ends with two wonderful affirmations, made all the more meaningful because Peter is applying teachings about the people of Israel to his Gentile audience. The first draws on Exodus 19:6, where Moses tells Israel you are now God's people because God says so. God has chosen you, so be holy as God is holy. The second quotes Hosea 2:23, which contrasts a past life and identity with the new life and identity granted by God. As commentator Fred B. Craddock beautifully puts it in *First and Second Peter and Jude* of the Westminster Bible Companion:

> These terms of sharp contrast—
> "once you were" but "now you are"—
> are often referred to as the language of
> conversion, and so it is. But it is also
> the language of confession appropriate
> for every gathering of the church, not
> in dramatic beating of the breast but in
> sincere gratitude and praise. The community of faith looks around at itself

and says, "This is the Lord's doing, and it is marvelous in our eyes."

**1 Peter 2:11-17.** The final verses of this passage deal with how Christians are to conduct themselves in this world. Above all, they are to follow God's ways, but they are also to follow the laws of the state insofar as they can. They will receive enough criticism as it is; there is no need to draw more by being bad citizens.

---

# INTERPRETING THE SCRIPTURE

### Called to Be Temples for God

First Peter 1 establishes that we are brothers and sisters in the family of God, as well as citizens in God's realm. In this lesson, we explore chapter 2 to see how Peter builds on these themes to establish that a Christian relationship with God never stops at the individual level. To be a Christian is to be part of a community of faith, and so Peter now addresses the church as a whole.

John 1:14 says that in Jesus, "The Word became flesh and lived among us." The Greek word translated "lived" here is literally "tabernacled." In the same way that God's glory and presence filled the Tabernacle in the wilderness, making that tent the place where God truly dwelt among the people, so God was present in Jesus Christ. Later, John also describes Jesus' body as being the real temple in which God was present with the people after the wilderness experience ended (John 2:21).

Using the same imagery for the community of faith, Peter refers to us as "living stones" that are to be "built into a spiritual house" (2:5). The image of living stones makes a deliberate reference to the idols that abounded in the culture surrounding the early Gentile church. Those stone figures were supposed to be the embodiment of a deity, yet they were in fact merely "dead" and profane artifacts. In contrast, Christians are "living stones" that truly carry the presence and the power of their God.

What's more, we are built upon "a cornerstone chosen and precious" (2:6). Christ is the one who holds the whole building together and makes it grow into a sacred temple dedicated to the Lord. Indeed, it is through our union with Christ, as the writer of Ephesians says, that "the whole structure is joined together and grows into a holy temple in the Lord; in whom you also are built together spiritually into a dwelling place for God" (Ephesians 2:21-22).

### A Priesthood of All Believers

First Peter 2:5 not only says the church forms a living temple but it also goes on to describe the community of believers as "a holy priesthood." This is an Old Testament image that occurs throughout the New Testament as well. There we find it associated with such acts as praising God, doing good and sharing what one has, worshiping God through every element of one's life, and proclaiming the good news (see Hebrews 13:15-16; Romans 12:1 and 15:15-16).

Peter himself uses the image of "priesthood," along with a few other metaphors, to connect our calling as God's people to our purpose in the world: "But you are a chosen race, a royal priesthood, a holy nation, God's own people, *in order that* you may proclaim the mighty acts of him who called you out of darkness into his marvelous light" (1 Peter 2:9, italics added). To paraphrase all of Peter's images, we Christians are called to be God's ministers.

Some people have difficulty speaking about the laity's call to ministry because the word "minister" has come to be associated so closely with ordained clergy. We think of it in terms of someone who is set apart for a particular and somewhat narrow set of tasks. That is never the way the word was intended in its usage in the early church years. It was always understood that being in ministry involves the entire covenant community because of the nature of ministry in a holistic sense. In the church, ministry is having care and oversight of the grace that God has given to us—and that task belongs to us all.

The Bible teaches that we are called and chosen for the purpose of service. God established the covenant community not to give us some kind of special status that exempts us from work but for the exact opposite. We are set apart primarily for the special purpose of being God's hands and voice in the world.

### Chosen to Be Christ to the World

Peter suggests that for the church to do all that it should do, it needs each member. Just as every stone is a necessary part of a building, so every Christian is an indispensable participant in the life of a church.

The implicit promise in this perspective is that God is always present to help things work as they should. Alone, none of us can begin to accomplish the church's mission. Together, however, we become the means by which God accomplishes amazing things.

Thus, in our communal life together we can count on certain divine promises and truths. Among these are:

1. *We don't have to be perfect for God to use our gifts.* Time and again, the Bible shows us God working through imperfect people. Within this current study, for example, we can look back at Gideon and Ezra as people who had some rather negative characteristics as far as leadership in the faith community goes. If God can work through such as these, the Bible reassures us, surely God can work through us.

2. *God can make all things happen.* All the stories we have studied so far affirm that God's power is real and that it breaks through all around us in surprising ways to accomplish what God wants. When situations seem hopeless, God still finds a way to work through the community of faith to bring deliverance, healing, and wholeness. Hear the good news in this! Even though the church has its share of problems and it is far from perfect, yet it remains—in some marvelous way that we can only credit to the grace of God—the body of Christ in the world.

3. *We each have gifts, and the community needs them all.* Peter wants us to see that every "stone" in Christ's church is needed. This affirmation serves as a challenge to each of us to seek God's gifts in ourselves and others, and it holds us all accountable for bringing those gifts to bear in God's service.

4. *It is in the whole community that we find all the gifts we need, not just in any one person.* Each of us stands in the midst of a community of people who are brothers and sisters, our family in Christ, who are also gifted in some way. Together as a whole, we are able to accomplish God's desires, as none of us could do alone. God tells us, in essence, "Only do what you can and that's enough—because if everyone does what he or she can, it will be more than enough."

So we end where we began this lesson: with an image of the church as the place where God dwells. Writing from the heart, Peter invites us to live into the picture of this building as he sees it—with doors and windows wide open, light streaming out into the world.

# SHARING THE SCRIPTURE

*Preparing Our Hearts*

Meditate on this week's devotional reading, found in Deuteronomy 10:10-15. In reminding the wilderness people of God's unwillingness to give up on them, Moses tells them that they are to fear, love, and serve God, and also keep the commandments because God has chosen them. How does the news that God has chosen you affect the way you relate to God and to others? Is this news as exciting and fresh as when you first heard it, or has it become so stale that the awesomeness of it no longer moves you? What does it mean to you to be chosen? In what ways will you love, serve, and obey God as a sign of this chosenness?

Pray that you and the adult learners will be aware of your special relationship with God, which empowers you to be God's heart, hands, and voice in the world.

*Preparing Our Minds*

Study the background from 1 Peter 2:1-17 and the lesson scripture, which is found in verses 1-10. As you read, identify that which distinguishes members of the Christian church from other groups.

Write on newsprint:
- ❏ information for next week's lesson, found under "Continue the Journey."
- ❏ activities for further spiritual growth in "Continue the Journey."

Plan an optional lecture using information from 1 Peter 2:1-3, 4-8 for "Explore Peter's Teachings on the Duties and Obligations of Christians."

## LEADING THE CLASS

*(1) Gather to Learn*

❖ Welcome the class members and introduce any guests.

❖ Pray that today's participants will recognize and give thanks for their place within the new covenant community.

❖ Brainstorm with the class answers to this question: **What attitudes and actions send signals that people are followers of Jesus Christ?** List ideas on newsprint.

❖ Review the list and ask the class to consider how the actions and attitudes they have listed differ from people who do not claim Christ.

❖ **Option:** If there are few differences listed between Christians and those who do not profess Christ, discuss with the group what that might say about the quality of witness Christians are making to others and what kinds of changes need to be made.

❖ Read aloud today's focus statement: **The way we live sends a clear signal about who we are and what we believe. What distinguishes members of the Christian church from other groups? Peter teaches that we are "a royal priesthood," a "holy nation," whose purpose is to declare God's mighty acts.**

*(2) Explore Peter's Teachings on the Duties and Obligations of Christians*

❖ Choose a volunteer to read 1 Peter 2:1-10.

❖ Note the two images used in verses 2-8: "newborn infants" and "living stones." Ask: **In what ways do you see Christians as "newborn infants" or "living stones"?** Use information from Understanding the Scripture to expand the discussion. If you prefer, use this information as the basis for a lecture.

❖ Point out that the idea of believers as a "spiritual house" or temple is found in other places in the New Testament. Ask volunteers to read aloud the following passages:

- 1 Corinthians 3:16-17
- 2 Corinthians 6:16a
- Ephesians 2:19-22

❖ Choose other volunteers to read aloud these passages from the Hebrew Scriptures that relate to today's passage.

- Isaiah 28:16    1 Peter 2:4, 6
- Psalm 118:22    1 Peter 2:4, 7
- Isaiah 8:14-15    1 Peter 2:8
- Exodus 19:6    1 Peter 2:9
- Hosea 2:23    1 Peter 2:10

❖ Conclude this portion of the lesson by discussing this question: **If all you had of the Bible was the passage from 2 Peter 2:1-10, what would you know about who Christ is and who you are in relation to him?**

*(3) Examine What "Being Chosen" Really Means in the Learners' Lives*

❖ Invite the class to read in unison today's key verse, 1 Peter 2:9.

❖ Solicit the students' ideas as to what it means to be "chosen." List these ideas on newsprint.

Ask these questions:

(1) **What happens when believers view chosenness as a sign of special privilege, rather than as a sign of obligation to obey and proclaim God?**

(2) **What solutions can you imagine to this problem?**

❖ Add to the conversation by asking a volunteer to read Genesis 12:1-3. Discuss why Abraham was blessed. (Be sure the students understand that he was blessed in order to be a blessing to others.)

❖ Choose someone to read Acts 1:8. Discuss the risen Lord's command that we are to be witnesses at home, in the wider community, and to the ends of the earth. Encourage the students to talk about how they as individuals and as part of God's church are proclaiming God's amazing deeds to others.

❖ Ask a student to read Acts 2:11, beginning with "in our own languages." Talk about the weight God gives to ensuring that everyone is able to hear the gospel proclaimed in his or her own language. (If you are in a geographic area where people speak more than one language, pursue this idea to see how your congregation can welcome those who do not speak this church's dominant language. Remember to include sign language for the hearing impaired in your discussion.)

❖ **Option:** Read or retell "Chosen to Be Christ to the World" from Interpreting the Scripture. Invite the adults to make comments on this reading, particularly on the idea in the final paragraph that the church is where God dwells.

*(4) Commit to Living Out Their "Chosenness" and Proclaiming God's Amazing Deeds to Others*

❖ Remind the students that both in the Hebrew Scriptures (see for example Exodus 19:3-6) and the New Testament (see for example 1 Peter 2:9) we read that God has chosen people who are God's treasured possessions. But this chosenness is, as we have seen, for a purpose: to bear witness to God's amazing deeds.

❖ Distribute paper and pencils. Ask the students to write five deeds of God that they will proclaim to others this week. These may be deeds as recorded in the Bible, or deeds God has enacted in their own lives.

❖ Invite each adult to read aloud at least one deed that she or he will tell someone else about.

❖ Encourage the students to echo your voice as you read this affirmation: **With God's help, I will proclaim to others the wonderful deeds of God so that they, too, might come out of the darkness and into God's marvelous light.**

❖ Suggest that the students put their papers in their Bibles so they may refer to their list of deeds during the week.

*(5) Continue the Journey*

❖ Pray that everyone who has participated in today's class will go forth believing they are chosen by God to proclaim the glorious works of God.

❖ Read aloud this preparation for next week's lesson. You may also want to post it on newsprint for the students to copy.

- ■ **Title: A Suffering People**
- ■ **Background Scripture: 1 Peter 4**
- ■ **Lesson Scripture: 1 Peter 4:12-19**
- ■ **Focus of the Lesson: Life tests us in many ways. How are we to respond to the trials and suffering that come our way? Peter believed that those who suffer as Christians are to rejoice as they follow Christ.**

❖ Challenge the students to complete one or more of these activities for further spiritual growth, which you will write on newsprint for the students to copy.

(1) **Talk with someone who has experienced Christ as a stumbling block. Perhaps this person was raised with rigid rules, or maybe experienced such hypocrisy that** he or she saw no value in the good news. **Share your faith and witness as to how God has worked in your life.**

(2) **Read again 2 Peter 2:1. Pray that God will reveal where these negative traits—malice, guile, insincerity, envy, and slander—are lurking in your life. Ask God to help you get rid of these traits.**

(3) **Reflect on examples of "chosenness" in your life. How have people who have wanted to be with you made you feel chosen and special? What parallels can you draw between those relationships and God's desire to choose you?**

❖ Sing or read aloud "We've a Story to Tell to the Nations."

❖ Conclude today's session by leading the class in this benediction, based on 1 Peter 2:9: **Go forth with the assurance that you are part of a chosen race, a royal priesthood, a holy nation, God's own people, in order that you may proclaim the mighty acts of him who called you out of darkness into his marvelous light.**

UNIT 3: THE NEW COVENANT COMMUNITY
# A Suffering People

---

## PREVIEWING THE LESSON

**Lesson Scripture:** 1 Peter 4:12-19
**Background Scripture:** 1 Peter 4
**Key Verse:** 1 Peter 4:19

### Focus of the Lesson:
Life tests us in many ways. How are we to respond to the trials and suffering that come our way? Peter believed that those who suffer as Christians are to rejoice as they follow Christ.

### Goals for the Learners:
(1) to open up Peter's teachings concerning how Christians are to respond when they suffer for the sake of the gospel.
(2) to acknowledge suffering as part of Christian living.
(3) to search for ways to stand in solidarity and support those who are suffering for the sake of the gospel.

### Pronunciation Guide:
Bithynia (bi thin' ee uh)
Pliny (plin' ee)
Trajan (tray' juhn)

### Supplies:
Bibles, newsprint and marker, paper and pencils, hymnals, Bible concordances

---

## READING THE SCRIPTURE

NRSV
1 Peter 4:12-19

[12]Beloved, do not be surprised at the fiery ordeal that is taking place among you to test you, as though something strange were happening to you. [13]But rejoice insofar as you are sharing Christ's sufferings, so that you may also be glad and shout for joy when his

NIV
1 Peter 4:12-19

[12]Dear friends, do not be surprised at the painful trial you are suffering, as though something strange were happening to you. [13]But rejoice that you participate in the sufferings of Christ, so that you may be overjoyed when his glory is revealed. [14]If you are

glory is revealed. [14]If you are reviled for the name of Christ, you are blessed, because the spirit of glory, which is the Spirit of God, is resting on you. [15]But let none of you suffer as a murderer, a thief, a criminal, or even as a mischief maker. [16]Yet if any of you suffers as a Christian, do not consider it a disgrace, but glorify God because you bear this name. [17]For the time has come for judgment to begin with the household of God; if it begins with us, what will be the end for those who do not obey the gospel of God? [18]And

"If it is hard for the righteous to be saved,
what will become of the ungodly and the sinners?"

[19]Therefore, **let those suffering in accordance with God's will entrust themselves to a faithful Creator, while continuing to do good.**

insulted because of the name of Christ, you are blessed, for the Spirit of glory and of God rests on you. [15]If you suffer, it should not be as a murderer or thief or any other kind of criminal, or even as a meddler. [16]However, if you suffer as a Christian, do not be ashamed, but praise God that you bear that name. [17]For it is time for judgment to begin with the family of God; and if it begins with us, what will the outcome be for those who do not obey the gospel of God? [18]And,

"If it is hard for the righteous to be saved,
what will become of the ungodly and the sinner?"

[19]So then, **those who suffer according to God's will should commit themselves to their faithful Creator and continue to do good.**

---

## UNDERSTANDING THE SCRIPTURE

**1 Peter 4:1-6.** This week's text is from the final part of 1 Peter, and it lifts up the current conditions faced by the original audience. Here we learn about their persecution and their suffering, and we read some of Scripture's most stirring words of hope.

Peter begins by reminding his audience that they are no longer to participate in the ways of the culture around them. While abstinence from their old way of life will no doubt lead to problems with folk around them, they can do no less than give up their old ways in light of all that Christ has done for them.

Underlying Peter's instructions is the implication that suffering for the sake of being loyal to Christ cannot be avoided until such time as the world itself is transformed. Until that day, Christians will receive the same hostile treatment that Christ himself did. As one means of enduring the current difficulties, Christians are

encouraged to remember that all who persecute them now will one day be judged by God—as will everyone, living and dead, who has heard the good news (4:5-6).

In addition, Peter hopes to bolster the faith and fortitude of his readers by helping them see that they are not alone in their current distresses. They are part of the community of faithful worldwide who also struggle in Christ's name. Even more, this whole body is joined with Christ himself because of his own experience of suffering.

So, until Christ comes again, Christians are to forego their old ways. The catalog of sins is explicit—"living in licentiousness, passions, drunkenness, revels, carousing, and lawless idolatry" (4:3)—but certainly not meant to be all-inclusive. Most likely, it reflects a traditional "vice list" such as we find in other Scripture passages such as Romans 1:29-31; 1 Corinthians 6:9-10; Galatians 5:19-21; and Revelation 21:8.

**1 Peter 4:7-11.** Peter then states that the time of accounting is not far off. Clearly he believes that the delay in Christ's return would not last much longer. So part of his message of encouragement is rooted in the conviction that God would soon make the world right.

Rather than argue for mere persistence until that day, however, Peter takes a more proactive approach. He knows that the fulfillment of God's new heaven and earth will not come until God's new age is finally established, yet he also believes that Christians can tap into elements of that new creation through their life as a community of faith. Accordingly, Peter lifts up four attitudes and actions that can help us do so. In their own way, these form a list of virtues that counter the vices described earlier.

First is the discipline of *prayer* (4:7). Peter is promoting the practice of prayer apart from the stressful circumstances facing some of his audience. Certainly prayer is a big help when things are going horribly wrong, but this verse addresses the need for a constant prayer life that one sustains over good times and bad. That is part of growing into a mature Christian; it is also a key way to prepare to meet the Lord in the event of a sudden return!

Peter follows this with the *love for one another* in Christ's community (4:8). As with prayer, this Christian virtue must be practiced constantly. The adage "love covers a multitude of sins" (4:8) introduces the element of forgiveness, which congregations must also practice on a regular basis. More is at stake than just how we treat one another right now, however. Peter maintains that in creating this loving and forgiving environment, the church foreshadows the way everyone will relate in God's future.

The third mark of life in the age to come is genuine *hospitality* (literally, "love of strangers")—that is, hospitality offered without complaint or resentment (4:9). Because Christians are themselves, in a theological sense, aliens wandering through a foreign land while in this world, we are to show the same acceptance and loving-kindness to others that God shows to us.

Finally, Peter writes of using one's gifts for the common good (4:10-11). The word used for "gift" here is the same used by Paul in 1 Corinthians 12, and it designates spiritual gifts in particular. While Paul speaks of several gifts, however, Peter mentions only two: speaking the words of God and serving. Whatever form these gifts take, they are to be used only in ways that add to the glory God receives through Christ over time (4:11).

**1 Peter 4:12-19.** Following this sermon-like section on the age to come, Peter returns to the problem of life right now. In light of all he has just said, he urges his audience to think of their current situation in a new way. Rather than being surprised at the "fiery ordeal" (4:12) of their persecution, he tells them to rejoice in it as a means of sharing Christ's suffering (4:13). Indeed, by suffering in Christ's name, the people of the early church share also in his grace and his glory (4:14, 16).

Peter also raises a caution, however, about misapplying these teachings. He is not saying that *all* suffering is worthwhile or brings blessing and glory to the sufferer. This status applies only to those suffering in the name of Jesus. It certainly is not in effect for those who "suffer" as a result of wrongdoing, such as criminal activity or meddling in the affairs of others (translated "mischief making," 4:15).

The final three verses confirm that Peter interprets the current sufferings as a sign that the final judgment is beginning (4:17). He hinted at this in the language of verse 12, in the sense that the image of a fiery ordeal is a sort of code phrase for the coming day of the Lord. Here, however, all is stated clearly. Looking ahead to the imminent return of Christ, Peter reminds his audience that, whatever they are going through, the punishment of their persecutors will be far worse (4:18). They are to take what comfort they can from this and stay faithful to God, who will in turn stay faithful to them (4:19).

# INTERPRETING THE SCRIPTURE

### Keeping the Text in Context

This week, we look at Peter's teachings on how Christians are to respond when they suffer for the sake of the gospel. It is important to remember this as the focus of the Scripture lesson. When the text speaks of suffering "in accordance with God's will" (4:19), too many times this is *misread* as saying that all suffering is God's will. The Bible as a whole makes clear that this is not so. To understand this Scripture passage rightly, we need to keep it in its proper context.

It helps to remember that 1 Peter was written during a time when the Christian church was threatened. The author intended these letters to encourage a frightened community and to help them hold fast to their faith under great pressure to recant it. Thus, when Peter speaks of suffering for the sake of the gospel, the words are accurately descriptive of what the church was experiencing.

### An Ancient Record

While we know that Peter's audience was either anticipating imminent persecution or already undergoing it, 1 Peter itself does not provide many details about the situation. Little documentary evidence remains regarding Roman-Christian relations in the earlier years of the church, so what we do have is very important.

One of the few official sources lies in correspondence between the Emperor Trajan and Pliny the Younger, governor of the province of Bithynia in A.D. 111–113. Their letters are the earliest we have on the subject, and scholars suggest they give a good picture as to what the church faced in Peter's day.

Pliny writes to Trajan both to advise him of actions already underway against Christians and to seek his guidance regarding future cases. Both his letter and the emperor's response show that no concentrated, statewide plan for persecution is in place.

Pliny begins by admitting that he has never actually witnessed an interrogation of those accused of being Christians. He is uncertain as to what lengths one should go in trying to prosecute these people. Pliny also questions whether children who claim to be Christians are to be handled in the same way as adult followers. He wonders about the kinds of punishments that should be meted out to those found guilty of unwavering allegiance to Christ, particularly if they have committed no criminal acts. He asks Trajan if there should there be a different standard of punishment for those who have renounced their faith in Christ.

One of Pliny's concerns, as seen in the translation of *Letters X.96-97* by Eugene M. Boring, is that he still has to pass judgment on those who are brought before him on charges. So he reports:

> I have handled those who have been denounced to me as Christians as follows: I asked them whether they were Christians. Those who responded affirmatively I have asked a second and third time, under threat of the death penalty. If they persisted . . . in their confession, I had them executed. For whatever it is that they are actually advocating, it seems to me that obstinacy and stubbornness must be punished.

He then goes on to describe a case of anonymous accusations and how he dealt with it:

> An unsigned placard was posted, accusing a large number of people by name. Those who denied being Christians . . . I thought necessary to release, since they invoked our gods according to the formula I gave them and since they offered sacrifices of

wine and incense before your image which I had brought in for this purpose along with the statues of our gods. I also had them curse Christ. It is said that real Christians cannot be forced to do any of these things.

Three additional pieces of information arise from Pliny's letter. The first is a brief description of common Christian practices, which the governor finds innocuous enough for an alternative religion:

[O]n a specified day before sunrise they were accustomed to gather and sing an antiphonal hymn to Christ as their God and to pledge themselves by an oath not to engage in any crime, but to abstain from all thievery, assault, and adultery, not to break their word once they had given it, and not to refuse to pay their legal debts. They then went in their separate ways, and came together later to eat a common meal, but it was ordinary, harmless food.

At the same time, we see that he did consider Christianity a potential threat only in so far as they might have a *political* agenda:

They discontinued even this practice in accordance with my edict by which I had forbidden political associations, in accord with your instructions. I considered it all the more necessary to obtain by torture a confession of the truth from two female slaves, whom they called "deaconesses." I found nothing more than a vulgar, excessive superstition.

Finally, the letter confirms that two of Peter's concerns were well-grounded. Christians may indeed be facing an increase in persecution, and many were already deserting the faith because of Pliny's actions.

### Suffering as Christians Today

Looking beyond their historical context, these words move us to consider the ways in which Christians today still suffer for the sake of the gospel. One may think of missionaries and other religious workers who are tortured and killed because of their ministries. Perhaps folk who suffer because of their efforts at peacemaking come to mind, such as those who are conscientious objectors during a time of war or those who put their lives at risk in conflict-torn parts of the world. There are many other examples as well.

Peter's words also challenge us to consider less dramatic, non-life-threatening ways that our own congregations may suffer for the sake of the gospel. For example, churches often take a stand on national and global issues that are unpopular and draw criticism. They may advocate for change in their local area that their neighbors oppose. The opportunities to speak out for justice and peace are endless, and thus so are the chances of becoming unpopular in some circles.

As we look across the world, we see many places where our brothers and sisters in Christ are suffering for the sake of the gospel. Once we become aware of this, it is natural to want to help. This is good, because they need all the support and encouragement they can get! Sending money is one option, of course, but there are other things we can do as well. We can learn more about the systems that oppress and hurt these servants of Christ, and we can work to change them. We can send letters or e-mails with a word of appreciation and encouragement, in order to build up their own strength and resolve. Most of all, we can pray for them diligently and earnestly, joining in saying as the apostle Paul once did, "I have heard of your faith in the Lord Jesus and your love toward all the saints, and for this reason I do not cease to give thanks for you as I remember you in my prayers" (Ephesians 1:15-16).

# SHARING THE SCRIPTURE

## Preparing Our Hearts

Meditate on this week's devotional reading, found in 1 Corinthians 12:20-26. In this section Paul writes about one body in Christ having many members. Verse 26 reminds us that, just as the entire human body feels badly if one part hurts, so it is with the body of Christ. Similarly, if all is well with a person, the entire body feels good. And so it is with the body of Christ. What is causing the body of Christ to suffer today? What is causing it to rejoice? In what ways do you help care for the entire body of Christ? What joy and sorrow do you feel as part of Christ's body?

Pray that you and the adult learners will be especially sensitive to those members of the body who are suffering because of their relationship with Christ.

## Preparing Our Minds

Study the background from 1 Peter 4 and the lesson scripture, which is taken from verses 12-19. Contemplate how we as believers are to respond to the trials and suffering that come our way.

Write on newsprint:

❏ information for next week's lesson, found under "Continue the Journey."
❏ activities for further spiritual growth in "Continue the Journey."

Prepare a lecture based on 1 Peter 4:1-6, 7-11 in Understanding the Scripture for "Open Up Peter's Teachings Concerning How Christians Are to Respond When They Suffer for the Sake of the Gospel."

Locate several Bible concordances. Your church library and local library should have these references. Many study Bibles (that is, those with footnotes, maps, and other helps) also include abbreviated concordances.

Check www.persecution.org for a list of countries where Christians are currently suffering and information about conditions in these countries.

## LEADING THE CLASS

### (1) Gather to Learn

❖ Welcome the class members and introduce any guests.

❖ Pray that those who have come today will open their hearts and minds to the message that God has for them this day.

❖ Read this information from www.persecution.org. **On April 2, 2008, Pastor Thumula Johnson and twelve members of his Gospel Mission team were distributing tracts and New Testaments in several villages in India. At the last village they intended to visit that day, the missionaries were harassed by the village head. When they tried to leave peacefully, their vehicle was surrounded by the village head and fifty other residents. For three hours the crowd tried to coerce the missionaries to confess, "Christ be brought down, hail Hindu gods." The missionaries were unwavering in their commitment to Christ, even when all of the New Testaments and other Christian literature they had was burned. Against their will, a Hindu ritual mark was applied to the heads of these missionaries, who themselves were Indian.**

❖ Discuss these questions:
    **(1) What motivates and empowers people such as Pastor Johnson to suffer for their faith?**
    **(2) What lessons can such people teach us?**

❖ Read aloud today's focus statement: **Life tests us in many ways. How are we to respond to the trials and suffering that come our way? Peter believed that those who suffer as Christians are to rejoice as they follow Christ.**

*(2) Open Up Peter's Teachings Concerning How Christians Are to Respond When They Suffer for the Sake of the Gospel*

❖ Present the lecture you have prepared on selected verses from Understanding the Scripture to set the stage for today's Bible text.

❖ Choose a volunteer to read 1 Peter 4:12-19.

❖ Invite the students to suggest what might have been going on among the people to whom Peter was writing.

❖ Read "An Ancient Record" from Interpreting the Scripture to get a firsthand look from the point of view of a powerful persecutor.

❖ Encourage the students to respond to Pliny's letter by answering these questions:

**(1) Why does the gospel of Jesus create both a lightning rod of anger for some and a source of comfort for others?**

**(2) Had you been living under Pliny's rule, do you think you would have remained steadfast in your faith? Why or why not?**

**(3) How would Peter's message have affirmed your faith?**

*(3) Acknowledge Suffering as Part of Christian Living*

❖ Read: **There are a variety of ways to view suffering. Some ascetics seek it out. Most of us try to avoid it at all costs. Some suffering is the result of poor choices. Some suffering is the result of unswerving devotion to God. All people have experiences that cause suffering, though people's interpretations of that suffering and their responses to it vary greatly.**

❖ Divide the class into groups of three or four. Give each person paper and a pencil, and each group a concordance. If you do not have enough concordances, enlist the help of students whose Bibles include a concordance.

❖ Ask the groups to look up the word "suffer" and other words that relate to it, such as "suffering." As one person calls out a verse from the concordance, another group member is to read the verse aloud. Each group member is to write what he or she has learned about suffering from this verse. Encourage each group to check at least five verses. Provide time for the group members to discuss what they have discerned about suffering from these verses.

❖ Call the class together and invite the groups to share any insights they have discerned from their Bible study.

*(4) Search for Ways to Stand in Solidarity and Support Those Who Are Suffering for the Sake of the Gospel*

❖ Read "Suffering as Christians Today" from Interpreting the Scripture.

❖ Look especially at the second paragraph of this reading and talk about ways that the class sees your own congregation as unpopular because of stances it has taken for peace and justice. If they cannot discern any unpopular stances, raise the possibility that the church is unwilling to take risks that might cause them to suffer.

❖ Invite the students to name countries in the world where Christians are oppressed. List these countries on newsprint. Include any information you have found in searching the Internet, particularly www.persecution.org.

❖ Encourage the students to pray silently for the countries listed and to ask God what they might do to help alleviate the pain of their fellow Christians.

*(5) Continue the Journey*

❖ Break the silence by praying that the adults will go forth ready to face opposition to their faith and support those who are experiencing such opposition.

❖ Read aloud this preparation for next week's lesson. You may also want to post it on newsprint for the students to copy.

- **Title: A Faithful People**
- **Background Scripture: 2 Peter 1:3-15**
- **Lesson Scripture: 2 Peter 1:3-15**
- **Focus of the Lesson: We all have faith in something or someone, but we often find it hard to develop this faith. How can we support and strengthen a growing and effective faith? Peter's second letter teaches that goodness, knowledge, self-control, endurance, godliness, mutual affection, and love all undergird a growing faith.**

❖ Challenge the students to complete one or more of these activities for further spiritual growth, which you will write on newsprint for the students to copy.

(1) **Do an Internet search to locate stories of Christians persecuted for their faith. See if there are ways that you can help these brothers and sisters in Christ, per-haps through prayer, financial contributions, or other means.**

(2) **Recall a time when you experienced personal suffering, which likely had nothing to do with suffering for Christ. How did you handle this situation? How did this event strengthen or challenge your faith in Christ?**

(3) **Do what you can to help someone who is suffering. This individual is likely not suffering for his or her faith but may be suffering in body, mind, or spirit because of poor choices, ill health, or events beyond personal control.**

❖ Sing or read aloud "Stand By Me."

❖ Conclude today's session by leading the class in this benediction, based on 1 Peter 2:9: **Go forth with the assurance that you are part of a chosen race, a royal priesthood, a holy nation, God's own people, in order that you may proclaim the mighty acts of him who called you out of darkness into his marvelous light.**

## UNIT 3: THE NEW COVENANT COMMUNITY
# A FAITHFUL PEOPLE

---

### PREVIEWING THE LESSON

**Lesson Scripture:** 2 Peter 1:3-15
**Background Scripture:** 2 Peter 1:3-15
**Key Verse:** 2 Peter 1:3

### Focus of the Lesson:
We all have faith in something or someone, but we often find it hard to develop this faith. How can we support and strengthen a growing and effective faith? Peter's second letter teaches that goodness, knowledge, self-control, endurance, godliness, mutual affection, and love all undergird a growing faith.

### Goals for the Learners:
(1) to unpack Peter's teachings about the faith of a godly person.
(2) to recognize the relationship between a deeply rooted faith and godly living.
(3) to discern and act in ways that promote growth in faith.

### Supplies:
Bibles, newsprint and marker, paper and pencils, hymnals

---

### READING THE SCRIPTURE

NRSV
2 Peter 1:3-15

³His divine power has given us everything needed for life and godliness, through the knowledge of him who called us by his own glory and goodness. ⁴Thus he has given us, through these things, his precious and very great promises, so that through them you may escape from the corruption that is in the world because of lust, and may become participants of the divine nature. ⁵For this very reason, you must make every effort to support your faith with goodness, and goodness with

NIV
2 Peter 1:3-15

³His divine power has given us everything we need for life and godliness through our knowledge of him who called us by his own glory and goodness. ⁴Through these he has given us his very great and precious promises, so that through them you may participate in the divine nature and escape the corruption in the world caused by evil desires.

⁵For this very reason, make every effort to add to your faith goodness; and to goodness,

knowledge, [6]and knowledge with self-control, and self-control with endurance, and endurance with godliness, [7]and godliness with mutual affection, and mutual affection with love. [8]For if these things are yours and are increasing among you, they keep you from being ineffective and unfruitful in the knowledge of our Lord Jesus Christ. [9]For anyone who lacks these things is shortsighted and blind, and is forgetful of the cleansing of past sins. [10]Therefore, brothers and sisters, be all the more eager to confirm your call and election, for if you do this, you will never stumble. [11]For in this way, entry into the eternal kingdom of our Lord and Savior Jesus Christ will be richly provided for you.

[12]Therefore I intend to keep on reminding you of these things, though you know them already and are established in the truth that has come to you. [13]I think it right, as long as I am in this body, to refresh your memory, [14]since I know that my death will come soon, as indeed our Lord Jesus Christ has made clear to me. [15]And I will make every effort so that after my departure you may be able at any time to recall these things.

knowledge; [6]and to knowledge, self-control; and to self-control, perseverance; and to perseverance, godliness; [7]and to godliness, brotherly kindness; and to brotherly kindness, love. [8]For if you possess these qualities in increasing measure, they will keep you from being ineffective and unproductive in your knowledge of our Lord Jesus Christ. [9]But if anyone does not have them, he is nearsighted and blind, and has forgotten that he has been cleansed from his past sins.

[10]Therefore, my brothers, be all the more eager to make your calling and election sure. For if you do these things, you will never fall, [11]and you will receive a rich welcome into the eternal kingdom of our Lord and Savior Jesus Christ.

[12]So I will always remind you of these things, even though you know them and are firmly established in the truth you now have. [13]I think it is right to refresh your memory as long as I live in the tent of this body, [14]because I know that I will soon put it aside, as our Lord Jesus Christ has made clear to me. [15]And I will make every effort to see that after my departure you will always be able to remember these things.

## UNDERSTANDING THE SCRIPTURE

**Introduction.** Second Peter was originally written and sent to certain Christians in Asia Minor who were struggling with concerns about end times and ethics. These readers had previously received 1 Peter (2 Peter 3:1) and one or more letters of Paul (3:15). The author identifies himself as Simeon (a variant of Simon) Peter, an eyewitness of Jesus' transfiguration (1:16-18). Now he is about to suffer martyrdom, as Jesus had prophesied (1:14; see John 13:36; 21:18-19).

For several reasons, however, most scholars do not think that the apostle Peter really wrote this letter. First, it was a common practice in the ancient world to write under the name of a famous person. This was not meant as an act of deception; rather, it was meant as a sign of respect and homage to the one whose name was used. In Peter's case, there are at least seven other manuscripts attributed to his authorship that we know he did not compose. Second, many ancient Christians doubted that Peter wrote this letter. Third, its style and vocabulary do not match 1 Peter, although that may be due to a change in secretary. (First Peter 5:12 records that letter as being scribed by "Silvanus," who may or may not be the Silas of Acts 15:22, 40; 16:19; 17:4). Finally, the letter seems to have been written some time after A.D. 64, when Peter died.

Certain clues indicate that the letter was written toward the end of the first century, but no later. For example, the author still expects Christ to return during his lifetime (3:14), and there is no sign that a formal church hierarchy has developed. Likewise, the author does not mention any of the heresies that cropped up during the early second century.

At the same time, the author addresses a particular problem that developed only a generation or two into the church's development. The original recipients of the letter were losing their hope in the Second Coming of Christ and the final judgment. With no judgment coming, they figured they might as well live as they liked. The author was concerned that they were no longer growing or moving forward in their Christian life, but were on the verge of giving it up altogether. This crisis sets the stage for the teachings that run throughout the letter.

**2 Peter 1:3-11.** These verses follow the salutation (1:1-2), and they constitute the beginning of the body of the letter. Taken as a whole, the section is a mini-sermon presenting the main themes that will be expanded by the rest of the book. As was common for formal exhortations in that day, it has three main parts.

Part 1 (1:3-4) lays the groundwork of God's saving activity in the past and ongoing support in the present. The author assures the people that the same God who called them through the divine "glory and goodness" is the God who even now gives them "everything needed for life and godliness" (1:3). They can count on the power of God to help them overcome the corruption of this world and thus to become more like God morally and ethically (that is, to "become participants of the divine nature," 1:4).

Part 2 (1:5-10) then lists the attitudes and actions that are the mark of Christians.

Verse 5 begins by urging Christians to "make every effort" to support their faith through a list of good qualities. The image is a particularly rich one in the original language, and worth considering.

The word translated "support" in verse 5 is based on a peculiar verb from Greek theater that describes the actions of one who provides for a chorus, the group of singers and dancers who comment on the action. This was often quite a large group, and they all needed to be costumed and paid. Thus, wealthy citizens who wanted to patronize the arts would take it on themselves to provide the necessary financial support—and their gifts were often quite lavish. Taken in this sense, verse 5 can be read as a strong command: "Don't just provide the minimum effort needed to support your faith. Make lavish and costly efforts to do so!"

Verses 5-7 then detail the elements that go into supporting one's faith. Notice that these are all practical and reasonable attributes to which anyone would want to aspire. What sets them apart in this context, however, is the joint goal of increasing one's faith (1:5) and helping one to become ever more effective and fruitful for Christ (1:8). Thus it is no surprise that the list begins with faith and ends with love. Along with countless other writers in the early church, this author sees those two attributes as summing up the whole goal of discipleship. Finally, going back to verse 3, we see that God gives us everything we need, but we have to put it to use.

Part 3 (1:11) of this mini-sermon grounds our present action in the future hope of entering Christ's eternal realm. Achieving a Christian lifestyle does not earn us entry into this realm, but it does confirm our "call and election" (1:10). In other words, it is the tangible sign of what God has already done for us, and it is all the proof we need that a place has been provided for us in the age to come.

**2 Peter 1:12-15.** The teaching ends with a personal statement from the writer.

Literarily, verses 12-15 fit a particular genre, called a "testament," most common in the Jewish writings of the intertestamental period (the time between the writings of the Hebrew Scriptures and the New Testament, roughly 200 B.C. to A.D. 50). In this type of writing, a famous figure leaves words of special importance to those who follow. These may be predictions, commands, or blessings. Some biblical examples include the blessing and charge of Jacob (Genesis 49), the blessing of Moses (Deuteronomy 33), Jesus' last discourse in John 13–17, or the Great Commission (Matthew 28:16-20). In each case, the essential points of a great person's life are summarized so that it can be remembered and followed many years later.

## INTERPRETING THE SCRIPTURE

### Christ as Ruler

Within the church's liturgical year, today we celebrate the reign of Christ over all creation. This theological setting provides a great framework for our text, which begins with a reference to Christ's "divine power" (1:3). This power, unlimited in the One who rules over all, is the reason we can trust Christ's promises and move forward in confidence as his people. We know that he is indeed able to give us "everything needed for life and for godliness" (1:3).

Moreover, the image of Christ as ruler provides a helpful analogy for our own place in his realm. In some ways, we are like the persons of old whom a queen or king would elevate to a noble rank and then endow with lands and resources. To press the analogy using the language of verse 10, as those whom Christ has graced:

(1) We have been called—that is, given a new name and a new title within his realm.

(2) We have been elected—that is, chosen and lifted up, given a status that we could not achieve on our own.

### Ourselves as Citizens

So then, now that we have been not only welcomed into Christ's realm but also given a place of honor there, what are we to do? The simple answer, as 2 Peter presents it, is *to act appropriately*. Out of our deep sense of gratitude and love for our Lord, we are to act in ways befitting his gift to us.

Verses 5-7 list some qualities of conduct that are fit for the citizens of Christ's realm: goodness, knowledge, self-control, endurance, godliness, mutual affection, and love. The list is deceptively simple in that these traits, which might seem easy enough to achieve on the surface, are nevertheless often lacking in the Christian community. Note that each quality is supported and strengthened by the next.

- *goodness* refers to acting in ways that are morally and ethically right. More than that, the term also carries a sense of excellence, indicating that such deeds are done exceptionally well.
- *knowledge* can signify general intelligence and practical discernment, but it can also refer to deeper insights into the things that are appropriate for Christians. It does connote knowledge that is ever-increasing or eventually full.
- *self-control* involves both the ability and the willingness to act in moderation at all times, as well as refraining from ungodly emotions and desires. Most scriptural texts further interpret this as the power to act with love on all occasions.

- *endurance* describes patiently persevering at a task. Biblical texts often use the term to refer to remaining steadfast in one's faith, especially under conditions of persecution or suffering, with the end result that such experiences are redeemed and transformed.
- *godliness* does not mean acting perfectly or in a holy manner. Rather, the term refers to a constant state of reverence and respect for God, especially as shown in acts of service to others.
- *mutual affection* (literally, *philadelphia*) is actually a term for the love that family members are to have for one another, especially in a close relationship like siblings. Here, the word indicates the love that we are to have for one another as brothers and sisters in Christ.
- *love* is the special Greek word, *agape*, that indicates the divine love shown by Christ. It is the unconditional love, described so beautifully by Paul in 1 Corinthians 13, that Christians are to have for all people, even their enemies.

What's interesting is that each of these attributes build on the one that follows. In a sense, then, the author presents a "top down" look at the way we are to act as God's citizens. The foundation for everything is what's named last—love. Everything else grows from that.

### Christian Evolution

If we work backwards through the list, we find a fascinating description of the evolution of a Christian life. As 2 Peter puts it, our development and growth in the faith goes through a number of stages before we can truly put our love into action. Here is a brief summary of what the list, taken from bottom to top, suggests.

As stated earlier, God's own love is the grounding for all the rest. The starting place for a life of discipleship lies in experiencing that divine love for ourselves and then being moved to share it with others. So the next step is sharing this love with others in the family of faith. Experiences of worship and fellowship in our communal life together are what lead to a deepening of a personal relationship with God.

Fortified by our growing relationships with God and with other believers, we find ourselves strengthened to be increasingly steadfast in our faith. Through a living connection with our Lord and with the support of a caring community, we grow in patience and trust. Most of all, we find ourselves better able to hold on to faith and hope when life falls apart, sometimes presenting us with suffering that seems almost unbearable.

The very experiences of life that test our endurance also enable us, in turn, to grow better at self-control. More patience helps us fight the desire for immediate gratification. Gratitude for God's steadfast care through difficult times can inspire us to make better choices from now on as a tangible form of thanks. Certainly the love of God expressed through the love of our faith community helps our own love grow—and as our love grows, we find less and less room in our hearts for anger, pride, or other emotions so completely disconnected from it.

Based on the list, only at this point do we begin to have a true understanding of what life in Christ is all about. Our experiences open up insights into the Scriptures and into the shared life of our community, as well as insights into our own call, that we could not reach otherwise. Moreover, the longer we live in Christ, the more our understanding grows. Few people would say that they understand all aspects of life and church, including the interpretation of Scripture, exactly the same way now as they did five years ago. We live, we learn, we grow—that is the blessing of life in the church.

Finally we come to the last trait of God's citizens, which is constantly to engage in actions that proclaim our membership in God's realm. As we grow in all the other traits, we are better and better equipped to put our faith into action in ways that not only express God's love for the world but also serve as a witness to it. No wonder the author follows this section by saying, "If these things are yours and are increasing among you, they keep you from being ineffective and unfruitful" (1:8)!

Notice that the text also says zealously pursuing these attributes will result in God providing entry into Christ's eternal realm (1:10-11). This is not to say that such actions will buy or earn a place in the age to come. I think, rather, the author means to say that disciples who pursue these goals will find they are able to participate in aspects of Christ's reign here and now.

---

## SHARING THE SCRIPTURE

### Preparing Our Hearts

Meditate on this week's devotional reading, found in Luke 19:12-26. This parable of the ten pounds includes elements of the parable of the talents found in Matthew 25:14-30, but there are differences, so do read carefully. As the parable in Luke relates to today's lesson, you will want to consider how you handle what has been entrusted to you. Are you living faithfully unto God? Are you taking what you have been given and adding value to that so as to enhance God's kingdom? Where could you be making a difference right now if you were more faithful?

Pray that you and the adult learners will recognize that God has provided you with what you need to live as godly believers.

### Preparing Our Minds

Study the background and lesson scripture, both found in 2 Peter 1:3-15. Consider ways in which we support and strengthen a growing and effective faith.

Write on newsprint:
❑ words shown in italics in "Ourselves as Citizens."
❑ information for next week's lesson, found under "Continue the Journey."
❑ activities for further spiritual growth in "Continue the Journey."

### LEADING THE CLASS

#### (1) Gather to Learn

❖ Welcome the class members and introduce any guests.

❖ Pray that those who have come today will be open to nudges by the Holy Spirit to develop their faith.

❖ Post a sheet of newsprint and write these words: **I have faith in** . . . Go around the room (unless the class is very large) and invite each person to complete that sentence quickly. The ideas may be theological, but they may also reflect one's culture or preferences. For example, one may say "I have faith in the future," another "government," and a third a favorite sports team.

❖ Raise this question: **Why do you think that most people have faith in something or someone?**

❖ Read aloud today's focus statement: **We all have faith in something or someone, but we often find it hard to develop this faith. How can we support and strengthen a growing and effective faith? Peter's second letter teaches that goodness, knowledge, self-control, endurance, godliness, mutual affection, and love all undergird a growing faith.**

#### (2) Unpack Peter's Teachings about the Faith of a Godly Person

❖ Read or retell "Introduction" in Understanding the Scripture to help orient the students before delving into today's reading.

❖ Choose someone to read 2 Peter 1:3-15 as if this person were Peter speaking to the church.

❖ Look again at 2 Peter 1:3, which is today's key verse. Ask the class to consider how God's divine power, as manifested through the Holy Spirit, has equipped them with what they need to live godly lives.

❖ Post newsprint on which you have written the italicized words in "Ourselves as Citizens" in Interpreting the Scripture. These words—*goodness, knowledge, self-control, endurance, godliness, mutual affection, love*—are from 2 Peter 1:5-7. Ask the class to try to define each word, and to write their ideas beside the word. Add ideas from "Ourselves as Citizens." Talk with the class about how these attributes lead one to demonstrate a virtuous life of faith.

*(3) Recognize the Relationship Between a Deeply Rooted Faith and Godly Living*

❖ Distribute paper and pencils. Invite the students to sketch a tree, showing its roots, trunk, branches, and leaves. (Remind them that artistic ability is not important.) Ask them to set this sketch aside.

❖ Brainstorm with the group answers to this question: **What creates a strong faith?** Write responses on newsprint, which you will leave posted. (Answers may include *spiritual disciplines, such as Bible study, worship, tithing, fasting, meditation, and journaling.* Answers may also include *mentors in the faith, parents, a strong church, a spiritual director or friend, opportunities to speak and enact a Christian witness, and life experiences that prompt one to rely on God.*)

❖ Brainstorm with the group answers to this question: **What are some signs of a godly life?** Write responses on another sheet of newsprint, which you will leave posted. (Answers may include *goodness, knowledge, self-control, endurance, godliness, mutual affection, and love,* as recorded in

2 Peter 1:5-7 and previously discussed. Signs also include how one's relationship with God is lived out in relationship to other people.)

❖ Encourage the students to review these lists to see which ideas apply to their own life. Then ask them to write words on their tree in appropriate places. For example, if a parent and strong church were foundational to a student's faith development, these words should be written in the roots. If a believing spouse continues to support their growth in faith, the spouse's name should be written on the trunk. Words on the branches and leaves could be those signs that one is living a godly life. These are the things that others can see as a witness.

❖ Ask the adults to talk with a small group about how they perceive a deeply rooted faith supports godly living, as well as ways in which godly living increases one's faith.

*(4) Discern and Act in Ways that Promote Growth in Faith*

❖ Read aloud this statement: **A Christian's words and works are two sides of the same coin.** Encourage the students to talk about how what we say we believe and how we act must be in synch in order for us to grow in faith.

❖ Read aloud these two verses from Frederick W. Faber's 1849 hymn, "Faith of Our Fathers." As suggested in *The United Methodist Hymnal,* "our fathers" has been changed to "the martyrs." For this lesson, the change more closely aligns the hymn to the church to which Peter wrote. After the reading, invite the adults to discuss how people who have lived godly lives in ages past can encourage them to act in ways that will promote growth in their own faith.

**Faith of the martyrs, living still,**
**in spite of dungeon, fire and sword;**
**O how our hearts beat high with joy**
**whene'er we hear that glorious word!**

Faith of the martyrs, we will love
both friend and foe in all our strife;
and preach to thee, too, as love knows
   how
by kindly words and virtuous life.

❖ Conclude this portion of the lesson by asking the class to speculate how the church of the early twenty-first century will be remembered for its faith.

### (5) Continue the Journey

❖ Pray that today's participants will go forth empowered by God's Spirit to live godly lives.

❖ Read aloud this preparation for next week's lesson. You may also want to post it on newsprint for the students to copy.

- ■ Title: A Hopeful People
- ■ Background Scripture: 2 Peter 3
- ■ Lesson Scripture: 2 Peter 3:1-13
- ■ Focus of the Lesson: Even in the toughest situations, an encouraging word from a friend can make all the difference in how we respond to challenges that confront us. How, then, can we encourage others to keep persevering when barriers seem insurmountable? Peter taught people to live as they awaited Christ's return.

❖ Challenge the students to complete one or more of these activities for further spiritual growth, which you will write on newsprint for the students to copy.

(1) Review the words on the tree you drew during the session. What areas seem sparse or weak? How can you deepen your faith and broaden your ability to live a godly life? Ask God for guidance so that you may grow into a spiritually sturdy "redwood."

(2) Practice a spiritual discipline that you may not normally use. Give it a try this week to see if it has the potential to increase your faith.

(3) Recall how other people have helped you this far in your spiritual journey. Think about actions you could take to help others to come to Christ and mature in their faith.

❖ Sing or read aloud "My Faith Looks Up to Thee."

❖ Conclude today's session by leading the class in this benediction, based on 1 Peter 2:9: Go forth with the assurance that you are part of a chosen race, a royal priesthood, a holy nation, God's own people, in order that you may proclaim the mighty acts of him who called you out of darkness into his marvelous light.

UNIT 3: THE NEW COVENANT COMMUNITY
# A HOPEFUL PEOPLE

---

## PREVIEWING THE LESSON

**Lesson Scripture:** 2 Peter 3:1-13
**Background Scripture:** 2 Peter 3
**Key Verse:** 2 Peter 3:9

### Focus of the Lesson:
Even in the toughest situations, an encouraging word from a friend can make all the difference in how we respond to challenges that confront us. How, then, can we encourage others to keep persevering when barriers seem insurmountable? Peter taught people to live as they awaited Christ's return.

### Goals for the Learners:
(1) to delve into Peter's encouraging teachings concerning the promise of Christ's return.
(2) to acknowledge areas in their lives where they need hope and encouragement.
(3) to encourage others who are facing difficulties and to devise a plan to give hope.

### Pronunciation Guide:
*parousia* (puh roo' zhee uh)

### Supplies:
Bibles, newsprint and marker, paper and pencils, hymnals

---

## READING THE SCRIPTURE

NRSV
2 Peter 3:1-13

¹This is now, beloved, the second letter I am writing to you; in them I am trying to arouse your sincere intention by reminding you ²that you should remember the words spoken in the past by the holy prophets, and the commandment of the Lord and Savior spoken through your apostles. ³First of all you must understand this, that in the last

NIV
2 Peter 3:1-13

¹Dear friends, this is now my second letter to you. I have written both of them as reminders to stimulate you to wholesome thinking. ²I want you to recall the words spoken in the past by the holy prophets and the command given by our Lord and Savior through your apostles.

³First of all, you must understand that in

days scoffers will come, scoffing and indulging their own lusts [4]and saying, "Where is the promise of his coming? For ever since our ancestors died, all things continue as they were from the beginning of creation!" [5]They deliberately ignore this fact, that by the word of God heavens existed long ago and an earth was formed out of water and by means of water, [6]through which the world of that time was deluged with water and perished. [7]But by the same word the present heavens and earth have been reserved for fire, being kept until the day of judgment and destruction of the godless.

[8]But do not ignore this one fact, beloved, that with the Lord one day is like a thousand years, and a thousand years are like one day. **[9]The Lord is not slow about his promise, as some think of slowness, but is patient with you, not wanting any to perish, but all to come to repentance.** [10]But the day of the Lord will come like a thief, and then the heavens will pass away with a loud noise, and the elements will be dissolved with fire, and the earth and everything that is done on it will be disclosed.

[11]Since all these things are to be dissolved in this way, what sort of persons ought you to be in leading lives of holiness and godliness, [12]waiting for and hastening the coming of the day of God, because of which the heavens will be set ablaze and dissolved, and the elements will melt with fire? [13]But, in accordance with his promise, we wait for new heavens and a new earth, where righteousness is at home.

the last days scoffers will come, scoffing and following their own evil desires. [4]They will say, "Where is this 'coming' he promised? Ever since our fathers died, everything goes on as it has since the beginning of creation." [5]But they deliberately forget that long ago by God's word the heavens existed and the earth was formed out of water and by water. [6]By these waters also the world of that time was deluged and destroyed. [7]By the same word the present heavens and earth are reserved for fire, being kept for the day of judgment and destruction of ungodly men.

[8]But do not forget this one thing, dear friends: With the Lord a day is like a thousand years, and a thousand years are like a day. **[9]The Lord is not slow in keeping his promise, as some understand slowness. He is patient with you, not wanting anyone to perish, but everyone to come to repentance.** [10]But the day of the Lord will come like a thief. The heavens will disappear with a roar; the elements will be destroyed by fire, and the earth and everything in it will be laid bare.

[11]Since everything will be destroyed in this way, what kind of people ought you to be? You ought to live holy and godly lives [12]as you look forward to the day of God and speed its coming. That day will bring about the destruction of the heavens by fire, and the elements will melt in the heat. [13]But in keeping with his promise we are looking forward to a new heaven and a new earth, the home of righteousness.

## UNDERSTANDING THE SCRIPTURE

**Introduction.** This text deals specifically with issues related to the delay of Jesus' triumphant return. The word that names this event is *parousia*, which the Greeks often used to describe the visit of a king or the manifestation of a god. It is the word most frequently used in the New Testament to denote the return of Jesus Christ at the end of time. (The phrase "Second Coming" is not found in the New Testament but was developed by later Christians.) The New Testament not only maintains that God in

Christ initially created the universe but it also continually insists that God in Christ will eventually come again to bring this universe to an end that includes "new heavens and a new earth, where righteousness is at home" (2 Peter 3:13).

**2 Peter 3:1-4.** Our quarter ends with a look at the final chapter of 2 Peter. Here we encounter the main crisis that led to the writing of the letter. Because the return of Christ has not come within the generation when it was expected, many members in the church are facing a crisis of faith. What if Jesus will never return? What hope have they then? And if they were wrong about that, what else in the gospel message might prove to be false?

Certain false teachers, here called "scoffers" (3:3), have decided to debunk the whole idea of a messianic return, and they are fueling the fears and doubts of others. These folk are perhaps cynical about the future by nature, but their skepticism definitely serves a selfish intent—they have an immoral lifestyle that they do not wish to change. They argue that the return will never happen so that they have a basis for continuing as they are.

**2 Peter 3:5-10.** The author responds by saying these folk are deliberately ignoring three things. First, that God not only created the world but God has already judged and destroyed it once with water (3:5-6). No one can doubt God's power to do so again.

Of course, the writer does not maintain that God will again destroy the earth with water. Rather, he speaks of a day when the world in which we live will be destroyed by fire (3:7) prior to God's re-creation of "new heavens and a new earth" (3:13). This image of a fiery end fits with several other passages throughout the Bible. For example:

- Moses says, "The LORD your God is a devouring fire" (Deuteronomy 4:24).
- The prophet Zephaniah speaks of "the day when . . . in the fire of [God's] passion all the earth shall be consumed" (Zephaniah 3:8).

- John the Baptist speaks of the burning of unfruitful trees and chaff with fire (Luke 3:9, 17).
- Paul writes that "the Lord Jesus [will be] revealed from heaven . . . in flaming fire" (2 Thessalonians 1:7-8).

Building on passages such as these, the writer of 2 Peter says that fire will destroy the world as we know it when Christ comes again.

Returning to the problem of the scoffers, the letter then says they also wrongly ignore the fact that God's time is not our time. God deals with eternity (3:8; see also Psalm 90:4); we do not. Because God does not experience time as we do, God's promise does not depend on the passing of time as we perceive it. Moreover, Jesus taught (and other biblical writers echoed) that "the day of the Lord will come like a thief" (3:10; see also Matthew 24:43; 1 Thessalonians 5:1-4; Revelation 3:3; 16:15), so we have no grounds to consider it late in coming as if it could somehow be expected at a certain time.

Thirdly, these scoffers conveniently ignore the very nature of God. They point to the passing of human time and accuse God of being slow to act. In reality, though, God is not slow but "patient"—delaying the return so that all may be saved (3:9).

**2 Peter 3:11-16.** Finally, our author says that the promise of Christ's Second Coming includes the establishment of "new heavens and a new earth" (3:13). Verses 10 and 12 try to describe what that day will be like, but the author does not want this to distract from the main point. Thus verse 11 says, "Since all these things are to be dissolved . . . what sort of persons ought you to be . . . ?" Verse 14 adds encouragement to strive during this period of waiting to avoid feeling anxious or afraid. This indicates that the author's purpose in providing descriptions of the Second Coming is solely to motivate the readers to live "lives of holiness and godliness" (3:11) and "to be found by [God] at peace, without spot or blemish" (3:14).

This "godliness" that Peter refers to here in chapter 3 was clearly described in chapter 1. "Godliness," as you will recall from last week's lesson (see "Ourselves as Citizens" in Interpreting the Scripture) refers to reverence and respect for God, especially as shown in acts of service to others. In verse 12, Peter writes of "waiting for and hastening the coming of the day of God." Spreading the good news to others is one means of hastening the day, as Jesus said in Matthew 24:14 when he foretold persecutions that Peter's readers were now experiencing. Those whose lives are marked with "holiness" live sanctified lives, consecrated unto God.

**2 Peter 3:17-18.** The final verses of this letter begin with a reminder not to get caught up in the false teachings that currently exist within the church (3:17). Next comes the positive encouragement to continue rightly in the life of faith by growing "in the grace and knowledge of our Lord and Savior Jesus Christ" (3:18). The letter then ends with a doxology to that same Christ, one that appropriately celebrates his exalted reign now and his eventual return to establish the new age at last.

## INTERPRETING THE SCRIPTURE

### The Power of God's Word

Today we begin a new church year and the season of Advent. During this liturgical period, we remember the gift of Jesus' birth, and we also anticipate the day when Christ will come again. In looking ahead to that return, we find that the passage for this week provides us with the same hope and encouragement that it did for Christians long ago.

If the language of this passage seems odd to us, it is because the author wanted to address a particular concern of his audience. The founding members of the church had expected Jesus to return as the triumphant Christ during their lifetime. This belief was so strong among the earliest Christians that Paul wrote to assure them that believers who die after their own conversion but before Christ's return would still be saved—all while assuming that he and most of his readers will be alive "until the coming of the Lord" (1 Thessalonians 4:15).

As time went on, however, and Christ did not return, a crisis of faith developed within the community. People began to wonder, having been wrong about this aspect of Christianity, what else they might have misconstrued. Was Christ ever coming back? And if not, what was the point of holding out against the powers-that-be?

Second Peter describes the rise of "scoffers" in the church (3:3-4)—people who not only questioned aspects of their faith personally but who also used their doubts to undermine the faith of others. Their influence added to the overall sense of crisis, so that more and more members began to fall away from the church. Losing faith that God's new age would ever come to transform this world, they lost hope. Worse, they lost all motivation for following Christ and gave themselves up instead to self-indulgence (3:3), urging others to join them (3:17; see also 2:2-3, 18-19).

The writer hastens to point out these cynics have overlooked a critical factor—God's word. By the power of that word, the world was created; by the same power, the world was destroyed and recreated at the flood. This same word has also decreed that the world will some day be destroyed and recreated again on a final day of judgment, this time by fire. The point is clear: only fools would choose to interpret this warning as a fanciful myth merely so they could keep indulging their immoral, libertine ways.

### God's Timing

The author also accuses the scoffers of equating God's timing with our own. They reason that because Christ's return has not happened within the timeframe of their expectations, it never will. From this, they even manage to reason that God does not care about the world or human affairs at all. They look back over the whole of history and deny any divine activity at all, whether for mercy or judgment (3:4).

The letter counters this thinking by pointing out the fallacy of equating God's sense of time with our own. Echoing Psalm 90:4, the writer reminds his audience that "with the Lord one day is like a thousand years, and a thousand years are like one day" (3:8). Moreover, God has a motive for this delay that fits right in with the divine nature—out of the sheer grace of God, judgment day is postponed until all have a chance to repent (3:9).

This letter was written to those who were despairing but not yet lost. The author hoped to rekindle their sense of trust and hope by focusing on the certainty of Christ's eventual return, thereby giving them a reason to live as Christians should. Thus he pleads with the community to "strive to be found by [God] at peace, without spot or blemish" when Christ returns (3:14).

### The Importance of Christ's Return

For us in the twenty-first century, the challenge takes a very different form. Whereas the earliest Christians were thrown into a crisis of faith when Christ did not return in their lifetime, we have grown to expect that he will not return during ours. Apocalyptic writings like those in 2 Peter seem fantastic to us, and more than a little weird. The writings tend to be so bizarre, in fact, that we find little connection between them and our own life of faith.

So what can we see in 2 Peter 3:1-13 that might make a difference for us? Perhaps we should start our search with the key points that the writer hoped to make.

First, the coming of the Lord will finally set the world right, once and for all. God loves us too well to let things continue forever as they are. Furthermore, we can draw hope and strength from knowing that it is God who will have the last say, not evil or suffering or even death. Anticipating God's final and complete victory gives us the confidence to stand against those powers now.

Second, the text points out that God's time is not our time—nor are God's motives what we tend to assume. We tend to look at events in terms of the effect on us personally, and so we perceive God to be unreasonably slow in bringing about the new creation. Look through God's eyes, says the writer, and you'll see things differently. God is not slow but "patient . . . not wanting any to perish, but all to come to repentance" (3:9).

Notice how a perspective of God's patience (3:15) transforms the delay of Christ's coming from a problem into an opportunity. Christians can actually "[hasten] the coming of the day of God" (3:12) by "leading lives of holiness and godliness" (3:11) that convince others of the goodness and power of God. The sooner everyone believes, says the writer, the sooner Christ will return.

### New Heaven and New Earth

The promise contained in 2 Peter 3 leads to two unmistakable conclusions. First, we have a legitimate reason to hope. God intends new life for us and for the world, and that new life will come one day in the form of a new heaven and new earth. Second, as the church, we have a great responsibility in this world. We exist within

God's plan and, accordingly, we are called to act in ways that embody it. This is the basis of—and the overall purpose for—our Christian calling.

We find the impetus and power to act in God's name based on the very hope described here. We wait with God's own patience, secure in the promise that one day there will be a "new heavens and a new earth, where righteousness is at home" (3:13). Hopefully, as we put our faith into action while we wait, we "grow in the grace and knowledge of our Lord and Savior Jesus Christ" (3:18).

In this Advent season, we anticipate the great hope of Christmas Eve and the joyous celebration of Christmas Day. The writer of 2 Peter reminds us that this is also a season of anticipating Christ's return—as is every season of the Christian life. And so we join in the joyous doxology: "To him be the glory both now and to the day of eternity. Amen" (3:18).

---

## SHARING THE SCRIPTURE

### Preparing Our Hearts

Meditate on this week's devotional reading, found in Psalm 42. The psalmist, like the people of Peter's community, longs to see God. Do you long for God? What steps have you taken toward God? How do you experience God's presence in worship, your prayer time, Bible study, meditation, and other spiritual disciplines? Recall a time when you strongly felt God's presence. What was the situation? How did you know that God was truly present? You may wish to write about this experience in your spiritual journal.

Pray that you and the adult learners will recognize God's presence in your life now and be prepared for the return of Christ in the future.

### Preparing Our Minds

Study the background from 2 Peter 3 and the lesson scripture, which is found in verses 1-13. Think about how we can encourage others to keep persevering even when barriers seem insurmountable.

Write on newsprint:

❏ Scripture passages for "Acknowledge Areas in the Learners' Lives Where They May Need Hope and Encouragement."

❏ information for next week's lesson, found under "Continue the Journey."
❏ activities for further spiritual growth in "Continue the Journey."

Plan a lecture for "Delve into Peter's Encouraging Teachings Concerning the Promise of Christ's Return."

### LEADING THE CLASS

#### (1) Gather to Learn

❖ Welcome the class members and introduce any guests.

❖ Pray that those who have gathered with the class today will come expecting God to work in their lives as you study and fellowship together.

❖ Brainstorm with the class answers to this question: **How can you encourage other people, especially when they face difficult circumstances?** Record their ideas on newsprint. Here are some possibilities to start or add to the list: *offer to take some concrete action to help someone; give specific words of praise for a job well done; add words of praise as you introduce someone; send an e-mail or card with encouraging words; remind other Christians of God's promises as recorded in the Bible; remind other believers that Christ will come again.*

❖ Read aloud today's focus statement: **Even in the toughest situations, an encouraging word from a friend can make all the difference in how we respond to challenges that confront us. How, then, can we encourage others to keep persevering when barriers seem insurmountable? Peter taught people to live as they awaited Christ's return.**

*(2) Delve into Peter's Encouraging Teachings Concerning the Promise of Christ's Return*

❖ Select a volunteer to read 2 Peter 3:1-13.

❖ Present a lecture to explain 2 Peter 3. Use information from all portions of Understanding the Scripture. As you speak, invite the students to look in their Bibles at any reference you are making to the text.

❖ Draw a connection between today's lesson and the first Sunday in Advent, as noted in the first paragraph of "The Power of God's Word." As an option, read part of the Gospel lesson for this Sunday (Revised Common Lectionary, Year C) from Luke 21:25-28, 36. Be aware that some in the class may not have associated Christ's second coming with the season of Advent.

❖ Invite the students to comment on how the inclusion of Christ's second coming within this season of the church year gives them a different perspective on Advent.

❖ Read or retell "The Importance of Christ's Return" from Interpreting the Scripture to see how 2 Peter can relate to the learners' lives today.

*(3) Acknowledge Areas in the Learners' Lives Where They Need Hope and Encouragement*

❖ Distribute paper and pencils. Invite the students to make a list of situations where they are longing for hope and encouragement in their lives right now. Assure them that they will not be asked to comment on this personal information.

❖ Point out that Peter wanted to provide hope for the people to whom he wrote about the day of Christ's return. Ask the adults to work with a partner. Assign each pair one of the passages, which you will list on newsprint, and ask them to be prepared to tell how this passage provides hope and encouragement as we await Christ's return.
- Matthew 24:29-31
- Acts 1:6-11
- 1 Corinthians 1:4-9
- 1 Thessalonians 3:6-13
- 1 Thessalonians 4:13-18
- Hebrews 3:12-14

❖ Draw the class together and encourage all of the teams to share their ideas with the class.

❖ Ask the students to refer again to their list of personal situations. Provide quiet time for them to meditate and write on their papers about the hope these Scripture passages give them as they face challenges and what appears to be a difficult or uncertain future.

*(4) Encourage Others Who Are Facing Difficulties and Devise a Plan to Give Hope*

❖ Ask the class to brainstorm names of people in the congregation or community who are confronting difficult circumstances. List these names on newsprint. *Make clear before you begin that only people whose situations are well known should be added to the list. Tell the class to be careful to observe privacy and confidentiality.*

❖ Zero in on one or more people that the class thinks it can help.

❖ Brainstorm ideas as a class (or in smaller groups, if you have selected several names) ways that you could help this individual or family. Make a realistic plan to assist. For example, if the Smiths lost everything in a fire, perhaps the class could spearhead a clothing collection or provide replacement school supplies for the children. If Mr. Anderson lives alone and has just returned from the hospital, class members may work out a schedule to sit with him and bring him meals.

❖ Make a chart showing who will do what, when they will do it, and any costs that will be involved. Likely, many items and food can be donated.

❖ Discuss how class members can help those facing challenges to know that this expression of love from the class is motivated by God's love for them.

*(5) Continue the Journey*

❖ Pray that today's participants will go forth with a renewed sense of hope for the future and a willingness to share that hope with others.

❖ Read aloud this preparation for next week's lesson. You may also want to post it on newsprint for the students to copy.

- **Title: The Lineage of David**
- **Background Scripture: Ruth 4:13-17; Matthew 1:1-17**
- **Lesson Scripture: Ruth 4:13-17; Matthew 1:1-6**
- **Focus of the Lesson: Genealogy is a popular hobby because people want to know who they are and where they came from. Why are we so fascinated with our family heritage? We want to be able to make connections, just as the Bible traces Jesus' human family through King David.**

❖ Challenge the students to complete one or more of these activities for further spiritual growth, which you will write on newsprint for the students to copy.

(1) Research a group that had tried to predict the date of Christ's return and was deeply disappointed when he failed to return "on schedule." Such groups include the Millerites, Adventists, and Jehovah's Witnesses. Try to learn how they determined the "end" date, what they did to prepare, and how they responded when the day came and went.

(2) Imagine you have been told that within one month you will meet Christ, either as a result of your own death or his second coming. What would you do within this month that you do not normally do? What changes can you make to become better prepared for Christ's return?

(3) Reach out to someone who has not yet said "yes" to Jesus. Encourage this person as tenderly as you can to turn to Christ and the hope he offers both now and eternally.

❖ Sing or read aloud "Lo, He Comes with Clouds Descending."

❖ Conclude today's session by leading the class in this benediction, based on 1 Peter 2:9: **Go forth with the assurance that you are part of a chosen race, a royal priesthood, a holy nation, God's own people, in order that you may proclaim the mighty acts of him who called you out of darkness into his marvelous light.**

# SECOND QUARTER
## Christ, the Fulfillment

DECEMBER 6, 2009–FEBRUARY 28, 2010

As this course begins on the second Sunday of Advent, we will be exploring prophecies made about the Messiah. Moving through the quarter, our lessons will draw connections between those prophecies and the fulfillment of them that we Christians find in the child born to Mary.

The four sessions in Unit 1, "The Promised Birth Fulfilled," examine the ancestors of Jesus and Isaiah's prophecies of Immanuel's birth, climaxing in the good news that Jesus is born. The lesson for December 6, "The Lineage of David" looks at Ruth 4:13-17 and Matthew 1:1-17 to investigate Jesus' genealogy. Isaiah 7:13-17 and Luke 1:26-38 are the basis for "Prophets Foreshadow Messiah's Birth," the lesson for December 13. "Emmanuel Is Born," which we will study on December 20, examines the uniqueness of Jesus' birth as seen from the perspective of Joseph and his encounter with an angel in Matthew 1:18-25. The unit concludes on December 27 with "Magi Confirm Messiah's Birth," rooted in Matthew 2.

Unit 2, "Evidences of Jesus as Messiah," includes five sessions that focus on events in Jesus' life that helped identify him as the Messiah. These events include his baptism, temptation, healing of persons who were unable to see and speak, a prayer of thanks to the Father, and rejection by people in his hometown of Nazareth. Matthew 3 is the background for the session on January 3, "Proclaimed in Baptism," in which we overhear not only John's proclamation about Jesus but also their conversation about baptism and God's affirmation of the Beloved Son. "Strengthened in Temptation," the session for January 10 from Matthew 4:1-11, considers the devil's challenges and Jesus' faithful responses. Jesus' compassion toward those who are suffering is seen on January 17 in Matthew 9:27-34 and 11:2-6 in "Demonstrated in Acts of Healing." Matthew 11:25-30, the text for January 24, includes familiar words that call those who are weary to Jesus, thereby giving evidence of who he is as "Declared in Prayer." The second unit ends on January 31 with "Revealed in Rejection," a lesson based in Matthew 13:54-58 and Luke 4:16-30, which shows how Jesus' former neighbors respond to him.

Unit 3, "Testimonies to Jesus as Messiah," considers the witness of specific people who confirm that Jesus is the Messiah. These people include a Canaanite woman, Peter, James, John, and a woman of Bethany. On February 7 we turn to Matthew 15:21-28 to see how Jesus was "Recognized by a Canaanite Woman," whom Jesus said had great faith. Matthew 16:13-27, the basis for the session on February 14, shows Jesus "Declared by Peter" as the Messiah, though Peter truly did not understand what messiahship entailed. The familiar story of the Transfiguration of Jesus found in Matthew 17:1-12, which we will study on February 21, allows us to glimpse Jesus' identity in "Witnessed by Disciples." The quarter concludes on February 28 with a story of extravagant love recorded in Matthew 26:6-13 where Jesus is "Anointed by a Woman in Bethany" prior to his Passion.

# MEET OUR WRITER

## DR. CRAIG KEENER

Craig Keener is Professor of New Testament at Palmer Theological Seminary of Eastern University in Wynnewood, Pennsylvania.

He has authored some fourteen books, of which the most relevant for this series of lessons is his *Commentary on the Gospel of Matthew* (Eerdmans, 1999; he published a simpler version with InterVarsity in 1997). Three of his commentaries (including Matthew) have won *Christianity Today* book awards. The best known of these, *The IVP Bible Background Commentary: New Testament*, gives relevant ancient cultural background for each passage in the New Testament, and has sold over 400,000 copies (including translations in various languages). His other commentaries include *1-2 Corinthians* (Cambridge, 2005); *The Gospel of John: A Commentary* (2 volumes; Hendrickson, 2003); *Revelation* (Zondervan, 2000); and a forthcoming two-volume commentary on Acts (Eerdmans).

His other books include works on the Holy Spirit (the most useful is *Gift & Giver: The Holy Spirit for Today* [Baker, 2001]); two books on African-American religion coauthored with Glenn Usry (InterVarsity, 1996, 1997); *Paul, Women & Wives: Marriage and Women's Ministry in the Letters of Paul* (Hendrickson, 1992), and others. He has also written over 150 articles and essays (including those at both academic and popular levels).

Craig is married to Dr. Médine Moussounga Keener, whom he met in graduate school at Duke University when she was an exchange student from the University of Paris. After finishing her Ph.D., she became a refugee for eighteen months during war in her home country of Congo. After reestablishing contact and a series of intervening adventures, they married. They have been working together to advance racial and ethnic reconciliation on both of their home continents.

Craig has also long been one of the few white ministers ordained in the National Baptist Convention, and is an associate minister at Enon Tabernacle Baptist Church in Philadelphia. Craig did his Ph.D. at Duke University, Durham, North Carolina, under D. Moody Smith.

Craig was converted from atheism as a young man. He contributes these lessons in gratitude to his aunt and uncle, Betty and Duane High, who have long taught Sunday school in The United Methodist Church, and whose prayers helped bring him into the faith.

# THE BIG PICTURE:
# GOSPEL GENRE

## What Are "Gospels"?

Understanding a work's genre helps readers know what to expect from the work, hence how to read it. For example, we read a history textbook with expectations that differ from our expectations for a science fiction novel. How would the Gospels' first audiences have understood the Gospels?

## Ancient Biography

When the first Gospel was published, with what would its first audience have compared it? We know that "gospel" means good news, but Christians have preached "good news" in various ways, narrating Jesus' death and resurrection, without creating the entire narrative works such as we have in the first four books of the New Testament. What then is the larger genre, or literary type, of these Gospels?

Most scholars today recognize that Matthew's genre is ancient biography. Throughout history, most people assumed that the canonical Gospels were biographies of some sort. For much of the twentieth century, scholars moved away from this assumption, because the Gospels differ from modern biographies. But as biblical scholars studied more ancient biographies, an increasing number of them recognized that the Gospels genuinely did belong to this category.

Like biographies, the Gospels focus on an individual; they belong to the precise range of length in biographies; they also employ sources (most obvious in the cases of Matthew and Luke) in a biographic rather than novelistic way. At the same time, they differ from modern biographies in the following respects: apart from a basic structure (such as birth before life and life before death) they are not overly concerned with the chronology of the events. Two of the Gospels open with Jesus' public activity rather than his birth. The Gospels unapologetically represent particular perspectives, not simply as much information as possible. All of these features, however, characterized ancient biographies, which differed from modern biographies in the same respects.

To classify a document as ancient biography does not settle all our modern questions about it. Most ancient biography was essentially historical in character; that is, biographers collected information from earlier historical sources. Granted, when sources were much earlier, they often contained conflicting information, and biographers had to make critical judgments as to what information was likeliest (or what they preferred for application purposes!) By contrast, when sources belonged to the past century or so (as in the case of the Gospels), their historical information is often much more reliable. Typically a greater abundance of preserved material was also available for recent characters.

We must remember that even ancient historians did not write the way modern historians do. They wrote with particular agendas, as the Gospel writers also clearly do. Ancient historians were more interested in cohesive and moving narratives and in rhetorical suitability than modern historians are. If historians knew that a speech was given on a particular occasion, they might even compose a speech appropriate to the occasion, rather than simply indicating that such a speech occurred. Because the sayings of famous teachers were often preserved, however, this practice would not apply to Jesus' sayings in the Gospels we are studying. Historians and biographers also were not free to invent events without serious challenge from their peers.

## Preservation of Information about Jesus

While the Gospel authors write from particular perspectives (as Christians, we affirm that God's Spirit inspired their perspectives), the writers did not simply make up stories to fit these perspectives but arranged significant genuine information. Paul's letters reveal that eyewitnesses remained in positions of leadership in the mid-first-century (see, for example, Galatians 2:9), during the church's rapid expansion. These eyewitness-leaders would certainly exert some control over what claims were "authorized" in the wider church. (Information circulated among the churches; see, for example, Luke 1:4; 1 Corinthians 1:11; Colossians 4:9, 16.) The basic message about Jesus was established and circulated while these eyewitnesses remained alive.

Moreover, disciples' primary task was to preserve and propagate the views of their school's founder. Even when a student grew to disagree with such views, the student remained obligated to report the views accurately and respectfully. Why should skeptics assume that Jesus' disciples alone among adherents of ancient schools would have forgotten or misrepresented most of his teachings?

Oral memory could be quite sophisticated, with storytellers able to recite stories, for hours. Orators often memorized speeches two hours in length before delivering them. The point in most of these cases was not verbatim recall, but the "gist." We do have examples of even greater feats of memory, though they were exceptional.

The importance of memory was even more central in education than elsewhere. Elementary students especially memorized bodies of information, including famous sayings. Moreover, students often took notes. Disciples of Jewish teachers may not have taken notes as often, but the sources we do have for them suggest that this was only because they demanded even greater rigor in oral memorization. Many Jewish sages gave their teachings in easily memorized form, as is the case with many of Jesus' sayings in the Gospels. Many of these sayings also reflect Aramaic figures of speech (not least, the title "Son of Man"), which differed from the common language of the later churches for whom the canonical Gospels were written. Disciples also paid close attention to the lives of their teachers, because teachers served as role models.

This is not to claim that the Gospel authors reported every detail the way we write history today. Ancients who memorized sayings also practiced paraphrasing them. Ancient writers exercised significant literary freedom for arrangement, allowing adaptations in wording and some details. This freedom was simply part of the genre of ancient biography (and history), and we cannot judge the Gospels in terms of genres that did not even exist in their day. What we can say is that the common story that the Gospels tell is the story of Jesus Christ, and that we can trust their message and the history in which it is grounded.

## The Message and Theology of the Gospels

Today some readers proceed on the assumption that all works are either historical or theological, either factual or ideological. This distinction does not hold completely true for modern history and biography, and certainly did not hold true for these genres' ancient predecessors.

Not surprisingly, writers had various literary interests. For example, to retain the attention and interest of their audiences, they often focused on the most interesting stories. This may be one reason Mark narrates the graphic scene of the paralytic being lowered through the roof, rather than devoting space to another story. "Action" and "adventure" are not, of course, the only criteria for inclusion in the Gospels. Matthew omits the graphic part about the roof, perhaps to save space for other stories, yet retains the basic story of the paralytic because of its important theological message.

The best writers were interested in producing cohesive compositions. One cannot thus focus on one passage in isolation, apart from the entire book in which it appears. In ancient settings, audiences would have heard Matthew read as a whole (or at least in large sections), rather than preached a passage at a time. To hear this Gospel the way Matthew intended us to hear it, then, requires us to hear each passage in light of its contribution to the entire Gospel. Every passage in Matthew reflects some themes that run through Matthew's entire Gospel, thus contributing to its larger story. The same is true for Luke, John, or other New Testament writings. When we examine passages in the following lessons, we will thus examine them in light of the entire biblical books in which they occur.

Such literary cohesiveness is compatible with ancient history and biography. We often speak of "plot" as applied to novels or dramas, but scholars have shown that basic plots and especially themes also run through ancient biographies and histories. To arrange a work cohesively does not mean that one invents one's content; it simply means that one writes well.

In history and biography, literary interests went beyond telling a good story and preserving information to communicating a message. Ancient historians and biographers often stated their interests up front. Most often these interests were moral: historical and biographic works provided both positive and negative moral examples that orators and teachers could use to promote good behavior. The Gospels certainly include plenty of moral examples: Jesus himself is the example par excellence, but we also have negative models like Herod and further positive ones like Mary, Joseph, or the woman who anointed Jesus.

Historians' interests were often political. As the Roman Empire expanded, many historians promoted the greatness of Rome; Josephus tries to make both Rome and his own people look good (blaming the war, for example, on extremists). These "political" interests were sometimes apologetic (that is, defenses). Greeks tended to look down on non-Greek civilizations, so Jews (like Josephus), Egyptians, Babylonians, and others wrote histories intended to demonstrate the greatness of their own traditions. The Gospels include such "politics." For example, although executed by Rome, Jesus' chief enemies were Jerusalem's own leaders. Likewise, foreign magi prove more open to God than Herod.

Their interests are also theological. Ancient historians often spoke of divine providence in history, and looked for patterns that revealed God's perspective. This was all the more true of Josephus, who, like other historians, did not balk at declaring God's purposes. Such perspectives are no less pervasive in his autobiography, or in other ancient biographies. That the Gospels communicate theology is obvious; the church has always listened to them to hear God's message.

Our modern division between information and perspective, or facts and faith, was not shared by ancient writers, and we should not impose it on the Bible. Where ancient historians and biographers differed from novelists and poets was not in their use of perspectives, but in their dependence on information. One can write a theological treatise without attention to historical information; one cannot write a history or biography that way. Ancient historians and biographers believed that they could communicate moral, political, or theological lessons by selecting genuine examples and retelling them a particular way.

## Publication

People often dictated brief letters off the top of their heads, but a finished literary composition like a Gospel was a major undertaking. A writer would produce a rough draft, often based on an earlier work (for example, Matthew uses Mark), then weave in other material. Through oral feedback at public readings, the writer would then revise the work, reworking it until it achieved a cohesive unity that most effectively communicated the writer's message. Such a work was not only time-consuming but also expensive. The cost of papyrus and scribes meant that producing a Gospel even the length of Mark would have cost thousands of dollars in today's currency.

You may have noticed that I have been using the term "audience" rather than "reader" for the ancient period. This is because most people in antiquity could not own personal copies of these books (even if they could read, which was often not the case), especially larger literary compositions like the Gospels. People lacked printing presses or copy machines, so books had to be copied painstakingly by hand. Most ancient Christians were familiar with the Gospels orally, from hearing them read in church.

For a person with sufficient education, writing a book was not nearly as hard as getting it "published." Normally a writer would circulate a book informally, especially through public readings, most often at banquets. Wealthy hearers who liked the book could order their own copies made, increasing the circulation. Naturally, such wealthy patrons usually favored contributions from their own social class, or at least not from less literate commoners. Early Christians, however, often tried to live by different values.

First-century churches met in homes, and naturally sometimes the larger homes belonging to their more affluent members. Like other group meetings, theirs included a common banquet, in this case, the Lord's Supper. As in synagogues, they included public readings along with their worship, not only of earlier Scriptures but also of apostolic writings. Like some non-Christian writers who had patrons, Luke apparently appeals to a patron, Theophilus, whose name may help the work circulate among his peers (Luke 1:3). But house churches in general would be interested in recollections about their Lord, or (especially in Diaspora churches he founded) letters of Paul, and similar writings.

Many had already written narratives about Jesus before Luke wrote his (Luke 1:1). Several Gospels, however, were apparently particularly well-written and rose to prominence over time, so that their "competition" was forgotten. Clearly Matthew and Luke believed Mark and some other shared material (usually called "Q") to be worthy of attention. Matthew became the favorite of the second-century church. Probably reflecting another line of eyewitness tradition, John achieved prominence among the four widely accepted by the church by the time of Irenaeus in the late second century.

## Conclusion

In contrast to some other works called "gospels" today, the four Gospels in our Bibles fit the model of ancient biographies. As ancient biographers, the Gospel writers wanted to communicate genuine information about Jesus in ways relevant to their audiences. They had access to plenty of written information about Jesus, since disciples transmitted oral information carefully, and many had also produced written accounts about Jesus from an early period. The skeptical assumption of some that Jesus' followers simply made up teachings, forgetting what he actually taught, contradicts what we know of ancient education.

The Gospel writers used their genuine information about Jesus to tell a cohesive story and present a theological and moral message. Their works would be circulated through public readings in some house churches or other settings, and those that generated the most interest circulated far more widely. Four of these most popular works, generally believed to reflect the authority of eyewitnesses themselves, became standard in the churches and became part of our Bible.

# CLOSE-UP:
# PROPHECIES OF JESUS FULFILLED

Since this quarter's lessons focus on Jesus as the fulfillment of prophecy, you may find it useful to compare prophecies with what may be seen as fulfillment. Although many additional prophecies are fulfilled, for our purpose as related to these lessons, we will focus on prophecies that appear to be fulfilled according to the Gospel of Matthew. We have also included some prophecies that Jesus quotes to show they have been fulfilled.

| Content of Prophecy | Hebrew Scripture | New Testament |
|---|---|---|
| Promised descendant of Abraham | Genesis 12:3 | Matthew 1:1 |
| Promised descendant of Isaac | Genesis 17:19 | Matthew 1:2 |
| Promised descendant of Jacob | Numbers 24:17 | Matthew 1:2 |
| Heir to David's throne | Isaiah 9:7 | Matthew 1:1, 6 |
| Place of birth | Micah 5:2 | Matthew 2:1 |
| Related to tribe of Judah | Micah 5:2 | Matthew 2:5-6 |
| Born to a virgin | Isaiah 7:14 | Matthew 1:18 |
| Massacre of infants | Jeremiah 31:15 | Matthew 2:16 |
| Fled to Egypt and returned | Hosea 11:1 | Matthew 2:14-15 |
| Proclaimed by one in the wilderness | Isaiah 40:3 | Matthew 3:3 |
| Ministry in Galilee | Isaiah 9:1-2 | Matthew 4:12-16 |
| Chosen by God to serve | Isaiah 42:1-4 | Matthew 12:15-21 |
| Reason for speaking in parables | Isaiah 6:9-10 | Matthew 13:13-15 |
| fulfills prophecy | Psalm 78:2-3 | Matthew 13:35 |
| Entry into Jerusalem | Isaiah 62:11 | |
| | Zechariah 9:9 | |
| | Psalm 118:26 | Matthew 21:1-11 |
| Betrayed by a friend for thirty | Psalm 41:9 | |
| pieces of silver | Zechariah 11:12-13 | Matthew 26:14-16 |
| False witnesses accuse him | Psalm 27:12 | Matthew 26:60-61 |
| Remained silent | Isaiah 53:7 | Matthew 26:62-63 |
| Suffered for others | Isaiah 53:4-5 | Matthew 8:16-17 |
| Crucified with sinners | Isaiah 53:12 | Matthew 27:38 |
| Scorned and insulted | Psalm 22:6-8 | Matthew 27:39-40 |
| Given sour wine to drink | Psalm 69:21 | Matthew 27:34, 48 |
| Buried among the rich | Isaiah 53:9 | Matthew 27:57-60 |
| Resurrection | Psalm 16:10 | Matthew 16:21; 28:9 |

# FAITH IN ACTION: PROCLAIMING THE MESSIAH

During this quarter we have explored prophecies of Messiah's coming and seen them fulfilled, examined evidences that point toward Jesus as the One who is the Messiah, and heard testimonies of those who encountered Jesus that help us confirm his identity. Given what we know, how can we keep this amazing news a secret? In response, we are called to proclaim who Jesus was. That proclamation may take many forms. Here are some ideas that you can use with the class to encourage them to go and tell the good news and to enact it for all to see.

(1) Spend time discerning what you believe to be true about Jesus. Remember that although Peter declared him to be the Messiah, Peter did not really understand what that meant for Jesus—or for himself. Before you tell others, you need to be clear about your own understanding of and relationship with Jesus. Review our lessons as needed.

(2) Talk with your own family as you gather for Christmas celebrations. Perhaps you will have a crèche or picture that you can use to illustrate the story of his birth. Then go on to tell what that birth means to the world—and to you as Jesus' disciple.

(3) Model your own actions after those of Jesus. Paul reminds us in Romans 8:9-11 that the same Holy Spirit who raised Jesus from the dead also dwells in you. Jesus himself told us to expect to be able to do greater things than he had done (John 14:12). So take action in faith, believing that God will do what needs to be done. Pray for the sick, comfort someone in need, feed the hungry, care for the poor and oppressed, show hospitality to those on the margins.

(4) Recall that Jesus was rejected by many who one would have thought would have been pleased to accept him. Help someone who is feeling rejected, perhaps due to a family breakup, loss of a job, or some other crisis. Witness as it seems appropriate.

(5) Help someone who is facing temptation. Do whatever you can to lead this person on a godly path. You may be able to speak about a similar temptation that you encountered and were able to overcome by God's grace.

(6) Try to get to know families in your church who present their children for baptism. Support them in whatever way you can to enable them to raise these children as Christ's disciples.

(7) Be a witness by volunteering your time to work with those who have a handicapping condition. Perhaps you can assist children who attend a school for the blind, or provide interpretation in sign language of a church service for those who are hearing impaired. Reach out to people whose mobility is limited and assist as you are able. Visit a veteran's hospital to cheer those who have been injured fighting for their country.

(8) Show your faith by giving generously to support God's work, even as a woman of Bethany used priceless ointment to anoint Jesus as a sign of her love for him.

# UNIT 1: THE PROMISED BIRTH FULFILLED
# THE LINEAGE OF DAVID

---

## PREVIEWING THE LESSON

**Lesson Scripture:** Ruth 4:13-17; Matthew 1:1-6
**Background Scripture:** Ruth 4:13-17; Matthew 1:1-17
**Key Verse:** Ruth 4:17

### Focus of the Lesson:
Genealogy is a popular hobby because people want to know who they are and where they came from. Why are we so fascinated with our family heritage? We want to be able to make connections, just as the Bible traces Jesus' human family through King David.

### Goals for the Learners:
(1) to examine Jesus' human ancestry.
(2) to glean truths from Jesus' ancestry that may apply to their lives.
(3) to recognize that God's working in Jesus' human ancestry to fulfill the promise of the Messiah affects how believers live.

### Pronunciation Guide:
Achan (ay' kan)
Aminadab (uh min' uh dab)
Amon (am' uhn)
Aram (air' uhm)
Asa (ay' suh)
Asaph (ay' saf)
Boaz (boh' az)
Hezron (hez' ruhn)
Hittite (hit' tite)

Jesse (jes' ee)
Moabitess (moh' uh bit es)
Nahshon (nah' shon)
Obed (oh' bid)
Perez (pee' riz)
Rahab (ray' hab)
Salmon (sal' muhn)
Tamar (tay' mahr)
Zerah (zihr' uh)

### Supplies:
Bibles, newsprint and marker, paper and pencils, hymnals, Bible dictionary

---

## READING THE SCRIPTURE

NRSV
Ruth 4:13-17

¹³So Boaz took Ruth and she became his wife. When they came together, the LORD

NIV
Ruth 4:13-17

¹³So Boaz took Ruth and she became his wife. Then he went to her, and the LORD

made her conceive, and she bore a son. [14]Then the women said to Naomi, "Blessed be the LORD, who has not left you this day without next-of-kin; and may his name be renowned in Israel! [15]He shall be to you a restorer of life and a nourisher of your old age; for your daughter-in-law who loves you, who is more to you than seven sons, has borne him." [16]Then Naomi took the child and laid him in her bosom, and became his nurse. **[17]The women of the neighborhood gave him a name, saying, "A son has been born to Naomi." They named him Obed; he became the father of Jesse, the father of David.**

Matthew 1:1-6
[1]An account of the genealogy of Jesus the Messiah, the son of David, the son of Abraham.
[2]Abraham was the father of Isaac, and Isaac the father of Jacob, and Jacob the father of Judah and his brothers, [3]and Judah the father of Perez and Zerah by Tamar, and Perez the father of Hezron, and Hezron the father of Aram, [4]and Aram the father of Aminadab, and Aminadab the father of Nahshon, and Nahshon the father of Salmon, [5]and Salmon the father of Boaz by Rahab, and Boaz the father of Obed by Ruth, and Obed the father of Jesse, [6]and Jesse the father of King David.

enabled her to conceive, and she gave birth to a son. [14]The women said to Naomi: "Praise be to the LORD, who this day has not left you without a kinsman-redeemer. May he become famous throughout Israel! [15]He will renew your life and sustain you in your old age. For your daughter-in-law, who loves you and who is better to you than seven sons, has given him birth."
[16]Then Naomi took the child, laid him in her lap and cared for him. **[17]The women living there said, "Naomi has a son." And they named him Obed. He was the father of Jesse, the father of David.**

Matthew 1:1-6
[1]A record of the genealogy of Jesus Christ the son of David, the son of Abraham:
[2]Abraham was the father of Isaac,
  Isaac the father of Jacob,
  Jacob the father of Judah and his brothers,
[3]Judah the father of Perez and Zerah, whose mother was Tamar,
  Perez the father of Hezron,
  Hezron the father of Ram,
[4]Ram the father of Amminadab,
  Amminadab the father of Nahshon,
  Nahshon the father of Salmon,
[5]Salmon the father of Boaz, whose mother was Rahab,
  Boaz the father of Obed, whose mother was Ruth,
  Obed the father of Jesse,
[6]and Jesse the father of King David.

## UNDERSTANDING THE SCRIPTURE

**Ruth 4:13-17.** Naomi, who earlier in the Book of Ruth felt abandoned by God, now found herself vindicated and blessed. Indeed, God vindicated Naomi, Ruth, and Boaz in ways beyond what they lived to see.

Ironically, Ruth was a Moabitess. Because of the corporate guilt of their people, the law

forbade Moabites to enter the "assembly of the LORD" (Deuteronomy 23:3). Ruth, however, left the corporate guilt of her ancestors by turning to Israel's God (Ruth 1:16), and God not only welcomed her but also made her great-grandson the king of Israel (4:17). The surprise ending of the Book of Ruth, a romance story, is that Israel's famous king, David, had some Gentile heritage—a point carried over into Matthew's genealogy.

**Matthew 1:1-2.** Ancient biographies often began with a person's ancestry; a noble ancestry would make the person about whom they wrote seem nobler. Jesus' ancestry delineated here evokes the entire history of Israel, from Abraham forward. By emphasizing this ancestry, Matthew reminds his audience that Jesus' mission is not an irrelevant afterthought to Israel's history, nor is Israel's history an irrelevant prologue to its Messiah. Rather, Jesus' mission is the climax of all that has gone before him and must be understood within that heritage.

Yet Jesus is even more than the climax for this history; he is its purpose and goal. It was through that heritage that God prepared the way for people to understand the one true God and Jesus' kingship ("Son of David"). Matthew's opening phrase, "an account of the genealogy" (literally, *biblos geneseos*), is actually a phrase taken from the standard Greek rendering in some genealogical lists in Genesis. In Genesis, however, the phrase lists the descendants of the person named; thus "the list of the descendants of Adam" (Genesis 5:1) is followed by his descendants. Matthew, however, does not list Jesus' descendants, but his *ancestors*, who are as dependent on him for their significance and purpose as we are on our ancestors. Jesus was the goal toward which God directed history.

Although many of Jesus' ancestors in the genealogy are significant, Matthew highlights two of them: Abraham and David (Matthew 1:1, 17). Jewish people considered all of themselves children of Abraham; by emphasizing Jesus' descent from Abraham, Matthew emphasizes that Jesus truly belonged to Israel's heritage and was one who truly fulfilled the highest ideals of Abraham's mission to bring blessing to the nations (compare Genesis 12:3; Matthew 3:9; 8:11). We treat "Son of David" below.

**Matthew 1:3-6.** In Matthew's day, most genealogies included only male ancestors (except occasionally a particularly illustrious woman). Because women appear so rarely in ancient genealogies, the four women Matthew mentions would quickly catch his audience's attention. Moreover, it is not the four famous matriarchs of Israel's history, including the three in Jesus' ancestry (Sarah, Rebekah, and Leah), that Matthew mentions.

Instead he notes Tamar, Rahab, Ruth, and "the wife of Uriah," that is, Bathsheba. Why these four? Some suggest that to prepare for the scandal of the virgin birth Matthew highlights their "immoral" connections. Yet Ruth did nothing immoral; the Bible mentions nothing immoral about Rahab except her title (which some associate with innkeepers), highlighting instead her faith. Although Matthew does emphasize Jesus' ministry to "sinners," sinful unions seem an unusual way to prepare for the virgin birth.

More likely, Matthew highlights these women's shared Gentile connections. We have already noted that Ruth was a Gentile. Tamar was apparently a Canaanite (Genesis 38:2, 6); Rahab was explicitly one. Canaanite women reflect no casual interest of Matthew's; he later mentions a Canaanite woman with great faith (Matthew 15:22). Matthew draws on an emphasis already found in the Old Testament, which contrasts Rahab with Achan (Joshua 6–7). The Canaanite Rahab betrayed her people by hiding the spies on her roof, hence rescued her family; the Israelite Achan betrayed his people by hiding Jericho's loot under his tent floor, hence destroyed his family (each family was presumably in on the secret). The Bible thus uses Rahab to show that God's concern with Canaanites was not ethnic but spiritual and moral. Even Canaanites who served God were welcome.

Bathsheba married into a Hittite household (2 Samuel 11:3), which Matthew emphasizes by calling her "the wife of Uriah" rather than simply "Bathsheba." Thus Matthew concludes with four women in the first part of his genealogy (in Matthew

1:3-6), all of them either Gentiles or (in the case of Bathsheba) with Gentile associations.

One common purpose of Jewish genealogies, however, was to emphasize the purity of one's Israelite ancestry. Matthew, by contrast, deliberately highlights the *mixed* nature of Jesus' royal line. Jesus was "Son of David," but three ancestors of King David and the mother of King Solomon have Gentile connections! Matthew will emphasize Gentiles frequently in his Gospel (for example, 2:1; 8:5; 28:19). He initiates this theme in the very opening of his Gospel by offering samples of some Gentiles in Israel's history who became part of God's people.

As Son of David, Jesus is the promised Messiah, the rightful king of Israel. Many of those who held political power did not wish to relinquish it for Jesus. Ironically, however, those who acknowledge Jesus as David's Son in this Gospel include the needy (9:27; 20:30-32), children (21:15), and even a foreigner (15:22)—people without power in Israel. Yet Matthew will further remind us that Jesus is more than what people expected David's Son to be; he is not only Israel's king but also David's own Lord (Matthew 22:42-46), the rightful Lord of humanity.

**Matthew 1:7-16.** Among Jesus' other royal ancestors in Matthew's genealogy, two bear special notice: Asa and Amon. Although translations normally obscure the point (assuming a transcriptional mistake rather than a connection with a Jewish midrash or explanation), Matthew's Greek for the names of these two kings is unusual. Instead of writing "Asa" and "Amon," he wrote "Asaph" and "Amos." These minor spelling changes probably hint at something more: Matthew reminds his audience that Jesus is not only the royal descendant of these kings but also the heir to other elements in Israel's history, such as the psalms (Asaph was a psalmist) and the prophets (like Amos).

**Matthew 1:17.** A comparison of Old Testament genealogies shows that Matthew leaves some out to make the genealogy fit his fourteen-generation pattern. Scholars debate the reason for this pattern, but probably Matthew at least found major turning points in Israel's history at something like (not exactly) this number of generations: Abraham, David, and the exile. Now Israel was well due for another significant event in salvation history: the coming of the Son of David. Some point out that in Hebrew, where letters doubled as numerals, the letters in David's name add up to "fourteen," implying another connection with David; others think that this apparent connection with David is simply coincidence.

## INTERPRETING THE SCRIPTURE

*The Centrality of David's Son*

As in ancient biographies more generally, a person's background could establish what to expect from the person (an expectation then adjusted up or down depending on his or her own behavior). Matthew's genealogy establishes royal expectations for Jesus.

Moreover, it shows us that Jesus is not just an afterthought in God's plan. He is not just one Christian doctrine to believe among others; he is not just another hero of the Bible among many. Jesus is the center of God's plan and purpose, the focal point of everything else that God planned in history. We are saved through depending on his death and resurrection; no one and nothing else could have accomplished this, including ourselves.

Moreover, it is not sufficient to simply acknowledge him in passing, as if he is an addendum to the rest of our lives. Jesus is

"Son of David," hence King of Israel. Jewish people expected David's son to be a conquering messiah. Yet Matthew redefines this messiahship, later showing that Jesus is greater than such a messiah, as the exalted "Lord" over all people (22:42-45).

Thus Jesus must be central not only in history but in our lives. If God's plan in Jesus is the goal of history, we who truly believe that ought also to base the major decisions in our lives on that larger plan. When we choose careers, we should consider how we can work to fulfill God's purposes in the world. When we decide how to use our resources and how to treat our neighbors, we should keep in mind God's larger purposes in Christ. Based on a living relationship with Christ through faith, we can work to make this world a better place, thus serving the One who has the right to rule our lives.

*God's Multicultural Plan*

Ruth's story highlights a special side of David's story. Because of the virgin birth (1:18), this is Jesus' royal lineage as "son of David," not his genetic one. Yet Matthew shocks his audience by reminding them of David's Gentile ancestors. Gentiles have always been part of God's plan, which is certainly good news for Jesus' followers today, most of whom are of Gentile ancestry.

Matthew illustrates this point by means of unions between persons of different ethnic groups. Sometimes the Old Testament warned against interethnic unions because marrying people who did not share Israel's commitment to God could (and often did) weaken Israel's commitment. This prohibition was, however, for spiritual, not ethnic purposes. (Thus, for example, Joseph and Moses both married interethnically when in exile from their own lands.)

Biblical examples of godly interracial marriages can encourage those whose marriages cross such boundaries today. I am from the United States and my wife is from Congo-Brazzaville in Central Africa; cultural differences sometimes compound the normal share of marital misunderstandings. Yet our unity in Christ is stronger than such differences, offering a vantage point to work for sensitive racial, ethnic, and cultural reconciliation.

Although Matthew uses marriage here to illustrate his point, other examples in the Gospel show that his concern extends far beyond marriage to cross-cultural sensitivity in general. Matthew probably wrote especially for Jewish followers of Jesus, and many scholars think that he wrote in the wake of Romans killing and enslaving tens of thousands of Jewish people. In such a setting, Matthew reminds his Jewish Christian audience that they must still seek to bring the good news about Jesus to everyone who will hear, including many Gentiles. If God can welcome Canaanites (like Rahab), God can also welcome even representatives of Rome (like the centurion of 8:5-13 or Jesus' execution squad in 27:54).

Today's world is torn by ethnic strife. Racism supported slavery in the United States and some Arab countries, and apartheid in South Africa; it undergirded terrible exploitation and sometimes destruction of Native Americans. Over the past century, ethnic conflict has often led to genocide, in Turkey, Nazi Germany, Rwanda, and elsewhere. Over half the countries in the world have ethnic minority populations of at least 10 percent, often with the majority culture misunderstanding, ignoring, and at worst repressing the minority cultures.

What does the gospel say to such conflicts? Matthew's Gospel repeatedly reaffirms the value of Gentiles (for Matthew's audience, those of foreign ethnicity and culture), reaching them with the good news and welcoming them among God's people. This theme is pervasive enough in this Gospel, and we will see it again. The same theme is prominent in Acts and Paul's letters, where again it is understood in terms of Jews and Gentiles. If God summoned the church to surmount a barrier once established in history by God, how much more would God summon us to surmount all other barriers established only by human selfishness? Followers of Christ must thus be ready to build cross-cultural relationships and work for racial and ethnic reconciliation.

### Preparing for the Great Commission

We have already noted that for Matthew, this emphasis on Gentiles is not an abstraction. David hired foreign mercenaries and ruled various peoples, but David's son will rule nations (Psalm 2:7-12). The women in the genealogy initiate a major theme in this Gospel (climaxed in 28:19). The magi come to worship (Matthew 2:1-2); God can raise children for Abraham from stones (3:9); Jesus relocated to a strategic place in "Galilee of the Gentiles" (4:15); he praised a centurion's faith (8:10-11) and that of a Canaanite woman (15:28); he delivered a demoniac in Gentile territory (8:28-32); he compared some Gentiles' past favorably to his own people (10:15; 11:23-24; 12:41-42); and he solicited Peter's confession of faith in Gentile territory (16:13).

More than this, Jesus promised that the good news would be announced among all peoples (24:14), and commissioned his disciples to make disciples for himself among all nations (28:19). Because the command to make disciples (carried out by "going," "baptizing," and "teaching") is the climax of Matthew's Gospel, it suggests the goal toward which Matthew has been aiming from the beginning.

Many people today dislike "missions" because it has often been implemented in a culturally insensitive way (starting with some of Paul's enemies who insisted that his converts be circumcised!). Without cross-cultural mission, however, Jesus' movement would not have spread to Gentiles, and probably would have perished within a century or two after the first-century destruction of Jerusalem. Jesus' cross-cultural commission reminds us that our spiritual responsibility extends beyond our own ethnic and national community, and that the movement of Jesus' followers extends beyond any one community to a global partnership of all believers in him. The seeds of this cross-cultural commission were rooted in the very lineage of Jesus himself.

## SHARING THE SCRIPTURE

### Preparing Our Hearts

Meditate on this week's devotional reading, found in 2 Samuel 7:8-17. Here we read about God's covenant with David. Notice that God's plan is to make a "house," that is, a dynasty, for David. This kingdom that begins with David and includes unnumbered ancestors will last "forever." Consider the role that family—ancestors and descendants—plays in your life.

Pray that you and the adult learners will give thanks to God for the family that has helped to make you who you are.

### Preparing Our Minds

Study the background from Ruth 4:13-17 and Matthew 1:1-17. The lesson scripture is taken from Ruth 4:13-17 and Matthew 1:1-6. As you read, consider why we are so fascinated with family heritage.

Write on newsprint:
❑ information for next week's lesson, found under "Continue the Journey."
❑ activities for further spiritual growth in "Continue the Journey."

Read the "Introduction," "The Big Picture," "Close-up," and "Faith in Action" articles for this quarter, all of which immediately precede this lesson. Decide how you will use the information from these supplemental resources as you lead this quarter's sessions. You may want to refer to some of this information during several sessions.

Plan the lecture suggested under "Examine Jesus' Human Ancestry" if you choose to use this option.

Locate a Bible dictionary or "who's who" to bring to the session.

## LEADING THE CLASS

### (1) Gather to Learn

❖ Welcome the class members and introduce any guests.

❖ Pray that an air of expectation will fill the hearts and minds of everyone who is present today.

❖ Discuss these questions. If the class is large, suggest that the students talk with a partner or small group after you read aloud each question.

(1) **Which of you has tried to research your family's roots, or have access to genealogical research that someone has done for your family?**

(2) **What interesting stories have you uncovered concerning your family's history?**

(3) **How have these stories helped you to better know your ancestors and yourself?**

❖ Read aloud today's focus statement: **Genealogy is a popular hobby because people want to know who they are and where they came from. Why are we so fascinated with our family heritage? We want to be able to make connections, just as the Bible traces Jesus' human family through King David.**

### (2) Examine Jesus' Human Ancestry

❖ Ask a volunteer to read Ruth 4:13-17.

❖ Use the information for this passage in Understanding the Scripture to help the adults better understand the role that Ruth, a Gentile from Moab, played in Jesus' human ancestry.

❖ Invite the students to look at Matthew 1:1-6 and call out, in order, the names of Jesus' ancestors that appear, beginning in verse 2. List those names on newsprint.

❖ Encourage the adults to identify, at least briefly, each of the people listed. Have a Bible dictionary on hand to help with the lesser-known names. Write a descriptive phrase or two next to each name.

❖ **Option:** Plan a lecture in which you identify each of the people listed in Matthew 1:1-6. The names in verses 2-6 are found in an extensive genealogy in 1 Chronicles 1–2. Actually, the first nine chapters of 1 Chronicles focus on genealogy. List the names on newsprint and write a descriptive phrase next to each name as you speak.

❖ Point out the information in Matthew 1:17, as described in Understanding the Scripture.

❖ Note that although males were usually listed, Jesus' genealogy in Matthew includes four women: Tamar, Rahab, Ruth, and Bathsheba (who is not named but referred to as "the wife of Uriah" in verse 6). Use information from Understanding the Scripture for Matthew 1:3-6 to help the students understand the importance of these four women.

❖ Highlight the significance of Jesus' relationship to David by reading or retelling the first two paragraphs of "The Centrality of David's Son" in Interpreting the Scripture.

### (3) Glean Truths from Jesus' Ancestry that May Apply to the Learners' Lives

❖ Read the first paragraph of "God's Multicultural Plan" in Interpreting the Scripture.

❖ Ask: **What difference does it make to you to know that Jesus had not only Jewish but also Gentile ancestors?**

❖ Distribute paper and pencils. Ask the learners to sketch a family tree of their direct ancestors, going back as far as they are able. As they did with the ancestors of Jesus, suggest that they write a descriptive phrase or two about each of their ancestors.

❖ Review the list of Jesus' ancestry made earlier in the session. Ask: **In what ways is Jesus' ancestry similar to your own?** (Focus here on the idea that as we trace generations of ancestors, most of us find that we are descendants of people from a variety of national, cultural, and ethic groups and possibly racial groups. Just as Jesus' family had some skeletons in the closet, so do most families, though many adults will not want to reveal this information. Some class members may be distantly descended from royalty.)

*(4) Recognize that God's Working in Jesus' Human Ancestry to Fulfill the Promise of the Messiah Affects How Believers Live*

❖ Point out that God's purpose in working in Jesus' human ancestors was to fulfill the promise of the Messiah.

❖ Help the class members think about what this fulfilled promise means in their own lives by reading this excerpt from "The Centrality of David's Son": **It is not sufficient to simply acknowledge Jesus in passing, as if he is an addendum to the rest of our lives. Jesus is "Son of David," hence king of Israel. . . . Thus Jesus must be central not only in history but central in our lives.**

❖ Discuss these questions with the class:
   **(1) How does your relationship to Jesus influence your decisions, particularly major ones such as career, spouse, or how you allocate your financial resources?**
   **(2) How does your relationship with Jesus shape your attitudes and behavior toward those who are "not like us"?**

*(5) Continue the Journey*

❖ Pray that all who have participated today will see themselves as part of the family of God and live as if Jesus is central to their lives.

❖ Read aloud this preparation for next week's lesson. You may also want to post it on newsprint for the students to copy.
   ■ **Title: Prophets Foreshadow Messiah's Birth**
   ■ **Background Scripture: Isaiah 7:13-17; Luke 1:38**
   ■ **Lesson Scripture: Isaiah 7:13-17; Luke 1:30-38**
   ■ **Focus of the Lesson: People often look for proof or signs that God is involved in our world. What proof do we have of such involvement? Isaiah prophesied of the coming Messiah who would be Immanuel (God with us), and Luke centuries later told how God sent the angel to reveal good news to Mary.**

❖ Challenge the students to complete one or more of these activities for further spiritual growth, which you will write on newsprint for the students to copy.
   **(1) Talk with people who have researched your family's history to learn what you can about your ancestors, their roots, and how their traits and choices have affected you.**
   **(2) Compile a list of reasons why you should "bless God" (see Ruth 4:14). Offer your list as a prayer of thanksgiving to God.**
   **(3) Share in the joy of a family that has recently welcomed a new child. Provide food, a gift, a card, babysitting service, or whatever is appropriate in this situation.**

❖ Sing or read aloud "Hail to the Lord's Anointed."

❖ Conclude today's session by leading the class in this benediction, adapted from Matthew 16:16: **Go forth now to love and serve the Messiah, the Son of the living God.**

UNIT 1: THE PROMISED BIRTH FULFILLED

# Prophets Foreshadow Messiah's Birth

---

## PREVIEWING THE LESSON

**Lesson Scripture:** Isaiah 7:13-17; Luke 1:30-38
**Background Scripture:** Isaiah 7:13-17; Luke 1:26-38
**Key Verse:** Isaiah 7:14

### Focus of the Lesson:
People often look for proof or signs that God is involved in our world. What proof do we have of such involvement? Isaiah prophesied of the coming Messiah who would be Immanuel (God with us), and centuries later Luke told how God sent the angel to reveal good news to Mary.

### Goals for the Learners:
(1) to explore Isaiah's prophecy and its fulfillment in Mary's acceptance of the angel's message.
(2) to identify signs of God's presence in their daily lives.
(3) to tell others ways that God is presently at work in the world.

### Pronunciation Guide:
Ephraim (ee' fray im)
*Maher-shalal-hash-baz* (may' huhr shal' al hash' baz)
*parthenos* (par then' os)

### Supplies:
Bibles, newsprint and marker, paper and pencils, hymnals, index cards

---

## READING THE SCRIPTURE

NRSV
Isaiah 7:13-17

<sup></sup>¹³Then Isaiah said: "Hear then, O house of David! Is it too little for you to weary mortals, that you weary my God also?

NIV
Isaiah 7:13-17

¹³Then Isaiah said, "Hear now, you house of David! Is it not enough to try the patience of men? Will you try the patience of my God

[14]**Therefore the Lord himself will give you a sign. Look, the young woman is with child and shall bear a son, and shall name him Immanuel.** [15]He shall eat curds and honey by the time he knows how to refuse the evil and choose the good. [16]For before the child knows how to refuse the evil and choose the good, the land before whose two kings you are in dread will be deserted. [17]The Lord will bring on you and on your people and on your ancestral house such days as have not come since the day that Ephraim departed from Judah—the king of Assyria."

Luke 1:30-38

[30]The angel said to her, "Do not be afraid, Mary, for you have found favor with God. [31]And now, you will conceive in your womb and bear a son, and you will name him Jesus. [32]He will be great, and will be called the Son of the Most High, and the Lord God will give to him the throne of his ancestor David. [33]He will reign over the house of Jacob forever, and of his kingdom there will be no end." [34]Mary said to the angel, "How can this be, since I am a virgin?" [35]The angel said to her, "The Holy Spirit will come upon you, and the power of the Most High will overshadow you; therefore the child to be born will be holy; he will be called Son of God. [36]And now, your relative Elizabeth in her old age has also conceived a son; and this is the sixth month for her who was said to be barren. [37]For nothing will be impossible with God." [38]Then Mary said, "Here am I, the servant of the Lord; let it be with me according to your word." Then the angel departed from her.

also? [14]**Therefore the Lord himself will give you a sign: The virgin will be with child and will give birth to a son, and will call him Immanuel.** [15]He will eat curds and honey when he knows enough to reject the wrong and choose the right. [16]But before the boy knows enough to reject the wrong and choose the right, the land of the two kings you dread will be laid waste. [17]The Lord will bring on you and on your people and on the house of your father a time unlike any since Ephraim broke away from Judah—he will bring the king of Assyria."

Luke 1:30-38

[30]But the angel said to her, "Do not be afraid, Mary, you have found favor with God. [31]You will be with child and give birth to a son, and you are to give him the name Jesus. [32]He will be great and will be called the Son of the Most High. The Lord God will give him the throne of his father David, [33]and he will reign over the house of Jacob forever; his kingdom will never end." [34]"How will this be," Mary asked the angel, "since I am a virgin?" [35]The angel answered, "The Holy Spirit will come upon you, and the power of the Most High will overshadow you. So the holy one to be born will be called the Son of God. [36]Even Elizabeth your relative is going to have a child in her old age, and she who was said to be barren is in her sixth month. [37]For nothing is impossible with God." [38]"I am the Lord's servant," Mary answered. "May it be to me as you have said." Then the angel left her.

---

## UNDERSTANDING THE SCRIPTURE

**Isaiah 7:13-17.** The immediate context in Isaiah, like the other birth annunciations in the Old Testament, refers to a child of the hearer's generation. God promises to give King Ahaz a sign (Isaiah 7:10-14): Before this child is old enough to know right from wrong, Assyria will overthrow the kingdoms Ahaz fears (7:15-17), that is, Aram and Israel (7:1-2, 5-9). The passage refers to Isaiah's own son, who will not be old enough to call, "My father" or "My mother" before Assyria had defeated those kingdoms (8:3-4).

Reading further in Isaiah's context, however, reveals why this passage is so appropriate. (This background is more relevant in next week's lesson, because Matthew 1:23, unlike Luke here, explicitly quotes the Isaiah passage.) Isaiah's children, with their symbolic names, were "signs" to Israel. "The-Spoil-Speeds-the-Prey-Hastens" (the meaning of *Maher-shalal-hash-baz* in 8:3) symbolized Israel's short-term deliverance but also pointed toward the future. For in the larger context, God would someday bring ultimate deliverance (9:1-5) through another child, a Davidic ruler who would also be called the "Mighty God" (9:6-7). The child "God-is-with-us" in 7:14 pointed to the ultimate example of God with us in the promised Messiah. Luke may know this larger context; Isaiah 9:7, like Luke 1:32-33, mentions David's throne and that the Messiah's kingdom will never end.

**Luke 1:26-27.** Gabriel comes to a virgin in an out-of-the-way village, in contrast to his appearance in the preceding passage (1:5-23) to an aged priest in Jerusalem. This passage (which mentions the previous miracle, 1:36) thus compares Mary with Zechariah. Ancient writers, including historians, often looked for patterns that they believed God or a deity had created in history. They also often compared characters as a way of highlighting points. Sometimes, as here, both characters could be positive, but one (here Mary) could be more positive than the other.

Both Zechariah and Mary are troubled by their encounters with Gabriel (1:12, 29); Gabriel urges both not to be afraid (1:13, 30), followed by the reason for the miracle (1:13, 30); the child's name (1:13, 31); and the announcement that the child will be great (1:15, 32) and have a mission (1:16-17, 32-33). Zechariah's son will be filled with the Spirit from the womb (1:15), and Jesus conceived through the Spirit (1:35). Zechariah and Mary each ask a question (1:18, 34) and receive proof or an explanation (1:19-20, 35-37). Yet Zechariah is struck mute for his unbelief (1:20), whereas Mary responds in faith (1:38). Such an accumulation of parallels leaves little room for us to assume coincidence here. Luke uses these contrasts to highlight Jesus' superiority to John the Baptist, with whom he is also paralleled (Luke 1:80; 2:40, 52).

**Luke 1:28-30.** In some respects, this passage resembles Old Testament annunciations of miraculous births. In some other respects, however, this passage goes beyond such parallels by echoing Old Testament passages about God's call. God promises divine enablement (Luke 1:28), as in some earlier biblical passages, and Mary responds with uncertainty (1:29), like many of her predecessors.

God or angels often told God's servants not to fear, as here. Gabriel, who has already announced Mary's favor in 1:28, also reaffirms it in 1:30. The term for "favor" can also mean "grace"; the initiative rested with God. Nevertheless, "finding favor" with someone was a common idiom in the Old Testament for pleasing them. Like Mary, Noah (Genesis 6:8), Moses (Exodus 33:17), and David (Acts 7:45-46) had "found favor" with God.

**Luke 1:31-33.** That Gabriel announces that Mary will bear and assigns the child's name echoes earlier biblical annunciations concerning Ishmael (Genesis 16:11, announced by the angel of the Lord); Isaac (Genesis 17:19); and most recently John (Luke 1:13; compare also "conceive and bear" regarding Samson in Judges 13:3). But because Mary is a "virgin" (*parthenos*), the passage probably also echoes Isaiah 7:14, where a young woman (in the standard Greek translation there, a *parthenos*) would bear a son, and the child would be named "Immanuel," or "God (is) with us."

**Luke 1:34-37.** In 1:34, Mary objects that she is a virgin. On one level, Mary might recognize that she is embracing shame in the eyes of people. If people knew that she was pregnant before marriage, this would bring shame, and traveling with her betrothed before the wedding (2:5) violated cultural standards, especially in rural Galilee.

Luke's emphasis, however, is not so

much on shame here as on believing God for the impossible (1:37). Gabriel resolves Mary's concern that she as a virgin cannot have a child, both by explaining and by providing evidence of God's work: God's own Spirit will form the child in her (1:35), and God had already performed a miracle for Elizabeth (1:36). The point, then, was that nothing would be impossible for God.

Some readers have compared Mary's virgin pregnancy with Greek myths about gods impregnating mortals. These stories, however, do not involve *virgin* conceptions or births. Parallels with earlier biblical annunciations show that the real background for this passage, as in Matthew, is in the Old Testament. Virgin birth goes beyond Old Testament examples, yet remains characteristic of the way God sometimes worked in the Old Testament. That both Matthew and Luke report a virgin birth indicates that the claim was well-established before either of them wrote.

Of course, we know—as Mary did—that virgin births are not the way God created our reproductive systems, and we cannot expect them to happen. Yet that objection underlines Luke's point: "Nothing will be impossible with God" (1:37). Even what is normally impossible need not be impossible to the universe's designer.

**Luke 1:38.** Mary does ask a question (Luke 1:34), but once she understands, she embraces God's call obediently (1:38). Receiving the promise that the Holy Spirit would come on her (1:35), Mary calls herself the "servant [*doulë*] of the Lord" (1:38, 48). The only other text in Luke's writing (or in the New Testament) that employs this particular feminine form for "servant" is in Acts 2:18, where it applies to God's female servants, on whom God pours out the divine Spirit (just as, in the same text, God does on the male servants). In Luke's larger narrative, Mary's experience of the Spirit thus foreshadows Pentecost, and she becomes a model for all Christians humbly receiving God's Spirit.

---

## INTERPRETING THE SCRIPTURE

### God's Sign

Luke does not mention God's "sign" until 2:12 (to the shepherds), though Isaiah mentions a sign to Ahaz. Yet as we noted above, Isaiah's son prefigures not only impending but also ultimate deliverance, through a son who would truly embody God with us. Mary receives not only a promise but also the sign of a virgin birth.

In contrast to the Greek term *parthenos* (which clearly identifies Mary here as a virgin), the Hebrew term in Isaiah is more ambiguous, yet as we have noted, has a messianic context that lends itself readily to what God did in Jesus' virgin birth. Christians can see the rendering *parthenos* in the Greek translation of Isaiah as providential.

Would we have trusted like Mary?

Although Western culture has often cultivated skepticism of supernatural activity, Christians in many cultures experience and report dramatic signs. Perhaps if we would learn to respond in faith to the signs God gives us, we could experience more of them.

### God Is Near the Humble

Zechariah is an aged priest serving in the temple; Mary is a very young woman in out-of-the-way Nazareth. (In view of Luke 2:24 and Leviticus 12:8, she and Joseph were also fairly poor.) From every human perspective of their day (age, status, gender, and location), Zechariah was the greater of the two, yet Luke emphasizes the opposite point: it is humble faith, not human status, which matters in God's sight. Zechariah and Mary each had their place, but God ultimately made a greater difference in history through Mary.

The comparison between Mary and Zechariah reminds us of the frequent biblical principle that God is near the broken and humble but far from the arrogant who do not depend on God. Of course, Zechariah is not arrogant in Luke's account, and he does receive God's blessing; but he is not as humble as Mary.

God surprised not only Mary (Luke 1:29) but also other people before calling them (Exodus 3:2-6; Ezekiel 1:28); Gideon doubted even an opening affirmation of his strength (Judges 6:12-13). When God called people in the Bible, especially to do something humanly difficult or dangerous, God also helped them. God often gave this same promise of being "with" God's servants (Genesis 26:3, 24; 28:15; 31:3; Exodus 3:12; Joshua 1:5; 3:7; Judges 6:12, 16; 1 Kings 11:38; Isaiah 41:10; 43:2; Jeremiah 1:8, 19). Later Luke reports the same promise to Paul (Acts 18:10). Luke's first report of the promise of God being with someone, though, comes to Mary (Luke 1:28).

Do we boast in our status or accomplishments? Or do we recognize that we can depend only on God and what God may do through us? Do we recognize that God does not see as we see, or value what we value (status, wealth, and so forth)? Some of us who have status may overlook people around us in menial jobs whom God may be using to change their world. We may overlook fellow-Christians in some parts of the world who are economically poor yet are much stronger witnesses for Christ than we are. We may learn from their example to depend on Christ's power rather than our status.

Likewise, if we have low status in the eyes of others, this does not tell us what God thinks of us. Mary's humble response to God's will shaped the course of history. The prayers of the humble may have greater ultimate influence to change the world than the strategies of rulers and generals who

think they control it. In the ultimate model of this pattern, our Lord embraced the lowly cross, and God has now enthroned him as humanity's rightful ruler.

### Mary as a Model

As we noted at Luke 1:38, Mary's ready embrace of God's Spirit and work in her life becomes a model for all of her son's followers. In the context of Luke's writing, Mary is only one of the women who provide a model. Although working within the constraints of the culture in which he was writing, Luke frequently affirms women, more frequently than most contemporary literature did. Luke later mentions women among the disciples (Luke 8:2-3). In contrast to many of his contemporaries, he affirms a woman in her role as a disciple—though disciples were often teachers in training—more than domestic roles traditionally assigned to women (10:38-42). Women prophesy and speak by the Spirit's inspiration (1:41; 2:36; Acts 21:9). Most important, one of Luke's key programmatic statements points to an ideal that goes even beyond the first-century examples Luke could offer: God's Spirit empowers both God's male and female servants (Acts 2:17-18).

Yet Mary is not a model only for women, any more than she is a model only for young people, residents of small towns, or people with limited economic resources. As noted above, Mary is a model for discipleship, prefiguring God's Spirit-empowered servants after Pentecost.

### A Model of Faith

Most people would not have responded with the ready faith Mary displays here. Indeed, Moses protested God's calling (Exodus 3:11–4:13); others like Gideon (Judges 6:15), Isaiah (Isaiah 6:5), and Jeremiah (Jeremiah 1:6) offered objections.

Yet hearing Gabriel's explanation that nothing was impossible for God (Luke 1:35-37),

Mary readily believed (1:38, 45). Luke elsewhere recalls that nothing is impossible with God (Acts 26:8), and offers examples of faith (Luke 5:20; 7:9; 8:48, 50; 17:19; 18:42; Acts 3:16; 14:9; 27:25). This pattern, of which Mary is Luke's first example, suggests that Luke invites us not simply to praise Mary's faith but to exercise faith ourselves. Faith does not, of course, mean that we will always get whatever we want. It does mean that we can trust God to fulfill God's purposes in our lives, including whatever God calls us to do.

God rarely calls us to do what we can do in our own strength; otherwise we would trust in our own strength. God normally calls us to do what we cannot do ourselves. The promise came to Sarah and Abraham when they were too old to have children. Before God exalted Joseph, God took him through slavery and prison in Egypt. Moses had nothing against Pharaoh's might except for God's Word. Jesus died unresisting on a cross, and after an unjust execution was raised only by God's power.

In Mary's case, faith involved both obedience to God's call and trust that God would fulfill God's own promise. As William Carey, an early Protestant teacher in India, put it, "Attempt great things for God; expect great things from God." I often find myself "attempting" more than "expecting," but biblical models of faith invite us to embrace both God's faithfulness and our responsibility. Every call from God, whether the sort of commandments given to all Christians or God's specific leading in your own life, involves both call and promise: our obedience and God's faithfulness.

How can we encourage our faith? In Mary's case, Gabriel cites the example of God's faithfulness to Elizabeth. The more we give heed to other examples of God's works in history, the most explicit being those given in Scripture, the easier it will be to trust God in our own lives.

## SHARING THE SCRIPTURE

### Preparing Our Hearts

Meditate on this week's devotional reading, found in Micah 5:1-5a. Even as the king is being humiliated during the siege of Jerusalem, the prophet promises that a new ruler will come forth from the clan of Judah in the small town of King David's birth, Bethlehem. The king was understood to be a shepherd (see Ezekiel 34), who provided peace and security for his flock. How does this prophesied leader provide you with a sense of peace, security, and continuity in God's plan?

Pray that you and the adult learners will perceive that God is involved in the world by exploring the events that occurred in Bethlehem two millennia ago.

### Preparing Our Minds

Study the background from Isaiah 7:13-17 and Luke 1:26-38. The lesson scripture is taken from Isaiah 7:13-17 and Luke 1:30-38. As you read, ponder the signs we have that God is involved in our world.

Write on newsprint:
- ❏ list of Bible passages found under "Explore Isaiah's Prophecy and Its Fulfillment in Mary's Acceptance of the Angel's Message."
- ❏ information for next week's lesson, found under "Continue the Journey."
- ❏ activities for further spiritual growth in "Continue the Journey."

Write on index cards or paper examples of God at work in the world for the activity under "Tell Others Ways that God Is Presently at Work in the World."

## LEADING THE CLASS

### (1) Gather to Learn

❖ Welcome the class members and introduce any guests.

❖ Pray that those who have come today will recognize signs of God's presence in the world.

❖ Read aloud this information that appeared on CNN's website on May 15, 2008: **Believing that he was doing the right thing because his government told him to kill Tutsis, Jean-Bosco Bizimana joined the rampage and killed the husband and five children of his neighbor, Iphigenia Mukantabana. For four years after this slaughter, Iphigenia did not speak with those neighbors. Then, after Bizimana had spent seven years in prison, a process was set in motion to allow perpetrators of such crimes to ask forgiveness. Iphigenia said that despite her family's killer's request for forgiveness, he would not have been forgiven had she not responded to him. "I am a Christian and I pray a lot," Iphigenia told CNN reporter Christiane Amanpour. Today, as a master basket weaver, Iphigenia works alongside Epiphania Mukanyndwi, the wife of Bizimana. These women are friends and share much together.**

❖ Ask: **What does this story reveal to you about the possibility of God's presence in the world?**

❖ Read aloud today's focus statement: **People often look for proof or signs that God is involved in our world. What proof do we have of such involvement? Isaiah prophesied of the coming Messiah who would be Immanuel (God with us), and Luke centuries later told how God sent the angel to reveal good news to Mary.**

### (2) Explore Isaiah's Prophecy and Its Fulfillment in Mary's Acceptance of the Angel's Message

❖ Ask a volunteer to read Isaiah 7:13-17.

❖ Use the information for this passage in Understanding the Scripture to help the students understand its historical context.

❖ Choose three volunteers to read Luke 1:26-38, which includes four background verses but will give a broader picture of the conversation between Gabriel and Mary. One reader will be the narrator, another will play the part of Gabriel, and the third will read Mary's words.

❖ Discuss these questions:

    **(1) What do you learn about Mary?**

    **(2) What do you learn about the child Mary will bear?**

    **(3) What do you learn about God?**

    **(4) How do you see Gabriel's words to Mary as a fulfillment of prophecy in Isaiah 7:13-17?**

❖ Note the biblical principle seen here that God is near the broken and humble. The idea of God being with those who serve God is also found in the following passages, which you will list on newsprint. Assign at least one person to look up each passage to find out to whom God (or an angel) was speaking and the nature of the situation. Invite each person to report to the class.

Genesis 26:2-3, 24; 28:13-15; 31:3

Exodus 3:11-12

Joshua 1:1-5; 3:7

Judges 6:11-12, 16

Isaiah 41:8-10; 43:1-4

Jeremiah 1:4-8

Acts 18:9-10.

### (3) Identify Signs of God's Presence in the Learners' Daily Lives

❖ Ask: **What assurance or sign do you have that God is present with you, even as with the biblical figures we have just encountered?**

❖ Distribute paper and pencils. Read aloud the fourth paragraph of "A Model of Faith" in Interpreting the Scripture. Invite the students to write William Carey's words at the top of their paper: **"Attempt great things for God; expect great things from**

God." Encourage them to make two columns and write in one what they are expecting and in the other, what they are attempting.

❖ Solicit comments from volunteers as to what they are expecting and attempting.

❖ Ask: **Think about what you are expecting and doing right now. What would you *not* be expecting or attempting to do if you did not believe that God was present in your life?**

*(4) Tell Others Ways that God Is Presently at Work in the World*

❖ Distribute index cards, each with one of the stories below that you have written prior to class, to four volunteer readers:

A Cambodian believer who has been praying for two years to be a good preacher now finds that God has given him confidence and alleviated his fear.

A 35-year-old British swimmer was without a pulse for about an hour after possibly being knocked out by a large wave. His mother believed, "everything was in place for a miracle." Miraculously, he quickly recovered and has no long-term medical problems.

A Christian pastor was accused by villagers in India of causing malaria and muteness in Charran, a man who "loved the Lord." The pastor encouraged villagers to pray for Charran and amazingly, in the presence of hospital doctors, he began to speak. Those who witnessed this event praised God and others have been inspired to hear the good news.

A pastor invited to speak to a rugby team in Fiji prior to a world championship competition was used by the Holy Spirit to bring ten young men to Christ.

❖ Encourage class members to comment on these stories and report on ways that they see God at work.

❖ Conclude by challenging those who are willing to tell others of God's presence in the world to raise their hands.

*(5) Continue the Journey*

❖ Pray that today's participants will wisely seek signs of God's presence in the world.

❖ Read aloud this preparation for next week's lesson. You may also want to post it on newsprint for the students to copy.

■ **Title: Emmanuel Is Born**
■ **Background Scripture: Matthew 1:18-25**
■ **Lesson Scripture: Matthew 1:18-25**
■ **Focus of the Lesson: People can feel all alone in their lives. Who can break down the walls that isolate us? Scripture proclaims that Jesus came to be God with us.**

Challenge the students to complete one or more of these activities for further spiritual growth, which you will write on newsprint for the students to copy.

**(1) Ponder Gabriel's words in Luke 1:37: "For nothing will be impossible with God." How have you experienced the truth of this verse? Where do you need to experience that truth now?**

**(2) Think about where you seek signs and omens for your life. How valid are your sources? Do these signs prove to be fruitful or do they lead to dead ends?**

**(3) Tell someone about the promised Messiah whose birth we will soon celebrate. Help this person understand that Jesus did not just arrive "by accident" but was promised by God and foretold by prophets centuries before his birth.**

❖ Sing or read aloud "Emmanuel, Emmanuel."

❖ Conclude today's session by leading the class in this benediction, adapted from Matthew 16:16: **Go forth now to love and serve the Messiah, the Son of the living God.**

## UNIT 1: THE PROMISED BIRTH FULFILLED
# EMMANUEL IS BORN

---

### PREVIEWING THE LESSON

**Lesson Scripture:** Matthew 1:18-25
**Background Scripture:** Matthew 1:18-25
**Key Verse:** Matthew 1:21

### Focus of the Lesson:
People can feel all alone in their lives. Who can break down the walls that isolate us? Scripture proclaims that Jesus came to be God with us.

### Goals for the Learners:
(1) to look with fresh eyes at Jesus' birth as told in Matthew.
(2) to consider what it means for the world, the church, and themselves to know that God is with us.
(3) to plan a way to share this good news with others.

### Supplies:
Bibles, newsprint and marker, paper and pencils, hymnals

---

### READING THE SCRIPTURE

NRSV
Matthew 1:18-25

18Now the birth of Jesus the Messiah took place in this way. When his mother Mary had been engaged to Joseph, but before they lived together, she was found to be with child from the Holy Spirit. 19Her husband Joseph, being a righteous man and unwilling to expose her to public disgrace, planned to dismiss her quietly. 20But just when he had resolved to do this, an angel of the Lord appeared to him in a dream and said, "Joseph, son of David, do not be afraid to take Mary as your wife, for the child con-

NIV
Matthew 1:18-25

18This is how the birth of Jesus Christ came about: His mother Mary was pledged to be married to Joseph, but before they came together, she was found to be with child through the Holy Spirit. 19Because Joseph her husband was a righteous man and did not want to expose her to public disgrace, he had in mind to divorce her quietly.

20But after he had considered this, an angel of the Lord appeared to him in a dream and said, "Joseph son of David, do not be afraid to take Mary home as your

ceived in her is from the Holy Spirit. **²¹She will bear a son, and you are to name him Jesus, for he will save his people from their sins."** ²²All this took place to fulfill what had been spoken by the Lord through the prophet:

²³ "Look, the virgin shall conceive and bear a son,

and they shall name him Emmanuel," which means, "God is with us." ²⁴When Joseph awoke from sleep, he did as the angel of the Lord commanded him; he took her as his wife, ²⁵but had no marital relations with her until she had borne a son; and he named him Jesus.

wife, because what is conceived in her is from the Holy Spirit. **²¹She will give birth to a son, and you are to give him the name Jesus, because he will save his people from their sins."**

²²All this took place to fulfill what the Lord had said through the prophet: ²³"The virgin will be with child and will give birth to a son, and they will call him Immanuel"— which means, "God with us."

²⁴When Joseph woke up, he did what the angel of the Lord had commanded him and took Mary home as his wife. ²⁵But he had no union with her until she gave birth to a son. And he gave him the name Jesus.

## UNDERSTANDING THE SCRIPTURE

**Matthew 1:18-19.** Ancient biographies often opened with relevant features of a person's background, such as the home in which they were nurtured or (in some unusual cases) special signs of future greatness at their birth. This passage both emphasizes the piety of Jesus' parents (hence his upbringing) and signs that from the beginning God had given Jesus a unique mission. This is especially clear because, as in Luke, Jesus was conceived through the Holy Spirit (1:18, 20). Although this means that Jesus was not physically the son of Joseph (hence of the Davidic line traced in 1:1-17), one's legal line was far more important. (Thus even many Roman emperors were "sons" of previous emperors only by adoption; but legal adoption made one fully a part of the new line.)

Ancient betrothal was more serious than modern engagements. It involved an economic arrangement between families, and often lasted a year before the wedding. Jewish tradition suggests that Galilean couples could not be alone together before their wedding (although Judean rules were apparently somewhat less strict, and with-

out Luke's account we might assume that Joseph and Mary were already in Bethlehem). Particularly significant for our passage, betrothal, like marriage itself, could be ended only by either death or "divorce."

Although specified in the law of Moses, the death penalty for adultery was no longer practiced in this period (if it had ever been implemented frequently). Adultery was, however, a matter of serious and permanent shame. Unfortunately, society had a double standard, punishing unfaithful wives more than unfaithful husbands. A spouse's or fiancée's sexual unfaithfulness could shame not only themselves but also their parents and the person to whom they were married or engaged. (Romans told of some scrupulous fathers who preferred their daughters' deaths to their defilement.) Jewish (as well as Gentile) law *required* a husband to divorce an unfaithful wife; a husband who failed to do so was regarded as enabling her guilt.

Because Galilean couples normally spent little time alone during their betrothal, Joseph probably did not know Mary well.

Yet even if he had known her well, and she had sought to explain the circumstances of her pregnancy, it would be asking a lot to expect Joseph to trust her story. Like us, Joseph knew that virgin births did not happen; they had never happened before, and only a unique act of God could make it happen then.

By "divorcing" Mary publicly, that is, before a court, Joseph could recoup some of his lost honor, and make clear that he repudiated any responsibility for her pregnancy. Moreover, Joseph could profit economically. If he had begun to pay a "bride price" (gifts to the bride's family to express gratitude for their expense in raising her), he would get this back. Any dowry (a Greek custom now practiced also in Palestine) her father had given her for the marriage would now become Joseph's possession. Yet Joseph chose instead to divorce her "privately," that is, giving her a certificate of divorce in front of two witnesses. Even at a cost to himself, Joseph wanted to minimize her shame.

**Matthew 1:20-23.** As in some other biblical annunciations of significant births (noted in the previous lesson), an angel of the Lord brings Joseph a message and announces the child's name.

The name "Jesus," like Joseph, Mary, and many other names in our Gospels, was a very common name in this period. (Those who have tried to identify tombs for Jesus or other Gospel characters based on names are either ignorant of this fact or simply out to make money.) "Jesus" in our Greek New Testament translates the same Hebrew name that appears in our Bibles as "Joshua." Because it means "the Lord is salvation," it was appropriate for one who would save his people from sins. Jewish people expected a promised deliverer from oppression; here, however, the object of salvation was their own sins. Before God would deliver Israel from captivity, Israel needed to return to God; while we may need deliverance from many other things, sometimes we may also need deliverance from ourselves.

Whatever other reasons God may have had for a virgin birth, Matthew lists only one: "to fulfill" Scripture (1:22). Matthew takes Scripture very seriously in its witness to Christ. Indeed, from this paragraph until the Sermon on the Mount, nearly every paragraph is built around at least one biblical text. The actual nature of his understanding of Isaiah, however, appears more complex than this affirmation. According to Matthew, Jesus' virgin birth was to fulfill Isaiah 7:14, which Matthew quotes in 1:23. As we explained more fully in the previous lesson, Isaiah's prophecy points immediately to Isaiah's own son. Isaiah's son was also a "sign" pointing to a greater ultimate deliverance of Israel. That ultimate deliverance would involve a son of David who would be the "Mighty God" (Isaiah 9:6-7; a divine title in Isaiah 10:21), an appropriate fulfillment of the name "Immanuel," "God is with us" (Isaiah 7:14). Matthew clearly has the larger context in mind; only a few chapters later, in Matthew 4:15-16, he quotes from Isaiah 9:1-2.

Sometimes Matthew offers his own Greek translation of the Old Testament, but here concurs with the standard one: Isaiah's "young woman" is a "virgin," and in this case, the Greek translation of the prophecy is literally fulfilled (Mary remains a virgin in 1:18, 20 and 25, framing the narrative). Of all the miraculous births in the Old Testament (starting with the matriarchs Sarah, Rebekah, and Rachel), this *virgin* birth would be the greatest of signs.

**Matthew 1:24.** Although the angel's message to Joseph came only in a dream, and the social risks of marrying Mary were great, Joseph obeyed the angel. (Among the Gospels, Matthew has a particular emphasis on dreams; see 2:12, 13, 19, 22; 27:19.) Most people in Joseph's day believed that dreams sometimes communicated divine wisdom. (Among "professionals," magi (2:1) were often known as dream interpreters.) Greeks often believed that a deceased person would communicate in a dream, but, as here, in Scripture revelatory dreams normally involved the voice of God or angels.

**Matthew 1:25.** Joseph's culture widely assumed that if a man and woman were alone together, they would quickly succumb to sexual temptation. If Joseph and Mary married at close to the average age in their culture (where women did not have "high school"), Joseph may have been in his late teens (18-20, though possibly older) and Mary perhaps around 16 (though possibly younger or older). Although in their culture age was more highly respected than youth, Matthew employs them as models of virtue.

Despite later tradition, there is no indication in the Bible itself that Mary remained a virgin after the point specified here, Jesus' birth. The most probable reason for mentioning Jesus' siblings later (and not here or en route to Bethlehem) is that they were born later to Mary and Joseph (compare Matthew 12:46-47; 13:55).

## INTERPRETING THE SCRIPTURE

### Commitment

By emphasizing the virtue of Jesus' parents, Matthew (like a good biographer) emphasizes his subject's virtuous upbringing. He also illustrates some moral principles that arise later in his Gospel. Thus this passage presupposes the importance of commitment in marriage. Underlining the danger of marital unfaithfulness, Matthew makes clear that even Jesus' warning against divorce (and Joseph's example) allows an exception for this reason (Matthew 5:32; 19:9). (1 Corinthians 7:15 allows an exception for abandonment; the common principle for these exceptions seems to be that we should work to nurture our marriages but are not held accountable if the spouse irreparably breaks it. Physical abuse fits the same category as adultery or abandonment.)

Sometimes we feel that biblical teaching about sexual fidelity is too harsh, but the God who designed us knows what is best for us. As Philip Yancey points out in his *Rumors of Another World*, God wants us to enjoy our sexual lives, but our sexuality is a delicate part of our personhood, meant to be expressed in marriage. True intimacy flourishes in the context of commitment, but trust becomes much more difficult when commitment is violated. Many of us have tasted the sting of betrayal, whether from abandonment by a parent, betrayal by a close friend, or others. Having felt the sting of betrayal, we should be careful never to inflict it on others, especially those who love and trust us the most.

Marriage requires commitment, and the Bible takes marital unfaithfulness very seriously. That Joseph, though being "righteous," was willing to divorce for what he believed to be marital unfaithfulness underlines the seriousness with which adultery was taken.

### Compassion

Yet Joseph's "righteousness" here is not simply that he took unfaithfulness seriously; law and custom expected this of him. Joseph's righteousness involves also compassion. Joseph could have regained some honor and probably profited financially by divorcing Mary in a court setting, but he chose not to do so. Matthew emphasizes that Joseph was going to divorce her privately, minimizing her shame, because he was "a righteous man" (Matthew 1:19).

Sometimes we think of righteousness as upholding an inflexible standard, without compassion for those who have violated it.

Joseph's example, however, reveals that righteousness involves not only upholding God's moral standard but also treating with compassion those who fail to meet it. Jesus modeled such compassion (9:13; 12:7). Jesus never compromised his standard in his teaching to his disciples. Yet he also never repudiated them when they fell short, just as he does not repudiate us when we fall short. We should keep in mind, however, that Jesus' goal in the Gospels, even in spending time with "sinners," was not just to love them (or us) as we were but to love us enough to help us to change and become better.

### Costly Obedience to God

When Joseph obeys the angel, he must know what is at stake. Matthew is not clear whether others besides Joseph are aware of her pregnancy, but if it is known that Mary was pregnant before the marriage, Joseph's failure to repudiate her would leave others with the assumption that he got her pregnant. He values God's honor more than his own, as well as true obedience to God's will over other people believing that he obeyed God's will.

Joseph and Mary could have dispelled any suspicions about Mary's virginity by having intercourse on their first wedding night. Weddings often lasted seven days, but a couple would normally have intercourse on the first night, and normally produce the blood-stained bedsheet to prove that the woman had been a virgin. Yet Joseph and Mary did not have intercourse till after Jesus was born, so that this might be not only a virgin conception but a virgin *birth*.

The couple's obedience is also expressed in self-control. Our culture, like Joseph's, often assumes that sexual self-control is impossible (and in contrast to Joseph's culture, often also assumes that it is undesirable). The self-control of this young couple, however, challenges our ready assumptions about what matters and what is possible.

Humans are not like most animals in heat; unlike most other creatures, we have intercourse face to face, and are capable of expressing romantic love at any time. God created us as relational creatures, with intercourse as a crowning sign of the intimacy that flourishes in the context of trust, hence commitment. This is also the best setting for nurturing children, and Jesus clearly grew up in such a household.

### The Savior, God with Us

Most important is what this passage tells us about Christ. God granted Jesus a special birth to signal his special mission. Sometimes when we teach about the moral model offered by Joseph and Mary, people feel bad about their behavior; but this passage also teaches us about an even more central character, the one who came to "save" us from "sins" (1:21). God has a new plan for the world, but first God wants to implement the plan in the lives of those who claim to follow God.

When Jesus came, he was God's presence among us, in a hidden way. We may be tempted to restrict God's presence with us to the Christmas story or to Jesus' earthly ministry, but such a perspective misses Matthew's point. Matthew tells us that Jesus remains God with us: "where two or three are gathered in my name," Jesus said, "I am there among them" (18:20). A familiar Jewish saying claimed that where two or three were gathered for the study of Torah, God's presence was among them. Jesus here assumes the role of God's presence. Finally, the Gospel closes by reminding us that Jesus, part of the Trinity (28:19), will be "with you" in your mission always, "to the end of the age" (28:20).

You may have heard the familiar complaint that if the Spirit were withdrawn from the church, much of our activity would continue as if nothing had changed! We need to live and serve in the recognition that Christ is really among us. Paul writes that God gave us the Spirit as a foretaste of our future inheritance. If we look forward to being with Jesus in the consummated kingdom, we should also live in submission to his kingship in the present.

Most of all, we should take courage.

Jesus did not simply give us instructions, then leave us to fulfill them completely on our own. Jesus is with us as savior (1:21-23), as Lord of the church (18:15-20), and as empowerer for the mission and purpose he has given us (28:18-20).

## SHARING THE SCRIPTURE

### Preparing Our Hearts

Meditate on this week's devotional reading, found in Galatians 4:1-7. Here Paul reminds his readers that they are heirs of God through God's Son, Jesus. What does it mean to you to know that you are an heir of God, a son or daughter who may call God "Abba! Father!" or, as we would say, "Daddy"? What difference does this relationship make in your life? Speak with someone else this week about your relationship with God the Father and Jesus. Encourage this person to seek out such a close, personal relationship for himself or herself.

Pray that you and the adult learners will cherish this very special relationship that they have with the Father through the Son.

### Preparing Our Minds

Study the background and lesson scripture, both of which are found in Matthew 1:18-25. Ask yourself: when people are feeling alone, who can break down the walls of isolation?

Write on newsprint:
❏ information for next week's lesson, found under "Continue the Journey."
❏ activities for further spiritual growth in "Continue the Journey."

Plan a lecture as suggested for "Look with Fresh Eyes at Jesus' Birth as Told in Matthew."

### LEADING THE CLASS

#### (1) Gather to Learn

❖ Welcome the class members and introduce any guests.

❖ Pray that all who are present today will experience the joy of knowing Jesus, God with us.

❖ Invite the students to recall a time in their lives when they seemed lonely. Perhaps a significant person had died, or a child had left home, or the loss of a job—even due to retirement—caused a rupture in relationships with friends and coworkers. Encourage a few volunteers to tell their stories briefly.

❖ Ask: **What role did your relationship with Christ play in helping you overcome this loneliness?**

❖ Read aloud today's focus statement: **People can feel all alone in their lives. Who can break down the walls that isolate us? Scripture proclaims that Jesus came to be God with us.**

#### (2) Look with Fresh Eyes at Jesus' Birth as Told in Matthew

❖ Select volunteers to read the parts of the narrator, the angel, and the prophet (1:23) in Matthew 1:18-25.

❖ Discuss these questions with the class:
**(1) What does this passage tell you about Mary?**
**(2) What does this passage tell you about Joseph?** ("Compassion" in

Interpreting the Scripture will provide you with information to add to the discussion.)

**(3) What does this passage tell you about Jesus?**

❖ Lecture briefly on information in Understanding the Scripture for Matthew 1:18-19, 20-23. Help the students understand customs related to betrothal, marriage, and divorce, as well as the meaning of "Jesus" and the issue of the virgin birth.

❖ **Option:** Read aloud Luke 1:26-38 and Luke 2:1-7. Invite the students to contrast Luke's version of Jesus' pre-birth story with Matthew's version. Note that Matthew focuses heavily on Joseph, whereas Luke's emphasis is on Mary. Ask the students to comment on what we would have lost had we had only one of these stories.

❖ Wrap up this portion of the session by asking the adults to report on any new insights they have seen regarding Jesus' birth.

*(3) Consider What It Means for the World, the Church, and the Learners to Know that God Is with Us*

❖ Discuss why God sent Jesus to be with us. Add ideas from "The Savior, God with Us" in Interpreting the Scripture to augment the discussion.

❖ Encourage the students to respond to this question: **How do you know that God is with you?** List their ideas on newsprint. Encourage brief stories that demonstrate how the adults perceive God to be acting in their lives.

❖ Distribute a hymnal, paper, and pencil to each adult. Set a time limit in which the students are to explore the hymnal to find ways that God is with us in Jesus. Suggest that the class members look first at Christmas music but that they may expand their search to other hymns. Ask them to jot down any ways they find.

❖ Call time and ask each student to report to a small group of three or four.

❖ Bring all of the groups together and ask: **In what ways did hymn writers demonstrate that God is with us in Jesus?** Students may want to retell the ideas in their words or quote some phrases from hymns. Ideas may include: Jesus as healer, teacher of God's wisdom, storyteller who teaches about the kingdom of God, peacemaker, righteous one, and bringer of justice.

❖ **Option:** If time permits, sing one of the carols or hymns that several students selected.

*(4) Plan a Way to Share This Good News with Others*

❖ Suggest that the students plan an activity to share the good news of Jesus' birth with others. Here are several ideas:

■ Go Christmas caroling as a class after December 25th. Perhaps the group will want to sing on streets near the church. Maybe they can arrange to go to a nursing home or other facility that would welcome visitors. Consider returning to the church for some light refreshments.

■ Provide food and/or gifts for a family in need or for persons in a facility, such as a domestic violence shelter. Include a New Testament among the gifts for each recipient.

■ Take homemade cookies to homebound members of the congregation. Share a word of testimony about what Jesus is doing in your lives.

❖ Determine who will participate in the activity, when it will be done, and where it will be done.

❖ Plan to gather whatever supplies are needed.

❖ Assign someone the job of coordinating the activity. For example, if you plan to deliver cookies, someone will need to call ahead to (a) be sure that the individual is able to eat cookies and (b) will be home when you plan to arrive. Remember that even those who are homebound may get out of the house if relatives are available to assist them.

❖ Remind the participants of the activity a day or two in advance. Even folks who are normally reliable may forget commitments during this busy holiday season.

*(5) Continue the Journey*

❖ Pray that those who have come today will be touched by the good news of Jesus' birth and share that news with others.

❖ Read aloud this preparation for next week's lesson. You may also want to post it on newsprint for the students to copy.

- **Title: Magi Confirm Messiah's Birth**
- **Background Scripture: Matthew 2**
- **Lesson Scripture: Matthew 2:7-9, 16-23**
- **Focus of the Lesson: People search for something meaningful in their lives. What is worth searching for? The magi searched for the new-born king, found him, and confirmed the truth of the Messiah.**

❖ Challenge the students to complete one or more of these activities for further spiritual growth, which you will write on newsprint for the students to copy.

(1) **Tell the story of Jesus' birth and what it means to you to someone who needs to hear this good news.**

(2) **Try recording your dreams for several nights. Keep paper and pencil handy by your bed. Do these dreams reveal anything to you? If so, how will you act on these dreams?**

(3) **Look up the word "dream" in a concordance. Check out where it appears in Matthew and read those passages to recognize the role that dreams play in this Gospel.**

❖ Sing or read aloud "That Boy-Child of Mary."

❖ Conclude today's session by leading the class in this benediction, adapted from Matthew 16:16: **Go forth now to love and serve the Messiah, the Son of the living God.**

UNIT 1: THE PROMISED BIRTH FULFILLED
# MAGI CONFIRM MESSIAH'S BIRTH

---

## PREVIEWING THE LESSON

**Lesson Scripture:** Matthew 2:7-10, 16-23
**Background Scripture:** Matthew 2
**Key Verse:** Matthew 2:10

### Focus of the Lesson:
People search for something meaningful in their lives. What is worth searching for? The magi searched for and found the newborn king, and confirmed the truth of the Messiah.

### Goals for the Learners:
(1) to look at the visit by the magi and the resulting effects on persons and events.
(2) to realize that Jesus is worth seeking and worshiping.
(3) to make a commitment to seek Christ daily.

### Pronunciation Guide:
Archelaus (ahr kuh lay' uhs)          *nezer* (neh' zer) or (nay' zer)
Epiphanes (i pif' uh neez)            Ramah (ray' muh)
Idumean (id yoo mee' uhn')            Sanhedrin (san hee' druhn)
Nazorean (naz uh ree' uhn)            Zoroastrian (zoh roh as' tree uhn)

### Supplies:
Bibles, newsprint and marker, paper and pencils, hymnals, optional map showing Jerusalem and Persia (Iran)

---

## READING THE SCRIPTURE

NRSV
Matthew 2:7-10, 16-23

7Then Herod secretly called for the wise men and learned from them the exact time when the star had appeared. 8Then he sent them to Bethlehem, saying, "Go and search

NIV
Matthew 2:7-10, 16-23

7Then Herod called the Magi secretly and found out from them the exact time the star had appeared. 8He sent them to Bethlehem and said, "Go and make a careful search for diligently for the child; and when you have found him, bring me word so that I may also go and pay him homage." [9]When they had heard the king, they set out; and there, ahead of them, went the star that they had seen at its rising, until it stopped over the place where the child was. [10]**When they saw that the star had stopped, they were overwhelmed with joy.**

[16]When Herod saw that he had been tricked by the wise men, he was infuriated, and he sent and killed all the children in and around Bethlehem who were two years old or under, according to the time that he had learned from the wise men. [17]Then was fulfilled what had been spoken through the prophet Jeremiah:

[18]  "A voice was heard in Ramah,
> wailing and loud lamentation,
Rachel weeping for her children;
> she refused to be consoled,
> > because they are no more."

[19]When Herod died, an angel of the Lord suddenly appeared in a dream to Joseph in Egypt and said, [20]"Get up, take the child and his mother, and go to the land of Israel, for those who were seeking the child's life are dead." [21]Then Joseph got up, took the child and his mother, and went to the land of Israel. [22]But when he heard that Archelaus was ruling over Judea in place of his father Herod, he was afraid to go there. And after being warned in a dream, he went away to the district of Galilee. [23]There he made his home in a town called Nazareth, so that what had been spoken through the prophets might be fulfilled, "He will be called a Nazorean."

the child. As soon as you find him, report to me, so that I too may go and worship him."

[9]After they had heard the king, they went on their way, and the star they had seen in the east went ahead of them until it stopped over the place where the child was. [10]**When they saw the star, they were overjoyed.**

[16]When Herod realized that he had been outwitted by the Magi, he was furious, and he gave orders to kill all the boys in Bethlehem and its vicinity who were two years old and under, in accordance with the time he had learned from the Magi. [17]Then what was said through the prophet Jeremiah was fulfilled:

[18]"A voice is heard in Ramah,
> weeping and great mourning,
Rachel weeping for her children
> and refusing to be comforted,
because they are no more."

[19]After Herod died, an angel of the Lord appeared in a dream to Joseph in Egypt [20]and said, "Get up, take the child and his mother and go to the land of Israel, for those who were trying to take the child's life are dead."

[21]So he got up, took the child and his mother and went to the land of Israel. [22]But when he heard that Archelaus was reigning in Judea in place of his father Herod, he was afraid to go there. Having been warned in a dream, he withdrew to the district of Galilee, [23]and he went and lived in a town called Nazareth. So was fulfilled what was said through the prophets: "He will be called a Nazarene."

---

## UNDERSTANDING THE SCRIPTURE

**Matthew 2:1-2.** In this narrative, Matthew introduces three new groups of people: the magi (NRSV, "wise men"; 2:1); King Herod; and Herod's own wise men, the chief priests and scribes (2:4). Through each of these characters, Matthew subverts traditional expectations: "pagans" who worship Jesus; a king of Israel whose behavior recalls Israel's pagan oppressors; and experts who know the Bible's teaching but neglect to take it seriously.

Magi were Persian astrologers (from the region of Iran). Scholars differ as to the meaning of the "star." Some propose a conjunction of celestial bodies, one portending a ruler and another associated with Judea, probably a few years before Herod's death in 4 B.C. (Jesus may have been born around 7 B.C.)

**Matthew 2:3-8.** Herod the Great (not to be confused with later members of his Herodian family in the New Testament) was an Idumean by birth, but ruled as "king of the Jews." His slaughter of Bethlehem's infants fits what we know of his character. He also acts like dreaded ancient Gentile kings, such as Pharaoh and Antiochus Epiphanes. So while the "pagan" magi worship Israel's true king, the current king of Israel acts instead like a "pagan" ruler!

Herod's own wise men can readily identify the place of the coming king's birth: Bethlehem, the town of the ancient ruler David, based on Micah 5:2. (Matthew recognizes that the "shepherd" the verse predicts is Jesus; see Matthew 9:36; 15:24.) This birthplace is appropriate for the "son of David" (Matthew 1:1).

The "chief priests and scribes" here belong to Jerusalem's "Sanhedrin," or city council. (Rome ruled its empire partly in collaboration with local elites on city councils.) These chief priests and scribes were not independent of Herod, since Herod had violently purged the older Sanhedrin of disloyal members, replacing them with his own loyalists. More significantly for Matthew's first audience, these chief priests and scribes foreshadow those later in his passion narrative, who seek the true king's execution.

**Matthew 2:9-12.** Bethlehem was so close to Jerusalem (only about six miles) that the star would only appear to move before them as they moved. The star may have indicated Judea, but they needed the Bible experts to find the specific town (2:5-6). Some believe that Matthew emphasizes the star's movement (2:9) to evoke the pillar of fire that moved before Israel in the wilderness.

Their joy in seeing the star's witness (2:10) fits joy over finding the treasure of the kingdom (13:44; compare 25:21, 23) or of Jesus' resurrection (28:8). Dignitaries could congratulate

a new king with gifts (2:11). Frankincense and myrrh were costly spices available especially in southern Arabia and east Africa, but they could have been acquired in Persia or along the route due to the caravan trade.

Herod is sure that the magi, with their obvious caravan (compare 2:3), cannot avoid him. Bethlehem was so close to Jerusalem that it was within visual range of Herod's palace called the Herodium. Moreover, the only major road north from Bethlehem, by which they could return home, led through Jerusalem. But guided by a divine warning, the magi take a different road, perhaps one south to Hebron.

**Matthew 2:13-15.** In an ironic reversal of the exodus (but similar to the stories of Joseph and others), Egypt becomes a place of refuge from oppression in Israel. Alexandria, on the Nile's north delta and not far from Judea, had a large Jewish population (perhaps even a third of Alexandria's possibly one million inhabitants). Although their night journey was potentially dangerous (especially due to robbers), the family should have been able to reach Egypt and remain there comfortably, using any of the magi's gold.

Matthew views their refuge in Egypt as setting the stage for their subsequent return, which evokes Israel's own exodus. In context, Hosea 11:1 refers to Israel's exodus from Egypt. Matthew surely did recognize the context (since, departing from the standard Greek translation, he even provides his own more accurate translation from the Hebrew). But Hosea 11 went on to speak of a new exodus, a new era of salvation. By identifying with Israel's heritage (as "son of Abraham," Matthew 1:1), Jesus also inaugurates a new era.

**Matthew 2:16.** Herod's behavior here fits how he acted whenever his power seemed threatened. His young high priest brother-in-law was becoming too popular, hence he had a drowning accident—in a pool that archaeology shows was only about three feet deep. On his deathbed, to ensure that his people would mourn for him when he died, Herod allegedly ordered nobles to be detained and executed at his death. (They were instead released, producing widespread celebration.)

Herod is particularly known for his own family life. Wrongly suspecting her unfaithfulness, he had his favorite wife strangled (though he afterward regretted it). Wrongly thinking that two of his sons were plotting against him, he had them executed. On his deathbed, he discovered that another son was genuinely plotting against him and had him executed as well. (In a probably apocryphal comment, the emperor Augustus was said to have remarked that it was safer to be Herod's pig than his son.) Most relevantly here, Herod's slaughter of the baby boys evokes Pharaoh's slaughter of Israel's baby boys, and perhaps Antiochus Epiphanes' similar activity. (The boys' age suggests that the magi arrived long after Jesus' birth—not alongside Luke's shepherds.)

**Matthew 2:17-18.** Far from merely dispassionately narrating this tragedy, Matthew laments in the language of Scripture. Jeremiah poetically claimed that Rachel (who was buried near Bethlehem) mourned when her children were carried off in captivity (Jeremiah 31:15). But Matthew also knows the rest of Jeremiah's context: after the tragedy of exile, God would restore Israel and establish a new covenant (31:16-40, especially 31:31-34). In the midst of the tragedy, God had nevertheless preserved the future deliverer, just as God once preserved Moses when Pharaoh killed Israel's babies.

**Matthew 2:19-23.** The assurance in 2:20 echoes God's assurance to Moses in Exodus 4:19, except that Moses' oppressor was Pharaoh and Jesus' was Herod. Herod died in 4 B.C. and was succeeded by Archelaus, who, despite having inherited his father's vices, lacked his administrative skills, rendering Judea unstable. The family thus moved to Nazareth. This was a small and relatively inconsequential town, but Matthew regards it as divinely significant, offering a Hebrew wordplay on its name. The likeliest of several proposals is that he plays on a prophetic name for the Messiah, namely *nezer*, the "branch" (see Jeremiah 23:5; 33:15; Zechariah 3:8; 6:12).

---

# INTERPRETING THE SCRIPTURE

### Devotion to Christ

Twice the passage emphasizes that the magi came to worship the king of the Jews (Matthew 2:2, 11), a model for post-resurrection disciples (28:9, 17). Magi's job description included honoring Persia's king; yet they could also be sent as goodwill ambassadors to other rulers, as here. In this case, they have faith to honor the newborn king identified by the star, even though he is not born in the Jerusalem palace where they expected him!

Matthew emphasizes that the magi bring costly gifts, just as later some give all they have for the kingdom (13:44-46) or in devotion to Jesus (26:7). A true disciple must love Jesus more than everything else (10:37-39; 16:24-26; 19:21). If this was true of magi who knew only that he would be a great king, how much more of us who know that he is also risen Lord and savior.

### Subverting Prejudice

Matthew's narrative subverts our expectations, hence challenges our prejudices. "Pagans" prove receptive to Jesus; Bible teachers neglect him; and Israel's king wants to eliminate competition. Of these three sets of characters, Matthew allows us to identify safely only with the magi. Those who search for truth today may find in them a ready model. Yet for those who already know Christ, the narrative is less about identifying with their quest than about affirming outsiders who are seeking truth (helping them find Christ in a "seeker-sensitive" way).

Matthew's mention of magi may have initially shocked his Jewish audience. Not only were magi Gentiles but they were also part of a Gentile religious system (whether of Persia's older polytheistic religion, or of Zoroastrian dualism). Moreover, they were *astrologers* following a star. Scripture forbade divination on pain of death, including astrology. Granted, by Matthew's day, when astrology was considered the current "science" from the east, Jewish people were more apt to accept that stars predicted the future. Nevertheless, followers of a star were hardly typical models of virtue. Moreover, the one passage where "magi" (as royal advisors and dream-interpreters) appear in the most common Greek rendering of his audience's Bible is not very flattering (Daniel 2:2, 10).

Yet these magi, of whom Matthew's audience would be intuitively suspicious, turn out to be the narrative's most positive new characters. By contrast, the king of God's people acts like a pagan king. Just as Matthew later reveals in Jesus' parable of the four soils (13:3-23), we cannot predict which kind of soil will bear fruit. Only God knows the heart and who will embrace the good news of Christ's love, so we should welcome everyone without prejudice.

By welcoming magi, Matthew is not endorsing astrology or divination. Although God had a higher standard for the covenant people, sometimes God worked with other peoples where they were to help them understand more about the true God (for example, 1 Samuel 6:1-18; compare Acts 19:15-17). On this one special occasion in history, a seeker-sensitive God testified to these Gentile astrologers, welcoming foreign dignitaries to celebrate Jesus' birth.

### Knowing the Bible without Obeying It

More troubling than the magi or Herod are the "chief priests and scribes"—Herod's Bible experts (2:4). These people, unlike Herod himself, knew the Bible and could answer biblical questions. They function as this narrative's closest equivalent to today's seminary professors, pastors, and Sunday school teachers. They knew that the magi were looking for the king (compare 2:2-3), and knew where the Bible said to find him (2:5-6). They did not, however, bother accompanying the magi to Bethlehem.

These experts illustrate that merely knowing the Bible is not enough if we do not take it seriously enough to obey its message. Indeed, a generation later, when Jesus was no longer a baby who could be ignored, this group's response proved even more hostile, perhaps revealing that the line between neglect and hostility is often thin.

Sometimes Christians have read "chief priests and scribes" in the Gospels in an anti-Jewish way—probably often so it will not challenge our own way of living. But Jesus and all his first followers were Jewish, so the problem with these leaders is not their Jewishness. Not only Jesus but most other Jewish groups resented abuses of power among many chief priests.

These elite people resembled other powerful groups throughout the Empire and often in our world (or relationships) today. Power corrupts, and people with power do not like to give it up. Power can of course be used for good (as Joseph of Arimathea illustrates). But do elite leaders or a crucified deliverer appeal more to us? What does our answer teach us about our own values?

### Jesus Was a Refugee

Herod's tyranny is little different from abuses of power common in many nations today. By citing the lament in Jeremiah, Matthew invites us not to recite the event dispassionately but to mourn such atrocities. The evening news should mobilize us to pray and work, not surrender in despair.

God preserved Jesus' family through their flight. This narrative illustrates that even from the very beginning, "the Son of Man has nowhere to lay his head" (8:20). God preserved Jesus, like Moses of old, to be a deliverer. Those within the narrative could see only the tragic injustice and suffering that we experience in this world; but in light of the larger picture of God's plan, there is hope even in the face of unspeakable tragedy (note Jeremiah 31).

Thousands of refugees suffer in today's world, usually neglected by our governments (but sometimes reached by the International Red Cross, World Vision, Doctors without Borders, and others). Years ago I panicked when Médine Moussounga, a friend from graduate school, sent me a letter that she might be killed. By the time I received it, her Congolese town had been burned to the ground. She and her sisters and mother fled into the forest, pushing her disabled father in a wheelbarrow. Often terribly ill without medicine, each was close to death at one time or another. Médine

often walked ten miles a day to get food for the family, through snake-infested swamps and fields of army ants. They spent eighteen months as refugees before we were able to reestablish contact. Later Médine, who is now my wife, read in my Matthew commentary that Jesus was a refugee. That Jesus had shared her sufferings offered new meaning to the suffering.

Five times Matthew here mentions "the child and his mother" (2:11, 13, 14, 20, 21), often in the context of Herod seeking to slay them. This description underlines how a brutal and powerful ruler felt threatened by a young mother and her baby. Exodus also tells of an evil ruler slaying children, while God preserved Moses, the future liberator. Even in the worst tragedies, God has a plan of hope for the future. Toward the narrative's end, Herod, who abused the power of life and death over others, now faced death himself (2:19-20). No tyrant's time is permanent; only God holds ultimate power.

## SHARING THE SCRIPTURE

### Preparing Our Hearts

Meditate on this week's devotional reading, found in Proverbs 9:7-12. We often refer to the magi, the subjects of today's session, as wise men. This passage from Proverbs speaks about true wisdom, which begins with "the fear of the LORD" (9:10). Wisdom gives those who seek it life. Where do you look for wisdom? How has "the knowledge of the Holy One" (9:10) given you "insight"? Where do you need new insight right now?

Pray that you and the adult learners will seek the insight that can only be found in God's wisdom.

### Preparing Our Minds

Study the background from Matthew 2 and lesson scripture, verses 7-9, 16-23.

Think about what is so meaningful that it is worth searching for.

Write on newsprint:
❑ ideas for "Make a Commitment to Seek Christ Daily."
❑ information for next week's lesson, found under "Continue the Journey."
❑ activities for further spiritual growth in "Continue the Journey."

Plan how you will present information about Herod and the magi in "Look at the Visit by the Magi and the Resulting Effects on Persons and Events."

### LEADING THE CLASS

#### (1) Gather to Learn

❖ Welcome the class members and introduce any guests.

❖ Pray that all who have come today

will be open to searching for that which gives true meaning in their lives.

❖ Read aloud this information from *Man's Search for Meaning,* first published in 1946 by internationally known psychiatrist and Nazi concentration camp survivor Viktor E. Frankl: **"Man's search for meaning is the primary motivation in his life. . . . A public-opinion poll was conducted a few years ago in France. The results showed that 89 percent of the people polled admitted that man needs 'something' for the sake of which to live. Moreover, 61 percent conceded that there was something, or someone, in their own lives for whose sake they were even ready to die. . . ."** Nearly 8,000 students at forty-eight colleges were asked on a survey conducted by Johns Hopkins University what they thought was "very important" and "16 percent of the students checked 'making a lot of money'; 78 percent said their first goal was 'finding a purpose and meaning to my life.'"

❖ Discuss these questions:
    **(1) Do you agree that meaning is "the primary motivation in life"? Why or why not?**
    **(2) What gives meaning to your life?**

❖ Read aloud today's focus statement: **People search for something meaningful in their lives. What is worth searching for? The magi searched for, found the newborn king, and confirmed the truth of the Messiah.**

*(2) Look at the Visit by the Magi and the Resulting Effects on Persons and Events*

❖ Introduce today's passage by reading or giving a brief lecture on material concerning Herod and the Magi, as found in Understanding the Scripture for Matthew 2:1-2, 3-8.

❖ **Option:** Use a map that shows Persia (modern Iran) in relation to Jerusalem. Estimate the number of miles the magi had to travel.

❖ Choose volunteers to read the parts of the narrator, Herod, the words of Jeremiah 31:15 (quoted in Matthew 2:18), and the angel. Ask this group to read Matthew 2:7-9, 16-23.

❖ Encourage the class to identify the events that take place in this passage and the effect these events have on various people. List ideas, which include the following, on newsprint:
    ■ Herod calls for the magi, who have arrived in Jerusalem, to learn about the star.
    ■ The magi proceed to Bethlehem to find Jesus.
    ■ The magi do not return to Jerusalem as Herod had told them to.
    ■ Herod orders the massacre of children under age two in Bethlehem.
    ■ Joseph, who had fled with his family to Egypt (2:13-15), returns to Palestine but now makes his home in Nazareth.

❖ Conclude this section by discussing these questions:
    **(1) What role did God's guidance through dreams play in this story?**
    **(2) What effect did the news of the Messiah's birth have on the following people: the magi; Herod; other children born about the same time in Bethlehem and their families; Joseph and his family?**
    **(3) Why do you suppose that this story only appears in Matthew?** (You may want to note Matthew's concern with Jesus as a new Moses. Like baby Moses, Jesus' life was in danger and his parents were forced to flee a tyrant who ordered the death of infants.)

*(3) Realize That Jesus Is Worth Seeking and Worshiping*

❖ Invite the students to talk informally with a small group about the Christmas gifts they had hoped to receive and the ones they actually got.

❖ Interrupt the discussion by asking: **How many of you were seeking a more intimate relationship with Jesus?**

❖ Encourage the adults to continue talking with their group about why it is so easy to ask for material things and so difficult sometimes for us to seek the One who is of incomparable worth. They may wish to consider how cultural influences, such as a drive for money and "things," impact what they seek and worship.

### (4) Make a Commitment to Seek Christ Daily

❖ Challenge the class members to use strategies for seeking Christ daily by posting these ideas on newsprint for them to consider.

- I will set aside regular time for prayer each day.
- I will read my Bible daily, lingering over words or phrases in which I feel God is speaking to me.
- I will do a good deed for at least one person each day as an expression of my love for Christ.
- I will share my love of Christ with others each day so that they too might come to know him.

❖ Distribute paper and pencils. Invite the students to write down at least one way that they will seek Christ each day during the coming week. Point out that the longer one engages in a specific action, the more likely it is to become a habit.

❖ Close by asking the students who feel ready to make a commitment to write this sentence, which you will need to read aloud, on their papers and then sign their commitment: **With God's help, I pledge faithfully to seek Christ each day with the diligence of the magi.**

### (5) Continue the Journey

❖ Pray that each participant will make a serious effort to search for Christ each day.

❖ Read aloud this preparation for next week's lesson. You may also want to post it on newsprint for the students to copy.

- **Title: Proclaimed in Baptism**
- **Background Scripture: Matthew 3**
- **Lesson Scripture: Matthew 3:1-6, 11-17**
- **Focus of the Lesson: Our actions reveal who we are. What actions disclose our identity? Jesus' willingness to be baptized and God's declaration confirming Jesus' identity provide us an example of how to relate to God.**

❖ Challenge the students to complete one or more of these activities for further spiritual growth, which you will write on newsprint for the students to copy.

(1) **Be aware of modern-day Herods who try to use people for their own benefit. Follow media stories of one of these "Herods," possibly a political dictator, to learn how this powerful person is impacting the lives of those who are powerless.**

(2) **Research the Feast Day of the Holy Innocents, which is commemorated on December 28 to recognize the children slaughtered under Herod's orders. Note especially the connection of "The Coventry Carol" with this day.**

(3) **Volunteer time or contribute money to an agency that helps families with children.**

❖ Sing or read aloud "We Three Kings."

❖ Conclude today's session by leading the class in this benediction, adapted from Matthew 16:16: **Go forth now to love and serve the Messiah, the Son of the living God.**

## UNIT 2: EVIDENCES OF JESUS AS MESSIAH
# PROCLAIMED IN BAPTISM

---

### PREVIEWING THE LESSON

**Lesson Scripture:** Matthew 3:1-6, 11-17
**Background Scripture:** Matthew 3
**Key Verse:** Matthew 3:17

### Focus of the Lesson:
Our actions reveal who we are. What actions disclose our identity? Jesus' willingness to be baptized and God's declaration confirming Jesus' identity provides us an example of how to relate to God.

### Goals for the Learners:
(1) to explore the act and meaning of Jesus' baptism.
(2) to find meaning in church practices, such as baptism, that symbolize a relationship with Christ.
(3) to begin or continue a relationship with Christ and to grow in that relationship through a visible or vocal confession of faith.

### Supplies:
Bibles, newsprint and marker, paper and pencils, hymnals, Bible commentaries

---

### READING THE SCRIPTURE

NRSV
Matthew 3:1-6, 11-17

¹In those days John the Baptist appeared in the wilderness of Judea, proclaiming, ²"Repent, for the kingdom of heaven has come near." ³This is the one of whom the prophet Isaiah spoke when he said,

> "The voice of one crying out in the
>      wilderness:
> 'Prepare the way of the Lord,
>      make his paths straight.'"

NIV
Matthew 3:1-6, 11-17

¹In those days John the Baptist came, preaching in the Desert of Judea ²and saying, "Repent, for the kingdom of heaven is near." ³This is he who was spoken of through the prophet Isaiah:

> "A voice of one calling in the desert,
> 'Prepare the way for the Lord,
>      make straight paths for him.'"

⁴John's clothes were made of camel's hair,

[4]Now John wore clothing of camel's hair with a leather belt around his waist, and his food was locusts and wild honey. [5]Then the people of Jerusalem and all Judea were going out to him, and all the region along the Jordan, [6]and they were baptized by him in the river Jordan, confessing their sins.

[11]"I baptize you with water for repentance, but one who is more powerful than I is coming after me; I am not worthy to carry his sandals. He will baptize you with the Holy Spirit and fire. [12]His winnowing fork is in his hand, and he will clear his threshing floor and will gather his wheat into the granary; but the chaff he will burn with unquenchable fire."

[13]Then Jesus came from Galilee to John at the Jordan, to be baptized by him. [14]John would have prevented him, saying, "I need to be baptized by you, and do you come to me?" [15]But Jesus answered him, "Let it be so now; for it is proper for us in this way to fulfill all righteousness." Then he consented. [16]And when Jesus had been baptized, just as he came up from the water, suddenly the heavens were opened to him and he saw the Spirit of God descending like a dove and alighting on him. [17]**And a voice from heaven said, "This is my Son, the Beloved, with whom I am well pleased."**

and he had a leather belt around his waist. His food was locusts and wild honey. [5]People went out to him from Jerusalem and all Judea and the whole region of the Jordan. [6]Confessing their sins, they were baptized by him in the Jordan River.

[11]"I baptize you with water for repentance. But after me will come one who is more powerful than I, whose sandals I am not fit to carry. He will baptize you with the Holy Spirit and with fire. [12]His winnowing fork is in his hand, and he will clear his threshing floor, gathering his wheat into the barn and burning up the chaff with unquenchable fire."

[13]Then Jesus came from Galilee to the Jordan to be baptized by John. [14]But John tried to deter him, saying, "I need to be baptized by you, and do you come to me?"

[15]Jesus replied, "Let it be so now; it is proper for us to do this to fulfill all righteousness." Then John consented.

[16]As soon as Jesus was baptized, he went up out of the water. At that moment heaven was opened, and he saw the Spirit of God descending like a dove and lighting on him. [17]**And a voice from heaven said, "This is my Son, whom I love; with him I am well pleased."**

---

## UNDERSTANDING THE SCRIPTURE

**Matthew 3:1.** That John lived in the wilderness (3:1, 3) evokes a life of complete sacrifice for God's mission. Jewish people remembered that God had led them through the wilderness after delivering them from Egypt. They also expected a future deliverance in the wilderness (Isaiah 40:3, quoted in Matthew 3:3; Hosea 2:14-15); some groups and prophet figures gathered followings in the wilderness. Its distance from civilization also made the wilderness a place of refuge, guerrilla warfare, and less interference from Roman or other soldiers.

**Matthew 3:2.** Matthew summarizes John's message here the same way he summarizes that of Jesus (4:17) and his followers (10:7): people must "repent," that is, turn back to God, to be ready for his coming "kingdom," that is, reign. Old Testament prophets often called Israel to "turn to" God. Although Jewish people understood that God reigned in the present, they also prayed daily for the consummation of his kingdom in the future. Unknown to John himself, the kingdom will come in two stages, because Jesus the king will come twice.

**Matthew 3:3.** The Isaiah quotation relates John's wilderness mission to the promise of a herald before the new exodus, the new salvation (see comment at 3:1). In Isaiah, the herald prepares God's way; Matthew thus hints in advance at Jesus' true status (see 28:18-20).

**Matthew 3:4.** Like his wilderness location, John's wardrobe and diet evoke sacrifice. His leather belt recalls Elijah (2 Kings 1:8), because John fills Elijah's role of preparing the Lord's way (Malachi 4:5; Matthew 11:13-14). Others ate locusts, but eating locusts exclusively was rare and austere.

**Matthew 3:5-6.** Despite powerful enemies (14:5-8), John enjoyed widespread popularity with the people. Gentiles converting to Judaism normally turned from their past Gentile sins and were baptized. Here, however, it is Jewish people who willingly come, on the same terms that Gentiles would have (see 3:9).

**Matthew 3:7.** Ancients believed that vipers' eggs hatched inside the mother, then the offspring chewed their way through their mother's womb, thereby killing the mother. Not only are these religious people not good children of Abraham (3:9); they are like parent-murderers! (In Luke, John addresses the crowds; Matthew focuses on members of the elite.)

**Matthew 3:8-10.** John here elaborates in greater detail his message of repentance (3:2). Those who truly turn from sin must demonstrate this repentance by a changed life. John compares them with trees that must bear good fruit or be used for firewood!

Most Jewish people believed that they were saved by virtue of being part of the covenant God made with their ancestors; they were chosen in Abraham. Like some earlier prophets, however (for example, Amos 3:2; 9:7), John assaults this sense of privilege. God will judge people by whether they have truly turned to God, not based on their ancestry! Greeks had stories of stones becoming people and vice versa, but John may use a play on words in Aramaic instead, where the word for "children" resembles the word for "stones." Thus he invites Jewish people to God on the same terms that Jewish people invited Gentiles, with baptism and turning from sin (3:6).

**Matthew 3:11.** John's message not only elaborates repentance but also the nature of the kingdom's coming king. Although the sort of people who carried or unlatched others' sandals were servants, and although Old Testament prophets were called God's "servants," John does not count himself worthy even to be the Coming One's servant. John recognizes that he prepares the way for someone divine (see 3:3).

Moreover, John's baptism was merely preliminary and preparatory for the Coming One's baptism. The Coming One would baptize in the Spirit, and it was clear from Scripture that only God could pour out God's Spirit (Isaiah 44:3; Ezekiel 39:29; Joel 2:28). Some people today think of fire baptism as positive, like Spirit baptism, but in the context of the immediately surrounding verses (Matthew 3:10, 12), it is clear that fire represents destructive judgment. John addresses Abraham's offspring or "brood of vipers" (3:7); some will repent and bear good fruit, hence receive the Spirit. Others will be cut down and thrown into, or baptized in, fire. John did not know that the fire baptism would come at a later stage (compare his confusion in 11:2-3).

**Matthew 3:12.** Unlike wheat, chaff was inedible. After harvest, farmers separated the two by throwing the wheat into the air, so that the wind (often the same term for "Spirit") would blow out the lighter chaff. Chaff was useless, and burned too quickly to be useful even as fuel. Earlier prophets used it as an image of judgment. But this chaff will burn eternally (in "unquenchable fire"), not quickly. Jewish views of hell varied (it could be temporary, or might annihilate the wicked), but for his religious hearers John focuses on the harshest view held in his day.

**Matthew 3:13-15.** When Jesus comes for baptism, John objects: he needs Jesus' Spirit baptism far more than Jesus needs his water baptism (3:11, 14). Jesus responds that his mission involves fulfilling righteousness (3:15), just as he fulfilled Scripture in identifying with Israel (for example, 2:15; 4:1-2), fulfilled the law by his teaching (for example, 5:17), and taught righteousness (5:6, 10, 20; 6:1, 33—the majority of uses of this term in the Gospels).

**Matthew 3:16.** The "opening of heavens" often signified a divine vision or revelation (Ezekiel 1:1; Acts 7:56), sometimes for something to descend from heaven (Genesis 28:12; John 1:51). Scholars have proposed various reasons why the Spirit is here symbolized as a dove. Although a few later Jewish sources portray the Spirit as a dove, more often they portray Israel as a dove (which does not make sense here). More relevantly, a dove was a herald of a new world in Genesis 8:11. In any case, if the Spirit is symbolized by a flying creature, a dove is the best option.

**Matthew 3:17.** A heavenly voice restrained Abraham from slaying his son Isaac (Genesis 22:11), who was Abraham's beloved son (Genesis 22:2). Some scholars thus think that the heavenly voice portrays Jesus as a sacrifice like Isaac. While this might be true in Mark, Matthew links the voice instead with Isaiah 42:1, by quoting it in such language at Matthew 12:18. If this is the case, the heavenly voice here confirms Jesus' mission as a suffering servant. In view of Isaiah's context, Jesus would thus be embracing the mission of Israel, again identifying with his people.

Although the allusion is clearer in Mark, some see also here an allusion to Psalm 2:7, widely used in a messianic context: "You are my Son." Thus Matthew would emphasize both the royal and suffering aspects of Jesus' calling. Many ancient rabbis viewed heavenly voices as a secondary replacement for the greater prophetic gift of old; but in this narrative, it supplements and confirms the prophetic message of John.

---

# INTERPRETING THE SCRIPTURE

### John's Lifestyle

John's message of repentance in light of the coming kingdom challenges us, especially if we are more attached to our present comforts than to hopes for a future vision of justice and peace. Yet John's lifestyle may challenge many of us even more than his message does, especially if we live in affluent cultures.

John lives in the wilderness, away from all the conveniences of society. (One wonders how most people in the modern West would do without electrical appliances, such as microwaves or televisions. I try to convince my son that not only prophets but all humanity lived without video games until our generation.) John wears just one pair of rough clothing associated only with the poor. His diet is likewise spartan, since he is limited to the sort of food easily available in the wilderness. Others ate locusts (the Dead Sea Scrolls even supply instructions for how to prepare them) but not as their entire diet.

John's whole life was devoted to the mission God had given him, a mission to wake up the rest of God's people to God's call for them. What are the values we live for? How important is God's kingdom to us? What sacrifices can we consider making to work for God's peace, justice, and truth in this world?

*John's Message*

John's baptism is meant to symbolize turning from sin, to prepare for the greater baptism in the Spirit given by Jesus. That is, the baptism is connected with a specific message, involving two elements: turning from sin and the coming of God's reign and its agent.

The message of turning from sin challenges the satisfaction of those who assumed themselves already children of the kingdom. Sometimes we look down on those who depended on their heritage in Abraham (3:9), but Christians often do the same sort of thing. The saying that "God has no grandchildren" is meant to remind us that merely growing up in a Christian family or attending church is not the same as genuinely submitting our lives to God's plan for us.

True repentance involves fruit. Since Martin Luther, Protestants have understood that it is what Jesus did for us rather than our own works that saves us. At the same time, most Protestant traditions (including Wesleyan, Calvinist, Anabaptist, and other traditions) also affirm that people who truly stake their eternal destiny on Christ will also truly *behave* as if they believe it. That is, faith is not simply a passing assent to a proposition; it is a relationship with God. It does not mean that we are perfect; it does mean that we recognize that Christ is our rightful king, lord, guide, and master.

A life truly devoted to God, such as those of John and Jesus, can be a stronger witness for Christ than many who accept the faith because they think it merely useful. When I was an atheist, I thought that if there was one religion that could not be true, it had to be Christianity. This was because most people in the U.S. claimed to be Christians, but I could not tell by their lives (with a few noteworthy exceptions) that they really believed in the teaching of Christ. If Christians did not take their gospel seriously, why should I? Happily, I discovered that I was wrong about Christ and also about many Christians. But the challenge of John's lifestyle and message remains important.

John does not announce merely repentance; he also announces the coming "reign of heaven," a Jewish expression for the reign of God. Many Jewish people expected that kingdom joyfully, recognizing that God would deliver Israel from oppression, fulfill promises, and establish peace and righteousness. Yet John warns that we must be ready for that kingdom, for people who do not live lives of peace and righteousness now do not really live like they want that kingdom in the future. John also announces the coming king who will establish that reign: the baptizer in the Spirit and fire. "I do not deserve even to be his servant" John essentially says (3:11). Our greatest task is to bear witness to one greater than ourselves.

*Jesus' Mission and Baptisms*

The heavenly voice apparently identifies Jesus' mission with that of Isaiah's suffering servant (Isaiah 42:1) in Matthew 3:17. This means that Jesus must identify with Israel, who is Isaiah's servant (Isaiah 41:8; 44:1-2, 21; 45:4; 48:20; 49:3). Thus Jesus must fulfill the mission where Israel had failed it (see Isaiah 42:19), and ultimately suffer on behalf of Israel (see Isaiah 49:5-7; 52:13–53:12).

Christians often wonder why Jesus would receive John's baptism, a baptism of repentance. (This is not the sort of story early Christians would have made up!) But if Jesus identified with us in our humanity, embracing even our human mortality and death, is it so surprising that he would also identify with us in this movement of baptism? Jesus' baptism identifies him with John's renewal movement for Israel, and ultimately with humanity. John's water baptism prefigures Jesus' Spirit baptism. By sharing our experience of baptism, Jesus prefigured his sharing our experience of suffering and death on the cross. As Jesus received the Spirit at his baptism, he is the one clearly qualified to baptize others in the Spirit.

Just as Christ identified with us in baptism, our baptism identifies us with Christ and what he was done for us. In Paul's language, we died with Christ to sin and selfishness (Romans 6:3-11); through faith in what Jesus did for us, and empowered by the Spirit, we can live a new life. This emphasis on transformation is appropriate, because baptism signifies repentance.

By the end of Matthew's Gospel, John's baptism involving repentance in light of God's reign is transformed. Now baptism is distinctly Christian, "in the name of the Father, Son, and Holy Spirit," because we understood that the king in God's kingdom includes Jesus, God's Son. No longer does he have only authority on earth to forgive sins (9:6); now he has all authority in heaven and on earth (28:18).

What about the other part of Jesus' mission that John announced—a baptism in fire? It is not possible to make the world completely righteous without addressing the unrighteousness that already pervades it. Nevertheless, well before that time, Jesus gives the Spirit to transform his followers so we can work for God's righteous purposes in the present world. If we have received the baptism that John wanted (3:14), it is so that, having been made ready for God's kingdom, we can join John in working to make the world more ready for God's kingdom.

---

## SHARING THE SCRIPTURE

### Preparing Our Hearts

Meditate on this week's devotional reading, found in Acts 8:26-38. Here we read the story of Philip, one of the seven chosen to serve the Hellenist widows (Acts 6:5), as he explains the words of Isaiah to a court official from Ethiopia who is returning home after worshiping in Jerusalem. The Ethiopian requested baptism, and Philip obliged. Baptism prompted the new convert to rejoice. Ponder what baptism means to you and how it has affected your life and identity.

Pray that you and the adult learners will give thanks for the opportunity to hear the good news and to put on Christ in the act of baptism.

### Preparing Our Minds

Study the background from Matthew 3 and lesson Scripture, verses 1-6, 11-17. Think about the kinds of actions that reveal who we are.

Write on newsprint:
- ❑ questions under "Explore the Act and Meaning of Jesus' Baptism."
- ❑ information for next week's lesson, found under "Continue the Journey."
- ❑ activities for further spiritual growth in "Continue the Journey."

Locate several Bible commentaries for use during the session.

### LEADING THE CLASS

#### (1) Gather to Learn

❖ Welcome the class members and introduce any guests.

❖ Pray that those who have gathered will prepare their hearts to be challenged by the Word of God.

❖ Read this joke that has circulated on the Internet: **A cop pulls over a driver. Instead of approaching the vehicle and asking for the license and registration, he calls for backup. When the backup arrives,** the police surround the car with their guns drawn and order the driver out of the car and onto the ground. As he's being hand-cuffed, the driver asks, "Why are you handcuffing me and pointing guns at me?"

"Because you're a carjacker!"

"No, I'm not! This is my car," replied the driver.

"Really?"

"Yes! Why would you think I'm a car-jacker?"

"Remember when you tailgated that old lady while flashing your high beams? Then you cut off a school bus and shot across three lanes without signaling? Then you nearly rear-ended the Volkswagen because they wouldn't speed up?"

"Uh. . . ."

"Well, I saw the Jesus bumper stickers and the Jesus fish on your car and said to myself, 'No true Christian would drive like that—he must have been carjacked!'"

❖ Point out that while we may laugh at this joke, its message about how others perceive our identity based on our actions is very serious. Invite several volunteers to tell stories (without identifying the people involved) where the actions of someone who claimed to be Christian did not live up to expectations.

❖ Read aloud today's focus statement: **Our actions reveal who we are. What actions disclose our identity? Jesus' willingness to be baptized and God's declaration confirming Jesus' identity provides us an example of how to relate to God.**

*(2) Explore the Act and
Meaning of Jesus' Baptism*

❖ Distribute paper and pencil. Read aloud Matthew 3:1-6, 11-17. Invite the students to either write down words that seem significant to them, or sketch a picture of the scene this passage describes. (They need not be artists.)

❖ Encourage them to talk about the words or scenes they chose by answering

questions such as these, which you may want to post on newsprint.

   (1) **Why are these words or scenes significant to you?**

   (2) **What do these words or scenes reveal about John the Baptizer, Jesus, or the kingdom of God?**

   (3) **Had you seen and heard John, would his message have pulled you closer to Christ or pushed you away? Explain the reason for your answer.**

❖ **Option:** One of the words some adults may have selected is "repent." Read or retell "John's Message" in Interpreting the Scripture to clarify the meaning of repentance and its relationship to baptism.

❖ Challenge the class members to raise questions about this passage. List these questions on newsprint.

❖ Divide the class into groups and distribute at least one Bible commentary to each group. Encourage the students to research answers to their own questions. To cover as much ground as possible, you may want to assign a particular question to each group. If you have only one commentary, ask one individual to read aloud the portion related to this passage. Suggest that adults who have study Bibles check the footnotes for clues to answers.

❖ Provide time for the groups to report their findings to the class.

❖ Use information from Understanding the Scripture, as appropriate, to fill in answers.

*(3) Find Meaning in Church Practices, Such as
Baptism, that Symbolize a Relationship
with Christ*

❖ Read or retell "Jesus' Mission and Baptisms" in Interpreting the Scripture to help the students understand how baptisms related to Jesus' ministry.

❖ Invite the students to recall a baptism they recently witnessed. What happened? How were they reminded of their own baptism and the vows they made or that were made on their behalf and professed during their confirmation?

❖ Distribute your denominational hymnal, if it includes at least one baptismal ritual. If several rituals are printed, such as in *The United Methodist Hymnal*, assign small groups to each review one of the rituals. Direct them to answer this question: **What does this ritual say to me about what my church believes about baptism?**

❖ Provide time for the groups to report back.

*(4) Begin or Continue a Relationship with Christ and Grow in that Relationship through a Visible or Vocal Confession of Faith*

❖ Invite the participants to read silently the confessions (or affirmations) of faith found in their hymnals.

❖ Distribute paper and pencils, if you have not already done so. Encourage the adults to write their own confessions of faith. (Some may prefer to focus on one in the hymnal and claim that as their own.)

❖ Solicit volunteers to read their confessions to the class.

❖ Note any common themes, as for example, a confession that Jesus is the Son of God.

❖ Ask the students to continue thinking how this vocal confession of faith may be expanded by some demonstration of faith. Encourage them to list actions they could take this week that will show forth their true identities as followers of Christ and children of God.

❖ Wrap up this portion of the lesson by challenging the adults to take action and to find at least one opportunity to share a portion of their confession of faith with someone else.

*(5) Continue the Journey*

❖ Pray that those who are present will talk and act in ways that demonstrate to others that they are followers of Christ.

❖ Read aloud this preparation for next week's lesson. You may also want to post it on newsprint for the students to copy.

■ **Title: Strengthened in Temptation**
■ **Background Scripture: Matthew 4:1-11**
■ **Lesson Scripture: Matthew 4:1-11**
■ **Focus of the Lesson: All of us face temptation in life. How can we overcome it? Jesus' experience of overcoming temptation set an example for us.**

❖ Challenge the students to complete one or more of these activities for further spiritual growth, which you will write on newsprint for the students to copy.

**(1) Write the word CHANGE, one letter at a time, vertically down a sheet of paper. Next to each letter write a word or phrase beginning with that letter that describes the difference the gospel has made in your life.**

**(2) Offer to support a family that has had a child baptized so as to help this child grow into the person God has called him or her to be.**

**(3) Spend time in meditation, focusing on areas of your life where you need to repent. Pray that God will empower you to turn around and make the changes necessary to live more faithfully as a disciple.**

❖ Sing or read aloud "When Jesus Came to Jordan."

❖ Conclude today's session by leading the class in this benediction, adapted from Matthew 16:16: **Go forth now to love and serve the Messiah, the Son of the living God.**

## UNIT 2: EVIDENCES OF JESUS AS MESSIAH
# STRENGTHENED IN TEMPTATION

---

### PREVIEWING THE LESSON

**Lesson Scripture:** Matthew 4:1-11
**Background Scripture:** Matthew 4:1-11
**Key Verse:** Matthew 4:10

#### Focus of the Lesson:

All of us face temptation in life. How can we overcome it? Jesus' experience of overcoming temptation set an example for us.

#### Goals for the Learners:

(1) to examine the event and meaning of Jesus' temptation in the wilderness.
(2) to identify situations that tempt them so as to be alert and ready to withstand temptation.
(3) to seek Jesus' help in dealing with temptation.

#### Supplies:

Bibles, newsprint and marker, paper and pencils, hymnals

---

### READING THE SCRIPTURE

NRSV
Matthew 4:1-11

¹Then Jesus was led up by the Spirit into the wilderness to be tempted by the devil. ²He fasted forty days and forty nights, and afterwards he was famished. ³The tempter came and said to him, "If you are the Son of God, command these stones to become loaves of bread." ⁴But he answered, "It is written,

'One does not live by bread alone,
 but by every word that comes from the mouth of God.'"

NIV
Matthew 4:1-11

¹Then Jesus was led by the Spirit into the desert to be tempted by the devil. ²After fasting forty days and forty nights, he was hungry. ³The tempter came to him and said, "If you are the Son of God, tell these stones to become bread."

⁴Jesus answered, "It is written: 'Man does not live on bread alone, but on every word that comes from the mouth of God.'"

⁵Then the devil took him to the holy city

[5]Then the devil took him to the holy city and placed him on the pinnacle of the temple, [6]saying to him, "If you are the Son of God, throw yourself down; for it is written,

> 'He will command his angels
>> concerning you,'
> and 'On their hands they will
>> bear you up,
> so that you will not dash your foot
>> against a stone.'"

[7]Jesus said to him, "Again it is written, 'Do not put the Lord your God to the test.'"

[8]Again, the devil took him to a very high mountain and showed him all the kingdoms of the world and their splendor; [9]and he said to him, "All these I will give you, if you will fall down and worship me." [10]Jesus said to him, "Away with you, Satan! for it is written,

> 'Worship the Lord your God,
>> and serve only him.'"

[11]Then the devil left him, and suddenly angels came and waited on him.

and had him stand on the highest point of the temple. [6]"If you are the Son of God," he said, "throw yourself down. For it is written:

> "'He will command his angels
>> concerning you,
> and they will lift you up in their hands,
> so that you will not strike your foot
>> against a stone.'"

[7]Jesus answered him, "It is also written: 'Do not put the Lord your God to the test.'"

[8]Again, the devil took him to a very high mountain and showed him all the kingdoms of the world and their splendor. [9]"All this I will give you," he said, "if you will bow down and worship me."

[10]Jesus said to him, "Away from me, Satan! For it is written: 'Worship the Lord your God, and serve him only.'"

[11]Then the devil left him, and angels came and attended him.

---

## UNDERSTANDING THE SCRIPTURE

**Matthew 4:1-2.** Mark, whose narrative is full of action, reports that the Spirit "drove" Jesus out into the wilderness (Mark 1:12); Matthew (4:1) and Luke (4:1), perhaps evoking God leading Israel in the wilderness, report the Spirit "leading" Jesus there. As Israel was tested forty years in the wilderness, so is Jesus tested forty days. Jesus thus identifies with his people (see earlier comments on 2:15—December 27; 3:15—January 3).

Through his narrative of these temptations, Matthew again links Jesus with Israel. He also teaches us about who Jesus really is (not a magician or a political figure, but a deliverer like Moses and especially God's own Son). Yet Matthew also makes Jesus a model for us of victory over temptation through God's Word. Believers are to pray that God will protect us in the face of testing

(6:13; 26:41). (The Greek term translated "tempt" here can mean "test." When God does it, the goal is testing, but when applied to the devil, who wants people to fail the test, "tempt" is appropriate.)

Whereas John had a restricted diet in the wilderness, Jesus eats even less. Jesus' sacrifice here evokes Moses, who fasted forty days and nights before delivering God's law from Mount Sinai. (Some scholars compare Jesus' teaching from the mountain in 5:1 with Moses giving the law from the mountain.)

**Matthew 4:3-4.** The tempter plays on Jesus' hunger to get him to use God's power for his own ends. Here and in 4:6, the tempter's words should be translated, "*since* you are God's Son." The devil can hardly deny Jesus' dramatic call in 3:17; but he can reinterpret it in different categories.

The people known for turning one substance into another were magicians.

Jesus will not, however, work magic, although he later multiplies food for others (14:19-21; 15:36-38). Here he simply depends on his Father to provide (which God does in 4:11). Each time the tempter seeks to redefine Jesus' mission as God's Son, Jesus returns to the foundation for knowing God's will: Scripture.

Just as Jesus identifies with Israel's testing in the wilderness, he quotes three commands from one section in Deuteronomy, all originally given to Israel in the wilderness. Israel failed these tests, but Jesus as Israel's champion succeeds on his people's behalf.

Jesus first quotes from Deuteronomy 8:3: God fed Israel with manna, so they would learn to depend on his word rather than on mere bread. The context of the verse is this: God led Israel forty years in the wilderness to test them (Deuteronomy 8:2), disciplining them like a parent disciplines a child (8:5). If God provided food for his "child" Israel, how much more would Jesus trust God's provision? (Interestingly, the context of some other texts Matthew has recently applied to Jesus also dealt with Israel's role as God's child: most obviously Hosea 11:1 in Matthew 2:15, but also in Jeremiah 31:20, shortly after 31:15, which is quoted in Matthew 2:18. Matthew probably assumes that his audience knows the Bible well enough to remember the contexts of verses he quotes.)

**Matthew 4:5-7.** Here the devil responds to Jesus' use of Scripture by quoting Scripture himself. He quotes Psalm 91:11-12 as a promise to the righteous, but he misapplies it. The context in Psalm 91:10 offers assurance that the angels will catch a person who *falls*—not one who deliberately throws himself or herself down to test the promise. Ironically, after Jesus resists the testing, God's angels *will* help him (Matthew 4:11).

Jesus responds by quoting Deuteronomy 6:16, close in context to his first quotation. This passage warns against testing God as Israel tested God at Massah, that is, where Israel demanded water as if God would not provide (Exodus 17:1-7). A psalm near the one that the devil quotes also mentions Massah as the place where Israel tested God although they had seen his work and should have known better (Psalm 95:8-9). (Deuteronomy 6:16 mentions testing God about God's provision, just like the context of Jesus' first quotation, in Deuteronomy 8:2-3, deals with God testing Israel over provision.)

**Matthew 4:8-10.** The devil here offers Jesus the promised kingdom without the cross—in return for worshiping him. Scripture actually said that God was sovereign over who ruled the kingdoms of the world (Daniel 4:32), but most Jewish people also believed that hostile angels governed Gentile nations (compare Daniel 10:20), and that Satan in some respect ruled this age because of human sin. Is Jesus called to rule the world? Other would-be messiahs sought political power without the cross, and that is a path that the devil offers Jesus.

Jesus' "Away with you, Satan," is significant, because Matthew later reports similar words in 16:23, where Jesus tells Peter, "Get behind me, Satan!" Why would Jesus apply similar words to his star pupil? Because Peter has just offered Jesus the kingdom without the cross—a false understanding of Jesus' messiahship (16:21-22).

At the cross, religious people likewise challenged him: if he was really God's Son, let him come down from the cross (27:39-43). (They echo the language of a widely circulated Jewish book called the Wisdom of Solomon [2:16-20], where the wicked similarly mock the righteous.) "He saved others," they mock, "he cannot save himself" (Matthew 27:42). Ironically, they spoke truth: he could not save both. Jesus knew his mission; as a song of Michael Card puts it, had people not nailed Jesus to the cross, his love would have held him there.

Jesus responds by quoting Deuteronomy 6:13, in the immediate context of his preceding quotation. The passage goes on to warn against idolatry more explicitly, the gods of the surrounding peoples (Deuteronomy 6:14) whose dominion the devil here offers. While Deuteronomy 6:13 enjoins "fearing" and "serving" only God, Jesus' quotation changes one verb, mixing in another familiar phrase from the Greek translation of Deuteronomy that reinforces the point: "worship" and "serve" appear together in Deuteronomy in repeated warnings against idolatry (Deuteronomy 4:19; 8:19; 11:16; 17:3; 29:26; 30:17).

**Matthew 4:11.** Jesus did not compromise with the devil to procure food or to procure angelic help. Now, victorious in testing, Jesus finally does receive angelic help and sustenance.

---

## INTERPRETING THE SCRIPTURE

### Callings Are Tested

The purpose of the Spirit leading Jesus into the wilderness is "testing." If Jesus did not escape it, we certainly cannot hope to evade it. Immediately after Jesus receives God's call (or a confirmation of it) in 3:17, the devil sets about to test that call.

Imagine that you have started teaching Sunday school, and you face opposition. Sometimes this could mean that God has a different ministry for you, but more often it means that you are being tested. Simply because things go wrong after we try to do something for God does not mean that God is not leading us! Far from it: everyone in the Bible (or at least everyone in the Bible that we know very much about) faced testing after God called them or gave them a promise.

Think of the years Abraham and Sarah waited for the promise. (Even at the end, though God had called Abraham "father of many nations," he has only one son with him.) Joseph's brothers bowed down to him, just as the dream said—but only years after he had suffered slavery and unjust imprisonment. After Samuel anointed David as king, David still faced years of pursuit by Saul before God's promise was fulfilled.

Some people in the Bible became terribly discouraged with their testing. Elijah, Job, and Jeremiah each even asked God to let them die, though they must have all been happy afterward that God did not grant their request. When Elijah learned that even fire from heaven had not convinced Jezebel, he wanted to give up; but his mission eventually succeeded.

Sometimes we put the people in the Bible on a pedestal, as if they were so different from us and had superior powers to endure their trials. "Elijah was a human being like us," James 5:17 says, yet God answered his prayers. Abraham and Sarah, models of faith for us, each laughed at God's promise (Genesis 17:17; 18:12) and once tried to fulfill it through Hagar. Joseph was still interpreting dreams even in prison (Genesis 40:12-19), but later, in good times, temporarily forgot the dream God had given him (Genesis 41:51). Moses temporarily doubted God's power and calling (Exodus 5:22-23). Some face even death before vindication (Hebrews 11:35–12:3). Many of those in the Bible lamented their testing and did not understand it; yet they discovered God's faithfulness in the end. That is one of testing's greatest purposes: it reminds us that God is ultimately in control, and we can trust God.

### Twisting the Calling

The devil could hardly convince Jesus that no heavenly voice had recently declared him God's Son (3:17). What he could do was to try to repackage God's call according to human categories. Magicians or those with special powers might claim to be children of deities; so the tempter suggests that Jesus act like a magician. Messianic figures sought to establish kingdoms; the tempter offers to give Jesus the divinely promised kingdom—without the cross. Yet Jesus understood that the true nature of his messiahship and kingdom involved the cross.

Sometimes temptation may involve denying God's Word (Genesis 3:1, 4). At other times, however, temptation may sneak in through the back door, where we least expect it, even through our religious or spiritual commitments. In this narrative, while the devil's strategy might question Jesus' sonship, his main strategy appears to be to seek to redefine it in terms more understandable to his contemporaries (even to Peter, later in the Gospel). Others sought power through magic, gathering followings, or political and military means (like some would-be messiahs of Jesus' era). Although we may seek power for good ends, we must not forget how it may tempt us, nor acquire it through immoral means. Indeed, once people have power, they often exploit it over others.

Like Jesus, our calling can be redefined. We can identify serving God with simply whatever that looks like in our church tradition, instead of considering the most biblical or effective ways to accomplish God's purposes in the world. We can also be tempted by power, initially with honorable motives, but then exploit our roles in selfish ways. Although we may need to make use of political structures, some Christians even exploit politics in local churches or denominations in ways that abuse others. Others put "spins" on information that distorts or slanders their opponents' purposes. All of these approaches stray far from Jesus' example, who openly confronted injustice yet also faced the cross, trusting his Father to vindicate him.

### Jesus Uses the Bible

Whatever the devil's test, Jesus always answers from Scripture, which outlines the true calling for a child of God. Jesus simply quotes Scripture, refusing to debate whether or not he will observe it. For Jesus, to know what Scripture says on a subject settles the matter; Jesus' obedience to Scripture is not even open to question.

Unfortunately, as any seminary professor can testify, the level of biblical literacy in the U.S. is declining. Some incoming students know little Scripture, yet it is difficult to use Scripture the way Jesus did unless we know it, in context. Knowing Scripture in context comes not just from memorizing Bible verses, as helpful as that approach may be. Those verses all belong to larger contexts, and may mean something quite different from what those quoting them assume. When as a young Christian I began reading forty chapters a day, so I could read through the entire New Testament every week (or through the Bible every month), within weeks I began to grasp the way each book of the Bible fit together. I also realized that I had been acting as if the Bible contained a lot of blank space between the "important" verses I had been quoting, and that most of my key verses did not mean exactly what I had been using them for!

Note that the devil also quotes Scripture, but out of context. Many people use the Bible these days, but we must make sure that we use it the right way, the way that is in keeping with the larger pattern of God's purposes in Scripture. Jesus knew the Bible well enough to tell the difference; we should do likewise.

### The Kingdom without the Cross

The devil, Jesus' disciple Peter, and, later, religious people at the cross all in a sense offered Jesus the kingdom without the cross. Clearly Jesus would have preferred to avoid the cross had it been possible; he prayed that he might escape it. Yet Jesus would not compromise his Father's mission and purpose for him, even in the face of death (26:39, 42).

Jesus' temptation is often our temptation as well. When Peter doubted that Jesus as the Messiah could be crucified, Jesus not only put Peter in his place but he also explained what it meant to be followers of a suffering Messiah: "If any want to become my followers, let them deny themselves and take up their cross and follow me. For those who want to save their life will lose it, and those who lose their life for my sake will find it" (16:24-25).

## SHARING THE SCRIPTURE

### Preparing Our Hearts

Meditate on this week's devotional reading, found in Hebrews 2:10-18. In verse 18 we learn that Jesus was tested and because of that testing he is able to help us. The writer of Hebrews also tells us that Jesus was able to destroy the dealer of death—the devil. Think about the kinds of tests you have faced in your own life. How have you responded to these temptations? What help do you need to overcome a current temptation?

Pray that you and the adult learners will be alert to tests and prepared to face them by the grace and power of God.

### Preparing Our Minds

Study the background and lesson scripture, both from Matthew 4:1-11. Ask yourself: recognizing that we all face temptation in life, how can we overcome it?

Write on newsprint:
- ❑ quotations found under "Identify Situations that Tempt the Learners So as to Be Alert and Ready to Withstand Temptation."
- ❑ information for next week's lesson, found under "Continue the Journey."
- ❑ activities for further spiritual growth in "Continue the Journey."

Select portions of Understanding the Scripture that you will highlight in the section entitled "Examine the Event and Meaning of Jesus' Temptation in the Wilderness."

### LEADING THE CLASS

#### (1) Gather to Learn

❖ Welcome the class members and introduce any guests.

❖ Pray that the participants will be strengthened in their resolve as they face temptations that beset all people.

❖ Read aloud this story that an anonymous author posted on the "He Invites" website: **Crack cocaine cost me my jobs, my money, and almost my life. My wife nearly left me. I went to group meetings, the hospital, and counselors and only learned more about how to deceive people. I tried to quit but couldn't. The thing about crack cocaine use is that it just does not seem to let you quit. You may go along doing fine when all of a sudden, "bam" you've got to have it. Nothing else matters. Arguing all the way, I finally went to church and learned that I could not trust in my self, but I could trust in God. I DID. The power of Jesus Christ has delivered me from crack cocaine, alcohol, pornography and even chewing tobacco. When the temptation comes, I just turn it over to Jesus. "The Lord knows how to deliver the godly out of temptations" (2 Peter 2:9, NKJV).**

❖ Encourage the adults to respond to

this story by telling stories they know of overcoming temptation, without mentioning the names of those involved unless they want to make a story of their own public.

❖ Read aloud today's focus statement: **All of us face temptation in life. How can we overcome it? Jesus' experience of overcoming temptation set an example for us.**

*(2) Examine the Event and Meaning of Jesus' Temptation in the Wilderness*

❖ Choose three volunteers to read the parts of the narrator, the devil, and Jesus from Matthew 4:1-11.

❖ Invite the class to identity the temptations that Satan threw at Jesus. Use information from the entire Understanding the Scripture portion that you have selected to explain how the devil tried to get Jesus to do his bidding.

❖ Note that the devil states "if you are the Son of God" (4:3, 6), apparently in an attempt to make Jesus reassess his calling and identity. Read "Twisting the Calling" in Interpreting the Scripture.

❖ Discuss these questions:

**(1) How did Satan try to "repackage" God's call on Jesus' life so that he would seem more like other people?**

**(2) How did Jesus assert his identity as God's Son?**

**(3) What lessons can we learn from the way Jesus handled temptation?**

❖ Direct the class members to look at 1 John 2:15-16. Compare these verses to Matthew 4:1-11. Ask: **How do they summarize the temptations that Jesus faced?**

*(3) Identify Situations that Tempt the Learners So as to Be Alert and Ready to Withstand Temptation*

❖ Encourage the adults to define the word "temptation." List their ideas on newsprint. (Words such as *enticement, seduc-*

*tion, allurement* should be included on the list.)

❖ Post some or all of these quotations related to temptation on newsprint. Invite volunteers to read them aloud.

■ **It is easier to stay out than to get out.** (Mark Twain, 1835-1910)

■ **He who has no mind to trade with the devil should keep from his shop.** (Robert South, 1634-1716)

■ **Our response to temptation is an accurate barometer of our love for God.** (Erwin W. Lutzer, 1941- )

■ **Pheasants are fools if they invite the hawk to dinner.** (proverb)

■ **Flee temptation and don't leave a forwarding address.** (anonymous)

■ **Temptation is the devil looking through the keyhole; yielding is opening the door and inviting him in.** (Billy Sunday, 1862–1935)

❖ Allow a few moments for the students to comment on ways that any of these quotations seem to be "on target" for them.

❖ Distribute paper and pencils. Challenge the students to meditate silently on these questions, which you will read aloud:

**(1) In what kinds of circumstances do I find myself tempted?**

**(2) How do I handle temptation under those circumstances?**

Some students may choose to write a response. Make clear that no one will be asked to reveal this confidential information.

❖ Conclude by pointing out that when we are aware of tempting situations we can be alert and ready to avoid or withstand them.

*(4) Seek Jesus' Help in Dealing with Temptation*

❖ Read "Jesus Uses the Bible" in Interpreting the Scripture.

❖ Point out that both Jesus and Satan quoted Scripture, but Satan used Scripture out of context. Note that we need to know our Bibles well in order to be sure that, like Jesus, we understand God's will and know how to withstand temptation.

❖ Discuss this question: **If we are to follow Jesus' model of relying on Scripture to turn aside from temptation, what does our congregation need to do to help all of our members become more biblically literate?**

❖ Make a list of opportunities that the church currently offers to help people become more familiar with the Bible. Be sure to include Sunday school, weekday Bible classes, short-term studies, retreats, DISCIPLE classes, and any other biblically based groups you sponsor.

❖ Talk about how the class might encourage others to become part of such groups as a way of preparing them for a life of discipleship. If such opportunities are not available, discuss how the class might inaugurate other Bible study activities, in addition to Sunday school. Wrap up by asking volunteers to work on such a project.

*(5) Continue the Journey*

❖ Pray that today's participants will look to Jesus when they face temptation.

❖ Read aloud this preparation for next week's lesson. You may also want to post it on newsprint for the students to copy.

■ **Title: Demonstrated in Acts of Healing**
■ **Background Scripture: Matthew 9:27-34; 11:2-6**
■ **Lesson Scripture: Matthew 9:27-34; 11:2-6**

■ **Focus of the Lesson: Although we live in a world where many people want to be able to explain all events scientifically, many mysteries remain. Who can we turn to when we are confronted by the inexplicable? Jesus performed healing miracles that led people to place their faith in him.**

❖ Challenge the students to complete one or more of these activities for further spiritual growth, which you will write on newsprint for the students to copy.

(1) **Compare and contrast the temptation stories of Jesus found in Mark 1:12-13 and Luke 4:1-13 with the account you read from Matthew 4:1-11.**

(2) **Recall that Jesus is able to rebuff the devil's temptations by quoting Scripture. Honestly assess your knowledge of Scripture. Challenge yourself to read and learn passages that are important to you.**

(3) **Read *The Temptations of Jesus* by Howard Thurman, noted author, educator, civil rights leader, and former dean of the chapel of Howard University.**

❖ Sing or read aloud "Lord, Who Throughout These Forty Days."

❖ Conclude today's session by leading the class in this benediction, adapted from Matthew 16:16: **Go forth now to love and serve the Messiah, the Son of the living God.**

## UNIT 2: EVIDENCES OF JESUS AS MESSIAH
# DEMONSTRATED IN ACTS OF HEALING

---

### PREVIEWING THE LESSON

**Lesson Scripture:** Matthew 9:27-34; 11:2-6
**Background Scripture:** Matthew 9:27-34; 11:2-6
**Key Verse:** Matthew 11:5

#### Focus of the Lesson:
Although we live in a world where many people want to be able to explain all events scientifically, many mysteries remain. Who can we turn to when we are confronted by the inexplicable? Jesus performed healing miracles that led people to place their faith in him.

#### Goals for the Learners:
(1) to explore how Jesus' healing acts were signs revealing his identity.
(2) to relate instances of healing in their lives.
(3) to recognize and give thanks to God who does marvelous things that we may not understand.

#### Supplies:
Bibles, newsprint and marker, paper and pencils, hymnals

---

### READING THE SCRIPTURE

NRSV
Matthew 9:27-34

27As Jesus went on from there, two blind men followed him, crying loudly, "Have mercy on us, Son of David!" 28When he entered the house, the blind men came to him; and Jesus said to them, "Do you believe that I am able to do this?" They said to him, "Yes, Lord." 29Then he touched their eyes and said, "According to your faith let it be

NIV
Matthew 9:27-34

27As Jesus went on from there, two blind men followed him, calling out, "Have mercy on us, Son of David!"

28When he had gone indoors, the blind men came to him, and he asked them, "Do you believe that I am able to do this?"

"Yes, Lord," they replied.

29Then he touched their eyes and said,

done to you." <sup></sup>³⁰And their eyes were opened. Then Jesus sternly ordered them, "See that no one knows of this." ³¹But they went away and spread the news about him throughout that district.

³²After they had gone away, a demoniac who was mute was brought to him. ³³And when the demon had been cast out, the one who had been mute spoke; and the crowds were amazed and said, "Never has anything like this been seen in Israel." ³⁴But the Pharisees said, "By the ruler of the demons he casts out the demons."

Matthew 11:2-6

²When John heard in prison what the Messiah was doing, he sent word by his disciples ³and said to him, "Are you the one who is to come, or are we to wait for another?" ⁴Jesus answered them, "Go and tell John what you hear and see: **⁵the blind receive their sight, the lame walk, the lepers are cleansed, the deaf hear, the dead are raised, and the poor have good news brought to them. ⁶And blessed is anyone who takes no offense at me."

"According to your faith will it be done to you"; ³⁰and their sight was restored. Jesus warned them sternly, "See that no one knows about this." ³¹But they went out and spread the news about him all over that region.

³²While they were going out, a man who was demon-possessed and could not talk was brought to Jesus. ³³And when the demon was driven out, the man who had been mute spoke. The crowd was amazed and said, "Nothing like this has ever been seen in Israel."

³⁴But the Pharisees said, "It is by the prince of demons that he drives out demons."

Matthew 11:2-6

²When John heard in prison what Christ was doing, he sent his disciples ³to ask him, "Are you the one who was to come, or should we expect someone else?"

⁴Jesus replied, "Go back and report to John what you hear and see: **⁵The blind receive sight, the lame walk, those who have leprosy are cured, the deaf hear, the dead are raised, and the good news is preached to the poor. ⁶Blessed is the man who does not fall away on account of me."

## UNDERSTANDING THE SCRIPTURE

**Matthew 9:27.** Mark reports only one blind man following Jesus with this cry (Mark 10:46-47). Perhaps Mark focuses only on the individual he knows, or perhaps Matthew, who omitted the healing of the blind man in Mark 8:23-25, compensates by adding another here.

More important is their cry: in faith, throwing themselves on Jesus' mercy, they recognize his identity as "Son of David," that is, the Messiah (see Matthew 1:1). Matthew reports them confessing Jesus' messiahship before Peter does (16:16). Desperate need sometimes generates radical faith.

**Matthew 9:28.** Although they had been crying after Jesus outside, they now followed him into the house. As in the parallel account in Matthew 20:30-31 (Mark 10:48) and in other miracle stories (Matthew 15:23-28; Mark 2:4-5; 5:27-28, 34; John 2:4-5), faith is persistent and refuses to be deterred. Jesus now asks whether they trust his ability to heal them, and they insist that they do (see further discussion at Matthew 9:29).

**Matthew 9:29.** Jesus touches their eyes to heal them; this fits a pattern of Jesus touching people who need help (for example, 8:15). (Jesus' touch can also communicate assurance; 17:7.) Although blindness was not unclean, elsewhere Jesus touches even those who are unclean, hence untouchable, according to the law (for example, 8:3; 9:18, 25). He is not ashamed to share with us in our brokenness, in order that he can make us whole (see 9:20-22 with Leviticus 15:25-27).

Jesus assures these blind men that they are being healed in response to their "faith." Healing is often connected with faith in the Gospels, including in Matthew (8:10, 13; 9:2, 22). Great faith can even move mountains (17:20; 21:21) and invite other miracles (21:22). Many people in the ancient world expected answers to their prayers based on their offerings or sometimes attempt to manipulate the deity by invoking special names and so forth. Jesus instead invites us to a relationship of trust in God's goodness and kindness (6:7-9).

**Matthew 9:30-31.** Jesus healed them. In Jesus' day, most healing claims involved individuals' prayers or, among Gentiles, temples of the healing figure Asclepius. We have relatively few reports of traveling wonderworkers from Jesus' day (many appear two centuries later), but there must have been some (compare Acts 8:9; 13:6; 19:13-14). Yet Jesus' miracles especially resemble those of some earlier biblical prophets. Some other Jewish "holy men" imitated Elijah's prayers for rain; some may have wished to follow his model of judgment (compare Luke 9:54); but Jesus followed Elijah's and Elisha's pattern of raising the dead, multiplying food, and so forth.

Ancients believed in many forms of supernatural activity, and attributed various sorts of feats to wonderworkers. What is striking is the fairly narrow range of most (albeit not all) of Jesus' miracles: most involve healing or deliverance. That is, most of Jesus' signs directly help people. These "signs" not only teach us about Jesus' power but also about his character.

Why does Jesus enjoin silence after performing the miracle? What scholars call the "messianic secret" is prominent in the Gospels and was noted already by the church fathers, though scholars differ on reasons for this mystery. One reason may be an attempt to limit the crowds (compare 13:2; Mark 1:45; 3:10; 5:24, 31). Another may be that, before Jesus' death and resurrection, people would be tempted to misinterpret his messianic mission (as they did in John 6:14-15). Nevertheless here, as in some other passages, those enjoined to silence could not keep the secret (compare Matthew 9:26; Mark 1:45). Even had they been able to restrain themselves, people who had seen them previously blind would surely demand to know how they now saw!

**Matthew 9:32-34.** Although most maladies Jesus cures in this Gospel are physical in nature, many also have spiritual causes that can be cured only spiritually. Jesus cares about the whole person and is ready to cure either kind of infirmity.

People responded to Jesus' cures in different ways. The crowds in 9:33 marveled at Jesus' extraordinary power. While they lack full understanding of his mission, their response is at least positive. By contrast, in 9:34 the Pharisees, representatives of the religious intelligentsia, attribute his undeniable power to demonic sources. This issue arises again in 12:24, where Jesus goes on to decisively refute it by pointing out that Satan would not assault Satan's own kingdom, as Jesus is doing (12:25-29).

**Matthew 11:2-3.** John's response to Jesus' miracles differs from that of the crowds or the Pharisees. Although John does not doubt that Jesus is a man of God who will tell him the truth when asked, John wonders whether he has been right in viewing Jesus as the Coming One (compare 3:15). After all, John announced that Jesus would baptize in the Spirit and fire (3:11), but he hears only of healings. John could not know that baptism in the Spirit awaited Jesus' resurrection, and baptism in fire a far distant future phase of his kingdom.

**Matthew 11:4-5.** Jesus' answer is, as often in the Gospels, a riddle, but one that John, who knows Scripture, should be able to solve. As in Matthew 4:4, 7, 10, Jesus' mission is defined by Scripture. Jesus here probably alludes to Isaiah 35:5-6, a passage involving Israel's restoration in the messianic era. This passage announced the healing of blind, deaf, lame, and mute. Similarly, Jesus alludes to Isaiah 61:1, which spoke of announcing good news to the oppressed in the time of the restoration. (Some scholars suggest that one text from the Dead Sea Scrolls also combines elements of these verses.) Thus, Jesus is in fact the one whom John prophesied. Even if some aspects of the restoration remain future, Jesus has already begun to fulfill other aspects in his earthly ministry.

**Matthew 11:6.** Jesus' riddle, together with Scripture and the miracles John's disciples have witnessed, are enough for John to recognize Jesus' identity. In turn, Jesus' identity is enough for John to rest assured that his own calling and life purpose, in preparing the Lord's way, have been fulfilled. John can have peace and rest secure in God's purposes.

The term translated "offended" here involves loss of faith, not mere dislike of something, and appears elsewhere in this strong sense. Others who misunderstood Jesus might stumble over him (13:57; 15:12); some might cause others to stumble (18:6-9; compare 16:23); and some would stumble over hardship (13:21; 24:10; 26:31). But John now can understand enough to remain firm.

## INTERPRETING THE SCRIPTURE

### Responses to Signs

People responded to signs of Jesus' identity in different ways. Blind men who had heard of his power hailed him "Son of David," and spread the news when he healed them. Likewise, seeing a mute man healed, the crowds were amazed. Some more prominent guardians of order attributed his signs to the devil. But only John, who would know the Scripture, fully understood the point of the signs: this healer was Israel's true king.

God provides signs to point us to Jesus, but God does not force our response. There are signs in our world today as well, but without faith we ignore them or dismiss them as coincidence.

### Miracles Today

We can thank God for the medical technology available in our day. Jesus multiplied fish and bread when no food was available but taught his disciples to trust God for food provided naturally (6:11; their next meal would in fact be the miraculous meal's leftovers, 14:20; 15:37). In the same way, God often works through natural means when they are available, and we can be grateful for this.

But God also is able to provide "signs"—not for the merely curious or hostile (16:1-4; 27:42) but also for those open to the truth. In many parts of the world today, the gospel is spreading through eyewitness claims of visible miracles, including healings of blindness and deafness. In the West, influenced by the radical Enlightenment, we are often skeptical of such reports, but Christians in other parts of the world, not dependent on our philosophic presuppositions, trust God to do what God did in the Bible.

We cannot explain why God heals some people and not others, any more than we can explain why God delivered Peter and not James (Acts 12:2-11). This is not due to God's lack of love for one person, since all of us ultimately die and all of us ultimately have hope of the resurrection. But we should not doubt that the one who designed us to begin with also is able to restore us and use this restoration to help others.

Western culture is even more uncomfortable with reports of demons and deliverance from them. Many cultures, however, do not share this reticence. Anthropologists objectively studying a wide range of societies find "spirit-possession" in a majority of them (though sometimes understood in various ways, including by anthropologists themselves). (One study found belief in spirit possession in 74 percent out of nearly 500 societies surveyed, most describing similar phenomena.) If we can believe in God and angels, why not also in hostile spirits? Some of course focus too much on spirits and find them everywhere. The central point is not evil spirits but trusting Jesus' power to deliver from them.

## Some Principles of Faith

Sometimes we struggle to have faith. Sometimes in the West this is because of our culture's long-term philosophic assumptions (though these are now waning in light of postmodern ways of thinking). Sometimes this is because we have so much already that we neglect learning to depend on the God who provides these things. But often it is also because we misunderstand what faith involves, thinking that we must have faith in our faith rather than in God!

What did faith involve in the Gospels? Faith did not mean disrespecting the Lord's prerogative to grant the request (Matthew 8:2). It did sometimes involve such desperation that one would do whatever necessary to get to Jesus (9:20-21; Mark 2:4-5). Godly faith involves not so much believing that our faith is great but believing in the great power and faithfulness of the One to whom we pray. Faith also means refusing to be

deterred; although God does have a right to refuse a request that is not for the best, sometimes obstacles are simply invitations to stronger faith. Either way, we continue to grow in trust, because the object of our faith is not ourselves, nor our request, but God. Moreover, God heeds a mustard seed of faith (Matthew 17:20). Initial faith need not be perfect for God to respond (compare Mark 9:24-27; Acts 12:5, 12-15). Nevertheless, we should embrace the opportunities presented by our smaller tests of faith so we will be ready for the larger ones.

Also, although many problems in the world are physical, the roots of many problems are also spiritual, as Jesus recognized. Some spiritual problems may be demonic; others may stem from the influence of sin in our lives or in society's structures. We cannot reduce everything to the same cause (physical, spiritual, relational, and so on). Whatever the specific case, it is important to recognize and deal with spiritual issues.

Thus Jacob struggled with an angel all night before facing his angry brother Esau (Genesis 32:22-32). When his attendant feared an army, Elisha helped him perceive heaven's armies (2 Kings 6:15-17). Others also recognized that the larger battle was spiritual (Daniel 10:18-20; Ephesians 6:12). We must often face our obstacles in prayer first. In some cases, spiritual battles may even involve spiritual powers like those that Jesus addressed.

## John's Doubts and Jesus' Assurance

Most people in the Bible, like us, sometimes had struggles to understand God's ways and to trust God, despite displays of God's power and mercy on other occasions. Jesus was healing the sick; but God's servant John was about to die in prison, and he found himself questioning whether he had fully understood God's mission. As it turned out, John's proclamation was correct; it was merely incomplete. Even the best teaching or prophecy cannot make us understand everything (compare 1 Corinthians 13:9).

God had already implied land and descendants for Abram (Genesis 12:1-2), but Abram needed reassurance. On receiving reassurance, he believed God's promise about a child (15:6) and then requested assurance about the land (15:8). Despite all this, in the next chapter he and Sarah resorted to Hagar as if God expected them to fulfill the promise by their own, natural means (16:1-2). Similarly, Jeremiah struggled with his calling (Jeremiah 15:10; 20:7-9, 14-18). Nevertheless, Abraham and Sarah, Jeremiah, and John persevered and grew in their faith.

Unlike some books, the Bible is realistic about its human heroes, whether John or others. They were human beings with struggles like ours. Yet God used them to fulfill God's purposes, and God can use us as well. Jesus did not condemn John for his limited understanding of God's plan. He encouraged John that God's plan was being fulfilled (Matthew 11:5), and that John would be blessed if he did not discard his faith (11:6). Afterward, Jesus told the crowds about John's strategic place in God's plan (11:7-11). Why not remind John himself? Perhaps because we are given enough to persevere in fulfilling God's will, but our ultimate reward must come with our Lord's final, "Well done" (25:21, 23).

## SHARING THE SCRIPTURE

### Preparing Our Hearts

Meditate on this week's devotional reading, found in Luke 5:27-32. Here we read about Jesus' call to Levi, known elsewhere as Matthew. Tax collectors were despised by Jews and Gentiles because they could add "profit" to the taxes they were employed to collect on behalf of the Roman government. Evidence of Levi's wealth is seen in the "great banquet" he was able to host in honor of Jesus. People were scandalized by Jesus' choice of such a "sinner." Identify someone whose confession of Christ shocks you. Why do you feel this way? Ask God to help you see this person through the eyes of Jesus.

Pray that you and the adult learners will be open to receiving and affirming whomever God calls.

### Preparing Our Minds

Study the background and lesson Scripture, both of which are found in Matthew 9:27-34 and Matthew 11:2-6. Think about who you can turn to when you are confronted by the inexplicable.

Write on newsprint:
❑ questions for group discussion in "Explore How Jesus' Healing Acts Were Signs Revealing His Identity."
❑ information for next week's lesson, found under "Continue the Journey."
❑ activities for further spiritual growth in "Continue the Journey."
Plan a brief lecture as suggested under "Explore How Jesus' Healing Acts Were Signs Revealing His Identity."

### LEADING THE CLASS

#### (1) Gather to Learn

❖ Welcome the class members and introduce any guests.
❖ Pray that all who have gathered will be open to the many ways that God moves in our lives, including those that cannot be explained.
❖ Read this true story found on the Order of Saint Luke website: **A friend had prayed for a pregnant woman who tests confirmed was carrying a fetus with many abnormalities. Throughout the pregnancy,**

ultrasound tests had verified the fetus was abnormal. Most of the babies with this syndrome do not live to their first birthday. Offered an abortion, the woman refused, even though she and her husband already had a disabled child. Much prayer surrounded this family. When the little girl was born, she was perfect.

❖ Ask: **How would you explain this baby's perfect health in light of medical tests that all showed serious, life-limiting problems?**

❖ Read aloud today's focus statement: **Although we live in a world where many people want to be able to explain all events scientifically, many mysteries remain. Who can we turn to when we are confronted by the inexplicable? Jesus performed healing miracles that led people to place their faith in him.**

*(2) Explore How Jesus' Healing Acts Were Signs Revealing His Identity*

❖ Choose a volunteer to read the story of Jesus healing two blind men as found in Matthew 9:27-34.

■ Present a brief lecture using material for Matthew 9:27, 28, 29, 30-31 from Understanding the Scripture to help the students see this story within the context of other healing stories.

■ Draw attention to other Gospel stories of blind persons being healed. Divide the class into groups. One group will research Matthew 20:29-34; a second group, Mark 8:22-26; and a third group, John 9:1-7. Encourage the groups to be prepared to discuss these questions, which you will post on newsprint, with the entire class:

(1) **What was the situation in which the blind person(s) encountered Jesus?**

(2) **How did Jesus respond to the one(s) needing healing?**

(3) **What happened?**

■ Call everyone together and allow time for group reports.

■ Wrap up this portion of the lesson by asking the adults to state how these healings may be understood as signs of Jesus' identity.

❖ Select a volunteer to read Matthew 11:2-6.

■ Point out that this passage concerns Jesus' identity. Jesus responds to the messengers the imprisoned John sent to him by quoting verses from Isaiah (26:19; 29:18-19; 35:5-6; 42:7; 61:1) in which the prophet sketches what God's liberating kingdom will be like. Invite five students to read these verses from Isaiah.

■ Ask:

(1) **According to Matthew 11:2-6, to whom has Jesus come and what has he done for them?** (Recognize that these reversals of fortune, most dealing with health issues, have come to those who are on the fringes of society.)

(2) **How do you see these actions as fulfillment of Isaiah's prophecies?**

■ **Option:** Select several biblical stories cited in Interpreting the Scripture and assign students to read these aloud. Then ask: **What is the common thread in these stories? What do they reveal to you about who Jesus is?**

■ Jesus blesses those who recognize who he is (11:6). Ask: **What examples can you give of persons blessed by Jesus?**

*(3) Relate Instances of Healing in the Learners' Lives*

❖ Encourage the learners to talk with a small group about a healing that they have experienced. Note that healings may be physical, mental, or emotional. Remind the students to listen to what is being said but not to pry into details that the speaker may not wish to reveal.

❖ Here is a discussion starter from the life of your editor, Nan Duerling. **In 1996 at the age of 49 I underwent two angioplasties and bypass surgery, all within three months of one another. Due to complications with the anesthesia administered for bypass, I needed to have an emergency tracheotomy and spent eight days on life support. I was in a full cardiac arrest for two minutes on the operating table. My beloved husband was told that I might not survive or could have long-term problems. Craig told them they didn't know me; I'd be just fine. He was there for every visitation time allowed in the surgical intensive care unit to encourage me. He called upon our church and faith-filled people around the country to pray for me. My full recovery astonished doctors. I have had no further cardiac events. I am able to write and edit, care for my elderly mother and mother-in-law who live with us, volunteer at church, volunteer in the field of animal-assisted therapy, and run a household. I believe without question that I was healed by God's grace. Thanks and praise be to the Great Physician!**

*(4) Recognize and Give Thanks to God Who Does Marvelous Things that We May Not Understand*

❖ Invite the students to read in unison today's key verse, Matthew 11:5. Recall that these words of Jesus were spoken in response to a question from John's messengers concerning Jesus' identity. Note information in the first paragraph of "John's Doubts and Jesus' Assurance" in Interpreting the Scripture to clarify why John raised questions.

❖ Read "Responses to Signs" in Interpreting the Scripture.

❖ Ask: **When confronted by healings or other miraculous signs of Jesus, both those you have witnessed and those you only have heard about, how do you respond?**

❖ Invite volunteers to offer a sentence prayer in which they give thanks to God for healings and miracles.

*(5) Continue the Journey*

❖ Pray that today's participants will go forth assured that Jesus' works reveal his identity as the Messiah.

❖ Read aloud this preparation for next week's lesson. You may also want to post it on newsprint for the students to copy.

■ **Title: Declared in Prayer**
■ **Background Scripture: Matthew 11:25-30**
■ **Lesson Scripture: Matthew 11:25-30**
■ **Focus of the Lesson: We admire those who are knowledgeable and seem to have all the answers to life. Where does that leave those who don't have everything all figured out? Jesus promised the truth and empowerment to those who follow and learn.**

❖ Challenge the students to complete one or more of these activities for further spiritual growth, which you will write on newsprint for the students to copy.

(1) **Visit someone who is ill, perhaps on your own or maybe as a member of a church team or animal-assisted therapy group.**

(2) **Encourage your church to assess its accessibility to people who have mobility, visual, or hearing issues. What changes can be made to make these folks feel more at home?**

(3) **Recall a significant event that has occurred during your lifetime. Try to remember whether or not you knew at the time that history was being made. Looking back on this event, how significant was it?**

❖ Sing or read aloud "When Jesus the Healer Passed Through Galilee."

❖ Conclude today's session by leading the class in this benediction, adapted from Matthew 16:16: **Go forth now to love and serve the Messiah, the Son of the living God.**

## UNIT 2: EVIDENCES OF JESUS AS MESSIAH
# DECLARED IN PRAYER

---

### PREVIEWING THE LESSON

**Lesson Scripture:** Matthew 11:25-30
**Background Scripture:** Matthew 11:25-30
**Key Verse:** Matthew 11:28

### Focus of the Lesson:

We admire those who are knowledgeable and seem to have all the answers to life. Where does that leave those who don't have everything all figured out? Jesus promised the truth and empowerment to those who follow and learn.

### Goals for the Learners:

(1) to examine Jesus' prayer of praise and the invitation to followers to learn from him.
(2) to realize that Jesus wants them to know him.
(3) to express in prayer praise to God and a willingness to know and learn from Jesus.

### Supplies:

Bibles, newsprint and marker, paper and pencils, hymnals, optional picture of a yoke

---

### READING THE SCRIPTURE

NRSV
Matthew 11:25-30
 ²⁵At that time Jesus said, "I thank you, Father, Lord of heaven and earth, because you have hidden these things from the wise and the intelligent and have revealed them to infants; ²⁶yes, Father, for such was your gracious will. ²⁷All things have been handed over to me by my Father; and no one knows the Son except the Father, and no one knows the Father except the Son and anyone to whom the Son chooses to reveal him.

**²⁸"Come to me, all you that are weary and are carrying heavy burdens, and I will give you rest.** ²⁹Take my yoke upon you, and

NIV
Matthew 11:25-30
 ²⁵At that time Jesus said, "I praise you, Father, Lord of heaven and earth, because you have hidden these things from the wise and learned, and revealed them to little children. ²⁶Yes, Father, for this was your good pleasure.

 ²⁷"All things have been committed to me by my Father. No one knows the Son except the Father, and no one knows the Father except the Son and those to whom the Son chooses to reveal him.

**²⁸"Come to me, all you who are weary and burdened, and I will give you rest.**

learn from me; for I am gentle and humble in heart, and you will find rest for your souls. ³⁰For my yoke is easy, and my burden is light."

²⁹Take my yoke upon you and learn from me, for I am gentle and humble in heart, and you will find rest for your souls. ³⁰For my yoke is easy and my burden is light."

## UNDERSTANDING THE SCRIPTURE

**Matthew 11:25-26.** When used for "praise," Jesus' term here (NRSV: "thank") especially involves acknowledgment of God's greatness. "Father" was a common title for God in prayer in antiquity; synagogue prayers often addressed "Our Father in heaven." Jesus took this respectful title to a new level of intimacy by calling God "Abba," that is, "Papa," setting a model for his followers (Mark 14:36; Romans 8:15). Those who could relate best to this "Father" here are "infants," not the independently minded. Jesus portrayed a relationship with the Father as one of dependence (Matthew 6:8; 7:9-11), inviting all disciples to become like little children in this sense (18:3-4; compare 23:9). Later Jesus welcomes children (18:2-5; 19:13-14) and the praise of "infants" (21:16).

"Lord of heaven and earth" was also a standard Jewish title for God in prayer. Those who recognize their own low status ("infants") were better off before this supreme ruler than those arrogant about their own intelligence (compare religious leaders in 23:4-9). We should recognize that Pharisaic sages (though probably not Sadducean aristocratic priests) valued humility, likely more than do most religious leaders today. Yet others who viewed themselves as wholly unlearned were in a better position to receive Jesus' message of the kingdom than even such sages.

This Gospel offers an example of God "revealing" truth to infants. Although the religious leaders failed to understand Jesus' identity, Simon Peter recognized him as Messiah. Thus Jesus announced that his Father had revealed this to Peter (16:17).

God's "hidden" treasures (13:35, 44) could be revealed to the lowly, not the proud.

**Matthew 11:27.** Jesus praises the Father for handing everything over to him. Elsewhere in Matthew's Gospel, we sometimes read about Jesus' authority (7:29; 10:1; 21:27), even authority on earth to forgive sins (9:6, 8). Yet ultimately, after Jesus' resurrection, the Father grants Jesus *all* authority in heaven and on earth (28:18).

Only Jesus knows the Father without mediation, and only those to whom Jesus reveals the Father will know him. The language of this passage sounds like the special way Jesus often speaks in the Gospel of John. In John's Gospel, the Father hands everything over to Jesus (John 3:35; 13:3; 17:2). The mutual knowledge of the Father and Son, and the knowledge of the Father through the Son, also figure prominently in John (John 10:14-15; 14:6-9). Such language would sound puzzling to someone who did not already know what it meant. Yet Jesus surely did sometimes describe himself as "the Son" (later Christians would not have invented the saying in Matthew 24:36, for example).

Because this passage derives from the material that Matthew and Luke share in common, it reflects very early material about Jesus' teaching. This suggests that the way Jesus often speaks in our latest canonical Gospel also reflects the way Jesus spoke on some occasions, at least privately among his disciples. Contrary to some of the passage's earlier critics, the language is not foreign to Jesus' Palestinian environment. The Dead Sea Scrolls use similar language about the knowledge of God. The language of only the Father and Son knowing each other also resembles Jewish language in texts about Wisdom, the closest traditional Jewish analogy to Jesus' role here. (Other Jewish sources did not have the Trinity, but could portray Wisdom as distinct from the Father, often as an attribute, yet in some sense divine.)

**Matthew 11:28.** The sage Joshua Ben Sira invited the unlearned (see 11:25, above) to come and learn from him, and accept the yoke of wisdom (Sirach 51:23-27, a book of the Apocrypha). But Jesus speaks with yet greater authority than Ben Sira. He speaks instead as divine Wisdom herself does, which invites hearers to come (Sirach 24:19-21), as Jesus also does repeatedly in the Gospel of John (for example, John 7:37). The rest that Jesus offers here is true Sabbath rest, compared with the Pharisaic interpretations of the Sabbath that follow (12:1-14).

**Matthew 11:29-30.** Paradoxically, one acquires rest from one's burdens (11:28) by accepting Jesus' yoke, a metaphor of service and labor. A yoke could involve a shared burden (as when yoking together two oxen), but the very poor could also use a yoke to pull loads themselves. What makes Jesus' yoke "light" is not that he demands less than other teachers (he does not; see 5:20), but that he does not load them down with senseless burdens that do not benefit them or others. (This contrasts with other teachers in 23:4, who "tie up heavy burdens, hard to bear, and lay them on the shoulders of others," though "they themselves are unwilling to lift a finger to move them.")

Instead, Jesus comes to serve and die for us (20:25-28).

Judaism employed the image of the "yoke" in a variety of ways. Negatively, it could refer to slavery or domination by an oppressive ruler. Positively, it could refer to God's dominion or to the rule of God's law. Because the paragraph that follows contrasts Jesus' and the Pharisees' interpretations of biblical law, Jesus' lighter yoke here might contrast with Pharisaic interpretation of the law. The Pharisees built a "fence" around the law, usually making it stricter, to prevent accidental violation (although they were also often interested in the law's intention). By contrast, Jesus focuses on the intention of the law and the principles behind it, principles that could be inferred only from a larger understanding of God's purpose. Many scholars argue that other teachers would have spoken here of God's yoke or the law's yoke. For Jesus to speak here of his own yoke makes sense, however, because of what he shares with the Father (11:27).

Jesus assures his disciples that because he is "gentle and humble in heart," they need not fear his yoke. The word translated "gentle" (or in some translations, "meek") appears as a virtue in the Beatitudes (Matthew 5:5) and in a prophecy used to describe Jesus as a "humble" king (21:5). When applied to a ruler or someone else in power, the term did not mean "easily intimidated" (as we sometimes think of "meek" in English) but a self-controlled use of power that enabled one to display compassion and mercy.

## INTERPRETING THE SCRIPTURE

### God's Greatness

When Jesus begins his prayer, "Father," he uses familiar language for prayer. Both Jesus and his Jewish contemporaries understood "father" in the usual sense of their culture: a dependable, loving, respected provider. In our day, some children have abusive or absent fathers, so it is important not to simply echo the term but to understand what the title was supposed to mean.

While we might be glad to praise God for

revealing truth to the lowly, we might be more reticent to praise God for withholding it from the proud. Jesus here offers an example, however, of trusting and praising God's wisdom in everything.

Jesus was pleased that God's selective revelation happened according to God's will (11:26); he always wanted what was pleasing to the Father (3:17; 12:18; 17:5). Jesus offers a model for how we too should relate to God, seeking always what pleases God.

### The Foolishness of Arrogance

Paul pointed out that God delights to show that the world's wisdom is foolishness, and to save those who "foolishly" trust the cross (1 Corinthians 1:17-31). Indeed, some scholars can pick apart the details of the biblical text, yet miss its heart because they do not know or care to know the God of whom the text speaks. Because human status is empty before the Creator who knows our hearts, only a posture of humility before God can receive God's most important blessings. When we seek to impress others (even with our religion, Matthew 6:1-18) rather than pleasing the One whose opinion ultimately matters, we act like practical atheists—disbelieving God on the deepest level of our hearts.

We tend to be awed by wealth, education, status, and celebrity. God delights to show that these benefits are of marginal importance, and can actually harm us if we become arrogant about them, as if we matter more than other people do. When John and Charles Wesley followed George Whitefield into the fields to preach the gospel to those alienated from the church, their social peers disdained them. Yet some historians believe that the Wesleyan revival turned England back from the brink of social chaos, preventing something analogous to the French Revolution. This movement helped undergird William Wilberforce and his colleagues as they worked, initially also to the disdain of their social peers, to abolish slavery in the British Empire. Many more are those who lacked status to begin with, yet through their prayers and sacrifices have worked to spread Christ's message and to change the world for good.

The inversion of wise and foolish in our passage resembles other reversals in the Gospel: for example, Persian wise men respond better to Jesus than Jerusalem's wise men (Matthew 2:1-11). In the immediate context, the towns privileged with his ministry would be punished more strictly than those who lacked the privilege (11:20-24). In condemning many of the religious leaders of his day, Jesus emphasizes that the humble will be exalted and those of high reputation brought low (23:12). Knowing their hearts, Jesus declared that these religious leaders wanted others to respect them for their services (23:5-7). Jesus warned his followers not to seek titles or marks of respect (23:8-10), for the greatest among them should be the others' servant (23:11).

While we are often ready to condemn the Pharisees of Jesus' day, we often display the same attitudes. Jesus did not say that the attitudes were all right so long as we are called Christians rather than Pharisees. Our status as God's servants is high enough; we do not need to compete with others to inflate it further.

### Religion or Relationship?

Religion or life itself can become the wrong sort of "yoke." Although the Pharisees followed their interpretation of the law joyfully, it offered little hope for the tax-gatherers and sinners Jesus was reaching (even the disciples would not have understood all of it). Nor did Jesus always agree with the interpretations of the Pharisees.

Thus, in the passage that follows this one, Jesus and the Pharisees differ over Sabbath rest (12:1-14), after Jesus promises "rest" here (11:28). Whereas the most scrupulous of

Pharisees may have wanted Jesus to heal on a different day than the Sabbath (12:10), Jesus believed that a person freed from an infirmity could rest better on the Sabbath. For Jesus, helping others who could then rest was legitimate on the Sabbath (12:11-12).

Knowing God includes knowing about God, but like any relationship, it also involves trust. Note that Jesus did not just teach about the law; he helped people in ways that could not be accomplished apart from God's power. His detractors wanted him to interpret sickness academically the way they did; Jesus cured the sickness. Jesus offers us not simply religion; he offers us a relationship with God. Sometimes it is easier for us to take refuge in religious tradition, in the clear rules of which we find comfort and sometimes self-justification. A relationship with God has its own demands—it too has a "yoke." But it also has a power to heal and transform supernaturally that mere religion cannot offer. And Jesus says that this relationship with his Father is available only to those to whom Jesus reveals the Father, to those who will humble themselves like utterly dependent children.

This passage also reminds us that it is Jesus who provides us a relationship with the Father (11:27). When our sin alienated us from God, Jesus gave his life so we could be forgiven (20:28; 26:28). We cannot make our own way to God; we must humble ourselves like little children and depend on God's gift (18:3; compare Mark 10:15). In Jesus' familiar language of John's Gospel:

"No one comes to the Father except through me" (John 14:6). In fact, this teaching, so counterintuitive to our culture, belonged to the apostolic message (for example, Acts 4:12; Romans 1:16); why would God have given the Son if other means for salvation had been available (Galatians 2:20)? Salvation is portrayed in various ways in the New Testament, but all involve a transition from one spiritual state to another, and always through Jesus.

*Jesus as a Compassionate Lord*

Jesus' description of himself as a compassionate ruler invites us to follow him. He is not only "gentle" but also "humble" in heart. A related term to this second adjective describes the appropriate response of disciples to Jesus (18:4), and the state that God exalts (23:12). Jesus did not have to pretend to be someone great or display his power. He knew his identity, hence was free to humble himself and let his Father exalt him (so also Philippians 2:6-11). Jesus' humility sets an example for us (2:5).

Humility is not self-deprecation or self-loathing; it also does not mean that one is easily intimidated. Humility means that we are secure enough in our identity that we are free to show grace to others rather than depending on their respect to prop us up. In the case of us as disciples, it also means recognizing who we are in contrast to who God is, a sober self-assessment that recognizes our limits as well as our God-given gifts and tasks.

## SHARING THE SCRIPTURE

*Preparing Our Hearts*

Meditate on this week's devotional reading, found in John 11:38-44. Jesus thanks his "Father" for having heard him just prior to calling Lazarus out of the tomb. In today's

passage from Matthew, note that Jesus also thanks his "Father." What does it mean to you to call God "Father"? What do Jesus' expressions of thanks to the Father suggest to you in terms of your own relationship with God?

Pray that you and the adult learners will thank the Father at all times.

### Preparing Our Minds

Study the background and lesson scripture, both of which are taken from Matthew 11:25-30. As you think about people who seem to have all the answers to life, ask yourself: where does that leave those who don't have everything all figured out?

Write on newsprint:
- ❑ information for next week's lesson, found under "Continue the Journey."
- ❑ activities for further spiritual growth in "Continue the Journey."

Plan a lecture for "Examine Jesus' Prayer of Praise and the Invitation to Followers to Learn from Him" as described in that section.

**Option:** Locate a picture of a yoke in a book or on the Internet.

### LEADING THE CLASS

### (1) Gather to Learn

❖ Welcome the class members and introduce any guests.

❖ Pray that those who have come today will be ready to release their cares and burdens to Jesus.

❖ Read these words aloud and discuss the final question: **Perhaps you admire detective Sherlock Holmes who after careful investigation can solve any mystery. He is well-versed in a wide variety of topics, many of which seem very arcane to the average person. Whether you are reading one of Sir Arthur Conan Doyle's short stories or watching Holmes on television, the story is always neatly wrapped up in about an hour. Some of us probably know a Sherlock Holmes in real life, someone who seems to have all the answers. How does it make you feel when you encounter one of these larger-than-life figures, especially if you don't have all the answers?**

❖ Read aloud today's focus statement: **We admire those who are knowledgeable and seem to have all the answers to life. Where does that leave those who don't have everything all figured out? Jesus promised the truth and empowerment to those who follow and learn.**

### (2) Examine Jesus' Prayer of Praise and the Invitation to Followers to Learn from Him

❖ Choose a volunteer to read Jesus' prayer and invitation, found in Matthew 11:25-30.

❖ Discuss with the participants what Jesus refers to when he says "these things" (here meaning Jesus' identity and the role he is to play) and why they think "these things" would be hidden from the wise but revealed to "infants" (that is, those who are vulnerable and dependent).

❖ Read aloud Matthew 11:27 again and invite the learners to comment on what this means and where they have seen these ideas before. (See Matthew 11:27 in Understanding the Scripture for information. You may want to have the students check some of the biblical references cited there.)

❖ Ask the students to read in unison today's key verse, Matthew 11:28.

❖ Help the class members understand that the burdens mentioned here could refer to the Pharisee's interpretation of the law that these religious leaders laid upon the backs of all of God's people. These burdens could also be the oppression that the people are experiencing under Roman rule.

❖ **Option:** Show a picture of a yoke (or a yoke itself) and explain how a yoke is used.

❖ Present a lecture, based on Matthew 11:29-30 in Understanding the Scripture and "Religion or Relationship?" in Interpreting the Scripture, in which you help the participants understand what Jesus means when he talks about a "yoke." Here is some information from a footnote of *The New Interpreter's Study Bible* for verse 30 that you may want to add: **"Verse 30 is better translated, 'My yoke is kind/good and its burden is small.' The use of imperial language to present God's empire is ironic. The gospel takes over the language of what it resists to present God's empire."**

❖ Ask: **After reading this passage, why would you want to know Jesus?**

*(3) Realize that Jesus Wants the Learners to Know Him*

❖ Invite the adults to respond silently as you lead them in this guided imagery activity.

■ **You have come to a quiet place that is special to you. Imagine the scene: perhaps a garden, beach, room in your home, or mountain trail. Take a few moments to be aware of the sights, sounds, and aromas you notice.** (pause)

■ **In the midst of this serenity, Jesus appears and invites you to ask anything you want to know about him. How do you respond?** (pause)

■ **Listen as Jesus answers you.** (pause)

■ **As he walks away, think about what you have learned about him. How will this new information deepen your relationship with him?** (pause)

❖ Ask: **What is the difference between knowing about Jesus and knowing Jesus?**

❖ Provide a few additional moments for silent reflection on these questions: **Can you honestly say that you know Jesus? If not, invite him into your heart and life right now. If you do know him, silently pray that you will continue to grow into a closer personal relationship with him.**

*(4) Express in Prayer Praise to God and a Willingness to Know and Learn from Jesus*

❖ Invite the class members to read in unison Psalm 100, a familiar song of praise.

❖ Discuss these questions:
   **(1) What reasons does this psalmist give for praising God?**
   **(2) What other reasons do you have for praising God?** (Students will most likely include their relationship with Jesus in their answers, but if not, be sure to add this important point.)

❖ Distribute paper and pencils. Encourage the students to each write a prayer in which they praise God, particularly for the gift of knowing Jesus as their personal Savior and Lord.

❖ Invite the students, as able, to stand in a circle. Encourage volunteers to read their prayers, or a portion of them. People may read at random, or you may ask them to go around the circle. Those who choose not to read aloud may say "pass."

*(5) Continue the Journey*

❖ Conclude the prayer time by asking God to help those who have come today to continue to grow closer to Christ and learn from him what the Father would have them to know.

❖ Read aloud this preparation for next week's lesson. You may also want to post it on newsprint for the students to copy.
   ■ **Title: Revealed in Rejection**
   ■ **Background Scripture: Matthew 13:54-58; Luke 4:16-30**
   ■ **Lesson Scripture: Matthew 13:54-58**
   ■ **Focus of the Lesson: People respond to rejection in different ways. What have we done when we have been rejected? Jesus faced rejection when he taught in the synagogue of his boyhood town of Nazareth, then he moved on to continue his ministry.**

❖ Challenge the students to complete one or more of these activities for further spiritual growth, which you will write on newsprint for the students to copy.

(1) Pray for someone who seems burdened and weary. Offer to do whatever you can to assist this person.

(2) Recall that Jesus uses the word "come" to call followers to him. Who can you invite to "come" with you to worship, Sunday school, a mission project, or other event that will enable that individual to experience Christ?

(3) Reread Matthew 11:25. The word that is translated in the NRSV as "thank" is also translated as "praise" elsewhere (see NIV). Make a list of at least ten reasons you have to thank and praise God. Review this list each day this week as part of your prayer time.

❖ Sing or read aloud "Come, All of You."

❖ Conclude today's session by leading the class in this benediction, adapted from Matthew 16:16: **Go forth now to love and serve the Messiah, the Son of the living God.**

## UNIT 2: EVIDENCES OF JESUS AS MESSIAH
# REVEALED IN REJECTION

---

### PREVIEWING THE LESSON

**Lesson Scripture:** Matthew 13:54-58
**Background Scripture:** Matthew 13:54-58; Luke 4:16-30
**Key Verse:** Matthew 54:58

**Focus of the Lesson:**
People respond to rejection in different ways. What have we done when we have been rejected? Jesus faced rejection when he taught in the synagogue of his boyhood town of Nazareth, then he moved on to continue his ministry.

**Goals for the Learners:**
(1) to review Jesus' teaching and rejection in Nazareth.
(2) to compare Jesus' experience of rejection with their own experiences.
(3) to commit to following Jesus even when rejection comes.

**Pronunciation Guide:**
Naaman (nay' uh muhn)
Sepphoris (sef' uh ris)
Zarephath (zair' uh fath).

**Supplies:**
Bibles, newsprint and marker, paper and pencils, hymnals

---

### READING THE SCRIPTURE

NRSV
Matthew 13:54-58

⁵⁴He came to his hometown and began to teach the people in their synagogue, so that they were astounded and said, "Where did this man get this wisdom and these deeds of power? ⁵⁵Is not this the carpenter's son? Is not his mother called Mary? And are not his brothers James and Joseph and Simon and Judas? ⁵⁶And are not all his sisters with us?

NIV
Matthew 13:54-58

⁵⁴Coming to his hometown, he began teaching the people in their synagogue, and they were amazed. "Where did this man get this wisdom and these miraculous powers?" they asked. ⁵⁵"Isn't this the carpenter's son? Isn't his mother's name Mary, and aren't his brothers James, Joseph, Simon and Judas? ⁵⁶Aren't all his sisters with us? Where then

Where then did this man get all this?" [57] And they took offense at him. But Jesus said to them, "Prophets are not without honor except in their own country and in their own house." **[58] And he did not do many deeds of power there, because of their unbelief.**

did this man get all these things?" [57] And they took offense at him.

But Jesus said to them, "Only in his hometown and in his own house is a prophet without honor."

**[58] And he did not do many miracles there because of their lack of faith.**

## UNDERSTANDING THE SCRIPTURE

**Matthew 13:54-56.** Even John nearly stumbled over the nature of Jesus' mission (Matthew 11:2-6); that others would do so need not surprise us. Although Jesus has been welcomed throughout Galilee, people from his home village are scandalized. They knew Jesus as a boy who grew up in a normal family among them, not as a prophet. Carpenters were often woodworkers; this was probably a common occupation in Nazareth when Jesus was growing up, since nearby Sepphoris, destroyed in his early childhood, was being rebuilt. The names of all his siblings were common. "Mary" was the most common Jewish woman's name in this period.

**Matthew 13:57.** Those closest to the truth usually missed it (2:1-12; 11:20-24), and this is also the case here. By this period, Jewish tradition generally affirmed that Israel rejected and even martyred most of its prophets. Even earlier, many failed to accept prophets from their own community (Jeremiah 1:1; 11:21-23; 12:6).

The rejection here fits the context. The following passage depicts the murder of the prophet John (14:1-12). Before the parables that precede this rejection, Matthew obliquely signals some level of trouble between Jesus and his family in 12:46-50, which is also apparent in verse 57: "except . . . in their own house." (This tension is more clearly seen in Mark 3:31-35 because of Mark 3:21). The parables set the larger tone for the rejection. Of four kinds of soil, only those who continued to listen to Jesus'

teaching, hence came to understand it, would persevere (Matthew 13:3-23). The kingdom would remain in this world in a way obscure except to those with faith (13:24-43).

**Matthew 13:58.** Mark claims that Jesus could not do a miracle in Nazareth because of their unbelief. Probably this means that Jesus refused to act as a magician (compare Matthew 4:3-4), since magicians normally demanded money rather than faith. Matthew, however, clarifies the wording: Jesus would not do a miracle there because of their unbelief.

**Luke 4:16.** Luke includes far more detail in the Nazareth rejection scene than do Mark or Matthew. In fact, although Luke almost always follows the sequence in Mark, in this case he moves the scene forward and makes it the Gospel's programmatic scene, introducing and defining Jesus' mission.

Other first-century sources show us that people read Scripture in synagogues on the Sabbath. In Palestine, one would stand to read and most sages would sit to expound the text.

**Luke 4:17.** Isaiah was one of the most popular books in this period; as a long scroll, it would be on two rollers. Townspeople would contribute money for community Scripture scrolls for local synagogues. Because Hebrew was written from right to left, one would unroll the scroll this way.

**Luke 4:18-19.** This passage from Isaiah 61:1-2 defines Jesus' mission. Throughout Luke's Gospel, Jesus does in fact bring hope especially to the poor (6:20; 7:22; 14:21; 16:22; 18:22; 19:8); does free the captives (especially from demons); heals the blind and challenges injustice. Although Jesus' hearers would know that the passage goes on to speak also of judgment, Jesus may break off the reading here because judgment belongs only to his future, Second Coming.

The passage also designates the source of Jesus' empowerment: God anointed Jesus with the Spirit (a point reiterated in Acts 10:38, which also mentions Jesus healing and freeing the devil's captives). The Spirit came on Jesus in Luke 3:22. After this the Spirit continued to lead and empower Jesus (Luke 4:1, 14). Jesus here provides the model for his followers' Spirit-empowered ministry in Luke's second volume (Acts 1:8; 2:17-18).

**Luke 4:20-22.** The attendant would give the scroll to the reader, who would afterward hand it back, as here. The initial response to Jesus is surprised but not yet hostile. The same is true of a synagogue exposition of Paul in Acts 13:42, until he appears to discount Jewish privilege in welcoming Gentiles (Acts 13:44-50).

**Luke 4:23-24.** Jesus cuts directly to the point, presumably because he knows what their response ultimately will be. They will not truly believe him unless they see the signs they have heard about elsewhere. "Doctor, cure yourself" was indeed a familiar proverb. Jesus responds with another commonplace fact: prophets were rejected by those in their own homelands.

**Luke 4:25-27.** Through the example of Elijah and Elisha, Jesus both challenges his hearers' assumptions and prefigures his own mission in the rest of the Gospel. Some of Jesus' miracles resemble those of Elijah and Elisha. He also faces rejection from some in his homeland and respect from some outsiders like these prophets did.

Luke has a significant interest in widows (Luke 2:37; 7:12; 18:3-5; 20:47; 21:2-3; Acts 6:1; 9:39-41), who in a male-centered culture were often vulnerable to legal oppression. Likewise, Jesus heals lepers (Luke 5:12-13; 7:22; 17:12-14).

Whereas everyone in Jesus' audience would affirm the importance of caring for widows, a different component in Jesus' examples stirs his audience's anger. Jesus speaks of miracles not only for others outside one's hometown, but for others outside one's homeland. The widow to whom God sent Elijah was from Zarephath, near where the oppressive Phoenician queen Jezebel was from! The one leper Elisha was reported to cleanse was from Aram (Syria), the very people warring against Israel at that time!

Jesus can infer that Israelite lepers were not cleansed (Luke 4:27) because shortly after Naaman's cleansing (2 Kings 5:1-19) we read of some Israelite lepers in Samaria (2 Kings 7:3). Ironically, it is a *Samaritan* leper who now epitomizes an outsider, and Jesus later heals him (Luke 17:15-19).

**Luke 4:28-29.** Although Jesus argued from Scripture, the crowd is angry that he appears to privilege Gentiles, enemies of his own people. This sets a pattern for Luke's work: the marginalized respond to Jesus' message, while insiders view him as a threat and an enemy. Likewise, in the Book of Acts, Paul has more success in the long run among Gentiles than among the leaders of his own people. When Paul preaches to crowds in the Jerusalem Temple, they listen to him—until he notes his mission to the Gentiles (Acts 22:21-22).

**Luke 4:30.** Luke does not tell us how Jesus evaded their intent. Perhaps his calm response brought them to their senses. The idea here probably resembles that in John 7:30 and 8:20: "his hour had not yet come." That is, however Jesus escaped the Father was protecting him for the rest of his mission.

# INTERPRETING THE SCRIPTURE

## Missing God's Work in Our Midst

We can fail to recognize the God who comes to us in the normal settings of our lives. Nazareth could not believe that the boy who grew up among them was a famous prophet. Still less could they have accepted the scandal of the incarnation, God embracing the limitations and even mortality of our humanity to reach us. On a general level, we often fail to appreciate God's gifts among us (spouses, friends, and so forth). More specifically, we may miss ways that God is seeking to speak to us in the routine patterns of our lives.

God works through Moses' old staff; through Elijah's cloak; or through a boy's few fishes and loaves. In Scripture, God can speak through a donkey, use improbable characters like the twelve sons of Jacob, Gideon, Hannah, or you and me. We are right to believe that God is "transcendent," far beyond us; but because God loves us, God is also "immanent," and comes to us in the very particularities and even brokenness of our human existence.

That those closest to the truth in Jesus' day usually missed it should provide a warning to us. Indeed, Jesus moves from rejection in the congregation in Nazareth (Luke 4:16-30) to confronting a congregation-attending demon in Capernaum (Luke 4:31-37). Being near the truth of the Bible or attending church services cannot substitute for believing biblical truth and acting as members of Christ's body, the church.

## Few Miracles and Unbelief

Peter had enough faith to begin walking on water (more than most of his modern armchair critics, including myself), yet not enough to sustain him without Jesus' compassionate intervention (Matthew 14:28-31). Jesus is often patient with our growing in faith, as he was with his disciples, never casting them aside (Matthew 6:30; 8:26; 14:31; 16:8; 17:20). But disciples are adherents or followers, who also persisted in learning from Jesus. By contrast, the disbelief in this account (Matthew 13:58) verges on disdain and rejection.

While lack of faith is not the only reason for lack of miracles, it is a prominent one. As Jesus' followers, we are in the situation of the disciples (not the hostile people in Nazareth), with opportunities to grow in our faith. Trusting God in the smaller opportunities prepares us for the larger ones. In some parts of the world, where Christians have less access to food or medicine, even prayer for daily bread (6:11) requires great faith. In other places, we can partner with these Christians in answer to their prayers and also look for our own opportunities to trust God more deeply in our daily lives before we face greater crises.

## Jesus' Mission

Jesus' mission, defined by Isaiah, includes both announcing good news and demonstrating it by restoring and healing, a mission that must depend on the power of God's Spirit for success. The focus of Jesus' mission was not the elite in Jerusalem but the poor, lepers, the blind, and others in need.

Isaiah's passage referred to the time of Israel's restoration. Many argue that it also echoes the justice principle of the levitical year of Jubilee. The fullness of restoration awaits a new world where evil will have no place. Yet as in Matthew 11:5 (paralleled in Luke 7:22), treated earlier, Jesus has inaugurated some of that restoration already in his earthly mission, a mission to be carried on by his Spirit-empowered followers. As Jesus says in Luke 4:21, "Today this scripture has been fulfilled." We should work to approximate what we can of the future kingdom for our king now. (For Jesus fulfilling other future hopes in the present, compare also Luke 19:5; 23:43.)

### Reaching Outsiders

In Luke's Gospel, Jesus ministers to and eats with the marginalized. In the Book of Acts, this pattern leads to the Gentile mission and table fellowship with Gentiles. Today, the majority of Christians are Gentiles, who can be very grateful that Jesus, Paul, and others took risks to spread the gospel to Gentiles.

Today, however, we still face the same temptations that Jesus' hometown congregation faced. We may not care about people far away, so long as we have God's blessings for ourselves. We may hold prejudices against other peoples, especially if those people have a history of conflict with our own people. We may not even care much about needy people elsewhere in our own communities, if they are different from us. Although church members do not usually throw annoying pastors, Sunday school teachers, or others over cliffs, some can still get annoyed about being reminded to care for others beyond their own circle. Before Christians today condemn the people of Nazareth, we must guard against the same attitudes among ourselves.

### Facing Rejection

We also learn from our Lord's boldness in challenging entrenched prejudices. While tact is usually advisable, some prejudices run so deep that confrontation is inevitable if people truly understand what we are trying to communicate. Although nonviolent toward others, Jesus was willing to face hostility and even a potential lynching to stand for God's purposes. On this occasion, God protected him from being killed. Toward the end of Luke's Gospel, Jesus does face death, yet his Father raises him. It takes great faith in God to stand for God's purpose and vision.

Jesus' mission often involved rejection, ultimately even the rejection of the cross. Jesus' suffering in Matthew's Gospel prefigures that of his disciples (compare 5:11; 10:22; 24:9). That most of us have experienced the pain of rejection, even from people we love, may give us sympathy for what Jesus suffered on a greater level. When we face rejection for his sake, however, we should remember that we share some of our Lord's suffering, and that he takes personally whatever such rejection we face (compare 25:45).

What are God's purposes worth suffering for in our day? The Nazareth account suggests some examples. The global church at which Jesus hinted in Nazareth now exists. For Christians to partner together and learn from one another across ethnic and cultural lines is essential. Likewise, we must still work to empower the marginalized, the needy, the unhealthy (by social and political means, but also by depending on God's power, as Jesus did, to do what humans cannot do).

Further, we must be ready to suffer for doing good, just as Jesus did. Suffering does not mean that we have done something wrong. No nation or individual will ultimately escape suffering, certainly including those who stand for justice for others. But like Jesus, we have ultimate hope in God's deliverance.

Christians suffer for Christ in many parts of the world, but it is possible anywhere. As a young Christian recently converted from atheism, I shared my faith, wanting others to know the truth and hope I had discovered. Sometimes, like one night after working at a street mission, I was beaten or had my life threatened for my testimony. But Jesus is worth our lives.

# SHARING THE SCRIPTURE

### *Preparing Our Hearts*

Meditate on this week's devotional reading, found in Isaiah 53:1-9. In these familiar words of the fourth and final Servant Song, we read in verse 3, "he was despised and rejected by others . . . he was despised, and we held him of no account." Isaiah applied these words to the servant whose identity has been unclear in terms of its Old Testament meaning. Christians have long seen in this despised figure the person of Jesus, "a man of suffering and acquainted with infirmity" (53:3). How is Jesus' identity revealed to you in his rejection?

Pray that you and the adult learners will recognize that Jesus comes to us not with the pomp of royalty but in the lowliness of one who is despised and rejected.

### *Preparing Our Minds*

Study the background from Matthew 13:54-58 and Luke 4:16-30. The lesson scripture focuses on Matthew 13:54-58. As you read, think about how you have responded to rejection.

Write on newsprint:
❏ information for next week's lesson, found under "Continue the Journey."
❏ activities for further spiritual growth in "Continue the Journey."

### LEADING THE CLASS

### *(1) Gather to Learn*

❖ Welcome the class members and introduce any guests.

❖ Pray that all who have come today will be open to the leading of the Holy Spirit as we continue to explore evidences of Jesus as the Messiah.

❖ Share this story from your editor with the group. As you read, ask them to think about rejection they have experienced and how they responded: **We were looking for a Curly-Coated Retriever when our breeder, also responsible for a Curly rescue group, called and said, "Nan, I have the perfect dog for you and Craig. I've just rescued him from a shelter. Do you want to meet him?" Well, actually, we were looking for a pure-bred dog with papers, but we ventured to meet this dog. His ribs were showing, yet he was as sweet and gentle as could be. Who could have possibly left this dear one in an outdoor kennel at a shelter in the middle of the night? We immediately said, "Yes, he's ours." Not knowing anything about him, we named him Noah, since Curlies are water dogs. Noah lived with us for eight years, during which time he helped me recover from serious heart disease; brought joy and laughter to my in-laws and my own mom, all of whom lived with us; and was always loving and loyal to us, despite a bitter rejection by a former owner. We are ever grateful that he rebounded from that rejection by being willing to trust people again. His death from cancer just before Christmas, 2004, was devastating to us, but we are extremely grateful for the privilege of being allowed to share our lives with him.**

❖ Provide a brief opportunity for class members to tell stories of response to rejection.

❖ Read aloud today's focus statement: **People respond to rejection in different ways. What have we done when we have been rejected? Jesus faced rejection when he taught in the synagogue of his boyhood town of Nazareth, then he moved on to continue his ministry.**

### *(2) Review Jesus' Teaching and Rejection in Nazareth*

❖ Choose a volunteer to read Matthew 13:54-58.

❖ Discuss these questions:

**(1) Why were the people of Nazareth missing God's work in their midst?** (Add ideas from "Missing God's Work in Our Midst" in Interpreting the Scripture, as appropriate.)

**(2) Matthew records that Jesus did few "deeds of power" (13:58) in Nazareth because of the people's unbelief. What lesson might you draw from this regarding why there are so few miracles performed today?** (See "Few Miracles and Unbelief" in Interpreting the Scripture for ideas to add to the discussion.)

❖ Note that Jesus faced rejection because his hometown neighbors "took offense at him" (13:57). Read aloud "Facing Rejection" from Interpreting the Scripture and then ask:

**(1) In what ways and under what circumstances have you been rejected for your beliefs?**

**(2) How do you handle people who "take offense" at your witness?**

❖ Read aloud another story of Jesus' rejection from Luke 4:16-30, today's background scripture.

❖ Divide the class into groups of three or four. Tell the groups to compare and contrast these two Gospel accounts by discussing these questions.

**(1) What similarities and differences do you see between the two stories?**

**(2) What information does one account provide that is not found in the other?**

❖ Bring the groups back together and ask each to share an interesting insight.

*(3) Compare Jesus' Experience of Rejection with the Learners' Experiences*

❖ Brainstorm answers to this question with the students: **Under what circum-** stances do people generally feel rejected? List their ideas on newsprint. Include rejections children may face, such as not being invited to a birthday party or being chosen last for a sports team or feeling that a sibling was always favored. Think also about rejections adolescents and young adults encounter, such as not being accepted by the college of their choice or being turned down for a date. Also consider rejections that adults experience, such as the loss of a job, a divorce, or not being accepted into the family of one's spouse.

❖ Invite volunteers to tell brief stories of rejections they encountered and how they responded to them.

❖ Direct the adults to look again at Matthew 13:54-58 to discover how the rejection Jesus experienced was similar to or different from the kinds of rejections the students have identified. Discuss their ideas.

*(4) Commit to Following Jesus Even When Rejection Comes*

❖ Read: **Burke Wilkinson wrote, "Rejection is the sand in the oyster, the irritant that ultimately produces the pearl." How does this saying relate to the way you might frame rejection?** (Help the class see that rejection can be a positive experience. Especially as they think about their relationship with Jesus, rejection may help them become more conformed to the image of the One who faced the ultimate rejection.)

❖ Distribute paper and pencils. Invite the students to look again at the newsprint on which they listed examples of rejection. Ask them to write a brief, confidential summary of a rejection they recently experienced.

❖ Bring the group together. Remind them that sometimes when we feel life is against us, we have great opportunities to grow in our faith as we continue to follow Jesus.

❖ Provide a few moments for the adults to write an additional sentence or two concerning how they will commit themselves to following Christ, even in the midst of rejection.

*(5) Continue the Journey*

❖ Conclude that quiet time by praying that everyone who has participated today will closely follow the Messiah, who was revealed in rejection.

❖ Read aloud this preparation for next week's lesson. You may also want to post it on newsprint for the students to copy.

■ **Title: Recognized by a Canaanite Woman**

■ **Background Scripture: Matthew 15:21-28**

■ **Lesson Scripture: Matthew 15:21-28**

■ **Focus of the Lesson: Family members face issues and often cannot find help. Where can we find resources to help? A Gentile woman came to Jesus, persistently seeking healing for her daughter, and Jesus healed the daughter.**

❖ Challenge the students to complete one or more of these activities for further spiritual growth, which you will write on newsprint for the students to copy.

(1) **Research the first-century synagogue to understand how Jesus was able to teach there.**

(2) **Browse the Internet to learn about how some Christians are rejected and persecuted even today. What actions can you take to support these people?**

(3) **Risk sharing your faith with a family member or friend whose attitudes are such that you will likely face rejection.**

❖ Sing or read aloud "Hallelujah! What a Savior."

❖ Conclude today's session by leading the class in this benediction, adapted from Matthew 16:16: **Go forth now to love and serve the Messiah, the Son of the living God.**

UNIT 3: TESTIMONIES TO JESUS AS MESSIAH

# Recognized by a Canaanite Woman

---

## PREVIEWING THE LESSON

**Lesson Scripture:** Matthew 15:21-28
**Background Scripture:** Matthew 15:21-28
**Key Verse:** Matthew 15:28

### Focus of the Lesson:
Family members face issues and often cannot find help. Where can we find resources to help? A Gentile woman came to Jesus, persistently seeking healing for her daughter, and Jesus healed the daughter.

### Goals for the Learners:
(1) to explore the account of the Canaanite woman and her faith.
(2) to describe a vibrant faith.
(3) to assess their faith and to pray that it will become even stronger.

### Pronunciation Guide:
Canaanite (kay' nuh nite)
Sidon (si' duhn)
Syrophoenician (si roh fi nish' uhn)
Tyre (tire)

### Supplies:
Bibles, newsprint and marker, paper and pencils, hymnals, optional map

---

## READING THE SCRIPTURE

NRSV
Matthew 15:21-28

²¹Jesus left that place and went away to the district of Tyre and Sidon. ²²Just then a Canaanite woman from that region came out and started shouting, "Have mercy on me,

NIV
Matthew 15:21-28

²¹Leaving that place, Jesus withdrew to the region of Tyre and Sidon. ²²A Canaanite woman from that vicinity came to him, crying out, "Lord, Son of David, have mercy on

Lord, Son of David; my daughter is tormented by a demon." [23]But he did not answer her at all. And his disciples came and urged him, saying, "Send her away, for she keeps shouting after us." [24]He answered, "I was sent only to the lost sheep of the house of Israel." [25]But she came and knelt before him, saying, "Lord, help me." [26]He answered, "It is not fair to take the children's food and throw it to the dogs." [27]She said, "Yes, Lord, yet even the dogs eat the crumbs that fall from their masters' table." [28]Then Jesus answered her, **"Woman, great is your faith! Let it be done for you as you wish."** And her daughter was healed instantly.

me! My daughter is suffering terribly from demon-possession."

[23]Jesus did not answer a word. So his disciples came to him and urged him, "Send her away, for she keeps crying out after us."

[24]He answered, "I was sent only to the lost sheep of Israel."

[25]The woman came and knelt before him. "Lord, help me!" she said.

[26]He replied, "It is not right to take the children's bread and toss it to their dogs."

[27]"Yes, Lord," she said, "but even the dogs eat the crumbs that fall from their masters' table."

[28]Then Jesus answered, **"Woman, you have great faith! Your request is granted."** And her daughter was healed from that very hour.

## UNDERSTANDING THE SCRIPTURE

**Matthew 15:21.** Jesus occasionally takes his disciples on "retreats" away from the crowds, and this sometimes requires him to take them into Gentile territory (16:13; Mark 3:7).

Tyre and Sidon were the most famous cities of Phoenicia, known for their trade, their production of expensive purple dye, and glass. Israel knew them also for other traditional reasons: they were associated with the Phoenicians, including the wicked Queen Jezebel. But this is not Jesus' first mention of these cities. Earlier he claimed that Tyre and Sidon would have been more responsive to his message than Galilean towns were (Matthew 11:21-22; also Luke 10:13-14). This woman (also from the region of Tyre in Mark 7:24-25) will quickly illustrate that point.

**Matthew 15:22.** Whereas Matthew has a "Canaanite" woman, Mark has a Greek Syrophoenician. Syrophoenicia (as opposed to Libophoenicia, around Carthage) included Tyre and Sidon. Since the time of

Alexander the Great, descendants of the Greek and Macedonian settlers held elite status there. Thus as a "Greek" Syrophoenician, this woman belongs to the ruling citizen class.

Those in the ruling citizen class profited from the labor of peasants in the surrounding countryside. One might say that members of her social class had been taking bread from other children's mouths; but now the shoe was on the other foot, and she came to a non-Greek, Jewish visitor as a suppliant. Jesus in a sense forces her to give up any sense of privilege belonging to her class. Just as need reduced the wealthy synagogue official Jairus and a marginalized woman with a flow of blood to the same status of supplication, so too this member of the local elite had to come as a suppliant.

Matthew, however, is more interested in the ethnic issue than in the class divide here. He does not report her Greek ancestry, but only that she is a "Canaanite," for she lives in a culture partly shaped by descendants of the ancient Canaanites and still worshiping Baal. The Canaanites were ancient enemies of the Jewish people. Matthew's audience may recall, however, two honored Canaanite women already in Matthew's opening genealogy (Tamar in 1:3; Rahab in 1:5).

It is noteworthy that this Gentile hails Jesus as "Son of David," hence Messiah, before Peter does (16:16), just as the Samaritan woman learns Jesus' identity before Peter's confession in the Fourth Gospel (John 4:25-29; 6:69). "Son of David" is a key title for Matthew (Matthew 1:1). Although suggested by the crowds (21:9), it appears in cries of faith from blind men (9:27; 20:30-31), children (21:15), and this Gentile woman (15:22).

**Matthew 15:23.** This is not the only place where the disciples seek to protect their important teacher from some petitioners. Later they rebuked those who brought children for Jesus to pray over (19:13). Likewise, the crowds tried to silence the blind men crying after Jesus in 20:31. In the other cases, however, Jesus welcomes the petitioners, whereas here he himself will raise obstacles (15:24, 26).

**Matthew 15:24-25.** By raising obstacles, Jesus may be partly testing her faith. This happens on other occasions in Scripture. The most significant parallel in Matthew's Gospel is probably Matthew 8:7, which should probably read, as in the TNIV, as a question: "Shall I come and heal him?" (The Greek in that verse reads more naturally as a question than a statement.) Jesus is there objecting to what the centurion seems to be implying, namely that Jesus should come to his house to heal the man. But strict Jewish piety forbade entering a Gentile's home (at least if the Gentile had any association with idolatry). The centurion responds by acknowledging that he does not need Jesus to come but only to speak the word, and Jesus praises the centurion's faith (8:8-10).

In the same way, this woman, desperate, refuses to be deterred. Indeed, she prostrates herself the way Gentiles normally did before their rulers or deities.

Yet in both these cases Jesus is expecting not simply perseverance, but also humility, to recognize Israel's prior status. Jesus' mission was first to Israel, and that was where he also first sent his disciples (10:6). Gentiles whom Jesus healed because of their extraordinary faith were exceptions, but they did point to the way more Gentiles could be welcomed in the future: through faith. They cannot approach Jesus like a Gentile wonderworker—most often, a magician—but through faith that he is an agent of Israel's true God. (Compare Elisha making Naaman dip in the Jordan rather than in the rivers of Naaman's own country in 2 Kings 5:10-12. In 2 Kings 5:17-18, Naaman ends up acknowledging the true God and even the "holy soil" of this God's land.)

**Matthew 15:26.** Although giving the children's bread to dogs may be simply an illustration, it is one that would sting. Granted, Greeks could keep small dogs as pets for their children (in contrast to Jews, for whom they were like rodents); children naturally took precedence over pets. Nevertheless, "dog" was an insult throughout ancient literature (associated with attachment to dung, corpses, other dogs' rear ends, and sometimes violence). In 15:24, Jesus raised an ethnic obstacle; now he raises the stakes even higher.

**Matthew 15:27.** The Canaanite woman responds with the humility of desperate faith. Accepting Jesus' illustration without complaint, she builds on it: While dogs should not eat the children's food, they are welcome to the crumbs. By acknowledging that even a crumb of Jesus' power is sufficient to perform the miracle, she confesses her great faith. In direct address, "Lord" can mean "Sir"; but in addressing the royal Son of David, even a crumb of whose divine power can heal, she recognizes Jesus as much more.

**Matthew 15:28.** The test is ended; Jesus

will not refuse such strong faith in his power. (The direct address "woman" means "Ma'am.") In the preceding narrative, Jesus has shown that it is the heart rather than tra-ditional external matters like unwashed hands that makes one unclean (15:1-20). Likewise, if this Gentile exercises faith in Israel's king, she shows a pure heart.

---

## INTERPRETING THE SCRIPTURE

### Lessons of Prayer and Faith

Jesus takes the disciples on "retreats" and himself goes aside to pray (Matthew 14:23; Mark 6:31-32). In the midst of our busy schedules, we sometimes need to get away from the pressing needs and be alone with God. Otherwise, the needs of the world can overwhelm us, but time in God's presence gives us perspective and equips us to keep working to make a difference. Nevertheless, when one's "retreat" is interrupted, as often happens in the Gospels, we should respond graciously.

Jesus' obstacles test the woman's faith, but he ultimately grants her request. Sometimes God's answer may be, "No," but sometimes we may give up too easily. When Elijah told Elisha to stay behind, he was testing Elisha; Elisha refused to leave, and received a blessing (2 Kings 2:1-15). When Jesus responded bluntly to his mother's request in John 2:4, she refused to be deterred (John 2:5) and received what she requested.

A desperate refusal to be deterred is a pattern in some other examples of faith. For example, the woman with the flow of blood should not be moving among the crowds, because she rendered unclean until evening anyone she touched (Leviticus 15:19); yet she had to get to Jesus. This is a case of scandalous faith, faith that will not be deterred no matter what anyone thinks (Mark 5:27-28). Finding the entrance to the house where Jesus was teaching too crowded, the paralytic's friends dug through the roof and lowered him in front of Jesus. They could not afford to be put off by any obstacles.

Jesus called their determination to get to him—their desperate trust that he and only he could help them—"faith" (Mark 2:5). Matthew leaves out some of these details, but his audience probably already knew the accounts in Mark.

As often in the Gospels, we also see that we can exercise faith on behalf of others for their healing and deliverance. The paralytic's friends have faith for him; the centurion has faith for his servant; Jairus has faith for his daughter; and this woman in Matthew 15 has faith for her daughter. All these examples of intercession also involve the characteristics of faith we see elsewhere, including determination that they must reach Jesus for help. As we can pray for our own desperate needs, we can also pray with the same commitment and fervor for those of people we love.

The object of faith is key. The desperate mother does not exhibit faith in her faith, or a generic faith that everything will work out, or faith that she has discovered the right formula or method to achieve her ends. She acknowledges Jesus as rightful king of Israel, of a nation that had subdued the ancient Canaanites before her. She recognizes that a mere crumb of his power is sufficient to heal her daughter. Some of us read this story and shrug, "That's easy. We know who Jesus is." But while it is easy for us when reading a Bible story, the deeper tests of faith come in crisis. Learning from the example of this woman and other people in the Bible can help us develop our own faith in Jesus to face the tests that will come our way.

*Demon Possession*

We commented on "spirit possession" in many societies in an earlier lesson. Many people who are willing to believe in God, a spirit, are more reticent to believe in super-human forces of evil. Modern Western culture has often taken an approach to reality that accepts only what is material. In contrast, many cultures have a wider view of the possibility of superhuman evil. While we often underestimate the potential of the human heart for evil, the effectiveness of cases like Hitler, Stalin, Pol Pot, and others on the one hand challenge those who relativize the notion of evil and on the other direct our attention to a superhuman dimension to evil.

Intense frustration, mental illness, brain disorders, and other factors could produce physical phenomena similar to those associated with possession in the Gospels. We would expect the invasion of a foreign spirit to cause psychological or psychomotor problems similar to split personalities, brain disorders, and so forth, but we should not suppose that all cases of these problems stem from a demonic presence. Although Matthew allows that demons can cause some other symptoms (Matthew 17:15), he also distinguishes between those symptoms and demons (Matthew 4:24). He does not suggest that demons are the only cause of such symptoms.

In his book, *Glimpses of the Devil*, noted psychiatrist M. Scott Peck dismisses many supposed cases of demonization today but does focus on a handful of cases in his psychiatric career that he could explain no other way. Jesus had the spiritual discernment to tell the difference; he both expelled demons and healed the sick.

*Jew and Gentile*

Gentile Christians may be troubled by the priority of the Jewish people here. Jesus' teaching may thus summon us to humble ourselves just as the woman did. True, the limitation to Israel (also 10:6) is later explicitly revoked (28:19); but we must recognize that the Christian faith did not start with Gentiles. If Jesus called his own people to look beyond parochial prejudices, he also summoned Gentiles to recognize that he came in fulfillment of Israel's heritage. In contrast to the Aryan Christianity promoted by Hitler's Reich Church (resisted by Dietrich Bonhoeffer and others), a Christianity cut off from its Old Testament and Jewish heritage is no Christianity at all.

Ultimately, the gospel has belonged to no one group of people: starting in Galilee, in the Middle East, it spread most abundantly at first into Syria, Turkey, and Egypt. It was enveloping the Roman Empire (though especially North Africa and the Greek-speaking East, and also Armenia) and East Africa (the kingdom of Axum) in the 300s. Christianity spread north in Europe, and to a lesser extent east in parts of Asia, and as Muslim Arab armies conquered much of the Middle East and North Africa, it was spreading in Russia. In the twentieth century the majority of Christians shifted from the West to Africa, Asia, and Latin America. No one region or people holds permanent possession of the gospel. Our one united heritage, however, lies in the history of Israel.

That this Greco-Phoenician woman (emblematic of Canaan), or a centurion (emblematic of Rome, though perhaps recruited locally in Syria), or a Samaritan leper or others came to Jesus by faith presented Matthew's audience with exceptions—the anomaly of "good" Gentiles. The point of these exceptions, however, was to suggest that there could be other exceptions, and that ultimately Jesus would welcome all who came through faith. We may think of groups of people that appear unredeemable to us—and remember that our group, whatever group that is, once appeared unredeemable to others. There is no people that cannot be transformed by God's grace—whether imperial Rome, Baal-worshiping Canaan, or ourselves.

As if to illustrate the point that scraps will be left over after the children have finished, Jesus soon afterward feeds a crowd of four thousand, with food left over for another meal (Matthew 15:32-38).

---

## SHARING THE SCRIPTURE

### *Preparing Our Hearts*

Meditate on this week's devotional reading, found in Isaiah 42:1-9. This passage includes the first of Isaiah's Servant Songs (42:1-4), in which we learn about the traits of the servant. The hymn in verses 5-9 praises Israel's Creator and Sustainer. Furthermore, the hymn talks about the covenant people whom God has called to be "a light to the nations" (42:6). Why do you think the early church connected this passage with Jesus?

Pray that you and the adult learners will be ever aware of who Jesus is and how he influences your lives.

### *Preparing Our Minds*

Study the background and lesson scripture, both of which are found in Matthew 15:21-28. Think about where you go to find resources when family members face issues.
Write on newsprint:
❑ list of scriptures under "Describe a Vibrant Faith."
❑ information for next week's lesson, found under "Continue the Journey."
❑ activities for further spiritual growth in "Continue the Journey."
**Option:** Find a map showing Tyre and Sidon.

### LEADING THE CLASS

#### *(1) Gather to Learn*

❖ Welcome the class members and introduce any guests.

❖ Pray that all who have come today will recognize the compassionate Jesus as he relates to their lives.

❖ Tell this story from Canadian christianity.com: **As a result of a routine visit to the doctor, a woman learned that her young, apparently normal, daughter had serious brain damage due to hydro-cephalus. The child would need to have risky brain surgery to install a shunt that would drain fluid. In the days prior to the surgery, the parents' lives "became an all encompassing cry to God" on behalf of their daughter. The child's name was lifted up in many prayer groups. And these prayers have truly been answered. While there are still soft spots in the girl's brain, the parents are determined to allow their nearly three-year-old daughter to be a "regular" kid. The mom, once a chronic worrier, has learned to renew her trust in God on a daily basis and to share the hope she experiences with others**.

❖ Discuss this question: **Where do you think parents of children with serious medical problems find the resources and courage to face each day?**

❖ Read aloud today's focus statement: **Family members face issues and often cannot find help. Where can we find resources to help? A Gentile woman came to Jesus, persistently seeking healing for her daughter, and Jesus healed the daughter.**

#### *(2) Explore the Account of the Canaanite Woman and Her Faith*

❖ Choose volunteers to read the parts of the narrator, Jesus, and the Canaanite woman in Matthew 15:21-28. Ask the class to read in unison the part of the disciples in verse 23.

❖ Read or retell the information on Matthew 15:21 and 15:22 in Understanding the Scripture. Be sure the students are acquainted with Sidon and Tyre. You may wish to locate these two cities on a map.

❖ Delve into the idea of "spirit possession" by reading or retelling "Demon Possession" in Interpreting the Scripture. Use this information to help the adults understand the serious nature of the Canaanite woman's daughter's illness. Also invite the students to comment on their understanding of demon possession.

❖ Encourage the participants to imagine themselves as Jewish bystanders who witnessed the encounter between Jesus and the Canaanite woman. Ask these questions:

(1) **What words would you use to describe this woman?**
(2) **How would you have treated her had she approached you?**
(3) **Why did you think Jesus seemed to treat her so harshly at first?**
(4) **Why do you think she was so persistent with Jesus?** (Be sure to note not only her concerns for her daughter but also her apparent belief that Jesus would be able to heal her daughter.)
(5) **How might the Canaanite woman be a role model for you?**

*(3) Describe a Vibrant Faith*

❖ Ask the students to read in unison today's key verse, Matthew 15:28.

❖ Brainstorm with them answers to this question: **How would you describe a "great faith"?** List their ideas on newsprint.

❖ Review the list with the group. Invite them to recall biblical stories in which people of faith are portrayed.

❖ Divide the class into groups and assign each group one of these stories highlighted in "Lessons of Prayer and Faith."

Write each key word and scripture text on a sheet of newsprint prior to the session. Ask each group to be prepared to report to the class how great faith was demonstrated in their story.

■ Elisha: 2 Kings 2:1-15
■ Centurion's servant: Matthew 8:5-13
■ Paralytic and his friends: Mark 2:1-12
■ Jairus and his daughter: Mark 5:22-24, 35-43
■ Woman with flow of blood: Mark 5:25-34

❖ Give each group an opportunity to report to the class.

❖ Wrap up this portion of the lesson by inviting the students to add ideas to their description of "great faith." If time permits, they may also choose to write a definition of "great faith," based on their own ideas and what they have found in the biblical stories.

*(4) Assess the Learners' Faith and Pray that It Will Become Even Stronger*

❖ Distribute paper and pencils. Suggest that the students review the list of Bible characters and ask themselves: "How is my faith like that of Elisha?" and so on, naming all the characters on the list. Encourage them also to identify and list ways in which their own behaviors and attitudes fit the description of "great faith" brainstormed earlier in the session.

❖ Change the slant of this activity by reading this quotation from Oswald Chambers (1874–1917): **Beware of worshiping Jesus as the Son of God and professing your faith in him as Savior of the world, while you blaspheme him by the complete evidence in your daily life that he is powerless to do anything in and through you.**

❖ Provide a few moments for the students to identify and list ways in which they need to grow in their faith so as to enable their "walk" to match their "talk."

❖ Conclude this portion of the session

by inviting the students to identify silently a situation in their own lives where, like the Canaanite woman, their only hope is in God. They are to focus on this situation as they turn to a neighbor in the classroom and say, "[name of classmate], great is your faith!" (Be sure that each person has a chance to hear Jesus' words.)

### (5) Continue the Journey

❖ Pray that those who have participated today will renew and strengthen their faith in Jesus.

❖ Read aloud this preparation for next week's lesson. You may also want to post it on newsprint for the students to copy.

- ■ **Title: Declared by Peter**
- ■ **Background Scripture: Matthew 16:13-27**
- ■ **Lesson Scripture: Matthew 16:13-27**
- ■ **Focus of the Lesson: Many people are curious about the Jesus of history. Who is Jesus really? Jesus affirmed that Peter's declaration of Jesus as the Christ, the Son of God, was a revelation by God.**

❖ Challenge the students to complete one or more of these activities for further spiritual growth, which you will write on newsprint for the students to copy.

(1) **Recall that the Canaanite woman exhibited great faith. In what situations in your own life do you need to approach Jesus with such solid faith? Speak persistently with him concerning these situations.**

(2) **Pray for a family member or friend who is facing medical challenges.**

(3) **Recognize that this story challenges sexism, racism, and exclusivism as Jesus chooses to heal the daughter of this Gentile woman. What barriers must you cross to help someone in need? What can you do to build bridges?**

❖ Sing or read aloud "Hymn of Promise."

❖ Conclude today's session by leading the class in this benediction, adapted from Matthew 16:16: **Go forth now to love and serve the Messiah, the Son of the living God.**

## UNIT 3: TESTIMONIES TO JESUS AS MESSIAH
# DECLARED BY PETER

---

### PREVIEWING THE LESSON

**Lesson Scripture:** Matthew 16:13-27
**Background Scripture:** Matthew 16:13-27
**Key Verse:** Matthew 16:16

#### Focus of the Lesson:
Many people are curious about the Jesus of history. Who is Jesus really? Jesus affirmed that Peter's declaration of Jesus as the Christ, the Son of God, was a revelation by God.

#### Goals for the Learners:
(1) to examine Peter's confession of faith.
(2) to compare Peter's answer to Jesus' question with responses people give today.
(3) to affirm their own faith.

#### Pronunciation Guide:
Caesarea Philippi (ses' uh ree' ih fil ip' i)    *petra* (pet' ra)
   or (ses' uh ree' uh fil' i pi)    *petros* (pet' ros)
*ekklesia* (ek klay see' ah)    *qahal* (kaw hawl')
Hades (hay' deez)    Sadducean (sad joo see' an)
*Kephas* (kay' fas)    *synagoge* (soon ag o gay')
Koine (koi nay')

#### Supplies:
Bibles, newsprint and marker, paper and pencils, hymnals

---

### READING THE SCRIPTURE

NRSV
Matthew 16:13-27

¹³Now when Jesus came into the district of Caesarea Philippi, he asked his disciples, "Who do people say that the Son of Man is?" ¹⁴And they said, "Some say John the Baptist, but others Elijah, and still others Jeremiah or one of the prophets." ¹⁵He said to them, "But

NIV
Matthew 16:13-27

¹³When Jesus came to the region of Caesarea Philippi, he asked his disciples, "Who do people say the Son of Man is?"
¹⁴They replied, "Some say John the Baptist; others say Elijah; and still others, Jeremiah or one of the prophets."

who do you say that I am?" [16]Simon Peter answered, **"You are the Messiah, the Son of the living God."** [17]And Jesus answered him, "Blessed are you, Simon son of Jonah! For flesh and blood has not revealed this to you, but my Father in heaven. [18]And I tell you, you are Peter, and on this rock I will build my church, and the gates of Hades will not prevail against it. [19]I will give you the keys of the kingdom of heaven, and whatever you bind on earth will be bound in heaven, and whatever you loose on earth will be loosed in heaven." [20]Then he sternly ordered the disciples not to tell anyone that he was the Messiah.

[21]From that time on, Jesus began to show his disciples that he must go to Jerusalem and undergo great suffering at the hands of the elders and chief priests and scribes, and be killed, and on the third day be raised. [22]And Peter took him aside and began to rebuke him, saying, "God forbid it, Lord! This must never happen to you." [23]But he turned and said to Peter, "Get behind me, Satan! You are a stumbling block to me; for you are setting your mind not on divine things but on human things."

[24]Then Jesus told his disciples, "If any want to become my followers, let them deny themselves and take up their cross and follow me. [25]For those who want to save their life will lose it, and those who lose their life for my sake will find it. [26]For what will it profit them if they gain the whole world but forfeit their life? Or what will they give in return for their life?

[27]"For the Son of Man is to come with his angels in the glory of his Father, and then he will repay everyone for what has been done."

[15]"But what about you?" he asked. "Who do you say I am?"

[16]Simon Peter answered, **"You are the Christ, the Son of the living God."**

[17]Jesus replied, "Blessed are you, Simon son of Jonah, for this was not revealed to you by man, but by my Father in heaven. [18]And I tell you that you are Peter, and on this rock I will build my church, and the gates of Hades will not overcome it. [19]I will give you the keys of the kingdom of heaven; whatever you bind on earth will be bound in heaven, and whatever you loose on earth will be loosed in heaven." [20]Then he warned his disciples not to tell anyone that he was the Christ.

[21]From that time on Jesus began to explain to his disciples that he must go to Jerusalem and suffer many things at the hands of the elders, chief priests and teachers of the law, and that he must be killed and on the third day be raised to life.

[22]Peter took him aside and began to rebuke him. "Never, Lord!" he said. "This shall never happen to you!"

[23]Jesus turned and said to Peter, "Get behind me, Satan! You are a stumbling block to me; you do not have in mind the things of God, but the things of men."

[24]Then Jesus said to his disciples, "If anyone would come after me, he must deny himself and take up his cross and follow me. [25]For whoever wants to save his life will lose it, but whoever loses his life for me will find it. [26]What good will it be for a man if he gains the whole world, yet forfeits his soul? Or what can a man give in exchange for his soul? [27]For the Son of Man is going to come in his Father's glory with his angels, and then he will reward each person according to what he has done."

## UNDERSTANDING THE SCRIPTURE

**Matthew 16:13.** Jesus again (compare 8:28; 15:21) brings his disciples into predominantly Gentile territory, perhaps deliberately eliciting Peter's confession in a setting that seems so at odds with what he confesses. (Compare the first post-crucifixion confession of Jesus as God's Son, 27:54). Until its recent renaming, Caesarea Philippi was known as "Paneas," for its famous grotto for the worship of Pan.

**Matthew 16:14-15.** Most opinions about Jesus involved prophetic figures, and indeed, Jesus did act in some respects like his predecessor John (as Herod Antipas noticed, 14:2), like Elijah, or like other prophets. Yet these opinions stopped short of Jesus' full identity, as his disciples by now should understand. While Jesus has not acclaimed himself, neither has he rejected those who call him "Son of David" (9:27; 12:23; 15:22).

**Matthew 16:16.** Peter, elsewhere the disciples' leading spokesman (15:15; 26:35), here recognizes that Jesus is Messiah and God's Son. God had already designated the Davidic line, especially the promised ruler par excellence, as God's son (2 Samuel 7:14; Psalm 2:7).

**Matthew 16:17-18.** Jesus affirms Peter's confession, noting that the revelation came from God, not from a purely human perspective (on such revelation, see 11:25). In Greek, Jesus then plays on Simon's nickname "Peter": you are *petros*, and on this *petra* I will build my church. In Koine Greek (and in the Aramaic word *Kephas* Jesus probably used here), in contrast to earlier Greek, *petros* and *petra* were interchangeable. Peter is not designated "Rocky" here arbitrarily, but because he has just confessed Jesus' identity. "Rocky" is foundational as the first to acclaim Jesus' identity, and all who follow his model will also be used to build the church.

The Old Testament often spoke of "building" God's people (Ruth 4:11; Psalm 147:2; Jeremiah 24:6). Here Jesus promises to build his people on the foundational recognition of his identity. Some today doubt that Jesus predicted the "church," but ancient teachers often established communities of disciples to carry on after them, and the renewal movement that produced Qumran's sectarian documents spoke of their own group as the *qahal* ("community"), a Hebrew term that the Greek version of the Old Testament translates as both *synagoge* and *ekklesia* (the word for "church" here). The "gates of Hades" translates an Old Testament expression (also familiar in Greek) meaning "the realm of death."

**Matthew 16:19.** The image of "gates" naturally relates to the image of "keys," but these keys involve God's kingdom rather than the realm of death. Keys to a palace were bulky; the official who carried them was a high official controlling access (for example, Isaiah 22:22). In contrast to a religious elite shutting people out of God's kingdom (Matthew 23:13), Peter was to provide them access by his message that Jesus was Christ and God's son. Matthew is not the only writer to recognize Peter's importance (for example, Galatians 2:7; Acts 2:14; 15:7).

Later rabbis spoke of their legislative authority as "binding" and "loosing." When Matthew uses these terms later in his Gospel, they are more judicial (18:15-18); if literal "binding" and "loosing" had to do with detaining and releasing, Jesus could apply the language to judicial assemblies of believers disciplining or exonerating accused members. The context here could suggest evaluating not those already in the community but those who wished to enter. In any case, the overall sense seems to be that the confession of Jesus' identity would continue to be foundational for facilitating and determining membership in the community.

**Matthew 16:20.** Jesus enjoins silence here, as often elsewhere. Rumors of Jesus' messianic claim would provoke quicker reaction from the authorities; would swell crowds beyond the possibility of control; and would prematurely promote a title the disciples themselves were not yet prepared to understand (see 16:21-22).

**Matthew 16:21-22.** Having accepted Peter's premise that Jesus is Messiah, Jesus now undercuts what Peter and others assumed that messiahship involved. Jesus defines his messianic mission in terms of suffering and death (16:21). Peter, just praised for his correct insight into Jesus' identity, presumably thinks that he carries this insight further by reproving Jesus' gloomy thoughts.

**Matthew 16:23.** Disciples were never to reprove their rabbis; Jesus rebukes Peter's rebuke. "Get behind me," or literally, "after me" orders Peter to return to his proper posture as a follower of Jesus rather than his leader. Jesus calls Peter "Satan" to evoke Jesus' earlier rebuke of Satan for offering the kingdom without the cross, as Peter now wants a non-martyred Messiah. In the span of a few verses, Peter falls from being "rock" to "stumbling block"! Jesus builds his church on Peter not because of the latter's perfection but because of his confession. When that confession diverges from the truth, it merits censure instead.

**Matthew 16:24.** Jesus cuts to the heart of the issue: Peter rejects the cross because he does not want suffering. Peter's concept of Messiah lacks the cross precisely because Peter wants to follow the expected triumphant Messiah, not a suffering one. Peter does not want to follow someone defeated and executed in this world because Peter does not want to face defeat and execution himself. Following Jesus in the time of miracles is pleasant; these same disciples abandoned him at Gethsemane.

Now Jesus warns that Peter must follow "after" Jesus (16:23), that is, return to the posture of disciple, and those who truly follow Jesus must follow to the cross. The person being executed normally carried the horizontal beam of the cross out to the site of their execution, often amid a jeering mob. To carry the cross was to follow Jesus to death, facing ridicule and scorn en route.

**Matthew 16:25-27.** In the final analysis, facing even death (16:24) is a small price to pay for following Jesus. If we follow him to the cross, we also share the hope of the resurrection. Everyone dies; but to die momentarily in hope of eternal life is better than temporarily preserving one's life only to lose it forever, popular as that approach to life may be.

Everything would come to light at Jesus' return, when he *would* come as triumphant Messiah. Jesus offers a foreshadowing of his coming in his transfiguration (16:28–17:8).

---

# INTERPRETING THE SCRIPTURE

### Jesus as Messiah

Peter's foundational confession of faith in Christ invites the church built on this rock to share the same confession. Some today regard Jesus as only a great prophet (Islam regards him as a very great prophet). Many secularists in the West affirm less about Jesus than this, denying prophets and any God behind them. Most scholars believe that Jesus performed miracles, a major source of his popularity. Many relate this to a category of ancient prophet modeled after Elijah and Elisha. Most believe that he was a sage. His sayings and parables resemble those of other Jewish sages of his day, though Jesus was often more radical than most teachers. But did Jesus claim to be more than this? Did Jesus claim to be Messiah?

The Synoptic Gospels themselves do not report Jesus openly revealing his identity in public among his own people before the Passion Week. Although often he provokes thought with riddles about his identity (especially in John's Gospel), he avoids being explicit enough for anyone to be able to accuse him of political claims. In private with his disciples, however, and in more public hints during the Passion Week, Jesus acted differently.

Certainly the disciples believed in Jesus' messiahship after they met him alive from the dead. Where did they get the idea? Likewise, Pilate certainly crucified Jesus on the charge of treason, as "King of the Jews." (This is not a charge Jesus' followers would have invented for him, unless every one of them had a death wish. Following someone crucified for treason could render the followers suspect as well.) Yet it is highly unlikely that Pilate or the disciples would have borrowed the idea from each other. Had Pilate gotten it from the disciples, they might have been crucified too. If Pilate believed that Jesus thought himself the Messiah, and Jesus' followers independently held the same view, is it not likely that the common source of the view was Jesus, just as the Gospels report?

### Jesus Warns of His Death

Peter's confession was right, but his understanding was wrong: Jesus was the Messiah but would bring victory through death, not conquest. Some today doubt that Jesus foreknew his death, thinking that his execution caught him by surprise. Yet even aside from the question of Jesus' prophetic insight, Jesus hardly could have not foreseen a death he provoked. When Jesus later overturns the tables in the Temple, he challenges the honor of the Sadducean high priestly establishment. Even a prophet like Jeremiah (who smashed a pot in the Temple) or Josephus' Joshua ben Ananiah (who simply announced its judgment) faced beatings. Jesus' more dramatic announcement of judgment would face harsher punishment still.

Jesus also knew both the Jewish tradition of prophets' martyrdom and that of intense suffering ("birth pangs") would precede the kingdom. Many also expected the bodily resurrection of the dead afterwards. Jesus' view is distinctive primarily in affirming that he would rise before others, befitting his unique role in the kingdom.

That the disciples continued to misunderstand, despite his warnings, indicates just how deeply their cultural presuppositions about messiahship and the kingdom controlled their thinking. How often do we miss plain biblical teachings about sacrifice, love of neighbor (including its often economic expressions), Christ's lordship, and so forth, because our presuppositions are so strong? Carried along by popular novels and movies, some North American Christians expect to escape great persecution or suffering (as if their generation and location would be uniquely excluded). On the other end of the theological spectrum, shaped by anti-supernaturalism or other cultural presuppositions, some assume that Jesus was only a great teacher or deluded visionary and not the Messiah.

Yet God causes many of us to understand that Jesus is truly God's Son (as God did for Peter, before he temporarily diverged from that view). We must recognize that Jesus' messianic mission involved suffering, and following him (to serve where the need is greatest) often involves the same.

### Counting the Cost

The "gates of death" may assail, but cannot prevail. In a context reminding disciples that following Christ may cost our lives (Matthew 16:24), it is essential for us to remember that no individuals' deaths will stop the church. Persecuted and even crushed in some parts of the world through history, the church has nevertheless persevered; death itself cannot stop it. God's purposes always have the final word. This message fits together with the message of the earlier prophets: Oppressive empires seem to control the world, but sooner or later all of them fall. God's people may be small and oppressed, yet they endure through history. In the end, God consummates the kingdom, which replaces all earthly empires.

Carrying Jesus' cross means facing whatever we need to face for him. We do not count death too high a price to pay to follow Jesus, because we recognized our lives as forfeit the moment we began following him. Since everyone faces death anyway, this is a small price to pay in view of eternal life. In many parts of the world, Christians do lay their lives on the line to serve Jesus and others in his name.

Ironically, when the time came for Jesus to carry his cross later in the Gospel, his disciples abandoned him. No disciple offered to share Jesus' cross, and the Romans had to draft a bystander to do what his own disciples who had seen his miracles were unwilling to do. Jesus never lowers the standards of God's demands, but he does show mercy on growing disciples. He forgave our spiritual predecessors so that he could make something stronger of them. Likewise, he gives us grace while forming us into his image. Given the realities of today's world, however, we should prepare our hearts, committing ourselves to faithfulness to Jesus and his purposes no matter what the cost to our earthly lives.

In Matthew's larger context, "denying" oneself means that we are prepared to suffer rather than to "deny" Jesus when persecuted (10:33). (If believers should share Christ courageously in the face of such harsh threats, it certainly has a message for those afraid merely of their neighbors' or colleagues' disapproval.) In fact, Peter, the disciple who does not want to think about future suffering in this passage eventually "denies" Jesus in the face of persecution (26:69-75). Failure to reckon with the commitment involved in following a crucified Christ can have long-term consequences. Though Peter repented deeply, all four Gospels publicly attest to his failure.

The Gospels thus emphasize that those who want to follow Christ are surrendering their lives to him. Some present salvation in terms of God having "a wonderful plan for your life" or inviting Jesus into your heart. These portrayals are true enough, but we need to understand what they really involve: Truly accepting Jesus means that we acknowledge his right to plan our future. Inviting Jesus into our heart means that Jesus rather than selfishness will be our Lord. It is Christ's work, not our own, that brings the gift of salvation; but part of that gift is a new life under God's kingdom or rule. Can we deny ourselves, acknowledging that God's way is truly the best way?

## SHARING THE SCRIPTURE

### Preparing Our Hearts

Meditate on this week's devotional reading, found in John 10:22-30. Read the words of Jesus aloud, listening to them as if you were one of the Jewish people with whom Jesus was speaking. What would you suppose about his identity? Would you believe his words? Think about people you know. If asked if Jesus were the Messiah, how would they answer? How do you answer?

Pray that you and the adult learners will recognize the Messiah and follow him.

### Preparing Our Minds

Study the background and lesson scripture, both of which are taken from Matthew 16:13-27. Ponder who you believe Jesus really is.

Write on newsprint:
- ❏ questions under "Examine Peter's Confession of Faith."
- ❏ information for next week's lesson, found under "Continue the Journey."
- ❏ activities for further spiritual growth in "Continue the Journey."

### LEADING THE CLASS

#### (1) Gather to Learn

❖ Welcome the class members and introduce any guests.

❖ Pray that all who have come today will explore their beliefs about who Jesus was—and is.

❖ Read what several historical figures have written about Jesus and invite the students to comment on what these writings reveal about who Jesus is.

- **The Christians . . . worship a man to this day—the distinguished personage who introduced this new cult, and was crucified on that account. . . . You see, these misguided creatures start with the general conviction that they are immortal for all time, which explains their contempt for death and self devotion . . . their lawgiver [taught] they are all brothers, from the moment that they are converted, and deny the gods of Greece, and worship the crucified sage, and live after his laws. All this they take on faith.** (*The Passing Peregrinus* by Lucian of Samosata, second century satirist)

- **Now, there was about this time Jesus, a wise man, if it be lawful to call him a man. For he was a doer of surprising feats—a teacher of such men as receive the truth with pleasure. He drew over to him both many of the Jews and many of the Gentiles. He was [the] Christ; and when Pilate, at the suggestion of the principal men amongst us, had condemned him to the cross, those that loved him at the first did not forsake him, for he appeared to them alive again the third day, as the divine prophets had foretold these and ten thousand other wonderful things concerning him; and the tribe of Christians, so named from him, are not extinct to this day.** (*Antiquities of the Jews* 18.3.3 by Pharisee and Roman historian, Flavius Josephus, A.D. 37–97)

- **Alexander, Caesar, Charlemagne, and myself founded empires; but upon what did we rest the creations of our genius? Upon force. Jesus Christ alone founded his empire upon love, and at this hour millions of men would die for him.** (Napoleon Bonaparte, 1769–1821)

❖ Read aloud today's focus statement: **Many people are curious about the Jesus of history. Who is Jesus really? Jesus affirmed that Peter's declaration of Jesus as the Christ, the Son of God, was a revelation by God.**

*(2) Examine Peter's Confession of Faith*

❖ Choose one person to read the part of the narrator, one to read the words of Jesus, and another to portray Peter in a dramatic reading of Matthew 16:13-27. Invite the class to read verse 14 in unison.

❖ Point out that these verses focus on three different points: Peter's confession, Jesus' prediction of his death and resurrection, and Jesus' explanation of the cost of discipleship.

❖ Post these questions on newsprint. Divide the class into three groups and assign each group a series of questions.

- **Matthew 16:13-20: What does this passage tell you about Jesus? What does it tell you about the beliefs of people who heard him? What does it tell you about Peter?** (Use "Jesus as Messiah" from Interpreting the Scripture to add other ideas.)

- **Matthew 16:21-23: How do Jesus' comments clarify what it means for him to be the Messiah? How would you characterize Peter's response? What causes Jesus to change his description of Peter from "rock" (13:18) to "stumbling block" (13:23)?** (Use "Jesus Warns of His Death" from Interpreting the Scripture to add other ideas.)

- **Matthew 16:24-27: What does Jesus mean when he calls followers to "take up [their] cross"? What does he mean when he tells followers to "deny" themselves? What would be your expectations of Jesus' repayment**

**to everyone?** (Use "Counting the Cost" from Interpreting the Scripture to add other ideas.)

❖ Call everyone back together and hear reports from each group. Add ideas from suggested portions of Interpreting the Scripture as appropriate.

*(3) Compare Peter's Answer to Jesus' Question with Responses People Give Today*

❖ Brainstorm with the class a list of contemporary answers to the question: **Who is Jesus?** List their ideas on newsprint. Note that the responses may be those that believers or nonbelievers would give. Answers abound and may include: *Messiah, prophet, teacher, moral example, fraud, blasphemer, Jewish man, king, God with us, Savior, healer, One who rose from the dead.*

❖ Review the list and ask the students to cite any scriptural evidence to support each response. (The adults need not quote chapter and verse, but encourage them to be as specific as possible. For example, the story of Jesus restoring sight to a man blind from birth supports the title of "healer." People who refused to believe in Jesus may have considered him a fraud or blasphemer.)

❖ Conclude by asking: **How would you say that contemporary people's responses to Jesus' question are similar to and different from the responses given by his contemporaries?**

*(4) Affirm the Learners' Faith*

❖ Read this quotation by twentieth-century author and scholar C. S. Lewis: **A man who was merely a man and said the sort of things Jesus said wouldn't be a great moral teacher. He'd be either a lunatic—on a level with a man who says he's a poached egg—or else he'd be the devil of hell. You must make your choice. Either this man was, and is, the Son of God, or else a madman or something worse.**

❖ Distribute paper and pencils. Provide a few moments of quiet time for the students to write their answer to Jesus' question: "But who do you say that I am?" (Matthew 16:15).

❖ Invite volunteers to share their responses. Affirm their answers, even if some responses are tentative or uncertain.

*(5) Continue the Journey*

❖ Pray that all who have come today will boldly confess Jesus as the Messiah, the Son of the living God.

❖ Read aloud this preparation for next week's lesson. You may also want to post it on newsprint for the students to copy.
- ■ **Title: Witnessed by Disciples**
- ■ **Background Scripture: Matthew 17:1-12**
- ■ **Lesson Scripture: Matthew 17:1-12**
- ■ **Focus of the Lesson: People sometimes seek special spiritual experiences. Which experiences are authentic? Three disciples experienced a spiritual encounter that confirmed Jesus as the Son of God.**

❖ Challenge the students to complete one or more of these activities for further spiritual growth, which you will write on newsprint for the students to copy.
- (1) **Write your own obituary. What would you want people to remember about you? What words or phrases might other people use to describe you?**
- (2) **Seek opportunities to bear witness to Jesus as the Messiah, especially to one who is searching for God.**
- (3) **Take a survey among family, friends, and neighbors by asking this question: Who do you say Jesus is? Compile the results. How many different answers did you get? What surprised you?**

❖ Sing or read aloud "His Name Is Wonderful."

❖ Conclude today's session by leading the class in this benediction, adapted from Matthew 16:16: **Go forth now to love and serve the Messiah, the Son of the living God.**

## UNIT 3: TESTIMONIES TO JESUS AS MESSIAH
# WITNESSED BY DISCIPLES

---

### PREVIEWING THE LESSON

**Lesson Scripture:** Matthew 17:1-12
**Background Scripture:** Matthew 17:1-12
**Key Verse:** Matthew 17:2

### Focus of the Lesson:
People sometimes seek special spiritual experiences. Which experiences are authentic? Three disciples experienced a spiritual encounter that confirmed Jesus as the Son of God.

### Goals for the Learners:
(1) to explore the disciples' experience on the Mount of Transfiguration.
(2) to identify times they have felt Jesus' presence in a special way.
(3) to look for places and situations where God is working.

### Pronunciation Guide:
theophany (thee of' uh nee)

### Supplies:
Bibles, newsprint and marker, paper and pencils, hymnals, optional information on retreat centers

---

### READING THE SCRIPTURE

NRSV
Matthew 17:1-12

¹Six days later, Jesus took with him Peter and James and his brother John and led them up a high mountain, by themselves. **²And he was transfigured before them, and his face shone like the sun, and his clothes became dazzling white.** ³Suddenly there appeared to them Moses and Elijah, talking with him. ⁴Then Peter said to Jesus, "Lord, it is good for us to be here; if you wish, I will

NIV
Matthew 17:1-12

¹After six days Jesus took with him Peter, James and John the brother of James, and led them up a high mountain by themselves. **²There he was transfigured before them. His face shone like the sun, and his clothes became as white as the light.** ³Just then there appeared before them Moses and Elijah, talking with Jesus.

⁴Peter said to Jesus, "Lord, it is good for

make three dwellings here, one for you, one for Moses, and one for Elijah." [5]While he was still speaking, suddenly a bright cloud overshadowed them, and from the cloud a voice said, "This is my Son, the Beloved; with him I am well pleased; listen to him!" [6]When the disciples heard this, they fell to the ground and were overcome by fear. [7]But Jesus came and touched them, saying, "Get up and do not be afraid." [8]And when they looked up, they saw no one except Jesus himself alone.

[9]As they were coming down the mountain, Jesus ordered them, "Tell no one about the vision until after the Son of Man has been raised from the dead." [10]And the disciples asked him, "Why, then, do the scribes say that Elijah must come first?" [11]He replied, "Elijah is indeed coming and will restore all things; [12]but I tell you that Elijah has already come, and they did not recognize him, but they did to him whatever they pleased. So also the Son of Man is about to suffer at their hands."

us to be here. If you wish, I will put up three shelters—one for you, one for Moses and one for Elijah."

[5]While he was still speaking, a bright cloud enveloped them, and a voice from the cloud said, "This is my Son, whom I love; with him I am well pleased. Listen to him!" [6]When the disciples heard this, they fell facedown to the ground, terrified. [7]But Jesus came and touched them. "Get up," he said. "Don't be afraid." [8]When they looked up, they saw no one except Jesus.

[9]As they were coming down the mountain, Jesus instructed them, "Don't tell anyone what you have seen, until the Son of Man has been raised from the dead."

[10]The disciples asked him, "Why then do the teachers of the law say that Elijah must come first?"

[11]Jesus replied, "To be sure, Elijah comes and will restore all things. [12]But I tell you, Elijah has already come, and they did not recognize him, but have done to him everything they wished. In the same way the Son of Man is going to suffer at their hands."

## UNDERSTANDING THE SCRIPTURE

**Matthew 17:1.** Although a "high mountain" was useful for getting away from the crowds, it also evokes Moses' experiences with God's glory on Mount Sinai. Matthew has earlier implicitly compared Jesus with Moses, for example, in 2:20 (see Exodus 4:19) and 4:2 (see Exodus 24:18), perhaps including his teaching from a mountain (Matthew 5:1; contrast the "level place" in Luke 6:17, though still in the hill country). Like the cloud or ascending the mountain, the "six days" may also represent an allusion to Moses on Mount Sinai, although the context is somewhat different (Exodus 24:15-16). (In 1 Kings 19:8, Elijah, who also appears here, similarly met God on Mount Horeb after forty days, evoking the example of Moses.)

**Matthew 17:2.** Greeks had stories of beings being transfigured, such as a story where Zeus becomes like lightning. Jewish people had accounts of angels, the righteous (sometimes after death) and divine theophanies, all sometimes envisioned as brighter than the sun. The most commonly recounted narrative about such glory known to both Matthew and his audience, however, was the story of Moses' transfiguration on Mount Sinai, as he witnessed God's glory.

**Matthew 17:3.** Some scholars think that Moses and Elijah appear because they represent the testimony of law and prophets to Jesus. Yet if so, Samuel (who is earlier than Elijah) or a major writing prophet (like Isaiah or Jeremiah) may have functioned better as a representative of "the prophets." Others think that Moses and Elijah appear here because it was thought that Elijah never died, and Moses' death was a matter of varied speculation in early Judaism. Possibly they both appear because Scripture had promised a prophet like Moses (Deuteronomy 18:15-19) and a sort of new Elijah (Malachi 4:4-5). Whatever the specific factors involved in the selection of these two witnesses, their appearance clearly suggests that Jesus' revelation is not meant to be contrary to prior biblical revelation but as a climax and epitome of it.

**Matthew 17:4.** Peter, who had rightly confessed Jesus as Messiah in 16:16 but spoken wrongly of the nature of that messiahship in 16:22, now misspeaks embarrassingly again. Important as the disciples were, they are not the heroes of the Gospels but were fallible people such as ourselves; Jesus is the hero. Peter's mistake here lay precisely in that misunderstanding: the honored prophets Moses and Elijah do not merit treatment equal to that of Jesus (see 17:5). The temporary "dwellings" Peter suggests may evoke the booths Israel built in the wilderness during the time of Moses, but they were also the sort of shelters people built more generally for workers in the fields (or, some suggest, for special visitors in the wilderness).

**Matthew 17:5.** The overshadowing cloud evokes the cloud of divine glory at Mount Sinai. The announcement of God's beloved and pleasing Son recalls God's very words about Jesus' identity and mission at his baptism, the only other instance of the "heavenly" voice in Matthew. Although Mark also includes both instances of the heavenly voice, Matthew connects them still more clearly by changing the wording of the first instance in Mark ("You are my Son") to fit the second ("This is my Son"). Whereas God spoke the Ten Commandments to Israel at Mount Sinai (Deuteronomy 4:12-13; 5:4-23), the voice here speaks of Jesus. Jesus has a higher role than Moses.

The voice here also adds a line, "Listen to him!" Although the phrase is not uncommon, in a context full of allusions to Moses it could evoke Deuteronomy 18:15: "The LORD your God will raise up for you a prophet like me from among your own people; you shall heed such a prophet" (literally, "Listen to him!"). Without dismissing the value of Moses and Elijah, the heavenly voice directs Peter's attention to Jesus. This "prophet like Moses" would be greater than Moses himself. Jesus had already helped the disciples understand that he was greater than the prophets (Matthew 16:14-16).

**Matthew 17:6-8.** People usually fell to the ground when confronted with overwhelming visions or revelations (for example, Daniel 8:17-18; 10:9; Ezekiel 1:28). As here, the revealer often also raised up those who fell down due to a revelation, or encouraged them not to be afraid (compare for example, Matthew 28:3-5; Daniel 10:10; Ezekiel 2:1). Jesus also assured them by touching them, as he often touched people (8:3, 15; 9:25, 29). That they afterward saw only Jesus by himself (17:8) fits the emphasis in this context that Jesus is greater than Moses and Elijah.

**Matthew 17:9.** Although Jesus kept aspects of his identity mostly secret (recently, 16:20), the secret would no longer be necessary after the resurrection. The disciples could understand his messiahship only in light of his death (16:21), and his death would make sense only in light of his resurrection.

**Matthew 17:10.** The prediction that Elijah would get things ready for the end appears in Malachi 4:5-6 and Sirach 48:10 (a book in the Apocrypha), and Jewish tradition expanded the idea further. Perhaps Elijah appeared in Malachi because apparently he had not died, or perhaps because he epitomized a prophet awakening Israel and turning the nation back to God. The disciples naturally asked about Elijah coming first because they had just seen Elijah on the mountain and wondered whether he was about to play his end-time role.

**Matthew 17:11-12.** Jesus takes the promise of the coming Elijah figuratively, of a prophet like Elijah rather than the literal return of Elijah himself (just as he would be a new prophet like Moses, not replacing the literal Moses). John was not like Elijah in terms of miracle-working (Jesus repeats Elijah's miracles instead) but in terms of turning people's hearts to God. Matthew's audience will remember that John's garb recalled Elijah (3:4). Ancient audiences were familiar with newer figures evoking older

ones (such as a new "Augustus," new "Nero," new "Alexander," and so forth.)

But as John, the new Elijah, was executed, so would Jesus, for whom John prepared the way, be executed. Jesus uses the opportunity to again begin preparing his disciples for the crisis their faith will soon face; Jesus' mission involved the cross. In the larger context of Matthew's Gospel, Jesus' suffering also foreshadowed that of his followers (16:21-24; compare 5:11; 24:9; 26:31).

## INTERPRETING THE SCRIPTURE

### Experiencing Jesus' Glory

Moses took his assistant Joshua onto the mountain (at least part of the way; Exodus 24:13; 32:17). Joshua would later carry forward Moses' work. Although Jesus had many followers, he spent the most time with those special followers who pressed into his inner circle. This included the twelve chosen witnesses, and among them, here, the three who were closest to Jesus on some occasions (Mark 5:37; Luke 22:8), and at least two of these became special leaders (Acts 3:1–4:19; 8:14-17; Galatians 2:9).

Moses had wanted to see God's glory (Exodus 33:18). God promised to show Moses the part of divine glory involving God's character (33:19) but not God's face (33:20). As God caused the divine glory to pass before Moses, God revealed the divine character to Moses: mercy, grace, avenging sin to three or four generations but demonstrating love to the thousandth generation (34:6-7).

Most modern Christians have not seen theophanies in the way that Moses did or the disciples did on the mountain; nor do we have an indication that these disciples (in contrast to Moses) witnessed such divine glory on a regular basis. Christians, however, have a benefit of divine glory that

Moses did not have. Paul says that the glory of the new covenant he preaches is greater than that of Moses. While Moses was transformed on the outside, the hidden glory of Christ's gospel transforms us on the inside (2 Corinthians 3:5-18).

Likewise, John says that the eyewitnesses beheld Jesus' glory, "full of grace and truth" just like the glory on Mount Sinai (John 1:14). But this glory communicated grace and truth even more fully than Moses' revelation (1:17). Whereas before no one (including Moses) had seen God fully, Jesus has now fully revealed God (1:18). Tracing the theme of "glory" through John's Gospel, we see that it was revealed in Jesus' benevolent signs, but ultimately at the point where he most fully shared our humanity: at the cross (12:23-24). That is to say, we have a deeper revelation of God's heart than Moses saw: God embraced our humanity and suffering and even shared our death to redeem us. No greater sign of God's love for us is possible. Considering Jesus' love for us and praising him for it is one way to experience his glory now.

### Jesus' Greatness

We may note that Jesus felt no need to reveal his identity prematurely (before the disciples were prepared to understand it), or to reveal it to those outside his circle who would not use the knowledge wisely. Ancients who wished to boast had to find acceptable ways to do it (such as "You forced me to boast" or, "I am merely offering myself as an example"). Jesus is concerned with pleasing his Father, not with human honor. The Father would exalt him in due time. Whereas Jesus humbled himself to embrace our humanity, we are sometimes more concerned with our reputation than with serving him.

We may also note clues regarding Jesus' identity here. Jesus' transfiguration evokes Moses but could evoke more than Moses. There is no suggestion here of Jesus being transformed by witnessing divine glory; rather, Jesus' own glory shines before the disciples, and they (rather than Moses) are the witnesses. Although Matthew may be content with the Moses allusion, the Gospel of John later develops the comparison with Moses so that the eyewitnesses who proclaim Jesus' message are the ones who, like Moses, beheld his glory (John 1:14), whereas Jesus is the incarnate revelation of God's glory. To grasp the multifaceted character of Jesus' mission, different New Testament authors present it in various complementary ways.

We further learn about Jesus' and the Father's character. Jesus is especially beloved by the Father and especially pleases the Father. We also see Jesus' compassion on his frightened disciples, whom he encourages here. The greatest sign of his love, however, is hinted at in his mention of his impending death. The reader of the entire Gospel of Matthew understands that Jesus dies not by tragic accident but on behalf of us whom he loved (Matthew 20:28; 26:28).

### A New Elijah

Many interpreters have used "typology" (studying the Bible to identify people and situations as prophesies that seem to be ful-

filled later) to make texts say whatever they want, turning real people in the Bible into nothing more than symbols or proofs for their favorite themes. By contrast, the Bible offers a different kind of "typology," namely through observing patterns in God's ways of working. Thus a prophet using figurative language (as prophets and psalmists often did) could promise a prophet like Elijah, just as another prophet could speak of a coming Davidic king as a new David (Ezekiel 34:23-24; 37:24-25) and the psalmist could speak of a royal priest like Melchizedek (Psalm 110:4).

This more restrained understanding follows the sort of literary connections we find within Old Testament documents themselves. Despite clear differences, some events in Joshua's ministry evoke those of Moses' (the parting of the Jordan recalls the parting of the sea). Elisha deliberately imitates Elijah (2 Kings 2:13-15). Some aspects of Moses' life mirror elements in Joseph's: Joseph brought Israel from Canaan to Egypt, and Moses brought them from Egypt to Canaan. Exiled from his homeland, Joseph married the daughter of a foreign priest; exiled from his homeland, Moses married the daughter of a foreign priest. Joseph was sold to Midianites; Midianites welcomed the fugitive Moses. Joseph, a slave, became a prince in Egypt; Moses, a prince of Egypt, identified with slaves.

Ancient historians (Greek as well as Jewish) looked for patterns they believed God created in history. While this approach can often prove subjective, over the course of the Bible we have some patterns repeatedly emphasized, as well as many inspired, prophetic interpretations of these patterns. One pattern that emerges frequently is that God's servants suffer before facing victory. This theme appears here as well.

### The Prospect of Martyrdom

When we think of success in life, we do not usually think of John the Baptist. After all, he was martyred by a ruler, leaving little political legacy. Yet John fulfilled his purpose in life: to prepare people for Jesus. It is easy to become discouraged that we are not making a bigger difference: Elijah himself despaired when, despite fire from heaven at Mount Carmel, Jezebel threatened to use her political power to have him killed (1 Kings 18–19). Power rather than truth continued in place. Yet Mount Carmel was a turning point, and over the next generation, much of Israel returned to its faith legacy in God and abandoned Baal. John faced uncertainties at least temporarily before he died (Matthew 11:3), yet from the larger standpoint of God's purposes he had achieved success.

It is important for us to remember that we are each a part in God's larger plan. To ignore our mission means that some lives may go untouched; but also our mission involves obeying faithfully, not always achieving results that the world quantifies as success. We must trust that the God who knows us knows both our calling and that of others, and is working out the divine purpose on the larger canvas of history. God, rather than ourselves, is the focus. For humans confronted with our own limitations, that focus can provide us great encouragement.

---

# SHARING THE SCRIPTURE

### Preparing Our Hearts

Meditate on this week's devotional reading, found in 2 Peter 1:16-21. In this passage, Peter, who was one of the eyewitnesses of Jesus' transfiguration, recounts that amazing event and in doing so supports his authority as an apostle. How do you think such an experience changed Peter? How have encounters on spiritual mountaintops changed you?

Pray that you and the adult learners will be open to the leading of the Spirit in your lives.

### Preparing Our Minds

Study the background and lesson scripture, both found in Matthew 17:1-12. Think about how you know when a spiritual experience is truly authentic.

Write on newsprint:
❑ information for next week's lesson, found under "Continue the Journey."
❑ activities for further spiritual growth in "Continue the Journey."

Plan a lecture for "Explore the Disciples' Experience on the Mount of Transfiguration" in which you explain key images and concepts discussed in Understanding the Scripture, such as high mountain, stories of transfiguration, cloud, and voice.

### LEADING THE CLASS

### (1) Gather to Learn

❖ Welcome the class members and introduce any guests.

❖ Pray that those who have gathered for today's session will seek experiences that connect them more closely to Christ.

❖ Read this commentary: **People seek spiritual experiences in our age, just as they did in the time of Jesus and long before that, stretching back to the experiences Adam and Eve had in the garden with God. Yet as rational people whose thinking is very much influenced by the eighteenth-century Age of Enlightenment, we may question the validity of so-called spiritual experiences. After all, there are people in psychiatric facilities who claim** to be Jesus himself. We may wonder about the validity of our experiences and those that others report.

❖ Discuss these questions and list ideas on newsprint.

**(1) How do we know spiritual experiences are real, especially when they are so difficult to talk about?**

**(2) What are the qualities of authentic spiritual experiences?** (Here are some possible criteria: *sense of knowing that one is experiencing God; love; truth; experience cannot be described in terms of time; awe; sense of the sacred; humility; heightened sense of creativity; experience is transformative.*)

❖ Read aloud today's focus statement: **People sometimes seek special spiritual experiences. Which experiences are authentic? Three disciples experienced a spiritual encounter that confirmed Jesus as the Son of God.**

*(2) Explore the Disciples' Experience on the Mount of Transfiguration*

❖ Invite the learners to close their eyes as you read today's Scripture passage from Matthew 17:1-12. Suggest that they try to imagine this scene as vividly as possible in their mind's eye and to be aware of voices.

❖ Invite the students to comment on what they saw and heard, describing the sights and sounds as specifically as possible. (For example, was the voice they heard booming or gentle?)

❖ Present the lecture you have prepared to help the adults better understand some key concepts and images in this story.

❖ Invite three students to role-play a conversation between Jesus, Moses, and Elijah, which is referred to in Matthew 17:3. What would Moses, generally thought to represent the law, and Elijah, generally thought to represent the prophets, have said to Jesus? (Encourage volunteers by pointing

out that no specifics of the conversation are given, so they can be free to use their imaginations.)

❖ Conclude by dividing the class into groups of three or four. Ask the students to talk within their groups about how they would have responded to this scene had they been Peter, James, or John.

*(3) Identify Times the Learners Have Felt Jesus' Presence in a Special Way*

❖ Read or retell "Experiencing Jesus' Glory" in Interpreting the Scripture.

❖ Point out that most Christians have felt Jesus' presence in a special way at least once.

❖ Give the students a few moments to recall one or more of these mountaintop experiences.

❖ Invite volunteers to tell about this experience. Note that sometimes an experience is too deep for words. Those who cannot describe their experiences in words may resort to describing the mood in terms of a color, or emotion, or place in nature, or a type of music.

❖ **Caution:** Some students may not recognize that they have had such experiences. Do not press anyone to participate, but remind the class that since only a handful of people has ever seen the transfigured Christ, their stories may seem more ordinary by comparison. That does not make their experience any less real or important.

*(4) Look for Places and Situations Where God Is Working*

❖ Read again Matthew 17:5. Solicit opinions as to what this means to the students. Refer to information about this verse in Understanding the Scripture to help unpack its meaning.

❖ Ask: **Where is there evidence in our congregation that we are listening to and heeding the voice of Jesus?** List ideas on newsprint. Look especially at what the congregation is doing in terms of mission, outreach to the community, spiritual formation, and discipleship-making within the congregation.

❖ Invite volunteers to share ideas that they believe God has laid on their hearts about new or expanded ministries. Talk about how the class might help bring these ministries to birth.

❖ **Option:** Consider the possibility of a class retreat for the purpose of praying and opening themselves to see and hear Christ more clearly. Present, if possible, a list of retreat sites that are accessible to your congregation. Even if you have no actual centers nearby, perhaps another congregation would allow you to use its sacred space to see and hear God in a fresh place. Talk with your pastor about possible retreat leaders. Many conferences/judicatory bodies have experienced people who will direct a retreat. Retreat centers generally have such persons as well. Talk with the class about any specific needs they have in terms of what they would hope to gain from such an event. Decide whether it will be one day (probably a Saturday) or overnight (possible a Friday night and Saturday). If the idea of a retreat excites the class, form a task force to investigate sites, leaders, and topics. Set a time for them to report back to the class for further action.

*(5) Continue the Journey*

❖ Pray that all who have participated today will seek spiritual experiences and then listen to Christ as they encounter him.

❖ Read aloud this preparation for next week's lesson. You may also want to post it on newsprint for the students to copy.

■ **Title: Anointed by a Woman in Bethany**

■ **Background Scripture: Matthew 26:6-13**
■ **Lesson Scripture: Matthew 26:6-13**
■ **Focus of the Lesson: People who truly love find ways to demonstrate that love. Can we ever give too much love? Jesus commended a woman who gave extravagantly out of her love for him as Messiah.**

❖ Challenge the students to complete one or more of these activities for further spiritual growth, which you will write on newsprint for the students to copy.

(1) **Browse the Internet searching for "pictures of the transfiguration of Jesus," or look through art books to find such pictures. Focus on one that appeals to you. How does this picture draw you into the scene and enable you to witness this amazing event?**

(2) **Recall some mountaintop experiences in your own life. Meditate on them or write about what happened, how you were affected, and how you believe your life was changed because of this event.**

(3) **Read Mark 9:2-8 and Luke 9:28-36. Compare and contrast these accounts with the one in Matthew 17:1-12. How does this story, told from the perspective of three Gospel writers, help you better understand who Jesus is?**

❖ Sing or read aloud "Christ, upon the Mountain Peak."

❖ Conclude today's session by leading the class in this benediction, adapted from Matthew 16:16: **Go forth now to love and serve the Messiah, the Son of the living God.**

UNIT 3: TESTIMONIES TO JESUS AS MESSIAH
# ANOINTED BY A WOMAN IN BETHANY

---

## PREVIEWING THE LESSON

**Lesson Scripture:** Matthew 26:6-13
**Background Scripture:** Matthew 26:6-13
**Key Verse:** Matthew 26:13

### Focus of the Lesson:
People who truly love find ways to demonstrate that love. Can we ever give too much love? Jesus commended a woman who gave extravagantly out of her love for him as Messiah.

### Goals for the Learners:
(1) to examine the narrative of a woman of Bethany who anointed Jesus.
(2) to identify themselves with the various people and attitudes in the narrative.
(3) to find a way to give extravagantly out of love for Jesus.

### Pronunciation Guide:
Gehazi (gi hay' zi)
synoptic (sin op' tik)

### Supplies:
Bibles, newsprint and marker, paper and pencils, hymnals

---

## READING THE SCRIPTURE

NRSV
Matthew 26:6-13

⁶Now while Jesus was at Bethany in the house of Simon the leper, ⁷a woman came to him with an alabaster jar of very costly ointment, and she poured it on his head as he sat at the table. ⁸But when the disciples saw it, they were angry and said, "Why this waste? ⁹For this ointment could have been sold for

NIV
Matthew 26:6-13

⁶While Jesus was in Bethany in the home of a man known as Simon the Leper, ⁷a woman came to him with an alabaster jar of very expensive perfume, which she poured on his head as he was reclining at the table.

⁸When the disciples saw this, they were indignant. "Why this waste?" they asked.

a large sum, and the money given to the poor." [10]But Jesus, aware of this, said to them, "Why do you trouble the woman? She has performed a good service for me. [11]For you always have the poor with you, but you will not always have me. [12]By pouring this ointment on my body she has prepared me for burial. [13]Truly I tell you, wherever this good news is proclaimed in the whole world, what she has done will be told in remembrance of her."

[9]"This perfume could have been sold at a high price and the money given to the poor." [10]Aware of this, Jesus said to them, "Why are you bothering this woman? She has done a beautiful thing to me. [11]The poor you will always have with you, but you will not always have me. [12]When she poured this perfume on my body, she did it to prepare me for burial. [13]I tell you the truth, wherever this gospel is preached throughout the world, what she has done will also be told, in memory of her."

---

## UNDERSTANDING THE SCRIPTURE

**Matthew 26:6.** Because lepers were unclean, it was highly unusual for a rabbi to be in the home of a leper (though given 11:5, Jesus may have already cleansed his leprosy). Jesus' presence may thus illustrate his customary refusal to marginalize the "unclean" (8:3; 9:11, 21-22, 25).

**Matthew 26:7.** Because John 11:2 seems to presuppose that John's audience is familiar with an anointing by Mary of Bethany, which fits the location here (Matthew 26:6), this woman left anonymous in the Synoptic Gospels (Matthew, Mark, and Luke) may well be Mary, sister of Martha. By not naming her, however, Matthew (following Mark 14:3-9) may implicitly invite us to connect her (as "the woman") with the other heroic women who appear later in the Passion narrative.

This woman's sacrifice for Jesus is a lavish one. Hosts usually offered high-status guests oil for anointing their heads (Luke 7:46) but not like this. Alabaster containers were semitransparent and looked similar to marble; they were useful for storing especially expensive ointments. To prevent the ointment's evaporation, people sealed the jar, so that someone using the ointment might need to break the jar's long neck and use the ointment immediately. Given its expense,

some think that the jar may have been a precious family heirloom. She sacrificially "pours out" the ointment (26:7) as Jesus sacrificially "pours out" his life (26:28; Matthew and Mark could have made the connection clearer by employing the same term, but they are similar).

This story differs in most details from the earlier anointing in Luke 7:36-50. (Major similarities are an alabaster vial of perfume and that the host's name is Simon, but Simon the Pharisee). This possibly suggests a mixing of two stories, perhaps the woman here following the earlier woman's model (as Jesus follows Mary's model in John 13:5). The story in John combines elements of both anointings. Because some have confused the two original stories, they have sometimes assumed that the woman here was known as "sinful"; this judgment is quite unfair to her. It is interesting, however, that whereas a Pharisee objected there, disciples object here in Matthew's account.

**Matthew 26:8-9.** The male disciples become "angry" here, as in 20:24. They accuse the woman just as the religious leaders earlier accused them (12:2; for other criticisms, see 9:11, 14; 17:24; 21:16) and became "angry" with Jesus (21:15). Their concern for the poor was not wrong.

It was customary to donate additional funds for the poor at Passover season, and Jesus certainly taught care for the poor. But they fail to understand this lavish display of love, declaring it a "waste" (Matthew's only other use of this term applies to "destruction" in 7:13).

In its context, this passage (26:6-13) displays three responses to the question, "How much is Jesus worth?" To Judas, he is worth thirty pieces of silver, the traditional price of a slave in the law (26:14-16). To other disciples, he is worth more, but they still object to the woman's extravagance (26:8). To the woman, however, Jesus is worth everything. The woman is clearly the model for Christian devotion in this passage. Not surprisingly, later in the Passion narrative, Judas betrays Jesus; the male disciples abandon him; but the female disciples follow to the cross and the tomb (27:55-56, 61), hence are made the first witnesses of the resurrection (28:5-10).

If much of Matthew's audience is tempted to identify with Jesus' venerated disciples, Matthew's story here forces them instead to identify with the women in the Passion narrative. The male disciples fail repeatedly (26:40, 43, 45, 51, 56), but the women provide a better model here. (Ironically, although women admittedly had less to fear from the authorities, ancient men usually considered themselves far braver than women.)

**Matthew 26:10-11.** Jesus responds because he knows the disciples' hearts, just as he earlier responded to members of the religious elite on the same basis (9:4; 22:18). Jesus' own disciples run the risk of becoming like the very religious elite that earlier opposed their master. (Since Mark 14:4 more generally remarks that "some" present complained about the waste, Matthew is going out of his way to underline this warning about disciples. Of course, given the gathering, his disciples may have been the primary persons present.)

Jesus commends her "good service," making her a model of discipleship, since he had earlier encouraged disciples to perform "good works" (the same expression in Greek). Jesus' response certainly does not diminish the importance of care for the poor. Such an attitude would contradict his teachings elsewhere in this Gospel (5:42; 6:2-4, 19-21; 19:21). In fact, Jesus' very words here allude to Deuteronomy 15:11, a verse that climaxes a section requiring care for the poor (Deuteronomy 15:1-10).

**Matthew 26:12.** One anointed guests' heads to show hospitality (Luke 7:46) and one anointed kings' heads extravagantly for their coronation (1 Kings 1:34, 39; 5:1). One also, however, anointed corpses for burial. Such long-necked flasks as the woman uses here are found in Jerusalem tombs of this period, probably dispensing their ointment at a beloved person's death. Jesus is anointed for his burial in advance, because by the time the Sabbath ends and the women arrive to anoint him, his body will no longer be there (Mark 16:1).

Those around Jesus in the narrative do not know how imminent this "burial" is. It is, however, obvious to us: immediately before this passage, Jerusalem's municipal elite are already plotting against him (Matthew 26:1-5), and immediately afterward, Judas joins the plot (26:14-16).

**Matthew 26:13.** Although unnamed in Mark and Matthew, this woman is granted a high honor: her story would be recounted throughout the world, that is, wherever the gospel would go (24:14). That was because her act would be preserved as part of the Passion narrative that Christians would always retell. Various ancient writers (such as Virgil and Ovid) spoke of their own fame being spread throughout the world through their writings—yet most are now forgotten by all but a few. This woman's sacrifice, however, remains a model for all followers of Jesus around the world, often read and recited.

# INTERPRETING THE SCRIPTURE

*The Woman and the Disciples*

The behavior of women in the Passion narrative, and Jesus' selection of women as the first apostles of his resurrection, should lay to rest the objections some have raised to the ministry of women. The Bible affirms the ministry of women in many places, as opposed to the two controversial passages that actually simply address local situations.

Yet a comparison of this woman with the male disciples reveals a theme in the Gospels that has implications even beyond gender roles—implications regarding power more generally. (Ancient histories and biographies often included theological, political, and other perspectives, and when those perspectives are inspired, as in the case of the Bible, we can certainly learn from them.) Herod abused his power against defenseless children, in contrast to outsiders who came to worship Jesus. The Sanhedrin refused to give up power to the rightful king of God's people. The ethnic heirs of the kingdom were reluctant to share it with ethnic outsiders. Those who responded most to Jesus were the poor, the sick, women, and moral outcasts such as tax-gatherers and sinners, rather than the social and religious "elite." Likewise, among the disciples, it was the women, rather than the men, who assumed the culturally expected role of leaders, who proved most faithful to the end.

God's kingdom inverts the world's values. (The same principle would have been true whatever groups were on top). This observation has implications for us in the church today. We humans have a tendency to become secure in our positions of power over others, whether as denominational leaders, seminary professors, pastors, Sunday school teachers, committee members, and so forth. Jesus reminds us that we have one master, and the rest of us are brothers and sisters (Matthew 23:6-10). When we become too secure with our positions, we should heed Jesus: "All who exalt themselves will be humbled, and all who humble themselves will be exalted" (23:12). To use our positions rightly, we must remember: "The greatest among you will be your servant" (23:11).

*Showing Devotion to Jesus*

Jesus honors this woman of Bethany and presents her sacrifice as a model for discipleship. We should consider various ways available to us to lavish our own devotion on Jesus, such as loving him from the heart, praying for him to show us more of his heart and will for our lives,; following whatever we know of his will in Scripture and from the leading of his Spirit.

Today we cannot lavish our love on Jesus by anointing his body in advance of his burial. Today we can instead lavish our love on him by caring for what he cares about, namely people. For us, caring for the poor may be precisely how we (in contrast to the woman) lavish our love on Jesus. We simply must not allow that duty or any other to consume us to the degree that we forget for whose honor we serve. As we give, serve, pray, wait, endure, and study, we should do all these things in Christ's name, lavishing our devotion on him in every way available to us. To us today as well as for this woman, the kingdom and its king are worth everything we have and are (13:44-46).

*Jesus Knows the Heart*

Jesus' sacrifice for us is much greater than anything we can give (26:26-29), but Jesus welcomes her gift and honors her more (26:10, 13). Even when others do not understand our motives, Jesus does, and he affirms what we do out of pure devotion to him. Jesus' close disciples had left their homes and livelihoods to follow him; hence they should have recognized sacrificial devotion. The criticism of some of Jesus' traveling associates, who had healed the sick and expelled demons (10:8), must have stung this woman's heart like Eli's misinformed criticism of Hannah hurt her centuries earlier (1 Samuel 1:12-16). But even men and women of God can be quite wrong. Jesus defended this woman against his own disciples who had left all to follow him.

Sometimes, when we are like this narrative's woman, others may fail to understand our good motives because our gifts or expressions of devotion do not conform to their own practices or expectations. Sometimes, when we are like this narrative's male disciples, we may fail to understand the motives or devotion of others. Sometimes (again like the disciples) we may convince ourselves that our motives or sacrifices are the best, but Jesus, who knows our hearts, knows otherwise.

Expressions of devotion are commendable, so long as they are from the heart. Paul, who practiced charismatic gifts, warned that such gifts were valuable only when used as expressions of love for other members of Christ's body. He sacrificed everything in the way of material possessions, yet warned that such sacrifice profited the person offering it only if her or his motivation was love (1 Corinthians 13:1-3). To deploy the other side of the same examples, I have sometimes observed Christian leaders who despised the spirituality of those practicing spiritual gifts or living sacrificially, as if these were not valuable expressions of devotion. Ideally, we should strive to honor our Lord with the best expressions of our devotion, recognizing that our Lord is the one whose opinion of our offerings matters most.

## How Much Is Jesus Worth?

In context (see 26:14-16), Matthew contrasts this woman's extravagant devotion with Judas' attempt to get what little he can out of Jesus. As disciples today, we must follow her example: seeking how much we can give to Jesus rather than what we can use him to get.

Some people may attend church or profess Christ solely for self-centered reasons, and would deny Christ if that proved more profitable. Of course, there is a legitimate sense of attending church or praying in order to get something: it is important to recognize our dependence on Christ and his strength from day to day. At the same time, faith that is cheaply bought or purely self-serving misses the point. Many people want to believe what is pleasant and convenient rather than what is true. Esau sold his birthright for a bowl of stew; Gehazi lost everything for two talents of silver and two changes of clothes (2 Kings 5:22-23); Judas abandoned eternal life for thirty pieces of silver.

If we truly believe that Jesus is who his disciples discovered him to be, then Jesus is worth everything. As he himself put it, "And everyone who has left houses or brothers or sisters or father or mother or children or fields, for my name's sake, will receive a hundredfold, and will inherit eternal life" (Matthew 19:29). The sacrifice is great, but the reward far exceeds the sacrifice. Whether people will make any sacrifice for Jesus depends on whether they genuinely believe his promise. His earliest disciples reflect a mixture of faith and fear; though Jesus reproved them, he never cast them aside, and in the end he developed them into what he had called them to be. By God's grace, the Lord will do the same with us.

# SHARING THE SCRIPTURE

## *Preparing Our Hearts*

Meditate on this week's devotional reading, found in Deuteronomy 15:7-11, which speaks about the sabbatical year. The law commends liberal giving to those who are in need. The law also promises God's blessings to ungrudging givers. Realistic in its understanding of the human condition, Deuteronomy 15:11 states: "there will never cease to be some in need on the earth." Where do you see people in need? What are you doing to address those needs? How have you experienced God's blessings as a result of your generous giving?

Pray that you and the adult learners will be mindful of the needs of the poor and give liberally to meet those needs.

## *Preparing Our Minds*

Study the background and lesson scripture, both found in Matthew 26:6-13. Ask yourself: can anyone ever give too much love?

Write on newsprint:
- ❑ questions for "Gather to Learn."
- ❑ questions for "Identify with the Various People and Attitudes in the Narrative."
- ❑ sentences to be completed for "Identify with the Various People and Attitudes in the Narrative."
- ❑ information for next week's lesson, found under "Continue the Journey."
- ❑ activities for further spiritual growth in "Continue the Journey."

**Option:** Plan the suggested lecture for "Examine the Narrative of a Woman of Bethany Who Anointed Jesus."

## LEADING THE CLASS

### *(1) Gather to Learn*

❖ Welcome the class members and introduce any guests.

❖ Pray that all who have come today will feel surrounded by the love of God and the love of their classmates.

❖ Encourage the students to work with a partner or small group to answer these questions, which you will need to read aloud or post on newsprint:

**(1) Under what circumstances in your life did you feel especially loved?**

**(2) What did someone do to demonstrate this special love for you?**

❖ Call the group together. Invite volunteers to comment on common themes they heard within their group.

❖ Read aloud today's focus statement: **People who truly love find ways to demonstrate that love. Can we ever give too much love? Jesus commended a woman who gave extravagantly out of her love for him as Messiah.**

### *(2) Examine the Narrative of a Woman of Bethany Who Anointed Jesus*

❖ Choose a volunteer to read Matthew 26:6-13.

❖ **Option:** Give a brief lecture based on the Understanding the Scripture portion in which you help the adults understand the meaning of anointing in general, and its specific meaning in this situation in Matthew 26.

❖ Talk about why Jesus defended the woman and accepted her lavish gift of anointing. Begin the discussion by reading or retelling "Jesus Knows the Heart" in Interpreting the Scripture.

❖ Select several volunteers to role-play this scene at the home of Simon. You will need someone to act as Simon, the woman, Jesus, and at least two disciples. Encourage them to use whatever facial expressions, body language, and voice they can to make this scene come alive.

❖ Point out that although she was criticized by the disciples, Jesus commended the woman for her action. Invite the class to read in unison Matthew 26:13, which is today's key verse.

❖ Discuss this question: **Where in today's world (including your own congregation) do you see people acting on Jesus' behalf in memorable and extravagant ways?**

❖ Conclude this section of the session by noting that some people use Matthew 26:8-11 as an excuse for not becoming involved in the plight of the poor. Read aloud Deuteronomy 15:7-11. Talk with the class about what Jesus meant when he said that the poor would be always with us. Consider whether he was simply stating a reality or telling people that the poor were not their concern. Talk with the class about how one's actions will differ, depending on their interpretation of what Jesus meant by his comment. Emphasize Jesus' concern for the poor by looking at the scriptures noted under Matthew 26:10-11 in Understanding the Scripture.

*(3) Identify with the Various People and Attitudes in the Narrative*

❖ Divide the class into three groups: Simon, the woman, and the disciples. Ask each group to view the story from the perspective of their character by answering the following questions, which you will post on newsprint:

(1) **Why do you think the woman anointed Jesus with such a lavish gift?**

(2) **What might be the real motivation for the disciples' response to the woman's action?**

(3) **Based on Jesus' comments, how do you think he was feeling about what the woman did?**

❖ Bring the class together and discuss the story from the perspective of each character. Encourage the students to comment on why the same action, seen from the point of view of a variety of people, seems to evoke such different responses.

❖ Note that part of the reason people respond differently may be explained by the tension between what constitutes a "necessary" action and what constitutes an "extravagant" one.

❖ Encourage the students to call out answers to complete these sentences, which you will post on newsprint: *(1) "An extravagant action is one that . . ." (2) "For an action to be considered 'necessary' it must meet the following criteria . . ."* Note seemingly contradictory answers, which may indicate a difference of opinion as to what is extravagant and what is necessary.

*(4) Find a Way to Give Extravagantly out of Love for Jesus*

❖ Read or retell "Showing Devotion to Jesus."

❖ Ask: **If you wanted to give or receive an extravagant gift, what would it be?** (If your group's extravagant ideas seem rather modest, suggest these "Most Extravagant Gifts" that Hitha Prabhakar wrote about on forbes.com for the December, 2006 gift-giving season: $100,000 jewel-encrusted ice bucket; private day spa for you and your guests for $100,000 at the Ritz Carlton; $8,800,000 pair of 60-carat diamond earrings; trip to space on Virgin Galactic for $1.8 million; Bentley Arnage car, starting at $170,000.)

❖ Mention that the woman of Bethany's gift was as extreme to most in her day as some of the gifts listed in *Forbes* are to us. Yet in evaluating her gift we need to focus on her motivation and the fact that Jesus believes she has anointed him for burial (Matthew 26:12).

❖ Distribute paper and pencils. Encourage the students to write about an extravagant way that they could serve Jesus. Their gift need not be expensive monetarily, but it may require a great deal of time and sacrifice. For example, they may decide to use a week of vacation to go where a natural catastrophe has destroyed homes to help people rebuild. They might choose to make a regular commitment to serve people who are poor, sick, or imprisoned. Suggest that the students be as specific as possible about what they intend to do.

❖ Choose volunteers to explain what they hope to do.

❖ Invite the class members to hold each other in prayer this week as they explore options for action and take steps to fulfill their commitment.

*(5) Continue the Journey*

❖ Pray that all who have come will show extravagant love for Jesus.

❖ Read aloud this preparation for next week's lesson. You may also want to post it on newsprint for the students to copy.

- ■ **Title: Mission to the Community**
- ■ **Background Scripture: Jonah 1:1–3; 3:1–9**
- ■ **Lesson Scripture: Jonah 1:1–3; 3:1–9**

■ **Focus of the Lesson: In a world filled with good and evil, persons are forced to choose between good and evil. What happens to people who turn from their wicked ways in sorrow? Jonah's plea to the people of Nineveh caused them to believe in God and fast, trusting that God would forgive them.**

❖ Challenge the students to complete one or more of these activities for further spiritual growth, which you will write on newsprint for the students to copy.

(1) **Take at least one action this week that shows extravagant love for Jesus.**

(2) **Write a prayer or poem, based on today's story, asking God to help you express your love for Jesus in a lavish, memorable way.**

(3) **Draw a picture of the scene of the woman anointing Jesus. Use this picture as a devotional aid as you pray for guidance to serve Jesus in an extravagant way.**

❖ Sing or read aloud "More Love to Thee, O Christ."

❖ Conclude today's session by leading the class in this benediction, adapted from Matthew 16:16: **Go forth now to love and serve the Messiah, the Son of the living God.**

# THIRD QUARTER
## Teachings on Community

MARCH 7, 2010–MAY 30, 2010

The theme of the spring quarter is "community." During these thirteen weeks we will explore what it means to live in community by studying the books of Jonah and Ruth, the teachings of Jesus, and the teachings of the early church. The lessons focus on the coming together of faithful people in response to God's call and examine how these people relate to one another.

The four sessions in Unit 1, "Community with a Mission," consider the Old Testament books of Jonah and Ruth. We will look at Jonah's mission to the community at Nineveh and the redemption of that community. We will also encounter the family as community in Ruth. The unit begins on March 7 with a session from Jonah 1:1-3 and 3:1-9 in "Mission to the Community," which identifies how a community can be influenced to change. "A Community to Redeem," the lesson for March 14 from Jonah 3:10–4:11, investigates Jonah's jealousy and anger in the face of God's will for Nineveh. Ruth 1:1-16, the background for the lesson of March 21, "Family as Community," recounts the beloved story of Ruth's faithfulness to her mother-in-law Naomi. The unit concludes on March 28 with "Acceptance in Community," based on Ruth 2–3, where we read of Boaz's favor toward Ruth.

Unit 2, "Teachings of Jesus," includes four sessions. On Easter, April 4, we look at John 13:21-30; 16:16-24; and 20:11-16 to see how "The Community Faces Pain and Joy." The lesson for April 11 from 1 John 2:7-17 reminds us of the importance of "Love within the Community." Love is necessary for "Connecting in Community," as taught by Jesus in Matthew 5:17-29 and 22:34-40, which we will study on April 18. As the unit ends on April 25 with "Inclusion in Community," a parable of Jesus, found in Luke 14:7-24, makes clear that everyone is invited to participate in the messianic banquet.

The five lessons in Unit 3, "Teachings of the Church," examine readings from Colossians, Philemon, and Jude. In the passages from Colossians, we will study the faithfulness of the community and how the community was established and chosen. Paul's letter to Philemon helps us look at how all are to be welcomed into the community. And the lesson from Jude examines a community at risk. On May 2, Colossians 1 explores how believers understand and live the truth as "A Faithful Community." Even in "An Established Community," there are situations in which one must distinguish truth from deceit, as we will see on May 9 as we study Colossians 2:1-19. "A Chosen Community," where everyone experiences a true sense of belonging, is the focus for the session from Colossians 3 on May 16. In "At Home in the Church," which we will study on May 23, Paul calls upon Philemon to do the right thing in regard to Onesimus. The unit closes on May 30 with a look at the Jude, where tempering judgment with mercy is very important when people are "At Risk in the Community."

# MEET OUR WRITER

## DR. MICHAEL FINK

Michael Fink moved to the beautiful mountains and lakes near Dandridge, Tennessee, in 2003 to take early retirement. Born in Sylacauga, Alabama, and reared in a Birmingham suburb, Mike was schooled in Alabama, Georgia, and Kentucky. He served churches in Kentucky, Indiana, and North Carolina; taught in colleges in North Carolina and Tennessee; and served for 25 years in various editorial, management, and staff capacities with a Christian publisher.

Dr. Fink has led Christian education conferences, consulted on Christian publishing, and ministered in twenty-three states in the United States as well as in ten foreign countries. He has coauthored one book, has contributed to five others, and has published Bible studies, sermons, poetry, and articles in numerous publications. He holds two master degrees and a Ph.D. in New Testament.

Since retiring, Mike has been an adjunct professor at Carson-Newman College in Jefferson City, Tennessee, and has worked part-time at a classic small-town hardware store—a great way to get to know people in a new location. A college major in mathematics has blossomed into a life-long attachment to computers, with a special focus on screening stocks and developing investment strategies. He has managed several portfolios for family members.

Mike's wife, Evelyn, is a preschool specialist who loves gardening, music, and shepherding their family of three daughters, two sons-in-law, and four grandchildren. Together Mike and Evelyn enjoy entertaining friends and boating in their kayak and pontoon boat on Douglas Lake. They like to travel and almost always have a book on cassette or CD playing as they drive. Since retiring, they have been in an almost continuous project of remodeling and upgrading their home; but Mike also has found time to take up golf again. Mike and Evelyn are active members of First Baptist Church in Jefferson City, Tennessee.

# THE BIG PICTURE:
# SEEING THE BIG PICTURE AND LITTLE PIECES OF COMMUNITY

Have you ever looked at a photograph in a newspaper through a magnifying glass? If you have, you will have discovered that what initially appears to be a uniform semblance of reality is actually thousands of small printed dots. If the photo is black and white, the dots are black on the white paper. Shades of gray are created by spacing dots close together or wide apart. If the photo is in color, dots of different colors are blended together to form a realistic picture. From a distance, the dots merge and recede into what becomes a meaningful image. Up close, the picture is revealed as a composition of a multitude of tiny pieces.

This principle is actually found pretty widely in our world. Wood block prints, jigsaw puzzles, tapestries, cross-stitches, engravings, impressionist art, computer printers, liquid crystal displays, animated scoreboards, digital watches, and a host of other things build meaningful symbols from smaller pieces that alone would be meaningless.

Even the Bible reflects this principle in some ways. Although we call it *"The* Bible," our *Protestant* Scriptures actually are a composition made up of sixty-six individual pieces. Admittedly, some of those pieces are large and bear great significance—Genesis, Exodus, Psalms, Isaiah, the Gospels, and Acts, for example. Many of the other books are small and often neglected. How many readers turn often to Nahum or Jude?

Our study this March-April-May quarter has three units. The second unit is a "big picture" study focused on some big ideas that are central to our faith community. The other two units focus on five of the smaller pieces of the big picture. While several of these small books share familiar stories (Jonah, Ruth, and Philemon, for example), we may not fully appreciate them until we view them in the context of the whole picture of Scripture. Without them, important biblical themes could lose their clarity. Even the brief Letter of Jude, whose place in the canon of the Scriptures has been questioned in almost every generation, may speak more piercingly than we might anticipate to the struggles we face today with immorality and godlessness.

This quarter we will be looking at both the big picture of the Christian community and at the little pieces that add important detail to how we view that community. At times we will move in close with a magnifying glass to see the smaller details. At other times we will step back to grasp the larger scope of the community's life. When we finish the study, we should have a better sense of the community we are striving to become as God's people.

## The Big Picture

The four lessons for April comprise a unit built around Jesus, his life, and his teachings. These lessons will help us gain perspective on four essential dimensions of the community that Jesus envisioned and inaugurated.

**1. The Great Event.** April 4 will be Easter, and Easter is a "Big Picture" time of the year. This one observance embodies the most significant aspects of what God has done for us through the death and resurrection of Jesus.

The events in what we call Holy Week comprise a sizeable block of the four Gospels (twenty-nine of their combined eighty-nine chapters). Beginning with the triumphal entry on Palm Sunday and continuing through the celebration of the resurrection on Easter, the week swings from high emotion to deep despair and back to joyful celebration. The disciples who had followed Jesus, deserted him, denied him, watched him die, mourned his loss, and grieved over their own faithlessness were staggered by the news of his resurrection. Jesus had tried to prepare them for these events, but preconceptions had clouded their understandings.

The events of that pivotal week became the defining moment for the new Christian community. Forgiven through Jesus' sacrificial death by means of crucifixion, hopeful because of the new life promised through the resurrection, and strengthened by the assurance of the abiding presence of the Holy Spirit, the disciples were being shaped into a fellowship of believers. Together their community of faith and hope could overcome its sorrows and celebrate its life under the guidance of the Spirit.

**2. The Great Bond.** Love is one of the central themes in the Johannine writings of the New Testament. That theme in the First Epistle of John will be examined on April 11. This rather small letter bears a large and pivotal message: "God is love" (1 John 4:8). That unsurpassable definition of God's nature may well be the greatest truth in Scripture.

First John, however, was not merely focused on God's nature. It also was concerned with the nature of those who accept God's love and follow in the footsteps of God's Son. God's love is the foundation upon which our relationships are founded.

John made clear that those who accept God's love must demonstrate love for others. The absence of love on the human level is evidence that God's love has not really penetrated into the hearts of those who claim to be followers. John's obvious conclusion was that the Christian community will be a community bound together by love. The nature, visibility, and scope of that love serve as the greatest evidence of fellowship with God and abiding in God.

**3. The Great Commandment.** On April 18 we will study what Jesus himself called "the greatest and first commandment" (Matthew 22:38). Surely when Jesus boils down the whole of what God expects of humanity, we ought to give careful attention. While it is true that he gave this teaching in response to those who were legalistically minded, Jesus demanded something that cannot really be commanded: "You shall love the Lord your God with all your heart, and with all your soul, and with all your mind" (22:37).

Those words did not even originate with Jesus; they came from the Old Testament book of Deuteronomy. By elevating them, Jesus not only summarized his own teachings but he also summarized the central requirement of the entire Judeo-Christian tradition—to love God completely.

Jesus was not content, however, to give just one commandment with one object. He gave a second commandment (22:39), which is so much like the first that we could almost say he gave one command ("love") and applied it toward two objects (first "love God," and second "love your neighbor"). That second commandment is a fundamental part of community-building.

In the Great Commandment Jesus defined the essential nature of the community of faith. He defined the objects of that community's devotion. He defined God's highest expectations of us.

**4. The Great Vision.** The last Sunday in April will draw this unit to a close by reminding us that God's love doesn't leave anyone out. The parable of Jesus that we will study probably will not be on anyone's favorite-parables list, but the vision it paints of God's banquet and those who will sit at the banquet table is a compelling and disturbing one.

The parable speaks of the kingdom of God and points to the role of each person in accepting or rejecting the invitation to be part of that kingdom. Some, who assume that their status already is established, will find themselves outside the banquet hall. Others, who have suffered rejection and ostracism, will find a place prepared for them at the table. Underlying these teachings from Jesus is an uncomfortable awareness that we often distort the Christian community. We try to populate it with righteous people like ourselves. We strive for positions of power and prestige. We turn away those who are not worthy, or we ourselves turn away from them and their need to be welcomed.

The picture of the Christian community this unit paints will show us how far we still need to go to transform our churches and our communities. Some things will need to be buried, and others raised to new life. Love will need to be more central as we comprehend the nature, depth, and breadth of the love to which God has called us.

## The Little Pieces

The other two units in this quarter are made up of "little pieces" that provide detail and texture to the scope of the Bible's message about community. The March unit is drawn from the Old Testament, and the May unit is drawn from the New Testament. I have called these "little pieces" because we will not be studying a Gospel or book from the Pentateuch in these units. No psalm, no great prophetic book, no sweeping book of history will be in view. No letter addressed to a major city like Corinth or Rome will be examined. But don't be caught off guard—these books still possess powerful messages that will challenge you in your life of faith and community.

**The Studies in March.** People who examine the major sweep of the Old Testament could easily reach the conclusion that God is pretty focused on Israel. Indeed, the Old Testament does center on Israel from the call of Abraham in Genesis to the expectations in the Minor Prophets of a redeemer-king who will fully establish Israel's power and prestige. At times God appears to be a warrior-God whose sole purpose is to elevate Israel and decimate Israel's enemies. God used the foreign powers to punish Israel when the nation went astray; but as soon as the nation turned back to God, the repressions and slaughter of the enemy resumed.

While we find occasional glimpses of God's wider purposes, two little Old Testament books provided a clear corrective to a narrow view of God's compassion and concern. Both of these are narrative books, but they are not narratives of great patriarchs, prophets, or potentates. The writers do not hit you over the head with prescriptive teachings or harsh judgmental pronouncements. They tell simple stories that expand our understanding of God's love and compassion.

The Book of Ruth falls in our biblical canon in the midst of the Former Prophets and the historical collections that span the time from Joshua to the post-Exilic period. The book itself is not prophetic; and while it is set as a historical narrative, the most important historical event it records is a local famine. No prophet speaks, no judge leads, and no king rules. Instead the book centers on a simple family transaction involving a minor law in the Old Testament. The focus is on a foreigner, a Moabite named Ruth. Having descended from Lot, the Moabites were distantly related to Abraham and the Israelites; but the relationship was never amiable. The story tells how one of these foreigners whose people followed other gods chose to follow God and became part of the Israelite community. The kicker, however, is that this obscure Moabite woman became the great-grandmother of King David. Thus, in the midst of a society exhibiting tendencies toward xenophobia (the fear of or contempt toward foreigners), a small glimmer of hope for greater inclusiveness emerges.

A similar outcome emerges in our study of the Book of Jonah. This story is about a prophet who fled from God's call to warn the feared enemies in Nineveh, the capital of Assyria, of coming judgment. The book ends with a question from God that rings as a clear declaration that God's compassion reaches beyond the boundaries of Israel: "Should I not be concerned about Nineveh, that great city?" (Jonah 4:11).

From these two small books a foundation is laid for Jesus' Great Commission (Matthew 28:19-20).

**The Studies in May.** The New Testament studies in May focus on Colossians, Philemon, and Jude. The first two are letters of Paul; but though they are minor letters in comparison with many other Pauline writings, they bear important messages.

To understand Colossians, think of the hundreds of small cities in the United States that thrived when the main U.S. highway ran through the center of town. When an interstate highway or a bypass skirted the town, however, the city core declined and the areas along the new routes flourished. Colossae was a once-thriving city that was bypassed by the newest Roman highway. As a result, the city was not prominent enough to warrant a visit from Paul (who focused on the strategic cities in each region he visited). Yet, the believers there played a significant role in Paul's ministry; and as a result, Paul wrote one letter to the congregation and a second personal letter to one of the members of the congregation. Both of these letters were cherished and eventually were included in our Scriptures.

Colossians, Philemon, and Jude are small works; but they offer insight for us in some important areas. Colossians helps us deal with theological controversy. Jude aids us in addressing moral controversy. Philemon demonstrates how Paul obliquely addressed one of the most insidious social institutions of his day—slavery—and gave us principles that can transform socially stratified people into a unified body in Christ.

A couple of years ago my wife and I were back in Nashville visiting the church of which we had been members for 25 years. After the morning worship service, a young woman with two young boys in tow approached me and asked, "Are you Dr. Fink?" I said I was, somewhat surprised, for few people have called me "Dr. Fink" outside of the years when I was a college professor.

The young woman went on, "I wouldn't have recognized you, and I'm sure you don't remember me. When my husband and I joined this church shortly after you moved away, I heard people talk about you. I've been hoping ever since that I would get a chance to meet you.

"When I was a high school senior, my parents and I visited Campbell University. The student recruitment officer who hosted us on that visit brought us to your class and asked if we could sit in. You said we could, and my parents and I sat at the back of the classroom. During that hour I decided that Campbell was where I wanted to study. I was so disappointed the next fall to discover that you had left the college, but I've always hoped that I could some day tell you how much sitting in your class for that one hour meant to me. I graduated from Campbell, went on to seminary, married, and now have these two children. My husband and I are working on the staff of Belmont University as ministers with college students."

Who would have thought that one small hour, one little part of a three-year stint as a college professor, could have been so significant? But there's another side to this story. After I retired and discovered that things went on quite well without me, I found myself like many retirees wondering whether I had made much of a difference at all through my work. Suddenly that ten-minute conversation, one little moment out of a lifetime, provided an affirmation that I needed and appreciated at a critical moment of transition in my own life.

Ruth, Jonah, Colossians, Philemon, Jude—little pieces indeed—but they are important pieces that enable us to see the big picture with the fullness and clarity we need to observe the hand of God at work among God's people.

# CLOSE-UP:
# PEOPLE OF COMMUNITY

We often hear of the biblical "superstars" of the faith, but what about those other folks who labored in the early communities of faith—the people who are more like us? We will try to get to know some whose names are mentioned in Colossians and Philemon.

**Apphia** (af' ee uh), whose name appears only in Philemon 2, is a leader in a house church. Scholars believe that she was likely the wife of Philemon and the mother of Archippus. Tradition says that she and her family were martyred during Nero's persecutions in Colossae.

**Archippus** (ahr kip' uhs) is associated with the church in Philemon's home in Colossae and may be his son (Philemon 2). In Colossians 4:17, Paul refers to a task that Archippus has "received in the Lord." Possibly he is being called to help set Onesimus free.

**Aristarchus** (air is tahr' kuhs), who Paul refers to as "my fellow prisoner" in Colossians 4:10, is "a Macedonian from Thessalonica" (Acts 27:2). His Macedonian heritage is also referenced in Acts 19:29, where he, along with Gaius, another companion of Paul, is dragged in the street during a riot at Ephesus. According to Acts 20:4, Aristarchus—along with Sopater, Secundus, Gaius, Timothy, Tychicus, and Trophimus—accompanies Paul to Macedonia and Greece.

**Demas** (dee' muhs), mentioned in Colossians 4:14, 2 Timothy 4:10, and Philemon 1:24, was both a fellow prisoner with Paul and also, according to 2 Timothy, one who deserted Paul and was "in love with this present world."

**Epaphras** (ep' uh fras), was "a servant of Christ Jesus" (Colossians 4:12) and a "fellow prisoner" with Paul (Philemon 1:23). He founded the church at Colossae (Colossians 1:7-8) and worked tirelessly for Christ in Laodicea and Hierapolis (Colossians 4:12-13).

**Jesus Justus** (jee' zuhs juhs' tuhs), or Jesus the Just, is mentioned only in Colossians 4:11, so we know nothing else about him.

**Nympha** (nim' fuh) is only named in Colossians 4:15, but she must have been an influential leader as the greetings are addressed to her "and the church in her house" in Laodicea.

**Onesimus** (oh nes' uh mus) is referred to by Paul as "the faithful and beloved brother" (Colossians 4:9) and "my child" (Philemon 10). Paul's letter to Philemon regarding Onesimus has been traditionally interpreted to mean that Onesimus was a slave who ran away from his master. Paul urges Philemon to receive him as a brother in Christ.

**Philemon** (fi lee' muhn) is the recipient of the letter from Paul bearing his name. He is appealed to throughout the letter, but mentioned only by name once in the New Testament, in verse 1. Paul refers to Philemon as "our dear friend and co-worker." He, along with Apphia and Archippus, host a church in their home.

**Tychicus** (tik' uh kuhs) appears in Acts 20:4, Ephesians 6:21, Colossians 4:7, 2 Timothy 4:12, and Titus 3:12. Acts 20 indicates that he was "from Asia." Tychicus apparently delivered several letters on Paul's behalf, including the ones to the Colossians, Ephesians, and Philemon. Since Paul was writing to the congregations in Ephesus and Colossae to correct doctrinal errors, he must have had confidence in Tychicus's ability to handle questions arising from these letters.

# FAITH IN ACTION:
# COMMUNITY ON A MISSION

In this quarter's lessons we are exploring the theme of community. What does it really mean to say that the church is a community of faith? Here are some questions to discuss with the class. You may want to divide into groups. If you do that, be sure each group has paper and pencils and that you provide an opportunity for each group to share its ideas, possibly on selected questions. Perhaps you could meet outside of class for some fellowship and frank discussion about your faith community and where you see it going. However you choose to do this activity, encourage the group to (a) see itself as a community, (b) assess their strengths and weaknesses, and (c) envision how they could become a more faithful community in the future.

(1) How do you define the word "community"?

(2) How do you see your church (or Sunday school class) living as a community?

(3) What differences are there between a community as a neighborhood and a community as a church?

(4) Jesus teaches that all are included in the community, as we study in the parable of the banquet in Luke 14. How does your church reach out to others to include them in community?

(5) If there are those who may not feel included in your faith community, what steps could you take to make them feel more at home?

(6) In what ways is your community growing spiritually?

(7) How has your faith community (either the congregation or class) grown numerically? If it is shrinking, why? What can be done to reverse that trend? (Recognize that sometimes new groups need to be formed to create communities that meet different needs. In some situations, the trend cannot be reversed.)

(8) As we see during Holy Week, the community can experience great pain and great joy. What examples can you recall when your faith community bonded together as a result of a serious loss (perhaps a building destroyed by fire or natural disaster) or a great joy (such as sending a member into ordained ministry or opening a shelter that welcomed the homeless)?

(9) First John describes the importance of living in the light of love. What examples can you name of ways that your faith community expresses its love, both to those within the church and to those outside?

(10) The church today experiences onslaughts from the culture at large in terms of values and behaviors, just as the early church did. In what ways does your congregation act as a counterculture, or alternative culture, that is rooted in the teachings of Jesus rather than the expectations of society?

(11) The congregations that we read about in the New Testament experienced their share of conflict, even as we do today. What methods of conflict resolution have worked for your congregation? How do these methods acknowledge in love that different people have different points of view?

(12) What changes would you like to see in your church to make it become a community that is more faithful to who you believe Jesus would have you to be and what you believe he would have you to do?

## UNIT 1: COMMUITY WITH A MISSION
# MISSION TO THE COMMUNITY

---

### PREVIEWING THE LESSON

**Lesson Scripture:** Jonah 1:1-3; 3:1-9
**Background Scripture:** Jonah 1:1-3; 3:1-9
**Key Verse:** Jonah 3:5

### Focus of the Lesson:
In a world filled with good and evil, persons are forced to choose between good and evil. What happens to people who turn from their wicked ways in sorrow? Jonah's plea to the people of Nineveh caused them to believe in God and fast, trusting that God would forgive them.

### Goals for the Learners:
(1) to introduce God's concern for the Nineveh community and God's plan of redemption using Jonah as a messenger.
(2) to value being given a second chance to complete a mission, especially when a wrong decision has been made.
(3) to name resistance to something they know they should do and to act.

### Pronunciation Guide:
Amittai (uh mit' i)
Nineveh (nin' uh vuh)
Tarshish (tahr' shish)

### Supplies:
Bibles, newsprint and marker, paper and pencils, hymnals

---

### READING THE SCRIPTURE

NRSV

Jonah 1:1-3

¹Now the word of the LORD came to Jonah son of Amittai, saying, ²"Go at once to Nineveh, that great city, and cry out against it; for their wickedness has come up before me." ³But Jonah set out to flee to Tarshish

NIV

Jonah 1:1-3

¹The word of the LORD came to Jonah son of Amittai: ²"Go to the great city of Nineveh and preach against it, because its wickedness has come up before me."

³But Jonah ran away from the LORD and

from the presence of the LORD. He went down to Joppa and found a ship going to Tarshish; so he paid his fare and went on board, to go with them to Tarshish, away from the presence of the LORD.

### Jonah 3:1-9

¹The word of the LORD came to Jonah a second time, saying, ²"Get up, go to Nineveh, that great city, and proclaim to it the message that I tell you." ³So Jonah set out and went to Nineveh, according to the word of the LORD. Now Nineveh was an exceedingly large city, a three days' walk across. ⁴Jonah began to go into the city, going a day's walk. And he cried out, "Forty days more, and Nineveh shall be overthrown!" **⁵And the people of Nineveh believed God; they proclaimed a fast, and everyone, great and small, put on sackcloth.**

⁶When the news reached the king of Nineveh, he rose from his throne, removed his robe, covered himself with sackcloth, and sat in ashes. ⁷Then he had a proclamation made in Nineveh: "By the decree of the king and his nobles: No human being or animal, no herd or flock, shall taste anything. They shall not feed, nor shall they drink water. ⁸Human beings and animals shall be covered with sackcloth, and they shall cry mightily to God. All shall turn from their evil ways and from the violence that is in their hands. ⁹Who knows? God may relent and change his mind; he may turn from his fierce anger, so that we do not perish."

headed for Tarshish. He went down to Joppa, where he found a ship bound for that port. After paying the fare, he went aboard and sailed for Tarshish to flee from the LORD.

### Jonah 3:1-9

¹Then the word of the LORD came to Jonah a second time: ²"Go to the great city of Nineveh and proclaim to it the message I give you."

³Jonah obeyed the word of the LORD and went to Nineveh. Now Nineveh was a very important city—a visit required three days. ⁴On the first day, Jonah started into the city. He proclaimed: "Forty more days and Nineveh will be overturned." **⁵The Ninevites believed God. They declared a fast, and all of them, from the greatest to the least, put on sackcloth.**

⁶When the news reached the king of Nineveh, he rose from his throne, took off his royal robes, covered himself with sackcloth and sat down in the dust. ⁷Then he issued a proclamation in Nineveh:

"By the decree of the king and his nobles:

Do not let any man or beast, herd or flock, taste anything; do not let them eat or drink. ⁸But let man and beast be covered with sackcloth. Let everyone call urgently on God. Let them give up their evil ways and their violence. ⁹Who knows? God may yet relent and with compassion turn from his fierce anger so that we will not perish."

---

## UNDERSTANDING THE SCRIPTURE

**Jonah 1:1-2.** The Book of Jonah is one of the twelve Old Testament books often called "the Minor Prophets." These prophetic writings were "minor" because of their length, not because of their lack of importance. Though four chapters long, Jonah is printed on just two pages in most Bibles. By contrast, Isaiah, with 66 chapters, is considerably longer. Yet Jonah's message is an essential one in helping God's people understand the scope of God's concern.

The prophetic nature of the book is signaled by the classic introduction, "the word of the LORD came to Jonah." Early in

Hebrew history, "seers" communicated revelations from God. Later the word "prophet" replaced the term "seer" (see 1 Samuel 9:9). Though the root meaning of the word "prophet" is unclear, it apparently came from a term meaning "to call" or "to announce" under the inspiration of God.

"Jonah son of Amittai" is mentioned only once in the Old Testament outside of the book bearing his name. Second Kings 14:25 places Jonah in the reign of the evil king Jeroboam II, who ruled over the Northern Kingdom from 786–746 B.C. Rather than being called to address the evils within his own country, Jonah was directed by God to "go at once" and "cry out against" Nineveh, the prominent capital of the ancient kingdom of Assyria (modern Iraq). To understand the "wickedness" of Nineveh, read Nahum 3.

**Jonah 1:3.** Jonah proved to be a reluctant prophet. Not only did he head west to the coastal city of Joppa (near modern Tel Aviv) rather than northeast toward Nineveh, but he also sought the impossible—to flee "from the presence of the Lord." Jonah's ultimate escape destination was Tarshish, a city of commercial fame brought about by the large seagoing vessels that bore the city's name. Though its exact location is not known, it represented somewhere far away—but not far enough!

**Jonah 3:1-2.** God gave Jonah a second chance, but not without some significant intervention. A mighty storm, a casting overboard by his fellow shipmates, a three-day stint in the belly of a large fish, and a desperate prayer to God for deliverance (Jonah 1:4–2:10) brought an opportunity for reconsideration. Jonah could not escape from God's presence; neither could he escape from God's commission. God commanded Jonah to "get up," "go," and "proclaim."

Jonah's commission did change in one respect. Rather than merely denouncing Nineveh for its wickedness (1:2), Jonah now had a specific message to proclaim to the citizens of Nineveh, a message that God would tell him.

**Jonah 3:3-4.** Given a second chance, Jonah obeyed God. He set out ("arose" in NASB), went, and began to proclaim God's message—according to the word of the Lord.

The size of Nineveh requires some explanation. The book of Jonah states that Nineveh was "an exceedingly large city, a three days' walk across." Modern excavations of the city reveal that the walls around the central palace fortress were about six miles in length, hardly a three days' walk. Much of the city obviously was outside the fortified palace, but how far was a three-day walk? Canals brought water to the city from the Zagros Mountains almost fifty miles away. Could that be the extent of the "city"? Perhaps the best understanding given the city's population (see 4:11) is found in the *New International Version*: "a visit required three days."

Jonah's message conveyed a timeline and an outcome. The number forty was commonly used in the Bible to denote the duration of critical situations, punishments, fasts, and vigils (see Genesis 7:4; Exodus 24:18; 34:28; Numbers 13:25; 1 Samuel 17:16; 1 Kings 19:8; and Matthew 4:2). Jonah's timeline of a pending crisis in forty days introduced enough tension to bring about a quick reaction from the people who heard his message.

The prediction that Nineveh would be overthrown did not state explicitly what agent would do the overthrowing. While the overthrow could have arisen from an internal rebellion or an opposing army, Jonah implied that God would be the agent. The Hebrew word used for "overthrown" is the same one used of Sodom in Genesis 19:21, 25, 29.

**Jonah 3:5-9.** The people's response to Jonah's message was dramatic. In Jonah's voice they heard the word of God, and they "believed God" and took seriously the warnings issued. Everyone—whether of high stature or low, old or young, rich or poor—accepted the message and demonstrated repentance through fasting and dressing in sackcloth.

Verse 5 indicates that the people "proclaimed" a fast, while verse 7 records that the king and his nobles "had a proclamation made." These separate actions draw upon two different Hebrew words. The people spontaneously responded to God's message with signs of genuine humility and repentance and called on others to join them. The king's response was no less sincere; but using his office, he formalized the response through a proclamation demanding observance by all the people and their animals as well.

The practice of fasting involved a broad range of expressions. It may have evolved from the natural human tendency to lose one's appetite when confronted with a crisis, such as the death of a loved one. It soon was associated, however, with a response to alienation from God. The extent of the fast (spontaneous, occasional, or ritual; food only or both food and drink; sunrise to sunset or longer; humbling oneself or afflicting oneself) varied from expression to expression. The fast in Nineveh appears to have begun spontaneously. Once the king issued a proclamation, the meaning and the extent of the observance certainly expanded.

Wearing sackcloth and sitting in ashes (or sprinkling ashes over one's head or smearing ashes on one's face) were cultural rituals of mourning. When these rituals were directed toward God, they became external signs of humility and repentance. Sometimes adding fasting to prayer was thought to increase the effectiveness of the prayer. Most of these elements were in the mix in Nineveh—fasting, sackcloth, ashes, and prayer.

The Assyrian king (perhaps understanding more clearly the implications of Jonah's message) recognized that rituals alone would not win God's approval. He also insisted that the people turn from their evil ways and from their violence. A change in the way the people lived was essential.

Once the people had done all they could do—repent, humble themselves, mourn, pray, turn away from evil—the outcome was up to God. Who could fathom what God might do? Who could anticipate where God's compassion might break out? Will God spare them from being overthrown (3:4) and perishing (3:9)? Verse 9 is a powerful release of the situation to God after all human efforts have been made.

---

## INTERPRETING THE SCRIPTURE

### The Scope of God's Concern

We can easily read the Old Testament and conclude that God is only concerned about the chosen people. God called Abram to be the father of a chosen nation. God made an exclusive covenant with Israel at Mount Sinai. God led the people to victory in their conquest of the Promised Land. God threw off persistent enemies and established a perpetual Davidic monarchy. On every hand Israel's enemies were devastated. Armies were slain, cities were destroyed, and false prophets were put to death in the name of a God who championed the cause of the chosen ones. The Book of Jonah provides a necessary and important check on such exclusivity.

Israel was strong in Jonah's day. Jeroboam II had expanded his control from Syria in the north to the Sea of the Arabah in the south, fulfilling God's word through Jonah (2 Kings 14:25, 28). Assyria, by contrast, was rather weak; and Jeroboam's campaigns in the north impinged upon areas of Assyrian interest. Thus, Jonah's prophecies of Jeroboam's victories were prophecies of Assyria's defeat. When the word of the Lord came to Jonah and commissioned him to go to Nineveh, God was sending Jonah into enemy territory.

Nineveh was located in modern Iraq. The remains of the ancient city are across the

Tigris River from modern Mosul, a city much in the news because of the war in Iraq. Imagine a modern Jew or an American sensing a call from God to go to Mosul to confront their wickedness! No wonder Jonah fled.

Imbedded in Old Testament books like Jonah and Ruth, but also peeking through in many other places, is an uncomfortable word about our enemies. That word reaches its zenith in Jesus' command, "Love your enemies and pray for those who persecute you" (Matthew 5:44). God is concerned for all people.

God's people are special only to the extent that they are engaged in showing God's love to the world. Even in a time of war, God's grace reaches out to all. Withholding that grace or claiming it exclusively for ourselves is our flight to Tarshish.

### The Breadth of Repentance

Repentance often is a shallow experience. People seem to regret more that they have been caught than that they have committed some misdeed. Falling back into old patterns and committing the same misdeed is rampant because many people interpret repentance to mean "determined not to get caught next time." Regret and remorse can only go so far in changing behavior.

Repentance is a central biblical concept. The basic Greek and Hebrew ideas of repentance are to change one's mind and to turn. Together these speak of both a mental and a physical aspect to repentance.

Regret and remorse are emotional feelings that often lead to shallow and short-term changes. Without the fundamental "change of mind" expressed by the Greek word for repentance, falling back into old patterns of behavior is easy. True change goes deep into the inner self and alters the way a person perceives self, others, actions, relationships, and God.

Most of us carry a strong tendency to try to please our parents. Trying to win their approval can be a strong motivator for change. While such motivation is not always healthy with earthly parents, something of that same drive is evident in change-of-mind repentance. Repentance means our desire to please God replaces the self-centeredness of our lives.

A change of mind can also lead to a change of direction, the "turn" represented in the Hebrew word for repentance. Like a North Star that provides a sure sense of direction, true repentance takes directions from God. Increasingly broader and deeper dimensions of our lives come under God's control as we follow God's guidance.

For a secular people, the Ninevites were amazingly responsive to Jonah's message. The power of a word from God affected the hearers deeply, and a response came immediately. The fasting and sackcloth were visible signs of a deep stirring within them. They mourned for the wickedness laid bare by Jonah's word from God.

The king's proclamation acknowledged that something more than grief was needed: "All shall turn from their evil ways and from the violence that is in their hands" (Jonah 3:8). The grief, the new way of looking at their deeds, and the turning away from their wickedness were evidences of true repentance.

### The Plan for Reconciliation

The Bible reveals God's plan for restoring relationships between God and sinful humanity. This plan focuses on what God has done and continues to do to redeem lost humanity. It highlights the initiatives that God has taken in creation, in covenant, in Christ, and in church. It focuses on sacrificial love that breaks down the barriers of sin and death.

You also may have heard of "the plan of salvation," the way God has provided for people who are estranged from God to be brought into relationship with God. This plan focuses on the recipients of the gospel message. It describes how a person is called to respond to what God has done in

Christ—accept the good news, believe in Christ, confess sins, become devoted to God, and so forth.

God also has a plan for bringing together God's initiative and humanity's response. This plan is what the apostle Paul called "the ministry of reconciliation" that God gave the church (2 Corinthians 5:18-20).

Though a reluctant agent of reconciliation initially, Jonah fulfilled this plan by bringing God's word to the people of Nineveh. He became God's ambassador. He made God's word known to the people, allowing God to make an appeal to the people through him. He entreated the people to be reconciled to God. Jonah was an important link in bringing together God's plan of redemption and the plan by which people might receive salvation.

The ministry of reconciliation is ours. While we engage in many worthwhile corporate activities to carry out this ministry, we often fall short in becoming individual agents of reconciliation. God does not call everyone to leave the safety of home for enemy territory to confront sinners with their wickedness. But each of us lives in the midst of broken lives. We are surrounded by people in need of compassion, love, forgiveness, redemption, and reconciliation. We have good news that can end despair and offer hope. To become links between God and humanity, we must become vulnerable to the discomforts that come with God's call. Unlike Jonah, however, we should rush to our ministry of reconciliation rather than flee from it. Who knows what God might do with our faithfulness in this ministry?

### The Opportunity in a Second Chance

Jonah messed up on his first opportunity to serve God in a ministry of reconciliation, and he suffered significant consequences. Interestingly enough, the hardened sailors on the boat to Tarshish were more ready to pray when the storm struck than was Jonah. Jonah slept through much of the storm and didn't pray until he was in the belly of the fish and his life was ebbing away (Jonah 2:7).

The Ninevites were more responsive to God's word to them through Jonah than Jonah was to God's word directly to him. Their response was quick and deep. Jonah had to get deep in the sea before he responded to God's call.

In spite of Jonah's reluctance and the mess he created for himself, God didn't give up on him. "The LORD came to Jonah a second time" (3:1) and gave Jonah another chance. Surely we too suffer the consequences of our disobedience; and just as surely, God doesn't give up on us. We are people who need a second chance and sometimes a third or fourth. Our obedience should be more like the immediate action to a commander's order than the response of a petulant child who continues the discussion to try to get his or her own way. Jonah failed on his first attempt, but when he had a second chance, he did as God commanded him, thereby fulfilling God's mission to the community at Nineveh. We, too, need to look for opportunities in the chances that God gives us to reach out to others.

---

## SHARING THE SCRIPTURE

### Preparing Our Hearts

Meditate on this week's devotional reading, found in Matthew 21:28-32. In this parable of the two sons Jesus teaches the importance of action. The son who indicated he would do as his father asked but did not was simply saying what he thought his dad wanted to hear. The other son, who initially refused to go work in the vineyard but "changed his mind and went" (21:29), was actually the one who "did the will of his father" (21:31). When have you said "yes" to God and then failed to act? When have you said "no" and then changed your mind?

Pray that you and the adult learners will be responsive to God's leading, changing your mind (repenting) as necessary to do God's will.

### Preparing Our Minds

Study the background and lesson scripture, both of which are found in two chapters of Jonah: 1:1-3 and 3:1-9. Think about how we are forced to choose between good and evil and what happens when people turn from wickedness.

Write on newsprint:
❏ information for next week's lesson, found under "Continue the Journey."
❏ activities for further spiritual growth in "Continue the Journey."

Read the "Introduction," "The Big Picture," "Close-up," and "Faith in Action" articles for this quarter, all of which immediately precede this lesson. Decide how you will use the information from these supplemental resources as you lead this quarter's sessions.

Plan an optional lecture as suggested under "Introduce God's Concern for the Nineveh Community and God's Plan of Redemption Using Jonah as a Messenger."

### LEADING THE CLASS

#### (1) Gather to Learn

❖ Welcome the class members and introduce any guests.

❖ Pray that today's participants will open their hearts to hear the good news and share it with others.

❖ Read this story from The Children's Court Centennial Communications Project: (http://www.cjcj.org/pdf/secondchances. pdf): **Derrick Thomas, perhaps best known**

as a Hall of Fame linebacker for the Kansas City Chiefs, was a graduate of the University of Alabama with a major in criminal justice and social work. He was also the founder of Third and Long, a foundation dedicated to helping inner-city children learn to read. As a teen found guilty of theft, his future did not look so promising. Having "beat the system" previously, Derrick was terribly upset when he learned that after repeatedly leaving the house when he was on home confinement, officials decided to lock him up in juvenile hall. Derrick claimed that this experience turned out to be "one of the most important breaks I ever got." Although he had other run-ins with the law as a teen, he turned his life around and was inspired to "make a difference on behalf of other troubled youth."

❖ Ask: **What does Derrick Thomas's story suggest to you about how people can respond when given a second chance?**

❖ Read aloud today's focus statement: **In a world filled with good and evil, persons are forced to choose between good and evil. What happens to people who turn from their wicked ways in sorrow? Jonah's plea to the people of Nineveh caused them to believe in God and fast, trusting that God would forgive them.**

#### (2) Introduce God's Concern for the Nineveh Community and God's Plan of Redemption Using Jonah as a Messenger

❖ Choose two volunteers, one to read Jonah 1:1-3 and the other to read Jonah 3:1-9.

❖ Encourage the students to put themselves in Jonah's sandals and answer these questions:
(1) **What caused you to run away from God?**
(2) **Why did you decide to act on God's command when you were given a second chance?**

❖ **Option:** Present a lecture based on Understanding the Scripture and "The

Scope of God's Concern" in Interpreting the Scripture to help the students learn more about Nineveh.

❖ Invite a volunteer to "interview" volunteers who play the role of the king of Nineveh and several ordinary citizens to learn what they believed about Jonah's God and why they responded as they did to his message.

❖ Wrap up this portion by talking about how Jonah's willingness to use his second chance offered the people of Nineveh an opportunity to repent and hope for new life.

*(3) Value Being Given a Second Chance to Complete a Mission, Especially When a Wrong Decision Has Been Made*

❖ Read or retell "The Opportunity in a Second Chance" in Interpreting the Scripture.

❖ Divide the class into groups of three or four. Encourage each person in the group to tell about a time when a parent, other family member, teacher, coach, employer, or someone else significant gave them a second chance to get something right. How did the students respond to this chance? What difference did it make in their lives?

❖ Bring everyone together and ask: **How have second chances in your life empowered you to give other people second chances?**

*(4) Name Resistance to Something the Learners Know They Should Do and Act*

❖ Distribute paper and pencils. Challenge the learners to write in confidence about some change they have been resisting in their own life and how they might take action to overcome this resistance.

❖ Call everyone together and invite the adults to affirm their commitment to take action by echoing these words of Paul: **"I can do all things through him who strengthens me"** (Philippians 4:13).

*(5) Continue the Journey*

❖ Pray that all who have come today will recognize that God gives second chances to those who repent and take action.

❖ Read aloud this preparation for next week's lesson. You may also want to post it on newsprint for the students to copy.

■ **Title: A Community to Redeem**
■ **Background Scripture: Jonah 3:10–4:11**
■ **Lesson Scripture: Jonah 3:10–4:5**
■ **Focus of the Lesson: When others receive some sort of benefit, deserved or undeserved, we can experience jealousy and anger and say, Why them? Is there another way to respond? Jonah came to realize that God is in control of things in the world and God's way of dealing with others differs from ours, but God's steadfast love abounds to all.**

❖ Challenge the students to complete one or more of these activities for further spiritual growth, which you will write on newsprint for the students to copy.

(1) **Use your influence to make a positive change within your church.**
(2) **Try fasting from food, television, or something else so that you can listen more closely for God and act on what you are inspired to do.**
(3) **Give thanks for second chances that God and people give to you this week.**

❖ Sing or read aloud "I Want a Principle Within."

❖ Conclude today's session by leading the class in this benediction adapted from Matthew 22:37, 39: **Go forth to love the Lord your God with all your heart, with all your soul, and with all your mind, and to love your neighbor as yourself.**

UNIT 1: COMMUNITY WITH A MISSION
# A COMMUNITY TO REDEEM

---

### PREVIEWING THE LESSON

**Lesson Scripture:** Jonah 3:10–4:5
**Background Scripture:** Jonah 3:10–4:11
**Key Verse:** Jonah 4:2

### Focus of the Lesson:
When others receive some sort of benefit, deserved or undeserved, we can experience jealousy and anger and say, Why them? Is there another way to respond? Jonah came to realize that God is in control of things in the world and God's way of dealing with others differs from ours, but God's steadfast love abounds to all.

### Goals for the Learners:
(1) to become familiar with the account of Jonah's anger at God's response to the city of Nineveh.
(2) to value the lives of all humans in spite of background and past actions.
(3) to commit to showing love, mercy, and forgiveness.

### Pronunciation Guide:
*manah* (maw naw')
Tarshish (tahr' shish)

### Supplies:
Bibles, newsprint and marker, paper and pencils, hymnals

---

### READING THE SCRIPTURE

NRSV
Jonah 3:10–4:5

¹⁰When God saw what they did, how they turned from their evil ways, God changed his mind about the calamity that he had said he would bring upon them; and he did not do it.

¹But this was very displeasing to Jonah, and he became angry. ²He prayed to the

NIV
Jonah 3:10–4:5

¹⁰When God saw what they did and how they turned from their evil ways, he had compassion and did not bring upon them the destruction he had threatened.

¹But Jonah was greatly displeased and became angry. ²He prayed to the LORD,

LORD and said, **"O LORD! Is not this what I said while I was still in my own country? That is why I fled to Tarshish at the beginning; for I knew that you are a gracious God and merciful, slow to anger, and abounding in steadfast love, and ready to relent from punishing.** ³And now, O LORD, please take my life from me, for it is better for me to die than to live." ⁴And the LORD said, "Is it right for you to be angry?" ⁵Then Jonah went out of the city and sat down east of the city, and made a booth for himself there. He sat under it in the shade, waiting to see what would become of the city.

**"O LORD, is this not what I said when I was still at home? That is why I was so quick to flee to Tarshish. I knew that you are a gracious and compassionate God, slow to anger and abounding in love, a God who relents from sending calamity.** ³Now, O LORD, take away my life, for it is better for me to die than to live."

⁴But the LORD replied, "Have you any right to be angry?"

⁵Jonah went out and sat down at a place east of the city. There he made himself a shelter, sat in its shade and waited to see what would happen to the city.

---

## UNDERSTANDING THE SCRIPTURE

**Jonah 3:10.** The deep, sincere, and comprehensive response of the people of Nineveh to Jonah's message changed their situation. Not only had the people listened to Jonah's message and accepted it as a word from God but they had also humbled themselves before God with fasting and desperate petition. So widespread was this response that not only the king and all the people participated but even their animals were denied food and water. The people all went into mourning mode by putting on sackcloth. They cast themselves down before God in hope of divine mercy.

What seemed to catch God's attention the most, however, were not the words of repentance, the acts of humiliation, or the breadth of the responses. God noticed "how they turned from their evil ways." Other than "the violence" mentioned in verse 8, these "evil ways" are unspecified—unless we draw from the prophecies of Nahum against Nineveh.

God withheld judgment against Nineveh. The declaration that the city would be overthrown was reversed.

**Jonah 4:1-4.** Jonah was not happy with this outcome. Indeed, "very displeasing" is a rather mild translation of a two-word

Hebrew expression that implies evil feelings were stirred up within Jonah.

We can only speculate about the cause of this extreme disappointment and anger. Perhaps his reasons were political. Nineveh was the enemy of his nation. Deep-seated animosity and prejudice is typical among enemies. Nineveh's downfall would have provided a welcome opportunity for continued peace and prosperity for Israel.

Perhaps his reasons were theological. God is a just God whose holiness is offended by sin. Surely the great evil in Nineveh deserved judgment by a just God.

Perhaps his reasons were personal. Jonah's integrity as a prophet depended on his prophecies coming true. If Nineveh wasn't overthrown in forty days, his stature as a prophet would be ruined.

Jonah also may have been upset with God for "forcing" him into the unwelcome role of prophet to Nineveh. So he "prayed" in that self-justifying "I told you so" fashion that is too much a part of our response to God's failure to do what *we* want. Jonah claimed that he had known all along that God was not really a God of justice. God was too "ready to relent from punishing" sinners. Instead, the Lord was "a gracious

God and merciful, slow to anger." *What a wimp!* Jonah thought. *With a God like that I would be better off dead!*

God responded to Jonah's angry prayer with a question, "Is it right for you to be angry?" The word "right" translates the basic Hebrew word for good or goodness. The only way to judge a human response is by contrasting it with the high standard of goodness. Falling short of that standard is a basic criterion for sin. God did not judge Jonah, as God had not judged the people of Nineveh. By the question, however, God let Jonah measure his own response against a different standard. That standard had nothing to do with the Ninevites and everything to do with Jonah.

**Jonah 4:5-8.** Jonah's spiteful anger didn't go away. Instead he took up a post east of the city to brood over his unfulfilled prophecy. "East of the city" would have been away from the Tigris River and its well-watered, fertile valley. The latitude of Nineveh (in modern Iraq) is similar to Nashville, Tennessee. The average temperature ranges from 45 degrees Fahrenheit in January to 92 degrees in July, but daily temperature swings of 30 to 40 degrees are not unusual. Facing such extremes, Jonah constructed a booth for shelter. "Booth" translates a word whose meanings range from "tent" to "hut" to "tabernacle." Jonah intended to wait out the forty days, hoping that by some chance God might withdraw grace and restore justice.

Even as God's prophet, Jonah still had much to learn about God. To help Jonah change his perspective, God gave him an object lesson. God caused a "bush" (NRSV; "vine" NIV or "gourd" KJV) to grow up quickly to provide shelter for Jonah. This garden plant may have been a castor bean or bottle gourd plant whose vine grows and withers rapidly. Providing shade from the burning sun, the plant changed Jonah's mood from very displeased (4:1) to "very happy" (4:6).

The next day, God acted again. God appointed a worm to attack the plant and cause it to wither. Then God sent a "sultry east wind" and a scorching hot sun that "beat down" on Jonah, so that Jonah too withered in great discomfort. Jonah's mood switched back to the death-wish mentality he had expressed before. The depression he had exhibited earlier became despair.

**Jonah 4:9-11.** Jonah had stopped praying (compare 4:1-3), but God had not stopped listening. God questioned Jonah again, and God's question paralleled the previous one (4:4). Only the focus changed. Previously God had questioned him about his anger over withheld judgment and offered grace. In the sheltering plant, God had offered grace to Jonah—one who had disobeyed God, fled from God's call, and pouted over God's graciousness to the Ninevites. In contrast to monumental issues, what good is there in anger over such an inconsequential matter as a dying plant? If Jonah can be so resentful toward God's magnificent grace offered to repentant sinners, why is withholding a minor grace from an unrepentant sinner not the very justice Jonah had expected of God?

The Book of Jonah ends with a question asked by God: "Should I not be concerned about Nineveh?" The question, however, is not just a question for Jonah. It is a question for every generation that reads this book. Is God's concern only for the chosen ones? What of the masses who do not know God? Would not "a gracious God and merciful, slow to anger, and abounding in steadfast love" (4:2) be concerned about 120,000 Ninevites or 900 million people in Africa or 1.6 billion Muslims? God's people cannot be bound by the exclusivity of being called by God, being chosen as God's people, being recipients of God's grace, or even being disciples of Jesus. The grace, the mercy, and the forgiveness given to us are our treasures to be shared with all humanity. "Mercy for us and justice for everyone else" is not a worthy slogan for God's people. Rather, "in Christ God was reconciling the world to himself, not counting their trespasses against them, and entrusting the message of reconciliation to us" (2 Corinthians 5:19).

## INTERPRETING THE SCRIPTURE

*Good and Bad Anger*

Understanding Jonah's anger is not easy because anger is a complex emotion, the causes of which are often hidden beneath the surface of consciousness. The complexity of the emotion is evident in the fact that over fifteen different Hebrew root words are used to describe the idea and are translated "anger" or "angry" in the *New International Version*.

All anger is not bad, and that explains why both God (Jonah 3:9, 4:2) and Jesus (Mark 3:5) can be described on occasion as angry. The Book of Jonah uses different Hebrew words to describe God's anger and Jonah's anger. The one used of God derives from the Hebrew word for nose or face and is the kind of anger evident in the flaring of the nostrils or a facial expression. The word used to describe Jonah's anger derives from a word for kindle or burn and describes a burning anger or rage and is quite different from God's being "slow to anger" (Jonah 4:2).

God's question to Jonah, "Is it right for you to be angry?" (4:4, 9) is an appropriate question for all occasions of anger. Often the recipients of anger have no clue as to the cause of the anger; and unfortunately, the person who is angry also often has no clue to the underlying reasons for an angry outburst. Because expressions of emotion can be delayed and the underlying causes for the emotion transferred, anger can be directed at the wrong people at the wrong time. The extreme anger Jonah displayed over the withered plant probably was this delayed/transferred kind of anger.

We have already probed some of the possible reasons for Jonah's anger about God's withholding judgment on Nineveh. Whatever the reason, we can note a couple of important things. First, God does not punish Jonah for his anger. As with David's honest expressions of his feelings in the Psalms, Jonah's complaints are accepted by God without punishment. Second, anger often carries us far beyond reason. To die over a withered plant is extreme. To be willing to die to bring God's grace and mercy to a people who do not know God would be worthy. But unless an angry person probes the reasons for the emotion—"Is it right for you to be angry?"—the anger often will be inappropriate for the time and the circumstances.

*Justice versus Mercy*

Christians marvel at the demonstration of God's grace through the life, death, and resurrection of Jesus Christ. The central message of the gospel is of a love so great that God was willing to sacrifice God's only Son so those who believe in him might have eternal life (John 3:16). Though that love is expressed for the whole world, we somehow have less passion about its application to those who do not quite measure up to our expectations.

Somehow unmerited grace just doesn't seem fair. If a person is going to be forgiven graciously, shouldn't that person have to do something that demonstrates sincerity and worthiness for such grace? Mercy that lets people off scot-free without any retribution or consequence seems unjust.

We want to think we have earned any benefits that come to us. Somehow our efforts, our devotion, or our character have made us worthy of reward. We tend to think highly of our merit and devalue the worthiness of others. Our faults or mistakes are minor, especially when compared with the "real sinners" of the world. Like Jonah, we think our disobedience pales in comparison with that of others. We deserve to be forgiven because God knows that deep inside we really are good people.

Jealousy eats at us when others get "unmerited" rewards or recognition. We wait with baited breath for the "mighty" to fall. We rejoice when they get their comeuppance and thank God that justice exists in the world.

These attitudes reveal that we are sinners falling short of God's glory (Romans 3:23). Whatever gradations we might give to sin, God sees all sin and all sinners the same. All are in need of grace. All are hopeless without the redemption that comes from God. Justice comes into play only when we fail to acknowledge that we, like all sinners, are in desperate need of God's mercy.

### God at Work among Us

We all have not been called to be prophets like Jonah, but the word of God comes to all of us—though probably not as directly as in Jonah's experience (see Jonah 1:1; 3:1; 4:4, 9). The word has come to us in the community of faith through Scripture, prayer, sermon, and service. I think the word of God also comes to us through many of the circumstances in our lives. The Book of Jonah indicates that God often is at work in the circumstances of life, guiding and directing people toward the will of God.

One Hebrew verb (*manah*) is used four times in the book of Jonah (though it is not translated in the same way). It first occurs in 1:17 where "the LORD *provided* a large fish." In 4:6, "the LORD *appointed* a bush." In 4:7, "God *appointed* a worm." Then in 4:8, "God *prepared* a sultry east wind." Similar circumstances occur with other verbs in 1:4, where "the LORD hurled a great wind," and in 2:10, where "the LORD spoke to the fish, and it spewed Jonah out upon the dry land." These

circumstances—as big as a storm at sea or as little as a bush, as big as a large fish that can swallow a man or as little as a worm—all were working in the plan of God to speak to Jonah, guide him, change him, and restore him in God's will and truth.

We certainly do not want to get into the habit of attributing to God every event in our lives, seeing tragedy as God's displeasure and success as God's blessing. On the other hand, if we are not open to the hand of God in the circumstances of our lives, we may miss important ways in which God is speaking to us and guiding us.

Brother Lawrence was a seventeenth-century lay brother among the Carmelites. He wrote a booklet that has become a classic in Christian devotion, *The Practice of the Presence of God.* Through his daily and often mundane experiences, Brother Lawrence trained himself to look for, discover, and celebrate the presence of God.

Such a focus does not come easily in the modern world where we are surrounded by so many distractions. Yet Jonah and Brother Lawrence remind us that the Spirit blows like a wind in our lives. We may scarcely feel it and hear it, and we do not always know where it comes from or where it goes (John 3:8). Times will come when God brings experiences, people, circumstances, and challenges into our lives as whispers of some new thing God has in store for us. Those new things may make us angry, may shake our traditional ways of thinking, or may send us into the pit of despair; but some marvelous aspect of God, of God's nature, or of God's will may come to us in a question like, "Is it right for you to be . . . ?" (Jonah 4:4, 9).

---

## SHARING THE SCRIPTURE

### Preparing Our Hearts

Meditate on this week's devotional reading, found in Matthew 9:9-13. After calling

Matthew, a man whose job as a tax (toll) collector would cause him to be hated by most people, Jesus announces that he had come to call those who are sinners, not the righteous ones. Jesus' dinner companions, "tax collectors and sinners" (9:10), highly offended the righteous Pharisees, who could not imagine that God would give such people a chance. In contrast, Jesus showed mercy and grace to those on the margins, and his attitude apparently caused jealousy and anger among the religious leaders. Who offends you?

Pray that you and the adult learners will be open to those in need of God's love and forgiveness, remembering that they, too, are ones for whom Jesus came and died.

### Preparing Our Minds

Study the background from Jonah 3:10–4:11 and the lesson scripture, Jonah 3:10–4:5. As you read this passage, think about whether there are other ways to respond to someone else's good fortune, rather than the jealousy or anger that people often exhibit.

Write on newsprint:
❑ information for next week's lesson, found under "Continue the Journey."
❑ activities for further spiritual growth in "Continue the Journey."

### LEADING THE CLASS

### (1) Gather to Learn

❖ Welcome the class members and introduce any guests.
❖ Pray that all who have gathered will experience the love and grace of God and share that gracious love with others.
❖ Read or retell "Justice versus Mercy" in Interpreting the Scripture.
❖ Encourage the class to talk about how this description does—or does not—ring true in terms of our response when others get something that we don't see them deserving. Probe their responses to see what motivates the jealousy that so often accompanies what we consider undeserved good fortune on the part of another.

❖ Read aloud today's focus statement: **When others receive some sort of benefit, deserved or undeserved, we can experience jealousy and anger and say, Why them? Is there another way to respond? Jonah came to realize that God is in control of things in the world and God's way of dealing with others differs from ours, but God's steadfast love abounds to all.**

### (2) Become Familiar with the Account of Jonah's Anger at God's Response to the City of Nineveh

❖ Select someone to read Jonah 3:10–4:5.
❖ Make a list of words or phrases on newsprint that the students would use to describe who God is, according to this passage.
❖ Discuss these questions:
(1) **Are any of the ideas we have brainstormed surprising? If so, which ones?**
(2) **Why are they surprising?** (Note that some students may be surprised to learn that people's actions are able to change God's mind.)
(3) **What implications do these ideas about God's nature have for how we relate to God?**
What changes, if any, should we make in terms of our actions and attitudes?
❖ Read or retell "Good and Bad Anger" in Interpreting the Scripture.
❖ Ask: **What emotions or attitudes formed the basis for Jonah's anger with God for sparing the Ninevites?**
❖ Provide a few moments of quiet time for the adults to think about situations in which they get angry with God, perhaps for extending mercy and grace to people they do not think are worthy.

### (3) Value the Lives of All Humans in Spite of Background and Past Actions

❖ Call the students together. Ask this question and list answers on newsprint:

Who are the modern-day Ninevites that certain Christians do not want to come before the throne of God's grace? (The broad answer is "people not like us." Specifically, though, these may be people who have been ostracized from the church for any number of reasons. List these categories of people.)

❖ Read this scenario and then ask the students how they would respond in this situation.

**Ellen Jones grew up in Friendlytown where your church is located. She never belonged to the church and was always the one who was somehow not like the rest of this small, close-knit community: pregnant at 16, a convicted shoplifter, deadbeat tenant who is always behind in her rent. Her now four-year-old daughter is ill and needs surgery, but Ellen's entry-level job offers no benefits. She has nowhere to turn. A church member who works at the same place as Ellen hears about her plight. How might the class as a group and as individuals respond so that Ellen may experience the love and value that God places on her life and the life of her daughter, despite past mistakes?**

❖ Conclude this part of the lesson by encouraging the students to think about people they know who do not feel valued. Distribute paper and pencils. Invite the students to write the answer to this question, which you will not discuss: **What can you do this week to help at least one of these people know that they are greatly valued by you and by God?**

*(4) Commit to Showing Love, Mercy, and Forgiveness*

❖ Read or retell "God at Work among Us."

❖ Refer to the list of modern-day Ninevites that the class brainstormed and ask:

**(1) Which of these groups of people are here in our community?**

**(2) How do we currently welcome them into the church—or do we?**

**(3) What other steps can we take to ensure that people who need to hear the message of God's redeeming love are able to do so?** (Note that in some cases the church may have to venture out to the people. Those who are incarcerated or ill with HIV/AIDS need to experience God's love even if they cannot physically get to the church building. Those who feel embarrassed by divorce, unemployment, lack of education, or other reasons need to know that the church will provide a safe, loving, non-judgmental environment for them.)

**(4) What biases might we as individuals and as a church need to overcome to be truly inclusive of all who long to experience God's love and forgiveness?**

❖ Invite the students to make a commitment to reach out to at least one group of people they have identified. Perhaps a small task force would be willing to suggest ways during a future class that would enable them to assimilate others into the class and church.

*(5) Continue the Journey*

❖ Pray that today's participants will go forth seeking to help others become part of the redeemed family of God by sowing God's love, mercy, and forgiveness.

❖ Read aloud this preparation for next week's lesson. You may also want to post it on newsprint for the students to copy.
- ■ **Title: Family as Community**
- ■ **Background Scripture: Ruth 1:1-16**
- ■ **Lesson Scripture: Ruth 1:1-9, 14, 16**
- ■ **Focus of the Lesson: When death changes family bonds, we long to strengthen ties to other relationships. What does it take to**

strengthen such relationships? Ruth made a loving commitment to her mother-in-law and accepted Naomi's God as her God.

❖ Challenge the students to complete one or more of these activities for further spiritual growth, which you will write on newsprint for the students to copy.

(1) Review today's key verse, Jonah 4:2. Use a concordance to locate other examples of this description of God's nature. Ponder what this description means in terms of your relationship with God and the way you treat other people.

(2) Gauge your own response to situations in which someone gets an apparently undeserved break.

Think about why you respond as you do, particularly if your response is negative.

(3) Read the short book of Nahum in which the prophet reports on the destruction of Nineveh, the capital of Assyria, by the Babylonians and Medes in 612 B.C. How is this view of Nineveh different from the city we see in Jonah?

❖ Sing or read aloud "Amazing Grace."

❖ Conclude today's session by leading the class in this benediction adapted from Matthew 22:37, 39: Go forth to love the Lord your God with all your heart, with all your soul, and with all your mind, and to love your neighbor as yourself.

UNIT 1: COMMUNITY WITH A MISSION
# FAMILY AS COMMUNITY

## PREVIEWING THE LESSON

**Lesson Scripture:** Ruth 1:1-9, 14, 16
**Background Scripture:** Ruth 1:1-16
**Key Verse:** Ruth 1:16

### Focus of the Lesson:
When death changes family bonds, we long to strengthen ties to other relationships. What does it take to strengthen such relationships? Ruth made a loving commitment to her mother-in-law and accepted Naomi's God as her God.

### Goals for the Learners:
(1) to explore Ruth's commitment to her mother-in-law, Naomi.
(2) to recall the feelings associated with a valued and meaningful relationship.
(3) to make a plan for strengthening relationships based on their relationship with God.

### Pronunciation Guide:
Ammonite (am' uh nite)              levirate (lev' uh rayt)
Chilion (kil' ee uhn)               Mahlon (mah' lon)
Elimelech (eh lim' uh lek)          Moab (moh' ab)
Ephrathite (ef' ruh thight)         Orpah (or' puh)
Kilion (kil' ee uhn)

### Supplies:
Bibles, newsprint and marker, paper and pencils, hymnals, optional meditative music and appropriate player

## READING THE SCRIPTURE

NRSV
Ruth 1:1-9, 14, 16

¹In the days when the judges ruled, there was a famine in the land, and a certain man of Bethlehem in Judah went to live in the country of Moab, he and his wife and two sons. ²The name of the man was Elimelech and the name of his wife Naomi, and the

NIV
Ruth 1-9, 14, 16

¹In the days when the judges ruled, there was a famine in the land, and a man from Bethlehem in Judah, together with his wife and two sons, went to live for a while in the country of Moab. ²The man's name was

names of his two sons were Mahlon and Chilion; they were Ephrathites from Bethlehem in Judah. They went into the country of Moab and remained there. ³But Elimelech, the husband of Naomi, died, and she was left with her two sons. ⁴These took Moabite wives; the name of the one was Orpah and the name of the other Ruth. When they had lived there about ten years, ⁵both Mahlon and Chilion also died, so that the woman was left without her two sons and her husband.

⁶Then she started to return with her daughters-in-law from the country of Moab, for she had heard in the country of Moab that the LORD had considered his people and given them food. ⁷So she set out from the place where she had been living, she and her two daughters-in-law, and they went on their way to go back to the land of Judah. ⁸But Naomi said to her two daughters-in-law, "Go back each of you to your mother's house. May the LORD deal kindly with you, as you have dealt with the dead and with me. ⁹The LORD grant that you may find security, each of you in the house of your husband." Then she kissed them, and they wept aloud. . . . ¹⁴ . . . Orpah kissed her mother-in-law, but Ruth clung to her. . . .

¹⁶**But Ruth said,**
**"Do not press me to leave you**
**or to turn back from following you!**
**Where you go, I will go;**
**Where you lodge, I will lodge;**
**your people shall be my people,**
**and your God my God."**

Elimelech, his wife's name Naomi, and the names of his two sons were Mahlon and Kilion. They were Ephrathites from Bethlehem, Judah. And they went to Moab and lived there.

³Now Elimelech, Naomi's husband, died, and she was left with her two sons. ⁴They married Moabite women, one named Orpah and the other Ruth. After they had lived there about ten years, ⁵both Mahlon and Kilion also died, and Naomi was left without her two sons and her husband.

⁶When she heard in Moab that the LORD had come to the aid of his people by providing food for them, Naomi and her daughters-in-law prepared to return home from there. ⁷With her two daughters-in-law she left the place where she had been living and set out on the road that would take them back to the land of Judah.

⁸Then Naomi said to her two daughters-in-law, "Go back, each of you, to your mother's home. May the LORD show kindness to you, as you have shown to your dead and to me. ⁹May the LORD grant that each of you will find rest in the home of another husband."

Then she kissed them and they wept aloud. . . .

¹⁴ . . . Then Orpah kissed her mother-in-law good-by, but Ruth clung to her. . . .

¹⁶**But Ruth replied, "Don't urge me to leave you or to turn back from you. Where you go I will go, and where you stay I will stay. Your people will be my people and your God my God."**

## UNDERSTANDING THE SCRIPTURE

**Ruth 1:1-5.** From the time when Joshua led the Israelites in the conquest of Canaan until Israel's first king, Saul, was anointed, the twelve tribes of Israel operated as a loose confederation. Their only central institution was the portable tabernacle where the ark of the covenant was housed. Only when the semi-independent tribes came under some kind of external threat did leaders arise. These leaders, called "judges," drew the tribes into concerted action to throw off the oppressor.

Ruth was the great-grandmother of David, Israel's second king (Ruth 4:13-22). Her story is set near the end of "the days when the judges ruled" (1:1). The account begins with a single family that decided to leave its homeland and settle in a neighboring country in hope of finding relief from famine.

Elimelech was an Ephrathite from Bethlehem in the tribal region of Judah. "Ephrathite" signifies that Elimelech's family came from a settlement called Ephrath (also Ephrathah), which predated Bethlehem but was later absorbed into it. This Ephrathite connection (see Genesis 35:19; 1 Samuel 17:12; Psalm 132:6; and Micah 5:2) probably emphasizes the family's ancient and aristocratic heritage.

Elimelech (whose name means "God is king") and his wife, Naomi ("my pleasant one"), had two sons, Mahlon and Chilion. The country in which they sought to escape the famine was Moab. Directly east and across the Dead Sea from Judah (in the region around modern Madaba, Jordan), Moab drew its name from a son born to Lot and his eldest daughter (Genesis 19:30-38). Moses conquered the area (Numbers 21:27-30), and it later was allotted to the tribe of Reuben (Joshua 13:9-16). In the time of David it was under the control of the Ammonites (1 Chronicles 19:6-9); and that situation probably prevailed during the time of Ruth as well.

Elimelech died in Moab, and his sons each married there. Mahlon and Chilion both married Moabite women named Orpah and Ruth. After being in Moab only ten years, Mahlon and Chilion also died. This left Naomi in a desperate plight—a widow in a foreign country with daughters-in-law who also were widows.

**Ruth 1:6-9a.** Famines occurred frequently in the ancient world, spawned by drought, blight, insect infestations, and warfare. The Hebrew root word for *famine* and its associated verb forms occur over 130 times in the Old Testament. Many of these recorded famines were localized, but some were extended (Genesis 41:27; 2 Samuel 24:13; 2 Kings 8:1) and extensive (Genesis 41:54; Acts 11:28).

Hungry people with few possessions move in response to every rumor of available food. News reached Moab that the famine in Israel had abated and food was available. Though she and her deceased family members had been treated kindly by her daughters-in-law, Naomi decided that the prospects in Judah warranted a return to her homeland, where a poor widow was more likely to receive assistance from her kin. So she and her daughters-in-law set out for Judah.

Perhaps Naomi, who was leaving a foreign country for her homeland, realized as her journey began that she was forcing the reverse situation upon her daughters-in-law. As Moabite widows, they probably would have a better chance of finding help among their own kin than in a foreign country. Returning to "your mother's house" (Ruth 1:8) would place each of them under their families' care. There they might find security and even perhaps a chance to remarry (1:9)

**Ruth 1:9b-13.** When kissed goodbye, the daughters-in-law tearfully persisted in their intentions to go with Naomi; but Naomi played out that scenario by making a reference to levirate marriage (Deuteronomy 25:5-6). According to Old Testament prescripts, if a man died without a male heir, the man's wife was not to marry outside the family. Rather, the deceased man's brother was to take her as his wife. Her first child in this new union would succeed to the name and privileges of the deceased husband and preserve the deceased's name in Israel.

Naomi had no more sons to fulfill the levirate law. If the daughters-in-law stayed with her, the only hope Naomi could see for them was for Naomi to marry again, have children, and hold them until their adulthood as potential husbands for the daughters-in-law. Practical woman that she was,

Naomi knew that none of those possibilities was realistic; and even if they were, would the daughters-in-law be willing to wait so long to resume their roles as wife and possibly mother?

Naomi concluded that God had thwarted her dreams, leaving her only with the bitter prospects of widowhood without descendants.

**Ruth 1:14-16.** Orpah finally was convinced. She kissed Naomi goodbye and returned to her parental home. But Ruth continued to cling to Naomi. The word "cling" translates the same Hebrew word used in Genesis 2:24 where "a man leaves his father and his mother and *clings* to his wife" (italics added). Ruth's commitment and devotion to her husband carried over to her mother-in-law. The bond of family created by marriage was not one she was willing to break. Ruth wed her future and her fortune to those of her mother-in-law.

When Naomi continued to encourage Ruth to follow the example of her sister-in-law and return to her parental home, Ruth sealed her commitment to stay with Naomi in a pledge so full of devotion and love that we often hear it quoted in wedding ceremonies. Ruth's pledge goes deep into the many dimensions of intimate relationships: community (not leaving, following, going, lodging), identity ("your people shall be my people"), and fidelity ("your God my God").

Hebrew religion often had its geographical, racial, and national dimensions. In later times, the rabbis prescribed ways in which a non-Jew could become a convert to Judaism. No such formula existed in Ruth's day, but her pledge to Naomi forms an almost stylized statement of what conversion encompasses. It involves entering into and becoming part of a new community. It involves adopting a new identity as a part of the people of faith. It involves pledging fidelity to God.

By her commitment, Ruth provided a new face for the faith of Israel. The face is an alien one, a Gentile one, and a feminine one. And because Ruth stands in the line of David's genealogy, she represents a significant broadening of our understanding of those who make up the people of God.

---

## INTERPRETING THE SCRIPTURE

### The Loss of Community

A sense of belonging—of being loved, accepted, and appreciated—is a very important part of human self-esteem. When a sense of belonging is missing, life can shrivel up like a plant lacking water. People who are plugged into meaningful relationships live longer, happier, more satisfying lives.

We find community on many levels. The most intimate level is the family—both the family into which we are born and the family formed if we marry. In the former, our sense of worth develops and is nurtured. When that goes well, we tend to thrive as confident and optimistic people. When it does not go well, we tend to struggle for acceptance and esteem throughout life.

In marriage, we often find a depth of intimacy and love that gives life profound meaning. When marriages fail, however, we can experience deep grief.

Community also can be found in other ways. The people with whom we live, work, play, and worship can become communities of support, encouragement, and acceptance for us. These communities supplement and enhance our sense of connectedness. They sometimes can replace deficiencies we find in other communities.

No community, however, is absolute and

permanent. Parents, spouses, children, friends, and co-workers die. Marriages break up. Jobs and employers change. People move away. Dissension and disagreement bring about the parting of ways. Catastrophes strip away our fixed points of reference.

How we handle the inevitable evolving and changing of our relationships is one of the essential tasks of life. Change can demoralize and defeat us, or it can challenge and inspire us. Will we withdraw from the fray or invest ourselves in forming new relationships?

Elimelech, Naomi, and Ruth provide inspiring examples of courageous people who faced difficult decisions—decisions that forced change upon them and caused them to move in new directions toward new relationships. The key, perhaps, is in seeing each loss of community as an opportunity for forming new communities.

### The Search for Community

Finding a new community in which we can develop meaningful relationships is not easy. Sometimes we fall into the trap of thinking, *If I could just change this aspect of my life, I would be happy.* The change we want might be in a marriage, a job, a neighborhood, a church, a club, or a group of friends. The lure of change is almost always more appealing than the circumstances we face when making the change.

Sometimes a new sense of community can come through redeemed relationships. Repentance, forgiveness, and recommitment can transform brokenness into wholeness. At other times, community can be found only by making a break with the past and forging into an unknown future.

God's call to Abraham was to go (Genesis 12:1). To Isaac it was to stay (26:2-3). To Jacob it was to go back (31:13). We find similar elements in the story of Ruth. Elimelech chose to go to a new country. Naomi chose to go back to Judah. Orpah chose to stay in Moab. Ruth chose a new country, a new companion, a new faith, and eventually a new husband. Though we tend to focus on Ruth, each character in the story was forced by the circumstances of his or her decision to find a new community or to reenter an old one under new circumstances.

Sometimes when we make changes, we find that the same problems arise in the new relationships. Why? Because a change in circumstances does not necessarily change us. Moreover, the problem may be more within us than in the circumstances. Before we make major changes, we do well to look honestly within ourselves for the reasons we want the change. If we haven't accepted our responsibility in creating the need for change, we likely will encounter problems in finding a new community. The prospects of success are almost always better when we are moving toward a new opportunity rather than away from an old problem.

Finding your way into a new community requires patience, persistence, initiative, and flexibility. I found this true when I retired and moved to a new community. We moved away from church members, friends, and co-workers who had been part of our lives for twenty-five years. Even our children and their families were farther away. The transition has not been easy. We still miss the old communities, but we also are finding that God has new opportunities for us here. While the search for that new place is behind us, the search for a new depth in relationships continues. And it will continue as our circumstances and our new communities themselves change over time.

### The Constancy of Faith

In the midst of change, God can be a sustaining force in our lives. My paraphrase of Psalm 46:6-7, from my unpublished collection entitled *The Poetic Psalter*, speaks of this transitory life and the constancy of God:
  "Though all the things we count as sure
    Are changing, failing, insecure,

And though the earth on any day
　　Could at God's voice just melt away,
We know the Lord is with us here,
　　A fortress mighty, steadfast, near."
From "Psalm 46," © 1996 by M. Michael Fink, Jr. Used with permission.

While many people and cultures have thought of their gods as tied to a place, a people, or a nation, Christians believe that God is far greater than even our best ideas. We do not need to go to a particular place to find God. We know God is not especially inclined toward one country, people, race, or sex over another. Those God chooses for special service are not elevated in God's affection but are accountable instruments by which God's love is spread to all people.

Elimelech did not leave God behind when he moved to Moab. Though Naomi certainly could have felt that God had abandoned her when her husband and sons died in Moab, we see her vibrant faith shine through. She knew that the Lord was still at work among the people back in Judah (Ruth 1:6); and even if she left her daughters-in-law behind in Moab, she knew the Lord would continue to deal kindly with them (1:8). Naomi's God was not a parochial God. Naomi's faith surely was an influence on Ruth.

Naomi's established faith had been tested by her circumstances, and she did not draw back from confessing her bitterness ("Call me Mara" or "Bitter," 1:20). Like her great-great-grandson, David, Naomi did not hesitate to speak her feelings openly and honestly to God. Honesty always preempts pretense.

Naomi's persistent faith saw her through the bad times and multiplied her joy when the good times returned. A "good-times-only" faith crumbles under adversity. A persistent faith, however, does not mean that all questions will be answered, all doubts erased, and all grievances addressed to our satisfaction. Not much is required to live by faith during good times. A robust faith is required to persist through the bitter times in life.

Ruth's absolute devotion to cling to Naomi reflects this same kind of persistent faith. Ruth was setting aside her natural family, her country, and its religion to stick with Naomi; but her devotion was not merely to Naomi. Her pledge was to the Lord, to whom she was accountable unto death (1:17).

A persistent faith in a constant God—that should be our goal! Let us not faint in times of trouble, but instead let us cling to "a fortress, mighty, steadfast, near." Let us not grow complacent in good times but instead let our faith be persistent, robust, and strong.

## SHARING THE SCRIPTURE

### Preparing Our Hearts

Meditate on this week's devotional reading, found in John 20:24-29. Probably you know the character in this story as "doubting Thomas," the disciple who was skeptical of the report of the other disciples who claimed to have seen Jesus. Yet there is another way to view this story: Jesus offers the "proof" Thomas seeks as a means of grace for him to believe. When have you needed an added measure of grace to believe in the risen Christ?

Pray that you and the adult learners will trust in God's grace to enable them to meet challenges to their faith.

### Preparing Our Minds

Study the background from Ruth 1:1-16 and the lesson scripture from Ruth 1:1-9, 14, 16. Think about what it takes to strengthen relationships when death changes our family bonds.

Write on newsprint:

❏ information for next week's lesson, found under "Continue the Journey."

❏ activities for further spiritual growth in "Continue the Journey."

Prepare to read aloud Ruth 1:1-5. You may want to consult the Pronunciation Guide.

Be prepared to discuss the suggested portions of Understanding the Scripture in the segment entitled "Explore Ruth's Commitment to Her Mother-in-law, Naomi."

Locate instrumental meditative music and an appropriate player if you choose to use music for "Make a Plan for Strengthening Relationships Based on the Learner's Relationship with God."

## LEADING THE CLASS

### (1) Gather to Learn

❖ Welcome the class members and introduce any guests.

❖ Pray that those who are participating in today's session will give thanks for the importance of family connections.

❖ Read or retell "The Loss of Community" in Interpreting the Scripture.

❖ Solicit comments concerning the importance of family and how, when one member dies, the family attempts to reconfigure itself. You may wish to reread this sentence and invite the students to respond: **Change [in our family relationships] can demoralize and defeat us or it can challenge and inspire us.** (Caution: Some class members may have recently experienced the loss of a loved one through death, divorce, or other crisis. Be sensitive to their needs to discuss—or refrain from discussing—their feelings.)

❖ Read aloud today's focus statement: **When death changes family bonds, we long to strengthen ties to other relationships. What does it take to strengthen such relationships? Ruth made a loving commitment to her mother-in-law and accepted Naomi's God as her God.**

### (2) Explore Ruth's Commitment to Her Mother-in-law, Naomi

❖ Read Ruth 1:1-5 aloud.

❖ Help the class realize what was at stake for Naomi, Orpah, and Ruth in the death of their husbands, particularly Naomi's husband, by reading or retelling in a brief lecture the information for Ruth 1:1-5, 6-9a in Understanding the Scripture.

❖ Choose volunteers to read dramatically the parts of a narrator and Naomi in Ruth 1:6-9, 14.

❖ Cover any other points from Understanding the Scripture (1:9b-13, 14-16) that you feel may be unfamiliar to the class.

❖ Ask the group to read in unison today's key verse, Ruth 1:16. Discuss these questions:

    **(1) What does this key verse tell you about Ruth's relationship with Naomi?**

    **(2) What do you think motivated Ruth to leave her homeland, people, and culture in Moab to go to her mother-in-law's home in Israel?**

    **(3) What influence might Naomi have had on Ruth that prompted her to be willing to adopt Naomi's God as her own?**

### (3) Recall the Feelings Associated with a Valued and Meaningful Relationship

❖ Encourage the students to think of a group that they previously or currently belong to in which they feel valued. This group could be a congregation, class, team, workplace group, civic organization, family, or other group.

❖ Post a sheet of newsprint. Ask the students to call out words or phrases to describe how they feel (or felt) when they are (or were) with this group.

❖ Talk further with the adults to see if they can identify why their relationship with this group was so meaningful. Perhaps the group shared a common vision that the students found affirming. Maybe the group served others in ways that were rewarding to them. Possibly their gifts and talents were valued and put to good use.

❖ Read or retell "The Search for Community."

❖ Point out that when we must find new communities, perhaps because we have moved to a new location, we usually try to avoid situations where we feel undervalued and seek those groups where we can feel as valued as we once did with another group.

❖ Invite volunteers to share stories of moving to new locations and searching for new communities. The final paragraph of "The Search for Community" is a helpful discussion starter if you have not already read it.

*(4) Make a Plan for Strengthening Relationships Based on the Learner's Relationship with God*

❖ Distribute paper and pencils. Ask the students to think of a relationship within their families or elsewhere that needs to be strengthened. Sometimes there has been a problem that needs to be resolved or an action that needs to be forgiven. In some cases, other priorities have taken precedence over the nurturing of a once-valued relationship.

❖ Encourage the adults to jot down ideas as to how they could, with God's help, strengthen the relationship they have identified.

❖ **Option:** Play instrumental meditative music as the students are working.

❖ Conclude this segment of the session by challenging the students to consider the options they have listed and begin to take action this week to commit themselves anew to this relationship.

*(5) Continue the Journey*

❖ Pray that those who have participated in today's session will do whatever possible to strengthen ties within their own families.

❖ Read aloud this preparation for next week's lesson. You may also want to post it on newsprint for the students to copy.

■ **Title: Acceptance in Community**
■ **Background Scripture: Ruth 2–3**
■ **Lesson Scripture: Ruth 2:5-12; 3:9-11**
■ **Focus of the Lesson: Most of us long for acceptance in our communities. How does one go about gaining acceptance? Ruth, who was a foreigner in a strange land, took the initiative to let Boaz know that she was willing to be part of the community.**

❖ Challenge the students to complete one or more of these activities for further spiritual growth, which you will write on newsprint for the students to copy.

**(1) Reach out to a family member who for whatever reason is disconnected from the rest of the clan. Help this person know that he or she is valued and does belong.**

**(2) Check census data or talk with longstanding members of your community to learn how your neighborhood has changed over time. You may be able to find a written history. How have these changes affected the community and enabled it to become what it is today?**

**(3) Offer to assist someone who has no one to help him or her. A homebound neighbor may appreciate a visit. Consider a ministry to a local nursing home where you visit patients who seldom have visitors.**

❖ Sing or read aloud "Happy the Home When God Is There."

❖ Conclude today's session by leading the class in this benediction adapted from Matthew 22:37, 39: **Go forth to love the Lord your God with all your heart, with all your soul, and with all your mind, and to love your neighbor as yourself.**

UNIT 1: COMMUNITY WITH A MISSION
# ACCEPTANCE IN COMMUNITY

## PREVIEWING THE LESSON

**Lesson Scripture:** Ruth 2:5-12; 3:9-11
**Background Scripture:** Ruth 2–3
**Key Verse:** Ruth 3:11

### Focus of the Lesson:
How does one go about gaining acceptance? Ruth, who was a foreigner in a strange land, took the initiative to let Boaz know that she was willing to be part of the community.

### Goals for the Learners:
(1) to explore the role of Boaz in demonstrating Ruth's acceptance in community.
(2) to appreciate expressions of respect for others and their possessions within community.
(3) to create communities of accepting hospitality.

### Pronunciation Guide:
Boaz (boh' az)                          *naarah* (nah ar aw')
Moabitess (moh' uh bite es)

### Supplies:
Bibles, newsprint and marker, paper and pencils, hymnals

## READING THE SCRIPTURE

NRSV
Ruth 2:5-12

⁵Then Boaz said to his servant who was in charge of the reapers, "To whom does this young woman belong?" ⁶The servant who was in charge of the reapers answered, "She is the Moabite who came back with Naomi from the country of Moab. ⁷She said, 'Please, let me glean and gather among the sheaves behind the reapers.' So she came, and she has been on her feet from early this morning until now, without resting even for a moment."

NIV
Ruth 2:5-12

⁵Boaz asked the foreman of his harvesters, "Whose young woman is that?"

⁶The foreman replied, "She is the Moabitess who came back from Moab with Naomi. ⁷She said, 'Please let me glean and gather among the sheaves behind the harvesters.' She went into the field and has worked steadily from morning till now, except for a short rest in the shelter."

⁸So Boaz said to Ruth, "My daughter,

[8]Then Boaz said to Ruth, "Now listen, my daughter, do not go to glean in another field or leave this one, but keep close to my young women. [9]Keep your eyes on the field that is being reaped, and follow behind them. I have ordered the young men not to bother you. If you get thirsty, go to the vessels and drink from what the young men have drawn." [10]Then she fell prostrate, with her face to the ground, and said to him, "Why have I found favor in your sight, that you should take notice of me, when I am a foreigner?" [11]But Boaz answered her, "All that you have done for your mother-in-law since the death of your husband has been fully told me, and how you left your father and mother and your native land and came to a people that you did not know before. [12]May the LORD reward you for your deeds, and may you have a full reward from the LORD, the God of Israel, under whose wings you have come for refuge!"

listen to me. Don't go and glean in another field and don't go away from here. Stay here with my servant girls. [9]Watch the field where the men are harvesting, and follow along after the girls. I have told the men not to touch you. And whenever you are thirsty, go and get a drink from the water jars the men have filled."

[10]At this, she bowed down with her face to the ground. She exclaimed, "Why have I found such favor in your eyes that you notice me—a foreigner?"

[11]Boaz replied, "I've been told all about what you have done for your mother-in-law since the death of your husband—how you left your father and mother and your homeland and came to live with a people you did not know before. [12]May the LORD repay you for what you have done. May you be richly rewarded by the LORD, the God of Israel, under whose wings you have come to take refuge."

**Ruth 3:9-11**

[9]He [Boaz] said, "Who are you?" And she answered, "I am Ruth, your servant; spread your cloak over your servant, for you are next-of-kin." [10]He said, "May you be blessed by the LORD, my daughter; this last instance of your loyalty is better than the first; you have not gone after young men, whether poor or rich. [11]**And now, my daughter, do not be afraid, I will do for you all that you ask, for all the assembly of my people know that you are a worthy woman."**

**Ruth 3:9-11**

[9]"Who are you?" he [Boaz] asked.

"I am your servant Ruth," she said. "Spread the corner of your garment over me, since you are a kinsman-redeemer."

[10]"The LORD bless you, my daughter," he replied. "This kindness is greater than that which you showed earlier: You have not run after the younger men, whether rich or poor. [11]**And now, my daughter, don't be afraid. I will do for you all you ask. All my fellow townsmen know that you are a woman of noble character."**

---

## UNDERSTANDING THE SCRIPTURE

**Ruth 2:1-7.** We do not know what happened to Elimelech's property when he moved to Moab. Perhaps he abandoned it because of the famine and hoped to return later and repossess it. Perhaps he sold it, planning to reclaim it later (Leviticus 25:25-28). With Elimelech's death, the property did not pass directly to his wife but rather to his male offspring. Mahlon, the eldest son, would have received two-thirds of his father's estate (Deuteronomy 21:15-17). The remainder would have gone to Chilion.

Though a widow could not inherit her husband's property, she was protected under the law of levirate marriage (Deuteronomy 25:5-10; Matthew 22:24-26), in which both the name and the inheritance of her husband were preserved through the widow's marriage to a brother of her deceased husband. This apparently was not possible or practical at Naomi's age. Numbers 27 provides that, without sons or daughters to preserve Elimelech's estate, the property would have passed to the nearest kinsman in his clan.

Boaz, a prominent rich man in Bethlehem (Ruth 2:1), was second in line as Elimelech's nearest kinsman. We are not sure whether Ruth was aware of this, but she did know of the Israelite law concerning gleaning (Leviticus 19:9; 23:22; Deuteronomy 24:19-22). Her desire to find "someone in whose sight I may find favor" (Ruth 2:2) may refer only to the gleaning or also may hint at a desire to find a suitable husband. The Book of Ruth, however, depicts Ruth's encounter with Boaz as the kind of happenstance that only God could set in motion. Ruth's gleaning just "happened" to put her in Boaz's fields, and "just then" Boaz arrived from Bethlehem (2:3-4).

When Boaz spotted Ruth, he inquired as "to whom does this young woman belong"—evidence that women in that society were assumed to be married, betrothed, or under the care of some male relative. The crew chief identified Ruth as "the Moabite who came back with Naomi" from Moab (3:6). He also noted that she was not gleaning merely as one of the poor, an alien, an orphan, or a widow—though she certainly qualified on those accounts. Rather she had asked permission to glean behind the reapers in the middle of the field before the sheaves had been removed. Not only had Ruth shown unusual boldness and initiative in requesting this privilege, but the crew chief also commended her for her hard and tireless work throughout the day.

**Ruth 2:8-23.** Boaz approached Ruth and demonstrated an immediate protectiveness over her. First, he called her, "my daughter," the same expression used by Naomi in 2:2. The Hebrew word for "daughter" (*bat* as in *bat mitzvah*) is a very general relational term.

The *New International Version*, for example, translates the word in its various occurrences as "daughter," "granddaughter," and "cousin," as well as "woman," "girl," "maiden," and "young woman."

Next, Boaz told Ruth to glean only in his fields and to follow closely behind the reapers. This choice location ensured a bountiful gleaning. Instructing the workers not to hinder her in any way, he also offered protection, security, and refreshment to her as she worked.

Then Boaz instructed Ruth to keep close to "my young women" (2:8; KJV uses "maidens"). Here (as well as in 2:5, 22-23 and 3:2) another Hebrew word (*naarah*) is used. This word focuses on youth, but being of marriageable age is generally implied. These young women assisted in the harvesting, probably providing water and other assistance to the workers. The term likely indicates that Boaz had not recognized Ruth as a widow when he first saw her (2:5).

Ruth's response to Boaz's generosity is significant. In humble gratitude, she prostrated herself before him. She offered no explanation of who she was, of her connection to Naomi, or of her being the widow of Mahlon. She seems to have been unaware that Boaz was a kinsman who might redeem her husband's property and name, at least until Naomi so informed her in 2:20. She positioned her gleaner status solely as a foreigner and later equated herself with Boaz's household servants (2:13). Her humility enhanced Boaz's generosity. Indeed, the favor she had hoped for (2:2) was being abundantly granted.

Boaz revealed that he knew more about Ruth than she realized. He knew of her marriage, her widowhood, her decision to adopt a new land and a new people, and her commitment to cling to Naomi as guardian and caregiver. He affirmed her decision to place herself in the hands of God as her refuge in time of trouble. Boaz shifted attention from his generosity to Ruth's deeds, commitment, and faith. He prayed that God would reward her fully for the hard choices she had made and still was facing.

**Ruth 3:1-18.** Ruth continued to glean in the fields of Boaz through the end of the barley and wheat harvests (2:23). Naomi, however, was worried about Ruth's long-term security (3:1). Naomi conceived a bold scheme that would force the obligation of a kinsman to the forefront. She instructed Ruth to gussy herself up and to approach Boaz stealthily after he had gone to sleep. While some sexual overtones are found in the account, the plan seems more one of creating a decisive moment for Boaz than of seducing him.

Naomi's plan worked as intended. When Boaz awoke at midnight, discovered a woman with him, and inquired who she was, Ruth recited the script prepared by Naomi. By asking him to "spread your cloak over your servant, for you are next-of-kin," Ruth clearly laid out Boaz's obliga-tions under the law. "Spreading the cloak" was a symbol of marriage, and "next-of-kin" affirmed that he was a kinsman who bore responsibility for redeeming Elimelech and Mahlon's property and progeny.

Boaz commended Ruth for her faithful-ness to her husband's interests and agreed to marry her. When Ruth reported the out-come to Naomi, Naomi recognized in the gift of six measures of barley the honorable intentions of Boaz. She encouraged Ruth to wait, for she knew that Boaz must first deal with the next-of-kin.

Through this marriage Ruth entered into the community; but even more significantly, she bore Boaz a son, who would become the grandfather of King David and a descen-dent in the messianic line of Jesus.

---

## INTERPRETING THE SCRIPTURE

### *The Importance of Community*

The Book of Ruth provides insight into the constructive workings of a community. Ruth and Naomi lived mobile lives; and, as in most societies, community began for them in the family. That family reached beyond the immediate family to an extended group of people who provided support and concern.

Their community also had several institu-tions that addressed the needs of its mem-bers. From the immediate family to the relatives who were kinsmen-redeemers to the provisions of levirate marriage, support was provided for widows and orphans. Laws also protected property rights while prescribing alms and gleaning rights for the poor, the disabled, and the aliens. The fact that Ruth—a poor woman, a childless widow, and an alien immigrant—found a place in Israelite society reveals much. The fact that some bold subterfuge was necessary shows that only rarely are societies ideal.

Some say that the sense of community is declining in American society. Surely the com-plexity and mobility of modern life contributes to this decline, but other factors also are at work. Sharing a core set of values provides cohesiveness for communities; but our secular, pluralistic society seems to be losing its value center. Individualism and the focus on per-sonal freedom and rights often drain away concern for the larger good of the community.

Many communities in our society are dysfunctional because they are caught up in bitter disputes over leadership, member-ship, and values. Struggles for power, authority, competitiveness, and exclusive-ness fracture communities and generate intolerant factions with intense commit-ments to narrow perspectives.

We still need stable and sustaining com-munities today. Identity, love, acceptance, achievement, and fulfillment grow out of participation in community. Each of us dis-covers who we are within some kind of com-munity. Each person finds self-value and self-worth in community and in turn learns to communicate a sense of worth and value for others. Each of us finds acceptance as we are affirmed by a community. Community status comes from actions, behaviors, and achievements that enhance the community; and we gain fulfillment by contributing to the larger good of communities.

Each of us should strive to find a place within a supportive community. We also should dedicate ourselves to ensuring that our communities are open, loving, and supportive, guiding each member toward healthy faith and maturity.

### Inclusiveness in the Community

The books of Ruth and Jonah bear special significance in the Old Testament because they preserve early traditions of God's concern for all people. This focus was especially important as Judaism developed.

From the time of David and Solomon, the people of Israel began to scatter from their homeland. At first this dispersion was a result of commercial and diplomatic interests. Later it was forced. When the Northern Kingdom fell to the Assyrians in 721 B.C., its people were deported and eventually lost their identity as they assimilated into the captor's culture. They sometimes are called the "ten lost tribes" because they lost contact with their native land, their religion, and their identity as Jews.

Later the Babylonians defeated the Southern Kingdom; and in three deportations between 598 and 582 B.C., they took all but the poorest citizens off into exile. Separated from their homes and religious institutions, the people in exile were determined to preserve their community. Grasping to maintain their identity as the people of God in a foreign culture, they focused on the law and its faithful observance as the cohesive characteristic of their identity. Over time, their outward focus on being a people destined to bless all the nations of the world turned inward. Their communities, their laws, their practices, and

their daily encounters became defensive—designed to preserve their distinct identity, their integrity as a people, and their separation from the corrupting influence of a pagan society. The results are seen in the New Testament, where legalism (the Pharisees), zeal (the Zealots), and withdrawal (the Essenes) produced communities dedicated to self-preservation and exclusivity.

Jonah's attitude toward the Ninevites symbolizes much of later Judaism and, if we are not cautious, can represent our own attitudes. Sometimes God must move boldly in redirecting us toward openness, concern, compassion, and acceptance. The message of Ruth is that commitment to God can come from surprising places outside the normal parameters of our communities. Our minds, our hearts, and our communities must be open to all who seek to make "your God, my God" (Ruth 1:16).

Edwin Markham expressed this inclusive sentiment poetically: "But love and I had the wit to win, / We drew a circle that took him in." What kind of circle is your church community drawing?

### Initiative in the Community

You would think that a community of believers living under the command to take the gospel into all the world would be naturally open and inclusive. You would think that the command to "go and tell" would be operative, but too often we act as if our commission is to issue an invitation to "come and see."

Initiative can be a delicate matter in a community. The initiative undertaken in trying to bring in outsiders not only varies from one community to another but it can also vary within the community itself. Some members of the community may be aggressive recruiters for new members. Other may show little concern for gaining new members and may even grow resentful if others bring in too many who "are not like us."

Newcomers change the dynamics within

a community. They bring new ideas, assumptions, and ways of doing things. The "we've always done it this way" crowd can become uncomfortable with the new. If the threat of the new or different becomes too great, communities can become mean and vicious both toward outsiders and insiders who take up the outsiders' cause.

Sometimes a sponsor or an advocate can be a means of decreasing the tension and smoothing the way toward a newcomer's acceptance. To some extent, Naomi began in this role for Ruth; but the cause certainly was taken up by Boaz. Many other biblical examples come to mind. Barnabas became an advocate for Paul as well as for John Mark. Peter became an advocate for Cornelius and thus for all Gentiles. Peter first and then James became strong advocates for the inclusion of Gentiles during the Council at Jerusalem.

An advocate can counsel the newcomer, anticipate and deal with opposition, commend and encourage the newcomer, and plan strategies for the newcomer's inclusion. An advocate who sticks with the task often becomes a pivotal influence in winning acceptance for a newcomer and integrating that person into the community.

Outsiders sometimes grow resentful of the barriers to inclusion in a community. They may shift all of the responsibility and the blame onto the "closed" community. A newcomer who waits, who grows resentful, or who withdraws because no one offers a welcome can lose important opportunities to gain acceptance in a community.

Ruth shows that initiative can be taken successfully by the outsider. She demonstrated boldness, persistence, hard work, humility, gratitude, and shrewdness. In trying to gain entrance and acceptance, the newcomer has more at stake; and inclusion should be so important that the newcomer is willing to take unusual initiative to gain admission into the community.

Barriers to acceptance in a new community can be many—class, sex, race, nationality, education, experience, and more. Willingness to take the initiative is important on both sides of the group's boundary, and persistence will pay off.

## SHARING THE SCRIPTURE

*Preparing Our Hearts*

Meditate on this week's devotional reading, found in Romans 12:9-18. After having written about new life in Christ, Paul goes on to describe what characterizes a Christian believer. In a nutshell, a believer practices selfless love. Verse 10 particularly speaks of loving each other "with mutual affection." As you ponder Paul's words, ask yourself how you exhibit the traits he describes. What changes do you need to make to bring your actions and attitudes better into line with the ideal Paul describes?

Pray that you and the adult learners will live lovingly in peace and harmony with all.

*Preparing Our Minds*

Study the background from chapters 2 and 3 of Ruth. The lesson scripture will focus on Ruth 2:5-12 and 3:9-11. Consider how one goes about gaining acceptance in a community.

Write on newsprint:
❏ information for next week's lesson, found under "Continue the Journey."
❏ activities for further spiritual growth in "Continue the Journey."

Prepare to read or retell Ruth 2:1-7 from Understanding the Scripture for "Explore the Role of Boaz in Demonstrating Ruth's Acceptance in Community."

Prepare to read or retell Ruth 3:1-8 from the Bible.

## LEADING THE CLASS

### (1) Gather to Learn

❖ Welcome the class members and introduce any guests.

❖ Pray that today's participants, especially those who are visiting, will feel accepted within the community of the class.

❖ Read aloud this story from http://www.crystal-reflections.com/stories /story_92.htm: **A married woman with three children was doing a "smile" project to complete a sociology class, the final course for her college degree. Soon after she and her family had entered a fast food restaurant two homeless men entered and ordered coffee, which is all they had money to buy. Moved by their plight, the woman added two breakfast trays to her order and took them to the men. As they, with tears in their eyes, thanked her, this non-church going believer responded: "I did not do this for you. God is here working through me to give you hope." This action, which affected many people, taught the woman the lesson of unconditional acceptance, which she said was "one of the biggest lessons I would ever learn."**

❖ Invite the students to respond to this story and briefly tell other stories of unconditional acceptance that they have witnessed.

❖ Read aloud today's focus statement: **Most of us long for acceptance in our communities. How does one go about gaining acceptance? Ruth, who was a foreigner in a strange land, took the initiative to let Boaz know that she was willing to be part of the community.**

### (2) Explore the Role of Boaz in Demonstrating Ruth's Acceptance in Community

❖ Read or retell Ruth 2:1-7 from Understanding the Scripture to set the stage for the first portion of today's lesson.

■ Choose a volunteer to read Ruth 2:5-12.

■ Invite the students to tell what they know about gleaning. Include a reading of Leviticus 19:9-10 in this discussion.

■ Invite the students to tell what they learn about Ruth from this passage.

■ Encourage them to state what they learn about Boaz.

■ Ask: **How do you see God at work in the lives of Ruth, Boaz, and Naomi?**

Build a bridge to the next section of today's Scripture lesson by reading or retelling the events that occur in Ruth 3:1-8. Select someone to read Ruth 3:9-11.

■ Use Ruth 3:1-18 in Understanding the Scripture to further explain Naomi's plan, Ruth's implementation of it, and Boaz's response.

■ Point out that while Ruth could have chosen to marry any man who would have her, the only way a male heir for Naomi could be recognized was if the marriage took place with one of Elimelech's close relatives. In such case, his line would be continued. Boaz takes on the responsibility of the kinsman-redeemer.

■ Conclude by asking:

(1) **Had you been a resident of Bethlehem (1:22) who was aware of Ruth's attempts to care for her mother-in-law, would you have welcomed this Moabite woman into your community? Why or why not?**

(2) **What might this story suggest about the way we extend (or withhold) acceptance of those who are "not like us"?**

### (3) Appreciate Expressions of Respect for Others and Their Possessions within Community

❖ Tell the students that the law giving Ruth permission to glean in the fields is found in what is called the Holiness Code, Leviticus 17:1–26:46. These chapters emphasize the importance of holiness for the whole community. Read aloud

Leviticus 19:1-4. Then divide the class and assign one of the following selected portions to each group for them to read:

- Leviticus 19:11-12.
- Leviticus 19:13-14.
- Leviticus 19:15-16.
- Leviticus 19:17-18.

❖ Call the groups together and discuss this question: **How would the lives of contemporary Christians become more conformed to the image of Christ if we adhered to these commands of the Holiness Code?**

❖ Sum up this portion of the lesson by noting that if we were to follow what we have read, we would show respect for others and strengthen our relationships within community.

*(4) Create Communities of Accepting Hospitality*

❖ Read aloud "Inclusiveness in the Community" in Interpreting the Scripture.

❖ Focus on the Edwin Markham quotation and the question that follows in the last paragraph: **What kind of circle is your church community drawing?**

❖ Talk about ways in which your church offers hospitality to visitors and newcomers. List specific actions on newsprint, such as sending visitors home with a loaf of bread or pie or other treat or helping a visitor in need find appropriate assistance.

❖ Ask: **As we look at what we are doing as a congregation, what else could we be doing to help those who come through our doors know that they are welcomed and accepted?** List these ideas on newsprint. You may want to focus on how this class can offer hospitality to newcomers.

❖ Challenge the class members to invite newcomers to attend worship and Sunday school next week, Easter Sunday. Suggest that the class agree to do something special to welcome those who come.

*(5) Continue the Journey*

❖ Pray that those who have participated today will feel accepted in the church community and extend that acceptance to others.

❖ Read aloud this preparation for next week's lesson. You may also want to post it on newsprint for the students to copy.

- **Title: The Community Faces Pain and Joy**
- **Background Scripture: John 13:21-30; 16:16-24; 20:11-16**
- **Lesson Scripture: John 16:16-24; 20:11-16**
- **Focus of the Lesson: Communities experience not only great pain and sorrow but also great relief and joy. Why should communities have hope? Jesus foretold his betrayal, death, and resurrection, and he taught that pain and sorrow will be replaced by relief and joy.**

❖ Challenge the students to complete one or more of these activities for further spiritual growth, which you will write on newsprint for the students to copy.

(1) **Invite people to attend Holy Week services with you. Reach out to let them know that even if they do not regularly attend church they will be welcomed and accepted.**

(2) **Study the Holiness Code found in Leviticus 17:1–26:46. Note the law regarding gleaning in 19:9-10, which is the provision that allowed Ruth to gather food for Naomi and herself. What parts of the Code do we Christians need to follow to better enable us to live a life of holiness?**

(3) **Be alert for ways that you can help someone who is on the margins of community, perhaps someone who is homeless or a stranger in a new place.**

❖ Sing or read aloud "Help Us Accept Each Other."

❖ Conclude today's session by leading the class in this benediction adapted from Matthew 22:37, 39: **Go forth to love the Lord your God with all your heart, with all your soul, and with all your mind, and to love your neighbor as yourself.**

UNIT 2: TEACHINGS OF JESUS

# THE COMMUNITY FACES PAIN AND JOY

---

## PREVIEWING THE LESSON

**Lesson Scripture:** John 16:16-24; 20:11-16
**Background Scripture:** John 13:21-30; 16:16-24; 20:11-16
**Key Verse:** John 16:16

### Focus of the Lesson:
Communities experience not only great pain and sorrow but also great relief and joy. Why should communities have hope? Jesus foretold his betrayal, death, and resurrection, and he taught that pain and sorrow will be replaced by relief and joy.

### Goals for the Learners:
(1) to highlight the internal source of the community's pain, its ensuing confusion, and its joy upon Jesus' resurrection.
(2) to identify causes of sorrow and joy.
(3) to support the community in times of pain and to join the community in expressing joy in good times.

### Pronunciation Guide:
Aramaic (air uh may' ik)                  Seder (say' der)
Rabbouni (ra boo' nigh)

### Supplies:
Bibles, newsprint and marker, paper and pencils, hymnals

---

## READING THE SCRIPTURE

NRSV
John 16:16-24

¹⁶**"A little while, and you will no longer see me, and again a little while, and you will see me."** ¹⁷Then some of his disciples said to one another, "What does he mean by saying

NIV
John 16:16-24

¹⁶**"In a little while you will see me no more, and then after a little while you will see me."**

¹⁷Some of his disciples said to one another,

to us, 'A little while, and you will no longer see me, and again a little while, and you will see me'; and 'Because I am going to the Father'?" [18]They said, "What does he mean by this 'a little while'? We do not know what he is talking about." [19]Jesus knew that they wanted to ask him, so he said to them, "Are you discussing among yourselves what I meant when I said, 'A little while, and you will no longer see me, and again a little while, and you will see me'? [20]Very truly, I tell you, you will weep and mourn, but the world will rejoice; you will have pain, but your pain will turn into joy. [21]When a woman is in labor, she has pain, because her hour has come. But when her child is born, she no longer remembers the anguish because of the joy of having brought a human being into the world. [22]So you have pain now; but I will see you again, and your hearts will rejoice, and no one will take your joy from you. [23]On that day you will ask nothing of me. Very truly, I tell you, if you ask anything of the Father in my name, he will give it to you. [24]Until now you have not asked for anything in my name. Ask and you will receive, so that your joy may be complete."

John 20:11-16

[11]But Mary stood weeping outside the tomb. As she wept, she bent over to look into the tomb; [12]and she saw two angels in white, sitting where the body of Jesus had been lying, one at the head and the other at the feet. [13]They said to her, "Woman, why are you weeping?" She said to them, "They have taken away my Lord, and I do not know where they have laid him." [14]When she had said this, she turned around and saw Jesus standing there, but she did not know that it was Jesus. [15]Jesus said to her, "Woman, why are you weeping? Whom are you looking for?" Supposing him to be the gardener, she said to him, "Sir, if you have carried him away, tell me where you have laid him, and I will take him away." [16]Jesus said to her, "Mary!" She turned and said to him in Hebrew, "Rabbouni!" (which means Teacher).

"What does he mean by saying, 'In a little while you will see me no more, and then after a little while you will see me,' and 'Because I am going to the Father'?" [18]They kept asking, "What does he mean by 'a little while'? We don't understand what he is saying."

[19]Jesus saw that they wanted to ask him about this, so he said to them, "Are you asking one another what I meant when I said, 'In a little while you will see me no more, and then after a little while you will see me'? [20]I tell you the truth, you will weep and mourn while the world rejoices. You will grieve, but your grief will turn to joy. [21]A woman giving birth to a child has pain because her time has come; but when her baby is born she forgets the anguish because of her joy that a child is born into the world. [22]So with you: Now is your time of grief, but I will see you again and you will rejoice, and no one will take away your joy. [23]In that day you will no longer ask me anything. I tell you the truth, my Father will give you whatever you ask in my name. [24]Until now you have not asked for anything in my name. Ask and you will receive, and your joy will be complete."

John 20:11-16

[11][B]ut Mary stood outside the tomb crying. As she wept, she bent over to look into the tomb [12]and saw two angels in white, seated where Jesus' body had been, one at the head and the other at the foot.

[13]They asked her, "Woman, why are you crying?"

"They have taken my Lord away," she said, "and I don't know where they have put him." [14]At this, she turned around and saw Jesus standing there, but she did not realize that it was Jesus.

[15]"Woman," he said, "why are you crying? Who is it you are looking for?"

Thinking he was the gardener, she said, "Sir, if you have carried him away, tell me where you have put him, and I will get him."

[16]Jesus said to her, "Mary."

She turned toward him and cried out in Aramaic, "Rabboni!" (which means Teacher).

# UNDERSTANDING THE SCRIPTURE

**John 13:21-30.** The Gospel of John offers an extended account of Jesus' last meal with his disciples (John 13–17). All four Gospels record that Jesus was giving hints of his death long before that Passover meal—indeed almost from the moment the disciples began to recognize who he was (see for example Mark 8:27-31; 9:30-32; 10:32-43; John 8:21-30).

Mixed into these accounts are glimpses of the deep struggle through which Jesus went as his "time" approached (John 7:6-8; Matthew 26:18). The betrayal by Judas and the denials Jesus foresaw among his disciples (John 13:36-38) deeply troubled him.

The disciples were out of touch with what Jesus was facing. Even when he openly declared, "one of you will betray me" (13:21), the disciples looked around wondering who would do such a dastardly deed. Peter asked the oft-called "Beloved Disciple" reclining next to Jesus to inquire who the betrayer might be. Even when Jesus identified Judas as the betrayer by dipping a piece of bread and giving it to Judas, the disciples seemed not to comprehend. So confused were they that they wondered aloud, "Surely not I, Lord?" (Matthew 26:22), perhaps reflecting that they too had been receiving bread dipped in the same bowl.

When Jesus dismissed Judas to "do quickly what you are going to do" (John 13:27), the disciples still assumed that some good motive was at work (like buying supplies or giving alms to the needy). The Gospel writer noted that "it was night" (13:30), and the dark hours were ahead.

**John 16:16-24.** The prospects of betrayal and denial were daunting, but Jesus introduced another foreboding prospect—his imminent departure from his disciples. In addition to the enigmatic statement in verse 16 that "you will no longer see me," the disciples recalled an earlier statement about Jesus' "going to the Father" (John 14:12, 28).

The emphasis on "a little while" in verses 16-19 is based on a Greek word meaning "very small." We get the words "micro" and "micron" from it. John used it with reference to a very short time. John had used the same word earlier in Jesus' telling his disciples, "In a little while the world will no longer see me, but you will see me" (John 14:19). In that context, the "you will see me" seems to have an end-of-time orientation because of "on that day" in the following verse—a frequent expression applied to the end-times.

We can understand how the disciples were confused by the world not seeing Jesus in a little while, the disciples not seeing him in a little while, the disciples seeing him in a little while, and the disciples seeing him at the end of time. From our side of Easter, we can understand these as references to Jesus' death ("no longer see me"), resurrection appearances to the disciples ("see me"), ascension ("going to the Father"), and future coming at the end of time ("see me").

These references to time introduce another contrast—a contrast in the feelings associated with the impending events. The death of Jesus would bring momentary rejoicing for his opponents but pain and sorrow for his disciples. His resurrection, however, would bring great joy for his followers.

Jesus likened this moment in salvation history to the birth experience. The impending death of Jesus was like a pregnant woman whose time has come. The pain and anguish of giving birth are real, consuming, and significant; but they suddenly are transformed into immense joy when the child is born. The resurrection and all it signifies for believers and their future brings that kind of joy—a joy that cannot be taken away.

After the resurrection and ascension, his followers lived for "a little while" in a time of not seeing Jesus. Lacking his physical presence, however, the disciples could live "in Jesus' name," assured that petitioning God in Jesus' name will bring the same responsiveness that they had experienced personally with Jesus.

**John 20:11-16.** All that the prophets of old had predicted and that Jesus himself had disclosed to his disciples happened. The brief hours between Thursday night's Passover supper with the disciples and early Sunday morning when Mary Magdalene went to the tomb must have seemed almost unending. John devoted two chapters to recording the fulfillment of the details Jesus had disclosed.

Jesus was betrayed and arrested (18:1-11). He was brought before the high priest for interrogation, during which Peter denied knowing him (18:12-27). Jesus then was taken before the Roman procurator, Pilate. Pilate's inquiry was a back-and-forth between him, Jesus, the Jewish leaders, and a bloodthirsty mob. Try as he might to appease Jesus' opponents, Pilate was unsuccessful in establishing Jesus' innocence. At last Pilate sentenced Jesus to death by crucifixion (18:28–19:16). Less than twenty-four hours after the last supper with his disciples, Jesus was dead and buried in a tomb by secret disciples (John 19:17-42). While the opposition rejoiced, the disciples were plunged into deep sorrow. No one saw Jesus for "a little while."

With the Sabbath over, Sunday morning found Mary Magdalene making her way to the tomb before sunrise. She possibly was accompanied by other women (Matthew 28:1; Mark 16:1; Luke 24:10; compare "we" in John 20:2). The Gospels agree that the women found an empty tomb, but other information about what was seen and by whom varies considerably.

The Gospel of John has several distinct features. First, Mary Magdalene was the first to encounter the risen Lord. Second, Mary Magdalene was not mentioned in the Gospel until the Crucifixion (19:25), and then only in the shadow of Mary, the mother of Jesus. Third, after discovering the empty tomb, Mary Magdalene ran to Peter and another disciple and informed them of the empty tomb. Fourth, only after Peter and the other disciple had left (believing but perplexed because they had not put all of the pieces together) did Jesus appear to Mary Magdalene alone. Fifth, the angelic messengers are mentioned in Mary's second visit to the tomb. Finally, when Mary first encountered Jesus, she did not recognize him. She thought he was the gardener. Only when Jesus called her by name did she recognize the indescribable truth and the principle message of Easter—her Lord and Teacher is alive!

---

## INTERPRETING THE SCRIPTURE

*Joy and Sorrow*

Most probably would agree that the birth, death, and resurrection of Jesus are the most significant events in his life. They are the focus of our Christian year, and two are commemorated this week. The three remind us that joy and sorrow often are intertwined in life. Advent with its eager anticipation of Christ's birth lifts our spirits. Lent with its fasting and penitence reminds us of the consequences of sin that led Jesus to the cross. Today we turn from the dark despair of crucifixion Friday to the joyous shout of the resurrection, "He is alive!"

Jesus' last week was Passover. That observance is a bittersweet remembrance for Jewish people. It recalls the bitterness of slavery in a foreign land. It also focuses on the deliverance of Israelites from their bondage under Moses' leadership and God's hand. The Passover meal, the Seder, eaten on the first night of Passover week, includes bitter herbs dipped in a sweet paste—another reminder of joy and sorrow intertwined in human experience.

An old joke tells of a person experiencing a rough time in life. A friend sought to encourage him by saying, "It could be worse." And sure enough, it did become worse! In reality our moods generally reflect the circumstances of our lives. If things are going well, we feel great. When things go badly, we plunge into despair. You don't have to be a manic-depressive personality to ride a roller-coaster of ups and downs in life. Even Jesus' spirit sagged when he sensed the imminent betrayal and denial of his closest followers.

Some bad things pass in a little while. Others fester and hold on for years. In good times and bad we all need a community that supports, encourages, prays for, and ministers to us. But we must not only be recipients of such support, we also must be support-givers. John Fawcett's hymn "Blest Be the Tie" reminds us: "We share our mutual woes, our mutual burdens bear; and often for each other flows the sympathizing tear." Monumental obstacles can be overcome when we join hands and hearts and draw strength from one another in the church.

### Hope

As individuals and as communities of faith, we must deal with the peaks and valleys of life. What we need to sustain us in the ups and downs is some confidence—some sense of hope—that overarches all the circumstances in our lives and renews our spirits.

In dealing with the sorrow that comes from bereavement, the apostle Paul contrasted believers with others "who have no hope" (1 Thessalonians 4:13). Paul affirmed that hope is an essential ingredient in coping with difficult fluctuations in life.

Easter provides the most powerful testimony to hope for the Christian community. What circumstances could engender more despair than what happened to Jesus between his praying in the garden and his dead body being laid in the tomb less than twenty-four hours later? The hopes of God's people for millennia, vested in him from his birth, were crushed. The pall of clouds that fell over the death scene seemed to symbolize that God was unwilling to look upon, and certainly would not intervene in, this execution.

When songwriter Rich Mullins contemplated this scene and Jesus' words, "Father, forgive them" (Luke 23:34), he wrote the lyrics of "Hope to Carry On." Mullins saw in the cross a sacrificial love that provides hope for carrying on no matter how difficult the circumstances.

Mullins could see hope in such a hopeless situation because of what happened on the first Easter morning. Darkness turned into light. Death turned into life. Despair turned into hope. Jesus was raised from the dead by the power of God.

Our hope is built on the foundation that beyond the temporal is something eternal, beyond the physical is something spiritual, and beyond death is life. Our hope is nourished in a community of faith built on victory over sin and death through our Lord Jesus Christ.

### The Last Shall Be First

Jesus' teachings and the Gospels themselves are filled with surprising reversals. What would seem to be reasonable, logical, and customary suddenly is turned topsy-turvy by a new perspective on what really is important.

The presence of itinerant and supposedly untrustworthy shepherds as witnesses to Jesus' birth would be one example of such a surprise. Another would be Jesus' appearing first to Mary Magdalene after the resurrection. In three of the four Gospels, Mary Magdalene is not even mentioned until she is listed among a group of faithful women mourning Jesus' crucifixion. Most of us would expect Peter to be the first to see Jesus after his resurrection—or at least James, John, or another of the Twelve. For a behind-the-scenes supporter of Jesus—and a woman to boot—to emerge as the first witness to his resurrection certainly is a surprising reversal.

Luke's Gospel first mentions Mary Magdalene as one of some women from

Galilee who were cured of evil spirits by Jesus and traveled with and provided support for him (Luke 8:2; 23:55). She is not mentioned again (and is first mentioned in the other Gospels, Matthew 27:56; Mark 15:40; John 19:25) until she appears at the cross where Jesus was crucified. Matthew (27:61) and Mark (15:47) explicitly identify her as one of the women who saw where Jesus was buried. All four Gospels place her at the tomb on Sunday morning and identify her as one of the first witnesses of the empty tomb. Matthew (28:1) mentions a resurrection appearance to Mary Magdalene and "the other Mary," but only John (20:1) and one of the endings added later to the Gospel of Mark (16:9) mention an appearance to Mary Magdalene alone.

Many have tried to find references to Mary Magdalene elsewhere in the Gospels. Some have tried to identify her with Mary, the sister of Lazarus; but that family was not from Galilee. Others have tried to tie her to the sinful woman forgiven by Jesus in Luke 7:37-50, but two verses later Luke introduced her by name without any reference to the previous account. Attempts to venerate her and create a special intimacy with Jesus have persisted even into the fiction of our own time, but all these do is offset the dramatic sense of reversal that the Gospels recount.

Though Jesus explicitly forbade it (Mark 10:42-45), the church has persisted in elevating some over others. Sometimes it is done on the basis of ministry, vocation, office, age, sex, race, experience, or some other criterion; but God continues to confound us by looking at the heart.

Mary's heart obviously was established early when Jesus cured her of evil spirits. She followed Jesus among a group of women who provided for Jesus and his disciples out of their own resources. She boldly stood as a sympathizer at the foot of the cross. She stayed near Jesus as he was moved from the cross to the tomb. As soon as the sabbath was over, she went to the tomb to mourn and minister to the burial needs. When the tomb was found to be empty and others had departed, she stayed at the tomb weeping. But when Jesus came to her, spoke to her, and revealed himself to her, she truly revealed her heart—and her joy—with her words, "My Teacher!"

Mary Magdalene was a woman taught by Christ. Our churches need more with humble hearts taught by Christ.

## SHARING THE SCRIPTURE

*Preparing Our Hearts*

Meditate on this week's devotional reading, found in Psalm 5. The writer, who has been harmed by the lies of enemies, turns to God for protection and deliverance. Center yourself and then read this psalm to see what words or phrases come to your attention. What comfort do you find here? What challenge? In what ways is this psalm of David your own psalm?

Pray that you and the adult learners will approach God with confidence and trust, knowing that God can deliver you from whatever oppresses you.

*Preparing Our Minds*

Study the background from John 13:21-30; 16:16-24; 20:11-16. The lesson scripture focuses on John 16:16-24 and John 20:11-16. Ask yourself: why should communities have hope?

Write on newsprint:
❑ questions for groups under "Identify Causes of Sorrow and Joy."
❑ information for next week's lesson, found under "Continue the Journey."
❑ activities for further spiritual growth in "Continue the Journey."

Plan any special accommodations you

will need to make in terms of class size and length as the congregation celebrates Easter.

## LEADING THE CLASS

### (1) Gather to Learn

❖ Welcome the class members and introduce any guests.

❖ Pray that all who have come today will join in praise to God for the resurrection of Jesus.

❖ Read this insight from blogger Viola Jaynes on www.spiritualthingsmatter.com, concerning her community, The Woodlands, Texas, about 75 miles north of Galveston, which was hit by hurricane Ike in 2008: **I was immensely touched and impressed that so many people were in high spirits following the storm. Everyone, including the ones who lost so much, were thankful for their lives and the lives of their loved ones. I saw one sign that read, "Landscaped by Ike," and another sign that humorously read, "Yard of the Month." I smiled when I read them because I realized that people somehow kept their sense of humor in the midst of all the destruction and tears. I spoke with many of my neighbors, and most were thankful because they knew it could have been so much worse. Some were not so fortunate. The pain of losing a life is immense. The pain of many who lost literally everything they own is devastating. This will take time to heal and, it will take time to restore things to normal once again.**

❖ Invite the class members to comment on this tragedy and others that they may be aware of in which people who had experienced great pain could also find joy and hope for the future.

❖ Read aloud today's focus statement: **Communities experience not only great pain and sorrow but also great relief and joy. Why should communities have hope? Jesus foretold his betrayal, death, and resurrection, and he taught that pain and sorrow will be replaced by relief and joy.**

### (2) Highlight the Internal Source of the Community's Pain, Its Ensuing Confusion, and Its Joy upon Jesus' Resurrection

❖ Solicit a volunteer to read John 16:16-24.

■ Look first at the key verse, John 16:16. Check in with the class to be sure that everyone can understand how such a statement would have confused the disciples. Add information from John 16:16-24 in Understanding the Scripture to explain this puzzling comment.

■ Consider Jesus' illustration of the woman in childbirth by asking: **How does this illustration help explain how pain and joy are intimately related? What other illustrations might you have used?**

❖ Read John 20:11-16 as expressively as you can. Encourage the students to close their eyes and imagine themselves as Mary. What do they see, hear, taste, touch, or feel? (Your purpose here is to help students experience this event for themselves, rather than just read it.)

■ Discuss the students' sensory perceptions and how these perceptions made the story more real to them.

■ Invite the students to comment on their emotions as they walked in Mary's footprints in the garden.

### (3) Identify Causes of Sorrow and Joy

❖ Divide the class into three groups and give each group a marker and sheet of newsprint. Assign groups the related questions as follows. If the class is large, assign several groups to each category. You may want to post the groups and questions on newsprint.

■ **Group 1—INDIVIDUALS: What kinds of situations often cause joy or sorrow in the life of an individual?**

■ **Group 2—CONGREGATIONS: What kinds of situations often cause** joy or sorrow that affects a substantial number of church members?

■ **Group 3—NATIONS: What kinds of situations often cause joy or sorrow that affects a substantial number of citizens?**

❖ Provide time for the groups to post their lists and report.

❖ Conclude by encouraging the adults to talk about how joy and sorrow may sometimes be intertwined. Also ask them to comment on how it is easier or more difficult to experience sorrow and joy alone or with some type of community.

*(4) Support the Community in Times of Pain and Join the Community in Expressing Joy in Good Times*

❖ Read or retell "Joy and Sorrow" in Interpreting the Scripture, particularly the final two paragraphs.

❖ Invite the students to look again at the lists they have generated to discern current instances of joys and sorrows where support is needed. For example, perhaps the loss of a familiar building or landmark was identified as a sorrow. Is there a church or other building within the area that has sustained damage and could be assisted? Perhaps the congregation is receiving confirmands or other new members into the fold who could be welcomed and nurtured by class members who want to share in this joy.

❖ Talk with the class about what they might do to help those who need hope in a time of sorrow or an opportunity to celebrate in time of joy.

❖ Ask all who are willing to offer some sort of support to whatever situation you have identified to repeat after you: **With God's help, we as Easter people will bring hope and share joy with those whom God commends to our care.**

*(5) Continue the Journey*

❖ Pray that all who have come today will allow the pain of Jesus' resurrection

and losses that they have suffered to turn to joy at the good news of life—resurrected and eternal.

❖ Read aloud this preparation for next week's lesson. You may also want to post it on newsprint for the students to copy.

■ **Title: Love within the Community**
■ **Background Scripture: 1 John 2:7-17**
■ **Lesson Scripture: 1 John 2:9-11, 15-17**
■ **Focus of the Lesson: Hate is rampant in our world, and we see evidence of that daily. Is there another way to live? John reiterates Jesus' teaching about love and exhorts believers to walk in the light of love.**

❖ Challenge the students to complete one or more of these activities for further spiritual growth, which you will write on newsprint for the students to copy.

(1) **Share with someone who is hurting the good news of Jesus' resurrection. Discuss, as appropriate to the situation, how we can live with hope because he lives.**

(2) **Do a comparative study of the resurrection accounts in Matthew 28, Mark 16, Luke 24, and John 20. What similarities and differences do you note among the people who are present and the events?**

(3) **Reflect prayerfully on Mary Magdalene's role in the resurrection story. What does the fact that God chose her to be a witness suggest about how God might use any of us, including you?**

❖ Sing or read aloud "In the Garden."

❖ Conclude today's session by leading the class in this benediction adapted from Matthew 22:37, 39: **Go forth to love the Lord your God with all your heart, with all your soul, and with all your mind, and to love your neighbor as yourself.**

## UNIT 2: TEACHINGS OF JESUS
# LOVE WITHIN THE COMMUNITY

---

### PREVIEWING THE LESSON

**Lesson Scripture:** 1 John 2:9-11, 15-17
**Background Scripture:** 1 John 2:7-17
**Key Verse:** 1 John 2:10

#### Focus of the Lesson:
Hate is rampant in our world, and we see evidence of that daily. Is there another way to live? John reiterates Jesus' teaching about love and exhorts believers to walk in the light of love.

#### Goals for the Learners:
(1) to explore John's contrast between hate and love, darkness and light, followed by Jesus' command to love.
(2) to determine if their actions are carried out within the spirit of love.
(3) to express some form of a loving action.

#### Pronunciation Guide:
*agape* (uh gah' pay)                    Laodicea (lay od i see' uh)
*eros* (air' ohs)                        *lectio divina* (lek' tsea oh  di veen' ah)

#### Supplies:
Bibles, newsprint and marker, paper and pencils, hymnals

---

### READING THE SCRIPTURE

NRSV
1 John 2:9-11, 15-17

⁹Whoever says, "I am in the light," while hating a brother or sister, is still in the darkness. **¹⁰Whoever loves a brother or sister lives in the light, and in such a person there is no cause for stumbling.** ¹¹But whoever hates another believer is in the darkness, walks in the darkness, and does not know the way to go, because the darkness has brought on blindness.

NIV
1 John 2:9-11, 15-17

⁹Anyone who claims to be in the light but hates his brother is still in the darkness. **¹⁰Whoever loves his brother lives in the light, and there is nothing in him to make him stumble.** ¹¹But whoever hates his brother is in the darkness and walks around in the darkness; he does not know where he is going, because the darkness has blinded him.

¹⁵Do not love the world or the things in the world. The love of the Father is not in those who love the world; ¹⁶for all that is in the world—the desire of the flesh, the desire of the eyes, the pride in riches—comes not from the Father but from the world. ¹⁷And the world and its desire are passing away, but those who do the will of God live forever.

¹⁵Do not love the world or anything in the world. If anyone loves the world, the love of the Father is not in him. ¹⁶For everything in the world—the cravings of sinful man, the lust of his eyes and the boasting of what he has and does—comes not from the Father but from the world. ¹⁷The world and its desires pass away, but the man who does the will of God lives forever.

## UNDERSTANDING THE SCRIPTURE

**1 John 2:7-11.** First John is one of three letters often classified with the Fourth Gospel and the Revelation to John as "the Johannine Literature." These writings are associated with the apostle John, who along with Peter and James formed the inner circle of Jesus' disciples. Because these books originated in the last decade of the first century, some scholars think they were written after the apostle's death by disciples or close associates of the apostle to preserve the apostle's teachings.

First John itself is addressed affectionately to believers, who variously are called "little children" and "beloved" and who relate to each other as brothers and sisters in a family. John encouraged them to maintain their faith and love in the face of opponents who have withdrawn from their fellowship over doctrinal and ethical issues. John exhorted the readers to walk in the light of truth and love.

John identified seven assertions made by the opponents that were contradicted by the way they lived (1:6, 8, 10; 2:4, 6, 9; 4:20). His basic principle is this: if you truly abide in Christ, you will live as Christ lived (2:6). For example, the opponents claimed, " 'I am in the light,' while hating a brother or sister" (2:9). This discrepancy between profession and practice revealed that the opponents were blindly stumbling in darkness.

The claim to "abide" in Christ (2:6) recalls Jesus' teachings recorded in John 15, where unfruitful branches are pruned away, where abiding in Christ is equivalent to abiding in

his love, and where Jesus commanded, "Love one another as I have loved you" (John 15:12). John affirmed that his teachings were grounded in this "old commandment that you have had from the beginning" (1 John 2:7; compare 2 John 5-6). This command to love was part of the tradition from Jesus that was passed on from the beginning in the proclamation of the disciples.

While the mention of "a new commandment" (1 John 2:8) could refer to John 13:34 (where Jesus' commandment was declared to be new), *"I am writing you* a new commandment" probably indicates that John was prescribing a new application drawn from Jesus' love commandment. The new commandment is valid because it was based on what "is true in him and in you," that is, in Christ and in his faithful followers.

First John 2:9 states the new commandment as an obvious implication when the love in the old commandment is displaced by hate. John focused on what hate indicates when found in the life of one who professes faith. The idea that hate could abide in a believer is so contradictory that John concluded such hate indicates darkness and blindness rather than light and truth. The triple implication of being in darkness, walking in darkness, and being blind offers little hope for those who have separated themselves from Christ (the light of the world), who live each day ("walk") in darkness, and who are blind and thus cannot see the light.

Love or hate for the brothers or sisters in the fellowship is the prime indicator of whether or not a person is abiding in Christ.

**1 John 2:12-14.** Spiritual blindness beset both those who have abandoned the fellowship of faith and love and those who demonstrated disobedience toward God and hate toward the family of faith. This blindness prompted John to launch into a litany that explained his intent in writing to the readers. The litany, whose poetic form may indicate it was adapted from another source, twice addresses each of three groups of readers—children, fathers, and young people.

In many ways, these groups represent the three generations represented within the church. "Little children" in verse 12 often was used figuratively in biblical times for the spiritual children of a teacher, apostle, or master. A different Greek word translated as "children" in verse 14 speaks more of younger children and expresses a stronger sense of fatherly intimacy. This instructional stage in life is when many come to "know the Father" (2:14) and come to faith in Christ as their Savior, experiencing the forgiveness of sins (2:12).

"Fathers" was a respectful title designating older members in a congregation who bore a spiritual parenthood for its members. These are affirmed for their long experience as people of faith.

"Young people" is derived from a root that speaks of young adults roughly between the ages of twenty-four and forty. This group generally was viewed as those who performed service within the congregation. They drew on their strength and knowledge of God's Word as they overcame the vexing temptations of life.

The application of John's message to young and old, experienced and inexperienced, new in the faith and mature in the faith is a comprehensive statement of what believers face daily. They are engaged in a struggle with "the evil one" (2:13-14) who entices them to sin. Jesus offers forgiveness, strength, and victory to those who will walk in the light of truth and love.

**1 John 2:15-17.** Earlier John had affirmed that the love of God manifests itself in those who obey God's Word. The expression "has reached perfection" (2:5) translates a Greek verb that means to complete, finish, accomplish, or fulfill. The verb's form denotes the progress of an action to a point of culmination and the continuation of its finished results into the present. In other words, when believers obey God's Word, all that God had sought to accomplish through divine love for humankind reaches its goal. That is why John could apply Jesus' commandment to love one another. When believers love one another, they fulfill God's love. To hate, on the other hand, interrupts the flow of God's love that is seeking to touch all people.

John admonished the community of faith not to love the world or the things of the world, pointing out that God's love in believers dispels such worldly love. John listed three aspects of this love of the world: desire of the flesh, desire of the eyes, and pride in riches. Each of these perceives something outside the self that a person wants to possess, control, or consume for selfish benefit. Giving in to such vices is selling out to transitory things that already are passing away. By contrast, those who do the will of God have latched on to that which lasts forever—eternal life with God.

## INTERPRETING THE SCRIPTURE

*The Testimony of Word and Action*

One of Jesus' central concerns about religious people was their hypocrisy. Our word

"hypocrite" is derived from a Greek word whose literal meaning is "judging another from below." We might view this as applying a lower standard to ourselves than the one we apply to others or as imposing a higher standard on others than we apply to ourselves. In Jesus' day, the word was widely used of theater actors who played a part, whose outward "show" bore little resemblance to their real selves.

Hypocrisy is not confined to religious leaders. It seems almost endemic to modern society. Politicians, business executives, media personalities, and sports figures join too many religious folks in displaying the symptoms. People go to extremes to hide their weaknesses, excesses, and deviancies from others. American media give so much attention to revelations of public downfalls that we often know more about a media star than we do about newsworthy happenings.

Jesus frequently spoke of judging others by the same standard that we want to be applied to us (Matthew 7:1-5). John followed the same principles as he laid out in 1 John—an anti-hypocrisy standard for personal integrity: People ought to live what they claim. Words and actions should correspond. Public image and private life should conform. Motives should be transparent in actions.

John was as concerned about the attitudes, actions, and behaviors of those within the church as those who had departed the fellowship. To avoid hypocrisy, those who claim to abide in Christ must live as Christ lived. They must walk in the light of truth. They must confess their sins and strive for righteous living. They must obey Christ's commands. They must love with the same self-sacrificing love exemplified in Jesus. Their lives must be a prayer to God, "Thy will be done."

The last paragraph has too many "musts." Personal integrity is rarely achieved by the imposition of rules and regulations. Instead, it flows from the heart. When our whole selves—heart, soul, mind, and strength—are fixed on Christ, our lives will be transformed by his daily guidance.

### The Correspondence of Love and Obedience

We tend to view love solely as an emotion driven by the beauty, value, and worthiness of the object that is loved. We have difficulty understanding how love can be commanded. Emotions and their associated feelings have subconscious origins that often mystify and surprise us. When we are smitten by love or attracted to something, we find the reasons for our feelings hard to describe.

Jesus commanded his followers to love, and his close disciple John also issued such a command to the readers of 1 John. So important is this love that John equated it with living in the light of truth.

You probably are acquainted with two of the Greek words translated "love" in the New Testament world. One word for "love" was *eros*, the root for the English word "erotic." While the English word focuses on sexual feelings and desires associated with love, the Greek word (which does not appear in the Bible) had a broader meaning. It spoke of a love and a desire to possess that was attracted by the object loved. *Eros* is a selfish or even greedy kind of love. It seeks to enhance the lover's life by gaining the benefits that come from the beloved.

Another Greek word for "love" was *agape*. This word often is used for God's love. Being expected to express that kind of love can be intimidating. Who can love as sacrificially as God loved humanity through Jesus? If love is the very nature of God and is the focus of God's activity toward humanity, whoever abides in God will abide in God's love and express *agape*.

First John advocates *agape*-love, which is "giving" love rather than "taking" love. It bestows value and worth on the beloved. This giving/bestowing is rather well expressed in the King James Version's translation of *agape* as "charity" (see 1 Corinthians 13). While the word "charity" can have overtones of condescension, the biblical concept is intertwined with grace and focuses on the unmerited aspect of the love.

The active orientation of love pushes us beyond warm, fuzzy feelings. It propels us into active expressions of concern for others. Sometimes we must attempt to love in this active way even when our "hearts" are not in it. Sometimes we must try to do good for people we don't even respect or like. Sometimes our love must be expressed unconditionally toward people whose attitudes, actions, and relationships are repugnant. Such love must be commanded because it would never occur spontaneously. Such gracious, giving, selfless love is the only truly transforming power in life.

We have received such love from Christ. As his followers, we must love as he loved, give as he gave, and sacrifice as he sacrificed so that the love of God can flow through us.

### The Power of Love and Hate

Hate is a dark and destructive emotion. We err, however, if we think of hate solely as an emotion. In the same way that love must be lived in order to be true, hate finds active expression in its efforts to denigrate, degrade, and destroy opponents.

Few of us own up to the emotion of hate or to our active expression of it. Because we keep our spiteful feelings bottled up inside, we think we don't hate. Because we hide our disdain and contempt for others behind smiles, we think we don't hate. Because our words of malice, scorn, and spite for others are spoken only among our friends, we assume we don't hate. We assume that ignoring, disregarding, and neglecting our enemies is benign.

Inactive love and inactive hate are substantially no different, especially when *agape*-love is our objective. Both are wasted feelings that fail to find expression in action and thus achieve no benefit and cause little harm other than to ourselves. Such static love or hate opens us to the judgment addressed to the church in Laodicea (Revelation 3:14-16).

Competing objectives lay claim on our love. We are drawn to love the world and the things in the world. The issues that create hate are based on worldly values—selfishness, greed, misunderstanding, disagreement, competition, pride, prejudice, power, control. When we seek worldly values, when we obey worldly principles, or when we desire worldly outcomes, we are loving the world and the things of the world—and hating God!

By contrast, Jesus calls us to a love so intense that it pushes all competing claims aside. The competition between two masters forces a choice of loving one and hating the other (Matthew 6:24). So sharp is this demand that even immediate family members and life itself must recede in the all-encompassing call to follow Jesus (Luke 14:26).

When believers love with *agape*-love, they fulfill God's love. This love cannot stop with fellow believers. Active love that seeks to accomplish good in the lives of others must even be directed toward our enemies (Matthew 5:43-48). To hate interrupts the flow of God's love that is seeking to touch all people. That interruption comes even when our hate is passive, because every negative feeling we have toward others impedes our expression of active love toward them. As the Christian community, we are called to live in the light and love of God.

## SHARING THE SCRIPTURE

### Preparing Our Hearts

Meditate on this week's devotional reading, found in John 13:31-35. Jesus' words to love one another as he has loved ring out loudly. Note in verse 35 that love—not any particular doctrine or creed that we may profess—identifies us as Christ's followers.

Try to view yourself through the eyes of a stranger this week. What would this person say about the way you love others, based on your driving, behavior at a sports event, interaction with your family at a restaurant, or other indicators? What changes do you need to make?

Pray that you and the adult learners will demonstrate love for one another in ways that become a model for others.

### Preparing Our Minds

Study the background from 1 John 2:7-17 and lesson scripture, verses 9-11, 15-17. Ponder this question: given all the hatred in our world, can you envision another way to live?

Write on newsprint:

❑ steps for *lectio divina* for "Explore John's Contrast between Hate and Love, Darkness and Light, Followed by Jesus' Command to Love."
❑ information for next week's lesson, found under "Continue the Journey."
❑ activities for further spiritual growth in "Continue the Journey."

Familiarize yourself with the information in Understanding the Scripture.

### LEADING THE CLASS

#### (1) Gather to Learn

❖ Welcome the class members and introduce any guests.

❖ Pray that all who have come today will experience the love of Christ and the adults who surround them.

❖ Read: **Hate crimes are perpetrated by an individual or group against people solely because they belong to a certain racial, religious, or ethnic group or because of their gender, sexual orientation, or age. Although the term "hate crime" did not enter our vocabulary until the 1980s, the Federal Bureau of Investigation (FBI) first began investigating hate crimes in the early 1920s when it opened its first case against the Ku Klux Klan, a white supremacist organization. Since 1992, the FBI has kept statistics on hate crimes. Numerous other countries also have laws on the books regarding hate crimes.**

❖ Ask: **What hate crimes are you aware of, either through the news media or as a result of knowing someone who has been targeted or having been targeted yourself? What do such crimes indicate about the degree to which hatred has festered in our society?**

❖ Read aloud today's focus statement: **Hate is rampant in our world, and we see evidence of that daily. Is there another way to live? John reiterates Jesus' teaching about love and exhorts believers to walk in the light of love.**

#### (2) Explore John's Contrast between Hate and Love, Darkness and Light, Followed by Jesus' Command to Love

❖ Help the students read today's passage using a modified version of an ancient technique, known as *lectio divina*, by following these steps. Distribute paper and pencils before you begin. Post newsprint showing the boldfaced words for the steps. Read the explanation of each word so that the adults will know what they need to do.

■ **Step 1—Prepare:** Prepare for the reading by asking the class to observe three to five minutes of silence as they come into the presence of God.
■ **Step 2—Listen:** Read aloud 1 John 2:9-11, 15-17 as the students follow along in their Bibles.
■ **Step 3—Discern:** Ask the students to review the reading silently, underlining words and phrases that "jump out" at them or writing these words on their papers.
■ **Step 4—Reflect:** Reflect on these selected words, perhaps repeating them silently to let them "sink in."

■ **Step 5—Pray:** Offer a prayer of thanksgiving, confession, lament, or some other form as a result of your reflections.

■ **Step 6—Obey:** Make a plan to obey whatever God is telling you to do as you continue to commune with God. You may wish to write this plan on your paper.

❖ Lead a discussion in which you ask the following questions:

(1) **What words in John's Epistle seemed most important to you? Why?**

(2) **What lessons is John trying to teach the church?**

(3) **How might these lessons apply to your own congregation?**

(4) **What comments puzzled you in today's reading?** (Use information from Understanding the Scripture to help answer questions.)

(5) **What changes do you feel God is leading you and your church to make, based on this reading?** (Think especially here about how the students and congregation could become more loving and more willing to reach out to others.)

*(3) Determine If the Learners' Actions Are Carried Out within the Spirit of Love*

❖ Read aloud "The Correspondence of Love and Obedience."

❖ Post a sheet of newsprint with the words "Walk in Light" in the left-hand column and "Walk in Darkness" in the right-hand column. Invite the students to give examples of actions that indicate someone is living by the light of God (that is, practicing *agape* love). Then encourage the students to give examples of actions that indicate that someone is stumbling in darkness (that is, acting with hatred toward another person or group.)

❖ Distribute paper and pencils as needed. Encourage the students to choose several positive actions (listed under "Walk in Light") they currently practice. Suggest they list other positive actions that they practice that may (or may not) be on the list the class created. Also encourage them to identify and list actions related to the darkness that they engage in. For each of these actions, suggest that the adults write a sentence or two about how they might move from darkness to light with God's help. Announce before the students begin that this work is confidential.

*(4) Express Some Form of a Loving Action*

❖ Remind the class that John was writing his epistle to a congregation, not to an individual.

❖ Ask the group to think of some ways that they could express God's love to visitors in the church, newcomers in the community, or to people in the neighborhood who have experienced hatred or ill-will, perhaps due to some form of prejudice.

❖ List ideas on newsprint.

❖ Invite each person to select at least one idea that he or she will try to implement in the coming week to make someone feel loved by God and your community of faith. Perhaps some students would be able to work together.

*(5) Continue the Journey*

❖ Pray that those who have come today will allow Christ's love to flow through them to all whom they encounter this week.

❖ Read aloud this preparation for next week's lesson. You may also want to post it on newsprint for the students to copy.

■ **Title: Connecting in Community**

■ **Background Scripture: Matthew 5:17-20; 22:34-40**

■ **Lesson Scripture: Matthew 22:34-40**

■ **Focus of the Lesson: People search for guidance in learning how to** express their love in positive ways. Is there an answer to their search? Jesus' answer is to "love the Lord your God with all your heart, and with all your soul, and with all your mind," and "love your neighbor as yourself."

❖ Challenge the students to complete one or more of these activities for further spiritual growth, which you will write on newsprint for the students to copy.

(1) Write a prayer in which you confess specific instances of failing to act in Christ's love. Ask for forgiveness and be assured that you have received it.

(2) Make a special effort this week to show love to a church member with whom you have had differences.

(3) Review 1 John 2:15-17. Make a list of the things of the world that you love. Ask God to help you overcome these desires and pride.

❖ Sing or read aloud "Where Charity and Love Prevail."

❖ Conclude today's session by leading the class in this benediction adapted from Matthew 22:37, 39: Go forth to love the Lord your God with all your heart, with all your soul, and with all your mind, and to love your neighbor as yourself.

## UNIT 2: TEACHINGS OF JESUS
# CONNECTING IN COMMUNITY

---

### PREVIEWING THE LESSON

**Lesson Scripture:** Matthew 22:34-40
**Background Scripture:** Matthew 5:17-20; 22:34-40
**Key Verse:** Matthew 22:37

### Focus of the Lesson:
People search for guidance in learning how to express their love in positive ways. Is there an answer to their search? Jesus' answer is to "love the Lord your God with all your heart, and with all your soul, and with all your mind," and "love your neighbor as yourself."

### Goals for the Learners:
(1) to explore the two greatest commandments.
(2) to examine their attitude of love toward God and others.
(3) to express love toward God and for others as we love ourselves.

### Pronunciation Guide:
*agape* (uh gah' pay)
*aheb* (aw habe')
Pharisee (fair' uh see)
Sadducee (sad' joo see)
Shema (shuh mah')

### Supplies:
Bibles, newsprint and marker, paper and pencils, hymnals

---

### READING THE SCRIPTURE

NRSV
Matthew 22:34-40

³⁴When the Pharisees heard that he had silenced the Sadducees, they gathered together, ³⁵and one of them, a lawyer, asked him a question to test him. ³⁶"Teacher, which commandment in the law is the greatest?"

NIV
Matthew 22:34-40

³⁴Hearing that Jesus had silenced the Sadducees, the Pharisees got together. ³⁵One of them, an expert in the law, tested him with this question: ³⁶"Teacher, which is the greatest commandment in the Law?"

³⁷He said to him, " 'You shall love the Lord your God with all your heart, and with all your soul, and with all your mind.' ³⁸This is the greatest and first commandment. ³⁹And a second is like it: 'You shall love your neighbor as yourself.' ⁴⁰On these two commandments hang all the law and the prophets."

³⁷Jesus replied: " 'Love the Lord your God with all your heart and with all your soul and with all your mind.' ³⁸This is the first and greatest commandment. ³⁹And the second is like it: 'Love your neighbor as yourself.' ⁴⁰All the Law and the Prophets hang on these two commandments."

## UNDERSTANDING THE SCRIPTURE

**Matthew 5:17-20.** The Sermon on the Mount (Matthew 5–7) is the most extensive record of Jesus' teaching and the most significant statement of what being a follower of Christ and a citizen of God's kingdom means. The sermon presents a significantly new way of relating to God and other people.

Jesus came to those who had long sought to fulfill their covenantal obligations by obeying God's law. Moses had been the nation's guide. He had gone to the mountaintop to meet God and to seal a covenantal relationship between God and Israel. The covenant obligated the people to obey God, and the Ten Commandments became the foundation for that obligation.

Throughout the remainder of Moses' life, God revealed life-encompassing expectations for the chosen people. The devout dedicated themselves to fulfilling all of God's expectations in every way. By the time of Jesus, the most devout and pious had cataloged all of the Old Testament laws and had spelled out in explicit detail how each should be carried out in daily life.

As often happens when the focus is placed on *what you do* rather than on *who you are*, the faith of Moses was gradually transformed into a burdensome legalism. The letter of the law took precedence over the intent of the law. The scrupulous observers of the law became haughty and judgmental toward those less scrupulous. Even the most pious sought loopholes that would keep them technically pure while leaving their selfish ambitions unbridled.

Jesus directly challenged this corrupted view of God's people. His opponents branded him as unfaithful to the covenant and intent on destroying the covenant law. Jesus countered with his own endorsement of the law.

Jesus affirmed the validity of the law while embracing its larger context. The law must be joined with "the prophets" (Matthew 5:17)—that part of the Old Testament that encompasses both historical and prophetic writing. The law was not static. It found vibrancy in the history of God's people as they struggled to apply divine principles in real-life situations. The law also found moral direction in the words of inspired prophets who disclosed God's intent and purpose for God's people.

Jesus also affirmed the relevance of the law. It was not just something out of the past. Rather, its "truth endureth to all generations" (Psalm 100:5, KJV), indeed, until "heaven and earth pass away" (Matthew 5:18).

Jesus affirmed the comprehensiveness of the law. Every "letter" or "stroke of a letter" even from "the least of these commandments" was important and deserved to be practiced and taught (5:18-19).

Jesus also pointed, however, to incompleteness in the law. The righteousness it produced in the devout scribes and Pharisees was not sufficient to gain entrance into the kingdom of heaven (5:20).

Scrupulous observance of the law by itself was not enough to bring one under the rule and reign of God. Something still was needed to "fulfill" the law (5:17).

Matthew 5:17 is a startlingly frank claim by Jesus. English translations often miss the pointed force of the Greek verb tense used. We could translate this verse, "Do not think that the explicit point of my coming was to destroy the law and the prophets. I came not to destroy but with the explicit purpose of fulfilling." The Greek word for "fulfill" means to bring something to completion or to finish something that has already begun. The rest of the Sermon on the Mount details the nature of that fulfilling.

**Matthew 22:34-38.** Jesus' views about the law and its role in righteousness were a constant point of contention with the scribes and Pharisees. The Sadducees also squabbled with him over particular theological views that they embraced. These opposition groups may be thought of as "parties" in the vein of modern political parties. These loose confederations bonded around particular views on religious and political issues and vied for the favor of the masses.

During the last visit to Jerusalem that culminated in his crucifixion, Jesus encountered increasing scrutiny from his opponents. They were intent on finding fault in his views and exposing him to the public as a fraud. The results of their questioning often produced the opposite effect. The crowds were astonished at Jesus' teachings and ability to confound his opponents.

Scholars devoted to the study of the Old Testament laws often discussed which of the commandments best summarized or captured the essence of the scriptural regulations. A religious scholar representing the Pharisees asked Jesus to address that matter. Matthew viewed the question as a "test," and he used a strong word found in Matthew 4:1-3 to describe the action ("tempted" 4:1) of the devil (called "the tempter" in 4:3).

The Greek word translated "greatest" in Matthew 22:36 is neither a comparative (greater) nor a superlative (greatest). Because the word can describe spaciousness, measurement, quantity, and intensity as well as rank, hints of comprehensiveness, breadth, value, and importance are present. Later Jesus added "first" to "greatest" in describing the commandment (22:38)

Jesus responded by quoting Deuteronomy 6:5, a part of the central Old Testament confession of faith called the Shema. Matthew, Mark (12:30), and Luke (10:27) record slight variations of the Shema. Matthew leaves out "might" and includes "mind." Mark and Luke include "mind" and "strength" but record them in a different order. This comprehensive command to love God with all of one's being is at the heart of faith. Significantly, the Synoptic Gospels all translate the Hebrew word for love (*aheb*) with the Greek word *agape*, which is the unselfish kind of giving love discussed in the previous lesson.

**Matthew 22:39-40.** Jesus did not stop with the first commandment, perhaps recognizing that people sometimes love God zealously and treat their neighbors cruelly. He offered a "second" commandment that is of the same nature or similar to the first—this time quoting Leviticus 19:18: "You shall love your neighbor as yourself."

On another occasion (Luke 10:25-37), Jesus clarified in the parable of the good Samaritan how extensive this command is, pushing it beyond the "your people" in Leviticus. Rather than focusing the command on the recipients of love ("Who is my neighbor?" 10:29), Jesus focused on the neighborliness of the one who shows love to anyone in need ("Which of these . . . was a neighbor?" 10:36).

By these priorities of loving God and loving neighbor, Jesus explained what is necessary to achieve the reign of God in our lives.

# INTERPRETING THE SCRIPTURE

### Kingdom Righteousness

When I defended my doctoral dissertation, the first question related to my interpretation of "righteousness" in Matthew 6:1. (The word translated "piety" in the NRSV is the Greek word for "righteousness.") One of my professors argued for a stronger Pauline understanding of the word. He thought I should have reflected that understanding more clearly in this passage from the Sermon on the Mount. Before I could reply, another professor on the committee challenged the first professor on his views. For the next forty minutes the two debated the issue while I watched silently. Theologically, righteousness can be a hot point of contention.

Righteousness also was a point of contention between Jesus and the devout Jewish leaders of his time. Jesus called his disciples to a righteousness that exceeded the righteousness of the scribes and Pharisees. Literally Matthew 5:20 states, "If your righteousness should not be present in greater abundance than that of the scribes and Pharisees, you certainly shall not enter the kingdom of heaven." Was Jesus merely calling for more acts of devotion? for more good deeds? for greater generosity? That certainly would be the case if piety is viewed exclusively as actions.

Righteousness, however, also has a relational dimension. In both the Old and New Testaments, righteousness is living so as to fulfill the expectations in relationships. With respect to God, the relationship is guided by covenant. With respect to other people, righteousness is guided by justice.

Jesus added another dimension to our understanding of righteousness when he focused on motives. Matthew 6:1-18 records a sharp criticism of the hypocritical ways righteousness was being practiced by many. Matthew 6:1 literally says that righteousness is something a person does, and the following verses address what have been called "the three pillars of Jewish piety"—almsgiving, prayer, and fasting. In each case, Jesus identified the temptation associated with any act of piety—the temptation to do it for show. Underlying motives are important.

Balancing deeds, justice, and motives is not an easy task. Doing the right thing for the right reason is the goal for which we should strive. In our time-sensitive society, we perhaps should add to the equation: righteousness is doing the right thing at the right time for the right reasons! When the command to love God and love neighbor was raised in Luke 10:25-28, the parable of the good Samaritan highlighted a person who acted spontaneously in such a righteous manner.

### Loving God and Neighbor

We dealt previously with love as something that can be commanded. We also dealt with the underlying meaning of *agape*-love. Matthew 22:34-40 raises the same matter, but this time the objects of the commanded *agape*-love are God and neighbor.

Perhaps the hardest characteristic of *agape*-love to apply to our love for God is the unmerited nature of *agape*. How could we ever imply that our love for God is not drawn by the merit of who God is, what God has done, and what God does for us each day?

The challenge in loving God is to surpass the kind of love that is given solely because of what we have received or might receive from God. Indeed, too much of our love for God is fickle. When times are good, we love God unreservedly. When times are hard, we question why God has forgotten or abandoned us. If our love for God is not constant through good times and bad times, we likely are loving with a "getting" rather than a "giving" kind of love.

We also would be naïve to pretend that other things do not compete with our affection for God. The Shema's command to love with all of the heart, soul, and might provides some natural measurements. What is the focus of our thoughts each day? What passions drive us? How do we spend our money, our time, and our energy? For what do we strive or sacrifice? These tangible focuses more truly reveal the nature and depth of our love for God than any profession of love we might make.

Our love of neighbor rarely reaches the level of *agape*-love either. Jesus pointed out in the Sermon on the Mount that loving those who love you is not especially meritorious (Matthew 5:46-48). The call to love your enemies and to pray for those who persecute you (5:44) is clearly a difficult challenge; but the greater challenge is to love every person without discrimination, paralleling God's treatment of the evil and the good, the righteous and the unrighteous (5:45). The reason equal application of love is difficult is that we highly value a love for others that returns some benefit to us. We naturally want to be loved back, to be appreciated, valued, and respected. If the good intentions of our love are not returned and our love falters or turns bitter, we know we have not yet achieved *agape*-love.

### Loving Self

In a time when self-esteem is viewed as an important aspect of mental health, we often find loving self treated as a third and equally important aspect of the greatest commandment. Some people almost treat love of self as a prerequisite for loving God and neighbor. If a person cannot love self, the thinking goes, the person has little to give in the way of love and is so needy for love that what love can be shown is inadequate and incomplete.

A more literal understanding of Matthew 22:39 might view self-centered love as natural and universally present. All of us are basically selfish to the core, looking out for our own good. The call to love others as we love ourselves is simply to transfer that same kind of protective self-interest onto our neighbors and to strive to love them with equal fervor.

Another possibility is to see loving your neighbor as yourself as an extension of the Golden Rule: "In everything do to others as you would have them do to you" (Matthew 7:12). This interpretation has special appeal since Jesus concluded the statement with "for this is the law and the prophets"—somewhat paralleling, "On these two commandments hang all the law and the prophets" (22:40). Loving others is putting into practice a radical kind of unselfish love that transforms relationships and invites a reciprocal setting aside of self by others.

First John also provides helpful commentary on the greatest commandment. John began with the affirmation that God is *agape*-love (1 John 4:16). The kind of love for which believers strive originates in God and in God's love for us. That kind of love transforms us, elevates us, and assures us of how truly valuable we are in God's sight.

God's love also becomes the model and the enabling power for our love—"We love because he first loved us" (4:19). So closely is our love tied to God's love that John concluded, "Those who say, 'I love God,' and hate their brothers or sisters, are liars; for those who do not love a brother or sister whom they have seen, cannot love God whom they have not seen. The commandment we have from him is this: those who love God must love their brothers and sisters also" (4:20-21).

Love for self originates in God's love for us. Such love evokes our full love and devotion to God. And the gracious love we experience compels us to love our neighbors and even our enemies with *agape*-love.

# SHARING THE SCRIPTURE

### Preparing Our Hearts

Meditate on this week's devotional reading, found in Romans 5:1-11. Here Paul writes about how believers are at peace with God, having been reconciled by means of Christ's atoning work on our behalf. All of this is the result of God's gracious love for us: "God proves his love for us in that while we still were sinners Christ died for us" (5:8). Memorize this verse. Think about it daily. What does it really mean in terms of how you live your life? How does knowing this verse affect your relationship with God?

Pray that you and the adult learners will be open to God's love in your life and willing to share that love with others.

### Preparing Our Minds

Study the background from Matthew 5:17-20 and 22:34-40. The lesson scripture is found in Matthew 22:34-40. Consider the kind of guidance you need in expressing your love for others in positive ways.

Write on newsprint:

❏ sentences to be completed for "Express Love toward God and for Others as We Love Ourselves."

❏ information for next week's lesson, found under "Continue the Journey."

❏ activities for further spiritual growth in "Continue the Journey."

### LEADING THE CLASS

### (1) Gather to Learn

❖ Welcome the class members and introduce any guests.

❖ Pray that all who have are present will experience the love of God and neighbor as the class fellowships and learns together.

❖ Ask this question and record answers on newsprint: **How can we express love to God and neighbor?** (Encourage the students to give concrete examples.)

❖ Add to the discussion by reading these words of Saint Augustine of Hippo (354–430) and asking how his ideas compare with those that the class has listed: **What does love look like? It has hands to help others. It has feet to hasten to the poor and needy. It has eyes to see misery and want. It has ears to hear the sighs and sorrows of men. That is what love looks like.**

❖ Read aloud today's focus statement: **People search for guidance in learning how to express their love in positive ways. Is there an answer to their search? Jesus' answer is to "love the Lord your God with all your heart, and with all your soul, and with all your mind," and "love your neighbor as yourself."**

### (2) Explore the Two Greatest Commandments

❖ Distribute paper and pencils.

❖ Choose a volunteer to read Matthew 22:34-40. Encourage the students to write the two laws that they hear.

❖ Ask two volunteers to read the sources from which Jesus quotes: Deuteronomy 6:5 and Leviticus 19:18. Again, ask the students to write the two laws that they hear.

❖ **Option:** Ask volunteers to read two other passages, Mark 12:30-31 and Luke 10:27, where these laws appear. Ask the students to write the laws they hear.

❖ Invite the students to note similarities and differences among the various quotations from the two commandments.

❖ Continue the discussion by reading or retelling Matthew 22:34-38 and 22:39-40 from Understanding the Scripture.

❖ Ask the class or small groups to discuss this question: **What challenges do you confront when asked to love God with**

**your whole being and to love your neighbor as yourself?**

*(3) Examine the Learners' Attitude of Love toward God and Others*

❖ Read aloud "Loving God and Neighbor" from Interpreting the Scripture.

❖ Read each of the following sentences and provide time for class members to respond. Likely, students will strongly agree or disagree, but probe their responses to see what attitudes lie at the root of each response. Encourage them to give examples to support their answers.

    **(1) Most of us prefer to love God when things are going well, but we raise a lot of questions with God if things are going poorly in our lives.**

    **(2) Other things do compete with our affection for God and most of the time God does not rank as number one in our lives.**

    **(3) Most of us treat people with the *agape*-love that Jesus practiced only when we think that love will be reciprocated.**

❖ Wrap up this portion of the session by encouraging the students to think silently about their own attitudes concerning love of God and love of neighbor.

❖ Ask volunteers to share any insights they have gleaned from this discussion and their quiet time.

*(4) Express Love toward God and for Others as We Love Ourselves*

❖ Read aloud "Loving Self" from Interpreting the Scripture.

❖ Invite the students to talk about their understanding of what it means to love themselves. (Be aware that some adults may have low self-esteem and think themselves unworthy of love. Do not engage in debate about this, but try to help the students recognize that because of God's love for each

of us we are able to have a healthy love for ourselves.)

❖ Distribute paper and pencils if you have not already done so. Read each of the following sentences aloud and ask the students to fill in the blank. You may wish to write these on newsprint. Tell the adults in advance that they will not be asked to share their answers with anyone.

    **(1) One action I could take to show that I love myself is . . .**

    **(2) . . . is a person who really needs to experience God's love. I could do . . . to help him or her experience God's love.**

    **(3) To demonstrate that God is really first in my life I will . . . during the coming week.**

❖ Challenge the adults to take action this week on each of the three ways of showing love that they have identified.

*(5) Continue the Journey*

❖ Pray that all who have come today will be aware of opportunities to love God, neighbor, and self in wholesome, positive ways.

❖ Read aloud this preparation for next week's lesson. You may also want to post it on newsprint for the students to copy.

    ■ **Title: Inclusion in Community**
    ■ **Background Scripture: Luke 14:7-24**
    ■ **Lesson Scripture: Luke 14:15-24**
    ■ **Focus of the Lesson: People send flimsy regrets to invitations without realizing that what they missed could have been a fantastic, life-changing event. Who is offering a life-changing event today? God is inviting everyone, anyone, to a banquet of food for the soul, and we had better not miss it!**

❖ Challenge the students to complete one or more of these activities for further spiritual growth, which you will write on newsprint for the students to copy.

(1) Write a prayer asking Jesus to teach you how to love as he loves.

(2) Recall ideas discussed in class and choose at least one way that you can put the love of God into action on behalf of someone else.

(3) Think about the command to "love your neighbor as yourself." Is it difficult to love yourself? If so, what new attitudes do you need to develop about yourself in order to fulfill this command?

❖ Sing or read aloud "Blest Be the Tie That Binds."

❖ Conclude today's session by leading the class in this benediction adapted from Matthew 22:37, 39: **Go forth to love the Lord your God with all your heart, with all your soul, and with all your mind, and to love your neighbor as yourself.**

UNIT 2: TEACHINGS OF JESUS
# INCLUSION IN COMMUNITY

---

## PREVIEWING THE LESSON

**Lesson Scripture:** Luke 14:15-24
**Background Scripture:** Luke 14:7-24
**Key Verse:** Luke 14:21

### Focus of the Lesson:
People send flimsy regrets to invitations without realizing that what they missed could have been a fantastic, life-changing event. Who is offering a life-changing event today? God is inviting everyone, anyone, to a banquet of food for the soul, and we had better not miss it!

### Goals for the Learners:
(1) to review the parable of the great banquet Jesus told at a dinner party.
(2) to identify God's life-changing events in their lives.
(3) to listen to God's invitation and to willingly accept the inclusiveness of God's community.

### Supplies:
Bibles, newsprint and marker, paper and pencils, hymnals

---

## READING THE SCRIPTURE

NRSV
Luke 14:15-24

¹⁵One of the dinner guests, on hearing this, said to him, "Blessed is anyone who will eat bread in the kingdom of God!" ¹⁶Then Jesus said to him, "Someone gave a great dinner and invited many. ¹⁷At the time for the dinner he sent his slave to say to those who had been invited, 'Come; for everything is ready now.' ¹⁸But they all alike began to make excuses. The first said to him, 'I have bought a piece of land, and I must go out and see it; please accept my

NIV
Luke 14:15-24

¹⁵When one of those at the table with him heard this, he said to Jesus, "Blessed is the man who will eat at the feast in the kingdom of God."

¹⁶Jesus replied: "A certain man was preparing a great banquet and invited many guests. ¹⁷At the time of the banquet he sent his servant to tell those who had been invited, 'Come, for everything is now ready.'

¹⁸"But they all alike began to make excuses. The first said, 'I have just bought a

regrets.' [19]Another said, 'I have bought five yoke of oxen, and I am going to try them out; please accept my regrets.' [20]Another said, 'I have just been married, and therefore I cannot come.' [21]So the slave returned and reported this to his master. Then the owner of the house became angry and said to his slave, **'Go out at once into the streets and lanes of the town and bring in the poor, the crippled, the blind, and the lame.'** [22]And the slave said, 'Sir, what you ordered has been done, and there is still room.' [23]Then the master said to the slave, 'Go out into the roads and lanes, and compel people to come in, so that my house may be filled. [24]For I tell you, none of those who were invited will taste my dinner.'"

field, and I must go and see it. Please excuse me.'

[19]"Another said, 'I have just bought five yoke of oxen, and I'm on my way to try them out. Please excuse me.'

[20]"Still another said, 'I just got married, so I can't come.'

[21]"The servant came back and reported this to his master. Then the owner of the house became angry and ordered his servant, **'Go out quickly into the streets and alleys of the town and bring in the poor, the crippled, the blind and the lame.'**

[22]"'Sir,' the servant said, 'what you ordered has been done, but there is still room.'

[23]"Then the master told his servant, 'Go out to the roads and country lanes and make them come in, so that my house will be full. [24]I tell you, not one of those men who were invited will get a taste of my banquet.'"

---

# UNDERSTANDING THE SCRIPTURE

**Luke 14:7-11.** Luke 14 provides insight into Jesus' social interactions. On occasion Jesus was criticized for socializing with tax collectors and sinners, even being called a glutton and a drunkard (Luke 5:30, 7:34, 15:2). Yet he also dined with upright Pharisees (7:36, 11:37, 14:1).

Luke 14 depicts Jesus using a favorite teaching method—the parable. This simple kind of story drawn from everyday life was popular with the crowds. It provided an oblique way of addressing significant but sometimes controversial issues. It drove home its point in vivid and memorable ways.

Luke 14 also gives evidence of the underlying uneasiness with which religious authorities received Jesus. From the first mention of the Pharisees in Luke 5:17-26 they are depicted as skeptical of Jesus' teachings, ministry, and scruples on religious matters (see 6:2, 7; 7:39; 11:38). "They

were watching him closely" (14:1), "lying in wait for him, to catch him in something he might say" (11:54).

Jesus also watched the Pharisees, observing how their behavior revealed much about their attitudes and motives. He previously had noted how the Pharisees loved "to have the seat of honor in the synagogues and to be greeted with respect in the marketplaces" (11:43). As he entered the home of the leader of the Pharisees, Jesus noticed this same vying for honor as guests chose seats at the dinner table (14:7). Jesus offered the guests practical advice through a parable about a wedding banquet.

Occasionally a parable may convey allegorical meanings, but generally the purpose of a parable is to convey one central truth. In this case, the truth is in verse 11: "All who exalt themselves will be humbled, and those who humble themselves will be exalted."

Note that the initial exalting or humbling

is the choice of the individuals themselves. The desire for privilege, power, and prestige is present in all people; but the esteem people have for themselves often influences how they conduct themselves in relationships. Because ego needs sometimes seem insatiable, humility must be deliberately chosen.

The ultimate exalting or humbling is stated in the future tense and passive voice ("will be") without reference to an agent. Such divine passives are frequently employed in Scripture with God as the implied agent. Jesus was pointing to a future reckoning where God will be the one exalting or humbling. A dinner host might have many criteria for seating people at the head table or elsewhere. For God, "humbling themselves" is a prominent criterion in both the human-divine and the human-human relationship.

**Luke 14:12-14.** Next Jesus turned his attention to the host. The host, as a leader of the Pharisees, would have been someone dedicated to the meticulous observance of the law. Because this was a sabbath meal (14:1), all preparations would have been made in advance. The Pharisees interpreted the commandment to keep the sabbath holy as forbidding all work on the sabbath.

Jesus focused attention on the host's guest list. A large part of social interaction is subtly self-serving. A host chooses guests from family, friends, and influential associates whose presence and good will benefit the host. Jesus, however, pointed the host toward a future reckoning—one beyond the social obligation created by hosting those who can repay your hospitality in kind. True blessedness comes from deeds of righteousness that cannot be repaid in kind but will be repaid in eternity. The righteous are those who have set aside self-interest and have invested in relieving the misery of the poor, the crippled, the lame, and the blind.

**Luke 14:15-20.** Upon hearing Jesus' reference to the blessedness that comes to the righteous at the resurrection, one dinner guest openly affirmed Jesus' theology of the future while subtly neglecting the criteria for righteousness that Jesus had stated.

The resurrection of the dead was a fundamental Pharisaic doctrine. At the end of time, God would reunite the body and spirit of the dead. The righteous would be raised to eternal life with God, but the unrighteous would face eternal punishment. Eating bread in the kingdom symbolized the messianic banquet in heaven for all of God's chosen ones. Of course, the Pharisees thought they would have prominent seats at the messianic table, having demonstrated their righteousness by their meticulous keeping of all the law. "Sinners" who failed to observe the law would be excluded from that banquet. This exclusive view of righteousness and salvation prompted Jesus to tell another banquet parable.

The occasion for a banquet could be a birthday, a wedding, or the celebration of a completed harvest, business deal, treaty, or building project. Note, however, that banquets are the province of the privileged. Servants might get leftovers from the banquet, and the poor might beg for scraps from the table. Neither would be invited to sit at the table.

In Jesus' day invitations were sent twice. Guests were initially invited so the host could plan a meal for the number who expected to be present. When the time came and preparations had been made, servants of the host were sent out to announce the banquet and call each guest to come. Generally, all who had accepted the invitation would attend, as it was considered poor manners to agree to attend and then renege.

In Jesus' parable the invited guests sent their "regrets." Each had an excuse, but none of them was a pressing or urgent matter. All of them were socially inexcusable snubs to the host. Their regrets signaled that they felt their social status was so secure they could reject the invitation and avoid any obligation to reciprocate for the host's invitation.

**Luke 14:21-24.** Matthew recorded a similar parable in which the servants announcing a wedding banquet are mistreated or even killed. In that case the host's anger was so great that he sent troops to destroy the invited guests before inviting others to come (Matthew 22:2-10).

Luke's host also was angered, but he sent out his servants to bring in the poor, the crippled, the blind, and the lame—the very groups mentioned in Luke 14:13. This was a reverse snub of sorts. Those attending the banquet gained a status above those who were not there. Matthew states this idea as, "those invited were not worthy" (Matthew 22:8).

Ultimate reversals (like Luke 14:11) were common features in Jesus' teachings. In this latter parable, those who were included excluded themselves. Those who were excluded were graciously included. Those whose status qualified them rejected the invitation. Those who had no merit or status were constrained to come in. By their responses they were granted a greater status than those who had been invited.

The Greek word for "compel" (14:23) can mean inner or outer compulsion, "urgently invite," or "strongly urge." The new guests were not necessarily forced against their wills, but in reality few of them would have crossed the threshold without strong urging.

---

## INTERPRETING THE SCRIPTURE

### The Twists and Turns of the Unexpected

One characteristic of Jesus' life and ministry is the degree to which the unexpected was at play. When the Jews looked for their long-expected Messiah, they did not look for one who would be born in a stable or die on a Roman cross.

While New Testament writers frequently emphasized how Jesus' coming fulfilled Old Testament prophecies, the actual fulfillment departed significantly from popular expectations. The divine plan took so many twists and turns that it seems almost no one fully understood it until after the resurrection. Indeed, the Holy Spirit continues to lead the church in discovering and rediscovering truths that contradict the "politically correct" views of our day.

Luke 14 shows that Jesus' teachings also followed a twisting and turning course involving the unexpected. Conventional wisdom says to arrive early and get the best seat. Grab the spotlight and gain notice. Get close to the rich, powerful, and influential if you want to win. Scratch the back of others, and they will scratch your back. Project the image of success and you will become successful.

By contrast, Jesus says that honor comes through humility, not from self-exaltation. Honor is bestowed, not grasped. Those who strive for positions of honor and power expose themselves to the danger of being disgraced. How much better to choose the lowest place and have the host invite you to a place of honor in front of all the guests. Prominence and status have little to do with the things that matter most from the view of eternity.

### Coming through the Back Door

One way of exalting yourself and advancing your own interests is to host a party, inviting important and prominent guests. The leader of the Pharisees likely had not gotten into his position as leader without ingratiating himself to a lot of the prominent religious, civic, and social elite in his community. Even by inviting Jesus he may have been trying to portray himself as a broad-minded, inclusive leader who was up-to-date on the latest fads and fashions. Anyone who could attract such a wide following as Jesus (12:1) must be someone worth knowing whose favor should be curried.

Much hosting and entertaining of others is a matter of creating subtle obligations. We don't come right out and say, "Now you owe me"; but implicit in polite society is the expectation that hospitality will be reciprocated. People who are always invited to parties but never throw one are likely to find themselves experiencing a gradually diminishing social life. Or people who never pick up the check when a group eats out regularly may find that they are starving their relationship with others in the group.

That kind of reciprocity is normal and rather innocent. But all of us have known or at least suspected some people of using social contacts to pave their way to the top. Quietly going through the back door, they think no one will notice their disguised self-interest.

I noticed recently a situation where a CEO (chief executive officer) was obviously in trouble and a member of the executive staff suddenly started having open houses, pushing community projects, and inviting groups into his home. It seemed pretty obvious that he was trying to line up support for his ascension to the top job. In another case, a friend learned that his boss was a motorcycle fan. He went out and bought an expensive cycle himself and then invited his boss to go for a ride. How disappointed he was when he found out that his boss was a Harley fanatic and he had bought a Honda. His boss wouldn't be seen on the same street with him!

With keen insight, Jesus went straight to the point of his host's motive in entertaining guests. He was building up obligations that would pay him back in the future with goodwill and continued support for his leadership. The problem with this approach is that earthly merit based on social, political, or religious obligations is not the most important thing from the view of eternity.

In contrast to courting the regard and approval of family, friends, and the favored, the leader should have been bestowing favor on the poor and needy around him—the very ones whom Scripture has shown to be close to the compassionate heart of God.

*Who's at the Table?*

Many people in our world suffer greatly because of discrimination and exclusion. False standards based on race, sex, class, education, appearance, and a host of other factors tend to divide the privileged from the deprived. Let there be no doubt that the Bible consistently reveals that God is on the side of the deprived.

This lesson's text, however, creates a problem of interpretation in this regard. Recall that a parable generally has only one main point. What is the main point of the parable in Luke 14:16-24? Is the parable being addressed to those who have been invited to the banquet or to those who were not? Obviously Jesus was not talking *to* the poor, crippled, lame, and blind. If that is true, the main point is not one of inclusiveness no matter how valid that concern might be.

Let me contend that this conclusion should make no difference to those studying this lesson, for all of us are people who already have been invited to the banquet— and that's the point! If you are one who attends church, participates in a Bible study class, and are studying this lesson, you've been invited. I don't care what denomination, age, race, sex, educational achievement, income level, disability, height, weight, or shoe size, you are part of the privileged!

That doesn't mean you are not disadvantaged in one way or another. It doesn't mean that you are not discriminated against in one way or another. It does mean a response is expected to the invitation: "Come; for everything is ready now" (14:17). Read that invitation six times, emphasizing a different word each time. Do you sense the immediacy of that invitation? What are you going to do with it?

Are you going to make excuses? *I'm too busy. I'm overworked. I've got more important things to do. I'm unhappy about what my church is doing. I don't like my pastor or my* *Sunday school superintendent.* Or make up your own excuse. The point is, if you don't pick yourself up and get to the banquet right now, when you do perhaps get there in the future you may find your seat taken by someone who was deprived, who had to be compelled to come, who could not cross the threshold without being pushed—but who is eating your supper!

That's what is important from the view of eternity!

---

# SHARING THE SCRIPTURE

## *Preparing Our Hearts*

Meditate on this week's devotional reading, found in Psalm 65:1-8. Attributed to David, this psalm gives thanks to God for a bountiful harvest. Even more, this is the God who forgives sin and invites people to come into the presence of the saving God in the holy temple. Make a list of all the reasons you have to be thankful to God. Challenge yourself to identify at least thirty reasons.

Pray that you and the adult learners will give thanks to God for the bounty they are experiencing in their own lives.

## *Preparing Our Minds*

Study the background from Luke 14:7-24 and lesson scripture, verses 15-24. Think about who is offering life-changing events today.

Write on newsprint:
❏ information for next week's lesson, found under "Continue the Journey."
❏ activities for further spiritual growth in "Continue the Journey."

Decide how you will present the background information suggested under "Review the Parable of the Great Banquet Jesus Told at a Dinner Party."

## LEADING THE CLASS

### *(1) Gather to Learn*

❖ Welcome the class members and introduce any guests.

❖ Pray that all who have come today will be open to everyone who claims the name of Christ.

❖ List on newsprint as many life-changing events as the group can identify. Possibilities include: *change in marital status (marriage, divorce, death of a spouse); birth or adoption of a child; child leaving home; move to another home, retirement home, assisted living, or nursing home; loss of job due to firing, layoff, or retirement; deployment of self or loved one for military service; imprisonment; serious illness and recovery.*

❖ Ask: **What are some of the positive and negative responses to life-changing events?**

❖ Read aloud today's focus statement: **People send flimsy regrets to invitations without realizing that what they missed could have been a fantastic, life-changing event. Who is offering a life-changing event today? God is inviting everyone, anyone, to a banquet of food for the soul, and we had better not miss it!**

*(2) Review the Parable of the Great Banquet Jesus Told at a Dinner Party*

❖ Use Luke 14:7-11 and 12-14 in Understanding the Scripture to set the context for Jesus' parable of the great banquet. You may wish to read or retell this information or create a brief lecture.

❖ Choose a volunteer to read Luke 14:15-24.

❖ Discuss these questions:

**(1) How would you have felt had you been the host and so many people who had accepted your invitation then failed to attend the banquet?** (Use the final two paragraphs in Understanding the Scripture for Luke 14:15-20 to clarify how invitations were issued and acted upon. Also note that "roads and lanes" at the edge of town would be where those who were disadvantaged lived.)

**(2) How would you have felt if you had been invited to a banquet unexpectedly after the originally invited guests had snubbed the host?**

**(3) How do you envision this banquet as being a life-changing event?**

**(4) What does this parable say to the church today? Are we accepting God's invitation or snubbing our host? What specific examples can you give to support your answer?**

*(3) Identify God's Life-changing Events in the Learners' Lives*

❖ Review the list of life-changing activities created during the Gather to Learn activity.

❖ Distribute paper and pencils. Invite the class members to list those events that they have experienced and write a sentence or two about why each event truly changed their lives.

❖ Bring the students together and encourage volunteers to share at least one event and the reason this event was life-changing. Probe to discover how the adults experienced God in these events.

❖ Wrap up this portion of the lesson by asking the students if they can draw any conclusions about such events. (Note that sometimes there are positive results, such as people growing stronger or increasing their faith. In other situations, people feel powerless and may lose their faith in God.)

*(4) Listen to God's Invitation and Willingly Accept the Inclusiveness of God's Community*

❖ Read "Who's at the Table" from Interpreting the Scripture.

❖ Provide time for the students to try reading silently, "Come; for everything is ready now" (14:17), six times, emphasizing a different word each time. Bring the class members back together and invite them to comment on insights they gained by accenting different words.

❖ Point out that this invitation requires an immediate response: Come, now! Ask the students to comment on how they respond to this invitation. Are they making excuses or are they hurrying to the banquet table? Point out that apparently the people in the parable thought their excuses were valid. Discuss the "valid" excuses contemporary Christians claim for failing to respond to Christ's invitation.

❖ Note that all kinds of people came to the banquet. Ask the participants:

**(1) Is our congregation one where everyone can come and feel at home? Why or why not?**

**(2) If not, what barriers need to be torn down in order to be truly inclusive?** (Think especially about barriers related to language, inaccessibility, age, economic status, difficulties in understanding the order of worship and terminology used, and other roadblocks that may cause people to turn away.)

❖ Conclude this portion of the lesson by challenging the class to work together to tear down these barriers so that all people may feel at home within this congregation.

### (5) Continue the Journey

❖ Pray that everyone who has come today felt welcomed and will go out to bring others in next week.

❖ Read aloud this preparation for next week's lesson. You may also want to post it on newsprint for the students to copy.

■ Title: A Faithful Community
■ Background Scripture: Colossians 1
■ Lesson Scripture: Colossians 1:1-14
■ Focus of the Lesson: There are people in communities of faith who lack the power to lead worthy lives. Where and how can we connect with God's strength and glorious power? Paul tells the Colossians that their power as a congregation of hope and faith has come to them by their acceptance of the word of truth, the gospel.

❖ Challenge the students to complete one or more of these activities for further spiritual growth, which you will write on newsprint for the students to copy.

(1) Organize, with the help of classmates and other church members, a dinner or party at the church or other venue for those who are homeless, hungry, or suffering in some other way. This event should be planned without expectation of reciprocation or even that people would listen to good news but should allow God's love to be felt by those who participate.

(2) Make a list of dinner parties and other social events that you host and attend. Who is on the guest list? Would these be the same people that Jesus would invite? Who do you need to add or delete?

(3) Invite someone who makes no claim to accept Christ to attend worship, Sunday school, or a church event, such as a Habitat for Humanity build, so as to experience the community of faith.

❖ Sing or read aloud "Come, Sinners, to the Gospel Feast," a hymn by Charles Wesley based on today's Scripture reading from Luke 14:16-24.

❖ Conclude today's session by leading the class in this benediction adapted from Matthew 22:37, 39: Go forth to love the Lord your God with all your heart, with all your soul, and with all your mind, and to love your neighbor as yourself.

## UNIT 3: TEACHINGS OF THE CHURCH
# A FAITHFUL COMMUNITY

---

### PREVIEWING THE LESSON

**Lesson Scripture:** Colossians 1:1-14
**Background Scripture:** Colossians 1
**Key Verse:** Colossians 1:9

### Focus of the Lesson:
Many people in communities of faith lack the power to lead worthy lives. Where and how can we connect with God's strength and glorious power? Paul tells the Colossians that their power as a congregation of hope and faith has come to them by their acceptance of the word of truth, the gospel.

### Goals for the Learners:
(1) to introduce Paul as a letter-writing teacher for the church at Colossae.
(2) to recognize that God is the source of their strength and power.
(3) to lead lives of prayer, thanksgiving, and good works in Christ's faithful community.

### Pronunciation Guide:
Colossae or Colosse (kuh las' ee)       Herodotus (heh rod' uh tuhs)
Epaphras (ep af ras')                   Laodicea (lay od i see' uh)
*epignosis* (eh pee' noh sis)           Phrygia (frih' gee uh)
*gnosis* (noh' sis)                     Xenophon (zen' uh fuhn)
Gnostic (nah' stik)

### Supplies:
Bibles, newsprint and marker, paper and pencils, hymnals, map that includes Colossae

---

### READING THE SCRIPTURE

NRSV
Colossians 1:1-14
¹Paul, an apostle of Christ Jesus by the will of God, and Timothy our brother,
²To the saints and faithful brothers and sisters in Christ in Colossae:
Grace to you and peace from God our Father.

NIV
Colossians 1:1-14
¹Paul, an apostle of Christ Jesus by the will of God, and Timothy our brother,
²To the holy and faithful brothers in Christ at Colosse:
Grace and peace to you from God our Father.

³In our prayers for you we always thank God, the Father of our Lord Jesus Christ, ⁴for we have heard of your faith in Christ Jesus and of the love that you have for all the saints, ⁵because of the hope laid up for you in heaven. You have heard of this hope before in the word of the truth, the gospel ⁶that has come to you. Just as it is bearing fruit and growing in the whole world, so it has been bearing fruit among yourselves from the day you heard it and truly comprehended the grace of God. ⁷This you learned from Epaphras, our beloved fellow servant. He is a faithful minister of Christ on your behalf, ⁸and he has made known to us your love in the Spirit.

⁹For this reason, since the day we heard it, **we have not ceased praying for you and asking that you may be filled with the knowledge of God's will in all spiritual wisdom and understanding,** ¹⁰so that you may lead lives worthy of the Lord, fully pleasing to him, as you bear fruit in every good work and as you grow in the knowledge of God. ¹¹May you be made strong with all the strength that comes from his glorious power, and may you be prepared to endure everything with patience, while joyfully ¹²giving thanks to the Father, who has enabled you to share in the inheritance of the saints in the light. ¹³He has rescued us from the power of darkness and transferred us into the kingdom of his beloved Son, ¹⁴in whom we have redemption, the forgiveness of sins.

³We always thank God, the Father of our Lord Jesus Christ, when we pray for you, ⁴because we have heard of your faith in Christ Jesus and of the love you have for all the saints—⁵the faith and love that spring from the hope that is stored up for you in heaven and that you have already heard about in the word of truth, the gospel ⁶that has come to you. All over the world this gospel is bearing fruit and growing, just as it has been doing among you since the day you heard it and understood God's grace in all its truth. ⁷You learned it from Epaphras, our dear fellow servant, who is a faithful minister of Christ on our behalf, ⁸and who also told us of your love in the Spirit.

⁹For this reason, since the day we heard about you, **we have not stopped praying for you and asking God to fill you with the knowledge of his will through all spiritual wisdom and understanding.** ¹⁰And we pray this in order that you may live a life worthy of the Lord and may please him in every way: bearing fruit in every good work, growing in the knowledge of God, ¹¹being strengthened with all power according to his glorious might so that you may have great endurance and patience, and joyfully ¹²giving thanks to the Father, who has qualified you to share in the inheritance of the saints in the kingdom of light. ¹³For he has rescued us from the dominion of darkness and brought us into the kingdom of the Son he loves, ¹⁴in whom we have redemption, the forgiveness of sins.

## UNDERSTANDING THE SCRIPTURE

**Colossians 1:1-8.** Colossae was a large and important city in the ancient world, gaining mention by early Greek historians like Herodotus and Xenophon. It was located in a region called Phrygia (located in modern-day Turkey) about one hundred miles east of the coastal city of Ephesus on the main trade route to the Euphrates River.

The city was relocated following an earthquake in A.D. 60, but even before then it had begun to lose its former prominence when trade was rerouted through neighboring Laodicea. The region was noted for its textiles.

Paul had never visited Colossae (Colossians 1:4; 2:1), but he had been informed about the church by Epaphras, a Colossian (4:12) who first brought the gospel to his fellow Gentile citizens there (1:5-7, 27). Epaphras had become a fellow prisoner with Paul (Philemon 23), perhaps in Ephesus. He appears to have informed Paul about a theological problem that was troubling the church, though Paul addressed the matter in such an oblique fashion that we can only sketch broad outlines of the issue.

Paul sought to build a positive relationship with his readers by affirming them for their faith (1:4), love (1:4), hope (1:5), and fruitfulness (1:6). He also affirmed their brother, Epaphras, as "a faithful minister of Christ" on their behalf (1:7).

Embedded in the affirmations are some veiled concerns, however. The mention of "faithful brothers and sisters" (1:2) implies that some were not so faithful. Having heard of "this hope before" implies a need to rehear "the word of truth" (1:5). "Bearing fruit among yourselves from the day you . . . truly comprehended the grace of God" (1:6) implies a time when the grace of God was not fully comprehended.

**Colossians 1:9-14.** Paul had assured the Colossians that he prayed for them with thanksgiving for their faith and love (1:3-4), but his ceaseless prayer for them (1:9) raised a hint of special concern. He wanted them to "be filled with the knowledge of God's will in all spiritual wisdom and understanding" (1:9), apparently concerned that they were facing issues that demanded greater understanding.

Some interpreters think this concern was for an early form of Gnosticism that was threatening the Colossian church. Though fully-developed Gnosticism did not emerge until late in the second century, Gnostic tendencies were present earlier. The Gnostics claimed a superior knowledge (their name is drawn from the Greek word for knowledge, *gnosis*), but Paul used a word in 1:9 that could be translated as "full knowledge" (Greek *epignosis*). All spiritual wisdom and understanding came from this full knowledge of God's will.

Gnosticism separated reality into opposing components—flesh and spirit or light and darkness being examples. The spirit took such a prominent role that many Gnostics thought the flesh was of little consequence and could be indulged without significant consequence. Paul's call for lives that are "worthy of the Lord, fully pleasing to him" and bearing "fruit in every good work" (1:10) strongly opposed that Gnostic tendency.

Paul prayed that the Colossians would be "made strong," would "be prepared to endure everything with patience" (1:11), and would give thanks joyfully to God (1:12). Their strength would come from the Lord's "glorious power," probably a reference to Christ's resurrection. Their patience and joy were grounded in the inheritance for which God had "enabled" (1:12) or "qualified" (NIV) them as saints who were living in the light.

The resurrection of the physical body was an abhorrent idea for Gnostics, who thought that only the spirit mattered. The Gnostics also claimed that light was something they solely possessed through their special knowledge. For Paul, light was part of God's kingdom. When God rescued believers from the power of darkness, redeemed them, and forgave their sins, God transferred them into Christ's kingdom. Redemption came through Christ and the forgiveness of sins, not from the knowledge of some mystical secrets, as Gnostics contended.

**Colossians 1:15-23.** The mention of God's beloved Son (1:13) prompted Paul to make a strong theological statement about Christ, whose nature apparently was at the center of the Colossian controversy. Paul combined and held together both the physical and the spiritual aspects of Christ: image and invisible, heaven and earth, visible and invisible (1:15-16). He affirmed that all things physical and spiritual were created and are sustained by Christ, who was before creation and who holds creation together

(1:16-17). He underscored Christ's human and divine nature: his physical death on the cross and resurrection balanced with "the fullness of God" dwelling in him (1:18-20). Christ played a unique role in reconciling all things and making peace through his death on the cross (1:20). All of these affirmations were designed to thwart the Gnostic insistence on separating the physical from the spiritual, the earthly Jesus from the heavenly Christ.

Paul continued his emphasis by claiming that reconciliation with God came about through the death of Christ's "fleshly body" (1:22). That death transformed those who were evil in thought and deed and hostile in their attitudes into a holy, blameless, and irreproachable people sustained by the hope promised in the gospel. The Colossians only had to continue steadfastly in the faith in which they had been securely established in Epaphras' bringing the gospel to them. Paul was committed to seeing that gospel proclaimed to every creature under heaven.

**Colossians 1:24-29.** Paul viewed his imprisonment as part of his commission from God and as suffering for the sake of the church. He appears to have assumed that some suffering was necessary before the word of God became fully known, and his suffering was picking up where Jesus' left off so that the necessary suffering would be completed.

Paul used Gnostic terminology in writing about "the mystery that has been hidden throughout the ages and generations" (1:26). The Gnostics thought that they alone had received this mystery, but Paul contended it had been revealed to God's saints—including the Gentiles. The mystery was that the same Christ who lived, died, and was raised to new life now indwells believers and provides them hope for the glory that is to be revealed at the end of time.

Paul proclaimed the good news of the Christ who came to reconcile to God those who are estranged. That proclamation included warning and teaching, and its goal was fully mature followers of Christ. All of Paul's energy was poured into the task of spreading this gospel to everyone.

---

## INTERPRETING THE SCRIPTURE

### A Community Searching for Truth

We often fail to take seriously the promise that Jesus made to his disciples that the Holy Spirit would "guide [them] into all the truth" (John 16:13). Some in the Christian community think they already have all of the truth. Their neglect of the Holy Spirit's role often leads them into a dogmatic faith that is closed to new insights and oppressively narrow in its understandings.

At the other extreme we find a secular society that often claims to have a monopoly on truth. Truth for them is supposedly objective and factual. It is based on scientific methods, logical deduction, and human insight. Their understanding has no place for transcendent realities, spiritual truths, or revealed wisdom. Recent books representing this view have adopted a decidedly anti-religious tenor. Some of their criticisms are justified. When our knowledge produces close-mindedness, when our faith results in exclusivity, and when our morality results in Pharisaic attitudes, we have veered far from the teachings of Jesus.

A faithful community is founded on truth. In Colossians Paul addressed a community searching for the truth. They had heard the gospel from Epaphras, but they were confused by opposing assertions of truth from those who claimed superior wisdom and knowledge. Paul sought to equip them for dealing constructively with this threat.

Paul did not ignore the opposing views that were challenging the Colossians. Indeed, Paul employed the vocabulary of the opponents. He filled his letter with their words—truth, knowledge, wisdom, understanding, and light—but he reoriented their meanings. For Paul, truth was the *truth of the gospel*. Knowledge was the *knowledge of God's will*. Wisdom and understanding were *spiritual* wisdom and understanding. Light came by being transferred into the kingdom of Christ.

Colossians 1:15-20 welds the spiritual emphases of the opponents (the invisible, heavenly thrones, dominions, rulers, and powers) with Christ, who was the firstborn of all creation, who created all things, and who embodied the fullness of God. But as in Philippians 2:5-11, Paul also emphasized that this exalted Christ was the incarnate Christ who humbled himself, who died on the cross, and who was the firstborn of the dead. Paul contended that God revealed in Christ Jesus is the ultimate source of truth.

As a community searching for truth today, we can learn from Paul. We must learn how to dialogue with secular views. We must draw from the best educational, scientific, psychological, and philosophical insights. And we must weld all of this to the revelation of God in Jesus Christ. Our search must be for the full knowledge and spiritual wisdom found in Christ.

*A Community Living Its Faith*

Paul sought to guide the Colossians to the full truth (*epignosis*) while steering them clear of the attitudes and actions that alienate people who need the gospel. To accomplish this he advocated basic Christian virtues like faith, love, hope, truth, patience, joy, and thankfulness. Paul knew that living the faith begins within. Conduct that is coerced or controlled by external forces will lack sincerity, promote hypocrisy, and wind up in a shallow, empty religion. Christian conduct flows from the heart.

Piety and devotion to God are important, but Christian virtues alone must never be our final goal. Paul encouraged the Colossians to put these virtues into practice. Christian virtues will find expression in active faith, love for all people, positive attitudes, honesty in relationships, and patient persistence in the face of difficulties. A virtuous life will be happy and joyful, founded on deep gratitude, with abundant grace shown to others.

The gospel bears fruit in bringing people to God, but it also produces fruitful disciples. Full knowledge, spiritual wisdom, and spiritual understanding will bear the fruit of good works. The danger is that good works will be performed to please others. Paul proposed another audience. The goal is a life pleasing to God, a life worthy of or befitting the Lord who redeemed us and forgave our sins.

As a community seeking to live our faith today, we can learn from Paul. We too must base our lives on Christian virtues. We must live out those virtues in our families, our churches, our work, and our relationships.

With our search for steadfast faith and maturity in Christ, we also need a dose of reality. Paul gave these instructions because the Colossians were not living up to these expectations. Neither do we. We are not perfect people. We are not always happy, joyful, loving, optimistic, and grateful. Our lives are not always worthy of the Lord and fully pleasing to him.

Paul is not calling us to fake it. He is calling us to steadfast faith and maturity in Christ. That kind of faith and maturity only is possible in a faithful community that loves and accepts us, warts and all. Such a community will regularly remind us of what God has done for us in Christ. It will encourage us when life is hard. It will lift us when we slip. It will enlist our gifts in worthwhile service. It will celebrate our victories. It will strengthen our resolve by being together, studying together, worshiping together, serving together, ministering together, and living out our days together.

Such a community can be faithful only to the degree that each of us is faithful. We must give as well as receive. We must serve as well as be served. We must love and be gracious and forgiving so that we can expect to be treated that way.

### A Community Sharing Hope

Hope is desperately needed in our world—perhaps more than ever. We are besieged by natural disasters and problems of our own making—hurricanes, droughts, floods, earthquakes, abject poverty, armed conflicts, devastating diseases, climate change, environmental disasters, hazardous products, governmental corruption, class and ethnic struggles, and economic shocks. Depression, mental illness, suicide, and desperation are commonplace and cry out for some glimmer of hope.

Often religion has been criticized for shifting attention away from real-world problems toward a pie-in-the-sky-by-and-by hope. Paul's hope certainly was tied closely to a future consummation; but he also recognized that hope is an element in helping believers remain "securely established and steadfast in the faith" (Colossians 1:23).

In light of this criticism, maybe we need to flip Paul's statement, "If for this life only we have hoped in Christ, we are of all people most to be pitied" (1 Corinthians 15:19). If we have hope only for some future life after death, what comfort can we find or give in light of the enormous despair around us?

Paul viewed hope as coming to people "in the word of truth, the gospel" (Colossians 1:5). "The hope promised by the gospel" (1:23) offers power to reconcile to God, transform lives, redeem the lost, comfort the weary, lift the burden of sin, and endure suffering patiently. Our gospel must underscore those dimensions of hope.

Perhaps the most significant aspect of Paul's understanding of present hope is the reality of "Christ in you, the hope of glory" (1:27). In this context Paul tied hope to a glorious mystery hidden through the ages. Paul claimed his role in making this mystery fully known. Ephesians 2:11-22 is an explication of the full significance of what "Christ in you" meant for Gentiles. In Christ God was creating one new humanity, bringing all people—Jew and Gentile—into one body by breaking down the wall dividing them. Through Christ all now have access in one Spirit to God. The possibility of Christ in you generates a dynamic hope for the present and the future.

---

## SHARING THE SCRIPTURE

### Preparing Our Hearts

Meditate on this week's devotional reading, found in Jeremiah 29:10-14. These may be familiar words to you. How comforting to know that God has plans for us that are for our "welfare" and will lead to "a future with hope" (29:11). Where in your life do you need to hear these words of assurance and hope? Are you hurting due to a broken relationship, financial worries, uncertainties about employment, illness, or some other crisis that may be discouraging you? Apply Jeremiah's words as a balm to your soul.

Pray that you and the adult learners will experience hope even in the face of crisis.

*Preparing Our Minds*

Study the background from Colossians 1 and lesson scripture, verses 1-14. Ponder where and how we can connect with God's strength and glorious power.

Write on newsprint:

❑ information for next week's lesson, found under "Continue the Journey."

❑ activities for further spiritual growth in "Continue the Journey."

Locate a map showing Colossae.

Look up the stories of some fallen leaders of the Christian faith, including those listed under "Gather to Learn." Be prepared to give a brief account of how or why each person has strayed from God's path and the consequences he or she faced.

## LEADING THE CLASS

*(1) Gather to Learn*

❖ Welcome the class members and introduce any guests.

❖ Pray that all who have gathered today will open their hearts and minds in the search for truth.

❖ Lead the group in listing on newsprint well-known Christian leaders who have fallen, often as a result of sexual impropriety or questionable financial practices. As examples, Ted Haggard, Jim Bakker, Jimmy Swaggart, Richard Roberts, and Paul Crouch have all been accused of inappropriate behavior. Ask: **Why do you think that certain individuals, even those who at one time were respected church leaders, are unable to lead lives that reflect biblical standards of morals and ethics?**

❖ Read aloud today's focus statement: **There are people in communities of faith who lack the power to lead worthy lives. Where and how can we connect with God's strength and glorious power? Paul tells the Colossians that their power as a congregation of hope and faith has come to them by their acceptance of the word of truth, the gospel.**

*(2) Introduce Paul as a Letter-writing Teacher for the Church at Colossae*

❖ Locate Colossae on a map. Use information from Colossians 1:1-8 in the Understanding the Scripture portion to help the class members become acquainted with this city to which Paul's letter was addressed.

❖ Choose a volunteer to read Colossians 1:1-14 as if he or she were reading this letter to the gathered church.

❖ Discuss these questions. Add any information you feel is helpful from Understanding the Scripture.

(1) **What does this letter tell you about the people of the church at Colossae?**

(2) **What do you learn about Epaphras, who founded the church?**

(3) **What is Paul's prayer for this congregation?** (Unpack the meaning of some of the words and ideas by reading the third and fourth paragraphs of "A Community Searching for Truth" in Interpreting the Scripture.)

(4) **How can you apply Paul's words to the Colossians to your own congregation?** (Check "A Community Living Its Faith" in Interpreting the Scripture for ideas.)

*(3) Recognize that God Is the Source of the Learner's Strength and Power*

❖ Read this story from www.cbn.com that illustrates God's power: **As a result of a car accident that left Donna Sikes with a severe concussion, she visited a chiropractor who recognized a problem. Because of concerns raised by her chiropractor, Donna went to several other doctors and was diagnosed with a tumor of the pituitary gland. Depressed, Donna considered suicide but recalling words from a 700 Club broadcast, she asked God for a miracle.**

She believed that God would meet her needs and so decided to have surgery to remove the tumor from her brain. The final MRI prior to this procedure showed no sign of a tumor! Another MRI was done; again, no sign of a tumor. Donna was not surprised because God had already told her that she was healed. Even her doctor described this as a miracle.

❖ Invite the students to comment on how Ms. Sikes might have connected with God's strength and power to enable this miracle to occur. (Consider possibilities such as prayer, reading Scripture, reading other books for encouragement, and worship.)

❖ Give volunteers an opportunity to share stories that demonstrate how God has been the source of their own strength and power. Ask them to comment on ways they have found to connect with God's strength and power.

*(4) Lead Lives of Prayer, Thanksgiving, and Good Works in Christ's Faithful Community*

❖ Invite the participants to read in unison 1 Colossians 1:9-12 from whichever translations they have.

❖ Distribute paper and pencils. Encourage the students to consider prayerfully ways in which they currently "lead lives worthy of the Lord" (1:10). List on paper a few words about what they are doing and the fruit that their lives are bearing as a result. For example: *I am helping an elderly neighbor with household chores. As a result, she is able to stay in her own home.*

❖ Invite volunteers to share what they have written.

❖ Conclude this portion of the lesson by challenging the students to seek God's wisdom this week so that they might find new ways to live faithfully and bear good fruit.

*(5) Continue the Journey*

❖ Pray that all who have come today will appreciate the ways in which their own community of faith lives as believers whose lives are worthy of the Lord.

❖ Read aloud this preparation for next week's lesson. You may also want to post it on newsprint for the students to copy.

■ **Title: An Established Community**
■ **Background Scripture: Colossians 2:1-19**
■ **Lesson Scripture: Colossians 2:1-10**
■ **Focus of the Lesson: People are deceived by all kinds of philosophies and human traditions that lead them away from the hidden treasures of knowledge and wisdom. Where can we find those hidden treasures? Paul tells the Colossians that knowledge and wisdom are in Christ Jesus and in the lives of those who are growing in Christ.**

❖ Challenge the students to complete one or more of these activities for further spiritual growth, which you will write on newsprint for the students to copy.

(1) **Use Paul's prayer in Colossians 1 to offer an intercessory prayer for missionaries, particularly ones your congregation supports.**

(2) **Consult a Bible dictionary or biblical who's who to learn more about Epaphras and his work. Identify some pillars of your own church and offer prayers on their behalf as they continue to lead the congregation.**

(3) **Talk with other Christians to discern how they understand the Bible to be a record of God's truth. How does their perception square with your own?**

❖ Sing or read aloud "Open My Eyes, That I May See."

❖ Conclude today's session by leading the class in this benediction adapted from Matthew 22:37, 39: **Go forth to love the Lord your God with all your heart, with all your soul, and with all your mind, and to love your neighbor as yourself.**

## UNIT 3: TEACHINGS OF THE CHURCH
# AN ESTABLISHED COMMUNITY

## PREVIEWING THE LESSON

**Lesson Scripture:** Colossians 2:1-10
**Background Scripture:** Colossians 2:1-19
**Key Verse:** Colossians 2:8

### Focus of the Lesson:
People are deceived by all kinds of philosophies and human traditions that lead them away from the hidden treasures of knowledge and wisdom. Where can we find those hidden treasures? Paul tells the Colossians that knowledge and wisdom are in Christ Jesus and in the lives of those who are growing in Christ.

### Goals for the Learners:
(1) to recall the meaning of the fullness of life in Christ found in Paul's letter to the Colossians.
(2) to explore their understandings and feelings about living in Christ.
(3) to encourage others to grow in Christ by modeling for them how to grow in Christ.

### Pronunciation Guide:
Laodicea (lay od i see' uh)
Pentateuch (pen' tuh tyook)
syncretism (sin' crah tiz um)

### Supplies:
Bibles, newsprint and marker, paper and pencils, hymnals, "treasure box"

## READING THE SCRIPTURE

NRSV
Colossians 2:1-10

¹For I want you to know how much I am struggling for you, and for those in Laodicea, and for all who have not seen me face to face. ²I want their hearts to be encouraged and united in love, so that they may have all the riches of assured understanding

NIV
Colossians 2:1-10

¹I want you to know how much I am struggling for you and for those at Laodicea, and for all who have not met me personally. ²My purpose is that they may be encouraged in heart and united in love, so that they may have the full riches of complete understanding, in

and have the knowledge of God's mystery, that is, Christ himself, [3]in whom are hidden all the treasures of wisdom and knowledge. [4]I am saying this so that no one may deceive you with plausible arguments. [5]For though I am absent in body, yet I am with you in spirit, and I rejoice to see your morale and the firmness of your faith in Christ.

[6]As you therefore have received Christ Jesus the Lord, continue to live your lives in him, [7]rooted and built up in him and established in the faith, just as you were taught, abounding in thanksgiving.

[8]**See to it that no one takes you captive through philosophy and empty deceit, according to human tradition, according to the elemental spirits of the universe, and not according to Christ.** [9]For in him the whole fullness of deity dwells bodily, [10]and you have come to fullness in him, who is the head of every ruler and authority.

order that they may know the mystery of God, namely, Christ, [3]in whom are hidden all the treasures of wisdom and knowledge. [4]I tell you this so that no one may deceive you by fine-sounding arguments. [5]For though I am absent from you in body, I am present with you in spirit and delight to see how orderly you are and how firm your faith in Christ is.

[6]So then, just as you received Christ Jesus as Lord, continue to live in him, [7]rooted and built up in him, strengthened in the faith as you were taught, and overflowing with thankfulness.

[8]**See to it that no one takes you captive through hollow and deceptive philosophy, which depends on human tradition and the basic principles of this world rather than on Christ.**

[9]For in Christ all the fullness of the Deity lives in bodily form, [10]and you have been given fullness in Christ, who is the head over every power and authority.

---

## UNDERSTANDING THE SCRIPTURE

**Colossians 2:1-5.** The apostle Paul was a Christian pioneer. He developed an intentional strategy for his missionary work, focusing on significant cities in the Roman world. He went first to the Jews in those cities and announced the gospel among them. From that base, he branched out to present the gospel to Gentiles. Later he corresponded with believers in many of these cities and offered them further guidance and direction.

From our perspective, Paul's concern for "all who have not seen me face to face" (Colossians 2:1) remains significant because we fit somewhat in that category. For those in Laodicea and Colossae, Paul's letters allowed him to multiply the efforts of his personal ministry (4:16). Though he could not be with them physically, through his let-

ters he could be with them "in spirit" (2:5). By this spiritual presence, he could both warn them of possible deceit (2:4) and commend them for their steadfast faith (2:5).

Paul wants to promote unity within the fellowship at Colossae. In chapters 1 and 2, he attempts to correct false teachings by countering some arguments (2:8-15) that those who would try to divide the Colossians may set forth. He pointed them to "God's mystery, that is, Christ himself" (2:2) as the source of the understanding and knowledge that would heal their fractured fellowship. In speaking of God's "mystery" (2:2), Paul used a term that normally occurred in the plural in Greek. "Mysteries" in many Greek religions were secret teachings and peculiar customs or ceremonies closed to outsiders. For Paul, the "mystery" was God's will and plan, which though hidden from human wisdom was openly revealed to all humanity in Jesus Christ.

**Colossians 2:6-10.** Paul warned the Colossians against the philosophy and deceit of those who threatened their community with supposed wisdom. The Greek word for "philosophy" is found in the New Testament only in this passage. Its root meaning is "love of wisdom," but Paul used it in a negative sense akin to false teaching. "Empty deceit" (2:8) denotes seduction through trickery that lures a person into sin.

"Human tradition" and "elemental spirits of the universe" evidently were aspects of the opponents' teachings. The word "tradition" is the same word used in the Gospels for the traditions preserved by the scribes and Pharisees. Paul employed the term in 2 Thessalonians 2:15 and 3:6 for traditions he had passed on to the church. By focusing on "human" tradition, Paul demoted the opponents' traditions to an inferior level.

"Elemental spirits" was the term used by the Greeks to describe the four basic elements from which they believed the natural world was created (earth, air, fire, and water). It also was used of the twelve signs of the zodiac. Having already elevated Christ above these elements of creation (Colossians 1:15-17), Paul reiterated Christ's superiority in 2:9-10. He called the Colossians to continue to live in the faith rooted, built up, and established in Christ, "who is the head of every ruler and authority" (2:10) and in whom "the whole fullness of deity dwells bodily" (2:9).

**Colossians 2:11-15.** To describe how believers come to fullness of faith in Christ (2:10), Paul tied the central aspects of Christ's redemptive work to central religious practices in Judaism—circumcision and baptism. This argument demonstrates a significant Jewish influence on the heresy Paul was addressing.

From the time of Abraham (Genesis 17), the physical circumcision of Jewish males had been the symbol of the covenant that God made with Abraham and his descendents. "The uncircumcised" was a derisive expression used of the Philistines and other opponents of Israel; but even in the Pentateuch, the physical symbol was recognized as incomplete without inner change (circumcision of the heart, Deuteronomy 10:16; 30:6; compare Jeremiah 9:25-26).

Baptism had its origins in ancient purification rites. In Judaism it came to the forefront as part of bringing Gentile proselytes into the Jewish faith. Proselytes were baptized and circumcised—the physical acts symbolizing the washing away of the pollution of their sins and their incorporation into the people of the covenant. John the Baptist was the forerunner of the Christian practice, emphasizing "baptism of repentance for the forgiveness of sins" (Mark 1:4).

For Paul, the Gentile Colossians had come to full faith in Christ by "a spiritual circumcision" (Colossians 2:11). Through their baptism, they had put off the body of flesh—a symbolic cutting away that paralleled circumcision. Through the power of God, believers were united with Christ, whose burial and resurrection were paralleled by the believer's baptism. Their trespasses were forgiven and the legal demand for punishment under the law was erased—both through the effect of the crucifixion. The crucifixion ultimately elevated Christ in triumph (2:15; see John 3:14-15; 12:32).

**Colossians 2:16-19.** Syncretism is the combining of various (and sometimes opposing) beliefs and practices into a new religious system. The Colossian heresy appears to have been a syncretism of pre-Gnostic and Jewish elements. Having emphasized the redemption the Colossians had in Christ, Paul issued a warning that points to a number of the opponents' beliefs. By his constant elevation of Christ, Paul seems to be countering the devaluation of Christ by the opponents.

From the Jewish aspects in the opponents' faith, criticisms were being leveled at the Colossians for their failure to observe food laws and celebrations promoted in the Jewish calendar. Scripture passages like Leviticus 11 and Deuteronomy 14 were the source of elaborate regulations of food that were allowed or prohibited. The designation of foods as "clean" or "unclean" was a ritual classification, not a sanitary one. The pollution and contagion of the unclean affected one's standing with the holy God.

Jesus significantly altered the views on this matter (Mark 7:1-23). Uncleanness was not acquired from outside but emerged from within. Paul consistently supported that view but on occasion called for sensitivity toward weaker believers (Romans 14:1-4, 14-23; 1 Corinthians 8:1-13). Paul classified these beliefs and practices as "a shadow" in contrast to the actual "substance" that belongs to Christ (Colossians 2:17).

The Colossian heresy also had ascetic and ecstatic dimensions. Added to the food restrictions ("Do not handle, Do not taste, Do not touch," 2:21) were the ascetic tendencies of "self-abasement" (2:18) and "severe treatment of the body" (2:23). Paul suggested that these had "no value in checking self-indulgence" (2:23). By "not holding fast to the head" (2:19) of the body (Christ), they separated themselves from God.

The ecstatic elements involved the worship of angels and visions. Rather than focusing on Christ as the intermediary between God and humanity, the opponents claimed wisdom that came from angelic intermediaries and visions. Rather than gaining wisdom, all they achieved was "a human way of thinking" (2:18). The only way to counteract this deviant theology was to hold fast to Christ.

## INTERPRETING THE SCRIPTURE

*Entering the New Life in Christ*

James S. Stewart, the gifted Scotsman some would call the best preacher of the twentieth century, wrote a book entitled *A Man in Christ*. Stewart developed his thesis from the more than eighty times that Paul used the phrase "in Christ" or "in Christ Jesus" in his epistles. From Paul's encounter with Christ on the Damascus Road to his death in Rome, his whole experience was an immersion of self into the person, character, work, and abiding presence of Jesus Christ.

We have a tendency to segment our lives—work, home, family, church, and recreation. Because the people, places, and things tend to shift and change from one segment to another, life often seems to lack a unifying element. Paul found the unifying element for his life in Jesus Christ.

A relationship with Jesus Christ might be called faith, salvation, vocation, daily walk, or Christian experience; Jesus Christ is the constant in whatever we call that relationship. Jesus is the binding force that holds together the segments of life for a Christian.

Colossians was addressed "to the saints and faithful brothers and sisters in Christ" (1:1). Paul had heard of their steadfast "faith in Christ Jesus" (1:4; 2:5). His goal was to "present everyone [to God] mature in Christ" (1:28). His hope of glory was "Christ in you" (1:27). But how does one become "in Christ"? How does one enter into this faith and relationship that unifies life and provides hope?

While Paul certainly had a theological understanding of these issues, in Colossians he chose to use two experiences to describe entry into faith in Christ. The first was "spiritual circumcision" (2:11). For Paul, "uncircumcision" (2:13) represented life in the flesh where people live in trespasses and sins and are dead to God. You might hear such persons described as lost, damned, self-destructive, codependent, or sowing their wild oats. For many, life is a self-centered, out-of-control kind of experience where immediate gratification and insensitivity to others dominates.

Paul described spiritual circumcision as putting off the body of flesh and turning away from a life of trespasses and sins. Whether sin is understood as evil deeds, selfish living, or falling short of the glory God intended, the turning away from sin and to Christ (often called "repentance") is the first step toward entering the "in Christ" relationship.

Physical circumcision provided a visible symbol of the covenant with God and of integration into a people of faith dedicated to God. Spiritual circumcision likewise draws people into a new covenant established through Christ and into a new community of faith dedicated to him.

The second experience Paul used to describe entering into faith in Christ was baptism. This ritual of purification symbolized spiritual burial and resurrection. The old dead and sinful self is buried in the baptismal waters, and the new alive and cleansed self is raised into life in Christ. Baptism also is a spiritual experience in line with spiritual circumcision. The physical act has no power in itself. Rather, it symbolizes what has transpired as the believer buries the old self and in the power of God rises to a new life in Christ. The power of God that raised Jesus from the dead transforms those who were spiritually dead. They rise to join other enlivened believers in the community of faith.

### Living the New Life in Christ

Paul admonished, "As you therefore have received Christ Jesus the Lord, continue to live your lives in him" (Colossians 2:6). Entering into the new life with Christ without living out that new life every day is like:

- getting married but each partner then going separate ways;
- having a job but never going to work;
- making a promise but then ignoring it;
- joining a club but never attending its meetings; or
- having a family but never seeing them.

Living in Christ is like living in an oxygen-rich atmosphere. The reality is present with us all of the time, though we may not be fully conscious of it. Whether we are sleeping or engaged in heavy exercise, we draw sustenance from the atmosphere. If we stop breathing, hold our breath, propel ourselves into the void of outer space, or in some other way cut ourselves off from the life-sustaining oxygen, we begin to see the signs quickly. If the condition continues, we eventually die.

Paul saw that all the "riches of assured understanding" and the "knowledge of God's mystery" were present to believers in Christ himself (2:2). "All the treasures of wisdom and knowledge" (2:3) were available to them—but not through human ways of thinking (2:18), human commands, or human teachings (2:22); not through secret knowledge, visions, rituals, or observances (2:16-18); and not through self-imposed piety, humility, or severe treatment of the body (2:23). Christ alone was the oxygen of their spiritual lives—ever present, life-giving, life-sustaining, and life-fulfilling.

Not only do believers live in Christ, but Christ is in believers. Just as oxygen is absorbed into the bloodstream and dispersed to every part of the body, Christ is in us. Every aspect of life is touched by his presence. No part of life can live and thrive without him.

### Holding on to the Faith

Life in the faith is not always easy. Sometimes it feels overwhelming and demanding. Sometimes it seems confusing and complex. Often it is challenged by culture, counterculture, and other cultures.

Sometimes people who seem a whole lot more knowledgeable and wise than we are mislead us. Sometimes people who seem a whole lot more devout disappoint us. Sometimes people who seem more charitable and loving act selfishly. Often the body of Christ seems divided by intractable theological, ethical, social, and political issues.

Paul cared a lot about theology and often argued vehemently for his point of view. Paul was concerned about racial and social distinctions and strongly contended that we are all one in Christ. Paul struggled with ethical issues of all kinds and sought to guide people to high moral principles. Paul also struggled with the politics of those who denied that he was an apostle, stirred up public opinion against him, spread false rumors about him, and even tried to kill him.

Yet, Paul centered his faith in Jesus Christ. He could still argue theology. He could still demand moral principles. He could still struggle with social issues. But when things became heated, when issues became confused, when opposition seemed overwhelming, and when imprisonment clipped his wings, Paul held fast to his center, Jesus Christ. Paul exalted Jesus.

Throughout Colossians Paul returned again and again to Jesus as the standard, Jesus as the example, Jesus as the solution. When times were tough, when issues were confusing, when disagreements were bitter—Jesus was the answer.

We need to hold on to the faith, but we must be cautious that we don't exalt the wrong aspects of our faith. We can still contend for theological, ethical, social, or political principles; but our lives must primarily be centered in following the life and example of Jesus Christ.

## SHARING THE SCRIPTURE

### Preparing Our Hearts

Meditate on this week's devotional reading, found in Ephesians 3:14-21. In this prayer, the writer asks that God strengthen the readers through the Spirit and enable them to know the love of Christ so that they may experience "the fullness of God" (4:19). Read verses 14-19 several times, from different translations if possible. Try to rewrite these verses in your own words as your own prayer. Use the doxology in verses 20-21 to conclude your meditation time.

Pray that you and the adult learners will recognize the work of the Spirit who enables you to grow in the knowledge and love of Jesus Christ.

### Preparing Our Minds

Study the background in Colossians 2:1-19 and lesson scripture, verses 1-10.

Contemplate where you might look for hidden treasures of knowledge and wisdom.

Write on newsprint:
❑ information for next week's lesson, found under "Continue the Journey."
❑ activities for further spiritual growth in "Continue the Journey."

Find a small box and write the words "treasure box" on it for the "Gather to Learn" activity. You may choose to put a "treasure" in the box, but that is not necessary.

### LEADING THE CLASS

### (1) Gather to Learn

❖ Welcome the class members and introduce any guests.

❖ Pray that all who have come today will discern truthful teachings of the church as you study together.

❖ Display the "treasure box" you have

brought. (Alternatively, ask the class members to imagine that you are holding a treasure box.) Invite the students to call out the kinds of treasures that may be hidden in this box.

❖ Ask the students to note roughly what percentage of their treasures were tangible items with monetary worth. Indicate that our lesson will explore another type of treasure.

❖ Read aloud today's focus statement: **People are deceived by all kinds of philosophies and human traditions that lead them away from the hidden treasures of knowledge and wisdom. Where can we find those hidden treasures? Paul tells the Colossians that knowledge and wisdom are in Christ Jesus and in the lives of those who are growing in Christ.**

*(2) Recall the Meaning of the Fullness of Life in Christ Found in Paul's Letter to the Colossians*

❖ Choose two volunteers to read Colossians 2:1-5, 6-10.

❖ Point out today's key verse, Colossians 2:8, and ask: **What teachings have you heard that in your opinion constitute "empty deceit" and "human tradition" rather than the truth of Christ?** (Be careful here to help the class distinguish between teachings that believers have honest disagreements about and those that have no biblical basis.)

❖ Divide the class into groups. Give newsprint and a marker or paper and pencils to each group. Challenge them to rewrite in their own words the important points that Paul is raising.

❖ Provide time for each group to report its findings.

❖ Use information from Colossians 2:1-5 and 6-10 in Understanding the Scripture to round out the discussion.

*(3) Explore Understandings and Feelings about Living in Christ*

❖ Read "Entering the New Life in Christ" from Interpreting the Scripture.

❖ Distribute paper and pencils. Invite the students to take the following two steps:
   ■ **Step 1:** List several statements of your own beliefs about who Christ calls you to be or what he calls you to do. (For example, Christ calls me to be an ambassador for him; Christ calls me to be a new creation in him; Christ calls me to love my neighbor as myself.)
   ■ **Step 2:** Write beside your statement of belief an example of how you are living out that belief.

❖ Bring the students back together and close this portion of the session by asking this thought question: **Based on the statements you have written and the examples you have given, what do you think Christ would say about the quality of your life in him?**

❖ Invite volunteers to comment on their answers after you have provided some quiet time for thought.

*(4) Encourage Others to Grow in Christ by Modeling for Them How to Grow in Christ*

❖ Read this excerpt from James Stewart's book, *A Man in Christ: The Vital Elements of St. Paul's Religion:* **"The only saving faith," said Luther, "is that which casts itself on God for life or death"; and Paul, whose faith was of that gallant kind, whose religion was a daily risk, who had no comfortable illusions about the forces antagonistic to Jesus, was the least likely of men to be seduced into the intricacies of speculations remote from the urgent realities of life. . . . Historical data and reminiscences you can rationalize: a living Lord you can only proclaim. There must, of course, have been considerable difference, both of matter and of manner, between the** apostle's preaching and the letters which he wrote; but let us not forget that he, Paul, was a preacher first and a writer second. And both spheres preaching and writing were ruled by one great fact—the fact of a living, present Lord; and by one all-decisive experience—the experience of union and communion with Him. This was the apostle's calling. This was his sole vocation and concern. This it was for which he had been born. He came to bring, not a system, but *the living Christ.*

❖ Discuss these questions with the class:

■ Do you agree with author James Stewart that Paul came to bring the living Christ?

■ If you agree, how does Paul model for us growth in Christ? (List these ideas on newsprint.)

■ As you consider Paul's model, how can you model a life that is "in Christ" for others? (You may wish to have the students answer this question aloud, or provide time for them to think silently about it.)

### (5) Continue the Journey

❖ Pray that today's participants will follow Paul's example and live their lives fully rooted in Christ.

❖ Read aloud this preparation for next week's lesson. You may also want to post it on newsprint for the students to copy.

■ Title: A Chosen Community

■ Background Scripture: Colossians 3

■ Lesson Scripture: Colossians 3:12-17

■ Focus of the Lesson: Sometimes people are confused about what it means to be chosen. What does it mean to be chosen by God? Paul teaches that our calling includes kindness and humility, forgiveness, love, the peace of Christ, thankfulness, and worship.

❖ Challenge the students to complete one or more of these activities for further spiritual growth, which you will write on newsprint for the students to copy.

(1) Be aware of teachings set forth by people who claim to be Christian that do not square with your understanding of the gospel. If possible, question the basis for these claims.

(2) Compare the countercultural teachings of the New Testament to the teachings that are often widely accepted as Christian in our society. Where do you note conflicting views? Which of these teachings will you choose to follow?

(3) Spend time alone with Jesus in prayer and meditation. How does this quiet time enable you to be more fully "in Christ"?

❖ Sing or read aloud "O Church of God, United."

❖ Conclude today's session by leading the class in this benediction adapted from Matthew 22:37, 39: **Go forth to love the Lord your God with all your heart, with all your soul, and with all your mind, and to love your neighbor as yourself.**

UNIT 3: TEACHINGS OF THE CHURCH
# A CHOSEN COMMUNITY

---

### PREVIEWING THE LESSON

**Lesson Scripture:** Colossians 3:12-17
**Background Scripture:** Colossians 3
**Key Verse:** Colossians 3:12

### Focus of the Lesson:
Sometimes people are confused about what it means to be chosen. What does it mean to be chosen by God? Paul teaches that our calling includes kindness and humility, forgiveness, love, the peace of Christ, thankfulness, and worship.

### Goals for the Learners:
(1) to unpack Paul's instruction about what it means to be chosen by God to be in community.
(2) to explore their own feelings of love and forgiveness within God's community.
(3) to choose words and deeds that express love and forgiveness in God's community.

### Pronunciation Guide:
*gnosis* (no' sis)                             *shalom* (shah lohm')
*Haustafel* (hous' tah fel)                    *Sophia* (se fee' uh)

### Supplies:
Bibles, newsprint and marker, paper and pencils, hymnals

---

---

### READING THE SCRIPTURE

NRSV
Colossians 3:12-17

¹²As God's chosen ones, holy and beloved, clothe yourselves with compassion, kindness, humility, meekness, and patience. ¹³Bear with one another and, if anyone has a complaint against another, forgive each other; just as the Lord has forgiven you, so you also must forgive. ¹⁴Above all,

NIV
Colossians 3:12-17

¹²Therefore, as God's chosen people, holy and dearly loved, clothe yourselves with compassion, kindness, humility, gentleness and patience. ¹³Bear with each other and forgive whatever grievances you may have against one another. Forgive as the Lord forgave you. ¹⁴And over all these

clothe yourselves with love, which binds everything together in perfect harmony. [15]And let the peace of Christ rule in your hearts, to which indeed you were called in the one body. And be thankful. [16]Let the word of Christ dwell in you richly; teach and admonish one another in all wisdom; and with gratitude in your hearts sing psalms, hymns, and spiritual songs to God. [17]And whatever you do, in word or deed, do everything in the name of the Lord Jesus, giving thanks to God the Father through him.

virtues put on love, which binds them all together in perfect unity. [15]Let the peace of Christ rule in your hearts, since as members of one body you were called to peace. And be thankful. [16]Let the word of Christ dwell in you richly as you teach and admonish one another with all wisdom, and as you sing psalms, hymns and spiritual songs with gratitude in your hearts to God. [17]And whatever you do, whether in word or deed, do it all in the name of the Lord Jesus, giving thanks to God the Father through him.

## UNDERSTANDING THE SCRIPTURE

**Colossians 3:1-4.** In Colossians 2 Paul used the image of baptism to help believers understand that they have been raised to a new life in Christ. Next Paul turned to the implications of that new life. The "so if" introducing 3:1 is best understood as affirming the reality of their having been raised in Christ at some time in the past (compare "since, then" NIV). "Above" and "where" are adverbs of place modifying the verb "seek," not adjectives modifying "things." The same is true of "above" in 3:2. The focus of the new life, whether in seeking it or in setting our minds upon it, is heavenward, where Christ has taken his place at the right hand of God. The new life currently is hidden with Christ in God, but that new life will be revealed openly when Christ appears in glory.

**Colossians 3:5-11.** Following the same dying and rising motif symbolized in baptism, Paul turned his attention to the dying part of that experience. What was it that was being buried symbolically in baptism? Paul's answer was, "Whatever in you is earthly" (3:5). Perhaps Paul's intention was to contrast the physical body with the spiritual body as he did in 1 Corinthians 15:42-44. If so, his imagery had three dimensions: dying and rising symbolized in the act of

baptism, dying and rising in the regeneration associated with salvation, and dying and rising at the end of the ages. The primary focus in this context, however, is the regeneration or transformation associated with salvation.

Paul next listed some of the aspects of the earthly body that must be put to death. These represented ways the Colossians once lived, but these vices now demonstrated disobedience that would engender the wrath of God. Colossians 3:5 includes two external and three internal vices. "Fornication" is unlawful sexual intercourse that includes unchastity and prostitution. "Impurity" is sexual immorality that renders one unclean before God. "Passion," "desire", and "greed" are internal desires that have gone astray and turned evil or excessive.

In verses 8-10 Paul changed his imagery but maintained an association with baptism. In some ancient baptismal observances, old clothes were removed before baptism and clean white garments were donned afterwards. Removing the old clothes symbolized stripping off the old self with its sinful practices, taking off or putting away such things as anger, malice, slander, abusive language, and lying. The new self that was put on was renewed in knowledge and shaped by the image of its Creator. This new self involves such a radical transformation that we can now say that Christ is in all and all human distinctions have been wiped away. Verse 11 states one of the clearest expectations in Scripture of what should happen in society through God's transforming power.

**Colossians 3:12-17.** If undressing symbolized stripping off the old self with its sinful practices, clothing oneself symbolized the new practices that reveal the transformed character of the redeemed. When God chooses us, sets us apart for service, and sustains us with love, God expects God's new creations to be different and to live differently.

In place of the sinful practices that characterized the old self, transformed believers will demonstrate "compassion, kindness, humility, meekness, and patience" (3:12). These are not merely character traits; they are active expressions in daily life as visible as the clothing we wear. Two—humility and meekness—are internal attributes that are visible in our demeanor. Three—compassion, kindness, and patience—are clearly relational in orientation and demonstrate a life focused on others rather than on self.

Three aspects of our relationship with God undergird this reorientation in the believer's life and demeanor—forgiveness, love, and peace. Because we have been graciously forgiven by God, we too must forgive (Matthew 6:12-15; 18:21-35). Because we have been deeply loved by God, we too must love (John 15:12-17; Luke 6:31-35; 1 John 4:7-11). Because we have experienced God's peace through Christ, we must live in peace with all people (John 14:27; Ephesians 2:13-19; Hebrews 12:14; James 3:18). To do otherwise would make us ungrateful people (Colossians 3:15, 17).

While the application of the principles of forgiveness, love, and peace are broad, Paul was especially concerned that the principles be applied within the fractured fellowship of the Colossian church. He urged them to let tolerance (3:13), harmony (3:14), and unity (3:15) prevail. Yet he held fast to the principle that these would come only as the peace of Christ ruled in their hearts (3:15), the word of Christ dwelled abundantly in their fellowship, and all wisdom (3:16, *sophia*, wisdom, rather than *gnosis*, knowledge) guided their teaching and instruction.

When their relationships, their instruction, their worship, their words, and their deeds were focused in the name of the Lord, their fellowship would become a living Eucharist—a giving of thanks to God through the Son.

**Colossians 3:18-25.** German scholars have a term, *Haustafel* (literally, "household table" or list of domestic duties), that they apply to sections of the Bible like Colossians 3:18–4:1. Such lists are found rather widely in ancient Jewish, Greek, and Roman writings. Many scholars think that these lists were part of the community's instruction given to converts prior to baptism. Some think that such lists were adapted from outside sources with little modification. Whatever the origin, an obvious need existed for instruction in how to live out one's Christian faith in a household that might include nonbelievers and slaves. Remember that the principles of forgiveness, love, and peace along with their expression through tolerance, harmony, and unity continue to provide the foundation for these instructions.

As was proper for that society, wives were urged to be subject to their husbands. The general instruction, however, was significantly qualified by "as is fitting in the Lord" (3:18). "Fitting" speaks of relationship or belonging to something. It was used frequently in the early church in expressions like "relates to," "pertains to," or "is in harmony with." It certainly adds an important priority for a wife committed to Christ. "In the Lord" parallels Paul's central motif, "in Christ." As one who in Christ is relating to her husband and family, a Christian wife would at least exercise the same virtues and avoid the same vices that Paul already had listed (3:12-15).

Husbands were instructed to love their wives with an unselfish *agape*-type of love. Such love is given, not taken; it shows initiative and concern for the well-being of another. "Never treat them harshly" translates a Greek expression that literally means "do not become bitter" against someone.

In quick succession, Paul turned to children (3:20), fathers (3:21), slaves (3:22-25), and masters (4:1). Children are to obey (or more literally "listen from below") to their fathers in all things. This is pleasing to God for those "in the Lord." Fathers are not to arouse, provoke, or irritate their children so that they should lose heart, or more literally, so that they lose their passion or are provoked to anger.

Paul's instructions to slaves are more extensive. He calls them to obedience, diligence, and trustworthiness. "Fearing the Lord," they are to work as though they work "for the Lord." Ultimately their reward will come from the Lord, and true justice ultimately will be applied without partiality. Masters, in like token, should treat their slaves justly and fairly, knowing that they too have "a Master in heaven" (4:1) to whom they are accountable.

## INTERPRETING THE SCRIPTURE

### A Chosen Community

We are "God's chosen ones, holy and beloved" (3:12). What a dynamic description of the Christian community! Those words remind us of several central concepts that guide our lives together in the church.

First, the Christian community exists at God's initiative. While churches may be formed for many reasons—some good and some bad—the impetus for the Christian community lies in God. While churches may be inclusive or exclusive based on many diverse criteria, the members of the Christian community are chosen by God. While churches may be narrow or expansive in their vision, God has an eternal and universal view that crosses time, space, gender, race, language, class, education, occupation, and age. Yet even the concept of being "chosen" raises theological issues that have caused divisions in the church.

Conflicting views of God's sovereignty and human free will have marked divisions that began during the Reformation and persist in denominational identities to this day.

Every group wants to claim that they are more "beloved" than any other group. How strange that the one body with many members and with Christ as its head battles over the limits to God's sovereignty and the effectiveness of human initiative.

In Colossians, Paul was addressing a community divided over theological issues. While he did not soft-pedal the theological differences, he did emphasize the things that bind the community together. He urged the Colossians to shed the emotions and deeds that accompany division (anger, malice, slander, abusive language, and lying). He called them to clothe themselves with the character traits that foster harmony (compassion, kindness, humility, meekness, and patience). All of these become expressions of the forgiveness, love, and peace we have received from God and are called to show toward one another.

Perhaps "holy" (rightly understood) best describes what being a chosen community means. Too often we shy from that description of the Christian community because it seems to imply perfection, purity, and sinlessness. In reality, the root understanding of "holy" is to be set apart for sacred use, to be consecrated to God, and to be dedicated to God's purposes. Our concern is not primarily to be right, but to be right with God and with the members of our holy fellowship. The objective is to become a member of the body of Christ, a beloved and holy people, set apart for God's service in our world.

### The Rule of Christ's Peace

To focus on the call to oneness in the Christian community (the body of Christ), Paul admonished the Colossians to "let the peace of Christ rule in your hearts" (3:15). Paul was not merely calling for the absence of warfare. Drawing on the Hebrew concept of *shalom*, he was urging the Colossians to establish relationships that are marked by such positive characteristics as wholeness, wellness, and harmony. Paul did not want them merely to banish contention from their fellowship; he wanted them to act constructively toward those with whom they disagreed in order to build a harmonious community.

Such efforts are difficult if not impossible from a human perspective. For that reason, Paul grounded this peace in Christ. Two images combine in this unifying "peace of Christ." The first was encountered in Colossians 1:20. Paul had written of the reconciliation that was made through the death of Jesus on the cross. God took the initiative in reconciling all things to God's self through this peace-making sacrifice. Paul's implication is this: those who have been reconciled to God through Christ cannot at the same time be un-reconciled with others for whom Christ died to make peace with God.

The second image of the "peace of Christ" draws on prophetic views of the messianic kingdom. Peace is an essential characteristic of the kingdom the messiah will establish. Early Christian thought also viewed peace as nearly synonymous with messianic salvation. Paul implies that those who live under the rule and authority of the king will enjoy peace and harmony in the kingdom.

Paul writes of peace over forty times in his letters, frequently coupling it with grace in the greetings of his epistles. "Grace" was a common greeting in Greek letters. By the addition of "peace," Paul elevated this call to reconciliation with God and with our neighbors.

### A Community in the Lord

Paul's identification with Christ was so complete that he often spoke of being "in Christ." That motif is frequently reflected in Colossians 3.

Dying and rising with Christ is a symbol of the believer's regeneration to a new life in Christ and is represented in the burial and rising of baptism. Living in Christ means to set your mind on the eternal "things that are above, where Christ is," (3:1) and to seek those things. The new life is so transforming that Christ is in all of those who are being renewed according to the image of their Creator, whether they are Greek or Jew, circumcised or uncircumcised, barbarian, Scythian, slave, or free (3:10-11).

Living in Christ or "in the Lord" (3:18) brings expectations about the way we conduct our lives. When the Lord forgives you, "you also must forgive" (3:14). The peace of Christ must rule in your heart (3:15), and the word of Christ must dwell in you richly (3:16). A wife's subjection must be "fitting in the Lord" (3:18), and a slave's work must be done as for the Lord (3:23-24). Even the slave's master must live in light of a Master in heaven (4:1). Paul sums up all of these connections with Christ in Colossians 3:17, "Whatever you do, in word or deed, do everything in the name of the Lord Jesus."

Living in this way is not easy in our world. We are expected to live with our feet on the ground, not our minds on the things above. A certain earthiness is required of the successful—whether it manifests itself in the greed of business success, the drive or passion for vocational achievement, the sexual prowess of a media idol, or the vague promises of a successful politician. When we practice compassion, kindness, humility, meekness, and patience—or work for peace in our world—many will label us "Christian wimps." When we practice patient love and humility in our marriages,

many will say we are selling out our rights. When we try to rear obedient and respectful children, many will say we're fighting a losing battle. When we work diligently and do our best at work, co-workers will call us apple polishers.

These are reasons that a community in Christ trying to live in the Lord is so essential in helping us become a living Eucharist—daily giving thanks to God through the Son.

## SHARING THE SCRIPTURE

### Preparing Our Hearts

Meditate on this week's devotional reading, found in Isaiah 41:4-10. In this prophesy that looks ahead to the restoration of Israel and the judgment against other nations, Israel is referred to as God's chosen servant (41:8-9). God has called Israel. The people of God need not be afraid; God is with them. In today's Scripture reading from Colossians we will see that as members of the church we are also chosen. How do you feel, knowing that God has chosen you? What questions does the notion of being chosen raise for you?

Pray that you and the adult learners will act in ways that exemplify the compassion and humility of those who are chosen by God.

### Preparing Our Minds

Study the background from Colossians 3 and lesson scripture, verses 12-17. Consider what it means to be chosen by God.

Write on newsprint:
❑ information for next week's lesson, found under "Continue the Journey."
❑ activities for further spiritual growth in "Continue the Journey."

### LEADING THE CLASS

#### (1) Gather to Learn

❖ Welcome the class members and introduce any guests.

❖ Pray that all who have come today will sense that they belong here today.

❖ Invite the students to talk about events in their lives that made them feel chosen. For example, perhaps one of the class members was elected homecoming queen years ago; another was asked to be a soloist in the choir; a third was interviewed by the media because of expertise in a particular subject. Encourage each volunteer to talk about what it meant to him or her to be chosen.

❖ Read aloud today's focus statement: **Sometimes people are confused about what it means to be chosen. What does it mean to be chosen by God? Paul teaches that our calling includes kindness and humility, forgiveness, love, the peace of Christ, thankfulness, and worship.**

#### (2) Unpack Paul's Instruction about What It Means to Be Chosen by God to Be in Community

❖ Set the stage for today's session by reading or retelling information in

Understanding the Scripture for Colossians 3:1-4 and 5-11.

❖ Select a volunteer to read Colossians 3:12-17.

❖ Distribute paper and pencils. Encourage the students to make a quick sketch of a person (even a stick figure) and write on the figure the characteristics with which God's people are to clothe themselves: *compassion, kindness, humility, meekness, patience, and love.* You may wish to read today's key verse, 3:12, and verse 14.

❖ Talk with the class about how they see these characteristics manifested in the lives of Christians. Consider especially, humility, meekness, and patience, which are often in short supply in our "me first/push ahead" society. Are there other characteristics that they would add to the list?

❖ Read "A Chosen Community" from Interpreting the Scripture and ask:

> (1) How do you see your church as "God's chosen ones, holy and beloved" (3:12)?
>
> (2) When outsiders look at your congregation, would they see you as you see yourselves? Why or why not?

❖ Conclude this portion of the session by noting that Paul was addressing a church divided by theological issues. Ask: **What barriers prevent the contemporary church, both locally and internationally, from becoming unified?**

*(3) Explore Feelings of Love and Forgiveness within God's Community*

❖ Ask a student to read again Colossians 3:13.

❖ Read aloud this story of Francis & Berthe Climbié from http://www.theforgivenessproject.com/stories/francis-berthe-climbie: **Francis and Berthe Climbié entrusted their seven-year-old daughter Victoria to the care of Marie-Therese Kouao, a relative who promised to take the child from her home in the Ivory Coast to** England to be educated. Tragically, Ms. Kouao tortured and killed Victoria. On the day that Francis and Berthe learned of Victoria's death they prayed that they would be able to forgive. Although Ms. Kouao expressed no remorse, the Climbiés forgave her, as well as her boyfriend, who did seek forgiveness. The Climbiés have established a school in the Ivory Coast in memory of their daughter. Their hope is that children from around the world will receive an excellent education here. Had such a school been available, Victoria would not have been sent away to be educated and would likely still be alive.

❖ Discuss these questions with the class or in small groups:

> (1) What can you learn from Francis and Berthe about forgiveness?
>
> (2) What do you think motivates people to offer forgiveness under such extraordinary circumstances?
>
> (3) How might the actions of the Climbiés, who experienced such a devastating loss, be a model for forgiveness within God's community of faith where conflicts often arise for much lesser reasons?

*(4) Choose Words and Deeds That Express Love and Forgiveness in God's Community*

❖ Read these words from Interpreting the Scripture: **Paul did not want them [the Colossian church] merely to banish contention from their fellowship; he wanted them to act constructively toward those with whom they disagreed in order to build a harmonious community.**

❖ Talk with the group about how they experience conflict and its resolution within their church or denomination. Consider questions such as these, but if your church is currently in the midst of a conflict you may need to modify this activity.

> (1) What kinds of issues or situations cause conflict and disunity?

(2) How do people try to come together to resolve their differences?

(3) What kinds of deeds and words have been used to express true forgiveness?

❖ Go around the room and invite each person to name an action or state several words that he or she would find helpful in situations where forgiveness is needed. For example, if someone asks for forgiveness, she might also suggest an activity (such as lunch) to "make things right." Or someone offering forgiveness may want to pray with the one who has wronged him. If a student chooses not to participate, he or she may simply say "pass."

❖ Challenge the students to recall these ideas when the need for forgiveness arises. Thank them for their participation by reminding them that they are all God's chosen ones and belong to the community of faith.

*(5) Continue the Journey*

❖ Pray that all who have come today will recognize that they belong to the community of faith and can help others experience this sense of belonging as well.

❖ Read aloud this preparation for next week's lesson. You may also want to post it on newsprint for the students to copy.

■ **Title: At Home in the Community**
■ **Background Scripture: Philemon**
■ **Lesson Scripture: Philemon 8-18**

■ Focus of the Lesson: Some people need someone to stand up for them and to be in their corner when the going gets tough. Where are all the places one can turn for help? Paul reminded Philemon that Paul was standing up for Onesimus because of their relationship in Christ.

❖ Challenge the students to complete one or more of these activities for further spiritual growth, which you will write on newsprint for the students to copy.

(1) **Read again Colossians 3:12-17. Which behaviors do you need to embrace? Ask God to help you take whatever action is needed.**

(2) **Offer forgiveness to someone who has wronged you.**

(3) **Write a prayer of confession concerning an action or attitude for which you need forgiveness. Ask God to forgive you. If possible, ask whomever you have hurt to forgive you as well.**

❖ Sing or read aloud "Forward Through the Ages."

❖ Conclude today's session by leading the class in this benediction adapted from Matthew 22:37, 39: **Go forth to love the Lord your God with all your heart, with all your soul, and with all your mind, and to love your neighbor as yourself.**

### UNIT 3: TEACHINGS OF THE CHURCH
# AT HOME IN THE COMMUNITY

---

## PREVIEWING THE LESSON

**Lesson Scripture:** Philemon 8-18, 21
**Background Scripture:** Philemon
**Key Verse:** Philemon 21

### Focus of the Lesson:
Some people need someone to stand up for them and to be in their corner when the going gets tough. Where are all the places one can turn for help? Paul reminded Philemon that Paul was standing up for Onesimus because of their relationship in Christ.

### Goals for the Learners:
(1) to explore Paul's plea for Onesimus based on their shared membership in Christ's community.
(2) to explore the feelings that result from standing up for someone.
(3) to take a stand or make plans to speak up for someone or a worthy cause.

### Pronunciation Guide:
Apphia (af ee' uh)
Archippus (ahr' kip puhs)
Aristarchus (air is tahr' kuhs)
Epaphras (ep af ras')

*koinonia* (coy-no-nee'-uh)
Onesimus (oh neh' sih muhs)
Philemon (fi lee' muhn)
Tychicus (tik' uh kuhs)

### Supplies:
Bibles, newsprint and marker, paper and pencils, hymnals

---

## READING THE SCRIPTURE

NRSV
Philemon 8-18, 21

⁸For this reason, though I am bold enough in Christ to command you to do your duty, ⁹yet I would rather appeal to you on the basis of love—and I, Paul, do this as an old man, and now also as a prisoner of Christ Jesus. ¹⁰I am appealing to you for my child,

NIV
Philemon 8-18, 21

⁸Therefore, although in Christ I could be bold and order you to do what you ought to do, ⁹yet I appeal to you on the basis of love. I then, as Paul—an old man and now also a prisoner of Christ Jesus—¹⁰I appeal to you for my son Onesimus, who became my son

Onesimus, whose father I have become during my imprisonment. ¹¹Formerly he was useless to you, but now he is indeed useful both to you and to me. ¹²I am sending him, that is, my own heart, back to you. ¹³I wanted to keep him with me, so that he might be of service to me in your place during my imprisonment for the gospel; ¹⁴but I preferred to do nothing without your consent, in order that your good deed might be voluntary and not something forced. ¹⁵Perhaps this is the reason he was separated from you for a while, so that you might have him back forever, ¹⁶no longer as a slave but more than a slave, a beloved brother—especially to me but how much more to you, both in the flesh and in the Lord.

¹⁷So if you consider me your partner, welcome him as you would welcome me. ¹⁸If he has wronged you in any way, or owes you anything, charge that to my account. . . . ²¹Confident of your obedience, I am writing to you, knowing that you will do even more than I say.

while I was in chains. ¹¹Formerly he was useless to you, but now he has become useful both to you and to me.

¹²I am sending him—who is my very heart—back to you. ¹³I would have liked to keep him with me so that he could take your place in helping me while I am in chains for the gospel. ¹⁴But I did not want to do anything without your consent, so that any favor you do will be spontaneous and not forced. ¹⁵Perhaps the reason he was separated from you for a little while was that you might have him back for good—¹⁶no longer as a slave, but better than a slave, as a dear brother. He is very dear to me but even dearer to you, both as a man and as a brother in the Lord.

¹⁷So if you consider me a partner, welcome him as you would welcome me. ¹⁸If he has done you any wrong or owes you anything, charge it to me. . . . ²¹Confident of your obedience, I write to you, knowing that you will do even more than I ask.

---

## UNDERSTANDING THE SCRIPTURE

**Philemon 1-7.** The Letter to Philemon is the shortest and most personal of the Pauline epistles. The letter itself is the only reference in the New Testament to Philemon. Onesimus, the subject of the letter, is referenced in Colossians 4:9 as "one of you." This indicates that Philemon likely lived in Colossae.

While titled in the Bible as if addressed to an individual, verse 2 shows that the church meeting in Philemon's house also was in view. The "you" in verse 3 is plural. Apphia probably was Philemon's wife. Archippus, mentioned in Colossians 4:17 as having a special task from the Lord, must have been a significant member of the church.

In contrast to other letters to individuals (Timothy and Titus), Philemon focuses on personal rather than ecclesiastical concerns. Yet the significance of the issue addressed has sweeping implications for the Christian community.

Since Paul had never visited the church (Colossians 1:4; 2:1), we are not sure how Philemon became Paul's "dear friend and co-worker" (Philemon 1). Philemon apparently had been converted to Christianity through the agency of Paul (Philemon 19), perhaps while Paul was in the region in Antioch of Pisidia (Acts 13:13-49).

After a greeting and a customary assurance of prayer for the recipients of the letter, Paul began to lay the groundwork for his appeal on behalf of Onesimus. First, he shifted to a singular "you" in verses 4-21, focusing specifically on Philemon. He affirmed Philemon for his "love for all the saints" that has "encouraged" and "refreshed" their hearts (Philemon 5, 7). Onesimus was now one of those "saints," though Philemon did not know it yet.

"Sharing" in verse 6 is the Greek word, *koinonia*, that strong fellowship binding the Christian community in one body. Philemon's faith was tied to that shared fellowship, but Paul implies that more "good" must be done for Christ before Philemon's faith can be fully "effective" (Philemon 6). We know that one aspect of that "good" was welcoming Onesimus.

**Philemon 8-16.** Paul came to the purpose of his letter in verse 8. He could have exercised authority as an apostle or as a facilitator in Philemon's faith and commanded Philemon's obedience. He preferred, instead, to make an appeal based on Philemon's love—a love that Paul already had affirmed. "Appeal" (Philemon 9) is the Greek word from which "Paraclete" is derived. It speaks of calling one alongside. Paul was calling Philemon to stand beside him in the matter of Onesimus just as Philemon would stand beside Paul as an "old man" and "prisoner of Christ Jesus."

Onesimus is mentioned first in verse 10; but Paul calls him "my child" and calls himself Onesimus's "father." Later Paul calls him "my own heart" (Philemon 12). This bond was forged during Paul's imprisonment, though the circumstances are unclear. If Onesimus were a runaway slave (the letter never states this explicitly), he may have been imprisoned in the same prison as Paul. Or he may have come to Paul's attention through Epaphras, another Christian from Colossae (Colossians 1:7; 4:12) who was imprisoned with Paul (Philemon 23).

Verse 11 makes a play on Onesimus' name (literally "useful"). Paul omitted the former status in which Onesimus had been useful to Philemon. Instead, he first speaks of Onesimus as having become "useless" to Philemon, either from having run away or

from having stayed away an extended time while on a mission for his master. With Paul's letter and Onesimus's return, the useless one had "now" become "useful"—both to Philemon and to Paul.

Paul implied in verse 13 that Philemon owed Paul some type of "service" during his imprisonment. To "be of service" is a verb form of the word from which "deacon" is derived. While no official status is implied here, Paul obviously wanted Onesimus to remain with him and to assist him as Philemon's representative. Reluctant to claim this right without Philemon's consent, and not wanting to force the issue overtly, Paul pointed to "the good deed" Philemon could perform voluntarily (Philemon 14).

Paul left the door open that Philemon might want Onesimus "back forever" (Philemon 15), but Paul stated a new basis for their relationship. "Forever" translates the Greek word for "eternal." In view of eternity, Onesimus could no longer be merely a slave. He would be "more than a slave" (Philemon 16); he had become "a beloved brother" through their common faith. Paul already had accepted Onesimus this way. Philemon could now have a beloved brother "both in the flesh and in the Lord," both in this life and in eternity.

**Philemon 17-21.** "Partner" in verse 17 shares a common Greek root with the word "sharing" in verse 6 (*koinonia*). If Paul and Philemon are partners in the gospel by virtue of their common faith, then Onesimus (who now shares that faith) also has become a partner. Paul asked Philemon to welcome Onesimus as Philemon would welcome Paul himself. "Welcome" means more than merely saying, "How do you do." It means to accept one into your home or your circle of acquaintances.

"If he has wronged you in any way, or owes you anything" begins a conditional sentence in Greek that implies the condition is true. Paul was accepting liabilities on behalf of Onesimus. He wasn't merely co-signing the note—he was assuming the debt. Yet Paul knew that he already had an offsetting balance with Philemon. Paul said what he claimed he would "say nothing about"—Philemon owed his own self to Paul, who had guided him to salvation.

Verse 21 strangely speaks of "obedience." Paul had approached the subject as an appeal to which Philemon could consent voluntarily. In the end, however, the imperative of the gospel demanded an acceptance of the common status of all who stand at the cross and before the empty tomb. Paul's statement in Colossians 3:11 summarizes this acceptance: There is no longer slave or free when Christ is all and in all.

**Philemon 22-25.** Paul concluded the Letter to Philemon with his usual greetings from others in his circle and with a blessing of the Lord's grace. But he added "one thing more" (Philemon 22). He asked Philemon to prepare a guest room for him, hoping that he might be released from prison and be able to fellowship with the church in Colossae. We need not doubt that Paul was making this request sincerely; but given his request that Philemon receive Onesimus as he would receive Paul himself, we cannot help but wonder if this was not a strong hint for Philemon to provide a guest room for this slave who now was as much a brother in Christ as was Paul.

---

## INTERPRETING THE SCRIPTURE

### Building Community

In Philemon, Paul was not addressing Pharisaic interpretations of Scripture or trying to prove that his understanding of the Bible was best. He was dealing with a thorny social issue—slavery—that was well-established in his time. Galatians 3:28 and Colossians 3:11 state Paul's principle on this issue, but laying out a principle and having it accepted are different matters.

The issue in Philemon is how to take principle to practice without rupturing the fellowship of the church. Paul did it by building a sense of community. Let's look at three dimensions of that effort.

### Affirming Our Bond in Christ

Paul often used the body as a model for the church. The body is a complex organism made up of many individual parts, but all of the parts are joined together in one. The parts have different functions designed for the good of the whole. Too often in churches we focus on the individual parts and their different functions. Too rarely do we grasp the wholeness of the body and the good that comes from the parts functioning together.

When we lose sight of our connectedness, envy, boasting, fault-finding, and competition can arise. Minor differences become major obstacles. Points of view replace a sense of direction. Particular gifts are showcased, and the weaknesses of others are exploited.

With our sophisticated understanding of human interactions, we easily could dismiss Paul as a manipulator who ingratiated himself to others to get his own way. Because we sometimes act insincerely to advance our cause, we may assume that Paul was doing the same in his letter. But if Paul was sincere (I see no reason to assume he wasn't), we may discover in his example a way to deal with today's complex issues.

In Philemon, Paul emphasized relationships. Note the relational descriptions that fill Paul's letter: brother, dear friend, co-worker, sister, fellow soldier, child, father, my own heart, beloved, partner, fellow prisoner, and fellow workers. These descriptors were applied to Timothy, Philemon, Apphia, Archippus, Onesimus, those listed in verses 23-24, and even Paul himself. This disparate group of slave and free, male and female, educated and uneducated, Jew and Gentile, young and old found their unity in Christ. So must we. We must affirm our bond in Christ, our interconnectedness and our unity under Christ, the body's head. Paul addressed a difficult and complex social issue by affirming such unity under the lordship of Christ.

### Incorporating the Disenfranchised

The church today is surrounded by disenfranchised and alienated people. The sources of this alienation are numerous: sex, age, ethnicity, education, occupation, and social or family status among others. Some are bound by their own barriers. Some are bound by limitations forced upon them. Some are classified, categorized, and ostracized by factors over which they have no control.

A central theme of Paul's ministry was, "Be reconciled to God" (2 Corinthians 5:20). Reconciliation with God is at the heart of removing disenfranchisement and alienation. The answer is not found in working your way out of your plight. Rather the answer comes in God's initiative through Jesus Christ, seeking to bring all persons into relationship with God. The Savior came to seek and to save those who were lost (Luke 19:10).

Paul recognized that reconciliation with God raises the necessity of tearing down "the dividing wall" of hostility (Ephesians 2:14) that separates human beings from one another. How does one accomplish within the community what God accomplished through Christ? Paul answered through his example.

First, Paul established a loving relationship with Onesimus. We do not know how Onesimus moved from bound slave to beloved "child"; but Paul obviously invested lots of time, energy, and love in developing, fostering, and expanding his relationship with Onesimus.

Second, many people escape disfranchisement and alienation by just one person seeing them as a child of God and helping them grasp the enormous freedom that accompanies that new self-understanding. Paul helped Onesimus experience the love of God. He also helped him discover that he was loved deeply and unconditionally by another human being who believed in him, saw his potential, and was willing to become his advocate.

Finally, Onesimus trusted Paul so much that he was willing, with Paul's encouragement, to return to Colossae and deal with whatever wrongs he had committed. Onesimus could have been put to death, thrown in prison, or reinstalled as a slave. The transforming love and support of Paul gave Onesimus the courage to deal with his new self-understanding in a positive way.

### Creating a Vision for the Church

Sometimes we expect people to do the right thing and they don't disappoint us. That's not always the outcome, but how much better to hold up the ideal and encourage people to strive for it than to accept defeat even before we make an effort. Yes, people are stubborn, prejudiced, set in their ways, and resistant to change. Yes, they sometimes pay lip service to the right and undermine it behind the scenes. Paul certainly was aware of these tendencies. Yet he forged ahead and advanced the ideal. He painted a picture of what should be and could be, and he trusted that people of faith would do their best to please God in their actions.

For Onesimus to find new standing in Colossae, Paul knew the church needed a dramatic new vision of what should be. Paul's strategy was subtle but effective.

Imagine how the church in Colossae would have responded if Paul had come for a visit. An important church leader instrumental in the conversion of Onesimus, Paul had been part of the Jerusalem Conference where church leaders worked out the basis for spreading the gospel to Gentiles (Acts 15). He had been a successful missionary and evangelist in neighboring Pisidia. He had bravely represented Christ in difficult circumstances and was in prison for his faith. If Paul had visited Colossae, imagine how the red carpet would have been rolled out and what a warm welcome he would have received.

Paul told the Colossians to prepare for such a visit, but the visitor would be the "child," not the father! Imagine the recollections of those who had heard Jesus' parables and their teaching about a father who sent his beloved son in his place. Would they remember the consequences for those who mistreated the son?

Paul said, "I'm hoping to come, so prepare a room for me. But for now, I'm sending my son. Welcome him as you would welcome me." What power lies in that vision of what ought to happen when a disenfranchised person becomes a child of God! What high expectations are raised by calling some alienated person "a beloved brother or sister!" When confronted by such a vision, will we not be inclined to "do even more than what I say" (Philemon 21)?

## SHARING THE SCRIPTURE

### Preparing Our Hearts

Meditate on this week's devotional reading, found in Colossians 4:2-9. At the close of his Letter to the Colossians, Paul mentions Onesimus, a major figure in this week's Scripture lesson. Note that Onesimus will accompany Tychicus to the church at Colossae to bring news about Paul and deliver his letter. Paul describes Onesimus as "the faithful and beloved brother, who is one of you" (4:9). Identify people in your own congregation who are "faithful" and "beloved" and serve God well by serving the church. Give thanks for these people.

Pray that you and the adult learners will be faithful servants of your own congregation.

### Preparing Our Minds

Study the background from the short book of Philemon and lesson scripture, verses 8-18. Consider where those who need someone to stand up for them can go to find support.

Write on newsprint:

❑ information for next week's lesson, found under "Continue the Journey."
❑ activities for further spiritual growth in "Continue the Journey."

### LEADING THE CLASS

#### (1) Gather to Learn

❖ Welcome the class members and introduce any guests.

❖ Pray that all who have come today will feel at home in this class, regardless of who they are or where they have come from.

❖ Read these two stories of acts of courage by people who chose to stand up for what they believed in, as found on the website http://www.bravenewtraveler.com/2008/09/15/10-revolutionary-acts-of-courage-by-ordinary-people:

■ **A 1989 photograph by Stuart Franklin of an unidentified, unarmed man standing before a line of tanks belonging to the People's Liberation Army on Tiananmen Square has become an international icon of a nonviolent act of courage.**

■ In 1930 Mahatma Ghandi organized a 248-mile trek to a seaside town where it was possible to make salt, in defiance of British salt laws. Thousands of Indians also participated in Ghandi's act of civil disobedience, which became a turning point of world opinion against British policies in India.

❖ Ask: **What motivates people to risk punishment—even their lives—to stand up for something?**

❖ Read aloud today's focus statement: **Some people need someone to stand up for them and to be in their corner when the going gets tough. Where are all the places one can turn for help? Paul reminded Philemon that Paul was standing up for Onesimus because of their relationship in Christ.**

*(2) Explore Paul's Plea for Onesimus Based on Their Membership in Christ's Community*

❖ Solicit a volunteer to read Paul's words to Philemon from Philemon 8-18.

❖ Ask these questions. You will find information in Understanding the Scripture for Philemon 8-16, 17-21 to add to the discussion.

(1) **What can you discern about the relationship between Paul and Onesimus from this letter?** (Note that Paul refers to Onesimus as his "child." The only other person Paul refers to in that way is Timothy.)

(2) **What can you discern about the relationship between Paul and Philemon?**

(3) **What can you discern about the relationship between Philemon and Onesimus?**

(4) **What can you learn from Paul about how to handle difficult situations within the community of faith?** ("Creating a Vision for the

Church" in Interpreting the Scripture may be helpful in this discussion.)

❖ Read: **Ignatius, the third Bishop of Antioch, wrote in his** *Epistle to the Ephesians*: "**I received, therefore,[4] your whole multitude in the name of God, through Onesimus, a man of inexpressible love,[5] and your bishop in the flesh, whom I pray you by Jesus Christ to love, and that you would all seek to be like him. And blessed be He who has granted unto you, being worthy, to obtain such an excellent bishop." Many scholars believe that this is the same Onesimus that Paul mentored. If so, what does that say to you about the importance of standing up for a member of Christ's community who needs someone to speak for him or her?**

*(3) Explore the Feelings that Result from Standing Up for Someone*

❖ Read "Incorporating the Disenfranchised" from Interpreting the Scriptures.

❖ Invite the class to identify some groups in our society who are seen as disenfranchised and alienated. List these on newsprint.

❖ Divide the class into teams and assign each team at least one group from the list. Ask each team to name people who have stood up for these groups. What did these people do and how successful were they?

❖ Provide time for the groups to report back. Perhaps the class as a whole will be able to identify additional groups of people.

❖ Discuss with the class times when they have stood up for a disenfranchised group or an individual who was being bullied or otherwise ostracized by others.

❖ Ask: **How does it feel to stand up for someone who is powerless or defenseless? Would you take such action again? Why or why not?** (Some students may have been involved in large social movements or blown the whistle on unethical business practices, but others may recall standing up to the neighborhood bully. Encourage the adults to think of whatever examples they can.)

*(4) Take a Stand or Make Plans to Speak Up for Someone or a Worthy Cause*

❖ Review the list of disenfranchised groups that you created in the previous section. Invite the students to add causes to this list that reflect Christ's concern for those on the margins.

❖ Place an asterisk (*) next to those groups (or causes you have added) that the students could potentially assist (or address) in your community. As an alternative, they may want to take on a cause that has far-reaching implications beyond the community, such as health care or immigration. Talk with the class members about what they could do to stand up for these groups or causes. Could they, for example, write letters to elected officials to support legislation that would aid a particular group? Could the students provide direct, volunteer assistance to these groups? Is there a way that through the church itself or another nonprofit organization the class could offer financial assistance?

❖ Close this portion of the session by challenging the students to work together (or individually) to stand up for people at the margins, just as Paul stood up for Onesimus.

*(5) Continue the Journey*

❖ Pray that today's participants will have the courage to do the right thing at all times.

❖ Read aloud this preparation for next week's lesson. You may also want to post it on newsprint for the students to copy.

■ **Title: At Risk in the Community**
■ **Background Scripture: Jude**
■ **Lesson Scripture: Jude 3-7, 19-21, 24-25**
■ **Focus of the Lesson: Some people, for whatever reason, cause problems within their communities. What can be done to resolve community problems? Jude reminds readers to contend for the faith entrusted to them, and to hold tight to their belief in Jesus Christ.**

❖ Challenge the students to complete one or more of these activities for further spiritual growth, which you will write on newsprint for the students to copy.

(1) **Mentor a younger Christian so as to help this person understand what it means to live as Christ's disciple.**

(2) **Help someone who has experienced a rupture in a relationship be reconciled.**

(3) **Act as a servant leader within your congregation, either as an elected official or informal leader.**

❖ Sing or read aloud "O God, Our Help in Ages Past."

❖ Conclude today's session by leading the class in this benediction adapted from Matthew 22:37, 39: **Go forth to love the Lord your God with all your heart, with all your soul, and with all your mind, and to love your neighbor as yourself.**

### UNIT 3: TEACHINGS OF THE CHURCH
# AT RISK IN THE COMMUNITY

---

## PREVIEWING THE LESSON

**Lesson Scripture:** Jude 3-7, 19-25
**Background Scripture:** Jude
**Key Verses:** Jude 22-23

### Focus of the Lesson:
Some people, for whatever reason, cause problems within their communities. What can be done to resolve community problems? Jude reminds readers to contend for the faith entrusted to them, and to hold tight to their belief in Jesus Christ.

### Goals for the Learners:
(1) to unpack Jude's message about judgment on false teachers.
(2) to discern faithfully the difference between false and true teachings.
(3) to plan ways to express mercy and to reclaim wavering or at-risk believers to the community.

### Pronunciation Guide:
Nephilim (nef' ih lim)

### Supplies:
Bibles, newsprint and marker, paper and pencils, hymnals

---

## READING THE SCRIPTURE

NRSV
Jude 3-7, 19-25

³Beloved, while eagerly preparing to write to you about the salvation we share, I find it necessary to write and appeal to you to contend for the faith that was once for all entrusted to the saints. ⁴For certain intruders have stolen in among you, people who long ago were designated for this condemnation as ungodly, who pervert the grace of our God into licentiousness and deny our only Master and Lord, Jesus Christ.

NIV
Jude 3-7, 19-25

³Dear friends, although I was very eager to write to you about the salvation we share, I felt I had to write and urge you to contend for the faith that was once for all entrusted to the saints. ⁴For certain men whose condemnation was written about long ago have secretly slipped in among you. They are godless men, who change the grace of our God into a license for immorality and deny Jesus Christ our only Sovereign and Lord.

⁵Now I desire to remind you, though you are fully informed, that the Lord, who once for all saved a people out of the land of Egypt, afterward destroyed those who did not believe. ⁶And the angels who did not keep their own position, but left their proper dwelling, he has kept in eternal chains in deepest darkness for the judgment of the great day. ⁷Likewise, Sodom and Gomorrah and the surrounding cities, which, in the same manner as they, indulged in sexual immorality and pursued unnatural lust, serve as an example by undergoing a punishment of eternal fire.

¹⁹It is these worldly people, devoid of the Spirit, who are causing divisions. ²⁰But you, beloved, build yourselves up on your most holy faith; pray in the Holy Spirit; ²¹keep yourselves in the love of God; look forward to the mercy of our Lord Jesus Christ that leads to eternal life. **²²And have mercy on some who are wavering; ²³save others by snatching them out of the fire; and have mercy on still others with fear,** hating even the tunic defiled by their bodies.

²⁴Now to him who is able to keep you from falling, and to make you stand without blemish in the presence of his glory with rejoicing, ²⁵to the only God our Savior, through Jesus Christ our Lord, be glory, majesty, power, and authority, before all time and now and forever. Amen.

⁵Though you already know all this, I want to remind you that the Lord delivered his people out of Egypt, but later destroyed those who did not believe. ⁶And the angels who did not keep their positions of authority but abandoned their own home—these he has kept in darkness, bound with everlasting chains for judgment on the great Day. ⁷In a similar way, Sodom and Gomorrah and the surrounding towns gave themselves up to sexual immorality and perversion. They serve as an example of those who suffer the punishment of eternal fire.

¹⁹These are the men who divide you, who follow mere natural instincts and do not have the Spirit.

²⁰But you, dear friends, build yourselves up in your most holy faith and pray in the Holy Spirit. ²¹Keep yourselves in God's love as you wait for the mercy of our Lord Jesus Christ to bring you to eternal life.

**²²Be merciful to those who doubt; ²³snatch others from the fire and save them; to others show mercy, mixed with fear—** hating even the clothing stained by corrupted flesh.

²⁴To him who is able to keep you from falling and to present you before his glorious presence without fault and with great joy— ²⁵to the only God our Savior be glory, majesty, power and authority, through Jesus Christ our Lord, before all ages, now and forevermore! Amen.

## UNDERSTANDING THE SCRIPTURE

**Jude 1-3.** Along with the epistles of James, Peter, and John, the Epistle of Jude is classified as a general or Catholic Epistle. That classification reflects that these letters were addressed to the church at large rather than to a congregation in a specific location. Jude addressed those who are "called," "beloved," and "kept safe for Jesus Christ" (Jude 1).

The writer identified himself as "Jude, a servant of Jesus Christ and a brother of James" (Jude 1). Tradition equates this James with the brother of Jesus (Mark 6:3; Matthew 13:55), who became a leader of the early church in Jerusalem (Acts 15:13) and authored the general epistle bearing his name (James 1:1). Though this would make Jude a brother of Jesus as well, Jude humbly classified himself as Jesus' slave. The same Greek name is translated Judas, Judah, Jude, and Judea in the New Testament.

Jude would have preferred to write a positive letter about "the salvation we share" (Jude 3), but instead he felt compelled by the situations facing the church to write a letter designed "to contend for the faith that was once for all entrusted to the saints" (Jude 3). Perhaps the seriousness of the situation caused Jude to skip the word of thanksgiving that was part of the traditional letter format in his time.

**Jude 4-7.** The objects of Jude's concern were people who had "secretly slipped in among" (Jude 4, NIV) the believers but who long before had been identified and condemned as ungodly. This previous identification may refer to the Old Testament law, which condemned their actions, or to the teachings of Jesus, who has warned of such deception (see Matthew 7:15-23). Claiming the all-sufficiency of God's grace, these deceivers perverted grace by viewing it as "a license for immorality" (Jude 4, NIV). By their deeds they were denying Jesus Christ, who if he were indeed their Master and Lord, would have transformed their lives into a closer likeness to his own.

To counteract the contention that God's grace provides a license for sin, Jude cited three examples of God's justice at work against those who failed to live by faith. First, God graciously saved the Israelites from their bondage in Egypt through the Exodus, but those who subsequently demonstrated their lack of faith through idolatry and disobedience were destroyed (Jude 5).

The second example is more difficult to understand because two traditions deal with fallen angels and both developed mainly outside the biblical text. Jude appealed to such an interpretation of Genesis 6:1-4. When the Old Testament was translated into Greek, the Hebrew words "sons of God" were frequently translated "the angels." These angels lusted after human women and chose to leave heaven, marry human women, and have children with them. Their children were giants called Nephilim (from the Hebrew word for "fallen"). A book called First Enoch explained how, as punishment, God imprisoned these fallen angels and sent the flood to destroy their offspring.

The third example is Sodom and Gomorrah (Genesis 18:16–19:29), which were destroyed by God's raining sulfur and fire on cities in which God could not find even ten righteous citizens. For a parallel to these examples, see 2 Peter 2:4-10.

**Jude 8-19.** Jude called the ungodly perverters of God's mercy "dreamers." They were as unaware of the implications of their sins as were those in the three examples just listed. Like the citizens of Sodom and Gomorrah, they defiled the flesh. Like the unfaithful in the Exodus, they reject God's authority. Perhaps by using the fallen angels as the justification for their lust, they slandered "the glorious ones" (Jude 8).

Verse 9 reflects a story drawn from a lost work called "The Assumption of Moses." The story and its source are recounted by an early third-century Christian scholar named Origen. We do not know much more about the story itself than what Jude records. This story obviously was known to Jude's readers, and he mixes it in with allusions to the Old Testament about Cain (Genesis 4), Balaam (Numbers 22–24), and Korah (Numbers 16). To all of these he added a quotation from First Enoch, perhaps because it summarized briefly a number of teachings from the Gospels about God's judgment (Jude 14-15).

Verses 12 and 16 contain a flourish of vivid descriptions of these self-centered, self-indulgent, self-important deceivers, who not only marred the community's love feasts by their grumbling and discontent but also endangered the community's life like a destructive hidden reef.

Jude concluded his refutation of the deceivers by pointing to predictions of the apostles. While Jude 18 parallels and may quote 2 Peter 3:3, the "predictions" (literally "words spoken in advance") align more closely with an oral tradition from which both writers may have drawn. These scoffers, who indulged in ungodly lusts and were devoid of the Spirit, were causing division in the community.

**Jude 20-25.** In conclusion, Jude turned from words contending for the faith to words exhorting the faithful, whom he called "beloved." In short, direct instructions he encouraged them to build their lives on the foundation of their holiest faith, to pray in the Holy Spirit, to guard themselves in God's love, and to anticipate the mercy of the Lord Jesus Christ awaiting them in eternal life. Their faith set them apart from the scoffers. The Spirit guided and empowered them in daily life. God's love protected them from the enticement of sin. The hope of mercy sustained them as long as they lived.

Three groups in the community's midst were in danger: those who were wavering; those on the brink of destruction; and those already defiled by unfaithfulness, disobedience, and godless behavior. Toward all three groups, Jude advocated demonstrations of mercy.

Ultimate hope for all, however, rested in God, who through our Savior and Lord Jesus Christ protects, sustains, forgives, and cleanses all who will stand in the presence of God's glory. To such a God as that, Jude offers a doxology of praise that spans all time and places (Jude 24-25).

---

## INTERPRETING THE SCRIPTURE

### Contending for the Faith

Jude's call to "contend for the faith that was once for all entrusted to the saints" (Jude 3) can sound like narrow intolerance and prejudice, particularly in our diverse, pluralistic society. Viewed from another perspective, however, it can be seen as essential action needed to protect the community and its well-being.

The difficult task in applying Jude's teachings is the lack of unanimity within the Christian community about what essential elements ensure the well-being of the community. Some argue for theological integrity; others for moral integrity; and still others for actively living out the principle of love without regard to theological or moral parameters.

Perhaps a few questions drawn from Jude would help identify some threats to the Christian community today.

■ *Perverting grace.* While grace is a wonderful and central concept of our faith, does grace have any limits? Do we use grace as a license or an excuse for doing wrong? Is costly grace made worthless by stripping it of the need for repentance and transformation?

■ *Denying the Lord.* When we declare that Jesus is Lord, what do we mean? Have we turned Jesus into a nice guy who had interesting things to say but generally can be ignored? Is what a person thinks about Jesus important? What does having faith in him mean? If he is Lord, what control have we given him over our lives, values, relationships, time, and money?

■ *Ignoring judgment.* Do we really believe in a final reckoning? Have we kept grace in proper tension with justice and righteousness? Has grace overshadowed our concept of God's wrath over evil and sin? Do we live the moment as if eternity hangs on it?

Jude sought to help his readers discern between true and false teachings. He wanted to counter the doctrinal errors of the Christian pretenders and to eradicate the corrupting practices that were contrary to apostolic teachings. His concerns were so strong that he was willing to fight for the faith that had been entrusted to Christ's followers.

### Contending for Moral Integrity

The relationship between faith and the way we live is often oversimplified. Faith can be feigned in good works; and good works can be performed by people without any faith. Jude's concern was whether sinful, corrupt, immoral practices can coexist with faith in Christ.

Jude knew that wrong teaching leads to wrong thinking and wrong behaving. By focusing on the true meaning of grace, on the true nature of Christ, and on the certainty of God's judgment, Jude first exposed the weak theological underpinnings of his opponents.

Jude then contended for moral integrity. We may be uncomfortable with the focus of Jude's moral concerns. Much that he condemned is endemic in our lax society. Licentiousness (Jude 4), sexual immorality and unnatural lust (Jude 7), defiling the flesh (Jude 8), and indulging ungodly lusts (Jude 16, 18) represent a degeneracy that once marked the godless world but has gradually crept into the church. We too have adopted a lenient view of grace and close our eyes to evil and corruption. We too see the authority of Scripture and tradition questioned and rejected by those "wiser" than our ancestors in the faith (Jude 8). We too see those who live like "irrational animals" (Jude 10) rather than like "those who are called, who are beloved in God" (Jude 1). We too see principled people slandered by those who neither understand nor accept the idea that they themselves might be falling short of God's intended goal for humanity (Jude 10). Somewhere along the way we have lost the connection between Jesus' grace shown toward the woman "caught in the very act of committing adultery" (John 8:4) and Jesus' words, "Go your way, and from now on do not sin again" (8:11).

Our generation is like waterless clouds, trees without fruit, wild waves of the sea, and wandering stars (Jude 12-13). But we will not recover our bearings by some self-righteous crusade for moral integrity. Rather we need to hear and heed Jude 20-21: "Build yourselves up on your most holy faith; pray in the Holy Spirit; keep yourselves in the love of God; look forward to the mercy of our Lord Jesus Christ that leads to eternal life."

### Contention Bathed in Mercy

The church is in the midst of great contention today. Disputes divide and split churches and denominations. Moral and ethical issues provide points of contention. Church bodies fight for dominance and control so that their theological and moral views will "win." Though not a complete catalog, here is a sample of some of the deep divides we face: war and peace, homosexuality and same-sex marriage, universal health care, immigration, stem cell research, brain function manipulation, abortion, poverty and economic justice, global warming and the environment, violence and gun control, and drug/alcohol abuse.

Developing a consensus in the Christian community about such divisive issues will not be easy. Unanimity likely will not be possible. Yet Jude provides a pattern for us in dealing with such problems. Clarifying the theological underpinnings and insisting on moral integrity (broadly defined to include honesty, patience, forgiveness, persistence, and goodwill) provide a start.

Jude concluded his letter with an emphasis on mercy, and that is an important element in dealing constructively with contentious issues. Jude first encouraged his readers to "look forward to the mercy of our Lord Jesus Christ" (Jude 21). This admonition recognizes that each of us will require mercy at the end of life's journey because none of us has lived a perfect life. We all have sinned and sinned grievously. We need mercy in the future because we are not perfect in the present— and we are not always right about everything. Our need for mercy should engender a sense of humility as we deal with contentious issues. We must always be open to the possibility that our views are not right on an issue. When we approach a contentious issue with humility and with openness that God may have more to reveal to us, we have taken the first step toward resolution.

Next, Jude advised that mercy be shown toward those who are wavering (Jude 22). Because so many issues are decided by democratic processes (a vote where one side wins and the other loses), people in the middle often become the focus of intense pressure, manipulation, and exploitation. Power politics, focused solely on winning, treats the wavering middle royally if it can be swayed and poorly if it can't be. Would not our contentions be altered if we treated the wavering ones with mercy—respecting their convictions, sharing with them in a search for truth, honoring their desire for integrity, appealing to the common good rather than to selfish needs, treating them as persons rather than as another vote?

Finally, Jude advised that we treat our opponents with mercy—even those we fear and whose actions we hate (Jude 23). Our society has lost much of its civility. In its place rabid partisanship has emerged that is satisfied with nothing less than destroying the enemy. Jude contended strongly against his opponents, but in the end he advocated merciful attitudes and actions toward those with whom he disagreed—even those he thought were undermining the church and its faith. This is the "love your enemies" principle expressed another way. Even though Jude thought he was right and his opponents were wrong, he recognized that people ultimately are changed by love, compassion, and mercy—not by force, intimidation, or negation.

Love, compassion, and mercy do not always win short-term; but God's truth will ultimately prevail. Perhaps we should leave winning to God and instead look to Jesus whose mercy has blessed us richly, even with eternal life.

---

## SHARING THE SCRIPTURE

### *Preparing Our Hearts*

Meditate on this week's devotional reading, found in 1 Timothy 6:3-10. Our session this week focuses on those who are at risk in the community. The passage from 1 Timothy has much to say about how people can be led from the truth by false teachers. It also speaks about the love of money, which has caused people to stray from the faith. As you read these verses from 1 Timothy, think about those things that tempt you to wander from your faith. What precautions do you need to take so as not to fall into the trap of temptation?

Pray that you and the adult learners will be aware of actions and attitudes that might cause people to fall away from the faith, and do all in your power to minimize these risks.

### *Preparing Our Minds*

Study the background, which is the entire book of Jude, and lesson scripture, verses 3-7, 19-25, which includes the key verses, 22-23. Think about what can be done to resolve problems created by a few people within a community.

Write on newsprint:
- ❏ information for next week's lesson, found under "Continue the Journey."
- ❏ activities for further spiritual growth in "Continue the Journey."

Plan the suggested lecture for "Unpack Jude's Message about Judgment on False Teachers."

Talk with your pastor during the week about ways in which the class could help inactive members return to church. Perhaps the pastor or membership secretary will be able to provide a list of names.

## LEADING THE CLASS

### (1) Gather to Learn

❖ Welcome the class members and introduce any guests.

❖ Pray that all who have come today will be open to the needs and concerns of other believers.

❖ Read this information to the class: **Whether Christians applaud his courage and stand by him or shun and threaten him, Bishop Gene Robinson is a lightning rod for conflict within the worldwide Anglican community. Since being elected as the first Episcopal bishop to profess openly that he is gay, Robinson has sparked such controversy that he was told in 2008 not to attend the Lambeth Conference, held once every ten years, where Anglican church policy and issues are discussed. He went there anyway, but was only able to witness outside the conference site. Despite death threats, Bishop Robinson intends to keep doing what he believes God has called him to do.**

❖ Talk with the class about ways in which the church can deal in a positive way with persons who for whatever reason cause turmoil and problems within the faith community.

❖ Read aloud today's focus statement: **Some people, for whatever reason, cause problems within their communities. What can be done to resolve community problems? Jude reminds readers to contend for the faith entrusted to them, and to hold tight to their belief in Jesus Christ.**

### (2) Unpack Jude's Message about Judgment on False Teachers

❖ Choose a volunteer to read Jude 3-7, 19-23 as the students follow along in their Bibles.

❖ Present a brief lecture, based on the Understanding the Scripture portion, to help the students understand Jude's purpose for writing, the concerns he raises, and the possibility that he may have been Jesus' brother, though this point is definitely not an established fact.

❖ Read "Contending for the Faith" from Interpreting the Scripture. Emphasize the three categories—perverting grace, denying the Lord, and ignoring judgment—that may be helpful in identifying threats to the Christian community today. Discuss the questions that accompany each of these three categories.

### (3) Discern Faithfully the Difference between False and True Teachings

❖ Note that much of the letter concerns false teachers who have "stolen in" (Jude 4) or "secretly slipped in" (Jude 4, NIV) and created problems among the believers because of their teachings. Also note that Jude gives numerous biblical examples to show how God deals with ungodly people. Ask: **What criteria do Christians use to determine whether a teaching is true or false?** (List these answers on newsprint. Recognize that answers may vary widely. Try to focus on criteria that most students can accept.)

❖ Invite the students to identify current teachings that they believe are false, or at least questionable. There may be honest disagreements among the students. Suggest that they think about these teachings in light of the criteria they have established. Here are two examples, with accompanying questions, which you may wish to read aloud:

■ **Prosperity gospel proponents teach that God wants believers to enjoy abundant success in every aspect of life, including finances. Hence, material goods are seen as an expression of God's favor on those who live authentic Christian lives.** (How does this theology square with Jesus' command to take up our cross, along with the notion of suffering for the sake of the gospel? How does it square with Jesus' concern for the poor?)

■ **Throughout church history various teachers have claimed to know when Jesus would return. These teachers would often attract a group who would sell their possessions and gather together to await the Lord's coming. So far, none of these teachers has proven to be correct.** (How do these teachings measure up against Jesus' statement in Matthew 24:36 that only God knows when that will be?)

*(4) Plan Ways to Express Mercy and to Reclaim Wavering or At-risk Believers to the Community*

❖ Suggest to the class that inactive members of the congregation may need to be encouraged to return. If you have a list of such people from your pastor (or membership secretary), read names and see if there are people in the class who would be willing to phone or visit at least one person or family. The purpose of this contact would be to let the inactive member know that he or she is missed, to listen to any concerns this person has, and to invite the individual to return. Encourage the callers to write notes about the conversation and to let the pastor know of their findings. There may be an illness or problem (at home or with the church) that the pastor needs to be aware of. Make clear that these calls are confidential, except for reporting to the pastor.

❖ Conclude this section by reading in unison the benediction found in Jude 24-25.

*(5) Continue the Journey*

❖ Pray that today's participants will go forth to help those who are struggling with

the faith to bring those who are at risk back into the fold.

❖ Read aloud this preparation for next week's lesson. You may also want to post it on newsprint for the students to copy.

■ **Title: Visible to God**
■ **Background Scripture: 1 Thessalonians 1**
■ **Lesson Scripture: 1 Thessalonians 1**
■ **Focus of the Lesson: People share many things through speech and action. What would be a positive witness in our world? For the Thessalonians, the example of their daily lives became a witness to the world, proclaiming their faith and their commitment to Jesus Christ.**

❖ Challenge the students to complete one or more of these activities for further spiritual growth, which you will write on newsprint for the students to copy.

(1) **Talk with someone you know who has left the church. Listen to the concerns this person raises. Do whatever you can to help this individual become reconciled to his or her congregation.**

(2) **List issues that you feel are causing controversy in the church today. Research at least two viewpoints on one particular issue. How do you evaluate both sides? Where do you stand?**

(3) **Identify the emotions that you experience when you consider the possibility of Christ's return in your lifetime. Why do you think you are experiencing hope, fear, or some other emotion?**

❖ Sing or read aloud "Go Forth for God."

❖ Conclude today's session by leading the class in this benediction adapted from Matthew 22:37, 39: **Go forth to love the Lord your God with all your heart, with all your soul, and with all your mind, and to love your neighbor as yourself.**

# FOURTH QUARTER
## Christian Commitment in Today's World

JUNE 6, 2010–AUGUST 29, 2010

During the summer quarter all of the lessons highlight the theme of commitment. The nature of commitment is the focus of the first unit, which features lessons from 1 Thessalonians. In the second unit we examine the foundation of Christian commitment as it is presented in 1 and 2 Thessalonians. The final unit, based on Philippians and Acts, will help us identify marks of commitment. As we look at Paul's teachings and record of his own experience, we will be able to glean ideas as to how we may live fully committed to Jesus Christ in the twenty-first century.

The four sessions in Unit 1, "The Nature of Christian Commitment," begin on June 6 with a lesson from 1 Thessalonians 1, "Visible to God," which concerns Christian witness in the world. On June 13 we turn to 1 Thessalonians 2 to explore motives for commitment in a lesson entitled "Pleasing to God." "Sustained through Encouragement," based on 1 Thessalonians 3 on June 20, examines how Christians support and encourage each other. The first unit closes on June 27 with a study of 1 Thessalonians 4:1-12 that spotlights commitment "Demonstrated in Action."

Unit 2, "The Foundation of Christian Commitment," begins on July 4 with a look at 1 Thessalonians 4:13–5:28 to help students find hope in "God's Cosmic Plan," which is foundational to commitment to Christ. The session for July 11, "Glory to Christ," based on 2 Thessalonians 1, helps believers find purpose in life while awaiting Christ's second coming. As people who are "Chosen and Called," Paul urges readers to stand firm in difficult circumstances, as explained in 2 Thessalonians 2 in the lesson for July 18. The unit ends on July 25 with a study of 2 Thessalonians 3, which explores how believers can find strength through "God's Own Faithfulness."

The five lessons in Unit 3, "The Marks of Christian Commitment," begin on August 1 with a careful look at Philippians 1, where those who are "Sharing God's Grace" can learn how to overcome the obstacles they face. The session for August 8 from Philippians 2:1–3:1a includes the familiar Christ Hymn, which challenges each reader to serve others by "Giving of Oneself" just as Jesus sacrificially offered up his life. Philippians 3:1b–4:1 is the background for the session on August 15, "Living into the Future," which teaches that Christ is the basis of the future in this life and the next. In the lesson for August 22 Paul writes in Philippians 4:2-14 about "Growing in Joy and Peace" as people bear one another's burdens, pray, comfort one another, and strengthen their commitment to Christ. The unit concludes on August 29 with an exploration of Acts 28 and Philippians 4:15-23, which stress that as believers are "Upheld by God" they are able to keep commitments, even as Paul did while he was in prison.

# MEET OUR WRITER

## THE REVEREND DR. DAVID A. deSILVA

David deSilva lives in Ashland, Ohio, where he serves as Trustees' Professor of New Testament and Greek at Ashland Theological Seminary and as music director and organist at Christ United Methodist Church. He is an ordained elder in the Florida Conference of the United Methodist Church, whose primary ministries are teaching, writing, music, and raising a family.

Dr. deSilva is the author of eleven books in the area of biblical studies, including *Seeing Things John's Way: The Rhetoric of Revelation* (Westminster John Knox, 2009), *4 Maccabees: An Introduction and Commentary* (Brill, 2006), *An Introduction to the New Testament: Context, Methods, and Ministry Formation* (InterVarsity, 2004), *Introducing the Apocrypha* (Baker, 2002), *New Testament Themes* (Chalice Press, 2001), *Honor, Patronage, Kinship, and Purity: Unlocking New Testament Culture* (InterVarsity, 2000), and *Perseverance in Gratitude: A Socio-rhetorical Commentary on the Epistle "to the Hebrews"* (Eerdmans, 2000). He has written several other books for devotional, small group, and retreat use, including *The Sacramental Life: Spiritual Formation Through the Book of Common Prayer* (Downers Grove: InterVarsity, 2008), *Praying with John Wesley* (Nashville: Discipleship Resources, 2001), and *Afterlife: Finding Hope in the Face of Death* (Nashville: Abingdon, 2003). He has also written or made video presentations for *Adult Bible Studies, Adult Bible Studies Teacher, DISCIPLE I & IV*, and, with Dr. Emerson Powery, *DISCIPLE Short Studies: Invitation to the New Testament* (Abingdon, 2007). He has contributed more than seventy articles to journals, collections of essays, Bible dictionaries, and Bible commentaries. This quarter marks his third contribution to *The New International Lesson Annual*.

David attended Princeton University, where he earned a Bachelor's degree in English, and then matriculated to Princeton Theological Seminary for the degree of Master of Divinity. In 1995, he was awarded a Ph.D. in Religion from Emory University in Atlanta. He is married to Donna Jean, his wife of nineteen years. Together they have three sons: James Adrian, John Austin, and Justin Alexander.

# THE BIG PICTURE: PAUL'S MISSION AND THE CITIES OF THESSALONICA AND PHILIPPI

Philippi received its name from Philip II of Macedon (the father of Alexander the Great), who took possession of the settlement in 356 B.C. The Philippi that Paul knew really took on its shape following the tumultuous civil war led by Marc Antony and Octavian (who would come to be known as the emperor Augustus) against Brutus and Cassius, the assassins of Julius Caesar. This war came to an end near Philippi in 42 B.C., and Philippi was chosen as the site for the settlement of the veterans of the victorious army. After Octavian defeated Antony near Actium in a second civil war (31 B.C.), Antony's soldiers were honorably located there, many of them having forfeited their claims to land in Italy. The city was strategically located on the north shore of the Aegean Sea, the smaller city of Neapolis serving, in effect, as Philippi's seaport.

Acts accurately describes Philippi as a Roman "colony" (Acts 16:12), as well as "a leading city" of Macedonia (though Thessalonica was the capital of this province). We should visualize a central city with a large amount of farmland surrounding it, the latter reflecting the original land grants to the veterans. At the time of Paul's visit, the population would have included the privileged descendants of these veterans, who became Roman citizens, Greeks (either descended from the inhabitants of the city before it was made a Roman colony, or attracted to the city for its commercial potential), and native Macedonians. The colony appears also to have had a sufficiently significant number of Jews at the time of Paul's visit to have a designated place for prayer. Josephus collects several decrees from the cities in the Eastern Mediterranean (for example, Halicarnassus and Sardis in *Antiquities* 14.10.23-24) that allow the Jews to construct prayer houses for their religious observances. In Halicarnassus, location by a river was important to the Jews, as also in Philippi (Acts 16:13).

Philippi was administered by Roman law, for a Roman colony was an extension of Rome itself. The citizens' identification of themselves as "Romans" (Acts 16:21) is a reflection of this pride in their political status. This provides important background to Paul's use of "political" language in this letter, calling the Christians there to remember that they are, first and foremost, a colony of the kingdom of God (Philippians 3:20). Paul may also be targeting this strong sense of political identity when he urges the Christians to display unity within their group (Philippians 2:1-4), civic unity being an essential component of conducting oneself appropriately in the body politic (*politeuesthai*, the verb used in Philippians 1:27).

Lying about one hundred miles west of Philippi along the Via Egnatia, the thriving commercial, port city of Thessalonica also enjoyed a long history before the advent of the Romans in 168 B.C. Perhaps because it was an important port city on the Aegean Sea, it was named the Roman capital of Macedonia in 146 B.C. It was not restructured as a Roman colony, however, so that more of its Greek identity survived into the Roman period than was true of Philippi. The city continued to be governed according to a Greek constitution, with a council comprised of local aristocrats and a gymnasium complex for the education of the young as well as the promotion of Greek culture, religion, and athletics. Like Philippi, Thessalonica had also supported Antony and Octavian against Brutus and Cassius in 42 B.C. The citizens especially revered Antony, although they quickly expressed their loyalty to Octavian after the defeat of Antony at Actium about ten years later.

Excavation has not yet yielded a clear picture of first-century Philippi comparable to the excavation of other cities, like Corinth. Archaeologists have found a Roman bath complex, a sanctuary dedicated to Dionysus in which women played a prominent role (both in terms of the priesthood and in terms of financial support), and a large theater that dates from the Greek period. They have also mapped out the forum (the administrative center of the colony) with its courtyard, council chamber, and temples, as well as a commercial center to the south side of the forum. Excavation of Thessalonica lags even further behind.

Paul claims that his Macedonian converts were famous throughout the region for having "turned to God from idols" (1 Thessalonians 1:8-10). Both Philippi and Thessalonica were cities full of idols from which to turn. Archaeology has also revealed a strong presence of the imperial cult in Philippi. There are inscriptions mentioning priests of the deified Julius, Augustus, and Claudius, and it is likely that the temples in the forum were dedicated to the emperors and Rome. In Thessalonica, inscriptions, carvings, and other archaeological finds also bear witness to the cult of Rome and her emperors, as well as shrines erected to honor other Roman benefactors. Coins minted at the turn of the era show the deified Julius on one side and Augustus on the reverse. An older temple was rededicated to the deified Augustus and his successors. The existence of an official called an *agonothete* suggests that athletic games or contests were held in the city in honor of the emperor on a regular basis. All of this adds up to a strong commitment to Roman imperial ideology in both of these cities.

The cult of the Roman emperors was not imposed upon the people by the emperors, but rather promoted locally in the eastern provinces of the empire as a means of showing loyalty and gratitude to the family of Augustus. The emperors were responsible for maintaining peace, which was a particularly valued commodity after the devastation of the civil wars that followed the assassination of Julius Caesar in 44 B.C. They were also the ultimate powers responsible for administering justice and for organizing relief in time of famine or other hardship. In short, they were considered to provide the kinds of benefits that were normally sought from the gods, with the result that showing them thanks in the form of worship was deemed entirely appropriate. The ideology of Rome as propagated through temples, statues, rites, coins, inscriptions, and literature expressed a hope that Rome would rule eternally in unbroken peace, with her emperors mediating the benefactions of the gods. In such a context, the Christian "good news" about a returning king who had been crucified as a revolutionary was not just a religious belief: it was a political claim.

Philippi also boasted cults of the traditional Greek pantheon (deities such as Zeus, Apollo, Dionysus, and Artemis), as well as cults imported from the East, like the Egyptian cult of Isis and Osiris or the Phrygian cult of the mother goddess Cybele. Such religious cults, all of which fall under the heading of "idolatry" as far as Paul is concerned, were important to the inhabitants of Philippi. Honoring the traditional gods secured their favor for the whole city's well-being. Engaging in the more exotic cults made for a more personal religious experience. The cult of Isis, for example, offered people a goddess who would protect them individually and also extend hope for their blessedness after death. The difference between these many cults and Christianity is that the former existed alongside other cults, but the latter would admit of no divinity except the One revealed through Jesus, which would become a major point of controversy between the Christian community and the world it left behind.

Evidence has also been uncovered in Thessalonica for the worship of the traditional Greco-Roman divinities (including the cult of Dionysus, which was prominent in this region), mystery cults like those of Isis, Osiris, and Sarapis, and the local cult of Kabiros. This last cult is a religious peculiarity of Macedonia and Thrace. As with most mystery religions, the details of the cult's beliefs and rituals are exceedingly difficult to discern with certainty, since we only have inscriptions, statues, and carvings as evidence rather than literary texts devoted to telling the myth or describing the worship. What seems to be clear is that Kabiros was a kingly figure murdered by his brothers but who lives on in the divine realm and whose return was expected by devotees. He served as an official patron deity for the city, and his favor was courted especially by craftspeople and merchants. The myth of Kabiros may have made the Christian mystery, which told of the death and expected return of another executed leader, seem less strange to the local population. It is interesting, however, that Kabiros would be the patron god of a Greek city, the preserver of the local order, while the message about Christ would be opposed as a revolutionary and dangerous one. It is probably the exclusivity of loyalty to this Christ and his Father, to the rejection of all the other gods celebrated within the civic order, that accounts for this difference in attitude: the kingdom of Christ, when it came, would leave no room for Roman imperialism or the cherished gods of the nations.

Acts gives detailed accounts of the initial evangelistic activity of Paul and his team in these cities (see Acts 16:6–17:1-10). Paul came into Macedonia during his second missionary journey, between A.D. 50 and 52. Philippi was the first Macedonian city evangelized by Paul and its church was the first planted on European soil. Acts 16:6-10 relates the dream vision of the Macedonian person, pleading with Paul to evangelize that region, and the way in which the Spirit pushed Paul's team in that direction. According to Acts, Paul began his ministry in Philippi by seeking out support in the Jewish community as a base for his ministry. He found this support in Lydia, who opened up her house to provide the emerging church with a place to meet for worship, prayer, teaching, and mutual encouragement. The initiative taken by Lydia also reminds us of the importance of women in the Philippian church (as elsewhere in Pauline circles). Two more such women will be named as Paul's co-workers in Philippians 4:2-3.

Paul's initial visit to this city ends in conflict, as locals charge Paul and Silas as Jews who were "advocating customs that are not lawful for us as Romans to adopt or observe" (Acts 16:21). This is not entirely untrue. Paul calls Gentiles everywhere to turn "to God from idols" (1 Thessalonians 1:9), which means abandoning traditional Greco-Roman piety and thus dishonoring the gods believed to ensure the well-being of the city and empire. These locals also played upon anti-Jewish sentiments. Jews enjoyed the status of "tolerated religion," but Roman officials were inclined to act against Jews who openly proselytized among Gentiles. Flogged and imprisoned without a trial, Paul turns his Roman citizenship, which ought to have protected him from such treatment, to advantage the next morning. He wins a public apology from the local magistrates and is escorted out of the city by them. While Paul may have left Philippi before he might have wished, he did not leave dishonored—something that would have been important for the church he left behind.

The Philippian church enjoyed a special place in Paul's ministry. Unlike other churches, Paul accepted money from the Philippian Christians in support of his ministry (Philippians 1:5; 4:10, 14-16, 18; 2 Corinthians 11:8-9). Despite their relative poverty, these Christians also contributed in an exemplary way to the collection Paul was taking up among his Gentile churches for the impoverished Christians in Jerusalem and Judea (2 Corinthians 8:1-4). Paul would visit the Philippians on at least two more occasions before his death. First Corinthians

16:5 and 2 Corinthians 1:16 refer to another visit to the Macedonian churches, and Acts 20:1-6 speaks of Paul's spending a Passover in Philippi just prior to his return to Jerusalem in A.D. 58. It is possible, though not certain, that Paul also visited the Philippian Christians after his imprisonment in Rome. There is a continuing witness to the health of the church in Philippi in Polycarp's letter to that community written in about A.D. 110. Paul's work in that city bore lasting fruit.

After leaving Philippi, Paul and Silas traveled westward along the Via Egnatia toward Thessalonica. Once again, initial outreach in the synagogue led to the formation of a fledgling group of believers in the house of Jason, a propertied convert, where the group could continue to be nurtured and to grow. First Thessalonians gives the impression of a primarily Gentile congregation (see especially 1 Thessalonians 1:9-10), but not necessarily exclusively so. Given the fact that he plied his trade while in the city to support himself (1 Thessalonians 2:9; 2 Thessalonians 3:7-9), and also received supplemental support from his friends in Philippi several times, he was no doubt active in the city for at least a few months (Philippians 4:16). The Christian group grew thanks to the hospitality of Jason and the leadership of Paul, until Paul was again forced to leave prematurely (1 Thessalonians 2:17). Paul departs Thessalonica for points west—Beroea, Athens, and eventually Corinth (Acts 17:10–18:17; 1 Thessalonians 2:17-3:6), where he would stay for eighteen months (Acts 18:11) and from whence he would write 1 Thessalonians.

Paul wrote 1 Thessalonians shortly after his departure from that city. After leaving under pressure himself, he was deeply concerned about the perseverance of his converts there, who had also fallen under the suspicion and hostility of their neighbors (1 Thessalonians 1:6; 3:1-5). Paul first sent Timothy back to Thessalonica to encourage the converts and find out how firm their faith had remained. Timothy returned with a positive report, as well as some questions the converts were asking (3:6). Paul's first letter responds further to the problem of the social pressure to abandon the faith and attempts to answer their concerns. The second letter continues to offer encouragement in the face of ongoing hostility and rejection by the believers' neighbors, clarification of expectations concerning the coming Day of the Lord, and instruction concerning the living of productive and respectable lives in the interim for the sake of the witness of the group.

Paul's letter to the church in Philippi comes from a later stage in the apostle's life, probably from the time of his detention in Rome in A.D. 60–62 (see Philippians 1:13; 4:22). These partners in ministry had sent Paul the gift of material support and encouragement through their emissary, Epaphroditus, and Paul writes to thank them for their friendship throughout his ministry. He also addresses two concerns that he had no doubt learned from Epaphroditus, namely the restoration of harmony in the congregation in the wake of a divisive quarrel between two leading figures in the church, and the strengthening of the congregation in the face of ongoing hostility toward the group kindled by its revolutionary message.

# Close-up:
# Cities of the New Testament

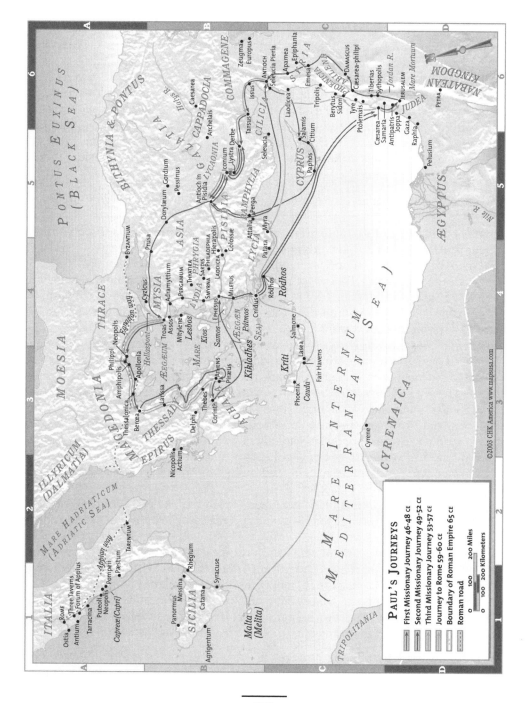

PONTUS EUXINUS
( BLACK SEA )

MOESIA

ILLYRICUM
(DALMATIA)

MARE HADRIATICUM
(ADRIATIC SEA)

ITALIA

Ostia • Rome
Antium • Three Taverns
Forum of Appius
Tarracina
Puteoli • Appian Way
Neapolis • Pompeii
Caprea (Capri) • Paestum
Panormus
Messina
Rhegium
SICILIA
Catana
Agrigentum
Syracuse
TARENTUM
Malta
(Melita)
TRIPOLITANIA

THRACE
BYZANTIUM
Egnatian Way
Philippi
Amphipolis • Neopolis
Apollonia
Thessalonica
Beroea
Larissa
MACEDONIA
THESSALY
EPIRUS
Nicopolis
Actium
Delphi
Thebes
Corinth • Athens
Cenchreae • Piraeus
ACHAIA

Prusa
Cyzicus
MYSIA
Adramyttium
Assos
Troas
Mitylene
Lesbos
PERGAMUM
THYATIRA
SMYRNA
SARDIS
Ephesus
Samos
Kios
EPHESUS
(AEGEAN SEA)
AEGEUM
MARE
Patmos
Kiklades
Krtti
Cnidus
Phoenix
Cauda
Lasea
Fair Havens
Salmone

HALYS R.
Dorylaeum • Cordium
Pessinus
Antioch in
Pisidia
PISIDIA
Iconium
Lystra • Derbe
PAMPHYLIA
Attalia • Perga
LYCIA
Patara • Myra
Rodhos
Ródhos

GALATIA
CAPPADOCIA
Caesarea
Archelais
LYCAONIA

Tarsus
CILICIA
Seleucia

CYPRUS
Salamis
Paphos • Citium

Zeugma
Europus
ANTIOCH
Seleucia Pieria
Apamea
Epiphania
Emesa
Laodicea
Tripolis
Berytus
Sidon
Tyre
Ptolemais
Caesarea
Samaria
Antipatris • Joppa
Gaza
Raphia
Pelusium

DAMASCUS
Caesarea-philippi
Tiberias
Scythopolis
Jordan R.
JERUSALEM
JUDEA
Mare Mortuum

COMMAGENE
SYRIA
ABILENE
PHOENICIA

NABATAEAN
KINGDOM
PETRA

AEGYPTUS
Nile R.

CYRENAICA
Cyrene

MARE INTERNUM
( MEDITERRANEAN SEA )

©2003 CHK America www.mapsusa.com

©2003 CHK America www.mapsusa.com

## PAUL'S JOURNEYS

First Missionary Journey 46-48 CE
Second Missionary Journey 49-52 CE
Third Missionary Journey 53-57 CE
Journey to Rome 59-60 CE
Boundary of Roman Empire 65 CE
Roman road

0      100      200 Miles
0    100   200 Kilometers

# FAITH IN ACTION: MAKING AND KEEPING COMMITMENTS

During this quarter we are exploring the nature, foundation, and marks of Christian commitment as seen in several New Testament communities and as practiced in today's church. To make these commitments even more personal, write the following questions on newsprint. Distribute paper and pencils, and invite the students to work alone to mull over or write answers. Provide time for the adults to work in groups to discern how they are making and keeping commitments, and what changes they feel called to make in light of their study of New Testament churches. If you do not have time to complete this activity in class, allow the students time to copy the questions and recommend that they consider them during the week ahead as part of their devotional time.

(1) What do you consider your top five priorities? List these in order of importance to you.

(2) What evidence (for example: time, money, emotional involvement) do you have to support your answers? List this evidence for each priority.

(3) Where do you see disconnects? In other words, you say that something is a high priority but you spend little time or money on that. Or, you indicate that something is a low priority but devote a lot to it. Do you need to make a greater investment of yourself here, or do you need to recognize that this priority is not as high—or as low—as you thought it was?

(4) In what ways do you live out your commitment to God? Where is this commitment ranked on your list of priorities? What does the amount of money you give to God (in relation to the money you have) say about your commitment? What does the time that you spend with God and on behalf of God in service to others say about the importance of your commitment? What might Jesus say to you about this commitment?

(5) How would you describe the level of your commitment to your community of faith?

(6) How do you make Christ visible to others, both inside and outside of the church?

(7) How much attention do you pay to the Holy Spirit? Are you committed to letting the Spirit enliven, encourage, sustain, and guide you? What examples can you give to support your answer?

(8) What kind of commitment have you made to God's creation? What daily choices do you make to help care for the earth and its creatures? Why is creation a priority for you—or is it?

(9) If you feel that your commitments and priorities are out of order, what changes will you make? Why are these changes important to you? What do you expect these changes to cost in terms of time, money, and investment of yourself?

(10) If your commitments are in keeping with God's will, Scripture teaches that you will feel joy and peace. Describe a scenario in which you found peace as a result of properly aligning your commitments.

Conclude this work by offering a prayer that God will continue to guide you to make commitments in keeping with who God calls you to be and what God expects you to do.

---

# UNIT 1: THE NATURE OF CHRISTIAN COMMITMENT
# VISIBLE TO GOD

---

## PREVIEWING THE LESSON

**Lesson Scripture:** 1 Thessalonians 1
**Background Scripture:** 1 Thessalonians 1
**Key Verse:** 1 Thessalonians 1:6

### Focus of the Lesson:

People share many things through speech and action. What would be a positive witness in our world? For the Thessalonians, the example of their daily lives became a witness to the world, proclaiming their faith and their commitment to Jesus Christ.

### Goals for the Learners:

(1) to recognize the faith of the Thessalonians as proclaimed by their lives.
(2) to evaluate their own Christian example.
(3) to proclaim their faith in God in positive ways.

### Pronunciation Guide:

Achaia (uh kay' yuh)
Cenchreae (sen' kruh ee)
*chairein* (khi' rain)
*charis* (khar' ece)

Macedonia (mas uh doh' nee uh)
*shalom* (shah lohm')
Silvanus (sil vay' nuhs)
Thessalonians (thes uh loh' nee uhns)

### Supplies:

Bibles, newsprint and marker, paper and pencils, hymnals

---

## READING THE SCRIPTURE

NRSV

1 Thessalonians 1

<sup>1</sup>Paul, Silvanus, and Timothy,

To the church of the Thessalonians in God the Father and the Lord Jesus Christ:

Grace to you and peace.

<sup>2</sup>We always give thanks to God for all of you and mention you in our prayers, constantly <sup>3</sup>remembering before our God and

NIV

1 Thessalonians 1

<sup>1</sup>Paul, Silas and Timothy,

To the church of the Thessalonians in God the Father and the Lord Jesus Christ:

Grace and peace to you.

<sup>2</sup>We always thank God for all of you, mentioning you in our prayers. <sup>3</sup>We continually remember before our God and Father

Father your work of faith and labor of love and steadfastness of hope in our Lord Jesus Christ. [4]For we know, brothers and sisters beloved by God, that he has chosen you, [5]because our message of the gospel came to you not in word only, but also in power and in the Holy Spirit and with full conviction; just as you know what kind of persons we proved to be among you for your sake. [6]And you became imitators of us and of the Lord, for in spite of persecution **you received the word with joy inspired by the Holy Spirit,** [7]so that you became an example to all the believers in Macedonia and in Achaia. [8]For the word of the Lord has sounded forth from you not only in Macedonia and Achaia, but in every place your faith in God has become known, so that we have no need to speak about it. [9]For the people of those regions report about us what kind of welcome we had among you, and how you turned to God from idols, to serve a living and true God, [10]and to wait for his Son from heaven, whom he raised from the dead—Jesus, who rescues us from the wrath that is coming.

your work produced by faith, your labor prompted by love, and your endurance inspired by hope in our Lord Jesus Christ.

[4]For we know, brothers loved by God, that he has chosen you, [5]because our gospel came to you not simply with words, but also with power, with the Holy Spirit and with deep conviction. You know how we lived among you for your sake. [6]You became imitators of us and of the Lord; in spite of severe suffering, **you welcomed the message with the joy given by the Holy Spirit.** [7]And so you became a model to all the believers in Macedonia and Achaia. [8]The Lord's message rang out from you not only in Macedonia and Achaia—your faith in God has become known everywhere. Therefore we do not need to say anything about it, [9]for they themselves report what kind of reception you gave us. They tell how you turned to God from idols to serve the living and true God, [10]and to wait for his Son from heaven, whom he raised from the dead—Jesus, who rescues us from the coming wrath.

---

## UNDERSTANDING THE SCRIPTURE

**1 Thessalonians 1:1.** Letters in the ancient world tended to begin with a salutation ("X to Y, Greetings"), followed by a thanksgiving or a "wish prayer" concerning the recipient, the letter body (disclosing its main purpose), and a brief closing expressing a wish for the recipient's well being. Paul followed this basic format but modifies the standard "Greeting" (*chairein*) to "Grace (*charis*) and peace to you," a clever and potent reminder to the hearers that they have left behind the world of "business-as-usual" and entered the sphere of God's favor and calling to wholeness, *shalom*. Silvanus (Silas, in Acts) and Timothy were both important co-workers of Paul, and

their presence in the salutation reminds us that Paul was not a maverick missionary but almost always worked as part of a larger missionary team as he planted churches all across the northeastern Mediterranean.

**1 Thessalonians 1:2-3.** Paul continues to follow the form of ancient letters by expressing a thanksgiving and mention of prayer on behalf of the recipients, although Paul's thanksgiving is richer and more elaborate than the perfunctory expressions common to ancient letters. Giving thanks to God for what the Thessalonians have done and continue to do is a strategic way of informing the believers that their choices and commitments, though opposed by their neighbors, have positive value in the sight of God. Paul speaks of their investment of their resources in the Christian venture (their "work of faith and labor of love," 1:3) and their commitment to persevere rather than cave in to outside pressure (their "steadfastness of hope," 1:3) as, in effect, the working out of God's desire for the group. Hence thanks are due to God as the source of their conversion and their ongoing commitment. By reminding the believers that God is indeed the source and sustainer of this spiritual journey, Paul helps confirm them in the conviction that, despite their neighbors' attempts to dissuade them from their faith, they have made exactly the right decisions by responding positively to the gospel.

**1 Thessalonians 1:4-5.** God's approval of the believers continues to be an important theme as Paul elaborates on this thanksgiving. The Thessalonian converts are where they are precisely because God has "chosen" them—selected them from among their neighbors for a very special privilege. That privilege is expressed in this letter mainly as deliverance "from the wrath that is coming" (1:10; see also 3:13; 5:9, 23), that is, from the pouring out of God's judgment upon a disobedient world and as entrance into God's kingdom and honor (2:12). Because of the firm expectation of the Day of Judgment, God's approval will be valued more heavily by the believers than their neighbors' disapproval. Paul often draws attention to the converts' experience of the Holy Spirit as an essential element of their coming to faith: they were not persuaded merely by clever words but by an encounter with God's own Self (see also 1 Corinthians 2:1-5; Galatians 3:1-5). Also important in this regard was the missionaries' own character and example, which withstood moral scrutiny, inspired trust, and manifested genuine, nurturing love (see further 1 Thessalonians 2:1-12).

**1 Thessalonians 1:6-8.** Paul and his team taught the Christian way of life by example as well as in speech, and their own example sought to reflect the example of Jesus. Ultimately, imitation of Jesus in his self-giving, other-centered, obedient attitude was the way to please God and to share in Jesus' resurrected life (Philippians 3:8-11), and it was this that Paul kept trying to inculcate among his converts (2:5-11).

Paul speaks of the "persecution" and "suffering" endured by his converts (1 Thessalonians 1:6; 2:14; 3:3-4). Martyrdom was quite common in the first century, though we find throughout the New Testament reference to the unofficial persecution of the Christian group. Their neighbors used insults, reproaches, physical affronts, manipulation of the law courts in suits, and economic boycott of the offenders' businesses to pressure the Christians to turn back from what the persecutors considered a deviant way of life and show themselves once more to be good citizens of the Greco-Roman world (see, for example, Hebrews 10:32-34; 1 Peter 4:3-4; Matthew 10:24-25; Luke 6:22). Paul's first challenge in addressing the fledgling church is to insulate the believers from the pressure, censure, and hostility they face as a result of their conversion. He must assure them that, despite all appearances, they are actually in a position of honor, privilege, and favor where God is concerned.

We find one such assurance here as Paul highlights what their conversion did for their fame beyond their city (1 Thessalonians 1:7-10). While the Thessalonian Christians' rejection of idols and commitment to Jesus may have cost them the respect and approval of their non-Christian neighbors, they have gained a positive reputation throughout the Christian circles of Macedonia and the newly founded churches in Achaia (Corinth and Cenchreae in Southern Greece), so that even as Paul spread the gospel he encountered people who had already heard about their conversion and their courage in the face of opposition. Paul informs them that they are even held up as exemplary in other Christian churches! The whole section thus takes on the tone of a congratulatory letter, as Paul seeks to encourage the believers, showing them that any loss of local reputation is compensated for many times over in the international fame and respect they have acquired.

**1 Thessalonians 1:9-10.** Why would their neighbors respond to their conversion with hostility? The answer can be found in the two components of the Thessalonians' conversion recalled in 1:9-10. First, in turning "from idols," the Gentile converts left behind all traditional expressions of piety, of loyalty and gratitude toward the gods and the emperor upon whose collective favor the well-being of the city depended, and of solidarity with their neighbors. To avoid all idolatry was to withdraw from most civic festivals and even social engage-ments, since "pagans" were scrupulous to acknowledge the gods at virtually every gathering. Second, in looking for the return of Jesus, the Christians were acknowledging the leadership of one who had been executed as an enemy of the state: his return would have been viewed by outsiders as a threat to the Roman peace. Most of the Christians' neighbors found security in the belief that Rome would rule forever and thus maintain peace. Christians would look suspiciously like revolutionaries who anticipated the downfall of Rome. Nevertheless, Paul reminds the believers that they have indeed set out on the wise and advantageous course, for it is the course that leads to experiencing Jesus' deliverance when God pours out God's wrath upon a rebellious and idolatrous world.

---

# INTERPRETING THE SCRIPTURE

### A Pastor's Perspective

First Thessalonians will give us several windows into Paul as "pastor" (alongside his larger pastoral team) of the congregations he founds, even after he has left them behind. A striking feature of the churches in both Thessalonica and in Philippi is their positive influence on Paul as their pastor. The church in Thessalonica is a source of great encouragement to Paul. When he spends time in prayer and calls them to mind, his heart is filled with delight and he is compelled to give God thanks for the fruit Paul's work among them has borne as God has tended and nourished what Paul planted. Later in the letter, we read how Timothy's report about what has transpired since Paul left the city under duress has brought encouragement to Paul's heart and reduced his pastoral anxiety (3:6-10). This appears to have had a renewing effect on Paul's own energy and vision for the work in which he is engaged.

Burnout is epidemic in the pastoral profession. Paul himself could easily have succumbed to such burnout, given the stressful circumstances of his life—always moving to new, unfamiliar surroundings, always putting himself out on public display for the sake of preaching the gospel, opening himself up to criticism, contradiction, and, all too often, verbal and physical assault. But the change he could observe in the lives of his congregations, the works of love and faithfulness he saw emerging among them and from them, all assured him that his labors and sacrifices were not in vain.

If pastors are to thrive in the work of ministry, they too need to see that their work is not in vain. If your pastors were to write a letter about how they remember you before God in prayer, about the emotional and spiritual effects your response to their ministry of the gospel has on them, what would they say? Are you a source of encouragement, an assurance of the effectiveness of their ministry?

## Exemplary Faith

The theme of following and becoming "examples" dominates the opening of this letter. At the core is the example of Jesus, about which Paul will have more to say in Philippians 2:1-11. As missionaries, Paul and his team sought to embody visibly that example, embracing hardship for the sake of obedience to God and as a witness to the value of God's promises; laying aside their rights, for example, to living off the support of the community, so that they could offer the gospel as a gift; assuming the more humble and nurturing role of nurses to the "babes" in Christ rather than exercising their authority with demands. The believers shaped their own lives after Paul's team's example, as it was customary not only to obey the words of a teacher but also to imitate his or her example. In turn, other believers in Macedonia and the neighboring province of Achaia who had heard of their faithfulness in the face of opposition and their commitment to works of love sought to imitate their praiseworthy, Christ-like virtues.

Paul holds together the two important themes of being "chosen" by God and falling in line with this imitative process of becoming like Christ and, to the extent that we do, becoming an edifying "example" to other Christians. In Romans, he will say more explicitly that God chose us to shape us after the image of God's Son (Romans 8:28-29). As in Paul's own case, embodying Christ's example allows other disciples to see and follow this example, thus being encouraged forward in their own process of becoming more like Jesus.

Asking ourselves in what ways, and to what extent, we embody Christ-likeness is a consistently useful self-examination exercise. To the extent that our speech and deeds reflect self-centered interests or the temporal pursuits and distractions of our society, we run the risk not only of our own spiritual harm but also of offering bad examples to our fellow believers. They may be discour-aged in their own walk—or at least not sufficiently emboldened to fuller discipleship—by what they observe in us. A well-known variation of this exercise is to ask consistently, "What would Jesus do?" Being able to answer this requires a deep familiarity with what Jesus actually did and the heart those deeds and words made visible to others.

Aspects of the disciples' example that Paul specifically elevates are their renunciation of idols, their commitment to serve the One God, and their setting their eyes on Jesus' return. They have become a stunning example of withdrawing their hope from empire and placing it fully in God. They no longer look to the domination systems of Roman politics, military power, and economics for their own peace and well-being, but to the love, light, and hope announced in the gospel. Here, too, is a healthful place for self-examination. How fully have we withdrawn our hope from the idols of nationalism, wealth, and power, to serve instead the God of all peoples who calls us to sharing and to service?

## Encouragement in Persecution

First Thessalonians, together with Timothy's visit, represents a kind of paradigm of "triage" first aid for disciples facing hostility and even persecution on account of their Christian commitments. The nature of Paul's team's response suggests several emotional and spiritual needs on the part of people who encounter serious opposition for their beliefs and commitments to an unpopular cause. One need is to know that God is still "in" what they are experiencing, that their experience of opposition is not a sign that they have stepped "out of line" with God's will. Another need is to know that they are not alone. Timothy's visit and Paul's letter were important reminders to them that they had not been abandoned in their trials. Paul thought it important also to communicate to them that others were watching their contest with admiration, thus affirming the positive value of the resistance and perseverance they were exhibiting. This is an important counterbalance to the message they were getting from their non-Christian neighbors.

Many more Christians are being persecuted globally by their neighbors for their commitment to Jesus than was the case even in the second century. Several organizations exist to help us become familiar with the situation of Christians in restricted nations and their needs. Christians who enjoy freedom from such persecution are in a strong position to extend the kinds of encouragement that Paul and his team offered to their friends in Thessalonica, and that Christians increasingly offered one another throughout the churches during the first centuries. This response could include at least prayer on behalf of our persecuted brothers and sisters, raising awareness in our influential Western nations about the plight of these Christians, and participating in relief efforts coordinated through denominational and independent agencies. The opportunity might occasionally arise to be in contact with such Christians (for example, in their travels or ours), affording the possibility of bringing encouragement directly to them, taking their stories back with us, and affirming for them the power of their example.

---

## SHARING THE SCRIPTURE

### Preparing Our Hearts

Meditate on this week's devotional reading, found in Titus 2:11-15. Here the writer, traditionally thought to be Paul, encourages Titus to tell the people to live exemplary lives. To be a good example, one must be "self-controlled, upright, and godly" (2:12) and also "zealous for good deeds" (2:14). Examine your own life. Do these words describe you? Can you think of specific examples to show that you are self-controlled, upright, and so on? If not, what changes do you need to make? Be aware of people for whom you have become an example of Christian living. What kind of example are you setting?

Pray that you and the adult learners will bear witness by your words and deeds to the living God who is made visible through you.

### Preparing Our Minds

Study the background and lesson scripture, both of which comprise chapter 1 of 1 Thessalonians. Think about what would constitute a positive witness in today's world.

Write on newsprint:
- ❑ questions for "Proclaim Faith in God in Positive Ways."
- ❑ information for next week's lesson, found under "Continue the Journey."
- ❑ activities for further spiritual growth in "Continue the Journey."

Read the introduction, "The Big Picture," "Close-up," and "Faith in Action" articles for this quarter, all of which immediately precede this lesson. Note that cities and areas mentioned in "The Big Picture" and lessons are found on the map in "Close-up."

Decide how you will use the information from these supplemental resources as you lead this quarter's sessions. You may want to substitute "Faith in Action" for an activity in a lesson of your choice.

### LEADING THE CLASS

#### (1) Gather to Learn

❖ Welcome the class members and introduce any guests.

❖ Pray that all who have come today will see Jesus in the life of each student.

❖ Call on volunteers to tell stories of people who have been a positive example for them. These people may be family members, coaches, teachers, mentors, or anyone else who has had an influence on at least some segment of their lives. What was it about this person that made him or her an unforgettable example?

❖ Summarize the stories by inviting the students to note common themes among the people who have been discussed. Are there certain behaviors and attitudes that are more likely to have a positive influence? If so, what are they? How do these behaviors and attitudes relate to life in Christ?

❖ Read aloud today's focus statement: **People share many things through speech and action. What would be a positive witness in our world? For the Thessalonians, the example of their daily lives became a witness to the world, proclaiming their faith and their commitment to Jesus Christ.**

*(2) Recognize the Faith of the Thessalonians as Proclaimed by Their Lives*

❖ Use information for 1 Thessalonians 1:1 in Understanding the Scripture to introduce Paul's letter.

❖ Read or retell "A Pastor's Perspective" from Interpreting the Scripture to enable the adults to better understand where Paul is coming from as he writes.

❖ Select a volunteer to read all ten verses of 1 Thessalonians 1.

❖ Ask these questions:
  **(1) Why does Paul give thanks for the people of the church at Thessalonica?**
  **(2) What specific characteristics did these people possess that made them such good role models?**
  **(3) Why was the congregation at Thessalonica so well-known among other Christian communities?**

❖ Use any information from Understanding the Scripture that you feel would be helpful to the class in becoming better acquainted with this church and Paul's admiration for its members.

❖ Read in unison today's key verse, this portion of 1 Thessalonians 1:6: **You received the word with joy inspired by the Holy Spirit.**

❖ Discuss these questions:
  **(1) If Paul were to visit our congregation today, what evidence would he have that we are joyful, Spirit-filled Christians?**
  **(2) What do you think he would say to us concerning how our lives proclaim our faith?**

*(3) Evaluate the Learners' Christian Example*

❖ Read "Exemplary Faith" from Interpreting the Scripture.

❖ Invite the students to be in an attitude of listening for God as you lead them in this guided imagery. Encourage them to relax and close their eyes.

  ■ **Imagine that you are in a quiet, secluded garden. Feel the sunshine warming your body. Hear the birds singing, and smell the fragrant blossoms.** (pause)
  ■ **In the midst of your quiet time, Jesus appears and takes a seat next to you on the bench. He challenges you with these words: to what extent do you think you really embody who I am? You pause for a few moments, struggling to find a suitable answer.** (pause)
  ■ **Hear yourself answer Jesus.** (pause)
  ■ **Listen as he responds to you. Does he commend you, take you to task, or challenge you to do better?** (pause)
  ■ **Open your eyes when you are ready.**

❖ Provide a few moments for the students to comment on any ideas that surprised or challenged them as they participated in this activity.

*4) Proclaim Faith in God in Positive Ways*

❖ Distribute paper and pencils. Tell the students that what they will be asked to do is confidential, so to be honest. Give the students a time limit (perhaps one minute) to write down every word they can think of to describe themselves. Use positive and negative words.

❖ Call time. Encourage the students to review their lists and then write a short paragraph in response to these questions, which you may want to write on newsprint:

　(1) **Suppose you were someone else reading this list. What impression would you have of the person who has your traits?**

　(2) **How might an onlooker rate the one who has your traits as a Christian witness?**

❖ Wrap up this portion of the session by challenging the class members to continue to view themselves through the eyes of other people, be aware of the witness they are proclaiming, and make adjustments as needed.

*(5) Continue the Journey*

❖ Pray that today's participants will go forth to proclaim Jesus Christ, the Son of God, through their words and deeds.

❖ Read aloud this preparation for next week's lesson. You may also want to post it on newsprint for the students to copy.

　■ **Title: Pleasing to God**
　■ **Background Scripture: 1 Thessalonians 2**

■ **Lesson Scripture: 1 Thessalonians 2:1-12**
■ **Focus of the Lesson: Many people shape their lives around significant goals to which they are committed. What should be the single, overall goal that shapes our life? Paul implies that all we do should grow out of an earnest commitment to please God.**

❖ Challenge the students to complete one or more of these activities for further spiritual growth, which you will write on newsprint for the students to copy.

　(1) **Let someone know how much his or her example has meant to you as you continue to grow in faith.**

　(2) **Watch yourself this week for any sign that you are losing self-control or acting in an ungodly way. Remember that others are watching you, and do whatever you can, with God's help, to change your behavior.**

　(3) **Pray that your congregation is able to make God visible to believers and those who do not yet know Christ.**

❖ Sing or read aloud "Lord, Speak to Me."

❖ Conclude today's session by leading the class in this benediction adapted from 2 Thessalonians 1:11: **Go forth with the assurance that we are always praying for you, asking that our God will make you worthy of his call and will fulfill by his power every good resolve and work of faith.**

## UNIT 1: THE NATURE OF CHRISTIAN COMMITMENT
# PLEASING TO GOD

---

### PREVIEWING THE LESSON

**Lesson Scripture:** 1 Thessalonians 2:1-12
**Background Scripture:** 1 Thessalonians 2
**Key Verse:** 1 Thessalonians 2:4

### Focus of the Lesson:
Many people shape their lives around significant goals to which they are committed. What should be the single, overall goal that shapes our life? Paul implies that all we do should grow out of an earnest commitment to please God.

### Goals for the Learners:
(1) to explore Paul's words about earnest commitment.
(2) to realize what it means to be earnestly committed to God.
(3) to make an earnest commitment to God a goal for life.

### Pronunciation Guide:
*euangelion* (yoo ang ghel' ee on)
Lystra (lis' truh)
Philippi (fi lip' i) or (fil' i pi)

### Supplies:
Bibles, newsprint and marker, paper and pencils, hymnals

---

### READING THE SCRIPTURE

NRSV
1 Thessalonians 2:1-12

[1]You yourselves know, brothers and sisters, that our coming to you was not in vain, [2]but though we had already suffered and been shamefully mistreated at Philippi, as you know, we had courage in our God to declare to you the gospel of God in spite of great opposition. [3]For our appeal does not spring from deceit or impure motives or

NIV
1 Thessalonians 2:1-12

[1]You know, brothers, that our visit to you was not a failure. [2]We had previously suffered and been insulted in Philippi, as you know, but with the help of our God we dared to tell you his gospel in spite of strong opposition. [3]For the appeal we make does not spring from error or impure motives, nor are we trying to trick you.

trickery, **⁴but just as we have been approved by God to be entrusted with the message of the gospel, even so we speak, not to please mortals, but to please God who tests our hearts.** ⁵As you know and as God is our witness, we never came with words of flattery or with a pretext for greed; ⁶nor did we seek praise from mortals, whether from you or from others, ⁷though we might have made demands as apostles of Christ. But we were gentle among you, like a nurse tenderly caring for her own children. ⁸So deeply do we care for you that we are determined to share with you not only the gospel of God but also our own selves, because you have become very dear to us.

⁹You remember our labor and toil, brothers and sisters; we worked night and day, so that we might not burden any of you while we proclaimed to you the gospel of God. ¹⁰You are witnesses, and God also, how pure, upright, and blameless our conduct was toward you believers. ¹¹As you know, we dealt with each one of you like a father with his children, ¹²urging and encouraging you and pleading that you lead a life worthy of God, who calls you into his own kingdom and glory.

**⁴On the contrary, we speak as men approved by God to be entrusted with the gospel. We are not trying to please men but God, who tests our hearts.** ⁵You know we never used flattery, nor did we put on a mask to cover up greed—God is our witness. ⁶We were not looking for praise from men, not from you or anyone else.

As apostles of Christ we could have been a burden to you, ⁷but we were gentle among you, like a mother caring for her little children. ⁸We loved you so much that we were delighted to share with you not only the gospel of God but our lives as well, because you had become so dear to us. ⁹Surely you remember, brothers, our toil and hardship; we worked night and day in order not to be a burden to anyone while we preached the gospel of God to you.

¹⁰You are witnesses, and so is God, of how holy, righteous and blameless we were among you who believed. ¹¹For you know that we dealt with each of you as a father deals with his own children, ¹²encouraging, comforting and urging you to live lives worthy of God, who calls you into his kingdom and glory.

---

## UNDERSTANDING THE SCRIPTURE

**Introduction.** In the introduction to this letter, Paul refers to the Thessalonian Christians' awareness concerning "what kind of persons we proved to be" (1:5), a topic he now takes up at length. It is possible that Paul responds to attacks on his character, most likely from the non-Christians in Thessalonica who might seek to erode the believers' commitment in part by trying to paint Paul as a cowardly charlatan like so many other peddlers of philosophies who had duped the converts for personal gain. However, it would be advantageous for him to remind the converts of his team's integrity and virtue for a number of reasons apart from responding to mudslinging, not least of which would be to reassure them of the confidence they could have in their teachers, and thus in the sincerity of the message they have received.

Since imitation of Paul and his co-workers was an important element of learning Christian discipleship (see 1 Thessalonians 1:6; 2 Thessalonians 3:7-9; 1 Corinthians 4:16; 11:1; Philippians 3:17), it would also be relevant to develop that pattern more fully by way of reminder. Paul's discussion of his own conduct reminds the converts of his moral example, which reinforces several more direct exhortations in the letter.

**1 Thessalonians 2:1-2.** Paul specifically recalls his ongoing commitment to preach the gospel as he had done in Thessalonica, despite the sufferings he and his team had just endured at Philippi (2:2), as proof of his courage and his sincerity. If he were engaged in preaching for personal gain, he would have given up this course of action long ago on account of the hardships it entailed.

It is tempting to think of "the gospel of God" (2:2) as simply a religious topic, but in the first century it would have had strong political resonances. The Greek word *euangelion* ("good news," "gospel") was used by non-Christians to speak of the significance of the birth of Augustus or the accession of the emperor Vespasian. In other words, the "gospel of God" had the overtones of the beneficent act of a world ruler on behalf of the people under that ruler. Paul announced a call to radical allegiance to this ruler, who "calls [people] into his own kingdom" (2:12) and offers pardon to those who now respond with loyal obedience (1:10).

**1 Thessalonians 2:3-4.** In all his actions, Paul seeks to please God rather than acquire the approval of mortals (2:4, 6). For many, peddling philosophy was a means by which to increase one's reputation, one's positive fame or honor. Only those who were free from such concern, however, could be either a true philosopher or a true Christian—especially when naming Jesus as Lord brings one into disrepute with most human beings. Paul is especially zealous to have his converts follow his example in this regard, calling their attention already to the One who looks on their hearts and actions (1:3), and whose approval counts for all eternity.

**1 Thessalonians 2:5-12.** Paul especially highlights his commitment to support himself as proof of his sincerity. Far from making money off the gospel, he believed so strongly in the message that he spent his own earnings to make it available (2:5, 9)!

He will also urge the believers to continue to work to support themselves and so that they might have means of relieving those in need (4:11-12; 5:14-15; see also 2 Thessalonians 3:7-13).

He recalls with highly personal language the emotional bonds and gentle, nurturing relationships that he formed with the believers, using the images of nurse and father (2:7-8, 11-12). Rekindling warm and loving feelings among his recipients and touching their hearts in this letter is another important way in which he reminds them that what they have gained in the church compensates them for what they have lost in the world. But Paul hopes his converts will also embody this quality toward one another, pouring themselves sacrificially into their "labor of love" for one another (1:3) so as to keep each one running forward toward the goal (see 3:12; 4:9-10; 5:11, 14-15).

Finally, Paul presents himself as an example of not allowing temporal desires like the desire for money, fame, or influence over others to distract one from the one important ambition of being found "worthy of God" (2:12) and being granted entrance into God's kingdom. This example intersects with the Thessalonian converts at the point of reputation (since concern for honor would lead them away from the group) and at the point of sexual purity (4:1-8). Greed and desire for power in the church also remain potent threats to completing the Christian race well in other first-century churches (see Philippians 2:1-4; 4:2-3; 1 Timothy 6:9-10; Titus 1:11).

**1 Thessalonians 2:13-16.** "Imitation," or falling in line with a pattern, again emerges as an important theme. Here, the emphasis falls on the pattern of the world's hostile response to those who respond faithfully to God, a pattern that establishes a new definition of "normal." Jesus' obedience to God brought him into conflict with, and rejection by, the authorities. The same fate befell the Jewish Christian community in Judea at the hands of non-Christian Jews. The same fate befalls Paul at nearly every turn as he preaches the coming kingdom of the crucified king. He now helps his converts see that what has befallen them since his departure from the city is not something unexpected that should cause them to question the choices they have made. Persecution is rather the "norm" for those who do what is virtuous and right in God's sight, and who seek God's approval for eternity rather than the approval of an impious world.

Paul's harsh words in 2:15-16, admittedly a far cry from his more sympathetic words in Romans 9:1-5, serve an important purpose. They remind the audience that those who oppose the progress of the gospel are the ones who displease God and who call down upon themselves God's judgment. Their hostile Gentile neighbors are hurting themselves more than the converts by their opposition since, like those who harass the churches in Judea, they will find themselves encountering God as Judge and Avenger (see also 5:3).

**1 Thessalonians 2:17-20.** In this section (which extends through 3:13), Paul comes to his chief pastoral concern, namely ensuring that "no one would be shaken by these persecutions" (3:3). Paul wants to assure the converts that he has not abandoned them, that he is as bereft as they are in the interim, and that he will come again in person as soon as possible to personally encourage them in the faith.

---

## INTERPRETING THE SCRIPTURE

### The Right Motives

If Paul is a model for imitation by believers, he is first and foremost here a model of evangelism. Evangelism means sharing the "good news of God," inviting other people to hear and respond to God's call to come "into his own kingdom and glory" (2:12). When I think of evangelism, the first images that come to my mind are of charismatic speakers surrounded by a stadium full of people—or nearly possessed speakers standing on street corners in major cities. I am not personally comfortable with imitating either pattern. But there is no one pattern for evangelism, and Paul himself probably combined several different models. The author of Acts shows Paul announcing the good news about God's call in Christ both in "religious" settings like the synagogue and in "public" settings like downtown Lystra or Mars Hill in Athens. But surely he did not cease to be an evangelist when he was busy at his trade, or when engaged in conversations with individuals or smaller groups.

Following Paul's example, we are all called to participate in evangelism, but not all in the same way. In 1 Thessalonians 2:1-12, Paul provides some universal guidance in regard to motives and manner, but not method, which can be left to individual gifting.

In regard to motive, he is unambiguous. He studiously purged himself of any self-centered motive when telling others about the gospel. Perhaps, in imitation of Paul, we should expand this to include purging ourselves of any "church-centered" motive for engaging in evangelism. That is to say, the goal or underlying motive for sharing the good news is not to swell our own church's membership, to deal with declining budgets through tapping fresh markets, or even to affirm ourselves as a growing church. The goal is to connect people with their God and Savior and to put them on the road to transformation by the Spirit—whether that would be best served through their participation in our own church or in another congregation. Our passion needs to be for the spiritual rebirth and renewal of the people to whom we go with the good news, not for reversing congregational decline.

Paul proved his other-centered motivation by working as a craftsperson to support himself, insofar as possible (he did receive support from his friends in Philippi while he evangelized Thessalonica), rather than opening himself up to the charge of fleecing the locals like so many other peddlers of philosophies. How can you and your local congregation engage evangelism in a way that similarly protects the purity of your motivations? One church did this by making it a policy not to ask visitors and newcomers to pledge during the first year of their involvement. Another group of churches manifested the same spirit by carrying out cooperative evangelistic and outreach efforts, demonstrating thus their unity and their sincerity—building God's kingdom rather than their own fiefdoms.

### The Right Manner

Paul distinguished himself from some other kinds of open-air philosophers in his day. Promoters of Cynicism, for example, had a distinctly "edgy" style. They were known for *openly* and brazenly challenging members of their audience and potential disciples for their manner of life, or their accommodation to the superfluous fashion, or their valuing of reputation and wealth. Rather than adopt a harsh, confrontational mode, Paul sought to bring the Thessalonians into Christian faith and practice by adopting a gentle, nurturing attitude toward them. He compares himself both to a nurse, a woman entrusted with the care of another's infant or toddler, and to a father, the traditional source of admonition and counsel in many Mediterranean wisdom traditions.

Paul and his team committed themselves to exhorting, encouraging, motivating, and shaping the converts. The process was far from impersonal. It was not just a matter of gaining assent to information or convincing someone to attend services. It involved an intimate sharing of life and self with those who were starting out on the path of discipleship. It required all the commitment of time, attention, and energy that goes into a close friendship, even into parenting.

The members of a growing congregation will have the same heart. Individuals who are more mature in their faith will take responsibility for the nurture of "younger" disciples. All will take seriously their calling to share with those outside the church what they have found in God and in the community of faith. All will look upon their investment of time, attention, and energy into the gentle nurture of new believers and growing believers as their best use of the same as members of one family in God.

### People-pleasers and God-pleasers

Many people like to please other people. They find safety in doing what is expected of them, and self-worth in the affirmation and approval they feel when others are "pleased" with them. Now, desiring to please others is not all bad. But it does present us with some very real dangers. If we are focused on other people's expectations, we may neglect God's expectations. If we seek affirmation and approval, we lose the freedom to follow God and conscience in our relationships, whether at home, at work, or in the sphere of public duty. We may fail to speak a word on God's behalf, or challenge a destructive behavior, or provide prophetic leadership.

If Paul were a "people-pleaser," his experiences of disapproval in Philippi (2:2) would have led him to cease his evangelistic efforts—if he had not done so long before! If he did attempt to preach the Christian message, he would have played to the expectations of his hearers rather than challenging those expectations and the value systems on which they were based. It is clear that Paul worked through these issues and decided that he would not be a people-pleaser, but a God-pleaser (1 Thessalonians 2:4, 6; Galatians 1:10).

Are there ways in which the desire to please others has held you back from doing as God desires, or walking in line with Jesus' or Paul's example? As I reflect on my own discomfort with evangelism, I realize that a lot of it stems from a "people-pleasing" mentality: the fear of what people will think of me, how I will come across, what social consequences might follow my attempts to share the gospel (or, at the very least, invite people to come where they will hear the gospel, for example, to accompany us to church). Paul's example challenges us to speak and to act with a view to advancing God's desires for others.

## SHARING THE SCRIPTURE

### Preparing Our Hearts

Meditate on this week's devotional reading, found in Galatians 1:1-10. As this letter opens, Paul is clearly concerned that the members of the church in Galatia have strayed from the truth to accept "a different gospel" (1:6). Moreover, Paul establishes his authority as an apostle. He is not interested in becoming popular with people but rather wants to win the approval of God. How about you? Are you adhering to the gospel message or wandering off track to find a religious experience that suits you better? How does your life measure up against the example of Jesus and the teachings of the Bible?

Pray that you and the adult learners will commit yourselves to pleasing God.

### Preparing Our Minds

Study the background from 1 Thessalonians 2 and lesson scripture, verses 1-12. Consider what the single overall goal that shapes your life should be.

Write on newsprint:
❏ information for next week's lesson, found under "Continue the Journey."
❏ activities for further spiritual growth in "Continue the Journey."

### LEADING THE CLASS

#### (1) Gather to Learn

❖ Welcome the class members and introduce any guests.

❖ Pray that those who have gathered will allow the Holy Spirit to show them the message that Jesus would have for them today.

❖ Read this story concerning Back on My Feet (http://backonmyfeet.org): **Back on My Feet (BOMF) is a non-profit organization that began in 2007 when Anne Mahlum, a twentysomething runner would pass by a homeless shelter in Philadelphia and realized that she could help make a difference in people's lives. Although BOMF does not offer food or shelter, it has developed a comprehensive program, based on three morning runs each week, to help homeless people gain confidence, experience perseverance, and work together as a team to find hope and a future. BOMF works with its runners to find links to job training, scholarships to further their education, and housing assistance. As of this writing, five shelters in Philadelphia are involved in Back on My Feet, and shelters in other cities are looking at the program to see how it might work for them.**

❖ Ask: **What does this story suggest to you about the impact commitment can have on one's life and the lives of others?**

❖ Read aloud today's focus statement: **Many people shape their lives around significant goals to which they are committed. What should be the single, overall goal that shapes our life? Paul implies that all we do should grow out of an earnest commitment to please God.**

*(2) Explore Paul's Words about Earnest Commitment*

❖ Select a volunteer to read about Paul's ministry in Thessalonica, as recorded in 1 Thessalonians 2:1-12.

❖ List on newsprint all the information the class members can learn about Paul from this reading.

❖ Divide the class into groups and give each group a sheet of newsprint and a marker to write their ideas. Encourage the groups to talk about why Paul would have written these comments. Are people criticizing him? If so, who? For what reason? What were they saying about him?

❖ Bring the groups back together and discuss what they discerned as they read between the lines of the Scripture passage. You may wish to add comments from "Introduction" in Understanding the Scripture and "People-pleasers and God-pleasers" in Interpreting the Scripture to recognize how Paul is different from those who speak in accordance with the expectations of their listeners.

*(3) Realize What It Means to Be Earnestly Committed to God*

❖ Read aloud the third and fourth paragraphs of "The Right Motives."

❖ Encourage the students to talk about:
   ■ how Paul's motivation for commitment to God appears to be other-centered.
   ■ how their congregation's motive for evangelism is other-centered, rather than church-centered. (If the group decides that their evangelistic efforts are more church-centered, discuss ways they could be more intentional about helping those outside the fold, as opposed to being primarily concerned about the church and its survival.)
   ■ the ways in which they as a church reach out to others to help them

make an earnest commitment to God.

❖ Invite several students to roleplay the following scenarios, which you will need to read aloud. Encourage others to respond:
   ■ **Scenario 1: Sam and his wife Jean have an opportunity to buy a larger dream home in an upscale community. However, if they buy this house they will no longer be able to give at least a tithe (ten percent) of their income to God. They made the commitment to tithe twenty-two years ago when they married. Hear Sam and Jean discussing whether or not they should proceed to purchase this new home.**
   ■ **Scenario 2: Tina is a gifted teacher who works in a suburban school. Her talents are much needed in a school where many of the students receive free or reduced-cost lunches. School officials are urging her to change schools. This would be a real transition and challenge for Tina. Hear Tina and her pastor discuss the pros and cons of such a move.**

*(4) Make an Earnest Commitment to God a Goal for Life*

❖ Distribute paper and pencils. Read aloud these words of Louis Cassels (1922-1974): **Jesus did not say, "Come to me and get it over with." He said, "If any man would come after me, let him take up his cross daily and follow me."** *Daily* **is the key word. Our commitment to Christ, however genuine and wholehearted it may be today, must be renewed tomorrow . . . and the day after that . . . and the day after that . . . until the path comes at last to the river.**

❖ Challenge the students to think of ways that they have taken up their cross daily during the preceding week. When have they acted as God called them to act, even when it meant hardship or difficulty for them? How did they feel after taking whatever action was necessary? If the students cannot think of any examples, were there times when God called but they chose not to respond? If so, what steps will they take to strengthen their commitment to God through Christ Jesus?

### (5) Continue the Journey

❖ Pray that today's participants will make their commitment to Christ a priority in their lives and act faithfully as they are motivated to please God.

❖ Read aloud this preparation for next week's lesson. You may also want to post it on newsprint for the students to copy.

■ Title: Sustained through Encouragement
■ Background Scripture: 1 Thessalonians 3
■ Lesson Scripture: 1 Thessalonians 3
■ Focus of the Lesson: The many demands of daily life make it hard to honor all our commitments. What can help us maintain lives that are faithfully committed to God? The text shows that Christian commitment is sustained in part through encouragement from others.

❖ Challenge the students to complete one or more of these activities for further spiritual growth, which you will write on newsprint for the students to copy.

(1) List at least two short-term or long-term goals that you have for your life. How are you working to fulfill each goal? What evidence supports your commitment to each goal? If you are not working diligently to meet the goals, what is preventing you from doing so?

(2) Identify at least one cause to which you are passionately committed. Do something tangible this week (spend time volunteering, give a donation, tell others about the cause) to support this cause.

(3) Be aware this week of situations where you find that you cannot please other people *and* please God. Choose words and actions that will enable you to keep your commitment to pleasing God.

❖ Sing or read aloud "Take My Life, and Let It Be."

❖ Conclude today's session by leading the class in this benediction adapted from 2 Thessalonians 1:11: Go forth with the assurance that we are always praying for you, asking that our God will make you worthy of his call and will fulfill by his power every good resolve and work of faith.

## UNIT 1: THE NATURE OF CHRISTIAN COMMITMENT
# SUSTAINED THROUGH ENCOURAGEMENT

---

### PREVIEWING THE LESSON

**Lesson Scripture:** 1 Thessalonians 3
**Background Scripture:** 1 Thessalonians 3
**Key Verse:** 1 Thessalonians 3:7

**Focus of the Lesson:**
The many demands of daily life make it hard to honor all our commitments. What can help us maintain lives that are faithfully committed to God? The text shows that Christian commitment is sustained in part through encouragement from others.

**Goals for the Learners:**
(1) to explore the importance of encouraging one another.
(2) to identify situations that cause them to feel discouraged and ways that they can experience encouragement.
(3) to encourage others to be faithful in their commitment to God.

**Pronunciation Guide:**
*euangelion* (yoo ang ghel' ee on)
Beroea (bi ree' uh)

**Supplies:**
Bibles, newsprint and marker, paper and pencils, hymnals

---

### READING THE SCRIPTURE

NRSV

1 Thessalonians 3

¹Therefore when we could bear it no longer, we decided to be left alone in Athens; ²and we sent Timothy, our brother and co-worker for God in proclaiming the gospel of Christ, to strengthen and encourage you for

NIV

1 Thessalonians 3

¹So when we could stand it no longer, we thought it best to be left by ourselves in Athens. ²We sent Timothy, who is our brother and God's fellow worker in spreading the gospel of Christ, to strengthen and

the sake of your faith, ³so that no one would be shaken by these persecutions. Indeed, you yourselves know that this is what we are destined for. ⁴In fact, when we were with you, we told you beforehand that we were to suffer persecution; so it turned out, as you know. ⁵For this reason, when I could bear it no longer, I sent to find out about your faith; I was afraid that somehow the tempter had tempted you and that our labor had been in vain.

⁶But Timothy has just now come to us from you, and has brought us the good news of your faith and love. He has told us also that you always remember us kindly and long to see us—just as we long to see you. **⁷For this reason, brothers and sisters, during all our distress and persecution we have been encouraged about you through your faith.** ⁸For we now live, if you continue to stand firm in the Lord. ⁹How can we thank God enough for you in return for all the joy that we feel before our God because of you? ¹⁰Night and day we pray most earnestly that we may see you face to face and restore whatever is lacking in your faith.

¹¹Now may our God and Father himself and our Lord Jesus direct our way to you. ¹²And may the Lord make you increase and abound in love for one another and for all, just as we abound in love for you. ¹³And may he so strengthen your hearts in holiness that you may be blameless before our God and Father at the coming of our Lord Jesus with all his saints.

encourage you in your faith, ³so that no one would be unsettled by these trials. You know quite well that we were destined for them. ⁴In fact, when we were with you, we kept telling you that we would be persecuted. And it turned out that way, as you well know. ⁵For this reason, when I could stand it no longer, I sent to find out about your faith. I was afraid that in some way the tempter might have tempted you and our efforts might have been useless.

⁶But Timothy has just now come to us from you and has brought good news about your faith and love. He has told us that you always have pleasant memories of us and that you long to see us, just as we also long to see you. **⁷Therefore, brothers, in all our distress and persecution we were encouraged about you because of your faith.** ⁸For now we really live, since you are standing firm in the Lord. ⁹How can we thank God enough for you in return for all the joy we have in the presence of our God because of you? ¹⁰Night and day we pray most earnestly that we may see you again and supply what is lacking in your faith.

¹¹Now may our God and Father himself and our Lord Jesus clear the way for us to come to you. ¹²May the Lord make your love increase and overflow for each other and for everyone else, just as ours does for you. ¹³May he strengthen your hearts so that you will be blameless and holy in the presence of our God and Father when our Lord Jesus comes with all his holy ones.

---

## UNDERSTANDING THE SCRIPTURE

**1 Thessalonians 3:1-5.** When Paul left Thessalonica, he left his converts in a difficult situation. They had stepped out of the behaviors expected of them by their neighbors in response to Paul's teaching, taking some real steps of faith and courage. But Paul left on account of the hostility against

him in the city, leaving the converts to fend for themselves, at least for a while, facing the hostility and suspicion of their neighbors while lacking the presence and encouragement of their teacher. In this section, which began properly in 2:17, Paul offers something of an explanation for why he did not come back to check on his friends and how they can know he has not abandoned them. Paul claims to have attempted to return to them in the interim, though circumstances prohibited him (2:18). Instead, he did the best that he could—he sent Timothy as a member of his team and as Paul's representative to check on the disciples and to encourage them in Paul's absence. Paul twice calls attention to the fact that Timothy's coming to them is the evidence of Paul's own deep concern for them (3:1, 5). Paul includes the detail that he preferred to be left alone in Athens (Silas and Timothy having remained in Beroea and being expected to join Paul as soon as possible; see Acts 17:13-15) so that Timothy could visit the believers in Thessalonica. If the Thessalonians were feeling forsaken as a result of his departure, Paul wants them to know that he would prefer to remain forsaken and alone so that they could know, through Timothy, that he is still "with" them in his heart and in theirs.

Paul continues to emphasize the predictability and normality of the society's negative response to the church members. When they chose to follow Christ, they chose, in effect, this destiny (3:3), namely to share in the hostility Christ endured, Christ's churches in Judea endured, and Christ's messengers endured. Paul had prepared the believers for this ahead of time (3:4), so that it should not catch them off guard or cause them to doubt the rightness or wisdom of their conversion. He introduces, however, yet another perspective on society's hostility by placing it in the context of the cosmic battle between Satan and the angels of God. The Tempter, Satan, is really the one behind the opposition to the believers. Their neighbors' disapproval and disavowal is a tool by which he seeks to defeat those who would respond to God's call, and thus diminish the kingdom of God (3:5). Satan had, in fact, been the one to thwart Paul's attempts to visit and encourage the converts (2:18), since Paul's return would

increase the likelihood of Satan's purposes being defeated. The believers are thus oriented toward their neighbors' attempts at "correction" to see in them not a legitimate critique of their new way of life but an attack of the evil one, God's cosmic enemy. Their commitment to resist the "temptation" to yield to that pressure will be measurably strengthened as they see behind it not just human beings but the Devourer of souls.

**1 Thessalonians 3:6-9.** Timothy had already returned to Paul with good news about the converts' commitment, with the result that 1 Thessalonians is not a letter of desperation (as if the converts were near to giving in to the temptation to revert to their old way of life), but rather one of encouragement to them to continue fighting the good fight. Timothy's visit also gave Paul an opportunity to learn about specific questions troubling the community (such as will be addressed in 4:13-18) as well as other specific information about the church.

Timothy's report reassures Paul that the converts remembered him and his team with love, warm affection, and deep commitment to the relationship (3:7). Paul shares that he too still suffers distress and persecution, but that the Thessalonian Christians' steadfast commitment gives him joy and strength in the midst of his trials (3:7-9; see also 2:19-20). Having heard Paul express how important to him is their ongoing Christian commitment, the converts will be moved to endure, in part, so as to continue to gladden the heart of the apostle who has meant so much to them, so that his labors and his suffering will not be "in vain" (3:5). It is noteworthy that Paul uses the verb form of the Greek word for gospel or "good news" (*euangelion*) to describe the action of Timothy reporting the news from Thessalonica. The news of the converts' firmness and love in Christ becomes, in effect, part of the good news of the coming of God's kingly reign in this world.

**1 Thessalonians 3:10-13.** Paul himself hopes still to return to Thessalonica to continue the work of shoring up their commitment to Christ and one another, and insulating them against the pressures of non-Christians (3:10-11). His letter will help serve those goals in the interim.

In the meanwhile, Paul points to two other essential resources for perseverance. One is the community itself, specifically the mutual love of believers manifested in mutual encouragement and in acts of kindness. Paul will return to this important resource throughout the letter (3:12; 4:9-10, 18; 5:11-15), since the building up of strong, close, personal, and meaningful relationships within the community of disciples is an important counterbalance to the loss of personal connections each believer has suffered on account of leaving behind his or her former way of life. In order for each individual convert to persevere, Christians must supply for one another the sense of belonging, of affirmation, of being loved and valued that their non-Christian neighbors have withdrawn from the converts.

A second motivation for perseverance is the end-time horizon of which Paul refuses to allow the converts to lose sight. History is rushing forward to the day of the "coming of our Lord Jesus" (3:13), the day on which those who have sought to please God will themselves experience the public approval and vindication of God in the sight of all (see also 2 Corinthians 5:9-10; 2 Thessalonians 1:6-10). Paul looks ahead to this day as the day on which his team's obedience and achievement will be manifested and rewarded (2:19-20), and he calls his converts to keep an eye fixed on that day so that they will so live in the present as to be found "blameless" (3:13). Steadfast endurance in the way of life taught by Paul, though it entails hardship in the present, remains the path to eternal safety and honor when God comes to judge. Paul introduces these topics here to help the Christians in Thessalonica decide afresh each new day that Christ's friendship is worth the world's enmity.

---

## INTERPRETING THE SCRIPTURE

### The Sacrifice of Encouragement

Paul and his team knew how vitally important it was to invest themselves personally in sustaining the faith of the recent converts in Thessalonica. They understood that their responsibility before God did not end with sharing the good news, with baptizing the new converts, or even with establishing free-standing congregations. They understood that they needed to continue to personally enflesh the love of God for these converts in their own ongoing acts of love and encouragement and solidarity.

In many liturgical traditions, the service of baptism invites the soon-to-be-baptized or their sponsors to make certain vows. The rite also invites the whole assembled gathering, as representatives of the whole congregation and even of the church of God in every place, to pledge themselves to take on certain commitments toward the new disciples. In the Book of Common Prayer, for example, the question is posed: "Will you who witness these vows do all in your power to support these persons in their life in Christ?" The response is given: "We will." Perhaps unfortunately, there is no follow-up discussion in the service concerning exactly what "all in our power" includes.

Paul and his team were committed to fulfill their own responsibility toward the converts in Thessalonica in the face of substantial personal and material cost. Paul speaks of the personal cost: he puts the converts' experience of encouragement ahead of his own, releasing Timothy to look after their emotional and spiritual needs while he remains alone in a new city, having just been hounded from the last two. Traveling from city to city, however, was a difficult business, proceeding by foot at about twenty miles per day, with the need to find provisions and lodging along the way (hence the importance of Christian hospitality throughout the early church). Paul and Timothy spared no expense, as it were, to make sure that the Thessalonians were on firm footing in their faith.

Doing all in our power for those whose faith God has, in part, entrusted to our nurture would certainly require us to make costly, sacrificial investment of our time, energy, attention, and even resources into another human being. A divorcee in a church I formerly attended lived a good example. She took in a young mother suffering domestic violence. This church member gave the young mother and her child a safe harbor from which to pursue some training, to find work and self-sufficiency, and to begin a fresh life. She brought this young woman into a loving community of faith that surrounded her with friendship, healing, and help. That more mature sister in Christ did, I think, all in her power to support the younger sister in her life in Christ, making good the promise of Jesus that those who come to him may leave family behind but will gain family a hundredfold (Mark 10:29-30).

### Faith-sustaining Relationships

Perhaps one of the surprises in 1 Thessalonians is the effect the converts have on Paul himself. In the midst of his own trials and experiences of hardship, Paul finds great encouragement hearing how these believers have remained faithful to the Lord to whom Paul and his team introduced them. Moreover, these believers have kept their warm affection for and devotion to their apostle, even in the wake of his untimely withdrawal from their midst. Paul sent Timothy back to Thessalonica in part for the sake of the converts (3:1), but also in part for his own sake, since their own

endurance in the faith meant so very much to him (3:5). Paul could endure many things (just scan 2 Corinthians 6:3-10; 11:24-29), but not the thought that Satan had undone his work among the Thessalonians.

We want our lives to have meaning, to have counted for something. We are often willing to go to extreme lengths and make significant sacrifices, but it is important that those sacrifices bear fruit. Paul provides us with an example of seeking that fruit in our relationships with other Christians, directing our investments of ourselves toward nurturing the faith of others, and allowing God to encourage us through the fruit that we see in the lives of those others. Biologists have listed "reproduction" as an essential characteristic of every living organism. This applies also to our faith. If it is a living faith, it will "reproduce" itself, bearing fruit by inviting and participating in the shaping of new disciples, or the ongoing strengthening and encouragement of established disciples.

While our obedience to God's call must not be dependent upon the results we can observe in others, we are reassured by the example of Paul here (as well as, for example, the promise of Jesus in John 15:5, 16) that our investment of ourselves in nurturing fellow Christians will indeed bear "fruit that will last." That fruit will provide us at critical points in our own journey with the assurance that our life's labor has not been in vain. From another angle, Paul's response to the converts' faith and affection suggests that we think about ways in which we can offer encouragement to those in Christian leadership, both through our own growth in commitment to discipleship and ministry and through our expressions of appreciation and affection for those who share with us not only the gospel but also their very selves.

### Blameless before the Lord

The stakes were high for the Thessalonian Christians. Persevering in their newfound faith meant estrangement from neighbors, associates, even family members, and the loss of any sense of being "at home" any longer in their world. Many forces, both internal and external, would draw the believers away from choosing to act consistently in line with the teachings of the Lord they had claimed, back toward behaving in ways that their neighbors would deem acceptable and that would bring them more temporal rewards. Failing to persevere, however, would mean leaving a place of favor in God's sight to return to a place of "wrath" at the coming accounting.

There is a goal for the Christian journey. Paul expressed this in terms of standing with confidence before Christ at his return—a confidence not born of arrogant pride, of course, but rather of responsive commitment to grow in those ways that please God. Paul also knew, however, that it could be hard to keep this goal in mind in the midst of competing pressures and desires. So he lays two responsibilities on the Christian community in this regard. First, we are challenged to help one another keep our focus on living to please God as our first priority (as in 4:18; 5:11). Second, we are challenged so to keep growing in our love for, and encouragement of, one another. As we provide one another with the emotional and relational support that can be seen and experienced, we are further emboldened to invest ourselves in our hope that cannot yet be seen or experienced. This love is directed first to "one another," but also to "all," again providing the visible and experiential witness to that faith and hope to which we invite the newcomer to Christ.

---

## SHARING THE SCRIPTURE

### Preparing Our Hearts

Meditate on this week's devotional reading, found in Acts 4:32-37. The believers of the early church shared whatever they had with each other. In our day, many would call this redistribution of wealth and property socialism. Whatever name is used to identify this way of living, it is clear that the first believers saw this as a model for how church members are to live. Try to put yourself in the midst of this congregation. How would knowing that people were going to help each other by sharing their possessions have made you feel had you been poor? How would you have felt if you had had property and wealth?

Pray that you and the adult learners will be willing to help care for and encourage others.

### Preparing Our Minds

Study the background and lesson scripture, both of which are chapter 3 of 1 Thessalonians. Consider what can help you maintain a faithful commitment to God in the face of many other demands that make it difficult to honor all of your commitments.

Write on newsprint:
❏ information for next week's lesson, found under "Continue the Journey."
❏ activities for further spiritual growth in "Continue the Journey."

### LEADING THE CLASS

### (1) Gather to Learn

❖ Welcome the class members and introduce any guests.

❖ Pray that those who have come today will feel sustained as they encourage one another.

❖ Read these words from Philip Kenneson's book, *Life on the Vine*: **Put bluntly, what most Christians need is not to be convinced that God needs to be "Number One" but to be helped to see what "seeking first God's kingdom" might actually look like in** terms of how we live day to day. **What does my commitment to remain faithful to God and God's kingdom mean for my commitments to my family, friends, neighbors, fellow workers and country?**

❖ Talk with the class to answer Kenneson's question. **What criteria do the students use to determine how they should act if they sense that a commitment to one's country, for example, is in conflict with a commitment to God?**

❖ Read aloud today's focus statement: **The many demands of daily life make it hard to honor all our commitments. What can help us maintain lives that are faithfully committed to God? The text shows that Christian commitment is sustained in part through encouragement from others.**

### (2) Explore the Importance of Encouraging One Another

❖ Choose a volunteer to read 1 Thessalonians 3:1-5.

❖ Read or retell 1 Thessalonians 3:1-5 from Understanding the Scripture to help the class understand why the church at Thessalonica would need encouragement.

❖ Select another volunteer to read information about Timothy's report from 1 Thessalonians 3:6-13.

❖ Read aloud "Faith-sustaining Relationships" from Interpreting the Scripture to discern how Paul finds encouragement from Christians he has nurtured.

❖ Close this part of the lesson by asking: **Even though our congregation is not experiencing the kind of persecution that the Thessalonians faced, what lessons can we learn from them and from Paul about how we might encourage one another?**

### (3) Identify Situations that Cause the Learners to Feel Discouraged and Ways that They Can Experience Encouragement

❖ Read aloud the final paragraph of "The Sacrifice of Encouragement."

❖ Talk with the students about how the divorced woman in this story was able to offer encouragement to someone else.

❖ Brainstorm with the class answers to this question: **What kinds of situations often cause people to feel discouraged?** List their ideas on newsprint and number each entry.

❖ Divide the class into groups and assign at least one entry to each group. The groups are to suggest ways to encourage people who are experiencing the assigned situation.

❖ Bring the groups together and ask a spokesperson for each group to report their ideas.

❖ Suggest that the students think of someone they could encourage by using one of the ideas they have heard. Distribute paper and pencils so that the students may record the name of the person they have identified and a few words about what they intend to do.

❖ Conclude this portion of the session by inviting the students to think quietly about a current situation that is discouraging them and where they might turn for help and encouragement.

❖ Call time by saying: **May you find the encouragement you need from friends who will surround you with the love of God, even as you encourage others.**

### (4) Encourage Others to Be Faithful in Their Commitment to God

❖ Read the final paragraph of "Blameless before the Lord" in Interpreting the Scripture.

❖ Repeat the two responsibilities Paul lays on the Christian community: (1) the challenge to please God as our first priority and (2) the challenge to grow in our love for and encouragement of one another.

❖ Discuss these questions, prompting the students to give concrete examples for each answer:

(1) **How are we as a church making God our first priority?**

(2) **How are we as a church showing our love for those within the church, and extending our love to those beyond our walls?**

(3) **What do we as a church do to encourage one another?**

(4) **Under what circumstances do we need to do more to encourage each other? To say this a different way, are there situations that many people prefer not to discuss—such as loss of a job, house foreclosure, infidelity, out-of-wedlock pregnancy, or hearing that a family is struggling to accept a son who has declared that he is gay—where we as a congregation fall silent and fail to offer encouragement? If so, what can we do to make those who come through our door feel that we will support them in any and all circumstances?**

❖ Challenge the students to look for opportunities this week to offer encouragement to anyone who seems to need it.

### (5) *Continue the Journey*

❖ Pray that all who have participated in today's session will go forth to encourage one another.

❖ Read aloud this preparation for next week's lesson. You may also want to post it on newsprint for the students to copy.

- ■ **Title: Demonstrated in Action**
- ■ **Background Scripture: 1 Thessalonians 4:1-12**

- ■ **Lesson Scripture: 1 Thessalonians 4:1-12**
- ■ **Focus of the Lesson: Strong commitment to a belief or cause usually leads one to take action that reflects the level of dedication. To what can we commit ourselves that would make our actions benefit others? The passage implies that Christian commitment is both reinforced and strengthened by concrete actions that grow out of our desire to please God.**

❖ Challenge the students to complete one or more of these activities for further spiritual growth, which you will write on newsprint for the students to copy.

(1) **Offer a word of encouragement to someone who may feel overwhelmed by his or her circumstances.**

(2) **List five people you know who need encouragement. In addition to doing whatever you can to help them, spend time in prayer for each person.**

(3) **Write a thank-you note to someone who has encouraged you. Let this person know how much his or her thoughtfulness meant to you.**

❖ Sing or read aloud "Be Still, My Soul."

❖ Conclude today's session by leading the class in this benediction adapted from 2 Thessalonians 1:11: **Go forth with the assurance that we are always praying for you, asking that our God will make you worthy of his call and will fulfill by his power every good resolve and work of faith.**

# UNIT 1: THE NATURE OF CHRISTIAN COMMITMENT
# DEMONSTRATED IN ACTION

---

## PREVIEWING THE LESSON

**Lesson Scripture:** 1 Thessalonians 4:1-12
**Background Scripture:** 1 Thessalonians 4:1-12
**Key Verse:** 1 Thessalonians 4:1

### Focus of the Lesson:
Strong commitment to a belief or cause usually leads one to take action that reflects the level of dedication. To what can we commit ourselves that would make our actions benefit others? The passages imply that Christian commitment is both reinforced and strengthened by concrete actions that grow out of our desire to please God.

### Goals for the Learners:
(1) to explore actions that grow out of our desire to please God.
(2) to experience ways to please God.
(3) to commit to a plan of pleasing God with dedicated lives.

### Pronunciation Guide:
Cynic (sin' ik)
*philadelphia* (phil ah del fee' ah)

### Supplies:
Bibles, newsprint and marker, paper and pencils, hymnals

---

## READING THE SCRIPTURE

NRSV
1 Thessalonians 4:1-12

**¹Finally, brothers and sisters, we ask and urge you in the Lord Jesus that, as you learned from us how you ought to live and to please God (as, in fact, you are doing), you should do so more and more.** ²For you know what instructions we gave you through the Lord Jesus. ³For this is the will of God, your sanctification: that you abstain

NIV
1 Thessalonians 4:1-12

**¹Finally, brothers, we instructed you how to live in order to please God, as in fact you are living. Now we ask you and urge you in the Lord Jesus to do this more and more.** ²For you know what instructions we gave you by the authority of the Lord Jesus.

³It is God's will that you should be

---

385

from fornication; [4]that each one of you know how to control your own body in holiness and honor, [5]not with lustful passion, like the Gentiles who do not know God; [6]that no one wrong or exploit a brother or sister in this matter, because the Lord is an avenger in all these things, just as we have already told you beforehand and solemnly warned you. [7]For God did not call us to impurity but in holiness. [8]Therefore whoever rejects this rejects not human authority but God, who also gives his Holy Spirit to you.

[9]Now concerning love of the brothers and sisters, you do not need to have anyone write to you, for you yourselves have been taught by God to love one another; [10]and indeed you do love all the brothers and sisters throughout Macedonia. But we urge you, beloved, to do so more and more, [11]to aspire to live quietly, to mind your own affairs, and to work with your hands, as we directed you, [12]so that you may behave properly toward outsiders and be dependent on no one.

sanctified: that you should avoid sexual immorality; [4]that each of you should learn to control his own body in a way that is holy and honorable, [5]not in passionate lust like the heathen, who do not know God; [6]and that in this matter no one should wrong his brother or take advantage of him. The Lord will punish men for all such sins, as we have already told you and warned you. [7]For God did not call us to be impure, but to live a holy life. [8]Therefore, he who rejects this instruction does not reject man but God, who gives you his Holy Spirit.

[9]Now about brotherly love we do not need to write to you, for you yourselves have been taught by God to love each other. [10]And in fact, you do love all the brothers throughout Macedonia. Yet we urge you, brothers, to do so more and more.

[11]Make it your ambition to lead a quiet life, to mind your own business and to work with your hands, just as we told you, [12]so that your daily life may win the respect of outsiders and so that you will not be dependent on anybody.

---

## UNDERSTANDING THE SCRIPTURE

**1 Thessalonians 4:1-8.** Paul calls the converts to dedicate themselves to live according to the apostle's instructions as the way "to please God" (4:1). The alternative to pleasing God is encountering God as the "avenger" of wrongdoing (4:6). The horizon of God's judgment, being approved or censured by God, again provides the backdrop for Christian ethics (see 3:13). Seeking to be honored before God's court, and fearing lasting disgrace there, the believers are likely to take Paul's instructions quite seriously.

God's will for the believers is their "sanctification" (4:3), a word that takes on rich meanings within both Jewish and Gentile cultures, in which purity and pollution were

living concepts. Being "sanctified" meant being moved from an ordinary state to a holy state, a state in which one could come into direct contact with the divine and be of service to the divine. Rituals like baptism were part of this process. The death of Jesus would later be interpreted in terms of a ritual sacrifice of consecration on behalf of believers (Hebrews 9:1–10:18). In the early church, however, becoming "holy to the Lord" was not merely a matter of ritual but also of character and behavior. To be sanctified, one must abstain from the defilements that God abhors, and those defilements are interpreted entirely in ethical terms in the New Testament (see Mark 7:14-23).

To be sanctified, however, is also to be set

apart from the ordinary. Paul uses holiness language to reinforce the church's social boundaries. As Christians pursue holiness, they leave behind the ordinary state that continues to characterize non-Christians. Paul focuses this discussion here on the sexual conduct that is to characterize the Christian group, distinguishing it from the non-Christian population. As a Christian abstains from extramarital sexual conduct, and also refuses to exploit his or her marriage partner as a means of getting sexual gratification (4:4, 6), he or she moves forward toward sanctification. There is some question as to how we are to read "your own body" in 4:4 (NRSV). The Greek reads "one's own vessel," which could refer to one's own sexual apparatus, one's body, or one's spouse (specifically the wife). Either way, Paul's intent is clear: sex within Christian marriage is a matter of intimacy, not physical gratification.

Paul characterizes the outside world as given over to the dishonorable state of being slaves to their passions (4:5). Greco-Roman philosophers also taught that one ought to exercise self-mastery so as to walk in line with virtue rather than being overcome and led into vice by one's own emotions, drives, and sensations. Sexual mores thereby furnish another line to draw between the sanctified and the outsiders. As Paul draws the inside/outside boundary more sharply in ways that also show the "outside" to be a place of greater dishonor or disadvantage, he strengthens the believers' perseverance within the church, despite the rejection they endure from their neighbors.

**1 Thessalonians 4:9-12.** With this section, Paul begins to respond to topics brought up by the converts and sent back to him via Timothy. What does it mean for us to show "sibling love" in the church? What about believers who have passed away—did they miss their reward? What about the timing of Jesus' return? These topics are taken up by Paul in turn at 4:9, 4:13, and 5:1. The "now concerning" at 4:9 and 5:1 is also used throughout 1 Corinthians (see 1 Corinthians 7:1; 8:1; 12:1; 16:1) where Paul is not bringing up these topics on his own but responding to the believers' questions.

Paul affirms the Thessalonian Christians in their practice of brotherly and sisterly love in language that also suggests familiarity with the "new commandment" that stands at the heart of John's community's understanding of the Christian ethic, namely Jesus' instruction to "love one another" (compare 1 Thessalonians 4:9 with John 15:12, 17 and 1 John 4:7-16). Paul uses the Greek word *philadelphia*, which means "brotherly and sisterly love," to describe the attitude that is to guide Christians in their interactions with one another. The early Christians were taught to regard themselves as born anew from God, with the result that they became sisters and brothers one of another (Matthew 12:46-50; 23:8-9; John 1:12-13; Romans 8:14-17; 12:10; Hebrews 2:10-11; 13:1). Indeed, some authors go so far as to say that the believer has left his natural inheritance behind in exchange for a new and more glorious one, which includes a new family (see 1 Peter 1:3-4, 14-19).

There was a well-developed ethic for kin (especially siblings) in the ancient world. Siblings were supposed to cooperate with one another rather than compete against one another. "Sibling rivalry" would have been regarded as an ugly thing. Siblings were supposed to be absolutely trustworthy and reliable in their support of one another. Harmony and unity were to be the watchwords of their relationships (Philippians 1:27–2:4; 1 Peter 3:8). These values were to be lived out in shared ideals and in the sharing of possessions (see Acts 4:32; 1 John 3:16-18). Siblings were to hide each other's shame (James 4:11; 5:9), to promote one another's honor (Romans 12:10), and to practice reconciliation, forgiveness, and patience toward one another (Matthew 18:15-17, 23-35; Colossians 3:13-14). Paul is content that the Thessalonians understand all this, and that they are manifesting sibling love toward one another both in and beyond their own congregation as they reach out to other congregations as well (4:9-10; see also 1:3). The fact that the Macedonian churches will distinguish themselves in the collection for the sisters and brothers in Judea despite their own lack of abundance will continue to testify to how deeply committed they were to fellow Christians, whether near or far, as family (2 Corinthians 8:1-5).

The second emphasis in this paragraph seeks to cultivate the presentation of a good face toward outsiders. While the believers are to be free from being swayed one way or another by the approval or disapproval of unbelievers, they are nevertheless urged to live in such a way as will not confirm out-siders' suspicions of them. Paul is drawing on philosophical traditions here, since Plato also commends the person who lives qui-etly, minds his or her own affairs, and avoids being a meddler. In urging believers to continue to work at their occupations, Paul seeks to distinguish Christians from Cynics. Unlike the Cynic, the Christian was not to become a parasite on the larger soci-ety, giving up his or her means of livelihood and choosing to beg. Rather, the Christian was to continue to contribute in meaningful and tangible ways to the life and welfare of society. Paul views labor as a noble way of life, since it provides freedom. He himself worked with his hands so as to be free to preach the gospel—and free from the con-straints of having to please patrons.

---

## INTERPRETING THE SCRIPTURE

### Putting It into Practice

If our witness is weak or our journey toward spiritual maturity slow, there is a good chance that this is not due to a lack of *knowledge* about Christ and about the call that Christ places upon the lives of his fol-lowers. Instead, it may be due to a failure to put into practice what we know. As Paul wrote to the Christians in Thessalonica, Christians whom he had personally trained in the way "to live and to please God" (4:1), the balance of his concern falls not on their being insufficiently informed but on their commitment to continue to let what they have learned form them.

Ultimately, our commitment to Christ is not made real in the beliefs that we hold or the words that we speak (though these are also important), but in the ordering of our lives around his commandments and the teaching of his apostles. At the close of his great ethical Sermon on the Plain, Jesus poses the rhetorical question, "Why do you call me 'Lord, Lord,' and do not do what I tell you?" (Luke 6:46; see also Matthew 7:21-23). The way to build a solid life, a life deeply rooted in God, is to act on Jesus' words, however countercultural or counter-intuitive—or counter to our own natural inclinations—that might be. The way to con-tinue to grow into a mature disciple formed in the image of Christ is to continue to allow the teachings of Paul and the other spiritual directors given to us in the Scripture to chal-lenge and chafe us, and in the end to allow them to win over our resistance to them.

Self-examination is an essential spiritual discipline, and Paul's opening words in this week's scripture offer a very useful focus for such self-examination. What is one thing you have learned, and "know by heart" as it were, about how to live so as to please God? Where do you see that specifically shaping your actions, responses, attitudes, or ambi-tions? Where do your actions not fall in line with your understanding? Now what will you do to close that gap? Repeat this exer-cise frequently, perhaps using paragraphs of Scripture as the basis for reflection.

## Holiness and Self-Mastery

What does God want for our lives? Paul answers here, "sanctification" (1 Thessalonians 4:3). "Holiness" is a key term in Scripture. From beginning to end, the call of God's people is to "be holy" as God is holy (Leviticus 11:44-45; 19:2; 1 Peter 1:14-16). Holiness means reflecting God's character and activity in the world, making the unseen God, as well as God's heart and actions, "visible" to the world. Matthew speaks of this character and activity in terms of God's completeness and ability to be generous and kind to all as God desires, not as they seem to deserve (Matthew 5:48). Luke speaks of this in terms of God's compassion and outreaching love (Luke 6:36). Paul speaks of holiness here in terms of refusing to pursue self-centered gratification, which is also foreign to the character of God, the *Giver* of all good, and he applies it specifically to that very powerful arena of human experience—sexuality.

Why should such a private matter be so rigorously regulated, both by social conventions of morality (such as the Greco-Roman ethicists would articulate) and by religious leaders such as Paul? Precisely because sexuality is so powerful a human force, one that engages us fully as embodied souls and carries commensurate power to harm another embodied soul. Within marriage, a spouse can feel used rather than honored by the attitude and practice of the mate. Infidelity causes the deepest, most personal wounds to the forsaken spouse. Adultery involving two Christian spouses from different couples can weaken the cohesion and witness of an entire congregation. Even "solitary" sexual acts like indulging in pornography and masturbation diverts sexuality from its proper, other-centered channels into stagnant pools of selfishness. All of these behaviors represent rifts—between people, or between our public and private faces, our old self and our new self in Christ—and rips and tears are the essence of un-wholeness, or "un-holiness." Everywhere Christians are urged to allow the Holy Spirit to empower mastery of the passions, including sexual passions that range outside of marriage or rage improperly within marriage (see, for example, Galatians 5:16-25; 1 Peter 4:1-4; Titus 2:11-14). Paul's words again lead us into the vulnerable but necessary ground of self-examination, confession, and repentance.

## Philadelphia

Cautions about harmful expressions of "love" are balanced in this lesson with encouragement to healthful, mutually fulfilling expressions of love, particularly the love that God desires to nurture between believers. This love is specifically named "the love of brothers and sisters," inviting people who are not related by blood to behave toward one another—to show the mutual investment of care, concern, and resources in one another—that characterize siblings at their best. Many of us come from dysfunctional families where we have *not* seen "sibling love" at its best. Some have perhaps been *most* hurt by brothers or sisters. But God is calling together one great family in which we receive the gift of sisters and brothers who will love us, and whom we will love, as God intended family to love one another.

Within the church, we make *philadelphia* real as we invest ourselves in a fellow believer's life as if he or she were our own brother or sister, talking, encouraging, sharing resources, regarding his or her burdens as our own and doing all that we can to help him or her shoulder them. We make *philadelphia* real as we allow and invite our fellow Christians into those spaces of our need and ask them for help. Rivalry, competition, trying to "win" some battle that will require a fellow believer to "lose"—these are out of place in the family of God, just as they would be out of place in a well-functioning family. And this family is not limited to the local congregation but includes Christians of every stripe near and far. It is part of our calling as family to educate ourselves about the needs of Christians beyond our church walls, and to discover ways to make *philadelphia* real in those relationships as well.

---

## SHARING THE SCRIPTURE

### *Preparing Our Hearts*

Meditate on this week's devotional reading, found in Hebrews 11:1-6. This familiar passage defines faith as "the assurance of things hoped for, the conviction of things not seen" (11:1). The writer continues with examples of the ancestors of faith, including Abel, Enoch, Noah, and Abraham and Sarah, among others. These people of God didn't just say they believed in God; rather, they put their beliefs into action. Think about the beliefs you profess. Think also about what you actually do. How well are your beliefs reflected in your actions?

Pray that you and the adult learners will demonstrate your beliefs in the way that you live and relate to others.

### *Preparing Our Minds*

Study the background and lesson scripture, both from 1 Thessalonians 4:1-12. Consider the kinds of commitments you are willing to make that would allow your actions to benefit others.

Write on newsprint:

❑ information for next week's lesson, found under "Continue the Journey."

❑ activities for further spiritual growth in "Continue the Journey."

Plan a brief lecture from Understanding the Scripture as suggested for "Explore Actions That Grow Out of Our Desire to Please God."

### LEADING THE CLASS

#### *(1) Gather to Learn*

❖ Welcome the class members and introduce any guests.

❖ Pray that those who have assembled this morning will focus their attention on the nature of Christian commitment.

❖ Encourage the students to recall a recent political election and ask: **How did people show their commitment to a particular candidate?** You may want to list responses on newsprint. These responses may include: *voting for that candidate, contributing to his or her campaign, making calls or doing other volunteer work on behalf of the candidate, attending a rally.*

❖ Conclude by asking: **Why do people think it is important to take action on behalf of a candidate (or cause) they strongly support?**

❖ Read aloud today's focus statement: **Strong commitment to a belief or cause usually leads one to take action that reflects the level of dedication. To what can we commit ourselves that would make our actions benefit others? The passages imply that Christian commitment is both reinforced and strengthened by concrete actions that grow out of our desire to please God.**

#### *(2) Explore Actions That Grow Out of Our Desire to Please God*

❖ Select a volunteer to read 1 Thessalonians 4:1-12.

❖ Read or give a brief lecture from Understanding the Scripture to help the class members recognize that sanctification (becoming holy) is God's will. Those who are sanctified are living in ways that are pleasing to God.

❖ Look first at the holiness Paul writes about in terms of sexual conduct. Read the second paragraph of "Holiness and Self-Mastery" in Interpreting the Scripture.

❖ Encourage the students to talk about how self-control, particularly in the area of sexual conduct, is an important way to please God. Be sure to note that it is through the Holy Spirit that such control is possible (4:8).

❖ Turn attention to Paul's encouragement for believers to love and care for one another as brothers and sisters. Read "Philadelphia" from Interpreting the Scripture.

❖ Talk with the class about how sharing resources and shouldering one another's burdens enable the church to invest in the lives of its members. Ask: **How does such behavior not only help those already in the church but also draw in those who are on the outside?**

### (3) Experience Ways to Please God

❖ Recruit volunteers to read the following Bible verses that will shed light on how we can please God. As each passage is read, list on newsprint ideas for pleasing God. Invite the class to add other ideas. They may or may not have an exact scripture to support their addition.

- Matthew 4:10 (worshiping and serving only God)
- Mark 16:15 (preaching the good news to everyone)
- Romans 12:1 (presenting oneself as a sacrifice to God)
- Romans 15:1-3 (pleasing others so as to build them up)
- 2 Corinthians 9:7 (giving cheerfully)
- Philippians 4:4 (rejoicing in the Lord)
- Colossians 1:10 (bearing fruit)
- 1 Thessalonians 5:17 (praying without ceasing)
- Hebrews 11:6 (having faith)
- 1 John 3:23 (believing in Christ and loving one another)

❖ Encourage the class members to review the list and discuss ways in which they see their congregation pleasing God.

You may need to create some questions related to ideas that have been listed. For example, you may ask:

(1) **In what ways is our church bearing fruit for Christ?**

(2) **What evidence do we have that we as a congregation give cheerfully?**

(3) **When visitors participate in our worship and activities, how would they see us rejoicing in the Lord?**

(4) **How do we as a congregation practice sacrificial living and giving?**

❖ Conclude this portion of the session by asking: **If Paul were to write to our church, what would he say about how we are—or are not—pleasing God?**

### (4) Commit to a Plan of Pleasing God with Dedicated Lives

❖ Read "Putting It into Practice" from Interpreting the Scripture.

❖ Distribute paper and pencils. Read the last paragraph of "Putting It into Practice" again, this time pausing to allow the students to write answers to the questions that our author raises.

❖ Challenge the students to write a sentence or two in which they state what they plan to do so as to live a life that is pleasing to God.

❖ Read these words from www.PracticeGodsPresence.com: **Each time we prayerfully read The Gospel the basic message becomes clearer and clearer: our Father's will for us is to follow the way and manner of Our Lord. We do this through the practice of the presence of God where we engage in continual conversation with Our Father; walk with Him in love, humility, simplicity, and faith; and think, say, and do what is most pleasing to Him. In this way, in the here and now, we become God's children who live in His gentle kingdom on earth as it is in heaven and we become reflections of His light and love.**

❖ Provide a few moments of silence for the students to reflect on how their plan will enable them to live in a way pleasing to God, a way that empowers them "to follow the way and manner of Our Lord."

*(5) Continue the Journey*

❖ Break the silence by praying that today's participants will go forth motivated to put their commitment to Christ into tangible actions.

❖ Read aloud this preparation for next week's lesson. You may also want to post it on newsprint for the students to copy.

■ Title: God's Cosmic Plan
■ Background Scripture: 1 Thessalonians 4:13–5:28
■ Lesson Scripture: 1 Thessalonians 5:1-11
■ Focus of the Lesson: Most people want to understand how they fit in and contribute to society as a whole. What is the context within which we obtain such an understanding? God's plan of salvation is embodied in the divine plan for all creation, which is directly related to Christ's return to earth.

❖ Challenge the students to complete one or more of these activities for further spiritual growth, which you will write on newsprint for the students to copy.

(1) Take action this week to demonstrate your love and concern for brothers and sisters in Christ. Such action may involve caring for them by giving of your time, talent, and treasure.
(2) Look up the words "holy" and "holiness" in a Bible concordance. Read some of the entries. Write your own definition or explain what it means to live a holy life.
(3) Research John Wesley's teachings on sanctification, which he also refers to as Christian perfection. What do you learn about sanctification from Wesley? What difference might his teachings make in how you live your life?

❖ Sing or read aloud "A Charge to Keep I Have."

❖ Conclude today's session by leading the class in this benediction adapted from 2 Thessalonians 1:11: **Go forth with the assurance that we are always praying for you, asking that our God will make you worthy of his call and will fulfill by his power every good resolve and work of faith.**

# UNIT 2: THE FOUNDATION OF CHRISTIAN COMMITMENT
# GOD'S COSMIC PLAN

---

## PREVIEWING THE LESSON

**Lesson Scripture:** 1 Thessalonians 5:1-11
**Background Scripture:** 1 Thessalonians 4:13–5:28
**Key Verse:** 1 Thessalonians 5:9

### Focus of the Lesson:
Most people want to understand how they fit in and contribute to society as a whole. What is the context within which we obtain such an understanding? God's plan of salvation is embodied in the divine plan for all creation, which is directly related to Christ's return to earth.

### Goals for the Learners:
(1) to examine Paul's words to the Thessalonians about God's master plan.
(2) to realize the meaning of Christ's return.
(3) to make or renew a commitment to Jesus so as to receive the gift of salvation and eternal life.

### Pronunciation Guide:
*Pax Romana* (pahks roh mah' nah)
*shalom* (shah lohm')

### Supplies:
Bibles, newsprint and marker, paper and pencils, hymnals

---

## READING THE SCRIPTURE

NRSV
1 Thessalonians 5:1-11

[1]Now concerning the times and the seasons, brothers and sisters, you do not need to have anything written to you. [2]For you yourselves know very well that the day of the Lord will come like a thief in the night. [3]When they say, "There is peace and security," then sudden destruction will come

NIV
1 Thessalonians 5:1-11

[1]Now, brothers, about times and dates we do not need to write to you, [2]for you know very well that the day of the Lord will come like a thief in the night. [3]While people are saying, "Peace and safety," destruction will come on them suddenly, as labor pains on a pregnant woman, and they will not escape.

upon them, as labor pains come upon a pregnant woman, and there will be no escape! <sup>4</sup>But you, beloved, are not in darkness, for that day to surprise you like a thief; <sup>5</sup>for you are all children of light and children of the day; we are not of the night or of darkness. <sup>6</sup>So then let us not fall asleep as others do, but let us keep awake and be sober; <sup>7</sup>for those who sleep sleep at night, and those who are drunk get drunk at night. <sup>8</sup>But since we belong to the day, let us be sober, and put on the breastplate of faith and love, and for a helmet the hope of salvation. **<sup>9</sup>For God has destined us not for wrath but for obtaining salvation through our Lord Jesus Christ,** <sup>10</sup>who died for us, so that whether we are awake or asleep we may live with him. <sup>11</sup>Therefore encourage one another and build up each other, as indeed you are doing.

<sup>4</sup>But you, brothers, are not in darkness so that this day should surprise you like a thief. <sup>5</sup>You are all sons of the light and sons of the day. We do not belong to the night or to the darkness. <sup>6</sup>So then, let us not be like others, who are asleep, but let us be alert and self-controlled. <sup>7</sup>For those who sleep, sleep at night, and those who get drunk, get drunk at night. <sup>8</sup>But since we belong to the day, let us be self-controlled, putting on faith and love as a breastplate, and the hope of salvation as a helmet. **<sup>9</sup>For God did not appoint us to suffer wrath but to receive salvation through our Lord Jesus Christ.** <sup>10</sup>He died for us so that, whether we are awake or asleep, we may live together with him. <sup>11</sup>Therefore encourage one another and build each other up, just as in fact you are doing.

## UNDERSTANDING THE SCRIPTURE

**1 Thessalonians 4:13-18.** One question brought back by Timothy concerned Christians who had died prior to the Lord's return. Did they lose out because they will not be able to meet Christ at his coming? Did they suffer the rejection of their peers in vain because they will not enjoy the benefits for hope of which they left behind their old way of life? It was vitally important for Paul to answer this concern. If death could indeed separate believers from their hope in Christ, those who remained alive would find considerably less courage to bear up under the pressures their neighbors were putting on them for fear of being the losers twice over, in this life and after death.

Paul's answer resonates strongly with Jesus' own teaching about the elect being gathered at the coming of the Son of Man (Mark 13:24-27), though Paul now makes the resurrection of the faithful dead an explicit feature of his end-time scenario. Paul sees in the resurrection of Jesus from the dead the first fruits of a great crop to be reaped from the realm of the dead (4:14; see, more fully, 1 Corinthians 15:3-34, 50-58), and the basis for our own hope. This hope, Paul claims, offers Christians a special resource as they grieve in the wake of death, a resource denied to the unbelieving world.

**1 Thessalonians 5:1-11.** The second coming, the Day of the Lord, was an important cornerstone of Paul's gospel and the converts' new faith. It would be quite natural, therefore, for the believers to inquire about the proximity of this event. Rather than attempting to lay out timetables or provide a series of signs preceding Christ's coming, Paul highlights the suddenness of the Day of the Lord. He uses two images to bring this suddenness home. The first is derived from a saying of Jesus, urging the disciples to remain watchful so that they will be prepared, unlike the householder who did not know when the thief was coming (Matthew 24:42-44). The image of the Lord coming "as a thief" became quite popular in the early church (1 Thessalonians 5:2; 2 Peter 3:10;

Revelation 16:14). The second is derived from Isaiah's oracle concerning the Day of the Lord in Isaiah 13:6-9, likening the arrival of that Day to the sudden onset of a pregnant woman's labor pains (5:3).

Knowing that the Day is coming, and coming suddenly, gives the believers an enormous advantage over those outside the church. Those outside are indeed saying "peace and security" (5:3) as Paul writes, for these two words were key slogans of Roman imperial rule. The *Pax Romana*, or "Roman peace," was the chief accomplishment of the emperors, and this "peace" was celebrated with altars, statues of the goddess *Pax*, and inscriptions on coins. Another common Roman coin reverse depicted "security" (*Securitas*) personified as a woman, presented as one of the benefits conferred by the emperors. Paul's gospel is indeed revolutionary in that he and his converts look forward to the overturning of this state of affairs at the Day of the Lord.

Although attaching oneself to Jesus has brought the converts into conflict with their neighbors and led to hardship, the real disadvantage, Paul states, lies with being at peace with that deluded society. In light of the coming crisis, the non-Christians are like drunken people groping about in the darkness at night, who finally fall asleep in a stupor and are completely overtaken by the calamity. Their opposition to the believers is a symptom of their ignorance and folly. Paul characterizes Christians and non-Christians here, moreover, in such a way as to highlight the contrasts and incompatibility between the two groups (light and darkness, day and night, sobriety and drunkenness), and thus to make the boundary lines clearer and stronger.

Unlike outsiders, the Christian is to "keep awake" (or "vigilant") and to "be sober" (5:6). The first verb is familiar from Jesus' instructions on the end time (see Mark 13:34-37). The second verb is often used as a metaphor to mean "exercise self-control." The need for vigilance and self-control is enhanced by Paul's introduction of military imagery into the passage with the inventory of armor (5:8). The image of warfare strategically influences the way the believers will think about the opposition they face, propelling them forward to seek victory beyond that opposition rather than succumb to it.

Paul concludes by urging the Christians to help keep their fellow believers on track and pressing forward (5:11; see also 4:18). A supportive and encouraging community is essential to individual perseverance in discipleship.

**1 Thessalonians 5:12-22.** The final section of 1 Thessalonians contains a series of general instructions. The first set of precepts addresses how believers are to treat those lay leaders who have the responsibility of guiding the congregation (5:12-13). A second set addresses the responsibility of every believer toward other believers, whether to admonish or sustain (5:14-15), and toward all. Here, Paul expresses in his own words a principle well attested in the Jesus tradition (see Matthew 5:38-48; Luke 6:27-36): rather than react with evil intent toward another's evil intent, let God's generosity and goodness guide your every deed (5:14-15). Even in a situation of persecution, Paul refuses to allow his converts to fail to apply this principle to their non-Christian neighbors as well as to fellow believers (5:15). By showing a generous heart, the believer might quite possibly defuse a nonbeliever's suspicion and hostility. A third group (5:16-18) calls for the Christian to make joy, prayer, and thanksgiving to God the hallmarks of every hour and of every situation. (See similar words in Philippians 4:4-7.) Joy and thanksgiving are not focused on or derived from the circumstances themselves but from holding to God's goodness and promises so firmly that these become a centering place of joy in the midst of all circumstances. The final set (5:19-22) encourages believers to allow the Spirit to move through and use them in corporate worship, while at the same time examining such manifestations against known standards (such as Scripture, Paul's instruction, and the inward testimony of the whole congregation) so as to discern their source.

**1 Thessalonians 5:23-28.** Paul concludes the letter with some liturgical elements, quite appropriate for the context of reading his letter in the gathered assembly of believers, as Paul solemnly commands (5:27). Making the text "public" has the effect of rendering all accountable to the Word rather than allowing some to subordinate the Word to their own ends and agendas. These liturgical elements include a benediction pronounced over the audience (1 Thessa-

lonians 5:23-24; compare Galatians 6:16; Ephesians 6:23; 2 Thessalonians 3:16) and a prayer for the favor of Christ to rest upon the congregation (1 Thessalonians 5:28; compare 1 Corinthians 16:23; 2 Corinthians 13:14; Galatians 6:18; Ephesians 6:24; Philippians 4:23; Colossians 4:18; 2 Thessalonians 3:18; Philemon 25). Paul's benediction strategically recalls themes from earlier parts of the letter, in particular God's desire that the believers be "sanctified" with a view to preparedness and preservation on the Day of the Lord. Paul thus leaves the hearers with these important themes ringing in their ears as the letter is rolled up and put away.

## INTERPRETING THE SCRIPTURE

*How Meaningful Is the Christian Hope?*

Our expression of our Christian hope takes many forms. At funerals, we may hear about the departed going to be "with the Lord" (as in Philippians 1:23) and joining his or her predeceased family, with the tacit expectation that the surviving family will also be reunited with the deceased someday. In our churches, we recite the creeds that affirm Christ's coming "to judge the living and the dead." In some circles, we hear about Jesus returning soon, and sometimes even about some more "signs" of his coming being fulfilled. The common denominator behind the various expressions is our hope that death will not have the final word on our lives but rather that *Jesus* will—and that his word will mean life for us forever.

Christians have been "encouraging one another with these words" (4:18) for two millennia. These beliefs help the grieving move through the grieving process armed with hope. They help disciples accept significant losses in this life for the sake of choosing what they have discerned to be the path of obedience to God. They help believ-

ers choose against self-centered inclinations in favor of a more virtuous, other-centered course of action. How real is this hope to you? Is life in this world more real than the hope of life in the kingdom? In what ways are you limited or hindered in your discipleship by any perception that this life is the real one, the "one you get"? In what ways are you freed for complete obedience and dedication to God by the assurance that God is greater than death?

*Getting Sober*

Paul looks out on a world that lives largely without regard for the One God's commandments, acting as if that God would never hold them accountable. He selects the image of "sleeping" as an apt metaphor for their state of mind as they keep God's judgment from their consciousness. He selects "drunkenness" as a similarly apt image for dulling one's own spiritual alertness through indulging the passions of the flesh, losing one's focus on the eternal race through temporal distractions, or having one's perception distorted through "drinking in" the values and ideology of the dominant, unbelieving culture.

It is easy indeed to become "intoxicated" in our culture. We too move within a political ideology that stresses "peace and security," that too often takes our attention away from the very real violence within our borders and inflicted beyond our borders, away from the terrible lack of peace as *shalom*, "wholeness," that threatens whole generations of urban youth. We are surrounded by the addictions of materialism and consumerism, being invited to keep chasing away our problems with new purchases and indulgences. We are offered the intoxicants of the pursuit of money, reputation, or advancement, and of self-gratification, whether our pride, our appetites, or our lusts. And we should not forget the very nonmetaphorical use of intoxicants that plagues so many families. All of these function as drugs to mask our pain, to distract us from the empty places God wants to fill with God's own love and Spirit.

From all such intoxicants the Christian is to abstain, so that he or she may be undistracted and unimpeded from preparing for the coming of the Lord, and unembarrassed about his or her past behavior when that Day arrives. Instead, the Christian is to remain awake and be sober (5:6). The privilege of knowing the truth about God comes with the responsibility of living in line with that truth. Being a child of the day means living in a manner befitting daylight, and especially in a manner befitting the Day of the Lord. "Let us live honorably as in the day," Paul writes, "not in reveling and drunkenness, not in debauchery and licentiousness, not in quarreling and jealousy. Instead, put on the Lord Jesus Christ, and make no provision for the flesh, to gratify its desires" (Romans 13:13-14). What are some of the worldly "intoxicants" that have a foothold in your life? How can you increase your spiritual sobriety, so as to live prepared to meet Christ without shame at his coming?

## Encouraging One Another

Paul's instruction in 1 Thessalonians 5:11 focuses our attention once again on each other. Throughout his letters, Paul urges believers to look after other believers, particularly with regard to doing whatever will help another remain faithful to Christ, grow in discipleship, and resist the snares of the Enemy. In this letter, Paul particularly singles out the experience of grief over the loss of loved ones as an opportunity for Christians to stand beside their grieving sisters and brothers, offering the gifts of presence, of support, and gentle reminders of the resurrection that injects hope into our grief (4:13-18). He also singles out the importance of remembering Christ's forthcoming visitation in judgment, calling believers to use this reminder to redirect one another's attention and goals away from what has value only in the sight of the drunken world toward what will have value in the sight of God.

An unfortunate side effect of the development of a professional clergy in the church has been the gradual abdication on the part of the laity—the unpaid ministers of the church—of their responsibility toward one another, depriving the whole church of their personal investment of service and support and replacing this with "contributions." All baptized Christians, however, are "ministers," channels for God's grace to flow within the church and beyond the church into the world. The role of the professional clergy is to *equip* the laity for ministry (Ephesians 4:11-13), not to do the work of ministry on behalf of the laity.

As we walk more and more in the ways that Paul teaches us to please God, we will find ourselves taking on roles that, perhaps, we have traditionally assigned to the paid church staff. We will learn how to come alongside the grieving or form long-term caring relationships (as developed, for example, through the excellent "Stephen Ministries" program). We will develop relationships of accountability, asking our seniors in the faith to help us in our weaknesses and offering help and accountability to our juniors in the faith in regard to theirs. We will dedicate ourselves to the work of outreach, both following up on parishioners we have not seen in attendance in some

time and inviting new souls into the fellowship of the congregation. When we see a need or opportunity to develop a new ministry, we will invest ourselves as God directs rather than waiting for someone else to make it happen. Paul's vision for the church is a vital and vibrant one indeed!

## SHARING THE SCRIPTURE

### Preparing Our Hearts

Meditate on this week's devotional reading, found in Joel 3:11-16. Here the prophet speaks about the coming "day of the LORD" (3:14). Many are "in the valley of decision" (3:14). Are you one of them? Or have you already sought refuge in the Lord? If you have, in what ways are you helping others to find hope as God's plan for the future continues to unfold?

Pray that you and the adult learners will seek salvation not only for yourselves but also help others to commit themselves to Christ.

### Preparing Our Minds

Study the background from 1 Thessalonians 4:13–5:28 and lesson scripture, 1 Thessalonians 5:1-11. Consider the context in which you want to fit in and contribute to society.

Write on newsprint:
❑ information for next week's lesson, found under "Continue the Journey."
❑ activities for further spiritual growth in "Continue the Journey."

Cut a sheet of newsprint into randomly shaped pieces to be used for a puzzle. Do this prior to class or have someone who arrives early do it for you. Be sure to have enough pieces for those who attend, plus two or three extra pieces for visitors.

**Option:** Prepare a lecture based on questions found under "Examine Paul's Words to the Thessalonians about God's Master Plan."

### LEADING THE CLASS

#### (1) Gather to Learn

❖ Welcome the class members and introduce any guests.

❖ Pray that all who have come today will open their hearts and minds to the leading of the Spirit.

❖ Distribute the pieces of newsprint you have cut so that each student has one piece. (If you have extra pieces, some adults will need to take another. If the class is extremely large, one person may have a single piece to represent several students.) Ask the students to gather around a table (or use the floor) and assemble their puzzle.

❖ Talk with the class about how most people want to fit together with others. Inquire about how they feel when they know where they fit in versus how they feel when they cannot find a comfortable place.

❖ Read aloud today's focus statement: **Most people want to understand how they fit in and contribute to society as a whole. What is the context within which we obtain such an understanding? God's plan of salvation is embodied in the divine plan for all creation, which is directly related to Christ's return to earth.**

#### (2) Examine Paul's Words to the Thessalonians about God's Master Plan

❖ Select a volunteer to read 1 Thessalonians 5:1-11.

❖ Discuss these questions:

**(1) What images does Paul use to describe the sudden arrival of "the day of the Lord"?** (Use information from the first paragraph of 1 Thessalonians 5:1-11 in Understanding the Scripture to help the students understand the biblical roots of these two images: a thief in the night and the onset of labor in a pregnant woman.)

**(2) Why is it important for believers to know that "the day of the Lord" will come suddenly?** (See the second paragraph of 1 Thessalonians 5:1-11 in Understanding the Scripture.)

**(3) What do Paul's words "keep awake and be sober" suggest to you about being prepared for "the day of the Lord"?** (See the third and fourth paragraphs of 1 Thessalonians 5:1-11 in Understanding the Scripture.)

**(4) What role does the community of faith play in preparing for "the day of the Lord"?** (See the fifth paragraph of 1 Thessalonians 5:1-11 in Understanding the Scripture.)

❖ **Option:** Answer these questions yourself and present them to the class as a lecture.

❖ Close this portion of the session by inviting the students to state ways in which they believe their congregation is encouraging its members to be prepared for Christ's coming.

*(3) Realize the Meaning of Christ's Return*

❖ Lead the adults in a unison reading of today's key verse, 1 Thessalonians 5:9.

❖ Divide the class into pairs or groups of three and suggest that they discuss what it means to them to know that God has destined them for salvation. How does that knowledge make them feel? With whom do they share such wonderful news?

❖ Read these comments about the Second Coming and ask the class to say how each one helps them better understand Christ's return and how we are to wait for it.

■ **The primitive church thought more about the Second Coming of Jesus Christ than about death or about heaven. The early Christians were looking not for a cleft in the ground called a grave but for a cleavage in the sky called Glory. They were watching not for the undertaker but for the uppertaker.** (Alexander Maclaren, 1826–1910)

■ **We are not a post-war generation, but a pre-peace generation. Jesus is coming.** (Corrie Ten Boom, 1892–1983)

■ **The only way to wait for the Second Coming is to watch that you do what you should do, so that when he comes it is a matter of indifference. It is the attitude of a child, certain that God knows what he is about. When the Lord does come, it will be as natural as breathing. God never does anything hysterical, and he never produces hysterics.** (Oswald Chambers, 1874–1917)

❖ Encourage the students to add any other ideas or images they have concerning the Second Coming.

*(4) Make or Renew a Commitment to Jesus So As to Receive the Gift of Salvation and Eternal Life*

❖ Provide a few moments for quiet reflection so that the students may consider their commitment to Jesus.

❖ Use the following portion of the Baptismal Covenant (as found in *The United Methodist Hymnal*) to call class members to make or reaffirm a commitment to Jesus.

**Do you confess Jesus Christ as your Savior,**

**put your whole trust in his grace,**

**and promise to serve him as your Lord,**

in union with the church which Christ has opened

to people of all ages, nations, and races?

If so, respond by saying, "I do."

*(5) Continue the Journey*

❖ Pray that all who have come today will feel hopeful as they consider their place in God's cosmic plan.

❖ Read aloud this preparation for next week's lesson. You may also want to post it on newsprint for the students to copy.

■ **Title: Glory to Christ**

■ **Background Scripture: 2 Thessalonians 1**

■ **Lesson Scripture: 2 Thessalonians 1:3-12**

■ **Focus of the Lesson: People often commit to someone or something because their commitment serves a purpose. What purpose does a particular commitment seek to fulfill? The text implies that God wants our Christian commitment to aim always at giving glory to Christ.**

❖ Challenge the students to complete one or more of these activities for further spiritual growth, which you will write on newsprint for the students to copy.

**(1) Act as a mentor for someone who is trying to fit in to the life of your congregation. Help this person see that he or she has a role to play as together you await the return of Christ.**

**(2) Turn to the word "day" in a Bible concordance looking for "Day of the Lord" or "Day of Judgment." Read these entries to learn as much as you can about what to expect on this day. Ask yourself: am I ready?**

**(3) Encourage someone who is in despair to find hope in salvation through Christ Jesus.**

❖ Sing or read aloud "I Know Whom I Have Believed."

❖ Conclude today's session by leading the class in this benediction adapted from 2 Thessalonians 1:11: **Go forth with the assurance that we are always praying for you, asking that our God will make you worthy of his call and will fulfill by his power every good resolve and work of faith.**

# UNIT 2: THE FOUNDATION OF CHRISTIAN COMMITMENT
# GLORY TO CHRIST

---

## PREVIEWING THE LESSON

**Lesson Scripture:** 2 Thessalonians 1:3-12
**Background Scripture:** 2 Thessalonians 1
**Key Verse:** 2 Thessalonians 1:11

### Focus of the Lesson:

People often commit to someone or something because their commitment serves a purpose. What purpose does a particular commitment seek to fulfill? The text implies that God wants our Christian commitment to aim always at giving glory to Christ.

### Goals for the Learners:

(1) to examine Paul's words about the judgment at Christ's return.
(2) to recognize the connection between their commitment to God and glorifying the name of Jesus Christ.
(3) to reaffirm their faith in Jesus Christ, who is worthy of glory.

### Supplies:

Bibles, newsprint and marker, paper and pencils, hymnals

JULY 11

---

## READING THE SCRIPTURE

NRSV

2 Thessalonians 1:3-12

³We must always give thanks to God for you, brothers and sisters, as is right, because your faith is growing abundantly, and the love of everyone of you for one another is increasing. ⁴Therefore we ourselves boast of you among the churches of God for your steadfastness and faith during all your persecutions and the afflictions that you are enduring.

⁵This is evidence of the righteous judgment of God, and is intended to make you worthy of the kingdom of God, for which

NIV

2 Thessalonians 1:3-12

³We ought always to thank God for you, brothers, and rightly so, because your faith is growing more and more, and the love every one of you has for each other is increasing. ⁴Therefore, among God's churches we boast about your perseverance and faith in all the persecutions and trials you are enduring.

⁵All this is evidence that God's judgment is right, and as a result you will be counted worthy of the kingdom of God, for which you are suffering. ⁶God is just: He will pay

you are also suffering. [6]For it is indeed just of God to repay with affliction those who afflict you, [7]and to give relief to the afflicted as well as to us, when the Lord Jesus is revealed from heaven with his mighty angels [8]in flaming fire, inflicting vengeance on those who do not know God and on those who do not obey the gospel of our Lord Jesus. [9]These will suffer the punishment of eternal destruction, separated from the presence of the Lord and from the glory of his might, [10]when he comes to be glorified by his saints and to be marveled at on that day among all who have believed, because our testimony to you was believed. [11]To this end **we always pray for you, asking that our God will make you worthy of his call and will fulfill by his power every good resolve and work of faith,** [12]so that the name of our Lord Jesus may be glorified in you, and you in him, according to the grace of our God and the Lord Jesus Christ.

back trouble to those who trouble you [7]and give relief to you who are troubled, and to us as well. This will happen when the Lord Jesus is revealed from heaven in blazing fire with his powerful angels. [8]He will punish those who do not know God and do not obey the gospel of our Lord Jesus. [9]They will be punished with everlasting destruction and shut out from the presence of the Lord and from the majesty of his power [10]on the day he comes to be glorified in his holy people and to be marveled at among all those who have believed. This includes you, because you believed our testimony to you. [11]With this in mind, **we constantly pray for you, that our God may count you worthy of his calling, and that by his power he may fulfill every good purpose of yours and every act prompted by your faith.** [12]We pray this so that the name of our Lord Jesus may be glorified in you, and you in him, according to the grace of our God and the Lord Jesus Christ.

## UNDERSTANDING THE SCRIPTURE

**2 Thessalonians 1:1-4.** After the traditional Pauline letter opening, the authors of this letter (Paul is once again joined by co-senders) craft a thanksgiving section that once more gives us a window into a Christian community's experience of being rejected, shamed, and abused by its non-Christian society. These experiences of persecution are current at the time of writing ("the afflictions that you are enduring," 1:4). Paul and his team are thus keenly aware that they need to help their converts understand these experiences in such a way that those converts will regard persevering in the face of hostility as advantageous and ennobling. This is the very opposite of the impression that the society is trying to make. Their non-Christian neighbors are still trying to make the converts see their departure from the dominant culture's way

of life as disadvantageous and shameful to them, so as to win them back.

The authors begin their task by praising the converts for the qualities they show as they bravely endure attack from outside, reporting that they are indeed spreading the good word about the converts' noble character throughout the churches of God (1:3-4). Their firmness and reliability in the face of opposition give them a claim to honor in the sight of God, the authors, and the "churches of God" beyond their city. In particular, Paul elevates their reliability in their relationships with one another—their love for one another, manifested in so many ways within a church that is under attack from outside. This love is an important contributing factor to the noble estimation God and the churches have formed of them (1:3). In short, they are doing everything "right" in God's eyes, which will come as a powerful encouragement since society has been trying to convince them they have been doing everything "wrong."

**2 Thessalonians 1:5-7.** The experience of persecution itself, however, is also ennobled by these authors as the means by which the believers are being fitted for God's kingdom itself (1:5). Jewish authors had already begun to view suffering affliction at the hands of the ungodly as a means by which God tested the commitment and character of the righteous and, like gold in the fire, proved their mettle and their worth (see Wisdom of Solomon 3:5 in the Apocrypha). Steadfast endurance in the face of hardships was not to be seen as society shaming them but as God shaping them and demonstrating their worth, with the result that they would enter into God's reward (see also Hebrews 12:5-11 and 1 Peter 1:6-7). The focus of the righteous sufferers is also strategically shifted by this concept. No longer are they concerned with their lost honor in the world's eyes or with escaping the heat but rather with proving themselves worthy of a greater honor ("worthy of the kingdom of God," 2 Thessalonians 1:5; "worthy of [God's] call," 1:11). Worldly ambitions are defused and the very human trait of being ambitious is itself harnessed to help believers persevere for eternal honor.

In what way, though, is the believers' suffering "evidence" of God's righteous judgment (1:5)? The authors are not suggesting that the persecutions came upon the believers because God judged the converts worthy of punishment, such that they had to pass through persecution before being "worthy" of the kingdom. Verses 6-8, which explain how God's justice will work out, lead away from such a reading. Rather, the believers' suffering is really a sign or proof of God's imminent vindication (positive judgment) of the believers and punishment (negative judgment) of those who afflict the innocent righteous. This too was a familiar topic in Jewish literature on suffering for righteousness or God's Law (see in the Apocrypha 4 Maccabees 9:8-9, 24, 31-32;

10:10, 21; 11:22-23; 12:11-14). Because God is just—and this is the underlying premise for the argument—the unjust affliction currently experienced by the believers is evidence that God's judgment will soon break in to set matters right, vindicating the faithful disciples and chastening those who afflict them.

**2 Thessalonians 1:8-12.** Part of Paul's strategy involves clarifying whose opinion really counts in the long run. The threat to Christian commitment is that the converts will begin to have regard for the opinion of their non-Christian neighbors concerning their adherence to Jesus and the "Christ cult." The danger is that they will begin to see themselves as pursuing a questionable, even shameful, course of action and will therefore turn away from Christ and the Christ-followers in order to regain the approval and affirmation of those outside the group. The sustained focus on the day of Christ's appearing and divine judgment in 1:6-12 offers a strategic and strong antidote to this potential poison.

The phrase "obey the gospel" (1:8) points again beyond a sense of "gospel" as a message to be believed toward a sense of "gospel" as an announcement about a significant political intervention. A new ruler is announced, and the question is implicitly posed: will you prove obedient to and receptive of his rule, or will he have to enforce his reign with military might (for example, "with his mighty angels" and "flaming fire")? The people outside the Christian group also keep themselves outside the sphere of God's favor and approval. They neither know God nor are obedient to God, particularly as God's will has been revealed in the gospel (1:8), with the result that they are themselves a dishonorable lot (lacking both in piety and justice, since they resist God's rule). Indeed, the very pressures they apply to the believers in an attempt to shame them into conformity with the dominant culture's values necessitate God's visitation of judgment upon their heads. Paul and his team hereby declare those pressures and persecutions of believers to be undeserved and unjust. The believers are thereby encouraged to withstand them, assured of God's approval of their walk and God's vindication of their honor against the outsiders.

God's court issues the only verdict—the only estimation of who is honorable and who censurable—worth considering, since God's opinion ascribes eternal honor or eternal disgrace. The believers can endure society's scorn since they know it will result in lasting honor when Christ returns as judge. Conversely, the nonbelievers' story moves in the opposite direction, from honor in worldly eyes to disgrace and criticism before God's court (1:9). In the meanwhile, the approval of God is mirrored in the esteem the converts enjoy in the eyes of their leaders (the authors) and of Christians around the Mediterranean (1:3-4).

## INTERPRETING THE SCRIPTURE

### The Crucible of Suffering

Suffering is an important topic in the Thessalonian letters. In both, Paul assigns a certain positive value to suffering that is quite foreign to our own cultural stance toward negative experiences. Suffering, for us, is something rigorously to be avoided, or, if encountered, alleviated as quickly as possible. This is deeply ingrained in our thinking, with the result that our capacity to follow Christ is often sorely limited. If being obedient to Christ's word or leading means putting ourselves in harm's way, we may be very reluctant to do so. If it means even the loss of our accustomed comforts, we may seek any excuse not to follow that path. But the larger truth of the matter is that our manner of following Christ is so congenial to the values of the society around us that we are unlikely to encounter the possibility of suffering on his behalf.

This is not the case for so many of our sisters and brothers around the world, from whose example we can learn much. They have organized their whole lives around Jesus, from trying to walk in his steps to meeting with other believers on a regular basis, even though this leads to conflict with their neighbors and repressive actions from their society. Nevertheless, they accept the cost of discipleship, believing that their own well-being ultimately depends on pleasing God rather than conforming to their society's expectations.

If we were fully to take Jesus' teachings and those of the apostles seriously, reordering our individual and common lives around them, would we rub against our society in significant ways? Would we no longer "fit in" and accept being treated as misfits? Whenever we take such steps and encounter such resistance, *then* Paul's words about suffering apply. It is important to clarify here that God is not *behind* the suffering. In the Thessalonians' case, the suffering comes from people who are committed to a way of life incompatible with the gospel of Jesus, and who react with hostility toward the Christians who threaten that way of life. But as the believers endure that suffering, God uses it to form their characters, clarify their commitments, and amplify their witness.

### According to Whose Standards?

As Paul draws attention to the coming visitation of Christ and God's judgment of humanity, he raises for his hearers the important matter of whose opinion really counts. Whose standards ultimately matter, such that we should try to live up to those standards? In the Thessalonians' situation, the more they valued the opinion of their society, the less likely they would be to persevere in following Christ. They would fall back into participating in the worship of the emperor and the traditional gods. Whether or not they ever believed in those gods again, they would erase their witness to the One God and to the fact that even the great Roman Empire was accountable to that God, and therefore subject to prophetic critique.

For us, the tendency is to accept a highly materialistic and hierarchical definition of "success" ("honor"). When we order our lives primarily around the acquisition of "more" and around the kind of superior "performance" that will get us recognized, affirmed, even promoted or better paid, we testify with our lives to the importance of these values. But we serve a Lord who taught his followers to seek greatness through serving others most fully and to seek wealth in heaven by keeping nothing for ourselves beyond life's necessities, so that others' lack of the necessities might be relieved. Living by those standards would leave us looking "small" in the eyes of many. But if we set our ambitions around living up to God's standards—living in a manner "worthy of the kingdom of God" or "worthy of [God's] call" (1:5, 11)—we will have to learn to accept coming up short in regard to many of our peers' standards. However, we would also never be too busy or tired to spend time and energy in communion with God, encouraging our own families and our fellow believers, or serving the mission of the church.

When confronting Israel for its toleration of the worship of Baal in its midst, Elijah challenged the people no longer to go through life limping between two opinions: either the Lord is God, and should be followed, or Baal is god, and should be followed (see 1 Kings 18:20-39). Jesus counseled his followers not to try to serve two masters, God and Wealth (see Matthew 6:24). Paul, in his own way, rings the changes on this theme as he calls the disciples to continue to order their lives fully with a view to the applause of heaven rather than the approval of worldly voices. To fail to make a clear choice threatens us with the loss of both.

*Reinforcing God's Standards*

Paul and his team perform a very important function reflected in both 1 and 2 Thessalonians, as well as Timothy's visit in person to the community. When the converts' neighbors are applying significant social pressure upon the disciples to make them feel like deviants who fail to measure up to "acceptable" standards, Paul vocally reminds them of that greater, invisible court of opinion that looks on with approval as the disciples persevere in faith, hope, and love. Paul and his team help the believers see their situation in the light of eternity, from the standpoint of God's judgment seat. It is vitally important that the perspective of the invisible God be brought to bear through visible representatives and in concrete relationships. Paul invites the congregation as a whole into continuing this service on one another's behalf, offering encouragement—and the social support that can be felt alongside and underneath such encouragement—of those behaviors and perspectives that keep the believers heading toward the prize of God's call.

If we are to grow in our awareness of the distance between what God affirms and what our society affirms, and to grow in our personal investment of ourselves in the former over the latter, we need to be attentive to this dimension of our lives together in the community of faith. Through what we praise, single out for special attention and honor, or show that we value, we nurture an environment that will either reinforce God's standards or the world's. We will foster a culture in which individual ambition is redirected toward excelling in embodying Christ's teachings or allowed to continue to run after those things that our society tells us are essential markers of a life worth living.

Do you reinforce worldly values by

admiring, speaking highly of, and treating with respect those who have wealth, prestige, and power as your society estimates these things? Or do you reinforce God's values by looking for, and praising instead, a Christ-like character, service to others locally and globally, and single-hearted devotion to doing what pleases and gives glory to God? In what ways might you need to change so as to free other believers to seek their self-worth in Christ and not the standards by which secular minds measure a person?

---

# SHARING THE SCRIPTURE

## *Preparing Our Hearts*

Meditate on this week's devotional reading, found in 1 Peter 5:6-11. This passage includes a theme that you will encounter in today's Scripture reading: suffering that leads to "eternal glory in Christ" (5:10). Notice that God does not cause us to suffer; neither are we to seek out suffering. Instead, suffering comes as a result of our relationship with Christ, for our opponent, the devil, is constantly after us. Yet Christ will "restore, support, strengthen, and establish you" (5:10). What specific application does this message have in your life this week?

Pray that you and the adult learners will recognize that even in the midst of suffering Christ is with you to strengthen you and call you into glory.

## *Preparing Our Minds*

Study the background from 2 Thessalonians 1 and lesson Scripture, verses 3-12. Think about this question: what is the purpose of making a commitment?

Write on newsprint:

❑ information for next week's lesson, found under "Continue the Journey."

❑ activities for further spiritual growth in "Continue the Journey."

## LEADING THE CLASS

### *(1) Gather to Learn*

❖ Welcome the class members and introduce any guests.

❖ Pray that all who have gathered today will be open to God's comfort and leading in their lives.

❖ Read this story from International Christian Concern (www.persecution.org): **Ahmadey Osman Nur, a 22 year old guest at a friend's wedding in Somalia, was shot and killed in September, 2008, because he dared to ask the Sheik who conducted the wedding in Arabic to translate a summary of the service into Somali, which the people in attendance could understand. Offended because Arabic is considered a "holy" language, the Sheik asked his bodyguard "to silence the apostate," for Nur had converted from Islam to Christianity. Several other Christians had also recently been martyred in Somalia. Nur would be remembered, according to his pastor, for his compassion to the elderly and also as the first in his area to memorize the entire book of the Acts of the Apostles, a book he cherished.**

❖ Ask: **If Christians in our community were threatened with death, how many do you think would remain committed to the faith? Why would some cling to Christ while others turned away from him?**

❖ Read aloud today's focus statement: **People often commit to someone or something because their commitment serves a purpose. What purpose does a particular commitment seek to fulfill? The text implies that God wants our Christian commitment to aim always at giving glory to Christ.**

*(2) Examine Paul's Words about the Judgment at Christ's Return*

❖ Choose someone to read 2 Thessalonians 1:3-12 as if reading to a congregation that is anxious to hear from Paul.

    ❖ Discuss these questions:

      **(1) What can you surmise about the situation of the congregation to whom this letter was addressed?** (Use information from 2 Thessalonians 1:5-7 to address this issue of persecution.)

      **(2) What dangers does Paul perceive for these Christians who are suffering?** (See 2 Thessalonians 1:8-12 in Understanding the Scripture.)

      **(3) How does this passage relate to you, especially if you live in a place where being a Christian does not bring scorn and persecution?**

❖ Encourage several volunteers to debate this statement: **The early church was stronger and better able to witness than most contemporary churches because its members knew and acted on the belief that in the end only God's opinion really counted.**

*(3) Recognize the Connection between the Learners' Commitment to God and Glorifying the Name of Jesus Christ*

❖ Distribute paper and pencils. Ask the students to list three things they intend to do this week. After they have completed their lists, ask them to list three things they would do if they knew that God's judgment were imminent.

❖ Discuss this question, without getting into the specifics of the students' lists: **If the two lists you just created were not identical, what other priorities have you put ahead of leading a life committed to God and prepared for the Second Coming of Christ?**

❖ Divide the class into groups and give each group a sheet of newsprint and a marker. Encourage them to list actions that they believe glorify the name of Jesus.

❖ Invite the groups to report their ideas. Here are some possibilities: *spreading the good news of Jesus, praising God in word and song, conducting ourselves in ways that demonstrate to others that Christ lives in us, testifying to what Christ has done in our lives.*

❖ Conclude by asking the students to think silently about how the lists they created independently were similar to and different from the list the group made. Suggest that they consider ways to commit themselves to more fully glorifying Christ through their actions.

*(4) Reaffirm Their Faith in Jesus Christ, Who Is Worthy of Glory*

❖ Distribute hymnals and ask the students to turn to "The Nicene Creed," an affirmation of faith that dates to the fourth century. Encourage the students to ponder the meaning of these words and what they believe as you read them aloud:

    **For our sake he was crucified under Pontius Pilate;**
    **he suffered death and was buried.**
    **On the third day he rose again**
    **in accordance with the Scriptures;**
    **he ascended into heaven**
    **and is seated at the right hand of the Father.**
    **He will come again in glory**
    **to judge the living and the dead,**
    **and his kingdom will have no end.**

❖ Invite those who wish to affirm their faith in Jesus Christ and commit their lives fully to him to read the entire affirmation of faith in unison.

*(5) Continue the Journey*

❖ Pray that today's participants will go forth to glorify Christ as a sign of their commitment to him.

❖ Read aloud this preparation for next week's lesson. You may also want to post it on newsprint for the students to copy.

■ Title: Chosen and Called

■ Background Scripture: 2 Thessalonians 2

■ Lesson Scripture: 2 Thessalonians 2:13-17

■ Focus of the Lesson: Commitments grow from a number of factors. What is at the heart of a commitment that makes a needed and lasting difference? The passage affirms that our Christian commitment grows from a response to being chosen by God and empowered by the Spirit.

❖ Challenge the students to complete one or more of these activities for further spiritual growth, which you will write on newsprint for the students to copy.

(1) Browse the website (www.persecution.org) of International Christian Concern, which is a human rights organization based in Washington, D.C., whose mission is to assist persecuted Christians around the world. Look for ways that you can help those who are suffering because of their faith in Christ.

(2) Offer an intercessory prayer on behalf of someone who needs to find purpose and direction in life.

(3) Think about your purpose in life. Consider who you are and what you do. What role does glorifying Christ play in your life? What role would you like it to play?

❖ Sing or read aloud "To God Be the Glory."

❖ Conclude today's session by leading the class in this benediction adapted from 2 Thessalonians 1:11: Go forth with the assurance that we are always praying for you, asking that our God will make you worthy of his call and will fulfill by his power every good resolve and work of faith.

## UNIT 2: THE FOUNDATION OF CHRISTIAN COMMITMENT
# CHOSEN AND CALLED

---

### PREVIEWING THE LESSON

**Lesson Scripture:** 2 Thessalonians 2:13-17
**Background Scripture:** 2 Thessalonians 2
**Key Verse:** 2 Thessalonians 2:15

#### Focus of the Lesson:
Commitments grow from a number of factors. What is at the heart of a commitment that makes a needed and lasting difference? The passage affirms that our Christian commitment grows from a response to being chosen by God and empowered by the Spirit.

#### Goals for the Learners:
(1) to review Paul's words to the Thessalonians about holding fast to the traditions he taught them.
(2) to enjoy some of the traditions Paul taught.
(3) to commit themselves to the call to believe in the good news of Jesus Christ.

#### Pronunciation Guide:
Antiochus (an ti' uh kuhs)
apocalyptic (uh pok uh lip' tik)
Caligula (kih lig' yuh luh)

eschatological (es kat uh loj' i kuhl)
*inclusio* (in kloo' zhee oh)
Pompey (pom' pee)

#### Supplies:
Bibles, newsprint and marker, paper and pencils, hymnals

---

### READING THE SCRIPTURE

**NRSV**

2 Thessalonians 2:13-17

¹³But we must always give thanks to God for you, brothers and sisters beloved by the Lord, because God chose you as the first fruits for salvation through sanctification by the Spirit and through belief in the truth. ¹⁴For this purpose he called you through our

**NIV**

2 Thessalonians 2:13-17

¹³But we ought always to thank God for you, brothers loved by the Lord, because from the beginning God chose you to be saved through the sanctifying work of the Spirit and through belief in the truth. ¹⁴He

proclamation of the good news, so that you may obtain the glory of our Lord Jesus Christ. **15So then, brothers and sisters, stand firm and hold fast to the traditions that you were taught by us, either by word of mouth or by our letter.**

16Now may our Lord Jesus Christ himself and God our Father, who loved us and through grace gave us eternal comfort and good hope, 17comfort your hearts and strengthen them in every good work and word.

called you to this through our gospel, that you might share in the glory of our Lord Jesus Christ. **15So then, brothers, stand firm and hold to the teachings we passed on to you, whether by word of mouth or by letter.**

16May our Lord Jesus Christ himself and God our Father, who loved us and by his grace gave us eternal encouragement and good hope, 17encourage your hearts and strengthen you in every good deed and word.

---

## UNDERSTANDING THE SCRIPTURE

**2 Thessalonians 2:1-2.** The authors come to their second concern, namely the correction of a misunderstanding of Christian understanding of the end time. The source of this misunderstanding, namely that "the Day of the Lord is already here," is not entirely clear, even to the authors. Was it revealed in a prophetic utterance ("by spirit"), or did it come through a false representation of Paul's words, spoken or written? Despite the insistence that the Day of the Lord will come suddenly and might well be very near, it has not yet arrived (2:1-2). The authors need to reaffirm both the certainty of Christ's return to reward the righteous, living or dead, and the lingering futurity of that event.

Many respected scholars interpret 2 Thessalonians as a letter written by a disciple of Paul, using 1 Thessalonians as a model, to address a new situation in one or more Christian churches using the deceased apostle's authority. Second Thessalonians 2:2 does suggest that letters written in Paul's name, but not actually written by Paul, might already have begun to be circulated before this letter was written. Some commentators have also suggested that the end-time viewpoints in the two letters—the expectation of the sudden appearing of the Lord in 1 Thessalonians and the expectation

in 2 Thessalonians that the Second Coming will be preceded by signs one can discern in advance—are incompatible, and so could not both come from Paul himself. The eschatological (end time) perspectives of the two letters, however, stand side-by-side elsewhere in the New Testament. For example, in Mark 13:28-37, the first half asserts that by careful observation of certain signs the disciples will know that the Son of Man is near; the second half cautions them that "about that day or hour no one knows" except the Father.

**2 Thessalonians 2:3-8.** As proof that the Day is still ahead, the authors revisit a basic end-time schedule of events that they share, to a large extent, with other Jewish apocalyptic groups. Before the end, there will be a widespread revolt against God's order and standards, and the emergence of a figure in whom the human and demonic revolt against God comes to fullest and final expression. The translation of this one's name from the Greek is the "Man of Lawlessness" (2:3).

Jewish and Christian apocalypses tended to look ahead to a single person or event in which all the evil and ungodliness now at work in the world, mostly under the surface and annoyingly elusive, would come to full and open expression. The Jews had witnessed many prototypes of such a person, as a line of Gentile overlords either desecrated or threatened to desecrate that which was most holy and symbolically important, namely the Temple of God in Jerusalem (Nebuchadnezzar, Antiochus IV, Pompey, Caligula), often along with shrines of other gods revered by conquered nations. Such figures entered apocalyptic lore as early as Daniel 7–8 and continue to be seen somewhat impersonally in Mark 13:14 and very personally in Revelation 13. The "Man of Lawlessness" is cast from the same mold, expressing this conviction that the enemy of God and God's people would come out into the open once and for all at some point—only to be destroyed once and for all. Even though the "Man of Lawlessness" may be seen as a fearsome figure, God is in control from beginning to end, and the lawless one is never a real threat to God's order.

At present, the "mystery of lawlessness" (2:7) is already at work, noticeably in the rejection of the gospel and the persecution of the believers. There is, however, an unnamed "restraining force" and "restrainer" (2:6-7) holding back the lawless one, but the coming of the lawless one cannot be far away. What the authors had in mind by this "restraining power" is far from clear. Some suggest the Roman Empire and its emperor, which, despite their faults, nevertheless maintained order and prevented lawlessness from running amok. The authors may also have had in mind some angelic power, since these are often depicted as exercising a restraining role in apocalypses (whether holding back the elements of judgment, or controlling the gate of the abyss; see Revelation 7:1-3; 9:1-3; 20:1-3). The converts are thus reminded that they are witnessing—and participating in—the opening acts of the end-time drama. The coming of Christ remains imminent, which renders the rebellion and advent of the lawless one all the more imminent, but they are still living out the "beginning of the birth pangs" (Mark 13:8). Nevertheless, the end

of the sequence is the same: the lawless one and all who have been duped by Satan fall under God's condemnation and perish at Christ's appearing (2:8, 11-12).

**2 Thessalonians 2:9-15.** What the "Man of Lawlessness" will bring out in full force openly in the future is already at work behind the scenes, namely the "mystery of lawlessness" (2:7). At the same time, Satan plies his deceptions upon those who have refused to embrace the truth of the gospel (2:9-10). The disciples' non-Christian neighbors—the very people trying to harass and shame them from continuing in their Christian walk—are in fact the victims of Satan's deceptions. Their rejection of the gospel and assault on the believers is part of the working of the "mystery of lawlessness" already active in the present time of the hearers, the beginnings of the final "rebellion" against God. These non-Christians, although acting and no doubt thinking of themselves as the guardians of traditional values, are actually spiraling downward to the abyss without even realizing their danger and doom. They are not, however, merely victims. In choosing against the gospel, they have refused to accept God's truth and have clung to disobedience as their preferred lifestyle (2:12). Therefore, they come not only under Satan's sway but God also seals their doom by giving them over wholly to that delusion (2:11).

The believers, however, are in a privileged position, even while they are being persecuted! They have received the necessary information to avoid falling prey to Satan's deceptions (2:3, 15). If they stand firm, holding onto the authentic message of Paul and his team, they will remain safe from this global deception (2:9-12) and enjoy deliverance and the fulfillment of God's good purposes for the converts (2:13), which includes obtaining a share in the honor ("glory") that Jesus himself enjoys (2:14). The section that began at 2:1 properly ends with 2:15, which returns to the words "by word" and "by our letter" (compare 2:2

and 2:15). The author has used a literary device called *inclusio* to indicate that the thanksgiving in 2:13 does not begin a new section, but rather completes the current section, which highlights once again the contrast between the converts (2:13-15) and those outside the church (2:9-12) so that those inside will not be tempted to revert to the lifestyle and worldview of those outside.

**2 Thessalonians 2:16-17.** Praying for the congregation, the authors call attention to the "eternal encouragement" ("comfort" may be too weak a translation here) and reliable, bright hope that God has given them (2:16). These gifts of God will enable the converts to keep swimming against the tide of their society because they have God's strength and the assurance of a greater future.

## INTERPRETING THE SCRIPTURE

### Which Story Shall We Live?

We have become much more aware of the power that our personal "story" exercises over our lives. One of the more obvious expressions of this awareness comes from the practice of counseling or psychology, where clients examine the story of their experience with their family of origin to discover ways in which their ongoing story (for example, their current relationships with spouse and children, or their continued wrestling with feelings of inferiority, or with overachievement, and the like) is limited and constrained by that earlier story. Another expression comes from the fundamental story "template" that we see all around us, and into which we are easily pressed: we get some degree of an education, take a job, work all our lives toward certain specified financial goals, and retire.

Paul invites us into a story of good news. God has selected us in love for a glorious destiny—deliverance from judgment and the enjoyment of a share in Jesus' own glory. This story invites us to live beyond the constraints imposed on our stories by a dysfunctional upbringing, offering healing and liberation instead. It invites us to live for a much grander goal, freeing us along the way to invest our time, energy, and resources far more fully in extending God's love to other people. It is a story that promises a happy ending with no regrets.

How fully has this story of God's good news taken root in your life and "invaded" the other stories that you have been living out? In what ways do the other stories continue to constrain you and work against God's story?

### Standing Firm and Holding Fast

Paul knows that diligence and determination are required in order to move forward toward God's good end for our story, and to resist being pulled back into the narrative plots that our families or our society would craft for us. Paul directs this diligence here toward holding onto the apostolic teaching and standing firm in the way of life and thinking that this teaching nurtures. This is not a call to conservatism in regard to all our church traditions pure and simple. We need to discern between essential "traditions" of the faith and those local or regional or denominational traditions that are "indifferent matters" in God's sight—comfortable, valuable perhaps, but not ultimately foundational.

However, many invitations to move away from those apostolic traditions confront us on a regular basis. The danger of being swayed by false, innovative teaching has been with the church since its inception. Sometimes this takes a radical form, as when the very hope in the resurrection from the dead comes under fire, since it does not fit into our modern, naturalistic worldview. Sometimes this takes a seductive form, as when we are told that God wants us to enjoy all of life's goodies, when the "gospel" of worldly success displaces the true gospel that invites us to become like Jesus in his obedient death so as to share also in his resurrection (Philippians 2:1-11; 3:8-11) or to pursue the path of self-denial and cross-bearing (Mark 8:34-38). Sometimes it takes a subversive form, as when the apostolic proclamation that God's kingdom would succeed and set right all the ills of human domination systems is made subservient to one human nation's exercise of its power.

Whatever the innovative departure from the teachings of Jesus and the apostles, Paul challenges us to keep ourselves so fully rooted in the tradition that we remain on course, not diverted by any of these detours. And "standing firm" is never just a matter of right doctrine but always includes right practice. We hold fast to these traditions most fully when we hold them not only in our heads but also in the very form and patterns of our daily lives.

### The Partnership of Prayer

This week's lesson passage closes with an example of a prayer that Paul and his team offered on behalf of the congregation to which they were writing. Praying on behalf of one another figures prominently in Paul's relationship with each of the congregations of disciples he planted and nurtured. On the one hand, Paul himself clearly made prayer on behalf of these communities of disciples a major component of his own prayer life (see, for example, Romans 1:9-10; Ephesians 1:16-19; Philippians 1:9-11; Colossians 1:3, 9-12; 1 Thessalonians 1:2-3; 2 Thessalonians 1:11-12; Philemon 4), as did other leaders like Epaphras (Colossians 4:12). On the other hand, Paul is consistently requesting that the congregations hold him and his team in prayer before God (Romans 15:30; Colossians 4:3-4; 1 Thessalonians 5:25; 2 Thessalonians 3:1-2; Philemon 22). When he instructs the congregations to make prayer a staple of their Christian discipline, he no doubt has intercession on behalf of others as well as praying for oneself in mind (Romans 12:12; Ephesians 6:18; Philippians 4:6; Colossians 4:2; 1 Thessalonians 5:17).

Prayer becomes a primary means by which each party keeps the other in view, considers the other's need, expresses care and concern for that other, and, in many ways, is led by God to provide for the other's need. As Paul prays for his converts' continued growth in maturity, he also is led to give them concrete guidance and direction to that end through his letters and his follow-up visits. As the Philippians, for example, keep Paul in their hearts and minds in prayer, God moves them also to invest themselves in supplying his physical needs from their own resources.

The kind of prayer Paul practices and encourages is a largely other-centered and God-centered exercise. Of course, we pray for our own concerns, seeking help to overcome the obstacles to our own spiritual growth and seeking guidance to walk in the ways that please God. But if our prayers remain focused on ourselves and our own, we have not yet prayed as Paul taught and modeled. A fuller practice of prayer trains us to become attuned to the needs and plight of our fellow believers. It directs our hearts toward that which God desires for others and for the larger community of faith. It exercises us in listening for God's leading and discerning God's prompting.

# SHARING THE SCRIPTURE

*Preparing Our Hearts*

Meditate on this week's devotional reading, found in Psalm 33:4-12. In this hymn the psalmist praises God both as the Creator of all and the Lord of history. Read verses 4-12 aloud as your own hymn of praise. Take a walk or do something else today to savor the beauty of God's created world. Ponder how blessed you are to know God. Give thanks for God's roles as Creator and Lord.

Pray that you and the adult learners will praise God for the marvelous works of creation and for the history of humanity over which God is Lord.

*Preparing Our Minds*

Study the background in 2 Thessalonians 2 and lesson scripture, 2 Thessalonians 2:13-17. Consider what makes a commitment so important that it grows.

Write on newsprint:

❑ information for next week's lesson, found under "Continue the Journey."

❑ activities for further spiritual growth in "Continue the Journey."

Plan the lecture as suggested for "Review Paul's Words to the Thessalonians about Holding Fast to the Traditions He Taught Them."

## LEADING THE CLASS

*(1) Gather to Learn*

❖ Welcome the class members and introduce any guests.

❖ Pray that all who have come today will be led to strengthen their commitment to Christ.

❖ Read this declaration by a young African pastor, found after he had been martyred in Zimbabwe (http://www.cwl inc.com/christian-commitment.htm): **I'm a part of the fellowship of the unashamed. The die has been cast. I have stepped over the line. The decision has been made. I'm a disciple of His and I won't look back, let up, slow down, back away, or be still. My past is redeemed. My present makes sense. My future is secure. I'm done and finished with low living, sight walking, small planning, smooth knees, colorless dreams, tamed visions, mundane talking, cheap living, and dwarfed goals. . . . I will not flinch in the face of sacrifice or hesitate in the presence of the adversary. . . . I won't give up, shut up, or let up until I have stayed up, stored up, prayed up, paid up, and preached up for the cause of Christ. I am a disciple of Jesus. I must give until I drop, preach until all know, and work until He comes. And when He does come for His own, He'll have no problems recognizing me. My colors will be clear!**

❖ Talk with the class about what they think motivates a person to have such a strong commitment to Christ.

❖ Read aloud today's focus statement: **Commitments grow from a number of factors. What is at the heart of a commitment that makes a needed and lasting difference? The passage affirms that our Christian commitment grows from a response to being chosen by God and empowered by the Spirit.**

*(2) Review Paul's Words to the Thessalonians about Holding Fast to the Traditions He Taught Them*

❖ Present a lecture based on 2 Thessalonians 2:1-2, 3-8, and portions of 9-15 in Understanding the Scripture to provide background for today's session and help the students become aware of "the Man of Lawlessness." This information will set the stage for the study of verses 13-17, which focus on believers being chosen for salvation.

❖ Select a volunteer to read 2 Thessalonians 2:13-17.

❖ Direction attention to these selected verbs in this passage (according to the New Revised Standard Version), which you may want to list on newsprint: *give (thanks), chose, called, obtain, stand (firm), hold (fast), loved, gave, comfort, strengthen.*

❖ Discuss these questions:

**(1) Which of these verbs refer to something that God (or Jesus) is responsible for doing?**

**(2) How do these divine actions affect believers in general and you in particular?**

**(3) Which of these verbs indicate something that believers are to do? How are you taking action?**

❖ Help the students become more aware of what they are to "stand firm on" and "hold fast to" by reading or retelling "Standing Firm and Holding Fast" in Interpreting the Scriptures.

### (3) Appreciate Traditions that Affect the Learners

❖ Divide the class into four groups. Give each group a sheet of newsprint and a marker. Assign each group three months of the year as follows: (1) January, February, March; (2) April, May, June; (3) July, August, September; (4) October, November, December. Ask each group to list as many activities as they can think of that the congregation regularly observes during each three-month period.

❖ Call the class together and ask each group to report. Post each list and invite the entire class to call out additions to the lists. Also invite the students to comment on why certain church traditions are especially dear to them.

❖ Close this portion of the session by asking these questions:

**(1) Which of these traditions are foundational to your faith?**

**(2) Which of these traditions are ones**

**that you may enjoy but are not truly essential to your faith?**

(If the students find it difficult to discern the difference between these two types of traditions, you may point out, for example, that celebrating Jesus' resurrection on Easter is foundational, though the exact way this congregation does that may be different from the way another congregation celebrates. As another example, hanging of the greens is a beloved Advent tradition in many churches but does not have any bearing on the teachings of the Christian faith.)

### (4) Commit to the Call to Believe in the Good News of Jesus Christ

❖ Read in unison "A Covenant Prayer in the Wesleyan Tradition," if you have access to *The United Methodist Hymnal* (page 607), as a sign of commitment to Christ.

❖ **Option:** Read aloud "A Covenant Prayer in the Wesleyan Tradition," phrase by phrase, and ask the students to echo these words:

**I am no longer my own, but thine.**
**Put me to what thou wilt, rank me with whom thou wilt.**
**Put me to doing, put me to suffering.**
**Let me be employed by thee or laid aside for thee,**
**exalted for thee or brought low by thee.**
**Let me be full, let me be empty.**
**Let me have all things, let me have nothing.**
**I freely and heartily yield all things to thy pleasure and disposal.**
**And now, O glorious and blessed God, Father, Son, and Holy Spirit,**
**thou art mine, and I am thine. So be it.**
**And the covenant which I have made on earth,**
**let it be ratified in heaven. Amen.**

### (5) Continue the Journey

❖ Pray that all who have come today will give thanks that God has called them and respond with renewed commitment to that call.

❖ Read aloud this preparation for next week's lesson. You may also want to post it on newsprint for the students to copy.

- ■ Title: God's Own Faithfulness
- ■ Background Scripture: 2 Thessalonians 3
- ■ Lesson Scripture: 2 Thessalonians 3:1-15
- ■ Focus of the Lesson: Many people keep their commitments even when it would be easier to do otherwise. What helps people stay committed under adverse circumstances? The text teaches that our ability to stay committed is grounded in God's own faithfulness to us.

❖ Challenge the students to complete one or more of these activities for further spiritual growth, which you will write on newsprint for the students to copy.

(1) Offer a prayer of thanks for each person in your Sunday school class. Ask God to bless these peo-ple who have been called to faith in Christ.

(2) Think about what you have been taught through the years concerning salvation in Christ. Have you come to understand any of these ideas in different ways—or challenge them completely? How do you see yourself standing firm in the faith, even if some of your understandings have changed?

(3) Encourage someone to make or renew a commitment in Christ Jesus. Provide support as this person struggles with issues of commitment and what they may mean in terms of changes in his or her life.

❖ Sing or read aloud "Jesus Calls Us."

❖ Conclude today's session by leading the class in this benediction adapted from 2 Thessalonians 1:11: Go forth with the assurance that we are always praying for you, asking that our God will make you worthy of his call and will fulfill by his power every good resolve and work of faith.

## UNIT 2: THE FOUNDATION OF CHRISTIAN COMMITMENT
# GOD'S OWN FAITHFULNESS

---

### PREVIEWING THE LESSON

**Lesson Scripture:** 2 Thessalonians 3:1-15
**Background Scripture:** 2 Thessalonians 3
**Key Verse:** 2 Thessalonians 3:3

### Focus of the Lesson:
Many people keep their commitments even when it would be easier to do otherwise. What helps people stay committed under adverse circumstances? The text teaches that our ability to stay committed is grounded in God's own faithfulness to us.

### Goals for the Learners:
(1) to unpack the narrative of God's faithfulness to us and explore what it means.
(2) to recognize examples of God's faithfulness in their lives.
(3) to develop ways to testify to God's faithfulness as the source of their commitment.

### Pronunciation Guide:
*atopoi* (ah' tay poy)

### Supplies:
Bibles, newsprint and marker, paper and pencils, hymnals

---

### READING THE SCRIPTURE

NRSV
2 Thessalonians 3:1-15

¹Finally, brothers and sisters, pray for us, so that the word of the Lord may spread rapidly and be glorified everywhere, just as it is among you, ²and that we may be rescued from wicked and evil people; for not all have faith. **³But the Lord is faithful; he will strengthen you and guard you from the evil one.** ⁴And we have confidence in the Lord concerning you, that you are doing and will go on doing the things that we command.

NIV
2 Thessalonians 3:1-15

¹Finally, brothers, pray for us that the message of the Lord may spread rapidly and be honored, just as it was with you. ²And pray that we may be delivered from wicked and evil men, for not everyone has faith. **³But the Lord is faithful, and he will strengthen and protect you from the evil one.** ⁴We have confidence in the Lord that you are doing and will continue to do the things we command. ⁵May the Lord direct

[5]May the Lord direct your hearts to the love of God and to the steadfastness of Christ.

[6]Now we command you, beloved, in the name of our Lord Jesus Christ, to keep away from believers who are living in idleness and not according to the tradition that they received from us. [7]For you yourselves know how you ought to imitate us; we were not idle when we were with you, [8]and we did not eat anyone's bread without paying for it; but with toil and labor we worked night and day, so that we might not burden any of you. [9]This was not because we do not have that right, but in order to give you an example to imitate. [10]For even when we were with you, we gave you this command: Anyone unwilling to work should not eat. [11]For we hear that some of you are living in idleness, mere busybodies, not doing any work. [12]Now such persons we command and exhort in the Lord Jesus Christ to do their work quietly and to earn their own living. [13]Brothers and sisters, do not be weary in doing what is right.

[14]Take note of those who do not obey what we say in this letter; have nothing to do with them, so that they may be ashamed. [15]Do not regard them as enemies, but warn them as believers.

your hearts into God's love and Christ's perseverance.

[6]In the name of the Lord Jesus Christ, we command you, brothers, to keep away from every brother who is idle and does not live according to the teaching you received from us. [7]For you yourselves know how you ought to follow our example. We were not idle when we were with you, [8]nor did we eat anyone's food without paying for it. On the contrary, we worked night and day, laboring and toiling so that we would not be a burden to any of you. [9]We did this, not because we do not have the right to such help, but in order to make ourselves a model for you to follow. [10]For even when we were with you, we gave you this rule: "If a man will not work, he shall not eat."

[11]We hear that some among you are idle. They are not busy; they are busybodies. [12]Such people we command and urge in the Lord Jesus Christ to settle down and earn the bread they eat. [13]And as for you, brothers, never tire of doing what is right.

[14]If anyone does not obey our instruction in this letter, take special note of him. Do not associate with him, in order that he may feel ashamed. [15]Yet do not regard him as an enemy, but warn him as a brother.

---

## UNDERSTANDING THE SCRIPTURE

**2 Thessalonians 3:1-5.** The authors create a transition between major topics (the futurity of the Day of the Lord and the problem of the "idle" in the Christian community) by expressing their prayers for the converts (2:16-17) and their requests for prayer on their behalf (3:1-2). Prayer—holding one another up in the presence of God and seeking God's timely and specific favors for one another—was a primary sign of partnership and means of pastoral care in the early church. A simple concordance search of Paul's letters shows the importance of prayer for the maturing of disciples, the

spreading of the gospel, and the safety and success of the missionaries. Prayer was regarded as effective. It was not a pious act of vague well-wishing but the securing of tangible and timely aid from the Almighty for one another.

The authors had already expressed their prayer that the congregation would experience the "eternal comfort" (encouragement) and "good hope" that God has given them (2:16-17), which would strengthen them to persevere against the onslaught of both internal and external resistance to their growth in discipleship. In a second prayer on behalf of the believers, the authors ask that the Lord will focus their hearts upon God's love for them and upon Christ's steadfast endurance (3:5). The latter points the hearers to Jesus' journey to the cross, reminding them that the way to glory is a cross-shaped path. The theme that connects both prayers is the confidence that God is at work in the converts. It is God who will establish them in the way of salvation (2:17); it is the Lord who undergirds their obedience to the apostolic tradition (3:4); it is the Lord who protects the converts from the evil one (3:3), whose activity was a prominent topic in 2:3-12.

The apostle's team needs prayer as well, and so prayer becomes an act of mutual caring and encouragement. First, the authors request prayers for the success of their preaching. The NRSV loses the vividness of the metaphor here: Paul wants to see the Lord's word "run" (3:1) like an athlete to victorious acclaim. The unimpeded progress of the word needs also to be met by the open reception of the word for what it is, thus the glorifying of the word as God's message of deliverance. But the team also faces opposition and so asks prayers for deliverance from those who will not respond in "faith" (3:2) but rather will cling to their deviant and wicked character and hinder the missionaries. The authors choose to describe the opponents of their work as *atopoi*, which means "out of place." This turns non-Christians' view of the Christians as "out of place," as deviants requiring correction, back upon the unbelievers' own heads.

**2 Thessalonians 3:6-10.** The third major concern guiding the authors is the report that some converts are "living in idleness" (3:6). The Greek adverb translated "in idleness" may also be rendered "in an unruly or undisciplined manner." Unfortunately, we have little information on why these believers are not engaged in fruitful labor. Were they unemployed persons who were attracted to the gospel but who then continued to live off the charity of the community? Were they formerly employed persons who came to believe that the closeness of the "end" meant that the ordinary business and rules of life no longer mattered, and so stopped working? Were they self-appointed spiritual directors of the community who gave up their mundane occupations so as to devote themselves full-time to regulating the lives (that is, meddling, being busybodies, 3:11) of their less spiritual sisters and brothers?

Certainty on this matter eludes us, but the authors' response is clear enough. Part of the "tradition" the converts received from Paul was not just instruction from his lips but instruction from his example. This is in keeping with the tradition of Greco-Roman philosophers who sought to teach not only by word but also by example how to live a life of virtue. Paul's example taught that it was a noble thing to work to support oneself and one's God-given mission (3:7-8; see also 1 Thessalonians 2:9-10). His explicit command, joined to his example, taught that it was also a necessary thing (3:10). Of course, Paul and his team would be the first to encourage charity toward those who were unable to support themselves or whose circumstances had forced them into want. Paul's thorough commitment to the relief work of taking up a collection for the poor in Judea demonstrates this. But to abuse charity to support an ignoble and idle lifestyle went beyond the pale, dishonoring charity itself. The authors assert that they worked with their own hands even though they had the authority as apostles to receive community support (3:9; see 1 Corinthians 9:1-18), so important was it to them that their example should encourage all to persevere in profitable labor.

**2 Thessalonians 3:11-15.** The authors may have been concerned that the presence of an idle, disorderly segment within the Christian community would bring legitimate criticism of the church from unbelievers on this point. Those who were idle could quickly become disruptive, unruly, even rebellious, and the church (already known to worship a crucified revolutionary) could not afford to be seen to promote this. Another concern would have been that the limited resources of the community for legitimate relief would be drained needlessly by such idlers, rather than multiplied by the work and contributions of every believer to bring relief to those in true need.

The authors rely not only on their authority but also on community support to enforce their values. The group is called to shame the idlers into shaping up (3:6, 14-15). By withholding fellowship (3:6, 14), but all in a spirit of brotherly and sisterly correction and love (3:15), they are to communicate that the idlers' way of life is not something the community will affirm or tolerate. The idlers, ideally, will feel shame before their sisters and brothers and, seeking to regain their fellow Christians' respect, will fall in line with the apostle's example.

**2 Thessalonians 3:16-18.** The letter closes with the normal benediction and wish for God's "grace" (3:18), God's favor and sustaining help, to be with the congregation(s). The letter purports to include Paul's own authenticating signature (3:17), a feature also seen in 1 Corinthians 16:21 and Galatians 6:11. This assumes a scenario in which Paul does not himself write down the words of the letter (leaving this to either Silvanus or Timothy) but adds a greeting in his own hand, both as a personal touch and as a certification that he is, indeed, behind the contents.

## INTERPRETING THE SCRIPTURE

### Teaching by Example

As we have seen already in regard to 1 Thessalonians 1–2, Paul was highly conscious and intentional about what his personal example would communicate about living the Christian life. Like any philosopher or religious teacher, he expected to teach both by word and example—and expected to be studied and imitated in this regard. I remember praying together with a slightly older brother in the faith, whose boldness and openness before God in prayer was a living example to me about how to pray. By following his example I enjoyed the benefits of a more immediate and open relationship with God in prayer. I know another brother who has boldly lived out his convictions about Jesus' call to the wealthy to "climb down" the corporate ladder, release more resources to charitable work, and recover more time for nurturing one's own faith and the faith of others (that is, for the things that really matter in life).

Our personal example will teach something about the faith. If we are not watchful, it might teach others that one can be a Christian and really live like anyone else would live, spending money the same way, engaging in business or the corporate ethos the same way, and so forth. What does your personal example teach? Is it fully consonant with what you would advise or teach others by word? For example, if you would lay emphasis on the importance of evangelism or working for social justice, does your own example reflect and model these emphases as well? What do you need to change to bring your example more fully in line with the values and beliefs you hold dear?

### A Christian Work Ethic

Paul certainly felt compassion for the poor, encouraging his converts to make the relief of need, both within and outside the church, a significant focus of their attention

(Galatians 2:10; 6:10). Because resources were quite limited, of course, he would always direct their attention first toward fellow Christians in need (see, for example, 1 Thessalonians 3:12; 5:15), most poignantly in the massive collection project he was organizing on behalf of the Christians in Jerusalem. The limits on resources also meant that the church could not afford to have people needlessly draining those resources when they were quite capable of working. This was Paul's own example, refusing to become a burden on the resources of the community but rather working at a trade so that he could contribute to the health of the community (in his case, by teaching and providing spiritual direction without requiring support) rather than siphon off its resources. By working themselves, the "idlers" would cease to drain the congregation's resources for genuinely necessary charity *and* have the wherewithal to contribute themselves to charitable endeavors.

Paul can be credited with nurturing a Christian work ethic that would be summed up much later by John Wesley in the famous dictum from his sermon "The Use of Money": "Having, first, gained all you can, and, secondly saved all you can, then give all you can." The purpose of engaging in a profession is not to gratify the frivolous desires that are fed by consumerism (and by every manufacturer and retailer eager to attract money). Nor is it to amass wealth that sits fruitlessly buried in the earth—or in a bank account or fund portfolio. It is to gather the wherewithal to do good to those in need after one's own needs and the needs of one's family have been met—indeed, thus truly treating Christian sisters and brothers in need like part of one's own family. Paul expresses this more fully in 2 Corinthians, where he discusses the collection at length: "God is able to provide you with every blessing in abundance, so that by always having enough of everything, you may share abundantly in every good work" (2 Corinthians 9:8).

*Church Discipline*

In addition to encouraging one another and praying for one another, the Christian community was an important force in encouraging individual believers to engage in behaviors consonant with the new life and end behaviors that were not in line with the gospel. Paul expects the community as a whole, and each "ordinary" believer individually, to intervene directly and constructively in the lives of those Christians whose way has strayed from the ways they learned about Christ. Jesus himself is remembered to have given instructions in this vein, charging disciples to approach the wayward sister or brother and gently explain the inconsistency, hoping to win her or him back to a way of life fully consonant with the faith (Matthew 18:15-20). James, similarly, charges each believer with the task of leading those who have fallen into sin back to the right way (James 5:19-20). This is always to be done in a spirit of gentleness and humility (Galatians 6:1).

In Thessalonica, Paul is especially concerned about these "idle" or "unruly" believers, both on account of their own failure to live according to Paul's more wholesome example, to the benefit of the group, and on account of the health of the reputation of the group itself. If the idle should persist in resisting the exhortations of their sisters and brothers, the community is called as a whole to respond by withholding that deeper level of fellowship until shame brings the idle around to acknowledge and embrace the norms of the group.

Putting this into practice is a tricky business. First, it is highly countercultural. Admonishing a fellow Christian about an affair he is having, or about the abuse he is inflicting at home, or some other such sin is likely to provoke the response "What business is that of yours?!" Our identity and responsibility toward one another as one family in Christ bumps hard against the society's definition of private and public, and the boundaries we erect between home and the "world outside." Second, it is easily abused. Whenever we discuss this facet of Paul's community formation in my classes, I hear as many stories of church leaders exercising totalitarian control over their flocks and employing "shunning" as an overt control mechanism as I do stories of churches applying the principle healthfully or neglecting it altogether.

Nevertheless, dealing directly with a member who has fallen into a sinful pattern, however uncomfortable this makes us, would be far healthier than many alternatives. For example, it directs energy away from grumbling *about* the person—a very prominent and destructive strategy for dealing with disapproved behavior in the church to this day—toward diagnosing a problem and giving those concerned an opportunity to address their behavior. It also offers a necessary antidote to our own blind spots in regard to our embeddedness in sin. We need each other to see what we often cannot bring ourselves to look at. Offered in a spirit of love—as to a sister or brother, not as to an enemy (3:15)—this kind of intervention can bring both the needed insight and support to help a fellow believer avoid making a shipwreck of his or her faith.

---

# SHARING THE SCRIPTURE

## Preparing Our Hearts

Meditate on this week's devotional reading, found in Psalm 89:1-8. In this prayer to protect and uphold King David, Ethan the Ezrahite sings of God's faithfulness and steadfast love. Write your own psalm in which you give thanks for the love God has so faithfully shown you. Consider that, like David, you are one of God's chosen ones.

Pray that you and the adult learners will gather strength as you experience God's continuing faithfulness.

## Preparing Our Minds

Study the background from 2 Thessalonians 3 and lesson scripture, verses 1-15. Think about what helps people stay committed under adverse circumstances.

Write on newsprint:

❏ information for next week's lesson, found under "Continue the Journey."
❏ activities for further spiritual growth in "Continue the Journey."

## LEADING THE CLASS

### (1) Gather to Learn

❖ Welcome the class members and introduce any guests.

❖ Pray that those who have come will be aware of the faithfulness of God that surrounds them.

❖ Read these words of Merv Rosell: **God could have kept Daniel out of the lion's den . . . he could have kept Paul and Silas out of jail . . . he could have kept the three Hebrew children out of the fiery furnace . . . but God has never promised to keep us out of hard places. . . . What he has promised is to go with us through every hard place, and to bring us through victoriously.**

❖ Invite the students to respond to Rosell's comments by citing other biblical stories they know that exemplify how God is with us in adversity. Other examples include: God leading the Hebrews as "a pillar of fire" and "pillar of cloud" as they fled Egypt with Pharaoh's troops in pursuit; the apostles being questioned by the Temple authorities for preaching when they had been forbidden to do so; Stephen as he is stoned to death for his faith; and Paul's numerous punishments and brushes with death for boldly proclaiming the name of Jesus.

❖ Read aloud today's focus statement: **Many people keep their commitments even when it would be easier to do otherwise. What helps people stay committed under adverse circumstances? The text teaches that our ability to stay committed is grounded in God's own faithfulness to us.**

*(2) Unpack the Narrative of God's Faithfulness to Us and Explore What It Means*

❖ Choose someone to read 2 Thessalonians 3:1-5, where Paul asks for prayer.

■ Read information from 2 Thessalonians 3:1-5 in Understanding the Scripture to help the students understand Paul's request for prayer.

■ Read in unison today's key verse, 2 Thessalonians 3:3, which emphasizes God's faithfulness and ability to strengthen those facing adversity and trials.

■ List on newsprint prayer concerns that the class members have.

■ Invite several volunteers to offer prayer on behalf of the people and situations that are listed.

❖ Select another volunteer to read 2 Thessalonians 3:6-15, in which Paul warns the congregation against being idle.

■ Begin a discussion about the work ethic Paul exemplifies by reading "A Christian Work Ethic" from Interpreting the Scripture.

■ Use the first paragraph of 2 Thessalonians 3:6-10 in Understanding the Scripture to explain why scholars believe some people were not engaged in productive work.

■ Invite the students to express opinions on John Wesley's dictum about

earning, saving, and giving, as found in the second paragraph of "A Christian Work Ethic." Ask:

**(1) What do you think Paul would say about Wesley's dictum?**

**(2) How does Wesley's work ethic differ from what seems to be the societal norm in the United States?**

*(3) Recognize Examples of God's Faithfulness in the Learners' Lives*

❖ Distribute hymnals. Invite the students to sing or read in unison the first verse and chorus of "Great Is Thy Faithfulness."

❖ Divide the class into groups of two or three. Allow time for each person to share a story of adversity from their own lives or the life of someone dear to them. Encourage them to talk about ways that God "came through" for them.

❖ Bring the class together again and ask: **What common themes did you notice as you listened to each other's stories?** (Possibly they will have noted—as was true with Merv Rosell's comments—that despite huge obstacles God was present with them. The situation itself may not have improved, but God's presence made it possible for them to deal with the adversity.)

*(4) Develop Ways to Testify to God's Faithfulness as the Source of One's Commitment*

❖ Follow these steps with the class members to help them develop ways to testify to God's faithfulness as the source of their commitment.

■ **Step 1:** Begin by defining the word "commitment." We have been talking about commitment for several weeks, so likely each person has formulated a personal definition. One broad definition would be a pledge to do something in the future. Another would be a devotion to a person or cause.

- **Step 2:** Zoom in on the idea of "commitment" by looking at it from the point of view of one's relationship with Christ. Ask: **What prompts you to make and keep a commitment to Jesus?**
- **Step 3:** Recall that the students have shared with small groups examples of God's faithfulness in their lives. Distribute paper and pencils. Encourage the students to write a short testimony concerning ways in which God's faithfulness to them undergirds their commitment to Christ.
- **Option for Step 3:** Collect these testimonies and have them typed and duplicated to share with the class at a future date. Students may choose to sign or not sign their names.

❖ Challenge the students to go forth to share their testimonies with others.

### (5) Continue the Journey

❖ Pray that those who have participated today will go forth knowing that God is able to strengthen and care for them in all circumstances.

❖ Read aloud this preparation for next week's lesson. You may also want to post it on newsprint for the students to copy.

- **Title: Sharing God's Grace**
- **Background Scripture: Philippians 1**

- **Lesson Scripture: Philippians 1:18b-29**
- **Focus of the Lesson: Under adverse circumstances, our commitments may be challenged. When, if ever, should circumstances lead us to compromise our commitment? As we remain faithful, God sustains us in all circumstances.**

❖ Challenge the students to complete one or more of these activities for further spiritual growth, which you will write on newsprint for the students to copy.

**(1) Make a list of ways that God has been faithful to you. Use this list when adversity weighs heavily upon you to remind yourself of God's faithfulness.**

**(2) Read a book by a Christian author who has undergone great adversity. How has this person relied on God to see him or her through a difficult time?**

**(3) Be an example to someone else in terms of your work ethic. Whether you are a paid employee or a volunteer, be the kind of worker whom others can emulate.**

❖ Sing or read aloud "God Will Take Care of You."

❖ Conclude today's session by leading the class in this benediction adapted from 2 Thessalonians 1:11: **Go forth with the assurance that we are always praying for you, asking that our God will make you worthy of his call and will fulfill by his power every good resolve and work of faith.**

UNIT 3: THE MARKS OF CHRISTIAN COMMITMENT
# SHARING GOD'S GRACE

---

## PREVIEWING THE LESSON

**Lesson Scripture:** Philippians 1:18b-29
**Background Scripture:** Philippians 1
**Key Verse:** Philippians 1:27

### Focus of the Lesson:
Under adverse circumstances, our commitments may be challenged. When, if ever, should circumstances lead us to compromise our commitment? As we remain faithful, God sustains us in all circumstances.

### Goals for the Learners:
(1) to examine Paul's message to the church in Philippians 1 about serving Christ in spite of circumstances.
(2) to analyze feelings about God's power to sustain them.
(3) to work toward never compromising their faith in God, no matter the circumstance.

### Pronunciation Guide:
Philippi (fi lip' i) or (fil' i pi)           Praetorium (pri tor' ee uhm)
*politeuesthe* (pah lee too' eh stheh)        *ta diapheronta* (tah dee ah fehr' ahn tah)
*politeuma* (pol it' yoo mah)

### Supplies:
Bibles, newsprint and marker, paper and pencils, hymnals

---

## READING THE SCRIPTURE

NRSV
Philippians 1:18b-29

Yes, and I will continue to rejoice, [19]for I know that through your prayers and the help of the Spirit of Jesus Christ this will turn out for my deliverance. [20]It is my eager expectation and hope that I will not be put to shame in any way, but that by my speaking with all boldness, Christ will be exalted now

NIV
Philippians 1:18b-29

Yes, and I will continue to rejoice, [19]for I know that through your prayers and the help given by the Spirit of Jesus Christ, what has happened to me will turn out for my deliverance. [20]I eagerly expect and hope that I will in no way be ashamed, but will have sufficient courage so that now as always as always in my body, whether by life or by death. ²¹For to me, living is Christ and dying is gain. ²²If I am to live in the flesh, that means fruitful labor for me; and I do not know which I prefer. ²³I am hard pressed between the two: my desire is to depart and be with Christ, for that is far better; ²⁴but to remain in the flesh is more necessary for you. ²⁵Since I am convinced of this, I know that I will remain and continue with all of you for your progress and joy in faith, ²⁶so that I may share abundantly in your boasting in Christ Jesus when I come to you again.

²⁷**Only, live your life in a manner worthy of the gospel of Christ, so that, whether I come and see you or am absent and hear about you, I will know that you are standing firm in one spirit, striving side by side with one mind for the faith of the gospel,** ²⁸and are in no way intimidated by your opponents. For them this is evidence of their destruction, but of your salvation. And this is God's doing. ²⁹For he has graciously granted you the privilege not only of believing in Christ, but of suffering for him as well.

Christ will be exalted in my body, whether by life or by death. ²¹For to me, to live is Christ and to die is gain. ²²If I am to go on living in the body, this will mean fruitful labor for me. Yet what shall I choose? I do not know! ²³I am torn between the two: I desire to depart and be with Christ, which is better by far; ²⁴but it is more necessary for you that I remain in the body. ²⁵Convinced of this, I know that I will remain, and I will continue with all of you for your progress and joy in the faith, ²⁶so that through my being with you again your joy in Christ Jesus will overflow on account of me.

²⁷**Whatever happens, conduct yourselves in a manner worthy of the gospel of Christ. Then, whether I come and see you or only hear about you in my absence, I will know that you stand firm in one spirit, contending as one man for the faith of the gospel** ²⁸without being frightened in any way by those who oppose you. This is a sign to them that they will be destroyed, but that you will be saved—and that by God. ²⁹For it has been granted to you on behalf of Christ not only to believe on him, but also to suffer for him.

## UNDERSTANDING THE SCRIPTURE

**Philippians 1:1-2.** Paul writes as a prisoner, probably in Rome, which would make the letter one of Paul's last (between A.D. 60 and 62). It is in Rome that one finds "the whole Praetorium" ("imperial guard," 1:13) and "the emperor's [Caesar's] household" (4:22) in their most impressive sense. In Rome, Paul was in chains under house arrest, awaiting a verdict of life or death (1:12-13, 19-26).

**Philippians 1:3-8.** The Philippians have held a special place in Paul's heart. This is the only church that he addresses as his "partners" (the deeper sense of the Greek words rendered "sharing" and "share" in

1:5, 7; see also 4:15-16), both in receiving the good news and supporting Paul's missionary endeavors to share that good news. The church in Philippi was a source of constant refreshment for his heart and his mission, giving Paul internal encouragement (1:3-4) and material aid (1:7; 2:25; 4:10-20), sharing in a "grace" relationship (1:7). The NRSV tries to clarify the Greek by adding the word "God's" before "grace," but this may actually obscure the point. Paul and the Philippian Christians enjoyed a reciprocal relationship of friendship, exchanging benefits both spiritual and material. It was in this kind of social relationship, whether between friends or between patrons and clients, that "grace" language was most at home in the ancient world. Paul's acceptance of monetary support from the Philippians was not just a sign of their devotion to the apostle but also a sign of the apostle's confidence in the church that they would not use gift-giving as leverage on the apostle, as a sign that they "owned" him, in effect. Paul dared not accept money from the Corinthian Christians, since he sensed (and rightly so) that such gift-giving would be misinterpreted and exploited by the patrons in the church.

**Philippians 1:9-11.** Paul concludes the letter-opening by sharing the content of his prayer for the church, namely that their love will continue to be combined with the God-given knowledge and insight that enables discernment of what is essential (*ta diapheronta*) to being found sincere and blameless at the last day (1:10). The NRSV does not precisely capture the meaning of *ta diapheronta* when it reads "what is best." It means, rather, "the things that really matter," those essentials of Christian faith and practice, as opposed to other issues about which Christians should be tolerant and not become divisive. Love coupled with such a focus provides a remedy for the inner-church quarrels, no doubt over indifferent matters, which were weakening the congregation (4:2-3).

**Philippians 1:12-18a.** While imprisoned and "off the circuit," as it were, other preachers have sought to distinguish themselves in the spreading of the gospel (most probably in Rome itself). Paul considers that some do this out of a sincere heart for God, but he knows that others do it out of a sense of rivalry with Paul, trying to replace him in the limelight of the churches. Thinking that Paul has the same spirit of reputation-seeking that the rivals do, the rivals believe their activity will grieve Paul as he watches others increase in fame at his expense (1:17).

Paul does not respond, however, as these rivals suppose. He is not drawn into a spirit of rivalry and competition on account of what other people are doing, but rather sets his eyes on what the Lord is doing. He sees that, whatever people's motives, the gospel is spreading even more since his imprisonment, and that is his only concern. The rivals are brought in here as negative examples, embodying strife, rivalry, and selfish ambition. Paul models how to rise above partisanship and rivalry. Discerning what really matters in the situation, he rejoices in the Lord (1:18). Paul draws attention to this aspect of his own situation in order to help the Christians in Philippi deal maturely with the emergence of rivalry and selfish conceit in their midst.

**Philippians 1:18b-26.** Paul defines his life as an opportunity to serve God (1:22). He does not demand comfort or safety but only seeks that the word of the Lord spread as a result of his life and that Christ be honored whether in his continued existence or his execution (1:20). His confinement has emboldened the witness of other Christians and allowed him to infiltrate the Praetorium itself with the knowledge of the gospel, and for that reason he does not chafe at his chains, though they no doubt chafed on him (1:12-14).

Paul regards death with confidence, not as an evil but as the gate through which he will pass to enter the brightness of the presence of the Lord (1:23). Dying is, therefore, "gain" (1:21). Early Christian leaders were well aware of the power of the "fear of death" in the lives of the people around them. The author of Hebrews regards the fear of death as the means by which Satan keeps people enslaved (Hebrews 2:14-15). Greco-Roman philosophers likewise recognized the fear of death as a great impediment to freedom. The person who feared imprisonment or death gave away his or her freedom to whoever had the power to imprison or kill them. Single-hearted dedication to Christ gave Paul back this freedom. Since the aim of his life was serving Jesus, no external circumstance would hinder his finding meaning in his life or fulfilling his deepest desires. Only the person who can say, "for me, to live means Christ" can also say "to die means gain."

**Philippians 1:27-30.** As in Thessalonica, so in Roman Philippi, the confession of Jesus as "Lord" and "Savior" (in a context where Augustus and his successors were already lauded with those very titles) and the expectation that he would come as king, brought Christians into conflict with their neighbors. The difference in the situation addressed by Philippians is that the addressees have been Christians for at least six years by this time, and possibly as long as ten to twelve, so that this hostility is not a new reality for them.

It was of utmost importance to Paul that his friends in Philippi match hostility from outside with internal unity, support, encouragement, and aid. If harmony and unity were to erode from within, the assaults from without would stand a better chance of achieving their objective, namely wearing down the believers and bringing them back into conformity with "good Roman values." He wants them to remain strong so that they will maintain their witness of courageous perseverance. As they face off with an unbelieving world, unafraid and unshaken, they testify with a voice more eloquent than words that Christ is worth everything and that God—and God's judgment—is real. In such a way, endurance of persecution becomes a proclamation of God's triumph over the world.

---

## INTERPRETING THE SCRIPTURE

*The Christ-centered Life*

Paul shares a great deal of his own heart in Philippians, continuing his strategy of teaching by example (see Philippians 3:17). In the Thessalonian letters, Paul focused attention on the example of his lifestyle. Here, he focuses attention on the example of his deepest desires and how these shape his general outlook. Paul shows himself to be astoundingly Christ-centered. He seeks to lift up Jesus, to promote Jesus, to bring honor to Jesus consistently in the midst of any circumstances and through all his speech and action. In regard to his present imprisonment awaiting trial, Paul is confident of the outcome—deliverance ("salvation") and freedom from being put to shame. It is not the circumstances in which he will find himself after the verdict that matter to him but rather his fidelity to bear witness to Christ and glorify Jesus with his own steadfastness. A verdict of "guilty" and sentence of death brings him no shame, since he would have kept his own faithfulness to Christ intact and used the occasion to testify to the excellence of the Lord.

Paul's goals and outlook—which he offers to us as a model to be internalized—are very different from the goals that our culture, and so many culture-driven preachers, hold out before us. One adult Sunday school group in our church recently worked through a popular "Christian" book that positioned readers to remain stunningly self-centered in its packaging of the gospel, a kind of variation on the theme of positive thinking helping people get what they want, from a parking space close to the entrance of the mall to a courtesy upgrade on an airplane to a bigger house. Paul's understanding of his best life now is entirely Christ-centered. There is no room for Paul's own personal preferences, no room for concern about Paul's enjoyment of particular creature comforts. Paul doesn't cloud his heart with such distractions. He seeks one thing: to bring honor to Christ by the way he lives, and the way he dies. One of the remarkable benefits about this focus is the sense of peace in the face of death that Paul enjoyed. Directing his entire being toward the One who had already crossed beyond death into resurrected life, Paul's deepest desires could not be thwarted or threatened by death, but only realized.

Clearly Christ is important to you, since you are undertaking the study of God's Word. What other things are important to you in your life? What do you want to get out of life before you die? To what extent would it be true for you to say, "to live means Christ"? Does your own death threaten your enjoyment or achievement of what is important to you, or have you come to a place in your life where you too can look at death with Paul's confidence?

### The Privilege of Suffering

Paul asserts that the experience of suffering for Jesus is an experience of God's gracious privilege, a sign of God giving the believers a special favor (1:29). To this, we might be conditioned to respond, "Don't do me any favors!" The insults, slander, vandalism, assault, and marginalization that would have been part and parcel of the experience of a targeted, deviant group are far from pleasant experiences. Why should the endurance of hardships encountered for the sake of Christ be thought of as a privilege?

Paul will say more about this in 3:7-16, in particular. Paul understood that God's primary aim for our lives was to make us more like Jesus. Almost every Christian knows and can quote the famous line from Romans, "All things work together for good for those who love God, who are called according to his purpose" (Romans 8:28). Few indeed keep that purpose clear in their contexts as they quote that verse: "For those whom he foreknew he also predestined to be conformed to the image of his Son" (Romans 8:29). Paul sought this "conform-

ing" in his own life, which for him meant enduring some share of the sufferings of Christ ("becoming like him in his death," Philippians 3:10). Suffering for the name of Christ has a way of clarifying our purpose and our intention, for example, to live for God's will, not for what people ordinarily crave (1 Peter 4:1-2). It nurtures in us the same commitment, focus, and obedience that characterized Jesus in his incarnation and death. The good news, of course, is that living the cross-shaped life of Jesus gives us assurance of living also the resurrected life with Jesus.

Once again, we need to remind ourselves that not all suffering should be considered "suffering for Christ." There is a great deal of suffering in the world that we are called to resist and to stamp out in the name of the just God who seeks the wholeness—the shalom—of all peoples. Some of this is far from our shores; some of it is within the homes of neighbors and fellow Christians, possibly even our own.

### Good Citizenship

Paul uses political language at a number of points in this epistle. In Philippians 1:27, he urges the disciples to "order their common lives as citizens" (politeuesthe) in a noble manner. In Philippians 3:21, he will draw attention to the location of their "body of his glory," also translated as "commonwealth" (politeuma), which is the divine realm, the place from which Christ will return. The Philippians would have been familiar with the Greek and Roman political virtues, having been taught to value harmony, solidarity, and unity as marks of the strong and honorable commonwealth, and to avoid factionalism, partisan strife, and civil unrest as attitudes and actions that bring weakness and disgrace to a city.

Paul reminds them here of their civic duty to another realm, the city of God. The seat of the kingdom of God—its capital, as it were—is located in the divine realm, and the Philippian congregation is a colony of that capital (much as Philippi itself was legally a colony of Rome, a "little Rome"). What will be the witness to the nobility and strength of the kingdom of God manifested by its citizenry in the here-and-now of Christian community?

As Paul will challenge his friends to embrace the core values of cooperation, of "pulling in the same direction," and banishing self-serving partisanship, his words continue to challenge us in our congregational life to live out a good witness to the nobility of God's people. "They'll know we are Christians by our love," the chorus of a well-known hymn, captures something of this ethic. If Christians within congregations and across denominations work together with a united front, we will move closer toward bearing that witness to the world that will testify to the power of God truly being at work in Jesus Christ (see John 17:20-23).

## SHARING THE SCRIPTURE

### Preparing Our Hearts

Meditate on this week's devotional reading, found in Acts 9:10-16. In this passage, which is part of the larger story of the conversion of Saul/Paul, we hear Ananias question God about Saul. God responds that Saul is a chosen instrument and that God "will show him how much he must suffer for the sake of my name" (9:16). Paul relates some of this suffering in his Letter to the Philippians. In chapter 1 he writes that his suffering and imprisonment have allowed him to spread the gospel. Think about your own view of suffering. Are there circumstances under which you view suffering as positive? How have you been able to spread the gospel in times when you were suffering?

Pray that you and the adult learners will commit yourselves with unreserved zeal to Christ and his cause, even if that commitment requires suffering.

### Preparing Our Minds

Study the background from Philippians 1 and lesson scripture, verses 18b-29. Consider if there is ever a time that circumstances should lead you to compromise a commitment.

Write on newsprint:

❑ information for next week's lesson, found under "Continue the Journey."
❑ activities for further spiritual growth in "Continue the Journey."

Plan a lecture as suggested for "Examine Paul's Message to the Church in Philippians 1 about Serving Christ in Spite of Circumstances."

### LEADING THE CLASS

#### (1) Gather to Learn

❖ Welcome the class members and introduce any guests.

❖ Pray that all who have come today will experience God's grace and renew their own commitments.

❖ Read this definition from *Merriam Webster's Collegiate Dictionary*: **"compromise: to adjust or settle by mutual concessions."**

❖ Note that some people find "compromise" to be negative, whereas others see it as neutral, and still others as positive, as these three quotations illustrate:
■ **Compromise is but the sacrifice of one right or good in the hope of retaining another—too often ending in the loss of both.** (Tyron Edwards, 1809–1894)
■ **Compromise makes a good**

umbrella but a poor roof; it is a **temporary expedient** (James Russell Lowell, 1819–1891)

■ **People talk about the middle of the road as though it were unacceptable. Actually, all human problems, excepting morals, come into the gray areas. Things are not all black and white. There have to be compromises. The middle of the road is all of the usable surface. The extremes, left and right, are in the gutters.** (Dwight David Eisenhower, 1890–1969)

❖ Talk briefly with the class about their perspective on compromise. How do they view this concept, particularly in light of their faith?

❖ Read aloud today's focus statement: **Under adverse circumstances, our commitments may be challenged. When, if ever, should circumstances lead us to compromise our commitment? As we remain faithful, God sustains us in all circumstances.**

*(2) Examine Paul's Message to the Church in Philippians 1 about Serving Christ in Spite of Circumstances*

❖ Present the lecture you have prepared from Understanding the Scripture for Philippians 1:1-2, 3-8, 9-11, 12-18a in order to set the stage for today's lesson.

❖ Choose a volunteer to read Philippians 1:18b-29.

❖ Focus on today's key verse, Philippians 1:27.

■ Encourage the class to talk about what a life that is lived "in a manner worthy of the gospel of Christ" looks like. What kinds of attitudes and actions mark the lives of believers?

■ Consider how they corporately, as a class and as a congregation, "are standing firm in one spirit, striving side by side with one mind for the faith of the gospel" (1:27).

❖ Look at Paul's comments about his suffering in verses 21-24. Note that while he would be relieved of suffering in death and be with Christ then, he feels he should remain alive to continue spreading the gospel. Ask:

(1) **In light of the obstacles that Paul faced, what motivated him to continue to preach the gospel?**

(2) **What would motivate you to endure what Paul endured for the sake of Christ?**

❖ Read or retell "The Christ-centered Life" from Interpreting the Scripture to wrap up this part of the lesson. Draw the students in by encouraging them to answer the questions in the final paragraph.

*(3) Analyze Feelings about God's Power to Sustain the Learners*

❖ Distribute hymnals. Ask the students to turn in the hymnal to a section that has a title such as "Strength in Tribulation" (pages 510-536 in *The United Methodist Hymnal.*)

❖ Divide the class into groups and assign each group several pages in the section you have identified in your church's hymnal. Ask the students to look at the words of their assigned hymns to discern how the hymn writer believes that God can sustain one in times of trouble.

❖ Ask each group to report to the class on at least one hymn that they found meaningful.

❖ **Option:** Sing at least one verse of several selected hymns as an affirmation of the students' belief that God will sustain them.

*(4) Work toward Never Compromising Faith in God, No Matter the Circumstance*

❖ Point out that Paul considers it a privilege to suffer for the sake of Christ. Read "The Privilege of Suffering" from Interpreting the Scripture.

❖ Distribute paper and pencils. Invite the students to write about how Paul may be an example for them. Suggest that they consider any current situations that would prompt some form of suffering or ostracism. For example, neighbors may be fighting the opening of a shelter at the church. To make this shelter a reality, some members will have to face opposition from other members of the community. What might Paul do in this case, for example?

❖ Provide an opportunity for volunteers to talk about how they see Paul as an example.

❖ Conclude this portion of the lesson by challenging the adults to write one sentence in which they express a commitment to remain strong in faith regardless of the situation.

### (5) Continue the Journey

❖ Pray that all who have come today will go forth to share the good news that God's grace sustains us even in the worst of circumstances.

Read aloud this preparation for next week's lesson. You may also want to post it on newsprint for the students to copy.

- **Title: Giving of Oneself**
- **Background Scripture: Philippians 2:1–3:1a**
- **Lesson Scripture: Philippians 2:1-13**
- **Focus of the Lesson: We live in a culture in which we are encouraged to pursue our dreams at any cost and to fight for our rights.**

Where can we find more to life than a selfish pursuit of our own happiness at the expense of others? God calls us, through Jesus' example, to find life in serving others.

❖ Challenge the students to complete one or more of these activities for further spiritual growth, which you will write on newsprint for the students to copy.

(1) **Encourage someone who is having a problem to remain strong in the faith.**

(2) **List ways that you have suffered because of your faith in Christ. Remember that suffering for Christ often entails resisting evil or injustice and proclaiming the gospel in the face of opposition.**

(3) **Use words from Philippians 1:3 to open a letter to a missionary, a person in the armed forces, someone who is ill, or another person who needs support.**

❖ Sing or read aloud "Praise, My Soul, the King of Heaven."

❖ Conclude today's session by leading the class in this benediction adapted from 2 Thessalonians 1:11: **Go forth with the assurance that we are always praying for you, asking that our God will make you worthy of his call and will fulfill by his power every good resolve and work of faith.**

UNIT 3: THE MARKS OF CHRISTIAN COMMITMENT

# GIVING OF ONESELF

## PREVIEWING THE LESSON

**Lesson Scripture:** Philippians 2:1-13
**Background Scripture:** Philippians 2:1–3:1a
**Key Verse:** Philippians 2:5

### Focus of the Lesson:

We live in a culture in which we are encouraged to pursue our dreams at any cost and to fight for our rights. Where can we find more to life than a selfish pursuit of our own happiness at the expense of others? God calls us, through Jesus' example, to find life in serving others.

### Goals for the Learners:

(1) to examine the life of serving others as described in Philippians 2.
(2) to be aware of our feelings when serving others.
(3) to commit to a servant lifestyle.

### Pronunciation Guide:

Epaphroditus (i paf ruh di' tuhs)

### Supplies:

Bibles, newsprint and marker, paper and pencils, hymnals

## READING THE SCRIPTURE

NRSV
Philippians 2:1-13

¹If then there is any encouragement in Christ, any consolation from love, any sharing in the Spirit, any compassion and sympathy, ²make my joy complete: be of the same mind, having the same love, being in full accord and of one mind. ³Do nothing from selfish ambition or conceit, but in humility regard others as better than yourselves. ⁴Let each of you look not to your own

NIV
Philippians 2:1-13

¹If you have any encouragement from being united with Christ, if any comfort from his love, if any fellowship with the Spirit, if any tenderness and compassion, ²then make my joy complete by being likeminded, having the same love, being one in spirit and purpose. ³Do nothing out of selfish ambition or vain conceit, but in humility consider others better than yourselves.

interests, but to the interests of others. **⁵Let the same mind be in you that was in Christ Jesus,**

6 who, though he was in the form of God,
did not regard equality with God
as something to be exploited,
7 but emptied himself,
taking the form of a slave,
being born in human likeness.
And being found in human form,
8 he humbled himself
and became obedient to the point
of death—
even death on a cross.
9 Therefore God also highly exalted him
and gave him the name
that is above every name,
10 so that at the name of Jesus
every knee should bend,
in heaven and on earth and under
the earth,
11 and every tongue should confess
that Jesus Christ is Lord,
to the glory of God the Father.

¹²Therefore, my beloved, just as you have always obeyed me, not only in my presence, but much more now in my absence, work out your own salvation with fear and trembling; ¹³for it is God who is at work in you, enabling you both to will and to work for his good pleasure.

⁴Each of you should look not only to your own interests, but also to the interests of others.

**⁵Your attitude should be the same as that of Christ Jesus:**

⁶Who, being in very nature God,
did not consider equality with God
something to be grasped,
⁷but made himself nothing,
taking the very nature of a servant,
being made in human likeness.
⁸And being found in appearance as a
man,
he humbled himself
and became obedient to death—
even death on a cross!
⁹Therefore God exalted him to the highest
place
and gave him the name that is above
every name,
¹⁰that at the name of Jesus every knee
should bow,
in heaven and on earth and under the
earth,
¹¹and every tongue confess that Jesus
Christ is Lord,
to the glory of God the Father.

¹²Therefore, my dear friends, as you have always obeyed—not only in my presence, but now much more in my absence—continue to work out your salvation with fear and trembling, ¹³for it is God who works in you to will and to act according to his good purpose.

---

## UNDERSTANDING THE SCRIPTURE

**Philippians 2:1-4.** Paul addresses at greater length the topic of harmony within the congregation announced in 1:27. On the basis both of the genuineness of their shared religious experience and the desire that they have to keep bringing joy to the heart of their imprisoned partner in the gospel (2:1-2), Paul calls the Christians to act as friends of one another, as siblings, and more—as well-ordered citizens of the commonwealth of heaven (see 3:20).

Paul speaks of the threats to unity in frank terms. One threat is "selfish ambition or conceit" (2:3). When this takes possession of a person, he or she will aim to increase his or her prestige and standing in a community. If anyone opposes or hinders such a person, the result is a competition in which victory can only be won at the cost of defeating the rival in a zero-sum game. Another threat is self-interest (2:4), considering what will be advantageous to oneself rather than advantageous to the whole community. Paul's remedy is radical and countercultural. Rather than claiming the recognition that may be one's due or seeking to make oneself greater in the eyes of others, the Christian is called to focus on honoring his or her fellow-believers. Rather than looking out for one's own interests, one is to consider what is in the interests of the circle of friends that Jesus has called together, who have been made sisters and brothers related by Jesus' blood. Competition and rivalry where cooperation and solidarity should exist (for example, among family) was regarded as a shameful thing in the ancient world. Paul cautions his partners not to forget their debts to each other as family, friends, and fellow-citizens of heaven.

**Philippians 2:5-11.** To drive this point home, Paul includes a poetic passage celebrating Jesus' demonstration of love and generosity toward humanity. Philippians 2:6-11 may constitute an early Christian hymn that Paul has woven into his letter. Other scholars would consider it an original Pauline composition. Either way makes little difference for its interpretation and for understanding Paul's strategy. Jesus refused to use his exalted status as an opportunity for personal gain but rather poured himself out completely for others in obedience to God. The example of one who "emptied himself" is a necessary remedy for people who are too full of themselves. Jesus, having a legitimate claim to being given preeminence, did not press that claim, but rather put God's will for God's people ahead of any desire for recognition of his own status. How much more should those whom Jesus saved, then, rid themselves of attempts to be acknowledged "first" in the community and cast off all conceit and selfishness!

Having the "mind of Christ," which is necessary for the genuine disciple, means setting aside our rights, claims, and entitlements in the service of others and the service of God, trusting God to vindicate us at the last day rather than trying to vindicate ourselves against every perceived slight and seeking God's triumph rather than our own in every argument.

**Philippians 2:12-18.** Paul expresses confidence that the Philippians will set aside any internal squabbling that might erode the peace of the congregation (2:12). As an aid, he invites them to refocus their energies on making progress in their own walk of discipleship. This is a matter of great seriousness to be engaged "with fear and trembling" (2:12), not because the outcome is in doubt, since God works together with and through the believer to cultivate that harvest of righteousness, but because this is the single most important business of life. The topic of Paul's prayer in 1:9-11 thus reemerges in the letter, as the believers are called away from divisive distractions back toward the things that matter.

Paul examines dissension under one additional lens, that of purity and pollution. The descriptors "blameless" and "without blemish" also figure prominently in discussions of clean and unclean animals and persons throughout Scripture. Both Jews and Gentiles had pollution taboos and purity codes, with the result that Paul's language would be equally effective for both. Murmuring against one's fellow-believers and engaging in controversies are diagnosed as defilements of the congregation. The intrusions of the unclean into the community of the holy ones ("saints," 1:1) is to be avoided because of the sanctity of the community and the One who dwells in its midst.

Paul closes his exhortation to unity by returning to the consideration of the joy that it would bring him (compare 2:1-2). He reminds the Philippians that he may in fact face execution, pouring out his own life as a libation over the Philippians' own faith offering, namely their steady response to the gospel. The hearts of the believers will likely be moved by this imagery, and by the fact that they can make their partner's sacrifice a more meaningful one by so simple an act as setting aside their internal differences.

**Philippians 2:19–3:1a.** Paul bolsters his exhortation with two further examples of commendable Christian behavior displaying the mind of Christ. Timothy distinguishes himself because he is "genuinely concerned for your welfare" and interests (2:20). The Greek suggests colorfully that "there is no one whose soul is equal to his." He thus stands in stark contrast with some unnamed others who are all "seeking their own interests, not those of Jesus Christ"

(2:21), which intentionally recalls the exhortation in 2:4. The second example is Epaphroditus, the Philippian Christian who brought Paul a gift from that community to assist him in his confinement (4:10-20). On the long journey, he fell ill and even came close to dying, all in the service of the congregation and of Paul (2:27). Having risked his life on account of "the work of Christ" (2:30), Epaphroditus became a living example of putting others' interests ahead of one's own, in a manner of speaking being obedient (almost) to the point of death. It is people who, like Epaphroditus, embody the mind of Christ that are to be held in honor (2:29), not those who insist upon recognition or having matters go their way.

## INTERPRETING THE SCRIPTURE

### Partnership

Throughout Philippians, a major motif is partnership in the gospel, specifically the partnership between a Christian leader or missionary and a congregation. This emerges most clearly in the opening and closing sections of the letter (1:1-11; 4:10-20). The motif continues to appear in other parts as well, as when Paul invokes the common bond and "partnership of spirit" (translated as "sharing in the Spirit" in the NRSV, 2:1) that they share as a motivation to act. Just how important this partnership has been to Paul, both in his missionary work as a free person and during his imprisonment, is evident from the letter. It has helped sustain him both emotionally and materially, with the result that the Philippians can rightly claim to have shared in Paul's work on behalf of the gospel. The emotional bond is so strong on the other side that Paul, in turn, can use it as leverage to get the Philippians to let go of any in-house strife they are fostering or tolerating as they focus together on their common bond of friendship (2:1-4).

Many churches seek out partnerships with missionaries or campus ministers or other persons engaged in ministry beyond the congregational setting. This partnership is most fruitful when it goes beyond being simply a financial commitment, when parishioners are personally and prayerfully involved in supporting that ministry. To what extent has your church been a source of refreshment and a safe place for some Christian worker beyond the congregation? To what depth have you been involved in supporting that worker's ministry through more personal investments of prayer, conversation, notes of encouragement, and the like?

### Christ-followers in a Rights Culture

"I've got a right to be here, same as you!" "I've got a right to be heard!" "Everyone has a right to good health care." "The public has a right to know the truth." "I've got my rights too you know." We live in a rights culture, a culture in which most people firmly believe that they are entitled to the enjoyment of particular goods and experiences, and in which claiming something as a "right" is a standard topic in debate (which may or may not ultimately stand up under scrutiny). We also live in a culture that defines happiness and fulfillment in terms of self-gratification, which has largely trained us to look out for our own interests and to set what we want for ourselves.

American Christians are "environmentally challenged," to put it mildly, when it comes to moving toward Christ-likeness. While it is not always the case, the conviction that we have a right to certain things, or the tendency to work for the gratification of our own interests, can show up in a wide variety of church disputes. "I want to enjoy *my* kind of music in church." "But I have a *right* to sing the hymns that I've always sung here." Sometimes we don't say it quite so explicitly but still experience a negative shift in our emotions and attitudes when something isn't going according to our liking in the church or we feel that we have some rights to something we're not getting.

Paul's advice and Jesus' example are, once more, radically countercultural. They train us to consider what will nurture or comfort the *other* rather than ourselves. The One who was equal with God refused to insist on enjoying what was his due, seeking how best and most fully to serve God's purposes for the restoration of others instead. How much more should we, who are certainly not equal with God, regard the nurture of our fellow sisters and brothers as worthy of the sacrifice of some of our own interests or of the insistence of some of our own right? The mind of Christ is formed in the believer in day-to-day interactions with fellow-believers. These interactions occur in the often trying and wearing circumstances of committee meetings, choir rehearsals, and administrative hassles, as well as in interactions with people outside the church and outside the Christian community. Paul urges us to keep coming back to Jesus' frame of mind as expressed in this elegant Christ hymn (Philippians 2:5-11) as our

touchstone whenever we find ourselves on the road to strife within the church. What, indeed, *would* Jesus do?

We have some responsibility as a congregation to reinforce the countercultural values taught by Paul and the example of Jesus, rather than reinforcing the self-seeking with our public words of praise. It is people who, like Epaphroditus, embody the mind of Christ that are to be held in honor (2:29), not those who insist upon recognition or upon having matters go their way. In the church, unlike the world, precedence and esteem cannot come because individuals have sought and fought for such recognition but only because they have, ironically, put others first out of a sincere love.

There is a danger that some will hear the words of the Christ hymn and Paul's exhortations from within a situation of abuse or oppression and apply these words directly to that situation. Having rights to pass over or relinquish is essential to embodying the mind of Christ. Being in a position to seek one's own interests is prerequisite to laying those aside for the sake of pursuing the interest of others.

*Cooperating with God*

This week's lesson passage closes with another very familiar line from Paul: "Work out your own salvation with fear and trembling" (2:12). Again, the second half of the statement is vitally important: God is at work in the believers, behind both the desiring and the doing of God's good pleasure (2:13). Paul crafts a vision of deep cooperation with God and with one another in our spiritual transformation.

It is, first of all, not a call to a privatization of spiritual growth, as if each one of us ought to attend to our own, personal, private spiritual life. A plural pronoun in the Greek stands behind the word "your." If the reader would permit a colloquialism, "y'all's salvation" would capture this better in English. Moreover, the word translated "own" often has a reciprocal sense when used in the plural, as it is here. Paul commissions his friends to invest themselves in working toward the spiritual maturity of each member of the congregation—each one his or her "own salvation" alongside everyone else's. It is, secondly, a process behind which God is standing and working at every turn. We are not left to our own devices or to run on our own steam. God guides, God impels, God empowers.

These words call us to intentionality in regard to progress in discipleship, particularly growing in Christ-likeness and in responsiveness to God. This involves spiritual disciplines that are practiced alone and in the company and strength of our fellow travelers. Such disciplines include regular, even daily, meditation upon Scripture; prayer, private, in small groups, and in corporate worship; silence, listening to God; fasting, withholding what is permissible so as to curb our illicit desires as well; retreating, withdrawing from busy-ness to give God extended attention and time; service, doing what our Lord commands. Through these and other means, we put ourselves in a position to discern how God is working within and among us, so as to cooperate with God for our own salvation.

---

# SHARING THE SCRIPTURE

### Preparing Our Hearts

Meditate on this week's devotional reading, found in Matthew 20:20-28. Here we see the mother of James and John asking Jesus to declare that her two sons will have prominent seats in the kingdom next to Jesus. She wants her sons to be given positions of prestige and power, but Jesus' kingdom is not about power and recognition. Note that this passage follows Jesus' third reference to his suffering, death, and resurrection. Service to others, which includes the possibility of laying down one's life, is the way of life in Jesus' kingdom. Do you seek the greatness of Jesus' servant?

Pray that you and the adult learners will give of yourselves to serve others.

### Preparing Our Minds

Study the background from Philippians 2:1–3:1a and lesson scripture, Philippians 2:1-13. Think about how life can be more than just a selfish pursuit of happiness at the expense of others.

Write on newsprint:

❑ information for next week's lesson, found under "Continue the Journey."
❑ activities for further spiritual growth in "Continue the Journey."

### LEADING THE CLASS

### (1) Gather to Learn

❖ Welcome the class members and introduce any guests.

❖ Pray that those who gather today will yearn to commit themselves more fully to Christ.

❖ Read these words from the Declaration of Independence of the United States of America: **We hold these truths to be self-evident, that all men are created equal, that they are endowed by their Creator with certain unalienable Rights, that among these are Life, Liberty and the pursuit of Happiness.—That to secure these rights, Governments are instituted among Men, deriving their just powers from the consent of the governed, —That whenever any Form of Government becomes destructive of these ends, it is the**

**Right of the People to alter or to abolish it, and to institute new Government, laying its foundation on such principles and organizing its powers in such form, as to them shall seem most likely to effect their Safety and Happiness.**

❖ Ask: **Are there ways in which the right to pursue life, liberty, and happiness has fragmented our society and pitted neighbor against neighbor or community against community? If so, what has caused this tear in the fabric of unity?**

❖ Read aloud today's focus statement: **We live in a culture in which we are encouraged to pursue our dreams at any cost and to fight for our rights. Where can we find more to life than a selfish pursuit of our own happiness at the expense of others? God calls us, through Jesus' example, to find life in serving others.**

### (2) Examine the Life of Serving Others as Described in Philippians 2

❖ Choose a volunteer to read Philippians 2:1-13.

❖ **Option:** If you have access to *The United Methodist Hymnal*, invite the students to turn to page 167. Tell the class that you will read verses 1-4 from your Bible; they will read verses 5-11 responsively from the hymnal with half of the students reading the regular print and half reading the bold print; and you will close by reading verses 12-13 from your Bible.

❖ Write these ideas from verses 6-11 in the left column of a sheet of newsprint: *did not exploit equality with God, emptied himself, being born, humbled, became obedient.* Write these words in the center column: *exalted, gave.* Write these words in the right column: *bend, confess.*

❖ Talk with the class about (a) the actions that Jesus took (left column), (b) the actions God took (center column), and (c) the response humans are expected to make (right column).

❖ Read aloud "Christ-followers in a

Rights Culture" from Interpreting the Scripture.

❖ Invite the class to look again at verses 1-4. Ask:

> (1) **How do these verses contrast with the expectations of a "rights culture"?**
>
> (2) **How do they compare with the actions that Jesus took (2:6-8)?**

❖ Read in unison Philippians 2:5, today's key verse, to emphasize the importance of having the mind of Christ.

❖ Conclude this portion of the lesson by asking the students to review 2:12-13 and then you will read or retell "Cooperating with God" from Interpreting the Scripture.

### (3) Be Aware of Feelings When Serving Others

❖ Read this excerpt from "Serving Others: An Evolution of Motivation," written by Carlton Deal for http://www.opensourcetheology.net/node/768: **Is serving for the church or is the church for serving? And how much does the answer matter? One thing I have discovered is this: serving others is my favorite act of worship. I feel God's pleasure in unselfish service maybe more than anything. Properly understood, I think serving is best enjoyed not because it's needed or because I should, but because Jesus is worth it. And I think I enjoy it, in part, because I am longing for the Kingdom to come in my heart as it is in heaven.**

❖ Discuss these questions:

> (1) **Do Carlton Deal's feelings about service reflect your own feelings? Specifically, do you feel that serving others is an act of worship? Why or why not?**
>
> (2) **If not, what other kinds of feelings do you experience when you serve others?**
>
> (3) **Are your feelings about service connected with what you are doing or who you are serving? Explain your answer.**

### (4) *Commit to a Servant Lifestyle*

❖ Point out that Paul clearly committed himself to a lifestyle of service to Christ by serving others.

❖ Invite the students to name other people whose lifestyles exemplify what it means to humbly and obediently serve God. The students should in a few sentences state why they believe the person they have named is a good role model.

❖ Distribute paper and pencils. Challenge the students to identify ways that they can live the lifestyle of a servant and write these ways on their papers.

❖ Close this portion of the session by asking the adults to write these words, which you will dictate, on their paper and sign their names if they are willing to make a commitment: **As one who seeks to have the mind of Christ, I pledge to live as an obedient servant of God by caring for those whom God calls me to serve.**

### (5) *Continue the Journey*

❖ Pray that all who are present will seek the mind of Christ so that they may give freely of themselves to serve others.

Read aloud this preparation for next week's lesson. You may also want to post it on newsprint for the students to copy.

- **Title: Living into the Future**
- **Background Scripture: Philippians 3:1b–4:1**
- **Lesson Scripture: Philippians 3:7-16**

■ **Focus of the Lesson: Many people are preoccupied with past failures or achievements. How can our lives achieve fresh focus? The Christian faith draws us into the future, preoccupied with God's mission in Christ.**

❖ Challenge the students to complete one or more of these activities for further spiritual growth, which you will write on newsprint for the students to copy.

**(1) Serve someone else this week who likely will be unable to offer you something in return. Providing food or other material goods is one way to serve. Taking action on behalf of another or listening to the other are also ways to give of yourself.**

**(2) Memorize Philippians 2:5-11 so that you can call to mind the humility and obedience of Christ.**

**(3) Talk with other Christians concerning their experiences as servants. What can you learn from them? What experiences can you share with them to assist them in their faith journeys?**

❖ Sing or read aloud "Jesu, Jesu."

❖ Conclude today's session by leading the class in this benediction adapted from 2 Thessalonians 1:11: **Go forth with the assurance that we are always praying for you, asking that our God will make you worthy of his call and will fulfill by his power every good resolve and work of faith.**

## UNIT 3: THE MARKS OF CHRISTIAN COMMITMENT
# LIVING INTO THE FUTURE

---

### PREVIEWING THE LESSON

**Lesson Scripture:** Philippians 3:7-16
**Background Scripture:** Philippians 3:1b–4:1
**Key Verses:** Philippians 3:13-14

#### Focus of the Lesson:
Many people are preoccupied with past failures or achievements. How can our lives achieve fresh focus? The Christian faith draws us into the future, preoccupied with God's mission in Christ.

#### Goals for the Learners:
(1) to investigate Paul's words about the value of knowing Jesus Christ.
(2) to contemplate the value of knowing Jesus Christ.
(3) to commit to learning more about Jesus Christ and to be willing to publicly acknowledge a relationship with him.

#### Pronunciation Guide:
Euodia (yoo oh' dee uh)                    *morph* (morf')
Judaizing (joo' day iz ing)                Syntyche (sin' ti kee)

#### Supplies:
Bibles, newsprint and marker, paper and pencils, hymnals

---

### READING THE SCRIPTURE

NRSV
Philippians 3:7-16

⁷Yet whatever gains I had, these I have come to regard as loss because of Christ. ⁸More than that, I regard everything as loss because of the surpassing value of knowing Christ Jesus my Lord. For his sake I have suffered the loss of all things, and I regard them as rubbish, in order that I may gain Christ ⁹and be found in him, not having a

NIV
Philippians 3:7-16

⁷But whatever was to my profit I now consider loss for the sake of Christ. ⁸What is more, I consider everything a loss compared to the surpassing greatness of knowing Christ Jesus my Lord, for whose sake I have lost all things. I consider them rubbish, that I may gain Christ ⁹and be found in him, not

righteousness of my own that comes from the law, but one that comes through faith in Christ, the righteousness from God based on faith. [10]I want to know Christ and the power of his resurrection and the sharing of his sufferings by becoming like him in his death, [11]if somehow I may attain the resurrection from the dead.

[12]Not that I have already obtained this or have already reached the goal; but I press on to make it my own, because Christ Jesus has made me his own. [13]Beloved, I do not consider that I have made it my own; **but this one thing I do: forgetting what lies behind and straining forward to what lies ahead, [14]I press on toward the goal for the prize of the heavenly call of God in Christ Jesus.** [15]Let those of us then who are mature be of the same mind; and if you think differently about anything, this too God will reveal to you. [16]Only let us hold fast to what we have attained.

having a righteousness of my own that comes from the law, but that which is through faith in Christ—the righteousness that comes from God and is by faith. [10]I want to know Christ and the power of his resurrection and the fellowship of sharing in his sufferings, becoming like him in his death, [11]and so, somehow, to attain to the resurrection from the dead.

[12]Not that I have already obtained all this, or have already been made perfect, but I press on to take hold of that for which Christ Jesus took hold of me. [13]Brothers, I do not consider myself yet to have taken hold of it. **But one thing I do: Forgetting what is behind and straining toward what is ahead, [14]I press on toward the goal to win the prize for which God has called me heavenward in Christ Jesus.**

[15]All of us who are mature should take such a view of things. And if on some point you think differently, that too God will make clear to you. [16]Only let us live up to what we have already attained.

---

## UNDERSTANDING THE SCRIPTURE

**Philippians 3:1-3.** Many scholars read Philippians 3:2 as a sign that the kind of Judaizing teachers that had upset the Galatian Christians had now made their way into the Philippian congregation. The fact that Paul provides no sustained argumentation against the Judaizers' message, however, makes this quite unlikely. Rather, Paul is recalling the Judaizing Christians as a negative example, a foil for Paul's own example that he will immediately go on to develop in 3:4-16. In order to cultivate the mind of Christ as one pursues the "prize of the heavenly [heavenward] call" (3:14), one must be entirely Christ-centered in one's focus and ambitions, and refuse to place one's confidence "in the flesh" (3:3). The Judaizers taught that physical circumcision had such value in God's sight that Gentile

Christians needed to accept this sign upon their own bodies. To Paul, however, this meant placing one's confidence in a mark in the flesh rather than relying fully on Christ's faithfulness to those who trust and seek him.

**Philippians 3:4-9.** Paul had enjoyed every privilege in the estimation of his fellow Jews. His parents had passed on to him a perfect pedigree in the house of Israel, and he himself had distinguished himself by his zeal for living out Torah's prescriptions (3:4-6). Nevertheless, he now considers all these credentials by which he formerly built himself up and measured himself against other people as "rubbish," that is, garbage and "dung" (3:7-8, KJV), because he had found that attaining Jesus and the life Jesus confers to be of immensely greater value than the precedence and esteem he was trying to forge for himself prior to encountering Jesus.

Paul's own example parallels Christ's example (see 2:5-11). Both had serious claims to recognition and preeminence, but both "regarded" these claims to be of less value than journeying where God commanded and discovering the reward that God had prepared for the obedient (2:6-7; 3:7-8). Following Jesus' example, Paul emptied himself of his claims to precedence on the basis of his heritage and his achievements as a pious Jew. Just as Jesus came to have his honor universally acclaimed only through the path of renouncing those claims, so also the follower of Jesus can only hope to enjoy the honor God bestows by giving up the attempt to make a name for himself or herself, both in the world and in the church.

**Philippians 3:10-11.** Paul shares here the passion that drives his own discipleship and ministry. The only prize he considers worth seeking and winning is Christ himself. Paul seeks intimate fellowship with Jesus, which entails being willing to embrace not only the power of Christ's resurrected life flowing into and through one's own service, but also "the sharing of [Christ's] sufferings" (3:10). Paul had his fill of sufferings (see 2 Corinthians 4:7-12; 6:3-10; 11:16-33), but it was precisely where his own resources and self-reliance failed that he discovered the power and encouragement that came from God alone. It was this power that sustained his faith in the face of crushing adversity and that empowered a ministry that changed the empire (see 2 Corinthians 4:7, 16-18). The Philippians themselves have been invited into this "sharing" through their endurance of hostile opposition from outside on account of their confession (1:27-30).

The process for attaining Christ and the prize of a resurrected life in the city of God entails "becoming conformed (*summorphizomenos*) into the likeness of Christ's death"

(author's translation, 3:10). Paul recalls the language of the Christ hymn, where the root meaning "form" (*morph-*) was also prominently featured ("the form of God" to "the form of a slave," 2:6-7). The fellowship of Christ's sufferings is thus not only the endurance of hardship out of loyalty and obedience to Jesus but also the relinquishing of the desire to be "first" in the community or to have one's own interests and will served. By giving up personal interests one can take the "form" of a servant to one's sisters and brothers, which is the only way also to be a servant of God.

**Philippians 3:12-16.** Paul provides a model of Christian maturity in action (3:15), continuing to explain what it means to refuse to place one's confidence in the flesh or in one's achievements as a basis for establishing a sense of self-worth and for claiming recognition from others. To this end, he shares his own mindset as he moves forward in discipleship, using images that are suggestive of an athlete running a race. Paul no longer speaks merely about leaving behind the pre-Christian credentials he leaned upon for recognition in a community and for his own self-worth, such as he listed in 3:4-6. "Forgetting what lies behind" (3:13) also includes his astounding accomplishments in the service of Christ.

Jesus is the driving force in this race. Jesus first took hold of Paul, and only on that basis can Paul hope to lay hold of the prize one day (3:12). Several times before, the reader has encountered a similar sentiment (see 1:6, 11; 2:12-13). This is another prescription against getting puffed up and insisting on recognition in the church. Ultimately, Jesus is behind our every success, every fruitful labor (see 1 Corinthians 4:7). What we have done must tend to recognition of Jesus' faithfulness toward the church, not our own accomplishments.

**Philippians 3:17–4:1.** Imitation of Christ, and of those disciples who model the mind of Christ in our midst, emerges again as an important medium for spiritual growth.

Paul laments the availability of too many contrary models, those "enemies of the cross" (3:18) within the church who have lost their focus on the heavenly prize and fallen back into the pursuit of earthly enjoyments. Paul has often encountered such people in his career—from the Judaizing missionaries in Galatia to the rival apostles in Corinth to the members of his team who desert him (2 Timothy 4:9-10) to worldly-minded Christians whose hearts remain fixed on the indulgence of the flesh and the fleshly mind. Paul's colorful description of them in 3:19 suggests that they serve the interests of their own person, whether that be a desire of the body, a craving for worldly honor gained in a worldly way, or any other temporal object of their heart. They are "enemies of the cross" because they resist the work of the cross in their own lives, refusing to take on the mind of Jesus therein revealed.

Paul's friends in Philippi are not to behave as such shallow believers do. As they conform themselves now to the mind of Christ, they confirm their commitment to Jesus' promise that he will himself return to transform their mortal bodies into his immortal likeness (3:21). They are encouraged not to turn aside from this great hope for the sake of satisfying any desire that belongs to the "body of our humiliation" (3:21), whether the desire to come out first in an argument, the desire to get one's own way, or the desire for recognition. Rather, as they conform themselves more to the mind of Christ, they receive the assurance that he will, in turn, conform them to his own "body of glory" (3:21) as he continues to work in them into eternity.

## INTERPRETING THE SCRIPTURE

### Letting Go of Failures

As Paul develops his personal example further, he lays a great deal of stress on "letting go" of what lies behind him. All of Paul's "letting go," however, points us to the surpassing value of what he is running forward to attain: Jesus Christ himself, and the heavenward call that Jesus laid upon Paul. The image of the race is most apropos. A runner wants to run "light." A runner doesn't want to have extra baggage, or a running suit that hinders movement. A runner wants to be able to maximize energy and output to push forward.

Paul doesn't talk specifically here about letting go of mistakes, failures, or lapses, though there is a hint of one failure that might well have hindered Paul as he moved forward in his Christian life. That is his pre-Christian activity as a persecutor of the church, the role in which Paul steps onto the stage of the early Christian drama (Acts 7:58–8:3) and to which Paul makes occasional reference (Galatians 1:13, 23-24; 1 Corinthians 15:8-10). Past failures represent a significant impediment for Christians, and so it seems prudent to give them some attention here.

The core of the gospel is the message that God offers us forgiveness in Jesus Christ, that God wants to pick us up off the floor, like the father his prodigal child, dust us off, and restore us to life within God's family. Indeed, Paul's monumental failure—thinking that he was most zealously serving God while he was seeking out Christians to bring them to trial before the Jerusalem courts—and subsequent calling by God taught him the depth of the measure of God's grace. When he writes that Christ reconciled us to God "while we were [God's] enemies," he knows very personally what that meant (Romans 5:10). Are there ways in which personal failures or unforgiven sins have stalled your forward progress in discipleship? How do you need to experience restoration, so that you can let go of those weights?

### Letting Go of Achievements

If letting go of failures is difficult, letting go of accomplishments may be even harder—and certainly sounds stranger! But a runner keeps his or her focus on the next steps of a race, straining ever forward toward the finish line, with his or her heart set on the prize to be enjoyed beyond the finish line. In such an enterprise, there is little room for looking back at how far one has traveled, taking pride in oneself in having made it halfway to the finish line, or boasting about being a better runner than one's fellow racers. All such thoughts would be dangerous distractions to the one who hopes to win the race. Rather, the person's whole being—mind, will, ambition, and strength—must be focused on what lies ahead.

When Paul writes from that prison late in his life as a Christian missionary that he forgets "what lies behind" (Philippians 3:13), he includes also his astounding accomplishments in the service of Christ. He had occasion to observe in Corinth the dangers of Christians holding on to those achievements. There, Christians used their spiritual knowledge, their spiritual gifts, their attachment to particular Christian teachers, and their service to the community as claims to enjoying privileged status over other Christians in the community. The result was a church that was deeply divided along several different fault lines.

Paul may perceive such a dynamic to be at work in the rift between Syntyche and Euodia, two prominent leaders of the community (see Philippians 4:2). Each one, reflecting on her service to the church in Philippi, her importance in the history of the growth of that congregation, and sacrifices made on behalf of the church, might well have felt that she had the right to have a say in where the church should go from there. Perhaps you yourself have heard—or thought—"after all I've done for this church, I can't believe anyone would oppose me on this!" In setting forward his own mind, Paul provides a potent remedy for this kind of competitive, self-focused, and ultimately divisive thinking.

Yet again Paul's vision for discipleship runs afoul of our cultural tendencies. We have a tendency to measure our self-worth (and, often, the worth of others) based on accomplishments. We often couple this with the expectation that those accomplishments will have some "trade-in value" when it comes to pushing for our own way in some settings. Paul, whose accomplishments surely dwarf those of many a Christian, models Christian maturity as a relinquishing of one's former claims to recognition and achievement for the sake of something better: moving forward undistracted toward Christ-likeness and our heavenly home. There is simply no place in this race for stopping to take pride in one's achievements along the road, or, even more to the point, insisting that the other runners run your way and to your rhythms on the basis of how much you've invested in running the race. Instead, all the focus is to be on Christ (3:8-11) and on the goal of the race, which is not winning petty power struggles on earth but rather being invited into the commonwealth of God in heaven (3:20).

### A More Productive Focus

And so Paul points us instead to what God is doing in, among, and through us in the present, and calls them to cooperate in seeing it done. The renunciations that Paul details in 3:7-13 are a necessary prerequisite to this new focus. We need to let go of the ways in which we have constructed our own "worth" in order to experience the new ways in which God will build us up in

Christ, giving us "worth" for eternity. This is something of what Paul means by becoming "right with God" through a Christ-centered faith rather than by means of (for him) the Torah-centered life.

A centerpiece of what God is doing in our present is conforming us to the likeness of his Son, or making us "like [Christ] in his death" (3:10), having the attitude, the character, the commitment, the faithful obedience in all circumstances that Jesus most fully exemplified for us as he took the form of a servant and accepted death on the cross. Sharing in Christ's death with a view to sharing also in his resurrection (3:10-11) brings baptismal language into Paul's example (see also Romans 6:1-4). Our focus as runners toward the prize is, in other words, on living out our own baptism, dying more and more to the "old person" formed in us by our nurture in a broken world, and coming alive more and more to the "new person" that is being formed in us as we respond to God's parenting. The question Paul would hold ever before us is not, "What have you accomplished so far?" but "Are you becoming more like Jesus?"

## SHARING THE SCRIPTURE

### Preparing Our Hearts

Meditate on this week's devotional reading, found in 1 John 4:7-12. Here the elder calls readers to love each other as a sign that they know God and the Son whom God sent. Think about how you express love for other people. Is your love confined to people you know, or people with whom you agree? Or may anyone see that God lives in you because your behavior reflects God's love? Be alert for feedback from others concerning how your light as a Christian is shining through to others as a result of the way you show God's love to them.

Pray that you and the adult learners will love others because God first loved you.

### Preparing Our Minds

Study the background from Philippians 3:1b–4:1 and lesson scripture, Philippians 3:7-16. Ask yourself: when I am preoccupied with past failures or achievements, how can I attain fresh focus?

Write on newsprint:

❑ discussion questions for "Investigate Paul's Words about the Value of Knowing Jesus Christ."
❑ information for next week's lesson, found under "Continue the Journey."
❑ activities for further spiritual growth in "Continue the Journey."

Prepare to retell "Letting Go of Failures" and "Letting Go of Achievements," both found in Interpreting the Scripture.

### LEADING THE CLASS

#### (1) Gather to Learn

❖ Welcome the class members and introduce any guests.

❖ Pray that those who are present today will prepare their hearts and minds to walk with Christ into the future.

❖ Encourage the students to name some successful companies that created products that failed. Here are several examples: *Ford Company's Edsel, 1957; Coca-Cola's New Coke, 1985; Apple Computer's Lisa, 1983; MacDonald's Hula Burger, 1962.* Note that all of these companies continued to exist long after their failures, which they learned from but did not dwell on.

❖ Read these words by James E. Sweaney and invite the students to respond to them: **Our mistakes won't irreparably damage our lives unless we let them.**

❖ Read aloud today's focus statement: **Many people are preoccupied with past failures or achievements. How can our lives achieve fresh focus? The Christian faith draws us into the future, preoccupied with God's mission in Christ.**

*(2) Investigate Paul's Words about the Value of Knowing Jesus Christ*

❖ Invite a volunteer to read Philippians 3:7-16.

❖ Retell "Letting Go of Failures" in Interpreting the Scripture. Read aloud the two questions that close this section and provide a few moments for the students to answer silently.

❖ Retell "Letting Go of Achievements" in Interpreting the Scripture. Ask: **How difficult is it for you to let go of achievements, especially in a culture that rewards accomplishments?** Again, provide a few moments for silent reflection.

❖ Read aloud these words from "A More Productive Focus" in Interpreting the Scripture: **A centerpiece of what God is doing in our present is conforming us to the likeness of his Son, or making us "like [Christ] in his death" (3:10), having the attitude, the character, the commitment, the faithful obedience in all circumstances that Jesus most fully exemplified for us as he took the form of a servant and accepted death on the cross.**

❖ Divide the students into pairs or groups of three to discuss these questions, which you will post on newsprint:

    **(1) How are you becoming more like Jesus?**

    **(2) How is the church helping you stay focused on this goal?**

    **(3) What additional help would you like to have from the church?**

*(3) Contemplate the Value of Knowing Jesus Christ*

❖ Distribute paper and pencils. Direct the students to fold the paper in half crosswise and tear it into two sheets. Ask each student to write an achievement of which they are proud on one sheet. If the adults do not want to be specifically identified, suggest that they use generic terms. For example, instead of saying "promoted to Vice President of XYZ Corporation" they might say "a promotion at work." Similarly, ask them to list a generic failure on the other sheet, such as "failure in a personal relationship" rather than "estranged from my older brother."

❖ Collect the slips of paper and redistribute them around the room. Call on people at random to read the sheet(s) before them. (The purpose in redistributing the sheets is to save students from any embarrassment in reading their own failures and achievements.)

❖ Collect the papers once again. Ask: **Did any of these accomplishments or failures surpass the value of knowing Christ? If so, which ones?**

❖ Provide a few moments of quiet so that the students may ponder just how important Christ is in their lives.

❖ Break the silence by asking anyone who wishes to do so to share the value of Christ that he or she experiences.

*(4) Commit to Learning More about Jesus Christ and Be Willing to Publicly Acknowledge a Relationship with Him*

❖ Distribute paper (and pencils, if you have not already done so). Tell the students to draw a line on the paper representing their faith journey. The line may be straight but more probably will zig and zag and perhaps look like a switchback at times. Tell them to think of this line as a race course. Suggest that they mark places on the line denoting experiences that have helped them become more conformed to the image of Christ. They may want to write a key phrase by each important point.

❖ Encourage volunteers to tell about an important event in their faith journey and in doing so publicly acknowledge their relationship with Christ.

❖ Conclude this section by inviting the students to read today's key verses, Philippians 3:13-14, in unison, beginning with "this one thing I do."

### (5) Continue the Journey

❖ Pray that today's participants will be able to set aside the achievements and failures of the past in order to press on with Christ into the future.

❖ Read aloud this preparation for next week's lesson. You may also want to post it on newsprint for the students to copy.

■ **Title: Growing in Joy and Peace**
■ **Background Scripture: Philippians 4:2-14**
■ **Lesson Scripture: Philippians 4:2-14**
■ **Focus of the Lesson: Many people grow restless under the demands life makes on them. How can we have peace and joy in life? God's peace and joy are rooted in following God's way.**

❖ Challenge the students to complete one or more of these activities for further spiritual growth, which you will write on newsprint for the students to copy.

(1) **Make a list of goals that have energized you and given you focus. How do these goals help you press forward toward Christ? If any do not help you on your faith journey, how might you reframe them—or even discard them?**

(2) **Devote special time this week to prayer and meditation. Renew your commitment to Christ on a daily basis.**

(3) **Read the Christian classic, *The Imitation of Christ*, by Thomas à Kempis. Consider ways in which you can imitate Christ.**

❖ Sing or read aloud "Jesus Is All the World to Me."

❖ Conclude today's session by leading the class in this benediction adapted from 2 Thessalonians 1:11: **Go forth with the assurance that we are always praying for you, asking that our God will make you worthy of his call and will fulfill by his power every good resolve and work of faith.**

## UNIT 3: THE MARKS OF CHRISTIAN COMMITMENT
# GROWING IN JOY AND PEACE

### PREVIEWING THE LESSON

**Lesson Scripture:** Philippians 4:2-14
**Background Scripture:** Philippians 4:2-14
**Key Verse:** Philippians 4:9

### Focus of the Lesson:
Many people grow restless under the demands life makes on them. How can we have peace and joy in life? God's peace and joy are rooted in following God's way.

### Goals for the Learners:
(1) to gain an understanding of Paul's exhortation about worrying in Philippians 4.
(2) to experience God's peace.
(3) to fill one's thoughts with things worthy of praise.

### Pronunciation Guide:
Epaphroditus (i paf ruh di' tuhs)      Syntyche (sin' ti kee)
Euodia (yoo oh' dee uh)                  Syzygus (soo' zdoo gus)

### Supplies:
Bibles, newsprint and marker, paper and pencils, hymnals

### READING THE SCRIPTURE

NRSV
Philippians 4:2-14

²I urge Euodia and I urge Syntyche to be of the same mind in the Lord. ³Yes, and I ask you also, my loyal companion, help these women, for they have struggled beside me in the work of the gospel, together with Clement and the rest of my co-workers, whose names are in the book of life.

⁴Rejoice in the Lord always; again I will say, Rejoice. ⁵Let your gentleness be known

NIV
Philippians 4:2-14

²I plead with Euodia and I plead with Syntyche to agree with each other in the Lord. ³Yes, and I ask you, loyal yokefellow, help these women who have contended at my side in the cause of the gospel, along with Clement and the rest of my fellow workers, whose names are in the book of life.

⁴Rejoice in the Lord always. I will say it

to everyone. The Lord is near. ⁶Do not worry about anything, but in everything by prayer and supplication with thanksgiving let your requests be made known to God. ⁷And the peace of God, which surpasses all understanding, will guard your hearts and your minds in Christ Jesus.

⁸Finally, beloved, whatever is true, whatever is honorable, whatever is just, whatever is pure, whatever is pleasing, whatever is commendable, if there is any excellence and if there is anything worthy of praise, think about these things. **⁹Keep on doing the things that you have learned and received and heard and seen in me, and the God of peace will be with you.**

¹⁰I rejoice in the Lord greatly that now at last you have revived your concern for me; indeed, you were concerned for me, but had no opportunity to show it. ¹¹Not that I am referring to being in need; for I have learned to be content with whatever I have. ¹²I know what it is to have little, and I know what it is to have plenty. In any and all circumstances I have learned the secret of being well-fed and of going hungry, of having plenty and of being in need. ¹³I can do all things through him who strengthens me. ¹⁴In any case, it was kind of you to share my distress.

again: Rejoice! ⁵Let your gentleness be evident to all. The Lord is near. ⁶Do not be anxious about anything, but in everything, by prayer and petition, with thanksgiving, present your requests to God. ⁷And the peace of God, which transcends all understanding, will guard your hearts and your minds in Christ Jesus.

⁸Finally, brothers, whatever is true, whatever is noble, whatever is right, whatever is pure, whatever is lovely, whatever is admirable—if anything is excellent or praiseworthy—think about such things. **⁹Whatever you have learned or received or heard from me, or seen in me—put it into practice. And the God of peace will be with you.**

¹⁰I rejoice greatly in the Lord that at last you have renewed your concern for me. Indeed, you have been concerned, but you had no opportunity to show it. ¹¹I am not saying this because I am in need, for I have learned to be content whatever the circumstances. ¹²I know what it is to be in need, and I know what it is to have plenty. I have learned the secret of being content in any and every situation, whether well fed or hungry, whether living in plenty or in want. ¹³I can do everything through him who gives me strength.

¹⁴Yet it was good of you to share in my troubles.

## UNDERSTANDING THE SCRIPTURE

**Philippians 4:2-3.** Paul addresses at last the most specific problem named within the congregation, asking Syntyche and Euodia to lay aside their differences and to end what appears to have become a divisive struggle. Encouraging them to "be of the same mind in the Lord" (4:2), Paul specifically recalls the language he used earlier to call the whole congregation to "be of the same mind" (2:2). Each one of these women will have reflected on their particular quar-

rel as they heard Paul's exhortations to unity and harmony, seeking one another's interests, and laying aside conceit and rivalry, topics that dominate Philippians (1:15-18; 2:1-11). It is probably also in part with a view to this quarrel that Paul expressed his prayer that his friends in Philippi would be able to discern what really mattered (1:10), redirecting the attention of Euodia and Syntyche away from the focus of their quarrel toward that which bound them and the whole congregation together, into which they could more profitably invest their energies.

Paul's follow-up exhortation in 4:3 demands special attention. Textual notes in both the NIV and NRSV preserve the suggestion that the Greek word translated as "yokefellow" (NIV) might be a proper name, Syzygus. This is highly unlikely, first since the name is not otherwise attested in Greek literature, and second because it is frequently used as a term of camaraderie. We are not able to discern the identity of this "loyal companion" or "yokefellow." Paul may in fact intend every person in that congregation to consider himself or herself a reliable yokefellow of the apostle, and thus entrusted with steering Syntyche and Euodia toward reconciliation. The responsibility of believers is not to take sides in a conflict between two of their fellow Christians, but to guide them toward reconciliation and harmony. Paul's description of each woman as someone who has struggled alongside Paul for the sake of the gospel, and as someone whose name is inscribed in the book of life, is also a subtle reminder to Euodia of Syntyche's worth and to Syntyche of Euodia's worth. Neither one of them should be competing against the other, or involved in a dispute seeking to win over the other. They are partners in the advancement of the gospel and partners in eternity, and need to regard one another in that light.

These verses incidentally remind us of the leadership role taken by women in Pauline circles, and of their importance in the spread of the gospel. Paul speaks of Euodia and Syntyche as he does his fellow evangelists and missionaries, indeed as part of a core group of Christian leaders in Macedonia.

**Philippians 4:4-9.** This section contains some of the most familiar verses from the letter. In this section, Paul is directing the focus of the congregation back toward their common ground. The first injunction, to "rejoice in the Lord" (4:4; see also 3:1), is a potent remedy for any divisive spirit.

Rejoicing in the Lord means taking delight in what God has done for the believer, in life as God's gift, and in the work of God through other members of the congregation and throughout the church universal. It is wholly centered on God, on the excellence of God's character, and on the splendor of God's gifts. It cannot coexist in the heart with selfish ambition or conceit, with rivalry or division.

Paul reminds the congregation of the astounding resource they have in God, a God who is near to them now and who stands ready to break into this age and usher in God's kingdom. Paul encourages his friends to frequent God's presence in prayer, laying before God the concerns of their hearts, so that they can move from anxiety to the "peace of God" that defies human understanding. Prayer is to be filled with gratitude, both for God's past provisions in time of need, and for God's nearness to hear new concerns and answer each in God's goodness and wisdom. Finally, Paul calls the hearers to focus their minds on that which is good. It is so easy to fixate on what is wrong, or allow the mind to be polluted with what is worldly or base. Training the mind to ponder what is honorable and pleasing in God's sight, one is more likely to do, and move others to do, these very things. And, indeed, "doing" is the final word of this series of exhortations: the instruction Paul has given in life and in speech is to be acted out in the daily lives of the believers (4:9).

**Philippians 4:10-14.** Paul closes Philippians with the theme of partnership, with which he also began the letter (see 1:3-7). There, Paul thanked God for their partnership. Here, Paul thanks the believers directly for the most recent symbol of their partnership, namely the unspecified gift (most likely money) that the congregation had sent to Paul through Epaphroditus.

In this "thank-you" note, Paul says that, although he appreciates the gift and the love that stands behind it (4:10, 14), he didn't really need the money. Paul is not belittling the gift, to be sure. He knows that the gifts provided by his friends in Macedonia spring not from their abundance but in spite of their own poverty and so represent precious sacrifices (see 2 Corinthians 8:1-5). In part, he wants to affirm to his friends that they and the personal concern that motivated the gift were more important to him than the funds themselves (Philippians 4:10, 17). In part, he is also still sharing his mind and heart with his friends, as he had earlier (see 1:12-26; 3:15-16). Indeed, he has advanced to such a deep dependence on Jesus that neither want nor abundance threatens to subvert his loyalty to God or derail the focus of his service. He uses a watchword of Stoic and Cynic philosophy here, translated as "content" in the NRSV (4:11). This term referred to the attainment of the independence of one's happiness from external things and circumstances, such that the philosopher's peace was no longer at the mercy of the conditions imposed upon him or her. It is often rendered as "self-sufficiency," but Paul gives this the important twist: this independence is achieved through complete dependence on Christ. This is the point of the famous claim of 4:13 in context. Paul also uses a technical term from the Greek mystery religions, translated as: "I have learned the secret" or "I have been initiated," 4:12). In these cults, initiates learn secret or hidden knowledge about the gods. As an initiate into Christ, Paul has learned the secret to attaining that independence and freedom for which the Greek philosophers earnestly seek.

---

## INTERPRETING THE SCRIPTURE

### Joy

Twice Paul has called the believers to "rejoice in the Lord" (3:1; 4:4). In the midst of his own suffering, Paul found delighting in the excellence of the Lord to provide a centering point that would keep him stable and staying the course (1:18; 2:17-18). He commends this focus to his friends in Philippi as well. Paul "rejoices in the Lord" when he abandons attempts to build up confidence in his ethnic identity, in his measuring up to human norms, and even in his achievements as a Christian missionary, seeking God's gift of confidence in Christ instead. Rejoicing in the Lord allows Paul to rise above the self-centered, divisive, competitive impulses that drive his rivals and could easily consume him as well, seeing instead the larger picture and how God's purposes are advancing in the midst of it all (1:15-18).

As his friends in Philippi focus their attention on the Lord and the joy that comes from knowing God, worshiping God, seeing God at work in their lives and in their midst, and looking for what God is doing, they will be much more likely to rise above any discord as well. As each becomes more fully attuned to God, he or she will necessarily become more closely attuned with one another and achieve harmony in their relationships. Rivalry and envy cannot coexist in the heart alongside delight; selfish conceit cannot coexist alongside rejoicing in the Lord. Rejoicing simply leaves no room for these less-noble impulses, as the focus is drawn away from the self to the Lord. Paul offers here perhaps one of his most potent prescriptions for centering our hearts on God and ordering our life together.

### Supplication

Anxiety has become a way of life among Americans. Anxiety seems only to have increased in recent years, with increased "security" around travel, increased violence in schools, and increased volatility in the job market. Our culture offers no cure, although it does offer to relieve the symptoms through a variety of medications.

Paul prescribes prayer as the cure for anxiety, in the tradition of the psalmist: "Cast your burden on the LORD, and he will sustain you" (Psalm 55:22). For this cure to have its effect, however, it is necessary to entrust the matter to God and to trust God with the outcome of the matter. When we worry, we tend to think that something undesirable will happen or that something desirable will fail to happen. Anxiety is attached to potential outcomes. Paul models a life of prayer that is attached to a particular Companion. In regard to one very significant prayer request, namely his impending trial, Paul shows a remarkable lack of concern about the outcome. That is because, whether he lives or dies, he knows he will still belong to God and experience God's presence and favor. It is the relationship with God that is important to him, and the security of that relationship gives him freedom from anxiety in the face of unknown outcomes.

*Peace*

The promise of a life centered on rejoicing in God and calm in the midst of unstable circumstances by a secure relationship with God is peace. Certainly Paul's peace in the face of a death sentence "surpasses all understanding" (4:7). Paul reveals more of the conditions that nurture this peace in the verses that open his "thank-you" note to the congregation (4:10-12). There he speaks of having learned the secret of contentment with much and with little, in lack and in abundance, and that secret is treasuring the presence of Christ and enjoying the strength that Christ's friendship brings. As long as you want that parking spot closer to the entrance of the store, or that courtesy upgrade, or that bigger home, or that promotion, or that contract, the peace of God of which Paul speaks will elude you. But if you want God, if you want fellowship with Christ, if you want God to work in your life to make you more like Jesus in any and every circumstance, you will not fail to get what you desire, and you will have peace in the process.

God also nurtures peace between us and our fellow Christians. We might balk at the idea that Paul wrote Philippians 1:27–4:1 largely to bring about the reconciliation of two people. Many of us have seen what can happen, however, when two leading figures in a congregation get into a disagreement about some issue. When that disagreement turns personal, it becomes an issue of ego and wounded pride compounded with a sense that one's tireless efforts for the church are unappreciated and unreciprocated. Such a situation is well worth the intervention of a timely and carefully crafted word—like Philippians.

Here we might focus on the role of this unnamed "loyal companion" (4:3) who is invited by Paul to come alongside these two women and help them find reconciliation and restored harmony with one another. Who would step forward in that congregation to respond to this anonymous invitation? Who will step forward in yours when two fellow believers are in a tussle, drawing (unwittingly or intentionally) others into that tussle? If God has called us to peace, it becomes our responsibility to help foster peace where quarreling or factions are on the rise—certainly not to add to the weight of one side, and not merely to stand by and watch from a safe distance.

*Something to Think About*

Just as it is true, from one perspective, that we are what we eat, so, from another perspective, we are what we put into our minds. In the words of a well-known maxim, "as a person thinks, so is she in her heart." Just as we try to teach our children to fill their bellies with good, wholesome things, so Paul reminds his friends and students to fill their minds with good, wholesome thoughts (4:8-9).

Being a "glass is half empty" sort of guy, I tend to focus on what is wrong, what is amiss, what is out of order, and what is unjust. But I've noticed that this comes at a real cost in terms of my attitude, of what I can healthfully bring to the table, even in terms of my availability to God. If we carry in our minds examples of what we have seen or heard about that was just, beautiful,

pious, what received commendation or uplifted the community, we ourselves are more ready to recognize these things around us, even call them into being and embody them ourselves. For this reason, reading the lives of the saints or devotional books like Jeremy Taylor's *On Holy Living* or other spiritual classics is an important part of our mental diet. Just as we eat right or take time to exercise, so we need to give time and attention to filling our time with the resources and activities that nurture ennobling thoughts.

---

# SHARING THE SCRIPTURE

### Preparing Our Hearts

Meditate on this week's devotional reading, found in Psalm 85:4-13. In this lament, the community cries out to God for mercy and restoration. The ideas of rejoicing and peace are present in this psalm, just as they are in Paul's letter to the Philippian church. When you are faced with problems that seem insurmountable, where do you turn to find joy and peace? Do you expect God to give you what is good, as the psalmist expects in verse 12? What techniques do you use to set aside the cares of a situation and focus on God's faithfulness and love?

Pray that you and the adult learners will be able to experience unbroken joy and peace in God, no matter what situations confront you.

### Preparing Our Minds

Study the background and lesson scripture, both found in Philippians 4:2-14. Think about how you can have peace and joy in your life.

Write on newsprint:

❑ information for next week's lesson, found under "Continue the Journey."

❑ activities for further spiritual growth in "Continue the Journey."

### LEADING THE CLASS

### (1) Gather to Learn

❖ Welcome the class members and introduce any guests.

❖ Pray that today's participants will open themselves to the joy and peace that only Christ can give.

❖ Mention that in recent memory serious economic problems, home foreclosures, wars on two fronts, concerns about the environment, and issues relating to public and personal security, among other situations, have challenged people in the United States and elsewhere. Ask:

(1) **How do you think most people respond to such serious, systemic troubles?**

(2) **What differences have you noted in the way Christians respond, compared to the way those who do not claim Christ respond?**

(3) **To what do you attribute these differences?**

❖ Read aloud today's focus statement: **Many people grow restless under the demands life makes on them. How can we have peace and joy in life? God's peace and joy are rooted in following God's way.**

*(2) Gain an Understanding of Paul's Exhortation about Worrying in Philippians 4*

❖ Enlist a volunteer to read Philippians 4:2-14 as if a member of the church at Philippi is reading Paul's letter to the congregation.

❖ Look at verses 2-3, where Paul returns to the theme of being "of the same mind in the Lord." Read or retell information in Understanding the Scripture for 4:2-3.

❖ Discuss these questions:
> **(1) What do these verses suggest about Paul's method of conflict resolution in the church?**
> **(2) What do they suggest about the role of women in the church?** (Note that the two women mentioned have "struggled beside" Paul and were obviously respected within their congregation.)

❖ Consider the next paragraph in the Scriptures, verses 4-7, where Paul commends prayer as the means by which one overcomes anxiety and finds "the peace of God."

❖ Read "Supplication" from Interpreting the Scripture. Encourage the class to contrast Paul's prayerful way of handling anxiety with the all-too-common American way: medications (legal and illegal) and alcohol. Read these two sentences again: **Anxiety is attached to potential outcomes. Paul models a life of prayer that is attached to a particular Companion.** Ask:
> **(1) Why do you think many people choose to worry anxiously about the outcome of some situation rather than "let go and let God"?**
> **(2) What can you do to help people cultivate a personal relationship with Christ?**

❖ End this section by encouraging the students to offer a silent, intercessory prayer on behalf of someone who is consumed with worry. Pray that this person will find peace in a relationship with Christ. End the prayer time with a brief prayer or simply with the word "amen."

*(3) Experience God's Peace*

❖ Read "Peace" from Interpreting the Scripture, which speaks about the peace of an individual and peace that occurs when opposing sides are reconciled.

❖ Talk first about individual peace. Point out that in Philippians 4:10-14 it seems clear that Paul experiences God's peace and joy no matter what the circumstances. This is the case because he "can do all things through [Christ] who strengthens [Paul]" (4:13). Encourage the students to speak about how Jesus' strengthening presence has enabled them to remain peace-filled when others were anxious or fearful. Invite the students to give specific examples of times when God's peace enabled them to respond positively to a difficult situation.

❖ Discuss how God nurtures peace between individuals, particularly in the midst of a church conflict. Talk about the qualities of a "loyal companion" who can come alongside those who are at odds and help them resolve their differences. You may wish to list ideas on newsprint. Some characteristics include: *being a good listener, both to the people involved and to God; being open-minded to hear all sides; being fair; being able to suggest a way forward that ensures the dignity of both parties; being able to diffuse conflict and keep others from taking sides.* If after you have created this list of characteristics the name of any church member(s) who might be able to mediate conflict should come to mind, assign someone to talk with each of these people to let them know that the class has discerned these traits within them. Encourage those who have been identified to step forward if a conflict arises.

### (4) Fill One's Thoughts with Things Worthy of Praise

❖ Invite the students to look again at Philippians 4:8-9. Lead them in making a list of examples of the kinds of behaviors that would be considered honorable, just, pure, pleasing, commendable, excellent, and worthy of praise. Write ideas on newsprint.

❖ Ask: **How might our community be different if all of the Christians who lived here focused on these things?**

❖ Distribute paper and pencils. Encourage the students to look again at this list and write ways that they can (and already do) embody the ideals mentioned in these verses.

❖ Challenge the students to live out these ideals in the coming weeks.

### (5) Continue the Journey

❖ Pray that each person who has come today will go forth in the peace and joy of Christ.

❖ Read aloud this preparation for next week's lesson. You may also want to post it on newsprint for the students to copy.

- ■ **Title: Upheld by God**
- ■ **Background Scripture: Acts 28; Philippians 4:15-23**
- ■ **Lesson Scripture: Acts 28:16-25a, 28-31**
- ■ **Focus of the Lesson: People struggle to keep commitments. How can we hold to our commitments?**

**In recognizing God's commitment and faithfulness to us, we are challenged to commit our lives to God's care.**

❖ Challenge the students to complete one or more of these activities for further spiritual growth, which you will write on newsprint for the students to copy.

(1) **Approach someone in your congregation with whom you have had a disagreement or power struggle. Do whatever you can to bring God's peace and harmony to the situation.**

(2) **Review Philippians 4:8-9. Practice the kinds of thoughts and actions of those who are committed to Christ as Paul lists them in this passage.**

(3) **Try to comfort and cheer someone who is filled with anxiety and worry. Do not belittle this individual's problems but try to show him or her that there is a different way to handle them through Christ.**

❖ Sing or read aloud "Rejoice, Ye Pure in Heart," based in part on Philippians 4:4.

❖ Conclude today's session by leading the class in this benediction adapted from 2 Thessalonians 1:11: **Go forth with the assurance that we are always praying for you, asking that our God will make you worthy of his call and will fulfill by his power every good resolve and work of faith.**

UNIT 3: THE MARKS OF CHRISTIAN COMMITMENT
# UPHELD BY GOD

---

## PREVIEWING THE LESSON

**Lesson Scripture:** Acts 28:16-25a, 28-31
**Background Scripture:** Acts 28; Philippians 4:15-23
**Key Verses:** Acts 28:30-31

### Focus of the Lesson:
People struggle to keep commitments. How can we hold to our commitments? In recognizing God's commitment and faithfulness to us, we are challenged to commit our lives to God's care.

### Goals for the Learners:
(1) to examine how Paul kept his commitments to Christ while a prisoner in Rome.
(2) to express how they feel about keeping to a task in the face of adversity.
(3) to commit to proclaim boldly God's work through Jesus Christ in all circumstances.

### Pronunciation Guide:
Appius (ap' ee uhs)
Puteoli (pyoo tee' oh lee)
Rhegium (ree' jee uhm)

### Supplies:
Bibles, newsprint and marker, paper and pencils, hymnals

---

## READING THE SCRIPTURE

NRSV
Acts 28:16-25a, 28-31
¹⁶When we came into Rome, Paul was allowed to live by himself, with the soldier who was guarding him.
¹⁷Three days later he called together the local leaders of the Jews. When they had assembled, he said to them, "Brothers, though I had done nothing against our people or the customs of our ancestors, yet I was

NIV
Acts 28:16-25a, 28-31
¹⁶When we got to Rome, Paul was allowed to live by himself, with a soldier to guard him.
¹⁷Three days later he called together the leaders of the Jews. When they had assembled, Paul said to them: "My brothers, although I have done nothing against our people or against the customs of our

arrested in Jerusalem and handed over to the Romans. ¹⁸When they had examined me, the Romans wanted to release me, because there was no reason for the death penalty in my case. ¹⁹But when the Jews objected, I was compelled to appeal to the emperor—even though I had no charge to bring against my nation. ²⁰For this reason therefore I have asked to see you and speak with you, since it is for the sake of the hope of Israel that I am bound with this chain." ²¹They replied, "We have received no letters from Judea about you, and none of the brothers coming here has reported or spoken anything evil about you. ²²But we would like to hear from you what you think, for with regard to this sect we know that everywhere it is spoken against."

²³After they had set a day to meet with him, they came to him at his lodgings in great numbers. From morning until evening he explained the matter to them, testifying to the kingdom of God and trying to convince them about Jesus both from the law of Moses and from the prophets. ²⁴Some were convinced by what he had said, while others refused to believe. ²⁵So they disagreed with each other; and as they were leaving, Paul made one further statement.

²⁸"Let it be known to you then that this salvation of God has been sent to the Gentiles; they will listen."

³⁰He lived there two whole years at his own expense and welcomed all who came to him, ³¹proclaiming the kingdom of God and teaching about the Lord Jesus Christ with all boldness and without hindrance.

ancestors, I was arrested in Jerusalem and handed over to the Romans. ¹⁸They examined me and wanted to release me, because I was not guilty of any crime deserving death. ¹⁹But when the Jews objected, I was compelled to appeal to Caesar—not that I had any charge to bring against my own people. ²⁰For this reason I have asked to see you and talk with you. It is because of the hope of Israel that I am bound with this chain." ²¹They replied, "We have not received any letters from Judea concerning you, and none of the brothers who have come from there has reported or said anything bad about you. ²²But we want to hear what your views are, for we know that people everywhere are talking against this sect."

²³They arranged to meet Paul on a certain day, and came in even larger numbers to the place where he was staying. From morning till evening he explained and declared to them the kingdom of God and tried to convince them about Jesus from the Law of Moses and from the Prophets. ²⁴Some were convinced by what he said, but others would not believe. ²⁵They disagreed among themselves and began to leave after Paul had made this final statement:

²⁸"Therefore I want you to know that God's salvation has been sent to the Gentiles, and they will listen!"

³⁰For two whole years Paul stayed there in his own rented house and welcomed all who came to see him. ³¹Boldly and without hindrance he preached the kingdom of God and taught about the Lord Jesus Christ.

---

## UNDERSTANDING THE SCRIPTURE

**Acts 28:1-10.** This scene comes from the middle of a larger narrative about Paul's tumultuous journey by sea to Rome. A few prisoners from Judea-Palestine are being taken under Roman guard to Rome, the soldiers commandeering passage on commercial ships carrying their own crews, cargo, and other passengers. Travel was rigorous in the first century. The Mediterranean was unsafe for travel during the winter months, such that Paul's trip to Rome is interrupted by the need to spend the entire winter off the seas. Indeed, the shipwreck narrated in Acts 27 is the result of not finding a harbor for the winter soon enough. Acts 28 opens with the entire ship's company stranded on the island of Malta, a small island south of Sicily. This part of the travel narrative is told from the vantage point of a "we," which has suggested to many that the author of Acts was actually a traveling companion of Paul at these points in the story (see 16:11-18; 20:7-15; 21:1-18; 27:1–28:15).

The ancients—both Jews and Gentiles—had a strong belief in *Nemesis*, that is, in people getting what was coming to them. This is evidenced by the natives' conjectures about Paul's crimes. Although not the first time such a mistake was made in Acts (see Acts 14:8-18), their quickness to believe that Paul was a god walking among them also suggests that the idea of the incarnation or the proclamation of Jesus as God-made-flesh would not have been all that foreign.

**Acts 28:11-15.** Syracuse is a city on the southeast coast of Sicily. Rhegium is a seaport at the southernmost tip of Italy's "boot." Puteoli is an important port city southeast of Rome. Christianity had spread to Rome and cities like Puteoli long before Paul's own arrival. A community of believers hosted Paul in Puteoli, and Christians from Rome came as far as Forum of Appius (a town approximately forty miles from Rome) and Three Taverns to meet the apostle and escort him back. Those distances would have represented two- or three-day journeys for pedestrian travelers each way.

**Acts 28:16-31.** Two of Luke's foremost interests as he composes the Gospel and Acts is to demonstrate, first, that the Christian gospel is indeed rooted directly in the "hope of Israel" (Acts 28:20), an outworking of the ancient and revered promises of God in the Scriptures, and, second, that the large percentage of Gentiles in this "Jewish" movement was itself a legitimate development. The final scene of Acts brings both points forcefully to the fore one last time. Paul spends an entire day explaining

the legitimacy of the much-slandered gospel "from the law of Moses and from the prophets" (28:23). After the mixed reception among the Jewish community in Rome, Paul cites Isaiah 6:9-10 as a scriptural warrant for the widespread Jewish rejection of the gospel. The consequence of this rejection was the open and unabashed offering of the promises of the God of Israel to the Gentile nations (28:28). The text from Isaiah is also familiar from the Jesus tradition, where Jesus himself is remembered to have cited it as an explanation for the rejection of his message and his disciples' preaching by their own fellow Jews (see Mark 4:12; Matthew 13:14-17).

**Philippians 4:15-16.** We are here again reminded of the unique relationship of "partnership" Paul enjoyed with this church among the many he had founded (4:15-16). This partnership was expressed, among other ways, through the Philippians' financial support of Paul's missionary endeavors and, now, in his imprisonment. Paul was careful, for example, not to accept financial support from the Corinthian churches, in part to distinguish himself from other peddlers of philosophies and religions by making the gospel "free of charge" (1 Corinthians 9:6-18), in part to maintain his independence from Corinthian patrons, so as to maintain his own claim to be *their* spiritual patron and father (1 Corinthians 4:14-15). Indeed, it was the Philippian disciples who helped finance Paul's mission to Corinth itself (2 Corinthians 11:8-9). Whenever the Macedonian churches are mentioned by Paul, it is with gratitude and praise (see 2 Corinthians 8:1-5).

**Philippians 4:17-23.** Although Paul is the direct recipient of the gift, the Philippians' act of sharing with Paul is also, mysteriously, a gift to God. It is a liturgical act, a sacrifice that has value in God's sight and has been accepted by God (4:18). Paul expresses confidence that God will also respond generously to the Philippians, in a strange twist of the normal flow of reciprocity. According to the "rules" of reciprocity in friendship and patronage relationships, Paul himself should return some gift to the Philippians, but he is in no position to think about such a return at the present time. God is, of course, in no way indebted by a gift, being the Giver and Source of all. Nevertheless God looks with favor on the generous act of God's children and will remember their own character when they call upon God for help in time of need (4:19). Thus, in God's economy, no generous act goes unrewarded. The view of God's provision articulated in Philippians 4:19 seems to be given fuller expression in 2 Corinthians 9:6-14. Paul's theology of money appears to have been that resources are provided by God to enable generosity, and also that God favors those who are themselves gracious towards the needs of others.

In his closing greetings, Paul mentions the "saints" or "sanctified ones" among Caesar's household that send their greetings to the disciples in Philippi along with Paul's own. This need not refer to actual family members of the emperor but rather any of the servants and clients that make up the extended household of a patron. Caesar's "household" would have been vast indeed in this sense. It is also, however, a sign of the fruitfulness of Paul's imprisonment, which he had claimed was advancing the gospel in these higher circles in the early part of the letter (1:12-13). One of the most remarkable qualities exhibited by Paul was his ability to turn virtually any circumstances of hardship into an opportunity to witness to the Christ who enabled him to endure all things.

Acts ends on an intentionally "upbeat" note, with Paul still actively preaching while under house arrest waiting for his appeal before the emperor's court. It is quite possible that this period of two years ended with the apostle's release to "be with Christ," as he himself wished in Philippians 1:23.

---

## INTERPRETING THE SCRIPTURE

### Speaking Boldly

If you, like me, are a reader located in a mainline denomination within Western Christianity, Paul's example in Acts 28 might challenge you most directly as he proclaims the kingdom of God and teaches about the Lord Jesus Christ "with all boldness" (Acts 28:30-31). Speaking the truth about Christ boldly has never come easily for me outside of the church or seminary or otherwise Christian context. When people have approached me about some spiritual concern or question, I'm in the game, but I remain uncomfortable initiating any conversation about faith in Jesus with someone whom I do not know to be a believer.

This is a place in which I have been too well formed by my schooling and social upbringing. Talking about your religion in a way that suggests another person should come over to it is just not "polite." But Paul's example shakes my complacency with myself. If our "good news" is true, we need to extend that invitation to others to acknowledge the reign of God and to live obediently to that reign, so that they too may encounter God peacefully at his visitation. I will probably never discover "boldness" proclaiming the gospel. But this much I can do: I can talk frankly about ways in which God has met me, ways in which Jesus has given me guidance or help. I can talk about the role God or the pattern of Jesus plays—or does not play fully enough—in the decisions I make. In other words, I can witness. A witness speaks of what he or she knows, has seen, has experienced. This is not threatening or confrontational. It is not judgmental. But it does provide opportunity for our conversation partner to learn, to be drawn, to be convinced by the Holy Spirit working alongside our witness.

### Redrawing Maps

The Book of Acts opens with Jesus announcing that by the power and guidance of the Holy Spirit the apostles would be his "witnesses in Jerusalem, in all Judea and Samaria, and to the ends of the earth" (1:8). The narrative plot of Acts unfolds in a way that shows this prediction to be fulfilled, first focusing on the growth of the church in response to the apostles' witness in Jerusalem (chapters 1-7), the spread of the gospel into Judea and Samaria (chapters 8-9), and the further spread of the gospel into the regions of Syria, Asia Minor, Macedonia, and Greece. Luke uses Paul's arrest and appeal to Caesar as the means by which to portray the preaching of the gospel in Rome (despite the appearance of Christians there long before, as Luke himself reveals). Rome? The central seat of world empire, pushed out to the margins as the "ends of the earth"? What a radical revision of the prevailing "map" of the political and economic realities of the day! But, for Luke, Jerusalem was the center of God's redeeming acts in history in the person of Jesus Christ. It was the true center in the human sphere, its centrality defined by God's actions, not human superpowers.

When I was an undergraduate, our university bookstore sold a humorous poster featuring a map of the world from the perspective of an alumnus or alumna. Of course, the university and its town were featured prominently in the center, ridiculously out of scale. There were the Eastern and Western U.S. seacoasts as places of business to which alums would tend to move, with hardly a hint of any other part of America. Europe, as a business partner and vacation spot for many alums, was present off to the right, with vestigial representations of the other continents. A few Pacific and Caribbean Islands were featured, oversized, representing more favorite vacation spots. It was funny, but in retrospect also a critique on our perspective. The plight of the poor in Asia and war-torn Africa, the hard-working but often struggling farmers across most of our Midwest, even the urban center directly to the south of us—all these fell off our radar.

The story of what God is doing in the world challenges our maps, forcing us, our city, even our nation out of the center and calling us to a broader view—a view that looks with God at what is of concern to God, not to the powers that be. Today, with the vital growth of the church in the southern hemisphere and in eastern countries, we perhaps find ourselves more "at the ends of the earth" rather than at the center of God's mission. Our own country is a fertile mission field for Spirit-filled and led Christians from Africa and Asia. We are called to a profound humility both in regard to decentralizing ourselves so that we can see what is of concern to God (and cooperate with that) and to seeking help from our sisters and brothers from foreign lands, remembering what is the height and depth and breadth of God's love for us, and vision for us, in Christ.

### Are You Hard of Hearing?

Paul's "last word" in Acts is a harsh one. He has diligently gone first to the Jewish population of each new city that he has visited, preaching the good news about Jesus first to them before moving out to the places where he would attract more Gentiles. Finally, in Rome, he rebukes the Jews for their lack of responsiveness to the gospel that he had encountered elsewhere and that, he claims, fulfills (or, perhaps better, re-enacts) the pattern of Isaiah's own calling to announce God's word to an unresponsive people. Paul would write about the "hardening" that has come over Israel "until the full number of the Gentiles has come in" (Romans 11:25) and about God's cutting out the shoots of the native vine to make room for the wild shoots of the Gentiles to be grafted into the people of God (Romans 11:17-24).

Other passages in the New Testament might be seen to feed "triumphalism"—the Gentiles "winning out" over the Jews—even more directly, such as the declaration in Hebrews 8:13 that the first covenant was nullified in favor of the second (the "new" covenant) or the conclusion to the parable of the wicked tenants that the vineyard would be given "to a people that produces the fruits of the kingdom" (Matthew 21:43). However, we cannot read these texts too comfortably. Unpopular as it may be to say, our "salvation" is not signed, sealed, and delivered. We are expected to show forth in our lives the "fruits of the kingdom." We are under divine scrutiny, to see if we will live in a manner worthy of the gospel, for "if God did not spare the natural branches, perhaps he will not spare you" (Romans 11:21).

Paul's recitation of Isaiah 6:9-10 leaves us with the question: Will *we* listen? Will *we* perceive and understand? Will *we* turn our hearts, thoughts, lives, hopes for ourselves fully over to God so that God can heal us? As you reflect on your study of Paul's letters to the churches in Thessalonica and Philippi, where has the Holy Spirit nudged you, made you feel uncomfortable, or suggested a new direction? How has the shape of your discipleship been challenged to expand or deepen? "Today, if you hear his voice, do not harden your hearts" (Hebrews 3:7-8).

---

# SHARING THE SCRIPTURE

### Preparing Our Hearts

Meditate on this week's devotional reading, found in Acts 9:23-30. These verses report on brushes that Paul had with death and how other followers of Christ befriended him. Paul kept his commitment to Christ by speaking boldly in his name. The other followers, though leery of Paul because of his background as a persecutor of the church, acted to protect him from the Jewish authorities who sought his life. How has God upheld you? How have other believers participated in God's plan to uphold you? How have you upheld others in Jesus' name?

Pray that you and the adult learners will be open to God's leading and ready to commit to whatever God calls you to do.

### Preparing Our Minds

Study the background from Acts 28 and Philippians 4:15-23. The lesson scripture is from Acts 28:16-25a, 28-31. Think about how you can hold on to commitments, even when it is a struggle to do so.

Write on newsprint:
❑ information for next week's lesson, found under "Continue the Journey."
❑ activities for further spiritual growth in "Continue the Journey."

### LEADING THE CLASS

#### (1) Gather to Learn

❖ Welcome the class members and introduce any guests.
❖ Pray that each one who has come to